Vietnam 2035

Vietnam 2035

Toward Prosperity, Creativity, Equity, and Democracy

World Bank Group

Ministry of Planning and Investment of Vietnam

WORLD BANK GROUP

1818 H Street NW, Washington, DC 20433
Telephone: 202-473-1000; Internet: www.worldbank.org

1 2 3 4 19 18 17 16

ISBN (print): 978-1-4648-0824-1
ISBN (electronic): 978-1-4648-0825-8
DOI: 10.1596/978-1-4648-0824-1

Cover design: Ministry of Planning and Investment of Vietnam and Bill Pragluski, Critical Stages, LLC.

Library of Congress Cataloging-in-Publication Data has been requested.

The State shall guarantee and promote the People's right to mastery; to recognize, respect, protect, and guarantee human rights and citizens' rights; and to pursue the goal of a prosperous people and a strong, democratic, equitable, and civilized country, in which all people enjoy an abundant, free, and happy life and are given conditions for their comprehensive development.

—Article 3 of the 2013 Constitution of the Socialist Republic of Vietnam

Contents

Foreword xvii
Preface and Acknowledgments xix
Executive Summary xxv
Abbreviations xxxiii

Part I Overview

Vietnam 2035: Toward Prosperity, Creativity, Equity, and Democracy 1

Introduction 3
Pillar 1 Economic Prosperity with Environmental Sustainability 17
Pillar 2 Equity and Social Inclusion 39
Pillar 3 A Capable and Accountable State 53
Summary and Conclusions 67

Part II Background Chapters

1 Thirty Years of Renovation and Vietnam's Aspirations for 2035 77

Main Messages 77
Đổi Mới: Motivation, Process, and Results 78
Future Opportunities and Challenges 91
Vietnam's Aspirations for 2035 99
Notes 104
References 105

2 Enabling Economic Modernization and Private Sector Development . . 109

Main Messages 109
Vietnam's Growth and Economic Modernization Record 111
Opportunities, Risks, and Challenges for Future Growth 119

Promoting Economic Modernization and Enhancing Competitiveness of the Private Sector . . . 133
Annex 2A Empirical Relationship among Political Connection, Firms' Access to Credit, and Profitability . . . 157
Annex 2B Growth Accounting to Identify Sources of Growth . . . 161
Notes . . . 163
References . . . 165

3 Building National Innovation Capacity . . . 169

Main Messages . . . 169
Innovation Capacity: Where Is Vietnam Today? . . . 172
Innovation: The Demand (or Firm) Side . . . 177
Innovation: The Supply Side . . . 186
By Way of Conclusion: Moving Toward an Innovation-Led Economy . . . 198
Notes . . . 199
References . . . 200

4 Managing Urbanization for Greater Economic Efficiency . . . 203

Main Messages . . . 203
Urbanization and Economic Transformation in Vietnam . . . 206
Vietnam's Urbanization in 3D: Density, Distance, and Division . . . 209
Causes of Low and Stagnant Density, Rising Distance, and Persistent Division . . . 221
Institutions and Infrastructure: Cities to Lead Vietnam's Transformation into a Modern Industrialized Nation . . . 228
Annex 4A Haiphong City: The Challenges and Promises of a Gateway in Transition . . . 238
Notes . . . 240
References . . . 240

5 Achieving Sustainable and Climate-Resilient Growth . . . 243

Main Messages . . . 243
Environmental Sustainability: A Key to Growth and Development . . . 245
Environmental Challenges in Vietnam Today and in the Future . . . 248
Underlying Causes and Priority Challenges . . . 262
Growing Sustainably Toward 2035: The Road Forward . . . 265
Notes . . . 276
References . . . 277

6 Promoting Equity and Social Inclusion . . . 281

Main Messages . . . 281
The Situation of Social Inclusion in Vietnam . . . 283
The Unfinished Agenda: Marginalized Groups and Equality of Opportunity . . . 287
The Emerging Agenda: Middle-Class Inclusion in a Market Economy . . . 301
Notes . . . 333
References . . . 334

7 Building Modern Institutions for an Effective State . . . 339

Main Messages . . . 339
The Role of Institutions . . . 341

Diagnosing Vietnam's Institutional Challenges 344
Toward Modern Institutions for an Effective State 356
Notes 366
References 367

Boxes

O.1 Potential benefits and risks of new technologies 11
O.2 Aspirations for 2035 14
O.3 State effectiveness and development: Confluence of Eastern and Western thought 54
O.4 Webs of state connections driving the pharmaceutical industry 57
O.5 Narrow interests block a master plan 58
1.1 A chronology of major market-oriented *Đổi Mới* reforms 81
1.2 The education philosophy of Vietnam under *Đổi Mới* 85
1.3 Vietnam's long-term growth trajectory relative to comparator countries 87
1.4 Changing attitudes of Vietnamese society toward the market and the state 92
1.5 The Trans-Pacific Partnership 95
1.6 Key features of aspirations for 2035 101
2.1 Enterprise reform in Vietnam 120
2.2 Global context: A golden period of growth? 122
2.3 A baseline scenario for income growth up to 2035 125
2.4 Low entrepreneurial confidence in Vietnam 129
2.5 Labor productivity growth in Vietnam, China, and the Republic of Korea 134
2.6 Secure access to land in Vietnam remains a binding constraint to firm growth 141
2.7 Deposit Insurance of Vietnam 143
2.8 Vietnam Asset Management Company 144
2.9 Trends in global production and trade networks 150
2.10 Vietnamese successes in ICT services industries 155
3.1 Four foundations of an innovation-led economy 170
3.2 Who are Vietnam's role models? 171
3.3 How a sound national innovation system promotes firm learning 175
3.4 Many policies exist only on paper 178
3.5 Firm upgrading in an MNC-dominated economy: Singapore 179
3.6 Efficiency and risk management in rice: An Giang Plant Protection Company in the Mekong Delta 182
3.7 Capital market development and exit facilitation: Brazil's *Novo Mercado* 184
3.8 Vietnam should strengthen staff capacity and promote the resolution of IPR infringements by civil measures 186
3.9 The United Kingdom research output and impact: Systematically evaluated under the Research Excellence Framework 189
3.10 Using research funds to promote progress on key thematic challenges of national importance: Mexico's *fondos sectoriales* 190
3.11 The Higher Education Reform Agenda, 2006–20 193
3.12 Rapid expansion of private higher education satisfies demand for skills in India 196
4.1 Underused industrial parks proliferate despite high costs 214
4.2 The Republic of Korea's secondary cities are important for manufacturing jobs 215
4.3 Some urban centers near the two metropolitan areas have been successful in attracting investment 217
4.4 Unplanned growth has been expensive in Latin America 223
4.5 Some advanced regional economies have adopted efficient systems of developing their cities 229

4.6	A portfolio of modern and livable cities	229
4.7	Shanghai moving away from GDP as a driving indicator of urbanization policy	232
4.8	Poland's spatial planning transition	233
4.9	Potential for high-speed rail	235
5.1	Gains from sustainable, inclusive, and resilient growth	247
5.2	Agricultural growth has a growing environmental footprint	249
5.3	Costs of poor sanitation	255
5.4	Sustainable Development Goals related to environmental issues	266
5.5	Co-management is crucial for sustaining marine fisheries	267
5.6	Payments for ecosystem services: A market-based approach to environmental management	268
7.1	State effectiveness and development: Confluence of Eastern and Western thought	343
7.2	Other countries' experience in managing talent in the civil service	361

Figures

O.1	Rapid and inclusive growth in Vietnam has yielded shared prosperity and strong gains in poverty reduction	6
O.2	The share of population over 65 will more than double between 2015 and 2035	12
O.3	By 2035, more than half the Vietnamese population will enter the global middle class	13
O.4	Income per capita growth scenarios for Vietnam to 2035	15
O.5	Keeping on course for catch-up: Vietnam and global comparators	18
O.6	Productivity growth has been trending downward	19
O.7	Firm-level asset productivity has declined sharply for the Vietnamese nonpublic enterprise sector	20
O.8	Urbanization in Vietnam appears to be on a path as strong as in the Republic of Korea and in China	34
O.9	Ethnic minority children face higher inequality of opportunity	40
O.10	Triangle of unequal opportunity for ethnic minority children	40
O.11	Large gaps in child health and nutrition by ethnicity persist	41
O.12	Total fertility rate has fallen over time, and the sex ratio at birth has increased sharply since 2005	44
O.13	A large gap in upper secondary school attendance remains between the poorest and richest 20 percent	46
O.14	Vietnam can follow the Republic of Korea's path in high school completion rates	46
O.15	The old-age dependency ratio will increase rapidly	48
O.16	As countries move to upper-middle-income status, pension coverage usually increases	49
O.17	The robust long-term correlation between prosperity and the quality of governance	54
O.18	Worldwide Governance Indicators, 2014	55
1.1	Vietnam: Reform, growth, and inflation, 1977–2015	80
1.2	Per capita GDP growth, 1991–2014	86
B1.3.1	Vietnam has performed well on its long-term income trajectory	87
1.3	Household poverty rate, Vietnam, 1993–2014	88

1.4 The Human Development Index in selected countries, 1990–2012 89
B1.4.1 Perceptions about the preferred economic system 92
B1.4.2 Perceptions of the pace of transition 92
1.5 Regional shares of global GDP (baseline scenario) 94
1.6 Change in Vietnam's real GDP as a result of the Trans-Pacific Partnership, 2015–35 96
1.7 Projections for surface air temperature increase 99
1.8 Income per capita growth scenarios for Vietnam to 2035 102
2.1 Strong growth has enabled Vietnam to narrow the income gap with the world average 110
2.2 Vietnam has had 25 years of fast, stable, and equitable economic growth 112
2.3 Large-scale sectoral shifts have been at play in Vietnam for at least 25 years . . . 113
2.4 Vietnam's structural changes are broadly consistent with global patterns 114
2.5 Consolidation of agricultural land has happened at a slow pace 115
2.6 In comparison with China, Vietnam has given heavy policy and investment attention to rice production—despite food consumption and expenditure patterns rapidly shifting away from rice 115
2.7 Livestock and aquaculture production is gaining share in agriculture 116
2.8 Rise of wage employment and its sectoral shifts, 2004 and 2012 117
2.9 Vietnam's exports have consistently grown faster than global and regional averages for the past 15 years, led by manufactured and high-technology products 118
2.10 Trade and investment liberalization has allowed industrial clusters to emerge with both local private and foreign-invested firms. 119
2.11 State-owned enterprises have seen a declining role in the economy since the early 2000s 119
2.12 The state has retained a virtual monopoly or oligopoly in several sectors 120
2.13 The number of newly registered domestic private companies has risen sharply since the 2000 Enterprise Law 121
B2.2.1 Global living standards took off after the eighteenth century 123
B2.2.2 Vietnam's share of global GDP relative to its share of global population has been recovering since the late 1980s 123
2.14 Labor productivity growth has been on a declining trend since the late 1990s 127
2.15 Low firm-level asset (capital and land) and labor productivity measures reflect Vietnam's long-inefficient state sector and worsening performance of private enterprises. 129
2.16 Domestic private firms are overwhelmingly small and mostly informal, preventing productivity gains through scale economies, specialization, and innovation 130
2.17 Large domestic private firms have, on average, been less productive than smaller private firms 130
2.18 Land and capital assets have been accumulated in sectors that have made the least productive use of them. 131
2.19 Labor productivity in agriculture remains low, even after growing strongly since 1990 132
2.20 Vietnam's ranking on the rule of law measure has declined since 1996, while its per capita GDP has increased sharply 140
2.21 Vietnam's performance on rule of law seems to be especially lagging on property rights 140
B2.6.1 Share of firms perceiving a low risk of land appropriation 141

2.22 Four global value chains—agribusiness, textiles and apparel, transport equipment, and electronics/ICT equipment—will continue to be export generators for Vietnam . . . 151
2.23 High import content of electronics exports . . . 153
2.24 Vietnam's Services Trade Restrictions Index scores are better than the Association of Southeast Asian Nations' average in all subsectors, reflecting progress on related regulations, 2012 . . . 155
3.1 Countries' research and development expenditure tends to rise with overall development level . . . 173
3.2 Vietnam performs better than expected on management practices, given its income level . . . 175
3.3 Vietnamese entrepreneurs view scientific institutions and university–private sector collaboration as lagging . . . 176
3.4 Managers in Vietnamese firms are strong on monitoring but weak on setting long-term targets, introducing new technologies, and reforming human resource policies . . . 180
3.5 Even the best firms in Vietnam fall below the average firm on the frontier benchmark . . . 181
4.1 Urbanization goes hand in hand with structural transformation . . . 207
4.2 Urbanization trends in Vietnam appear as strong as in the Republic of Korea and in China . . . 207
4.3 Urbanization and the transition from slow to fast growth in China . . . 208
4.4 Urbanization and the transition from slow to fast growth in Vietnam . . . 208
4.5 Vietnam's urban population growth in the global picture . . . 210
4.6 Low-density spatial expansion can dampen agglomeration economies . . . 210
4.7 Productivity is higher in industrial zones than in neighboring cities . . . 212
4.8 Industrial zone occupancy rates are lower, the farther from the center, in the Ho Chi Minh City region . . . 213
4.9 Fragmented and stealth urbanization in Ho Chi Minh City metropolitan region . . . 215
4.10 Share of Vietnam's population, by city size, 2009 . . . 216
4.11 Change in share of Vietnam's population, by city size, 1989–2009 . . . 216
4.12 Urban wage premiums are small outside Hanoi and Ho Chi Minh City . . . 217
4.13 Urban and rural poverty headcount rates are falling . . . 219
4.14 More households have a permanent home . . . 220
4.15 After receiving Class I status in 2009, Thai Nguyen's local receipts nearly doubled . . . 224
5.1 Making water available in the future means addressing today's water exploitations . . . 250
5.2 Vietnam has lost an alarming percentage of "primary" forest over the past 20 years, although its overall forest cover is around 40 percent . . . 251
5.3 The prominence of aquaculture in Vietnam's economy requires close coordination, biosecurity investments, and efforts to stem water pollution and water use in fisheries . . . 253
5.4 Wastewater treatment needs low-cost solutions, regulatory certainty, and market incentives . . . 255
5.5 The economic implications of Vietnam's wastewater cleanup gives pause . . . 256
5.6 Fine particulate matter, driven by industry and coal-fired power plants in the north, is approaching Chinese levels . . . 257
5.7 Projected reduction in aquaculture income as a result of impacts of climate change without adaptation . . . 260

5.8 In only one decade, the three measures of carbon dioxide emissions—greenhouse gas emissions, per capita emissions, and carbon intensity of GDP—increased by 50 percent 261
5.9 Urban areas have seen a rapid increase in motorcycle ownership, 2000–11 262
5.10 Developing in each region a single coordinated multisectoral plan, similar to the Mekong Delta Plan, will facilitate better coordination with the center 273
6.1 Poverty has plummeted in Vietnam in the past two decades 284
6.2 Vietnam has managed to contain the rise in inequality even as its economy grew rapidly 284
6.3 Vietnamese citizens express high rates of satisfaction with public amenities 286
6.4 Vietnam's 52 ethnic minorities are much more likely to be poor than the Kinh–Hoa ethnic majority 287
6.5 Poverty rates vary by ethnic group, 2009 288
6.6 The historically poor in Vietnam are much more likely to be poor today 288
6.7 Individual ethnic groups with higher migration rates are economically more successful 290
6.8 Ethnic minority children lag the Kinh's near-universal primary completion rate 291
6.9 Ethnic minority children score lower on tests than Kinh but show large gains with time in school 291
6.10 Large gaps in child health and nutrition by ethnicity persist 292
6.11 Ethnic minority children face inequality of opportunity, 2010–14 292
6.12 Triangle of unequal opportunity for ethnic minority children 292
6.13 Disability rises quickly after age 65, with two-thirds of those age 80 reporting some form of disability 295
6.14 Wealthier countries are more likely to report being a good place to live for people with intellectual disabilities, 2014 295
6.15 Most children with severe disabilities in Vietnam never attend school, 2009 295
6.16 Employment rates vary widely across disabilities 296
6.17 Percentage of population without permanent registration in four major urban centers 298
6.18 Net school enrollment rate by school level and *hộ khẩu* status 298
6.19 Vietnam runs close to India and China as having the world's highest sex ratio at birth 300
6.20 By 2035, more than half the Vietnamese will have entered the global middle class 302
6.21 Even with rapid change over the last 25 years, family farming still employs the largest share of Vietnamese workers 304
6.22 The nongovernment minimum wage in Vietnam is high relative to the median wage, compared with other countries 305
6.23 Vietnam—following labor code changes in 2012—is more restrictive in hiring and dismissing workers than France and China 306
6.24 The high frequency of wildcat strikes is a symptom of a weak industrial relations system 308
6.25 A large gap in upper secondary school attendance remains between the poorest and richest 20 percent 310
6.26 Over the past 25 years, Vietnam has greatly expanded access to education 311
6.27 Vietnam excels in international tests, scoring above many rich countries 312

6.28 Vietnam can follow the Republic of Korea's path in high school completion rates 314
6.29 Vietnam needs to sustain its progress in raising life expectancy of its citizens 316
6.30 The poor use grassroots health care, while the rich use higher level hospitals 316
6.31 Creating a basic road map to strengthen primary care entails many steps...... 318
6.32 Out-of-pocket health expenses push many Vietnamese into poverty 319
6.33 Reliance on out-of-pocket health expenditures declines as countries develop and move toward universal health care 320
6.34 The current approach to expanding insurance coverage is unlikely to achieve 100 percent coverage by 2035 321
6.35 The old-age dependency ratio will increase rapidly......................... 325
6.36 The Vietnamese people expect the state to be their primary source of support in old age... 326
6.37 Pension coverage should increase as Vietnam moves to upper-middle-income status, 2013................................... 327
6.38 Vietnam currently has low pension spending, but this is expected to rise quickly in coming years 327
6.39 Vietnam has a large "missing middle" of old-age support................. 328
6.40 Social assistance coverage and generosity vary across provinces but were in line with or slightly above East Asia Pacific neighbors 329
7.1 There is a long-term correlation between good governance and prosperity, 1996–2013 342
7.2 Corruption is a continuing challenge....................................... 345
7.3 Rule of law continues to be weak 346
7.4 Where private business interest ends and government begins is still being negotiated in Vietnam 348
7.5 Transparency and preferential access to information are major hindrances to economic efficiency... 350
7.6 Corruption in public administration is a widespread concern 352
7.7 A comparative assessment shows relatively weak protection of property rights in Vietnam 353
7.8 Membership of mass organizations and other voluntary groups is growing 354
7.9 Vietnam has low levels of transparency..................................... 355
7.10 Comparative ratings show relatively low judicial independence in Vietnam 356
7.11 Vietnam's legislature and judiciary do not constitute strong checks on the executive 357
7.12 A strengthened center will serve Vietnam well in streamlining resources and operations... 359

Maps

4.1 Urban expansion in the Ho Chi Minh City agglomeration 211
4.2 Many industrial zones are empty in the periphery of Ho Chi Minh City metropolitan region.................................. 213
4.3 Industrial output values per km^2 are highest in Hanoi and Ho Chi Minh City.....216
4.4 Hanoi's street space is ill suited for urban transport 227
6.1 Geography alone does not explain poverty in Vietnam 289

Tables

O.1 Logistics Performance Index rankings 28
1.1 Average annual growth in real GDP 94
1.2 Overview of the Trans-Pacific Partnership and Free Trade Area of the Asia-Pacific impacts on Vietnam, 2015–35 96
B2.3.1 Structure of the economy, supply side 126
B2.3.2 Structure of the economy, demand side 126
2.1 Sources of growth in Vietnam, 1990–2013 128
2.2 Sectoral GDP and productivity growth, 1990–2035 128
B2.5.1 Labor productivity growth in Vietnam, China, and the Republic of Korea 134
2.3 Logistics Performance Index rankings 156
2A.1 Main results 158
2A.2 Selected agribusiness sectors and upgrading potential in Vietnam 159
2A.3 Vietnamese unit prices for key export crops compared with world averages 160
2A.4 Main global motor vehicle parts suppliers in Vietnam 160
2A.5 Classification of sectors for investment 161
2B.1 Sources of GDP growth in Vietnam 162
3.1 Vietnam's ability to identify, adapt, and invent new technologies and to become more productive and diversify into new goods is weak 172
3.2 Vietnam is far behind comparator countries in patenting activity, reflecting weak research and development activity 174
3.3 Workforce skills suffer from structural deficiencies in the tertiary education system 176
3.4 Vietnam is weak in ease of paying taxes and starting a business, protecting investors, and resolving insolvency—all essential to doing business 183
3.5 Vietnam's doctoral students are an increasing presence in the United States, but their numbers fall short of Asian competitors 191
3.6 The share of the age cohort attending tertiary education has grown in many national systems 192
3.7 University faculty have improved qualifications, with one in six faculty now having a doctorate and more than half a master's degree 193
4.1 Urbanization of land and people, 1995–2015 210
4.2 Occupancy rates of industrial zones with comparable zoning and boundary definitions 212
4.3 Access to services is converging for urban and rural residents 220
4.4 Criteria assessment of cities upgraded from Class II to Class I 224
4.5 Types of master plans and plans in Vietnam 225
B5.2.1 The downside of agricultural growth is a large and extensive environmental footprint 249
B5.3.1 The estimated cost of poor sanitation-related impacts is US$780 million 255
5.1 Vietnam has a high and increasing exposure to gradual-onset impacts of climate change 258
5.2 Climate change and sea-level rise will affect yields and production of key crops 260
5.3 Cumulative inflation surpassed tariffs and percentage increase show that real electricity prices are among the lowest in the region 264
5.4 Trade-offs should be balanced with the urgency required for the measures 276

6.1 Vietnam has experience dramatic improvements in a range of social indicators.... 285
6.2 Countries have different criteria in setting minimum wages 309
6.3 Comparator countries averaged a 0.7 percent increase in total health expenditure, with out-of-pocket expenses decreasing 9 percent, 1990–2015.... 321
6.4 Alternative routes to 100 percent insurance coverage 322
6.5 International experience indicates that strong accountability matters most in delivering health care—not public or private provision 323
6.6 Vietnam has a high social contribution rate for pensions.................. 328
7.1 A demographic snapshot of the civil service 361

Foreword

After 30 years of economic reforms since the launch of *Đổi Mới* in 1986, Vietnam has recorded significant and historic achievements. From a poor, war-ravaged, centrally planned economy, which was closed off from much of the outside world, Vietnam has become a middle-income country with a dynamic market economy that is deeply integrated into the global economy. Vietnam's economic growth has been not only rapid but also stable and inclusive, translating into strong welfare gains for the vast majority of the population. This is an impressive record of success—one that the Vietnamese people take justifiable pride in, while appreciating the support of the international community.

But 30 years of success from reforms raises expectations for the future. The country's ambitions are aptly captured in the Vietnamese constitution, which sets the goal of "a prosperous people and a strong, democratic, equitable, and civilized country." There is a firm aspiration that by 2035, Vietnam will be a modern and industrialized nation moving toward becoming a prosperous, creative, equitable, and democratic society.

Motivated by these aspirations, in July 2014, the Government of Vietnam and the World Bank Group jointly initiated the *Vietnam 2035* report.

The report recognizes six key transformations that will help Vietnam achieve its goals for 2035: (1) to enable economic modernization with a competitive private sector firmly in the lead; (2) to improve the country's technological and innovation capacity; (3) to reshape urban policies and investments for more dynamic cities and urban centers; (4) to chart an environmentally sustainable development path with increasing adaptation and resilience to changing climate patterns; (5) to promote equality and inclusion among marginalized groups for the development of a harmonious middle-class society; and (6) to establish a modern rule-of-law state and a democratic society.

Vietnam 2035 structures these transformations and the reform agenda around three key pillars: balancing economic prosperity with environmental sustainability; promoting equity and social inclusion; and enhancing the capacity and accountability of the state.

We are delighted by the close partnership between the experts of Vietnam and the World Bank Group and other international scholars that has characterized the preparation of the report, *Vietnam 2035: Toward Prosperity, Creativity, Equity, and Democracy.* We hope that the Government of Vietnam, the World Bank Group, and other development partners will continue the effective collaboration in incorporating the report's relevant recommendations in the Socio-Economic Development Plan 2016–20 and the Socio-Economic Development Strategy 2021–30, as well as in the oversight and evaluation of the implementation process.

Nguyễn Tấn Dũng
Prime Minister
Socialist Republic of Vietnam

Jim Yong Kim
President
World Bank Group

Preface and Acknowledgments

The report, *Vietnam 2035: Toward Prosperity, Creativity, Equity, and Democracy,* is a joint initiative of the Government of Vietnam and the World Bank Group formally forged between Prime Minister Nguyễn Tấn Dũng and President Jim Yong Kim in July 2014.

The report was written by a Vietnamese–World Bank Group team under the supervision and guidance of Deputy Prime Minister Vu Duc Dam; Minister of Planning and Investment Bui Quang Vinh; Axel van Trotsenburg, World Bank Group Vice President for East Asia and Pacific; Victoria Kwakwa, Country Director for Vietnam; and Sudhir Shetty, World Bank Group Chief Economist for East Asia and Pacific. Gratitude for insightful advice is extended to members of the Steering Committee for the Vietnam 2035 Report: Prof. Nguyen Xuan Thang (President, Vietnam Academy of Social Sciences), Nguyen VanTung (Vice Chairman of the Office of Government), Nguyen Ngoc Bao (Vice Chairman, Economic Commission of the Central Committee of the Communist Party of Vietnam), Bui Thanh Son (Vice Minister of Foreign Affairs), Truong Chi Trung (Vice Minister of Finance), Nguyen Toan Thang (Deputy Governor), and Prof. Bui Tat Thang (President, Development Strategy Institute).

The Ministry of Planning and Investment was assigned by the Government of Vietnam to coordinate the line ministries, agencies, and research institutes, and to collaborate with the World Bank Group in the preparation of the report. A joint Vietnam–World Bank Group coordination team was established, which was led by Dr. Cao Viet Sinh (former Vice Minister of Planning and Investment), Victoria Kwakwa (Country Director), and Sandeep Mahajan (Lead Economist).

The Government of Australia, the Korea International Cooperation Agency (KOICA), and the U.K. Department of International Development (DFID) provided financial support for the report, which is gratefully acknowledged.

The report benefitted from invaluable comments from World Bank Group peer reviewers Ted Chu (Chief Economist), Mario Marcel (former Senior Director), Martin Rama (Chief Economist), and Ana Revenga (Senior Director), as well as reviewers who provided comments on the concept note and decision draft. We extend special thanks for the insights and recommendations on the Overview and chapters of the report from an advisory panel that comprised David Dollar (Brookings Institution), Ravi Kanbur (Cornell University), Homi Kharas (Brookings Institution), Danny Leipziger (Growth Dialogue and George Washington University), Vikram Nehru (Carnegie Endowment for International Peace), Mari Pangestu (Columbia University), Graham Teskey (Abt

JTA), and Mme Ton Nu Thi Ninh (Former Vice Chairwoman, Committee for External Affairs, National Assembly of Vietnam).

The report benefitted from the synergies between international expertise and local in-depth knowledge through effective team collaboration and valuable contributions of international and local consultants. The preparation process was broad-based and consultative, with active engagement of Vietnam's government ministries and agencies, academic research institutions, and international experts in numerous workshops and focus group discussions. Public engagement in the preparation of the report was facilitated through an online website, on-line discussions, live chats, as well as a national essay competition in Vietnam.

The English version of the report was edited by Bruce Ross-Larson and a team at Communications Development Incorporated that included Jonathan Aspin, Joe Caponio, and Mike Crumplar. Production and publication of the English version was managed by Rumit Pancholi, Susan Graham, and Patricia Katayama of the World Bank Group's Publishing and Knowledge Division, External Communications.

The Vietnam 2035 report has seven chapters and an Overview written by individual chapter teams, whose members are listed below in alphabetical order of their surnames.

Overview

Lead authors: Dr. Cao Viet Sinh (former Vice Minister of Planning and Investment), Gabriel Demombynes (Senior Economist), Victoria Kwakwa (Country Director), Sandeep Mahajan (Lead Economist), and Sudhir Shetty (Chief Economist).

Core team: Prof. Hoang The Lien (former Vice Minister of Justice), Dr. Nguyen Quang Thai (Secretary General, Vietnam Association of Economists), Nguyen Van Vinh (Vice President, Development Strategy Institute [DSI]), Pham Chi Lan (former Vice President of the Vietnam Chamber of Commerce and Industry), Dr. Vo Tri Thanh (Vice President, Central Institute for Economic Management [CIEM]), and Doan Hong Quang (Senior Economist).

The Overview builds on background papers and notes prepared by Manu Bhaskaran (Centennial Asia Advisors), Claus Brand (Consultant), David Dapice (John F. Kennedy School of Government, Harvard University), Do Thien Anh Tuan (Lecturer, Fulbright Economics Teaching Program), Sebastian Eckardt (Senior Economist), ImpactECON, LLC, Nguyen Xuan Thanh (Director, Fulbright Economics Teaching Program), and Dr. Vu Thanh Tu Anh (Director of Research, Fulbright Economics Teaching Program).

Thirty Years of Renovation and Vietnam's Aspirations for 2035

Lead authors: Prof. Bui Tat Thang (President, Institute for Development Strategy), Sandeep Mahajan (Lead Economist), Ray Mallon (Consultant), Nguyen Van Vinh (Vice President, DSI), and Dr. Vo Tri Thanh (Vice President, CIEM).

The chapter builds on background papers and notes prepared by Dr. Nguyen Duc Thanh (Director, Vietnam Institute for Economic and Policy Research), Dr. Nguyen Quang Thai (Secretary General, Vietnam Association of Economists), and Prof. Tran Dinh Thien (Director, Vietnam Institute of Economics).

Capable research assistance was provided by Dang Huyen Linh, Vu Thu Trang, Nguyen Dang Hung, Nguyen Thi Huong Giang, and Nguyen Thi My Hanh (DSI).

Enabling Economic Modernization and Private Sector Development

Lead authors: Mona Haddad (Practice Manager), Sandeep Mahajan (Lead Economist), Pham Chi Lan (former Vice President of the Vietnam Chamber of Commerce and Industry [VCCI]), and Pham Thi Thu Hang (Secretary General, VCCI).

Core team: Doan Hong Quang (Senior Economist), Claire Honore Hollweg (Economist), Steven Jaffee (Lead Rural Development Specialist), Nguyen Van Lan (Senior Operations Officer), and Daria Taglioni (Senior Trade Economist).

The chapter builds on background papers and notes prepared by Alwaleed Fareed Alabatani (Lead Financial Sector Specialist), Guillermo Arenas (Consultant), Reyes Aterido (Consultant), Ruth Banomyong (Consultant), Dr. Dang Kim Son (former Director of the Institute of Policy and Strategy for Agriculture and Rural Development [IPSARD]), David Dollar (Brookings Institutions), Dang Hung Vo (Consultant), Mary Hallward-Driemeier (Senior Principal Specialist), Stacey Frederick (Consultant), Gian Thanh Cong (Consultant), James Hanson (Consultant), Tanja Goodwin (Private Sector Development Specialist), Claire Honore Hollweg (Economist), Victor Kümmritz (Consultant), Dr. Le Dang Doanh (former President, CIEM), William Mako (Consultant), Miles McKenna (Consultant), Martha Martinez Licetti (Lead Specialist), Martin Molinuevo (Consultant), Ben Shepard (Consultant), Dr. Nguyen Do Anh Tuan, (Director, IPSARD), Dr. Nguyen Dinh Cung (President, CIEM), Dr. Nguyen Thi Tue Anh (Vice President, CIEM), Georgiana Pop (Senior Economist), Timothy Sturgeon (Massachusetts Institute of Technology), Prof. Tran Van Tho (Waseda University, Japan), Vu Kim Hanh (Director, Center for Business Research and Support), Deborah Winkler (Consultant), Dr. Vu Thanh Tu Anh (Director of Research, Fulbright Economics Teaching Program), Chunlin Zhang (Lead Private Sector Development Specialist), and Ezequiel Zylbeberg (University of Oxford).

Capable research assistance was provided by Gian Thanh Cong (Consultant).

The chapter team is grateful for useful comments and advice from: Danny Leipziger (Growth Dialogue and George Washington University), Catherine Martin (Principal Strategy Officer), and Daniel Street (Operations Officer).

Building National Innovation Capacity

Lead authors: Dr. Banh Tien Long (former Vice Minister of Education and Training), Michael Crawford (Lead Education Specialist), Dr. Le Dinh Tien, (former Vice Minister of Science and Technology), and William Maloney (Chief Economist).

The chapter builds on background papers and notes prepared by Nicholas Bloom, Raissa Ebnerb, Kerenssa Kayc, Renata Lemosd, Raffaella Sadune, Daniela Scurf, and John Van Reeneng (World Management Survey), Hyunho Kim (Chonnam National University), Dr. Hyungsun Kim (Inha University, Korea), Dr. Nguyen Van Duong (Senior Expert, Ministry of Education and Training), Mr. Nguyen Vo Hung (Head of Reform Policy and Technology Market Department, Vietnam Institute of Science and Technology Policy), Mr. Nguyen Manh Quan (Vice President, Vietnam Institute of Science and Technology Policy), Dr. Pham Thi Thanh Hai (lecturer, Hanoi National University), Joonghae Suh (Korea Development Institute), Dr. Tran Thi Ha (former Director General, Education Department, Ministry of Education and Training) and Deok Soon Yim (Science and Technology Policy Institute).

The team is grateful for comments and advice from: Prof. Dr. Hoang Van Phong (Chairman, National Council for Science and Technology, former Minister of Science and Technology) and Dr. Tran Ngoc Ca (head of office, Office of Science and Technology, Vietnamese Embassy in Washington, DC).

Managing Urbanization for Greater Economic Efficiency

Lead authors: Dr. Huynh The Du (Fulbright School of Public Policy), Somik Lall (Lead Urban Economist), Dr. Nguyen Do Anh Tuan (Director, IPSARD), and Madhu Raghunath (Senior Urban Specialist).

The chapter builds on background papers and notes prepared by Luis Blancas (Senior Transport Specialist), David

Bulman (Consultant), Dr. Dang Kim Khoi (IPSARD), Edward Leman (Consultant), Dr. Nguyen Anh Phong (IPSARD), Truong Thi Thu Trang (Deputy Head of Faculty, IPSARD), and Pablo Vaggione (Consultant).

The chapter team is grateful for useful comments and advice from: Zoubida Allaoua (Senior Regional Advisor), Judy Baker (Lead Economist), Abhas Jha (Practice Manager), Danny Leipziger (Growth Dialogue and George Washington University), Paul Vallely (Senior Transport Specialist), and Anna Wellenstein (Practice Manager).

Achieving Sustainable and Climate-Resilient Growth

Lead authors: Diji Chandrasekharan Behr (Senior Natural Resources Economist) and Prof. Truong Quang Hoc (former Director of the Center for Research Resources and Environment, Vietnam National University).

Core team: Anjali Acharya (Senior Environmental Specialist), Prof. Bui Quang Tuan (Director, Vietnam Institute for Regional Sustainable Development), Todd Johnson (Lead Energy Specialist), and Prof. Nguyen Trung Thang (Vice Director, Institute of Strategy and Policy on Natural Resources and the Environment).

The chapter builds on background papers and notes prepared by Tijen Arin (Senior Environmental Economist), Christophe Crepin (Sector Leader), Richard Damania (Lead Economist), Franz Gerner (Lead Energy Specialist), Sarath Guttikunda (Consultant), Steven Jaffee (Lead Rural Development Specialist), Iain Menzies (Senior Water and Sanitation Specialist), Tae Yong Jung (Yonsei University), Sung Jin Kang (Koera University), Joo Young Kwak (Yonsei University), and Truong Thi Thu Trang, Dang Kim Khoi, Kim Van Chinh, Nguyen Thi Cam Nhung, Nguyen Van Lam, and Pham Kim Dung (all IPSARD).

Capable research assistance was provided by Nguyen Phuong Nga (Consultant).

The chapter team is grateful for useful comments and advice from: Carter Brandon (Lead Economist), Christophe Crepin (Sector Leader), Richard Damania (Lead Economist), Douglas J. Graham (Senior Environmental Specialist), and Iain Shuker (Practice Manager).

Promoting Equity and Social Inclusion

Lead authors: Prof. Dang Nguyen Anh (Director, Institute of Sociology), Gabriel Demombynes (Senior Economist), and Philip O'Keefe (Lead Economist).

Core team: Michael Crawford (Lead Education Specialist), Puja Vasudeva Dutta (Senior Economist), Prof. Giang Thanh Long (Director, Institute of Public Policy), Dr. Nguyen Thang (Director, Center for Analysis and Forecast), Dr. Nguyen Thi Lan Huong (Director General, Institute of Labour, Invalids and Social Affairs), Truman Packard (Lead Economist), Achim Daniel Schmillen (Economist), and Owen Smith (Senior Economist).

The chapter builds on background papers and notes prepared by Reena Badiani-Magnusson (Senior Economist), Kari Hurt (Senior Operations Officer), and Vu Hoang Linh (Economist).

Capable research assistance was provided by Tran Thi Ngoc Ha (Consultant).

The chapter team is grateful for useful comments and advice from Ravi Kanbur (Cornell University) and Ana Revenga (Senior Director).

Building Modern Institutions for an Effective State

Lead authors: Prof. Hoang The Lien (former Vice Minister of Justice), Jonathan Pincus (Rajawali Foundation, Indonesia), and Charles Undeland (Senior Governance Specialist).

Core team: Soren Davidsen (Senior Public Sector Specialist), Dr. Nguyen Van Cuong (Deputy Director, Institute of Legal Science), and Tran Thi Lan Huong (Senior Public Sector Specialist).

The chapter builds on background papers and notes prepared by Maridel Alcaide (Consultant), Dr. Bui Nguyen Khanh (Deputy Director, Institute of State and Law), Noah Buckley (Consultant), Professor Yoon Je Cho (Consultant), Dr. Duong Thanh Mai (former Director, Institute of Legal Science), Prof. Nguyen Nhu Phat (Director, Institute of State and Law), Prof. Pham Duy Nghia (Fulbright School of Public Policy), Dr. Thang Van Phuc (former Vice Minister of Home Affairs), Vu Hoang Quyen (Senior Economist), Vu Thanh Tu Anh, David Dapice, Nguyen Xuan Thanh and Do Thien Anh Tuan (Fulbright Economic Teaching Program, Vietnam).

The chapter team is grateful for guidance and advice from: James Anderson (Country Manager), Robert Taliercio (Practice Manager), and Graham Teskey (Principal Technical Lead, Governance, Abt JTA).

Additional editing of the report was handled by a Vietnamese editorial team with participation of Dr. Cao Viet Sinh (former Vice Minister of Planning and Investment, team leader), Prof. Hoang The Lien (former Vice Minister of Justice), Dr. Nguyen Quang Thai (Secretary General, Vietnam Association of Economists), Nguyen Van Vinh (Vice President, DSI), Pham Chi Lan (former member of Prime Minister's Economic Advisory Board), Dr. Vo Tri Thanh (Vice President, CIEM), and Doan Hong Quang (Senior Economist).

The administrative coordination was carried out by the Administration Office of the Vietnam 2035 Steering Committee set up at the DSI. The Committee included: Prof. Bui Tat Thang (President), Nguyen Van Vinh (Vice President), Nguyen Thi Huong Giang, Bui Thi Thuong, Dang Huyen Linh, Dinh Thi Ninh Giang, Doan Thanh Tung, Le Quang Dao, Nguyen Quoc Truong, Nguyen Thi My Hanh, Nguyen Dang Hung, Nguyen Quynh Trang, Pham Le Hau, Pham Le Hoang, Pham Minh Thao, Pham Thanh Hien, and Vu Thu Trang.

In addition, administrative activities were coordinated with by the officials of the Government Office, including: Le Hong Lam (Director, Department for International Relations), Nguyen Huu Lam Son (Expert), Ho Anh Tai (Expert, Department for International Relations).

Administration and communications activities from the World Bank Group side were managed by Bo Thi Hong Mai (Senior Communications Officer), Tran Kim Chi (Communications Associate), Vu Lan Huong (Communications Associate), Nguyen Hong Ngan (Communications Officer), and Vu Thi Anh Linh (Program Assistant).

It is with great pleasure that the Ministry of Planning and Investment and the World Bank Group introduce the report *Vietnam 2035: Toward Prosperity, Creativity, Equity, and Democracy* with the hope that Vietnamese leaders and policy-making agencies will find it useful.

Bùi Quang Vinh
Minister of Planning and Investment
Socialist Republic of Vietnam

Axel van Trotsenburg
Vice President for East Asia and Pacific
World Bank Group

Executive Summary

The year 2015 marks 70 years since Vietnam's Declaration of Independence, 40 years since Reunification, and just short of 30 years from the launch of *Đổi Mới*, which catapulted the nation from the ranks of the world's poorest to one of its great development success stories. Critical ingredients of success have been visionary leaders, a sense of shared societal purpose, and a focus on the future. Starting in the late 1980s, these elements were fused with the embrace of markets and the global economy, setting the nation on the path to becoming the middle-income country that it is today. Its spectacular growth since then, one of the fastest in the world, has all but eliminated extreme deprivation and lifted tens of millions of people out of poverty.

Looking forward to 2035, which will mark 60 years since Reunification, Vietnam now aspires to modernity, industrialization, and a higher quality of life. These aspirations and the supporting policy and institutional agenda stand on three pillars: balancing economic prosperity with environmental sustainability, promoting equity and social inclusion, and bolstering the state's capacity and accountability. The rapid growth needed to achieve these aspirations will be sustained only if it stands on faster productivity growth and reflects the costs of environmental degradation. Productivity growth, in turn, will benefit from measures to enhance the competitiveness of domestic enterprises, scale up the benefits of urban agglomeration, and nurture a creative and innovation-led economy. Maintaining the record on equity and social inclusion will require lifting marginalized groups and delivering services to an aging and urbanizing middle-class society. And to fulfill the country's aspirations, the institutions of governance will need to become modern, transparent, and fully rooted in the rule of law.

Balancing Economic Prosperity with Environmental Sustainability

The goalposts for Vietnam's future economic success are set broadly and aspirationally—the 2013 constitution sets the objective of a "prosperous people and strong country," marking little deviation from its 1992 version. Party and government documents couch the income objectives in similarly aspirational terms, with an annual gross domestic product (GDP) per capita growth target of 7 percent (equal to around 8 percent annual growth). Growth rates in this range would produce by 2035 an upper-middle-income country on the cusp of high income—at the level of Malaysia or the Republic of Korea in the mid-2000s. But this target is extremely ambitious, far surpassing

Vietnam's past growth and with few global precedents.

The Vietnamese qualities of thrift, discipline, and hard work will have to be deployed in full measure for the country to stay close to its aspirations. The national savings rate needs to remain high while the investment rate rises slightly. Discipline and hard work can help counter the projected rapid aging of the population. But more is needed. Productivity and innovation will eventually have to become the main drivers of growth. That will require policies to tackle the stagnation in productivity and long-term investments, especially in urban infrastructure and innovation capabilities.

What explains the stagnation in productivity? Public investment is not as efficient as it needs to be because of uncoordinated and often incoherent investment decisions of a fragmented state structure. There also is little doubt that most state-owned enterprises (SOEs) are inefficient producers. So widespread inefficiencies in state investment perpetuate the weak productivity trends across the economy. But they do not fully explain the decline in productivity growth, reasons for which are especially worrisome. A steady erosion in the productivity growth of the domestic private sector leaves it just as inefficient as the state sector—for two reasons. First, the institutional foundations for an advanced market economy are insufficiently developed, undermining private property rights and competition in product markets. Second, factor markets are governed by an unclear mix of allocation by markets and by fiat. Commercialized state institutions—whereby the state is directly involved in economic activity through SOEs and indirectly through the influence of vested interests—have ensured that land and capital allocations are guided as much by arbitrary administrative decisions as by efficient market signals.

Productivity is also hurt by malfunctioning land markets in at least two other ways. First, the urbanization of land is outpacing the urbanization of people, reducing urban population density and suppressing productivity gains from urban agglomeration. Second, obstacles to consolidation of small landholdings in agriculture are depressing small-landholder profits and sector productivity.

The sustainability of Vietnam's long-term growth is further threatened by environmental stresses. Growth in the past 25 years has imposed significant environmental costs. Rapid depletion of natural resources is a particular concern. Environmental pollution from urban and industrial wastewater leaves waterways toxic, while urban water and air pollution are beginning to pose serious health hazards, especially near Hanoi and Ho Chi Minh City, and particularly for children. Vietnam is also one of the countries most vulnerable to climate change, with settlements and economic activity in the Mekong Delta at especially heightened risk. Exacerbating the risks is rapidly growing energy consumption, increasingly reliant on coal-powered electricity generation. In recent years, Vietnam's increase in greenhouse gas emissions has been one of the world's fastest.

The reform agenda to unleash strong and sustainable economic growth will have four essential elements:

1. *Create an enabling environment for domestic enterprises.* The immediate emphasis needs to be on ensuring more competitive and productive domestic enterprises. Restructuring and equitizing SOEs will remain important, but will not be enough—fixing the nascent and weak domestic private sector commands even greater policy attention. This will involve strengthening the institutional foundations of the market economy, with emphasis on protecting property rights and enforcing competition policies. A stable, well-regulated, and inclusive financial sector and transparent and functioning land markets will also be crucial. A more capable and confident domestic private sector will deepen links with foreign firms, enabling the transfer of technology and know-how that are critical for higher productivity growth. More rewarding participation in global value chains will also come from a stronger services sector and

more extensive transport and network connectivity across the country and with trading partners. Finally, a more market-driven and commercial approach will be needed to modernize agriculture. Commitments under major international trade agreements (the Trans-Pacific Partnership in particular) offer a real opportunity to carry out many demanding and politically sensitive reforms.

2. *Spur learning and innovation.* Sustaining high growth over an extended period will depend on an aggressive agenda to spur learning and innovation. Neither enterprises nor knowledge and research institutions are currently motivated to focus adequately on this agenda. A national innovation system can improve the situation. On the demand side, it will encourage firms to seek out the best available knowledge and strengthen the technical and financial support to facilitate their learning. On the supply side, such a system will help build the skills of the workforce beyond its current proficiency in basic education, while raising the quality and relevance of research and advanced training in universities and government research institutes.

3. *Reshape urban policies and investments.* For Vietnam to succeed in its growth and economic modernization ambitions, its cities need to do more to nurture private enterprise and innovation, support the growth of industrial clusters integrated with global value chains, and attract and agglomerate talent. Playing this role credibly will involve reshaping policies and investments to amplify economic density in and around large metropolitan areas such as Ho Chi Minh City, Hanoi, Haiphong, and Da Nang, as well as a network of dynamic secondary cities; reduce the distance to markets to enable specialization; and equalize access to services between migrants and urban residents. Fulfilling this agenda will require functioning land markets, coordinated urban planning, and improved connective infrastructure.

4. *Sustain the environment.* There are three core elements of the reform agenda to sustain the environment: protect the quality of natural resources (air, land, and water); build climate resilience in economic planning, sectoral policies, and infrastructure investments; and find ways to tap more clean energy sources, including through regional power trade. Such a sustainable, inclusive, and resilient growth path calls for strong policies and institutions to coordinate actions and investments, smart investments (with private participation) that internalize environmental and climate costs, and more accessible data and information for decision making and monitoring progress.

Promoting Equity and Social Inclusion

Vietnam's emphasis on equity and social inclusion has always been strong. And it is one of the few countries to achieve high growth with equity. Its record rests on a foundation established by equitable land distribution in the late 1980s, effective delivery of basic services such as health and education, and public policy choices that equalized fiscal transfers across provinces with different levels of development. Vietnam wants to maintain that record. Its central socioeconomic philosophy—a market economy with socialist orientation—captures the balance in its preferences for equity and market-led growth.

Past performance and societal preferences notwithstanding, sustaining the positive equity trends is not something that Vietnam can take for granted, especially as the forces of urbanization, globalization, and the rising skill intensity of production take firmer root. Looking toward 2035, Vietnam needs to pursue a dual agenda for equity and social inclusion.

The unfinished inclusion agenda is ensuring equality of opportunity. While Vietnam has taken long strides in lifting living standards since *Đổi Mới*, significant groups remain marginalized, and the gaps in opportunity for children are wide between poor and wealthy households. An ethnic minority child is four times more likely than a Kinh child to die before her first birthday. More than half the children with severe disabilities never attend school.

Such exclusion stands in stark contrast to the fortunes of those at the top: over the last decade, the number of millionaires in Vietnam has tripled while malnutrition rates among ethnic minority children have hardly budged. Rectifying such inequities will require renewed efforts. Four elements of the equality of opportunity agenda for 2035 are key:

1. *Reduce the barriers to opportunities for ethnic minorities.* Targeted initiatives in education, nutrition, and sanitation can close the large gaps in opportunities for ethnic minority children. An approach of experimentation and evaluation, building on new insights from behavioral economics, could develop effective interventions in these areas. Policy actions would also become more effective through greater voice for ethnic minorities.

2. *Make people with disabilities full participants in society.* Vietnam has made strong commitments to the inclusion of people with disabilities but lags severely in implementation. Following the example of other countries, it can realize these promises by regularly monitoring commitments and by creating opportunities for people with disabilities and their families to be their own advocates through social organizations.

3. *Delink the household registration system from access to public services.* At least 5 million Vietnamese lack permanent registration in their place of residence and thus have limited access to public services, including schooling, health care, and such administrative services as registering a vehicle and applying for a birth certificate. While the force of the system has waned, it remains a source of inequality of opportunity and an effective tax on migration. Phased reform of the *hộ khẩu* system would place all citizens on an equal footing.

4. *Reduce gender gaps.* More opportunities for women in public leadership roles could be created by eliminating gender discrimination in the retirement age and using affirmative action as a short-term measure. Also critical is reducing the imbalance in the sex ratio at birth, now one of the world's highest, with 114 boys born for every 100 girls. The preference for sons would be reduced through expanding the pension system, reforming the population policy, and campaigning to highlight the value of daughters.

Two social megatrends will shape the emerging inclusion agenda unfolding in Vietnam. The first is the rise of the middle class, which will be increasingly urban and employed in the formal sector. By 2035 more than half of the Vietnamese people will be part of the global middle class (up from just over 10 percent today), with needs distinct from those of the mass of rural poor that characterized Vietnam in the past. The second is an extreme demographic shift, with the size of the elderly population climbing dramatically—making Vietnam one of the most rapidly aging countries in the world —and the working-age share of the population shrinking. Around 2035, the old-age dependency ratio—the number of people 65 years of age or older for every 100 people aged 15–64—will have risen to almost 22 (from under 10 today), while the working-age population will begin to decline in absolute terms. Four elements of the middle-class and aging population agenda are key:

1. *Expand the pension system to cover a majority of the population.* Given the challenges of rapid aging, expanding coverage to those in the informal sector will be possible only through a diversified system and a major reform to make it financially sustainable, including raising the retirement age.

2. *Ensure that nearly all children complete upper-secondary school with job-relevant skills.* One policy priority will be ending the exam-based allocation of upper-secondary-school places and replacing it with universal secondary-school attendance. Another is to continuously improve the quality and relevance of what students learn, to help them develop the noncognitive and complex problem-solving skills they need for a competitive labor market.

3. *Establish effective representation of workers through independent unions.* Vietnam needs to move toward an industrial relations system suited to a mature market economy, where the interests of workers, employers, and the state are more properly represented in a true bargaining process, following the recent commitments in a Trans-Pacific Partnership side agreement. In addition, labor market regulations could better balance the protection of workers with the flexibility to promote a vibrant formal sector.

4. *Achieve universal health coverage with a rebalanced delivery system.* Ensuring access to good quality health services without imposing financial hardship will entail both reforming the insurance regime and shifting health care from its current focus on hospitals toward high- quality primary care at the center of an integrated system.

Bolstering the State's Capacity and Accountability

Political and institutional reforms need to keep pace with Vietnam's development. Evidence from a large number of countries indicates that state effectiveness, or the capacity of government to set objectives and attain them, is closely associated with better development outcomes. State effectiveness rests on three supporting pillars: a well-organized government with a disciplined, meritocratic bureaucracy; an adherence to market rationality in economic policy making; and mechanisms to ensure checks and balances in the government and broad public participation. All three legs of the state effectiveness tripod are necessary for satisfactory results. Reforming state structures but rejecting market discipline, or assigning a larger role to the market mechanism while insulating government decision making from the community, are unlikely to generate positive outcomes.

The relationship between state effectiveness and development outcomes is evident in Vietnam. Many early achievements emerged from the country's state capacity, which was unusually strong for its level of income. Today, the productivity stagnation and the weak environment for private-sector development are attributable to gaps in state effectiveness. Vietnam's unique history has produced state institutions that are commercialized and fragmented and face insufficient scrutiny by citizens.

State commercialization in Vietnam refers to the continued strong engagement of the state in economic activity directly through SOEs, particularly through large state economic groups, and indirectly through very close links with an exclusive segment of the domestic private sector. Vietnam is not alone in having influential vested interests, but the degree to which relationships to the state are integral to economic success appears to be unusually high. State fragmentation refers to the lack of clear hierarchy and assignment of roles and responsibilities both within the central government and between the center and the provinces—and the inertia and inefficiencies this generates in formulating and implementing policy. Horizontal and vertical fragmentation of power has resulted in overlapping mandates with conflicting rules and decisions. The result is often gridlock or decisions that are suboptimal from society's point of view. The absence of merit-based management of public servants exacerbates the adverse effects of commercialization and fragmentation of the Vietnamese state on the quality of public administration.

Vietnam's legal framework provides some space for citizens to participate in governance. "Government of the people, by the people, and for the people" and "People know, people discuss, people do, and people monitor" are well known affirmations in the constitution. In practice, there is a gap between these statements and the actual space that is available for citizens to influence decisions. Citizen participation in social organizations not sponsored by the government is growing rapidly, but this does not mean a corresponding improvement in the quality of their participation. Election processes and mechanisms for engaging citizen organizations are not robust enough to provide true citizen representation, and Vietnam lacks a system of effective checks and balances between the three branches of government. Access to information, which is key to citizens exercising their voice to hold the state accountable, is still lacking.

The result is a government that often finds it difficult to articulate coherent economic policies, that is open to extensive bargaining among state institutions and between the state and private sectors, and that is shielded from public scrutiny of policy decisions and public reaction to the consequences of economic policy.

Modernization of Vietnamese institutions will involve an overhaul of the state and its relationships to the market and society. Efforts to enhance state capacity and accountability will need to move concurrently on a three-point agenda:

1. *Develop a more rationally organized government structure with a meritocratic bureaucracy.* The government needs more rational organization, and greater coherence on roles and responsibilities among state institutions. This will involve decentralization embodying clearer functional assignments for the different levels of government, with corresponding adjustments in the intergovernmental financial framework that clarify and improve accountability and overcome inefficiencies in coordination and use of public resources. The center of government could be strengthened to improve policy coordination and oversight of execution of policies by public agencies. A clearer allocation of powers and responsibilities is needed among central bodies to have greater effectiveness and accountability. Public administration practices need to be reformed to ensure that merit drives the deployment of human resources by the state.

2. *Apply market rationality to economic policy making.* State–market relations will have to be characterized by a clearer division between the public and private spheres. Specifically, government agencies involved in economic regulation should not engage in business of any kind, to avoid the appearance and reality of conflicts of interest. The state's role in the economy needs to be transformed from a producer to an effective regulator and facilitator, focusing on providing a level playing field in the economy with enforcement of free and fair competition and more secure and transparent property rights, particularly around land issues. This will require the state not only to significantly reduce its SOE portfolio and strengthen corporate governance of the remaining SOEs but also to stop giving preferential treatment to SOEs and closely linked private companies. In addition, there needs to be an independent and more capable, trained, and meritocratic judiciary to enforce rules and provide the level playing field. Creating the space for a genuinely independent private sector will require reduced state control over business and professional organizations, including the Vietnam Chamber of Commerce and Industry. Allowing these organizations to operate as authentic representatives of independent business interests would give voice to the domestic private sector and enable these groups to do more in monitoring government policy.

3. *Strengthen state accountability.* The state can be organized in a way that provides for genuine checks and balances among the executive, legislature, and judiciary. The National Assembly could be transformed into a professional body (consisting of full-time deputies and supported by expert staff), with oversight of all the state's operations. The judiciary needs to be similarly strengthened, with emphasis on its independence from the executive and enhanced transparency in its functioning. A large and diverse set of citizen organizations could be allowed to participate in decision making and hold the state accountable. The state could provide a legal framework to promote the right of citizens to associate. It could also adopt legislation requiring public bodies to be transparent and provide mechanisms for citizens to interact effectively with the state by enhancing citizen access to accurate and timely information and by providing greater media independence.

Abbreviations

3D	three dimensional
AFTA	ASEAN Free Trade Area
AIIB	Asian Infrastructure Investment Bank
ALTC	aged and long-term care
ASEAN	Association of Southeast Asian Nations
CEO	chief executive officer
CMI	climate moisture index
CVT	continuously variable transmission
DIV	Deposit Insurance of Vietnam
EAP	East Asia and Pacific
EDB	Economic Development Board
FDI	foreign direct investment
FSQL	Fundamental School Quality Level
GCM	global climate model
GDP	gross domestic product
GERD	gross expenditure for research and development
GRI	government research institute
GSO	General Statistics Office
GVC	global value chain
HDI	Human Development Index
HSR	high-speed rail
ICT	information and communications technology
IFC	International Finance Corporation
ILO	International Labour Organization
IMF	International Monetary Fund
IPCC	Intergovernmental Panel on Climate Change
IPR	intellectual property rights
IT	information technology

KOSIS	Korean Statistical Information Service
LMIC	low- and middle-income country
LPI	Logistics Performance Index
MARD	Ministry of Agriculture and Rural Development
MDC	matching defined contribution
MITI	Ministry of International Trade and Industry
MOET	Ministry of Education and Training
MOHA	Ministry of Home Affairs
MOHRSS	Ministry of Human Resources and Social Security
MOLISA	Ministry of Labour, Invalids, and Social Affairs
MONRE	Ministry of Natural Resources and Environment
NAFOSTED	National Foundation for Science and Technology Development
NBSC	National Bureau of Statistics of China
NCCD	National Coordinating Council on Disability
NDC	Nationally Determined Contribution
NHSO	National Health Security Office
NIS	national innovation system
NPL	nonperforming loan
OECD	Organisation for Economic Co-operation and Development
OOP	out-of-pocket
PAR	Public Administration Reform
PCI	Provincial Competitive Index
PES	payments for environmental services
PFES	paying for ecosystem services
PISA	Programme for International Student Assessment
PPC	Provincial People's Committee
PPP	purchasing power parity
R&D	research and development
R&E	research and exploration
S&T	science and technology
SBV	State Bank of Vietnam
SDG	Sustainable Development Goal (of the United Nations)
SME	small and medium enterprise
SOE	state-owned enterprise
SRB	sex ratio at birth
SSF	State Shareholding Fund
STI	science, technology, and innovation
STRI	Services Trade Restrictions Index
TFP	total factor productivity
TiVA	Trade in Value-Added
TPP	Trans-Pacific Partnership
UCS	Universal Coverage Scheme

UN	United Nations
UNDP	United Nations Development Programme
UNICEF	United Nations Childrens' Fund
VAMC	Vietnam Asset Management Company
VAT	value-added tax
VCA	Vietnam Competition Authority
VGCL	Vietnam General Confederation of Labour
VHLSS	Vietnam Household Living Standards Surveys
VLSS	Vietnam Living Standards Surveys
VPI	Vietnam Productivity Institute
WDI	World Development Indicators
WGI	Worldwide Governance Indicators
WTO	World Trade Organization

Part I

Overview

Vietnam 2035

Toward Prosperity, Creativity, Equity, and Democracy

Introduction

Shaking off the legacy of colonization and long, brutalizing conflicts is hard—and forging an uninterrupted pathway to modernity, perhaps even harder. Only a handful of nations have succeeded at both. Their winning formula? Usually some combination of strong leadership and good governance, a sense of common purpose and future orientation, a reliance on markets to allocate resources, and active engagement with the world on trade, investment, and knowledge flows (Commission on Growth and Development 2008). Since the launch of the *Đổi Mới* (economic renovation) reforms in the late 1980s—to move from a closed, centrally planned economy to a globally integrated, socialist-oriented market economy—Vietnam has deployed these ingredients to good effect.

To any external observer, Vietnam is a major development success story. One of the world's poorest countries at the onset of the reforms, it has, in a single generation, leapfrogged to middle-income status, while achieving social outcomes typically seen at much higher incomes. Vietnam's economic growth since the early 1990s has been among the fastest in the world, and its pace of poverty reduction almost unprecedented. But the Vietnamese people, keenly aware of the big challenges left, are not yet ready to declare success. And for countries as for people, success needs to be measured not only against ability, effort, or even the performance of peers, but also against ambition.

The Vietnamese people have always set a high bar for success. The 1992 constitution exemplified this early on by setting forth the goal for the state to build "a prosperous life for its people, a strong country, and an equitable, democratic, and civilized society, ensuring the well-being, freedom, and happiness of all citizens as well as conditions for their all-round development." Success thus defined was both multifaceted and aspirational. There is also the strong sense that the journey may be just as important as the destination. The tenets of thrift, discipline, and hard work are cherished means to higher living standards in the Vietnamese value system, not to be diluted or lost along the way. So are societal values of equity, compassion, filial responsibility, respect for social norms and the rule of law, and the authority of elders and teachers.

The motivations that fuel Vietnam's ambitions are both external and internal. Externally, the driving force is Vietnam's neighborhood—the world's most dynamic region. Vietnamese mind-sets are steeped in the rapid ascents of Japan and the East Asian Tigers. They not only serve as powerful examples but also stoke fears of being permanently left behind. Internally, there is pride in a rich past—justifiable for a society with one of the world's longest continuous histories and civilizations.[1] As recently as the early 19th century, Vietnam was a regional powerhouse, with a much larger economy than those of Thailand, Malaysia, or the Philippines (The Maddison Project database, 2010). The drive to reclaim the country's place in the community of nations is accordingly strong.

Energized by past success but by no means content, Vietnam now aspires to modernity, industrialization, and a higher quality of life. The aspirations reflect an emphasis on clean water and clear blue skies; a healthy, secure, learned, and equitable society; and an effective state accountable for improving material welfare.

Achieving these aspirations will require bold and decisive action, both to grasp the opportunities and to manage risks. The notable opportunities are an emergent domestic middle class, proximity to a rapidly rising China, and megaregional trading agreements—particularly the Trans-Pacific Partnership (TPP), in which Vietnam is the only lower-middle-income member. The major risks are the rapid aging of the population, the less hospitable global economy, and the threat of climate change, to which Vietnam is heavily exposed. Global technological and business innovations, powered by the information revolution, will remain disruptive—presenting more opportunities and risks, with Vietnam's net benefits depending on its responses.

The country's aspirations and the supporting policy and institutional agenda thus stand on three pillars: balancing economic prosperity with environmental sustainability, promoting equity and social inclusion, and bolstering the state's capacity and accountability. The rapid growth needed to achieve these aspirations will be sustained only if it stands on faster productivity growth and reflects the costs of environmental degradation. Productivity growth, in turn, will benefit from measures to enhance the competitiveness of domestic enterprises, scale up the benefits of urban agglomeration, and nurture a creative and innovation-led economy. Maintaining the record on equity and social inclusion will require lifting marginalized groups and delivering services to an aging and urbanizing middle-class society. And to fulfill the country's aspirations, the institutions of governance will need to become modern, transparent, and fully rooted in the rule of law.

A Record of Strong and Equitable Growth, with Emerging Concerns

Vietnam is a major development success story. Its per capita GDP growth since 1990 has been among the fastest in the world, surpassed only by China. Growth has also been remarkably stable and inclusive, which, with major gains on human development, has contributed to impressive progress in alleviating poverty and improving nonincome dimensions of welfare. But declining productivity growth, insufficient progress in including marginalized groups in the country's development (ethnic minorities in particular), and degradation of the environment call into question the durability of the current development model. Vietnam's governance structure could also be at an inflection point. The institutions that were adequate to carry the country to its lower-middle-income level are now exposing gaps that, unless addressed with boldness and urgency, are likely to impede the journey to upper-middle-income status.

In 1986 an impoverished Vietnam, on the brink of an economic crisis, embarked on a path of economic renovation (*Đổi Mới*). It was an explicit recognition that the "fence-breaking" reforms of the previous decade—opportunistically initiated to test the limits of central planning—had shown promise and that the situation was dire enough to demand a more systematic approach. Annual inflation was running at more than 400 percent (Rama 2014), the real economy on a downward slide and heavily dependent on foreign aid (Tran 2015), food in short supply, the budget chronically short of resources (Vu et al. 2015), and the vast majority of the population in poverty.

Đổi Mới thus began a process of macroeconomic stabilization, unshackling the economy from state controls and gradually but steadily integrating with the global economy.[2] More durable foundations for a market economy were built over time. And in competently managing the transition from a planned to a market-economy structure, Vietnam succeeded where many countries that had been part of the former Soviet Union have failed.

Four aspects of the approach to reforms proved most effective. First, Vietnam chose to be pragmatic and flexible, both in the sequencing and the pacing of reforms. Reforms were introduced incrementally, after extensive consensus building, and wholesale shock therapies were avoided (Rama 2008). And if internal or global experience suggested course correction, the system proved adaptable. Second, Vietnam played to its strengths by focusing on labor-intensive production and agriculture. Third, the emphasis on building human capital was early and effective. Vietnam already had relatively high levels of literacy and life expectancy (Arkadie and Mallon 2003). The human-capital base was further expanded following *Đổi Mới*, enhancing the returns on the market-oriented reforms that followed. Fourth, where a domestic consensus was harder to forge, Vietnam used its commitments under external trade agreements to good strategic effect, particularly to usher in some of the more complex enterprise reforms. Each of these four aspects of the approach remains important for the next generation of reforms—a subject of this report.

Less than three decades after the start of the *Đổi Mới* reforms, Vietnam has built up an impressive record of strong economic growth that has also been equitable and stable, as shown in figure O.1. GDP growth per capita has averaged 5.5 percent a year since 1990 (panel a), yielding a three-and-a-half-fold increase in average income. Only China performed better. Growth has benefitted from its remarkable stability (panel b) and a strong external orientation of the economy. External trade has been a major driver (panel c), much of it powered by strong foreign direct investment, with the stocks standing at more than $250 billion, sourced from a diverse group of more than 100 countries. And growth has been inclusive, as seen in a fairly small increase in the Gini coefficient (panel d) and the faster income growth of the bottom 40 percent (panel e). As a result, poverty has fallen rapidly (panel f).

Vietnam in 2015 is an unrecognizably transformed, dynamic, middle-income economy. Social outcomes have improved dramatically across the board. Using a variety of international and national poverty lines, poverty has fallen rapidly since the launch of *Đổi Mới*. The $1.90-a-day poverty rate fell from 50 percent in the early 1990s to 3 percent today. Not only are incomes higher, but the Vietnamese population is better educated and has a higher life expectancy than most countries at a similar per capita income. In recent international tests, Vietnamese students outperformed the average for countries in the Organisation for Economic Co-operation and Development (OECD), with remarkably little variation across income groups and urban–rural locations. The maternal mortality ratio has fallen below the upper-middle-income country average, while under-five mortality has fallen by half, to a rate slightly above that average. Access to basic infrastructure has also improved substantially. Electricity is now available to almost all households, up from less than half in 1993. Access to clean water and modern sanitation has risen from less than 50 percent of all households to more than 75 percent.

In some areas, however, Vietnam has fallen short. Labor-productivity (output per worker) growth has been on a declining trend since the end of the 1990s, seen across most industrial subsectors, as well as in mining, finance, and real estate. In agriculture, labor productivity has grown robustly, but its level is still lower than in most of the region's middle-income countries. With almost half the workforce still engaged in agriculture, Vietnam has too many workers on its farms. Remedies include consolidating agricultural landholdings (which are too fragmented and small) and moving

FIGURE O.1 Rapid and inclusive growth in Vietnam has yielded shared prosperity and strong gains in poverty reduction

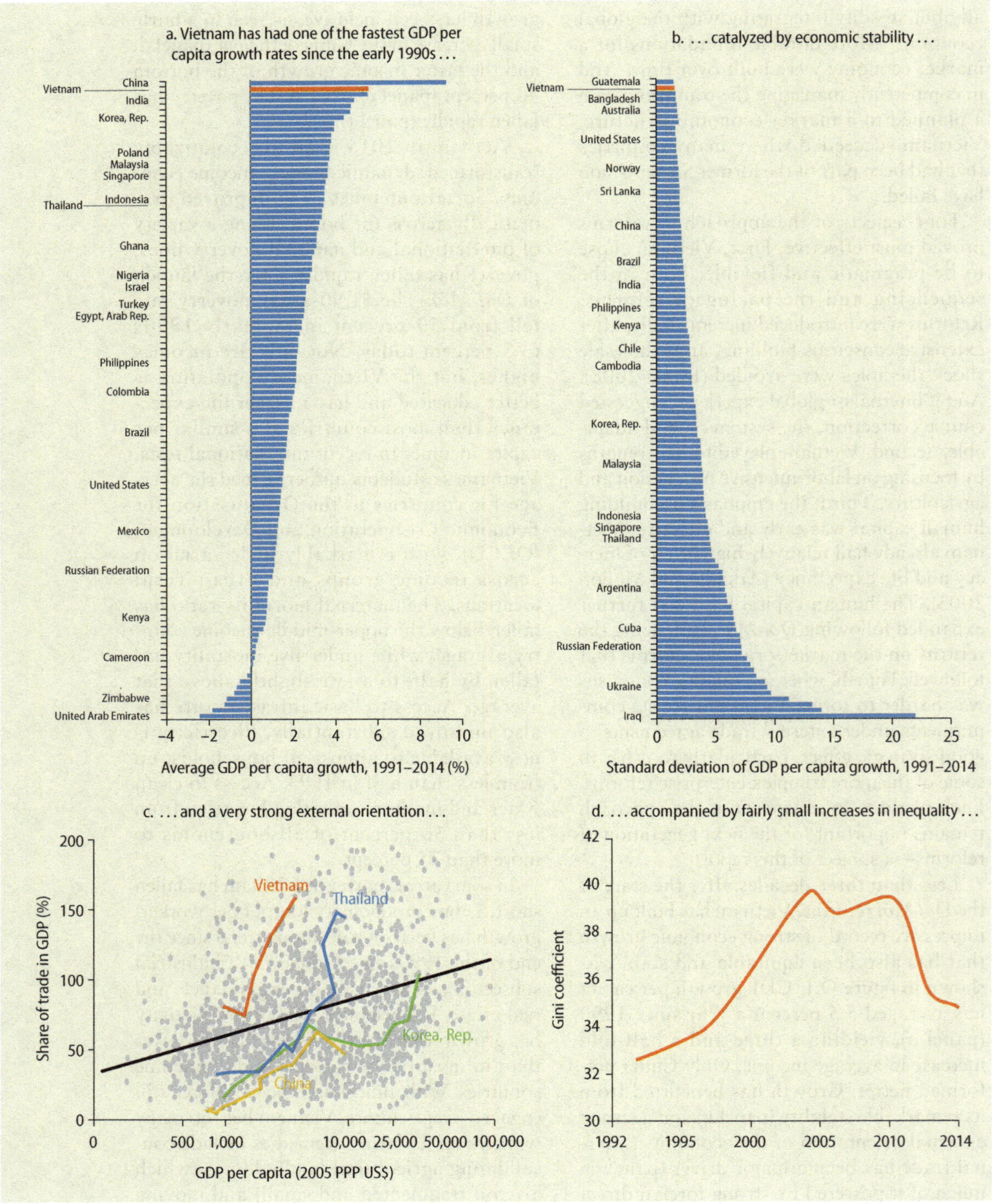

(figure continues next page)

FIGURE 0.1 Rapid and inclusive growth in Vietnam has yielded shared prosperity and strong gains in poverty reduction *(continued)*

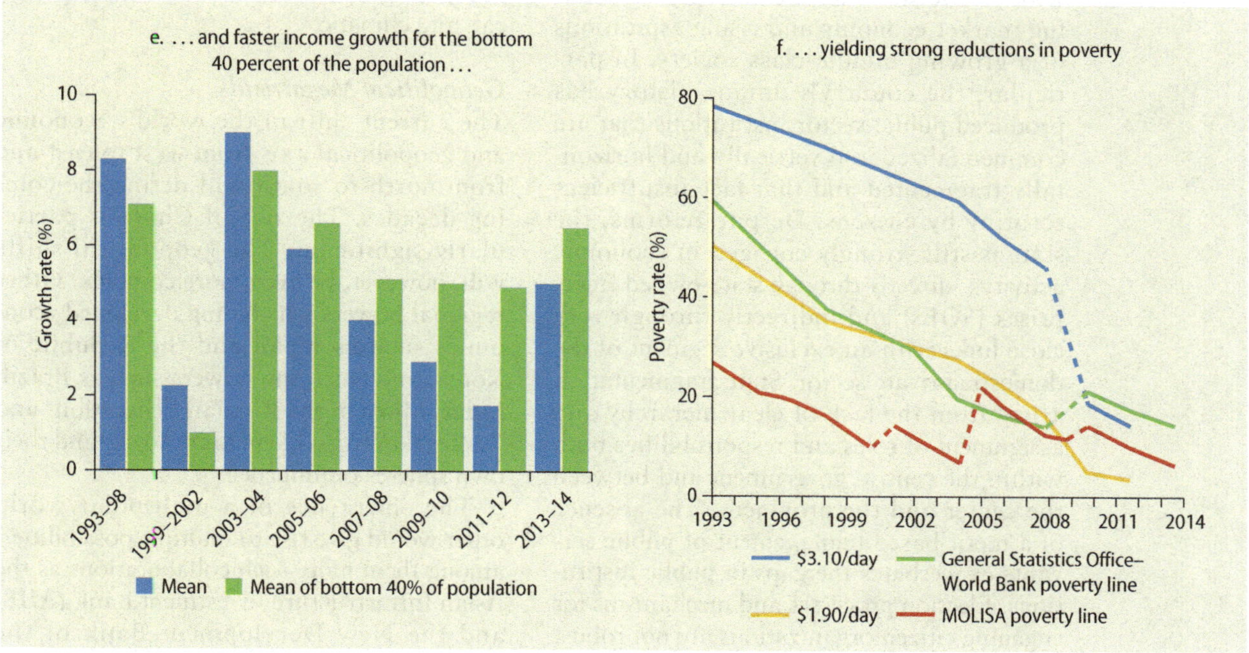

Sources: World Development Indicators; General Statistics Office of Vietnam; Penn World Table 8.0; and World Bank and Ministry of Planning and Investment of Vietnam calculations.
Note: Dotted lines in panel f indicate periods when substantial changes were made to poverty lines or methodologies. MOLISA = Ministry of Labour, Invalids and Social Affairs; PPP = purchasing power parity.

farmers to the more productive industry and service sectors. But it does not help that job creation in manufacturing has plateaued at a relatively low level and that services involve mostly informal activity.[3]

Although Vietnam has avoided the large increases in inequality in other fast-growing countries, the differences between rich and poor are still significant. While members of ethnic minorities have experienced gains in welfare since the early 1990s, they face a growing gap relative to the majority population. With 15 percent of the population, they now make up half the poor. And in recent years, progress for ethnic minorities has stalled on poverty reduction, child mortality, and nutrition. Many ethnic minority citizens remain largely disconnected from the country's larger economic success.

Growth has to a large extent come at the cost of the environment. Vietnam's greenhouse gas emissions have grown the fastest in the region, while the environmental quality of its air, land, and water has deteriorated considerably. Water and air pollution have reached serious levels, especially near Hanoi and Ho Chi Minh City, posing major health risks. In addition, a large part of Vietnam's protective mangrove forests has been destroyed, while overfishing has seriously depleted the nearshore fisheries, posing threats to livelihoods. Removing natural forests in some upland areas has contributed to more frequent and severe flooding of lower altitude farms and human settlements. Finally, Vietnam is one of the world's most vulnerable countries to climate change, with adaptation challenges accordingly severe, especially in the Mekong Delta. With almost all large-scale hydropower potential tapped and with limited development of other renewable sources, greater reliance on coal is a growing threat to environmental sustainability and to energy security.

Last but not least, Vietnamese institutions have failed to keep up in important ways with the needs of an increasingly demanding market economy and rising aspirations of a growing middle-class society. In particular, the country's unique history has produced public-sector institutions that are commercialized and vertically and horizontally fragmented and that face insufficient scrutiny by citizens. Despite reforms, the state is still strongly engaged in economic activity—directly through state-owned enterprises (SOEs) and indirectly through very close links with an exclusive segment of the domestic private sector. State fragmentation arises from the lack of clear hierarchy and assignment of roles and responsibilities both within the central government and between the center and the provinces. The absence of a merit-based management of public servants exacerbates the gaps in public institutions. Election processes and mechanisms for engaging citizen organizations are not robust enough to provide true citizen representation, and Vietnam lacks a system of effective checks and balances between the three branches of government.

Opportunities and Risks

Global Megatrends and External Risks and Opportunities

Vietnam's location on the easternmost edge of the Indochinese peninsula makes it a vital link between East, Southeast, and South Asia. The physical connection to these Asian regions and the maritime connections to the rest of the world have shaped Vietnam's history and will remain crucial for its future. But geography very likely will not be destiny in the same way that it was in the past. After all, the hyperconnectivity of the modern world (which Vietnam has signed on to) overcomes many of the binds of geography. Moreover, future opportunities and risks are projected to be largely supraregional. That will require geopolitical and economic outreach well beyond the neighborhood.

Four global megatrends will be important for Vietnam to consider in the next two decades:[4] geopolitical, economic, technological, and climatic.

Geopolitical Megatrends

The current shift in the world's economic and geopolitical axis from west to east and from north to south will define the coming decades. The rise of China is particularly significant. The geopolitical shifts will, however, be even more complex. Other regional powers—including developed economies such as Japan and the Republic of Korea, and emerging powers such as Brazil, India, Mexico, the Russian Federation, and Turkey—are also likely to try to expand their own spheres of influence.

The emergence of a multipolar world order would give rise to multiple possibilities, among them more such collaborations as the Asian Infrastructure Investment Bank (AIIB) and the New Development Bank of the BRICS states (Brazil, Russia, India, China, and South Africa). There could also be tensions or even conflicts among the rising powers, or among rising and existing powers.

Cooperative relations with a rising China will remain essential. Vietnam is one of the signatories to and founding members of the AIIB. Its infrastructure financing needs over the next several decades will run into tens of billions of dollars a year. With most bilateral partners reducing their presence in Vietnam, the AIIB could cover some of the emerging financing gap.

Of the geopolitical risks particularly relevant for Vietnam are maritime issues with China that go beyond just territorial concerns. The maritime waters have considerable economic and strategic value, containing a wealth of fish stocks and energy and mineral reserves. They are also critical for shipping and communications. With the Middle East in turmoil, the geopolitics of energy will also have implications for Vietnam both as a producer and exporter of crude oil and as a rapidly growing consumer of petroleum products.

In the midst of this fast-evolving world order, Vietnam will need to continue building its alliances judiciously with a clear eye on its long-term economic and political interests.

Global Economic Megatrends

The global economy is projected to grow at an average of 3.2 percent annually between 2015 and 2035, with continuing expansion in trade integration, urbanization, and technological advances the main drivers. The rise of China, India, and members of the Association of Southeast Asian Nations (ASEAN) matched by the (relative) decline of the United States, Europe, and Japan would be the most apparent shift in the global economic structure in coming decades.[5] China clearly is the biggest part of this story. In this report's projections, it would overtake the United States as the world's largest economy (in market prices) around 2032. It has been the world's largest exporter since 2009, and the second-largest importer of goods. It is set to become an important source of investment financing for emerging economies, particularly regionally.

Trade with China already accounts for 20 percent of Vietnam's total, up from 10 percent in 2000. The significant flow of foreign direct investment into Vietnam is linked, in part, to a shift in low-wage production from China. As real wages in China continue their sharp rise, many of its production bases will continue to look southward in search of lower wages—the "China+1 strategy." Vietnam's proximity to southern China, home to many of these production networks, gives it a meaningful competitive edge. Producers can benefit from its low wages and from being part of the Chinese supply chains at the same time—a highly attractive combination. The agglomeration of a nascent electronics-industrial cluster in the north-central parts of Vietnam (around Hanoi) is an early sign of these possibilities. Moreover, with a rapidly emerging middle class, the Chinese consumer market (the world's fastest growing) will be increasingly attractive for Vietnamese producers.

Growth prospects in East Asia will also be underpinned by the ongoing shift toward multilateral (often regional) trade agreements. The ASEAN integration—starting with the ASEAN Economic Community that became a functioning trading bloc in 2016—can bring considerable economic benefits. Estimates for Vietnam range from a 1 to 3 percent cumulative increase in national income (ERIA 2012 and Thanh 2015). Even so, ASEAN integration is seen in Vietnam as a stepping stone for locking in even more promising partnerships beyond the region (Thanh 2015). Especially noteworthy is the TPP. Also significant are the Free Trade Area of the Asia-Pacific and the Regional Comprehensive Economic Partnership, each in less advanced negotiations than the TPP.

The TPP agreement includes the world's largest and third-largest economies (the United States and Japan), with TPP countries accounting for 36 percent of world GDP and more than a quarter of all world trade. Vietnam is well positioned to benefit. According to this report's analysis, implementing the TPP could add a cumulative 8 percent to Vietnam's GDP by 2035. Others have estimated double-digit gains for Vietnam, many times larger than for any other TPP country (Petri and Plummer 2014). Vietnam could also usefully leverage commitments under the TPP to lock in policy reforms that might otherwise be politically harder to carry out.

Top-down multilateral trade integration is likely to be complemented by important subregional collaborations, including that within the Greater Mekong Subregion. Dwindling and increasingly unpredictable water supplies along with a rising demand for water and energy will require greater regional cooperation for energy and water security.

New Technological and Business Megatrends[6]

Technological innovations, fueled and supported by the information revolution, will disrupt production and trading patterns across the world. Advances in digital technologies ranging from three dimensional

(3D) printing, programmable microcontrollers, and second-generation computer numerical control milling and routing make it easier and less expensive to manufacture customized high-quality products. Major advances in renewable energy (particularly solar) are posing a growing challenge to conventional and usually environmentally more damaging energy sources. Next-generation genome sequencing and other advances in the biomedical field are set to open a trillion-dollar industry in the next decade, enhancing and extending human life. Advanced robots are being deployed on shop floors at an exponential rate, boosting productivity and driving costs down.

The information revolution is also enabling major disruptive innovations in business models. The Internet eradicates many of the information advantages of colocation and cost sharing. Raw materials and other inputs to various degrees of preprocessing are available for sourcing on the Internet. Online platforms such as Alibaba.com, Etsy, and Maker's Row make it possible for manufacturers to search for customers without having to spend a lot on advertising and distribution. Crowdfunding sites such as Indiegogo and Kickstarter can aid in attracting finance.

For the most part, these trends bring upside opportunities. But some unintended consequences have to be managed. Skill-intensive and labor-efficient technology is set to eliminate the more routine middle-income vocations while complementing highly skilled and thus higher-income jobs. Already, new technologies have displaced handicraft producers in numerous industries ranging from textiles to metalworking. The progress of technology may also increase inequality in society, as those leveraging technology gain higher incomes. The gap between labor productivity and wages may also widen. Some even raise the specter of premature deindustrialization in the developing world, partly because of automation (Rodrik 2015).

Vietnam, with its well-deserved reputation as a dynamic and adaptable economy, can view these disruptive innovations with optimism (box O.1). But to maximize the benefits, long-term investments will have to upgrade the technical skill sets of the next generation, and the domestic business environment will have to be the focus. Some technologies will have associated risks that require careful management.

Global Climate Change

Climate change is among the most consequential global issues. Greenhouse gas emissions are on a path to a 3.5–4.0 degrees Celsius (°C) warmer planet by the end of the century. Climatic conditions, heat, and other weather extremes considered highly unusual or unprecedented today could become the new normal. The impact of global climate change is already being felt, with the number of category 4 and 5 storms having risen sharply over the past 35 years. The Arctic Sea's ice has shrunk to its lowest on record, and global sea levels have risen about 10–20 centimeters in the past century, with an accelerating rate of shrinking. Rising sea levels increase the risk of storm surges and the fluctuations in precipitation.

Vietnam has been ranked among the five countries likely to be most affected by climate change. A high proportion of its population and economic assets are in coastal lowlands and deltas. Temperature increases in Vietnam have averaged about 0.26°C per decade since 1971, (Nguyen, Renwick, and McGregor 2013) twice the global average.[7] On current trends, annual average temperatures will (depending on the location) be 0.6–1.2°C higher by 2040 relative to 1980–99 (MONRE 2012). The predictions show intensified heat and cold waves, and 28–33 centimeter increases in sea level around Vietnam's shores.[8] Seasonal variability in precipitation is also projected to increase, with the wet season getting wetter and the dry season drier. Extreme rainfall and flooding would also become more likely, particularly in the northern region, including Hanoi, with increased risk of landslides in mountainous areas. A southward shift

BOX O.1 Potential benefits and risks of new technologies

Solar energy. Solar energy is largely available year round, especially in southern and central Vietnam. The potential market for solar panels and water-heating systems is significant, but progress is slow due to high development costs. Solar panels have been installed in the Nha Trang and other urban areas along the south-central coast and in rural, mountainous, and other remote areas that are difficult to reach with grid electricity.

Social mobility, analytics, and cloud services. These services present opportunities to catch up with the developed countries, if close cooperation among scientists, enterprises, and the government is established for the long term.

Genomics and life sciences. Potential benefits come from genetically modified foods and other advances in the life sciences. Improved varieties of corn can be used as feed to fatten hogs, which should have strong commercial prospects, especially with Vietnam forecast to consume 33 kilograms of pork per person by 2020 (more than China and the European Union). Genetically improved crops could also reduce the country's feed imports, which quadrupled between 2011 and 2014. Environmental and consumer groups are demanding more transparency on health risks and increased regulation of such products.

E-commerce. Opportunities are abundant, as foreign companies enter the market and local e-commerce firms consolidate. E-commerce sales were estimated at more than $15 billion in 2015, driven by rapid Internet uptake and even faster adoption of smartphones. A lack of apps for purchasing online, slow online payment growth, and concerns over the security of online purchases need to be rectified, and logistics services for traceable and timely shipping of small packages upgraded. E-commerce logistics are more demanding and operationally complex than those for import-export operations—the current setup in Vietnam.

Additive manufacturing (3D printing). This technology can broaden opportunities but undermine Vietnam's traditional manufacturing. As it advances, manufacturing will likely turn small-scale, widely distributed, and customizable, prompting investors from developed economies to relocate production back home.

has been seen in the typhoon trajectory in the past five decades. If this continues, Ho Chi Minh City would be at greater risk of being directly hit. Coastal erosion and salinity intrusion are other unfolding risks likely to accelerate.

Agriculture, particularly rice production, is projected to be hit hard, most severely around the Mekong Delta, where much of the land area is less than 2 meters above sea level (Wassmann et al. 2009). Climate change could reduce annual rice production by 3–9 million tons by 2050, and highly productive areas of coffee plantations may become unsuitable for the purpose (Bunn et al. 2015). The marine ecosystems in Vietnam are also likely to be severely affected. And climate change impacts are also likely to have adverse health consequences, including water- and vector-borne diseases and diarrheal illnesses (Coker et al. 2011). Flooding would compound the risks. The poor and elderly would be especially vulnerable to heat extremes, compounded by the rapid increase in Vietnam's elderly population.

Domestic Trends, Risks, and Opportunities

Demographic Megatrends

Over the past two decades, Vietnam cashed in its "demographic dividend"—the economic growth boost generated by a bulge in the share of the population of working age. The dividend is now nearly spent; the working-age share peaked in 2013 and is now in decline. Based on United Nations (UN) projections, the absolute number of people of working age will start to fall soon after 2035. More important, Vietnam reached a turning point in the size of its older population in 2015 and will become one of the world's fastest-aging societies. The number of Vietnamese older than 65 years will grow from 6.3 million today to 15.5 million. The share of the population older than 65 years will rise from 6.7 percent in 2015 to 14.4 percent in 2035 (figure O.2), transforming it from a young to an aged society.

This demographic transformation has stark consequences. First, the decline in the working-age population will mean that a key driver of Vietnam's rapid per capita growth will diminish, making human capital deepening and other sources of productivity growth even more vital for sustaining robust growth. Second, serious fiscal challenges will be driven by the rising burden on the pension and health systems. Third, institutional arrangements for the provision of care to the old-age population will quickly become a major concern.

FIGURE O.2 The share of population over 65 will more than double between 2015 and 2035

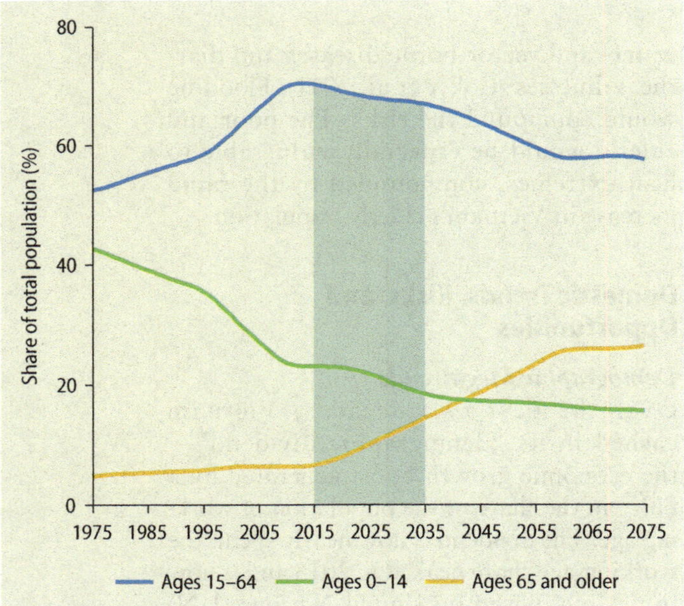

Source: UN 2015.

Vietnam's Emerging Middle Class

Vietnam's rapidly emerging middle class, also increasingly more urban, will offer another significant opportunity. Vietnam is a country of 90 million people, the 14th most populous on the planet. Its $200 billion economy is likely to be close to the trillion dollar mark (in 2015 prices) by 2035, with more than half the population projected to join the ranks of the global middle class with consumption of $15 a day or more in 2011 purchasing power parity (PPP) terms (figure O.3), compared with 11 percent today, giving new potency to the domestic market as a driver of growth.

In addition to being a major opportunity, a rising urban middle class will shift expectations and bring new challenges. The majority of that population will aspire to formal jobs and will want to gain high-quality skills through tertiary education. And the expansion of wage employment without well-functioning industrial relations institutions will expose the economy to the risk of substantial worker-employer conflict, evident in the large increase in strikes since 2006. The urban middle class will also demand greater political openness and more accountable government, which the existing system would struggle to meet.

Unfinished Economic Modernization Agenda and Rising Political Economy Challenges

Perhaps the biggest and most important opportunity—necessary for all other opportunities and to mitigate risks—lies in completing the unfinished economic modernization and structural transformation agenda. Part of this relates to maximizing the gains from the ongoing structural transformations that have been a major contributor to growth since the early 2000s. With agriculture still accounting for almost half the labor force, and with significantly lower labor productivity than in the industry and services sectors, future gains from structural transformation could be substantial.

FIGURE O.3 By 2035, more than half the Vietnamese population will enter the global middle class

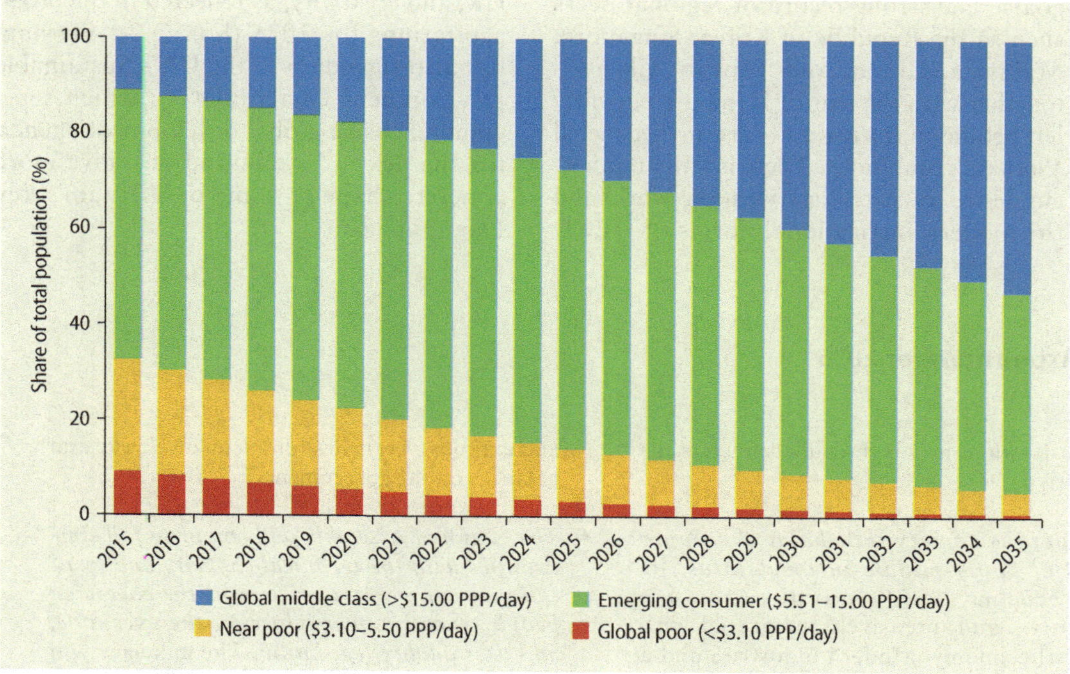

Source: General Statistics Office of Vietnam.
Note: Figures here reflect the projected distribution of per capita consumption, based on 2014 VHLSS data, assuming 4 percent annual growth in per capita consumption. PPP = purchasing power parity.

The transformation from state to private ownership of the economy is even less advanced. The state-owned enterprises and commercial banks continue to inhale too much oxygen out of the business environment, undermining economywide efficiency and crowding out the productive parts of the private sector. The state also wields too much influence in allocating land and capital, giving rise not only to opportunities for corruption by handing over arbitrary power to officials but also to heavy economywide inefficiencies. So, adjusting the role of the state to support a competitive private sector–led market economy remains a major opportunity. And while global integration has advanced well, with Vietnam embedding itself in global value chains, the benefits are constrained by the absence of links with domestic firms.

Many policy actions to grasp these opportunities are well known. What has been mostly lacking is follow-up action. It may well be that the political economy of some of the needed reforms has become a binding problem. Reforms are likely to face greater resistance than in the past, from interest groups that perhaps have more to lose now than 25 years ago. And the benefits are more uncertain than they were when reforms warded off widespread economic crisis. Deploying homegrown and politically feasible solutions—a strength of the first-generation reforms—will remain important for next-generation reforms.

Aspirations for 2035

By 2035, 60 years after Reunification, Vietnam aspires to become a modern, industrialized economy—next in a succession of East Asian economies to have made the transformative journey to upper-middle or high-income status. The many achievements since the launch of the *Đổi Mới* reforms have certainly contributed to the ambitious goals. The strong record of regional peers such as the Republic of Korea, Singapore, Malaysia, China, and Taiwan, China—together with the fear of being permanently left behind in the region—has further fueled Vietnam's ambitions. There is still an inherent desire to "catch up" with the world and the modern institutional norms of OECD countries for living standards, the rule of law, and creativity, as reflected in the broad aspirations for 2035 (box O.2). Vietnam has also signed up to the UN's Sustainable Development Goals (SDGs), which set a comprehensive global development agenda for the next 15 years and will give more concrete shape to some of Vietnam's key long-term goals.

BOX O.2 Aspirations for 2035

Vietnam's aspirations may be broadly defined in the following ways:

- *A prosperous society will be at the upper reaches of upper-middle-income status.* Its market economy will be private sector–led, competitive, and intensively integrated with the global economy. Modern industries and a knowledge-based economy, housed in an efficient and well-connected network of modern cities, will drive growth.

- *A modern, creative, and democratic society will be the driving force for future development.* The emphasis will be on creating an open and free environment that promotes learning and innovation for all citizens, who will be guaranteed equal access to development opportunities and the freedom to pursue their vocations, while fulfilling their responsibilities without compromising national and communal interests.

- *A rule-of-law state will be effective and accountable.* It will clarify the relationship between the state and the citizenry and between state and market. It will perform its basic functions effectively, including developing and enforcing legislation, managing international relations, ensuring public safety and national security, and ensuring that markets function freely while addressing market failures. It will develop strong social institutions to ensure that the power belongs to the Vietnamese citizens and protect their right of pursuing creativity. It will develop clear lines of responsibilities between the legislative, judiciary, and executive branches for adequate checks and balances on the government.

- *The National Assembly will comprise full-time deputies with the technical capacity and institutional autonomy to represent the sovereign people, exercise oversight over the executive, and pass quality legislation.* The judiciary will similarly be suitably positioned, with autonomy and strong capacity to resolve disputes in a more diverse society and economy. The executive will be well integrated horizontally and vertically, with clear functions for central and subnational authorities.

- *A civilized society will make every citizen and every political and social organization (the entire political system) equal before the law.* Underpinning this will be robust, diverse people's social organizations that can exercise fundamental rights, including the people's direct democratic rights and the rights to information and association.

- *A responsible member of the global community of nations will build global alliances and fulfill global responsibilities for peace and security while proactively seeking regional and global opportunities for economic integration.*

- *A sustainable environment will protect the quality of Vietnam's air, land, and water.* It will build climate resilience into economic planning, social policy, and infrastructure investments to reduce the most severe risks posed by climate change. It will develop diverse, clean, and secure energy sources.

The Ninth Party Congress adopted the phrase "socialist-oriented market economy" as the official way to describe Vietnam's economic system in April 2001, codified in the 2013 revision of the constitution. The 2011–2020 Socio-Economic Development Strategy set forth the objective "to become a basic industrialized country with the foundation of a modern and industrial country by 2020."

Despite broad acceptance, the precise definition of the term "modern and industrial" economy has not been announced (Tran 2015). While any definition would be arbitrary, this report sets forth five specific quantitative criteria for meeting that objective:

1. A GDP per capita of at least $18,000 (in 2011 PPP)
2. A majority (over 50 percent) of the Vietnamese population living in urban areas
3. A share of industry and services in GDP at more than 90 percent and in employment at more than 70 percent
4. A private-sector share in GDP of at least 80 percent
5. A score of at least 0.70 on the UN's Human Development Index

How well is Vietnam positioned to become a modern, industrial economy by 2035? Its GDP per capita—at $5,370 (in 2011 PPP) in 2014—would need to grow at a minimum of 6 percent a year to reach the $18,000 mark by 2035 (figure O.4). This would be significantly higher than the average per capita growth rate of 5.5 percent between 1990 and 2014—and well above the 3.8 percent average for all middle-income countries over the same period. A lower and more feasible (but still ambitious) per capita growth rate of 5.0 percent (Vietnam's average over the last 10 years) would take its GDP per capita to just under $15,000 by 2035 and put Vietnam on par with Brazil in 2014, well poised to reach $18,000 by 2040. A growth path of 7 percent (Vietnam's aspirational growth target) would take per capita GDP to $22,200, roughly the income of the Republic of Korea in 2002 or Malaysia in 2013. This higher growth rate would also enhance Vietnam's

FIGURE O.4 Income per capita growth scenarios for Vietnam to 2035

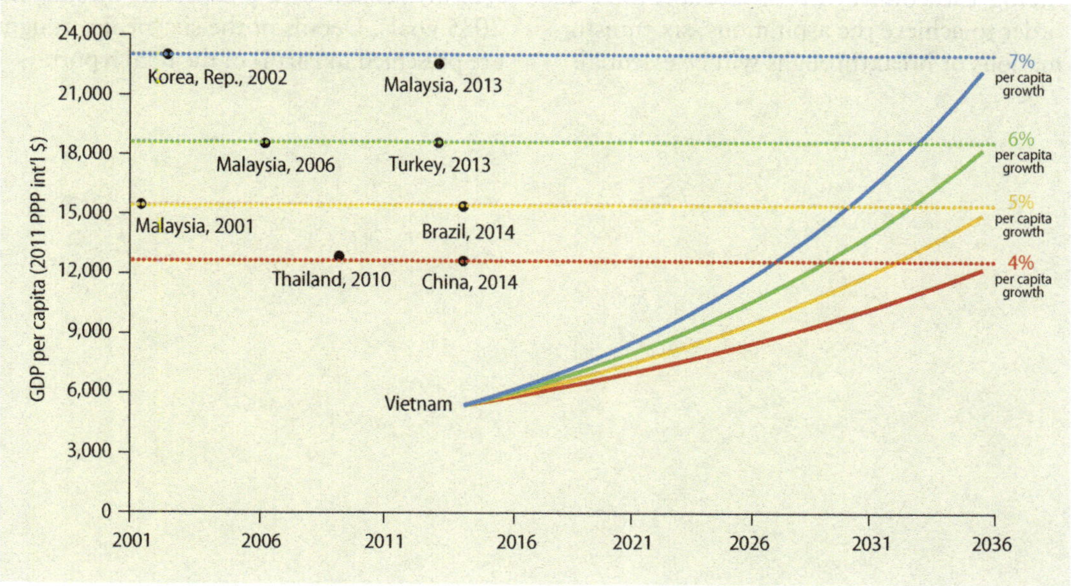

Source: World Development Indicators, and World Bank Group and the Ministry of Planning and Investment of Vietnam calculations.
Note: PPP = purchasing power parity.

chances of catching up with Indonesia and the Philippines.

Also in 2035, at least 54 million of Vietnam's 108 million citizens would be urban residents, almost 25 million more than today. The urbanization rate, now at around 33 percent, would need to increase 2 percent a year to meet this target, matching the pace of the past 20 years. The nonagriculture sector has grown at twice the pace of the agriculture sector since 1990. This 2:1 ratio of growth rates is also projected over the next two decades, even with agriculture growing at its potential 3.0–3.5 percent. That would ensure a 90 percent share of the nonagriculture sector in the economy. The 80 percent private-sector share in GDP, if feasible, would involve a departure from the past. With the share of the public sector in GDP stuck at around 33 percent since the onset of the *Đổi Mới* reforms, this would involve a more meaningful attempt to restructure the SOEs (including equitizing bigger chunks of them) and providing a bigger stimulus to the private sector.

Thirty years of *Đổi Mới* reforms have brought many successes. Vietnamese development aspirations for 2035 are bold and significant, but the challenges and risks facing the country are also enormous. In order to achieve the aspirations, six transformations or breakthroughs will be essential:

1. Enabling economic modernization with a productive and globally competitive private sector firmly in the lead
2. Building the country's technological and innovation capacity for a creative society
3. Managing urbanization and other forms of spatial transformation to achieve economic efficiency
4. Charting an environmentally sustainable development path with enhanced capacity for climate resilience
5. Promoting equality and inclusion of the marginalized groups for the development of a harmonious middle-class society
6. Building a modern, rule-of-law state with a democratic society and a fully established market economy

The six breakthroughs serve as the foundation for realizing the 2035 aspirations, and may be summarized in three pillars: economic prosperity balanced with environmental sustainability; equity and social inclusion; and a rule-of-law state with high capacity and accountability. The rest of this report is organized around these three critical aspirations for 2035. It covers both the feasibility and challenges of realizing these aspirations under current conditions and lays out a pathway for reform to enhance the prospects of meeting the 2035 goals. Details of the six breakthroughs are presented in Part II of the final report.

Pillar 1 Economic Prosperity with Environmental Sustainability

Vietnam is on a trajectory of rapid growth. Past performance has stoked ambitions of even faster growth over the next 20 years, and Vietnamese leaders are keen to see per capita growth accelerate from its average of 5.5 percent since 1990 to around 7.0 percent. This will require the ratio of gross capital formation to GDP to pick up to around 35 percent (from 31 percent currently) and stay at that level for at least a decade—and the gross national savings rate to stay at 35 percent. But, above all, productivity growth, which has been on a long-term declining trend, will require greater attention.

The reform agenda will be demanding, given that the decline in productivity growth has been broad based. The government will need to prioritize reforms with more immediate payoffs such as strengthening the microeconomic foundations of the market economy. The reforms with medium-term impacts would support ongoing structural transformations and the deepening of global integration by developing a market-oriented and commercialized agriculture sector, strengthening Vietnam's position in global value chains, and building more resilient and credible macroeconomic institutions. Those with longer-term gestation would seek to create more robust learning and innovation structures, promote efficient urban agglomeration, and ensure environmental sustainability.

Vietnam's Long-Term Growth in a Global Perspective

"Catch-up growth"—in which latecomers benefit from investment and transfer of technology and know-how from richer countries—has produced extraordinary episodes of economic success in East Asia and elsewhere since the end of World War II. Some economies—like Japan, the Republic of Korea, Singapore, and Taiwan, China—sustained high growth for some five decades and were propelled to high-income status. Others—like Brazil, the Arab Republic of Egypt, Indonesia, Mexico, and Thailand—showed promise for two or three decades, but then became mired in the "middle-income trap." China's ascent, albeit incomplete, seems on a trajectory similar to the first group's—and to Vietnam's.

Having grasped the catch-up opportunities, Vietnam is strongly positioned on its long-term income trajectory relative to its global comparators. A long-term comparison with China is striking on two counts. First, growth accelerations in both countries, although 13 years apart (starting around 1977 and 1990), begin at roughly the same per capita income of around $1,100 (2005 PPP). Second, 24 years into its growth acceleration (2014), Vietnam had kept up with China over the equivalent period (to 2001) (figure O.5, panel a).

The story remains broadly similar when looking at other successful economies (those with at least a three-and-a-half-fold increase in per capita income in the first 25 years of their growth accelerations) and considering a 50-year period. The starting points for the growth accelerations were close, with Thailand at $835 (2005 PPP) at the lower end and Taiwan, China, at $1,365 at the upper end. About a quarter century into its growth acceleration, Vietnam's position is broadly at par with those successful economies (figure O.5, panel b).

What happens from here on is even more important. At roughly 25 years into their growth accelerations—where Vietnam is now—the economies that made it into the high-income ranks pulled ahead of the rest. The Republic of Korea and Taiwan, China, maintained their growth records of the first

FIGURE O.5 Keeping on course for catch-up: Vietnam and global comparators

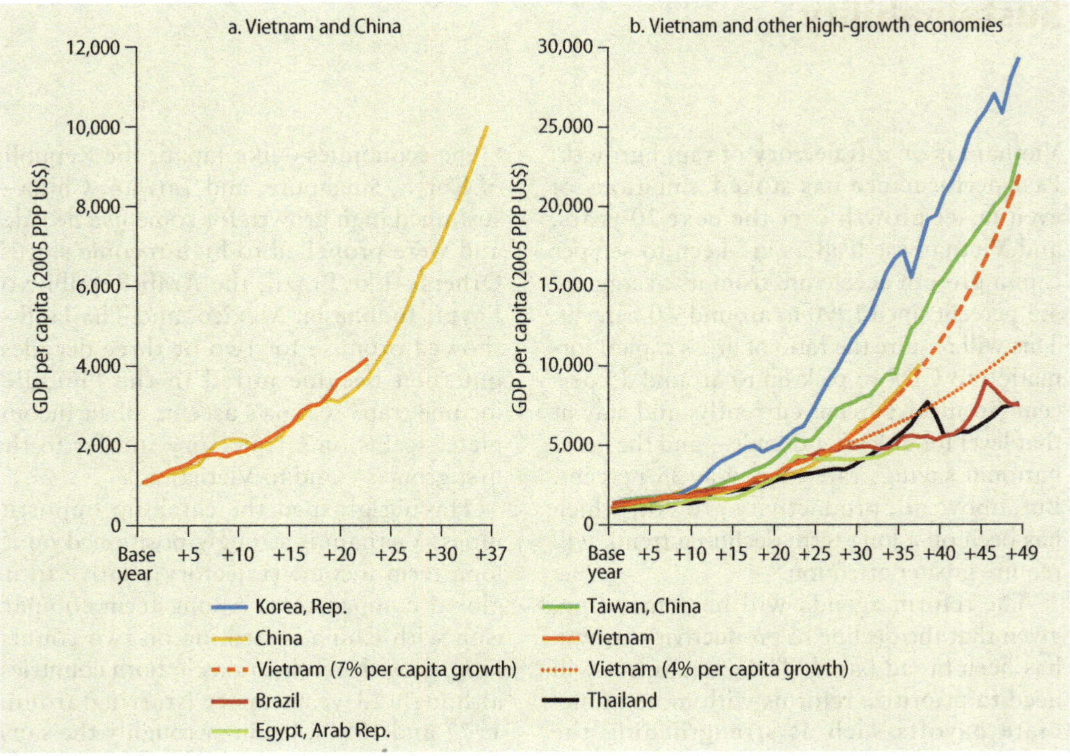

Source: Calculations based on data from Penn World Table, Version 8.0.
Note: Base years are 1951 for Taiwan, China, and Brazil; 1958 for Thailand; 1962 for the Republic of Korea; 1969 for the Arab Republic of Egypt; 1977 for China; and 1990 for Vietnam. PPP = purchasing power parity.

25 years over years 25–50, but Brazil, Egypt, and Thailand started to see growth rates fall.

Vietnam is thus seemingly at a critical juncture. Decisions at this stage matter for meeting long-term income aspirations. If the country can carry out the reforms to pull up its GDP growth to its 7 percent per capita target, it would match the trajectory of China and by 2035 stand a strong chance of reaching the incomes of the Republic of Korea and Taiwan, China, in the early 2000s. At the higher reaches of upper-middle-income status, it would be strongly positioned for the final ascent to high income. It would also have a stronger chance of catching up with or even overtaking its middle-income neighbors such as Indonesia and the Philippines. But if Vietnam's per capita growth slips to around 4 percent a year, that will be good enough only to take its average income close to that of Thailand or Brazil today, and its chances of catching up with the neighboring wealthier middle-income countries would be lower.

What will determine Vietnam's path? Productivity is fundamental. Economists generally agree that countries' inability to break out of the middle-income trap (whether or not they have been growing fast) is almost entirely attributable to stagnating productivity (Eichengreen, Park, and Shin 2011; Agenor, Canuto, and Jelenic 2012). Summarizing the importance of productivity in development economics, Nobel Prize–winning economist Paul Krugman notes, "Productivity isn't everything, but in the long run it is almost everything. A country's ability to improve its standard of living over time depends almost entirely on its ability to raise its output per worker." (Krugman 1994) Here, though, the story becomes less rosy for Vietnam.

Trends in Productivity Growth: A Cause for Concern

Behind Vietnam's impressive growth since 1990 are some worrying signs. Two stand out in comparing the 1990s with 2000–13. First, GDP growth was a full percentage point lower in the second period (at 6.6 percent) than in the 1990s. While this slowdown was in part a reflection of the weaker environment following the 2008–09 global financial crisis, a slowdown in labor-productivity (output per worker) growth that started in the late 1990s was also a contributing factor (figure O.6, panel a). In fact, an acceleration in labor-force growth prevented an even steeper decline in GDP growth after 2000. Second, decomposition of labor-productivity growth in the two periods shows that, since the early 2000s, the contributions of capital deepening (panel b) and structural transformation from agriculture to manufacturing and services (panel c) have picked up markedly. Conversely, growth in total factor productivity, which accounted for the bulk of labor- productivity growth in the 1990s, collapsed in the post-millennium period, and labor-productivity growth fell in a majority of the sectors. Labor productivity actually declined in mining, public utilities, construction, and finance—all sectors in which SOEs have kept their dominant role.

Driven by multiple objectives (profit not high among them) and by distorted incentives, SOEs have stayed unproductive.

FIGURE O.6 Productivity growth has been trending downward

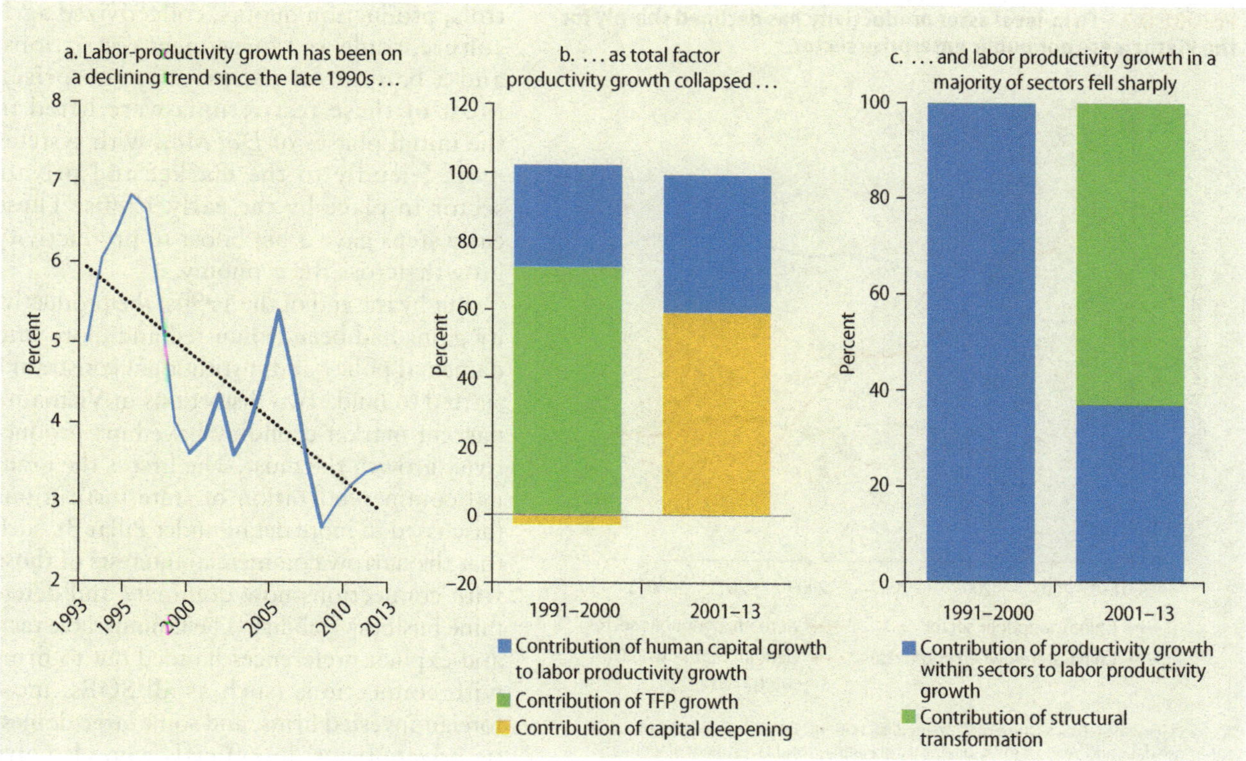

Source: Calculations based on General Statistics Office of Vietnam data.
Note: Panel a displays a 3-year moving average. In panel b, capital deepening is measured as the change in the ratio of capital stock to GDP.

Measures of firm-level asset (capital and land) productivity (figure O.7) and labor productivity throughout the 2000s capture their inefficiencies. Despite a long-running (albeit uneven) SOE equitization process, the public sector's presence in production and its control over factor markets remain pervasive. The state still retains a majority stake in more than 3,000 SOEs, which account for about a third of GDP (same as in 1990) and close to 40 percent of total investment. The state sector also maintains a virtual monopoly (or oligopoly) in critical sectors such as fertilizer, mining, utilities, banking, construction, and agriculture. Under growing pressure to restructure, it has at least sought to ensure that its feeble productivity does not deteriorate further.

Domestic private enterprise gives even more cause for concern. Driven by reforms to first legalize and then facilitate private enterprise, the private sector grew exponentially after the late 1980s.[9] But its growing presence has been marked by worsening productivity, so much so that there is little daylight between the productivity of labor and that of assets in the domestic private and SOE sectors (see figure O.7). Vietnamese private firms, on average, were using their assets more productively than their Chinese counterparts in the early 2000s, but by 2014 their asset productivity had fallen to less than half that of their Chinese peers. Vietnamese private firms are overwhelmingly small and informal, which prevents productivity gains through specialization and economies of scale. And the relatively few large domestic private firms (especially those with more than 300 employees) tend to be even less productive than the smaller private firms (on both asset and labor productivity).

FIGURE O.7 Firm-level asset productivity has declined sharply for the Vietnamese nonpublic enterprise sector

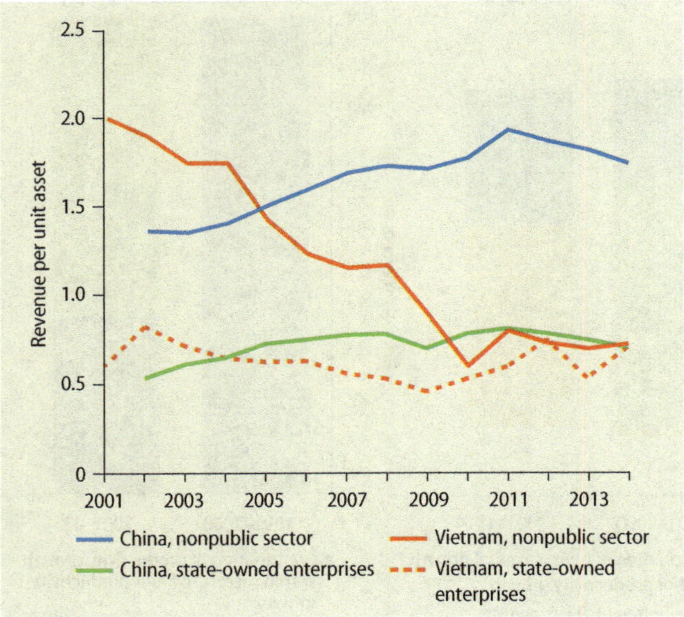

Sources: General Statistics Office of Vietnam data, National Bureau of Statistics of China enterprise data, and World Bank and Ministry of Planning and Investment of Vietnam calculations.
Note: Asset productivity is revenue per unit of assets.

What explains these trends, and why do they differ between the two periods? The initial pickup in productivity growth in the 1990s reflected Vietnam's move toward a market-economy structure and the removal of many distortions (multiple price controls, production quotas, collectivized agriculture, trade and investment restrictions, and a ban on formal private enterprise). Most of these restrictions were lifted in the initial phases of *Đổi Mới*, with systems more friendly to the market and private sector in place by the early 1990s. These early steps gave a big boost to productivity growth across the economy.

But by the end of the 1990s, the productivity gains had been exhausted and more fundamental policy and institutional constraints started to bind. Two distortions in Vietnam's nascent market economy have hurt productivity growth the most. The first is the gradual commercialization of state institutions (discussed in more detail under Pillar 3), such that the narrow commercial interests of those with connections now dominate and determine business viability. The innumerable tacit and explicit preferences handed out to firms with connections (such as all SOEs, most foreign-invested firms, and some large domestic private firms) by officials who also give inadequate attention to economic efficiency make it very difficult for many private firms to thrive, even if they are productive.

Commercialization of state institutions has produced an uneven and partial approach to market reforms, leading to two imbalances. In the first, a warm embrace of markets as the mechanism for resource allocation has coincided with a much more cautious and ambiguous approach to giving up state control of production and to accepting domestic private ownership of productive assets. This has spawned an entrepreneurial business class within (or closely connected to) the state rather than outside it and permitted a continuing heavy presence of SOEs in many sectors.

In the second, the market embrace has itself been two-speed. Impressive progress in liberalizing product markets and integrating them with the global economy under international trade agreements has been accompanied by a more subdued and muddled approach to developing and liberalizing factor markets, as seen in the largely inefficient allocation of land and capital. For example, significant assets (land and capital) were accumulated in the construction, real estate, and banking and finance sectors between 2001 and 2013, even though these sectors were among the least productive. Allocations are likely influenced by arbitrary administrative decisions and connections, at heavy economic cost—as substantiated by a considerable literature. A 2008 study finds that the allocation of bank credit is related to connections and that the most profitable private firms do not even attempt to get bank loans (Malesky and Taussig 2008). Updating the analysis to 2013, this report finds that the results hold. Provinces with a high density of SOEs provide less credit to private firms and require more time to issue land-use rights certificates than other provinces (Van Thang and Freeman 2009, for example). Easier access of SOEs to credit, land, and export quotas in the garment and textile sector has reduced the profitability and viability of private firms (Nguyen and Le 2005).

Another distortion in Vietnam's market economy that has hurt productivity has been the relative neglect of building critical market institutions. The greatest weaknesses are in those responsible for protecting private-property rights and ensuring free and fair competition. These institutional shortfalls have impeded the emergence of large, competitive, private firms and further discouraged small household firms from entering the formal sector (Malesky and Taussig 2009), even though switching from informal to formal activity can raise firms' productivity and profitability (Boly 2015).

The adverse impact on the performance of domestic private firms, while unsurprising, has been substantial. With noncompetitive and state-controlled factor markets and inadequately developed formal market institutions, firms turn to informal institutions and networks and often find illegitimate means to enter the market, grow, and become more profitable (Steer and Sen 2010). There is no reason to believe, however, that those who are more adept at garnering political capital or exploiting connections are also necessarily better at running businesses.

A Reform Agenda to Reignite Productivity Growth

The imperative to improve productivity growth is therefore clear and strong. GDP growth since the early 2000s has been led by forces that compensated for weak and declining productivity growth but are now reaching their natural limits. Rapid labor-force growth made up for low and declining labor-productivity growth economywide. Large-scale structural transformations offset the low and declining labor-productivity growth at the sectoral level. And an acceleration in capital accumulation counterbalanced the low and declining growth in total factor productivity. In the next phase of development, each of these compensatory factors is projected to have a sharply diminished impact, exposing overall economic growth much more to the weak productivity trends. Moreover, the global context is likely to be far less hospitable than before the global financial crisis.

Vietnam's advantage is being at an early enough stage of development to reignite productivity growth without compromising its 2035 income objectives. At a similar stage of development (the late 1970s), the Republic of Korea saw a major acceleration in its labor-productivity growth, which is encouraging since it suggests that a turnaround in such growth is possible. But it also highlights how demanding the agenda for institutional reforms is. Some of that country's reforms launched in the late 1970s and early 1980s—macroeconomic stabilization, agricultural modernization, and greater emphasis on competition and market deregulation—strongly and quite quickly helped improve productivity growth. But others—in the areas of higher education, research and development (R&D), and urbanization—operated with a significant lag, having begun many years earlier.

Reforms in Vietnam would need to be not only comprehensive (given its broad-based slide in productivity growth) but also carefully sequenced with a fixed eye on long-term growth. The agenda, accordingly, can be broken down into three broad (and overlapping) time horizons.

- *Reforms with immediate impacts.* Strengthening the microeconomic foundations of the market economy would have to be the immediate priority, with the payoffs most significant over the next five years. This should help stem the declining trend in productivity growth and, by enabling greater and more efficient participation of the private sector, provide a strong growth stimulus for the next decade or so.
- *Reforms with impacts in the medium term.* These would comprise measures that are also carried out without delay, but their impact would be felt the most between years five and ten. These would aim to support the ongoing structural transformations and deepening of global integration (including the capital account) by modernizing and commercializing agriculture, strengthening Vietnam's position in global value chains, and building more resilient and credible macroeconomic institutions.
- *Reforms and investments with impacts mostly in the long term.* These could be phased in over the next two or three years, with payoffs expected only with a significant lag. They take into account the fact that the current growth model (supported by the short- to medium-term reforms) is likely to start hitting diminishing returns no later than a decade or so from now, as the economy reaches the upper-middle-income level and environmental degradation reaches its limits. The longer-term focus would be on spurring learning and innovation, promoting urban agglomeration, and ensuring environmentally sustainable development.

The impacts of the reforms are not mutually exclusive. Functioning land markets and strong microinstitutions will be just as important after a decade as they are in the next three years, although the short-term impact will be felt more acutely because of the current distortions that will get eliminated. Elements of stronger macroeconomic institutions will be needed in the next two or three years to ensure fiscal consolidation and greater efficiency of spending. The environmental agenda can also have some immediate payoffs through more efficient pricing systems that internalize environmental costs.

Reforms with Immediate Impacts: Strengthening the Microeconomic Foundations of the Market Economy

The immediate priorities have to be stronger microeconomic market-economy foundations. SOE reforms stay an important part of this agenda, but are no longer enough: creating better enabling conditions for the private sector, such as strengthening market institutions and liberalizing factor markets, takes precedence.

Strengthening Market Institutions

The evidence is compelling that well-functioning markets require well-defined rules of the game, enforced transparently and predictably. The agenda calls for strong market institutions whose role is especially important in the early phases when markets are underdeveloped and small distortions can have amplified effects. The emphasis in Vietnam will have to be on enforcing competition policies and ensuring the security of property rights. Restructuring the SOE sector and leveling the playing field for all enterprises—private or public, domestic or foreign—is an important part of this agenda (discussed under Pillar 3).

Liberalizing Factor Markets

Vietnam's financial sector is still relatively underdeveloped, with the banking sector saddled with deep-seated structural problems and capital markets still in their infancy. Land markets are even less developed and complete. Moreover, as noted, state influence on credit and land allocations seems excessive, leading to significant economic inefficiencies. Labor market regulations are less onerous (Pillar 2), but even those are not free of policy concerns. The *hộ khẩu* household registration system (which, among other problems, impedes rural–urban migration) is less burdensome than in earlier years but still imposes efficiency costs (Pillar 2).

Building Financial Markets

The financial sector has expanded rapidly since the early 1990s, but still has wide scope to take on an even bigger role. It has done a reasonably good job of mobilizing savings but fallen short in allocating credit to its most productive uses and providing an inclusive payment system. Much of the lending, especially by state-owned commercial banks, has gone to SOEs, or increasingly to private companies with connections, crowding out lending to productive segments of the domestic private sector. Financial inclusion has increased since the early 1990s, but remains an issue for less well-off Vietnamese, especially those in rural areas.

The banking sector is struggling, having taken a big hit after the global financial crisis toppled the real estate market (where the banks had heavy exposure). Banks' average return on assets has fallen steeply since the crisis (from 1.8 percent in 2007 to 0.5 percent in 2012). Their reported nonperforming loans (NPLs) have risen and are generally considered understated. And their provisions are lower than in middle-income peer countries in East Asia. Many of the NPLs and restructured loans are related to SOEs. Moreover, cross-ownership of banks by each other and by enterprises (including SOEs) remains significant. Compliance with Basel Core Principles is improving but still low, and many banks lack Basel II's capital requirements for market and operational risks—even as the country looks to move toward Basel III. On-site inspections, particularly of the state-owned commercial banks, have been limited, and consolidated supervision of banks is lacking. Off-site monitoring also needs to be improved.

Three items are on the agenda for the financial system over the next 20 years.

Reducing the risk of major financial crisis. Vietnam's response to potential financial crises could be accelerated if the government strengthens the National Monetary Advisory Council. The council could meet regularly, supported by a dedicated technical team to provide timely reports and drafts of notifications and instructions to banks. Information on the financial system could be improved by better off-site data and supervision from the State Bank of Vietnam (SBV). Improving the capacity for crisis management and the framework for bank resolution will improve the crisis response in the event of illiquidity or insolvency in the banking sector. This could be further strengthened by firming the resources of the Deposit Insurance of Vietnam (DIV) and legally enabling it to undertake a purchase and assumption transaction of failed banks' assets. This measure would require both a gradual shift in the DIV's funds from banks to government debt and legal changes that permit the government to borrow from the SBV on behalf of the DIV in large crises, under well-defined conditions.

Developing a larger, more diverse, stable financial sector. This requires steadily increasing bank capital and developing the broader financial sector. The first challenge is resolving the large NPL overhang in banks. A good starting point would be confidential audits (including operational audits) by reputable international firms and strong application of prudential norms, without regulatory forbearance. For banks deemed sound and viable, NPL resolution would involve direct sales of collateral related to the NPLs and transfers of NPLs and collateral, under a more robust legal framework, to a strengthened Vietnam Asset Management Company for management, recovery, and sale. The banks deemed insolvent would be closed, merged with viable banks, or sold (either directly or through the company).

Improving future performance in the banking sector will depend on better enforcement of improved regulation and supervision of risks taken by banks (with closer attention to state-owned banks) and by other sellers of assets such as insurance and pension firms. One major improvement would be to apply macroprudential supervision and better off-site supervision. A second would be a gradual shift toward international regulatory and accounting norms. Moving toward Basel III would mean higher requirements for capital, including capital for market and operational risks, and reduced incentives for excessive risk-taking by banks (in a context where some banks are struggling to meet even Basel II requirements). Third would be to gather more information on business groups, which could help reduce connected lending.

Deepening the capital markets (starting with the market for government debt) will also need changes to the legal and accounting frameworks to bring them in line with international standards. That would make foreign investment through the capital market more attractive. As in most developing countries, developing contractual savings institutions (such as insurance companies) has only begun in Vietnam, but their role will increase over the next 20 years as the economy modernizes. Generating investor interest in insurance companies will depend on improved clarity of company accounts, compliance with international accounting and reporting standards, improved corporate governance, and a strengthened Insurance Supervisory Authority.

Increasing financial inclusion. Vietnam has done fairly well in lending to individuals[10] relative to other lower-middle-income countries, but not as well in deposits and remittances.[11] Remittances in Vietnam tend to go through financial institutions, with much less use of mobile phones and money-transfer operators. Alternative uses of mobile phones would improve financial inclusion in remittances and deposits at lower cost. Although Vietnam would need major changes in regulation—for finance and telecommunications—this approach would take advantage of the country's large number of mobile phone subscriptions. A good international example is Kenya's M-Shwari, which launched in 2012, and by end-2014 had 9 million accounts, total deposits of $45 million, and outstanding loans of nearly $18 million—and its deposit holders can apply for short-term loans. Financial inclusion in Vietnam would also require higher-quality credit information on borrowers.

Developing Land Markets

Land, according to the Vietnamese constitution and law, is owned by the public and managed on its behalf by the state. Land-use rights for specified periods are issued to individuals, who are allowed under the law to transfer these rights to other individuals. The state may take back the land and annul the rights in the national interest, based on compensation according to law.

The overall legal framework for individual rights to land use is subject to the interpretation of numerous overlapping laws, and its implementation is equally riddled with a plethora of implementing regulations and overlapping mandates. This is just at the national level—provincial and municipal administrations issue their own instructions on land use and transfers.

The markets for trading land-use rights are, in effect, missing (Cung 2015). Functioning primary markets for land-use rights are virtually absent. The role of the markets is played by state agencies, often using ill-defined administrative procedures. And the "price" for issuing land-use rights bears little resemblance to a true market-determined price.

Secondary land markets, more prevalent, operate under multiple constraints. Market mechanisms are rarely deployed in cases involving reclassification of land use from agricultural to nonagricultural land. In such cases, land-use planning decisions by local administrations (and not demand-supply conditions or local preferences) determine the reclassified purpose of land use. Moreover, the "seller" or the individual giving up land-use rights, often a farmer, is unlikely to receive fair compensation: the benefit from the transaction is mostly captured by the local government and by the "buyer," who often receives the land at prices below what a functioning secondary land market would have produced.

The missing land markets are problematic from several angles. For one, their absence, alongside weak property rights, fosters a patronage-based business model.[12] Their lack undermines efficiency in other ways, too. A land-use right holder who would like to change land use to a more rewarding economic activity will find the administrative costs high, often prohibitively so, and the processes time-consuming. The lack of land markets also creates distortions in urbanization patterns (see the later section "Using Cities to Power the Drive to Modernity and Industrialization"). The development of transparent and functioning land markets, therefore, is an important and urgent policy priority.

Reforms with Impacts in the Medium Term: Managing Structural Transformations and Deepening Global Integration

The medium-term emphasis will have a threefold focus. First is modernizing and commercializing agriculture, which engages almost half the workforce in a country almost 70 percent rural. Second is strengthening participation in global value chains to maximize the chances of strong productivity gains, given the heavy and probably increasing reliance on external markets. And third is building more resilient and credible macroeconomic institutions, which will become more critical with the impending demographic shifts, huge spending needs in infrastructure and social sectors, and greater capital account integration with the global economy.

Modernizing and Commercializing Agriculture

A move to industrialize more deeply and modernize services is not incompatible with a sharp focus on agriculture. The sector is—and will remain for the foreseeable future—an important area of Vietnam's comparative advantage, and will have to perform at its high potential to support economic modernization.

While the agricultural sector has progressed enormously since the late 1990s, emerging concerns over the quality and sustainability of its growth model require immediate policy attention. Sectoral labor productivity remains much lower than in comparator countries, despite rapid gains since the 1990s. The fragmented, smallholder-dominated character of the sector with heavy state involvement contributes to this outcome. Another important factor is the dominance of rice in its use of the best land and much of the country's irrigation capacity. Economic issues include low smallholder profitability, heavy underemployment among agricultural workers, uncertain food safety, low value addition, price-discounted commodities in international markets, gaps in multimodal farm-to-market connectivity, limitations in storage and cold-chain logistics, and limited technological or institutional innovation. And some agricultural growth has come at the expense of the environment.

Agriculture is at a turning point. Major opportunities will be in domestic, regional, and international markets, yet the sector will no longer be able to compete on the basis of low-cost, labor-intensive natural-resource use. The sector will also face growing domestic competition—from cities, industry, and services—for labor, land, and water. Future growth will depend on increased efficiency and innovation.

Change is also needed in the structural patterns of production and supply-chain organization, which are highly fragmented, with limited collective action at farmer level and weak vertical coordination. This fragmentation has contributed to unnecessary transaction costs, unrealized economies of scale in certain functions, and poor incentives to produce and maintain higher-quality produce and raw materials. Similarly, change is warranted in the "state management" model—that is, in the technical and regulatory services provided by the state, in public investments and expenditures in the sector, and in the policies applied to foster farmer and agribusiness investment. Demand-driven agriculture needs flexibility. It cannot be centrally planned.

If Vietnam's agriculture follows global patterns, it will see two transformations. The first will modernize production methods, change the patterns of land use (such as less rice, more value-added crops, and more livestock), and increased collective action in organizing farm services. The second will modernize the agro-food system by processing agricultural commodities (crops, livestock, and harvested fish) into value-added food products.[13]

Signs of these shifts are already emerging in some areas or corridors in the agro-food complex. But how efficiently these processes occur, how inclusive they are, how disruptive they are, and whether they follow a straight or convoluted path will depend heavily on public policy.

For example, the government could facilitate a more vibrant market for agricultural land and support farmer shifts from rice monocropping to mixed cropping, including livestock and aquaculture or other forms of specialization. It will want to deploy regulations, incentives, and facilitative services—combined effectively—to stimulate and monitor a "greener" agriculture and a system for food safety and consumer protection that inspires confidence. Supply chains capable of tracing the movement and physical condition of perishable products—like frozen fish from an origin in the Mekong Delta to a consumption market in Western Europe or North America—would contribute to strengthening both trade competitiveness and food safety. There will be greater demand for information and for technical and financial instruments, to better manage risks associated with agriculture. The government will need to facilitate these types of services. Improved educational and vocational training services, for instance, will quicken the adoption of improved farm and post-harvest technologies. Creating and maintaining a favorable environment for agroindustrial and agribusiness investment and operations will also be critical for adding value to food products and rebranding them for quality and sustainability. Vietnam can draw on and adapt to many international examples of good practice.

The government has played a major and, in some areas, leading role in the past development of agriculture. Some of its functions —including land-use planner, farm manager, commodity trader, and technology supplier —will be less important or even detrimental as agriculture moves toward a more flexible, market-driven, and knowledge-based system. The government can undertake less direct investment in agriculture if it promotes private agricultural services and facilitates private investment efficiently, including through public-private partnerships. That should free resources to achieve excellence in applying environmental, phytosanitary, animal health, and food-safety regulations. The government will, though, have a continuing role in supporting farmer organizations, in maintaining rural infrastructure and other elements that influence farmer and agribusiness transaction costs, and in coordinating their activities.

Leveraging External Trade Opportunities

Vietnam has gained much from external trade. Deepening its participation in global value chains (GVCs) has given it a real headstart over other emerging market competitors for the potentially even more rewarding opportunities from proposed multi- and bilateral free-trade agreements, such as the TPP. Not only is Vietnam's export basket much bigger than before, it is also much more diversified, reflecting a transition from exporting primary commodities to low- and medium-tech manufactured goods (apparel, furniture, and footwear), and then to more sophisticated products (machinery and electronics).

Growth in service exports, however, has been lackluster. Nor does the current GVC model in Vietnam fully exploit the opportunities. It relies heavily on foreign-invested firms operating final-stage assembly operations, with limited backward links to domestic suppliers in key manufacturing activities and little transfer of technology between foreign and local firms, which often lack the capacity to absorb higher technologies or jump to more sophisticated tasks or value chains. A striking feature of Vietnam's export-oriented manufacturing operations is the relatively high value of imported components going into final assembly—an estimated 50–60 percent for garment and footwear exports, for example. Most accessories and parts going into the export-oriented production of smartphones and tablets also come from abroad.

So, while retaining final-assembly production for large-scale job creation in manufacturing (at least in the medium term), Vietnam could simultaneously deepen the participation of domestic suppliers into the final-assembly process by developing more comprehensive networks of dependable tier-1 and tier-2 suppliers, as China has done. This may better position it to begin moving into more sophisticated products in existing GVCs, increasing the value-added share in existing GVCs by moving into more sophisticated tasks, and shifting into new supply chains with higher value-added shares.

Reforms would first promote competitive private firms capable of establishing production links with foreign-invested firms. The key to moving up the value chain in each of the early industrializers in East Asia has been a vibrant domestic private sector. Eventually, as Vietnamese firms absorb know-how and become globally more competitive (through technological upgrading and scale economies), the country could aim for some of its firms to be at the head of GVCs, where returns are far higher. Apple, for instance, retains more than 45 percent of the wholesale price of a new iPhone as gross profit.[14] Samsung (Republic of Korea), Huawei (China), and Tata Group (India) are other examples.

The second policy imperative is to develop a modern service sector, a critical input for manufacturing, especially on the export side. This is one area where Vietnam lags behind its competitors. The absence of a functioning modern financial sector is a major handicap. Lack of access to early-stage financing limits the development of a dynamic entrepreneurship start-up ecosystem. Insurance, telecommunications, and transport and logistics are also lagging. This gap will be felt even more as Vietnam climbs GVCs and as the value content of its trade goods rises.

Service activities such as R&D, design, and engineering should be developed as a way of upgrading participation in GVCs (see the section "Spurring Learning and Innovation to Sustain Rapid, Long-Run Growth"). Modern services are also a direct source of exports, growth, and job creation. If the country can upgrade its human capital base and its information and communications technology (ICT) infrastructure and connectivity, it can become a regional powerhouse in IT-enabled sectors.

Regulatory reforms will be essential to energize services. Foreign ownership restrictions in strategic services such as banking, telecommunications, media, electricity transmission and distribution, road freight, rail transport, air transport, and port operations are either prohibitive or much more onerous in costly approvals than they are in comparator countries (World Bank 2012). The restrictions need to be rationalized and eased, allowing market mechanisms to predictably allocate investment among domestic and foreign investors alike. Addressing gaps in dispute resolution is another priority. Foreign service firms are wary of the legal system, and often specify dispute settlement by arbitration in such jurisdictions as Singapore. Vietnam can also be more proactive in engaging partner countries to lower the barriers to service trade within ASEAN.

Finally, as Vietnam integrates more fully and profitably into GVCs, it can also boost its connectivity. Firms that participate in value chains need to move goods across borders cost-effectively and reliably, in order to keep inventory carrying costs low and comply with the strict requirements of lead firms for on-time delivery. Connectivity has three key attributes, each requiring policy attention.

Institutional connectivity. The "software" side of things includes trade facilitation, structural and regulatory reforms, and transport and logistics facilitation. Vietnam performs relatively well on the World Bank's Logistics Performance Index (LPI), ranking 48 among 160 countries on the overall rating and the highest among the lower-middle-income countries (table O.1), although still lagging regional upper-middle-income countries such as China, Malaysia, and Thailand. Its rankings have improved since 2007 across the board, except for customs procedures.[15] Health and sanitation performance standards inspections are underperforming, below Vietnam's ASEAN peers.

Physical connectivity. A well-connected country has abundant and high-quality physical infrastructure, especially international gateways and multimodal interfaces, including ports, airports, road and rail links, as well as ICTs. It also includes energy, which is vital to the continued success of manufacturing firms, and can be traded among neighboring countries. Vietnam comes out well on the infrastructure component of the LPI ranking (44), but many transport aspects require attention.

Current modes are overloaded in and around the major economic clusters and these do not connect well to each other or to major trade gateways, reflecting lack of coordination to develop economic zones and transport corridors (World Bank 2013). Key issues include poor road conditions (see the section "Using Cities to Power the Drive to Modernity and

TABLE O.1 Logistics Performance Index rankings

	Overall LPI	Customs	Infrastructure	International shipments	Logistics quality and competence	Tracking & tracing	Timeliness
Vietnam, 2007	53	37	60	47	56	53	65
Vietnam, 2014	48	61	44	42	49	48	56
China, 2014	25	27	26	10	32	23	31
Malaysia, 2014	28	38	23	22	35	29	36
Thailand, 2014	35	36	30	39	38	33	29

Source: World Bank's Logistics Performance Index (LPI).

Industrialization"), grossly underdeveloped freight-rail and inland-waterway infrastructure, and supply-demand mismatches in deepwater maritime port infrastructure.[16] Although expressways require further investment, transport expenditures need to be rebalanced from road transport (the most costly form of domestic freight transport) to multimodal facilities (for handling and storing goods in high-capacity warehousing) to take advantage of more cost-effective modes such as rail and inland waterways. Rebalancing from capital to maintenance expenditures in transport is also needed.

People-to-people connectivity. The third attribute refers to ease of movement of people across borders (for service provision, education, and tourism). Vietnam has abolished caps on the number of foreign workers that foreign firms can hire, and has new procedures for them to obtain work permits. Managers, executives, and specialists who enter the country as intra-corporate transferees are allowed to stay for an initial three years, subject to extension. But there is still wide scope to better meet global businesses' need to bring in specialist international staff.

Developing institutions for Macroeconomic Management

Stability of aggregate price levels, predictability of relative prices, and sound management of public resources are all critical for efficient domestic markets and long-term competitiveness. Vietnam has had episodes of high inflation, and public and publicly guaranteed debt has built up fast. The efficiency of public expenditure has also been low in several key areas (World Bank and Ministry of Finance of Vietnam 2015), while coordination between the main institutions of macroeconomic management, both at the center (Ministry of Finance, Ministry of Planning and Investment, and the SBV) and between central and provincial governments, is relatively weak. Resolving these emerging issues and meeting the anticipated needs of a more open and sophisticated economy require sustained investments in resilient, credible, and well-coordinated institutions for macroeconomic management.

Managing Monetary Policy

Some of Vietnam's peers pursue very different monetary policies but still follow sound principles. Chile, the Republic of Korea, South Africa, and Thailand pursue more classical inflation-targeting strategies, while Singapore maintains low and stable inflation by tightly managing its nominal effective exchange rate. Their central banks have been assigned price stability as the primary mandate. An operationally independent decision-making body, following a transparent framework, conducts monetary policy. Decision makers are responsible to the government for fulfilling their mandate, and they use comprehensive model-based monetary and economic analysis to assess the policy stance and communicate their decisions.

The central lesson for Vietnam is that it needs to overcome the current multiplicity of objectives for the SBV (Brand 2015). To do this, the Vietnamese authorities can further develop the SBV's close management of the exchange rate or, preferably, focus on domestic inflation. Both options require a clear price stability mandate and swift development of operational and analytical capabilities of SBV staff. The SBV could assign the conduct of monetary policy to an operationally independent Monetary Policy Committee, which requires that a host of analytical and organizational aspects be resolved first, including requirements for appointing committee members, frequency of meetings, briefing requirements, structure of policy debate, and external communication. In taking monetary operations further, an operational target consistent with monetary policy will need to be chosen, and monetary instruments will need to be market oriented. Having a sound framework for managing liquidity and forecasting items on the central bank balance sheet is also crucial.

The SBV could pursue price stability to help safeguard macroeconomic stability if it had more operational independence. But central bank autonomy goes hand in hand with transparency and accountability. Stipulating regular external reporting to political stakeholders and the public could ensure the SBV's accountability for its mandate. And to ensure that the conduct of monetary policy is unobstructed by concerns about fiscal dominance, the SBV would need to be prohibited from quasi-fiscal operations.

Vietnam thus needs to reduce the SBV's myriad objectives and strengthen its operational and research capacity. The current low-inflation global environment provides an opportunity for getting the monetary policy framework right before global monetary conditions tighten.

Strengthening Budgetary Institutions

The expected economic and social transformations over the next 20 years will give rise to complex fiscal challenges. Deeper global integration and further transition to a market-based economy will increase exposure to macroeconomic shocks and volatility, underscoring the importance of prudent macrofiscal management to maintain fiscal buffers to cope with shocks while ensuring a sustainable debt trajectory. Vietnam will also have to manage the transition from accessing mostly concessional external financing to relying on domestic and global capital markets to meet its fiscal financing needs. While broadening the scope of funding sources, this will intensify refinancing, interest-rate and exchange-rate risks, and expose the country more directly to the scrutiny of global capital markets and private creditors, placing additional demands on prudent fiscal management and transparency, and the country's creditworthiness more broadly.

The fiscal system will also be asked to adjust to profound social changes, particularly to accommodate the emerging demands of an aging population and a rising, increasingly urban middle class (Pillar 2). These trends reinforce the importance of a budget process that prioritizes sound spending and aligns fiscal resources to evolving social needs. They also emphasize the more self-reliant and autonomous model of subnational and municipal finances.

As Vietnam embarks on the next phase of budgetary reforms, the interlinkage between fiscal policies and institutional arrangements will become even more important, pointing to four key reform priorities.

Maintaining fiscal discipline and rebuilding resilience to domestic or external shocks (or both). Public and publicly guaranteed debt, having increased rapidly over the past few years, now exceeds 60 percent of GDP. While the risks of acute debt distress remain manageable, fiscal buffers to handle future macroeconomic shocks are wearing thin, a matter of concern given rising vulnerabilities, including those potentially emanating from contingent liabilities associated with SOE debts (at about 50 percent of GDP).

Strengthening macrofiscal management requires three main institutional measures. First, a credible fiscal consolidation plan, institutionally anchored in a medium-term budget framework, is crucial to stabilize and then gradually reduce public debt. Second, the budget should be more comprehensive, since many fiscal and quasi-fiscal activities are not yet reflected in the core budgetary sphere.[17] Third, the government's debt-management function will have to be upgraded to enhance the coordination and consolidation of debt-management responsibilities, which remain fragmented across functional departments in the Ministry of Finance, the Ministry of Planning and Investment, and the SBV.

Mobilizing resources for development. A fair, transparent, and efficient tax system that minimizes distortions and generates adequate revenue for the budget is crucial. Vietnam's current revenue to GDP ratio—about 25 percent on average over the past 10 years—is commensurate with its income. But its continuing economic transformation will shift the revenue potential of different taxes, which tax policy needs to accommodate.

For example, trade-related revenue (about 10 percent of total revenue) will decline sharply due to commitments under free-trade agreements. In contrast, the revenue potential of personal income tax is expected to rise as wage employment formalizes. Efficient land and property taxes could become a more important revenue source, especially locally, and strengthen incentives for more efficient land use. Tax-policy reforms need to be accompanied by further modernization of the tax administration, based on risk-based compliance management and modern technologies (including e-filing). Environmental taxes should play an increasing role, not only from a fiscal perspective but also to encourage energy efficiency by reflecting the costs of externalities from natural-resource use.

Improving strategic allocations of resources and service delivery. The fiscal system will need to cope with aging-related expenditures in the pension and health systems. And demands of a growing urban population will require smart investments in urban transport, solid waste management, water and sanitation, and health and education. The focus will have to be on adjusting the composition of spending and enhancing its allocative and operational efficiency, by instituting a clearly articulated fiscal strategy underpinned by a robust, multiyear budget framework, as envisioned in the Budget Code amendments adopted in 2015. Incorporating performance information and regular spending reviews in budgetary decision making could also inform allocation decisions and help in strategically realigning public spending.

Reforms of intergovernmental fiscal relations should continue to empower local authorities to respond to local needs, financially and administratively, while strengthening accountability mechanisms and performance incentives. Measures could include clarifying expenditure responsibilities, expanding revenue autonomy, and putting in place a prudent framework for municipal borrowing while strengthening interjurisdictional coordination across provinces.

Enhancing information management. A final priority relates to developing robust monitoring and evaluation systems, for fiscal policy to be guided by evidence-based decision making. This is the direction taken by most rising middle-income economies, especially in Latin America. Vietnam has invested heavily in its public financial management system and capabilities, strengthening basic transaction-related controls and capturing data more efficiently. Yet fragmented organizational responsibilities hamper full use of these systems for timely and comprehensive reporting and the disclosure of key fiscal information. Beyond technological changes, organizational and process changes may be required to ensure that financial and nonfinancial data are shared, processed, analyzed, and used well in decision making.

Reforms and Investments with Impacts in the Long Term: Developing an Innovation-Driven, Urban-Based, and Environmentally Sustainable Economy

Structural transformation is unlikely to be as rewarding after Vietnam reaches upper-middle-income status (around the end of the 2020s at its current pace). The returns from adapting imported technology and know-how will diminish. And the exploitative use of natural resources will certainly reach its limits. These checks require policy makers to make critical choices in three areas with longer-term gestations—developing an innovation-driven economy that is housed in modern, efficient, and competitive urban structures and is environmentally sustainable.

Spurring Learning and Innovation to Sustain Rapid Long-Run Growth

Developing an innovation-driven economy will demand an unambiguous commitment to cultivating and upgrading a dynamic private sector. It will also demand far-reaching reforms in the education and training systems for generating higher-order human capital. And more generally, it will demand a competitive societal climate that values openness to new ideas and stimulates risk taking and technology upgrading. All three were critical to the rapid growth of Japan, the Republic of Korea, and Singapore—examples that Vietnam holds up for its own growth ambitions.

Vietnam's national innovation system is weak and contributes little to output or growth. Still missing is a critical mass of dynamic and innovative firms that provides the demand side for innovation. Moreover, firms' capacity to adopt and carry out new research is underdeveloped. Also largely absent are longer-term strategic views on firm and product upgrading and the human resources necessary for innovation. These needs reflect the lack of competition in product markets and the low capabilities of firm managers (Bloom and Van Reenen 2007; Maloney and Sarrias 2014).

On the supply side, research institutes and universities provide too little research, and what is produced is mostly deficient in quality and relevance. Too few domestic knowledge institutions produce human capital with truly world-class skills and knowledge. The research and graduate (PhD) training systems are separate, so the virtuous circle where good research in universities also produces high-quality PhD holders barely functions in Vietnam. Government funding for R&D is spread thinly across more than 600 small government research institutes that produce very little valuable output. The allocations, small and fragmented as they are, are abstractly linked to meeting high-level socioeconomic goals in long-term government planning documents. It is seldom clear what government-funded R&D's concrete contribution to these goals is supposed to be, and it is nearly impossible to measure success (or lack thereof). There are few links between universities or think tanks and the private sector. And the separate systems for research institutes and research universities creates duplication, inefficiencies, and dispersion of scarce resources.

Impressive gains in access to higher education have been made, but a long agenda remains. Tertiary education fails to meet demand for high-quality degree programs. Public universities are hampered by a lack of de facto autonomy, which impedes setting or changing curricula without external approval, raising adequate revenue, or developing full-time, high-quality faculty. Faculty salaries (tightly regulated for public institutions) are inadequate, limiting the talent that universities can draw on and obliging staff to take multiple teaching jobs, often at different institutions. Private universities have more freedom to set their curricula and tuition levels, but cannot expand enrollments to match student demand.

A more consistent partnership between the government and the private sector is needed, as is greater ambition in reforming the university and research system. If improvements begin now, the system can be strong as the need for it grows. Today, few firms are fundamentally held back by the lack of indigenous R&D capacity, but as firms become more knowledge-intensive, they will be.

Placing Enterprises at the Center of Innovation

SOEs are sheltered from competitive pressures by government support, which applies minimal pressure on them to innovate and remain dynamic, so the SOE restructuring agenda in Pillar 3 is relevant here. Foreign-invested firms have the option of outsourcing their R&D production to countries with more developed science and technology systems. But spillovers within Vietnam from R&D carried out in such firms are weak, hampered by the generally low level of absorptive capacity of Vietnamese firms and concerns about security of intellectual property rights. The response requires improving the firms' absorptive capacity and securing intellectual property rights. Domestic private enterprises are either too small to need innovation or are so preoccupied by the business environment that the paucity of innovation capacity is not holding them back. (The reform agenda to tackle this challenge was seen earlier in the response to the obstacles faced by the domestic private sector.)

Improving Enterprise Capacity for Technological Learning

The emphasis here will be on helping firms improve their capacity for "technological learning," to know how to use processes and technologies for production that are in use elsewhere but new to Vietnam. This gradual process gives an advantage to the fastest-learning firms and readies them to seek frontier knowledge, new to the world. A broad system of firm extension paired with private-sector organizations, such as chambers of commerce and banks (as in Japan and Singapore), can help identify high-potential, high-growth firms that may merit further support. As firms become more sophisticated, they need higher-order and more tailored knowledge from universities and government research institutes. They also need a market-driven system of venture capital/private equity to finance high-risk and high-return innovation activities.

Ensuring Relevant Skills and Knowledge

Raising the quantity, quality, and relevance of research, knowledge production, and advanced training of human capital—while creating and deepening connections to global knowledge networks—requires the government's research institutes, and especially its higher education institutions, to achieve a new dynamism in teaching and research. The reform path includes many of the same elements that other countries have successfully used:

- Investing more in producing research, knowledge, and advanced human capital
- Evaluating the quality and relevance of all research outputs and related activities
- Rewarding the best and most productive researchers through merit- based allocation and awarding them enough resources
- Balancing the promotion of basic research and thematic research on national priorities
- Uniting the research and university-based graduate education systems and building strong domestic graduate education through strong PhD programs
- Accessing the global knowledge frontier through international links

Continuously Improving the Quality and Relevance of Skills

Improving the quality and relevance of skills in the labor force calls for greater responsiveness and dynamism in tertiary education—in four areas. First, workers should raise their skills by completing more and better education in a wider range of economically useful disciplines, entering firms as lifelong learners to stay current with the leaders in their sectors and industries. Second, students would see an expanding range of choices of high-quality, relevant degree programs, as externally determined enrollment quotas would disappear when a greater range of providers compete to give potential students the best programs at the best prices. Third, private universities and colleges would proliferate as tuition caps are lifted and those institutions that best meet the needs of students are allowed to easily expand. As part of this, financial aid would become routinely available to qualified but needy students so expansion does not harm equity. And fourth, information systems would provide aspiring students with essential facts about each university or college, such as the employment success of graduates, their salaries on graduation by degree program, and faculty qualifications.

Using Cities to Power the Drive to Modernity and Industralization

By enabling agglomeration economies, cities enhance productivity and spur innovation and economic diversification. Rising population and economic densities enable savings in transport and communication costs, lead to frequent interactions, enable finer specialization and knowledge spillovers, and heighten competition in product and labor markets. Cities create viable markets for specialized business services, freeing firms to focus on their core competencies and take creative ideas to commercial scale. Cities are also instrumental in matching skills with job opportunities, and density allows for an integrated "thick" labor market. Just as many Indian children who grew up to become software engineers lined up to move to Bangalore, a flourishing Ho Chi Minh City can help Vietnamese children find the firm that wants them—and will pay for their skill set.

Evidence from today's developed countries and rapidly emerging economies substantiates the tight link between economic development and urbanization fairly conclusively (figure O.8). No country in the industrial age has sustained economic development without rapid urbanization. International evidence suggests that doubling a city's population raises its productivity by 5 percent.

Over the past three decades, Vietnam has undergone an extensive urban transformation that has driven its structural transformation and economic development. In 1986, Vietnam had fewer than 13 million urban residents; it now has 30 million of them, and urban areas contribute over half of national GDP. Alongside rising economic density, the country also has an impressive record in keeping rural–urban and regional disparities in check through central transfers aimed at poorer areas that has allowed for the expansion of basic services and infrastructure. Even in cities, slums and urban segregation appear less of a challenge than in many other developing economies.

As Vietnam embarks on an even more ambitious growth trajectory, cities should be prepared to play a greater role in nurturing a burgeoning domestic private sector, supporting the growth of firm clusters that integrate into GVCs, and providing the logistics support and managerial capabilities to enhance productivity and accelerate growth. Policies and investments can be reshaped so that *economic density* is amplified around large metropolitan areas as well as secondary cities with demonstrated potential; *economic distance* to large markets is reduced to enable specialization; and *social division* in access to services between migrants and urban residents is dissipated to encourage human-capital development for social inclusion and greater agglomeration economies.

Reshaping policies is important as there are signals that the current urbanization model is constraining economic transformation. The main signal is the land conversion–based urban development model, with industrial zones developed ahead of demand and a proliferation of small, fragmented urban expansions that are not well connected to transport networks and service delivery nodes. The area of land for industrial zones increased by around 77,000 hectares from 2000 to 2010, with major fiscal implications as zones need to be serviced with roads and infrastructure. This could still be a worthwhile use of public resources if the economic

FIGURE O.8 Urbanization in Vietnam appears to be on a path as strong as in the Republic of Korea and in China

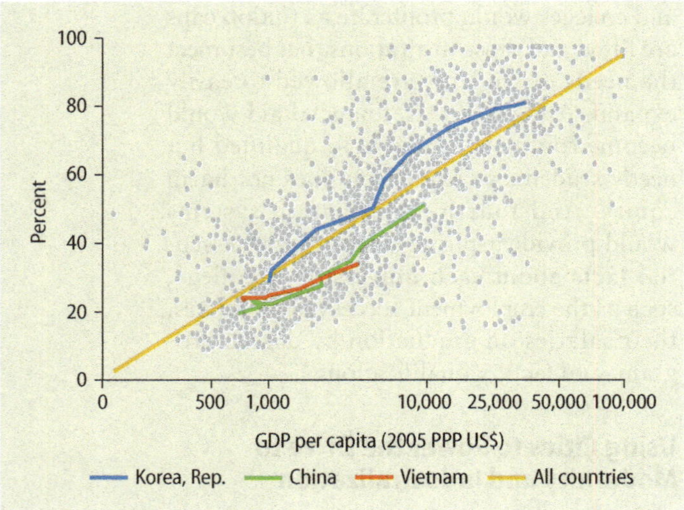

Sources: Calculations based on the World Development Indicators database and Penn World Table, Version 8.0.
Note: PPP = purchasing power parity.

returns were there. But this is not yet the case, with an average occupancy rate in industrial zones of less than 50 percent. Small, fragmented development of urban industrial and residential land poses an even bigger problem: 70 percent of the land occupied by industry in Ho Chi Minh City is in areas outside formally approved industrial zones, damping economic density. Urban areas need to be developed at scale.

The second signal is the limited connectivity between cities and markets as well as unreliable supply chains and high logistics costs. Logistics costs account for 21 percent of GDP—against an estimated 19 percent in China and 15 percent in Thailand—primarily driven by unreliable supply chains. At the greater metropolitan level, bottlenecks hamper economic efficiency and diminish their attractiveness to prospective homeowners and businesses. It takes nearly two hours to travel from the central business district of Ho Chi Minh City to the center of Binh Duong New City even at off-peak hours, a distance of only 40 kilometers. Weak regional connections add to the economic distance, with Vietnam's provinces and cities more like independent oases rather than parts of an integrated marketplace.

The third signal that Vietnam's spatial transformation is being thwarted relates to social division, where migrants to urban areas have considerably lower access to urban services and lower wages (see Pillar 2). Without *hộ khẩu,* migrants face numerous difficulties in applying for a job, trying to get a loan, registering a business (or motorbike), buying or renting a house, and signing up for medical insurance.

Two main sets of policies could be addressed for Vietnamese cities to better enable economic growth: upgrading institutions and expanding connective infrastructure.

Upgrading Institutions

Enable land markets. Land markets need to emerge and flourish. Reforming land institutions, like strengthening land registration and bringing in market land valuation, is a priority to reduce excess and fragmented urban land conversion. Increasing the transparency of land pricing by establishing mechanisms to regularly publicize land values obtained in auctions and individual land sales is a good start. These efforts could be tied to local-government fiscal reforms that promote broader use of land and property taxes as an alternative to land-conversion fees.

Enhance coordination. Local governments are rewarded for business expansion within their boundaries, undermining potential clustered development or economies of scale in infrastructure investment. The city classification system encourages local infrastructure development and fragments urban development. Institutions need to be strengthened for integrated urban planning—within and across sectors and at the corridor, metropolitan, and regional levels.[18] Urbanization is at a critical juncture, and its proper management requires a "whole-of-government" approach. The mandates within line ministries need to be reviewed and aligned with international best practices.

Strengthen urban planning capabilities. There is an urgent need to strengthen capabilities in urban planning departments to integrate socioeconomic realities in developing physical plans. Master plans and other physical plans could be linked to the budget process; if plans can be supported by key investments, their credibility will rise. Coordination mechanisms that can align provincial and city plans are essential, because the socioeconomic development plans, urban master plans, and sector infrastructure plans are prepared by different departments often running on different schedules and using inconsistent data and projections for planning. The timing of planning could be synchronized and the number of plans within a territorial space cut heavily (ideally to two or three). Vietnam also needs a professional cadre of urban planners who can plan and manage cities. A greater emphasis on this discipline is required in university education and in the talent that ministries and provinces hire.

Expanding Connective Infrastructure

Mainstream integrated transport and logistics planning. The government could push to mainstream integrated planning for transport and logistics across modes, geographic areas, and public-sector functions. One primary reason for transport modes to be misaligned on supply and demand and relative to each other is that they are planned individually, largely decentralized, and fragmented.

Improve road quality and logistics. Congestion in major urban areas has led to bans on trucks operating within city limits. The limited capacity of bridges and roads and the overall condition of transport infrastructure increase costs. Road access to big ports—Hai Phong and Cai Mep–Thi Vai being the priority—could be rebuilt, and key road corridors and expressways need more investment.[19]

Expand the level and quality of urban transport services. These are closely tied to refinements in urban planning.

In addition, there is a need to synchronize policies for rural and urban development; currently, these policies are developed in isolation. This is unfortunate and is leading to a growing perception that rural and urban areas are in competition—for example, for water resources—or that urban development has been predatory—for example, in inequitable land acquisition and compensation policies. It is important to see that rural-urban relations are the venue for the structural transformation of the economy. A symbiotic relationship between rural areas and a hierarchy of urban areas will likely determine how inclusive Vietnam's future urbanization will be.

In implementing projects and supporting investments, the authorities may want to recalibrate the roles of the state and the market in managing the urbanization process. In particular, they could:

- Refocus the role of the state and improve its capabilities in areas that only the government can manage. These areas include strengthening the capacities and coordination of urban planning, augmenting public finances, improving social services, and increasing investment in infrastructure to support urban plans.
- Redistribute responsibilities, powers, and resources among national, local, and metropolitan governments to ensure that issues addressed at the regional scale are not undermined by local interests.
- Relax the state's control of and involvement in activities managed more efficiently by markets, particularly land markets, where regulation has produced costly distortions. The solution is not new regulations but fewer restrictions.

Achieving Environmentally Sustainable Development

The sustainability of Vietnam's long-term growth is threatened by the environmental problems that have built up. These hazards are expected to worsen at an increasing pace between now and 2035 as the current model of economic growth, industrialization, and urbanization further strains the country's limited land, water, and energy resources. One of the lessons of development is that the environmental quality of water and the air is important not only for ecosystem health and the quality of life in general, but also for income growth. Four environmental challenges stand out for the last of the longer-term gestation responses.

Four Environmental Challenges

Deteriorating natural resources. The nation depends on natural resources much more than most other countries in the region. This is most evident in employment, with more than half the labor force depending on agriculture. In the mountainous northwest and central areas, poorly planned expansion of agriculture has eroded soil and removed biodiverse natural forests, degrading the land. The soil erosion has, in turn, contributed to more frequent and severe flooding of lower-altitude farms and human settlements. A significant portion of the protective mangrove forests has been destroyed, resulting in estimated losses of $34 million a year, while overfishing has seriously depleted nearshore fisheries resources, threatening the livelihoods of several hundred thousand people. Agricultural output has risen, but at the cost of increased land use and of chemical fertilizers and pesticides. Without regulatory and institutional checks, the next 20 years are likely to see greater competition over scarce arable land, more conversion of forests for agriculture, and even faster depletion of these precious natural resources.

Deteriorating environmental quality. The quality of land, water, and air has worsened considerably. Water pollution has reached serious levels, especially near Hanoi and Ho Chi Minh City. Air quality has also declined due to growth in fossil fuel use for power generation, industrial energy, and transport. A high incidence of respiratory infections among children under age five is observed, due to poor air quality, and an estimated 4,000 premature deaths annually are related to coal-fired power generation. In urban areas, environmental pollution from urban and industrial wastewater has resulted in toxic waterways with impacts on economic production, and unknown—but likely severe—impacts on human health.

Threats from climate change. Vietnam is among the countries most vulnerable to climate change given its location, share of population in low-lying deltas, and dependence on climate-vulnerable sectors. Forecast changes in precipitation, temperatures, and sea level all point to substantial risks in high-density and economically important areas. The country's response must consider the demographics, socio- economic context, political dimensions, and biophysical landscape when allocating resources and coordinating land and resource planning and use, in a climate-resilient approach to development.

Rapidly growing energy consumption. Energy use is growing faster than in any country in the region, led by electric power. Reflecting current trends and policies, the share of coal for power generation will rise from 32 percent in 2014 to 54 percent by 2030. Around 60 percent of coal used for electrical generation will be imported. The intensity of energy consumption (the amount of energy used per unit of economic output) is also among the highest in the world, and inefficient energy use is one of the main reasons. The energy policies adopted over the next few years—on energy efficiency, renewables, natural gas, and coal—will largely determine the trajectory of the energy sector and of associated issues.

Making the Right Choices

Given the confluence of these four challenges, Vietnam is at a juncture where the right choices can help it avoid the irreversible environmental degradation and major environmental remediation costs facing some other countries. A low-carbon growth path prioritizes investments that take account of environmental costs and results in inclusive and resilient growth, and is a more sustainable and affordable long-run option. It requires strong institutions to monitor and enforce plans, policies, and regulations for sustainable natural resource and environmental management; incentives for sustainable investments (with private participation) that benefit the environment and the poor; and improved access and use of information for decision making, monitoring, and transparency and accountability.

Strong policies and institutions. Much of sustainable growth is about policies that address market failures and "get the prices right" by introducing targeted incentives such as environmental taxes, pricing environmental externalities such as carbon, creating tradable property rights, and reducing inappropriate subsidies. Such growth also requires reduced resistance to change with, for example, information on the economic value of environmental services provided by natural assets.

Vietnam needs well-coordinated public institutions that can correct the market failures related to the environment, and can enforce regulations and standards. They are especially needed in the Mekong Delta, which is highly vulnerable to climate change and is institutionally complicated, with planning and implementation across several ministries and agencies with little coordination of investment decisions by provinces. Institutions also need to ensure that agricultural promotion policies do not conflict with environmental goals. For example, some locations have subsidies to expand their fish-processing capacity or boat building while making efforts to conserve fisheries.

Climate-smart investments. One move would be to accelerate the restructuring and equitization of SOEs in natural resource sectors, as well as in energy and heavy industry. This would also require enforcing standards, such as food safety and biosafety in aquaculture or improved energy efficiency (especially on the demand side). The government can establish public goods and services to enable greater private involvement in such investments. Better pricing of energy products (particularly electricity) will improve the efficiency of their use while attracting greater private investment. Private investment could be permitted in renewables other than hydropower. It will also significantly increase the proportion of electricity produced for renewable sources through the development of hydro, wind, solar, and biomass, in conjunction with the expansion of cleaner natural gas.

Information systems. Disclosure and harmonization of information must underpin effective management of natural resources and mitigation of environmental pollution and land degradation. The systems must enhance the data and information used for managing natural resources, and make the information understandable and accessible to the broader public. Vietnam could accelerate the adoption of technology in upgrading the environment-related information systems. But it must first update, scale up, and further harmonize the information platforms that already exist.

The net cost of sustainable and climate-resilient growth is usually modest in the long run. The up-front capital investments are often recouped through subsequent savings from low operating costs or new markets, and an improved skill base (if suited to the needs of the market economy). Most estimates indicate that investments to decarbonize energy systems often pay for themselves.

Pillar 2 Equity and Social Inclusion

Equity is a deeply held value of the Vietnamese people. The preamble to the Constitution of the Socialist Republic of Vietnam sets the goal of "a prosperous people and a strong, democratic, equitable, and civilized country." And Article 50 stipulates, "The State shall create equal opportunities for citizens to enjoy social welfare."

Vietnam's economic growth, particularly in the 1990s, rested heavily on the equitable distribution of land-use rights in the early years of *Đổi Mới,* driving a rapid increase in agricultural production. The government channeled substantial resources from this growth to fund pro-equity spending, which helped the country avoid the spike in inequality experienced in some other fast-growing countries. But past performance is no guarantee of future results, and signs of growing inequality are emerging. Looking to 2035, Vietnam faces a dual agenda: one unfinished, for equality of opportunity, and one emerging, for a rising middle class and aging population.

Underpinning both agendas is the need for a new vision of social policy. Historically, and especially in planned economies, social sectors have been considered "nonproductive." This view is changing. The social sectors are very much productive and becoming increasingly central to realizing the goals of knowledge-based and globally competitive upper-middle-income countries. Education contributes to productivity growth. Labor-market institutions balance productivity growth and societal welfare. Reforming the *hộ khẩu* system can help realize the full potential of structural change from low-productivity rural employment to formal-sector urban work. An adequate social safety net allows people to take entrepreneurial risks with the confidence that they will not face destitution if their business fails. And universal health coverage ensures that people are productive students and workers, channeling otherwise high precautionary savings to more productive uses.

The Unfinished Agenda: Ensuring Equality of Opportunity

Vietnam's move from collectivism toward a market economy has created incentives that allow talented, entrepreneurial, and hard-working individuals to flourish. But it also leads inevitably to some inequality in outcomes—the result of interaction between opportunities, effort, and luck. While inequality in outcomes is expected in a market economy, inequality of opportunity is inherently unfair and incompatible with the ideals in the constitution. Equality of opportunity prevails when social outcomes are independent of circumstances at birth. It can be understood as a "level playing field," giving all children an equal chance at success. Despite significant social achievements, profound inequality of opportunity remains.

The discussion here focuses on inequality of opportunity for three marginalized groups: ethnic minorities, people with disabilities, and urban migrants. Members of these groups—who collectively make up one in four Vietnamese—have faced particular challenges, despite strong government commitments to their full inclusion in society. The discussion also reviews gender equity, focusing on the imbalance in leadership positions and the sex ratio at birth.

Ethnic Minorities

The single greatest equity challenge is the persistent and substantial gap in socioeconomic outcomes between most members of the country's 52 ethnic minorities and other Vietnamese. This divide is driven in part by steep disadvantages in opportunities among ethnic minority children (figure O.9).

FIGURE O.9 Ethnic minority children face higher inequality of opportunity

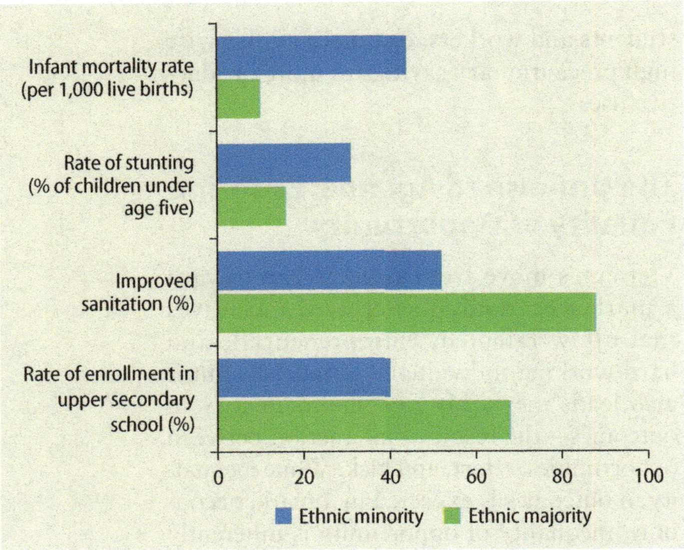

Sources: General Statistics and Multiple Indicator Cluster Survey.

FIGURE O.10 Triangle of unequal opportunity for ethnic minority children

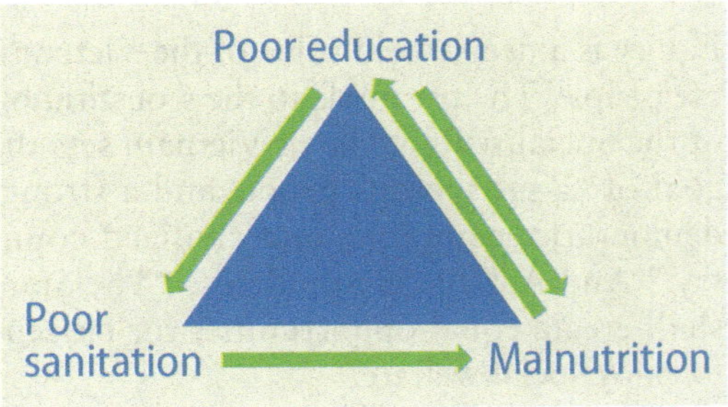

Over the long term, migration will likely be a pathway to economic integration for many ethnic minorities, which points to a need to focus on providing equality of opportunity for the next generation of ethnic minority children, so that they will be equipped to lead prosperous lives wherever they end up in adulthood. Three interrelated circumstances generate a triangle of inequality of opportunity for ethnic-minority children: poor education, malnutrition, and low access to sanitation (figure O.10).

The higher poverty among ethnic minorities can be attributed in substantial part to low educational attainment. The modest ethnic minority enrollment at tertiary and upper-secondary levels is a consequence of many factors, including childhood malnutrition, in turn driven by poor sanitation. Completing the cycle, children who grow up in poor households with less-educated parents are much more likely to drop out of school early, be malnourished, and lack adequate sanitation. In these three areas, focused policy interventions could close the opportunity gap.

Improving education access for ethnic minority children is the first policy priority, to be addressed by expanding current government initiatives: high-quality early-childhood education programs; placing teaching assistants who know the local mother language in the first few years of primary school to ease the transition for children who do not learn Vietnamese at home; and financial support—including cash transfers to households, conditional on school attendance—to make it possible for children to attend upper-secondary school.

Improving nutrition is the second priority. A vast literature has shown that early-childhood nutrition has substantial effects on early cognitive development and readiness to learn in school. Despite existing programs, high rates of malnutrition persist among ethnic minority children (figure O.11, panel a). The National Nutrition Program in Thailand, which reduced malnutrition rates by more than 75 percent in 10 years, shows what a concerted national effort can achieve. Such a campaign in Vietnam could include promotion of exclusive breastfeeding of infants under six months old, coupled with extension of maternity leave for women in wage employment. It could also introduce a comprehensive program to fortify basic foods with vitamin A, iron, selenium, and zinc. And it could develop new varieties of bio-fortified rice and maize and provide free nutritional supplements to women of childbearing age.

FIGURE O.11 Large gaps in child health and nutrition by ethnicity persist

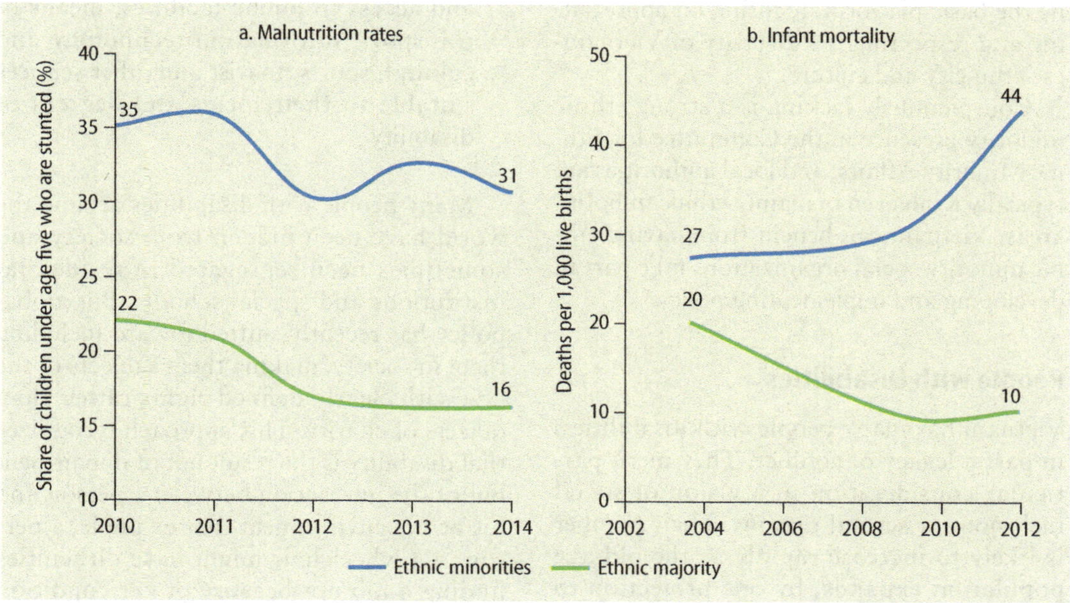

Sources: Analysis of National Institute of Nutrition Surveys and UNICEF's Multiple Indicator Cluster Survey (MICS) 2006, 2011, and 2014 reports.
Note: For the nutrition figures, the ethnic-majority group includes only Kinh, while in the infant-mortality figures it includes both Kinh and Hoa. Figures shown are point estimates based on household survey data. As with any survey-based estimate, they are subject to sampling error. The sampling error—and thus the confidence interval around the point estimate—is larger for ethnic minorities because their sample size is small within the survey. The MICS reports do not specify the confidence interval for point estimates.

The third policy priority is sanitation. Major drivers of malnutrition are poor hygiene practices and lack of access to improved sanitation facilities. In communities without improved latrines, children are often exposed to bacteria, viruses, fungi, and parasites that cause intestinal infection. The high rates for diarrhea and parasitic infection are two leading causes of morbidity in the northern mountains, and lack of access to sanitation is one reason for the persistently high infant mortality rates among ethnic minorities (figure O.11, panel b). And stunting rates for children below the age of five are high precisely among the ethnic minority communities most likely to lack such facilities. A targeted sanitation program, with incentives to promote communitywide behavior changes, can do much to achieve universal use of improved sanitation among ethnic minorities.

In developing education, sanitation, and nutrition programs for ethnic minority children—and programs to address ethnic minority poverty more generally—the government could benefit from experimenting, monitoring, and evaluating, since the evidence on what works is thin. Pilot approaches could be carefully evaluated before programs are expanded to scale. And for all three points of the triangle, initiatives could draw on promising new insights from behavioral economics. Choices about sending children to school, feeding infants, and constructing latrines are determined by a variety of factors other than cost-benefit calculations. Interventions in all three areas that seek to "nudge" behavior can be effective and cost-efficient.

Policies and programs to achieve equality of opportunity for ethnic minorities need to tackle prejudice and stereotyping and getting ethnic minority voices heard. Although the legal framework is adequate in recognizing equality of status between ethnic minorities and Kinh, prejudice against minorities is still common (World Bank 2009). Education can be the basic platform, focusing on appreciating and respecting the diversity of Vietnamese ethnicity and culture.

Conspicuously lacking is a strong ethnic minority presence in the Committee for Ethnic Minority Affairs, and local authorities are typically Kinh even in mainly ethnic minority areas. Vietnam can benefit from having ethnic minority social organizations take part in developing and implementing policy.

People with Disabilities

Vietnam has many people with disabilities, in part a legacy of conflict. They merit particular consideration in a vision of social inclusion for several reasons. Their number is likely to increase rapidly as the old-age population expands, by one projection to more than 12 million by 2035. As Vietnam reaches upper-middle-income status, it will face the rising expectations of people with disabilities and their families for greater inclusion. And given greater resources, it could meet the promise of its commitments to inclusion. Foremost among them are the Law on Disabilities, passed in 2010, and the UN Convention on the Rights of Persons with Disabilities, which Vietnam ratified in February 2015. Protecting people with disabilities is also in the constitution.

The UN Convention's purpose is "to promote, protect and ensure the full and equal enjoyment of all human rights and fundamental freedoms by all persons with disabilities, and to promote respect for their inherent dignity." The Law on Disabilities guarantees the following rights to people with disabilities:

- To participate on an equal basis in social activities
- To live independently and integrate into the community
- To enjoy exemption from or reduction of certain contributions to social activities
- To be provided with health care, functional rehabilitation, education, vocational training, employment, legal assistance, and access to public facilities, means of transport, information technology and cultural, sports, tourist and other services suitable to their forms and degrees of disability

Many people with disabilities around the world have been hidden from society and sometimes been segregated in residential institutions and special schools. But global policy has recently shifted toward including them in society, making them subjects of the law with clearly defined rights rather than objects of charity. This approach recognizes that disability is the result not of impairment but of the interaction between a person and his or her environment. For example, a person in a wheelchair might have difficulties finding a job not because of her condition but because of such barriers as staircases in the workplace. And a child with a disability might have difficulties going to school due to the attitudes of teachers and school officials who cannot adapt to students with particular needs.

On paper, Vietnam's policies for people with disabilities are highly inclusive. But there are substantial shortcomings in implementing a broad agenda. More than half the children with severe disabilities never pass through the doors of a schoolroom. Getting them into schools is crucial to provide them with basic opportunities to participate in society and to engender attitudes of inclusion among others.

One simple step would be to regularly monitor policy implementation. A mechanism for this is, in fact, one of the government's commitments under the UN Convention on the Rights of Persons with Disabilities.

Another step would be to create space for social organizations for people with disabilities. In other countries, such people and their families have advocated for themselves through their own organizations. Such campaigns have guided governments on policy implementation and ensured that they follow through on commitments.

Urban Migrants and the *hộ khẩu* System

Urban migrants are a third group lacking equality of opportunity, due to the *hộ khẩu* system. More than 5 million Vietnamese do not have permanent registration where they live, 2.7 million of them in Ho Chi Minh City. Although the registration system has less force than it once did, it perpetuates inequality of opportunity. Citizens in major urban centers without permanent registration face difficulties in access to services for health, schooling, social protection, and utilities as well as challenges in employment and social connections. Applicants for permanent registration face steep hurdles, including large unofficial payments to local officials, such that some people live in major cities as temporary residents for several years.

The broad objective of policy reform could be to further loosen the link between service access and permanent registration status. One option is to make it easier to obtain permanent registration. Many countries have some form of local registration for service access, and in most of them, obtaining local residence requires some proof of residence, such as a property title or lease. What distinguishes Vietnam's *hộ khẩu* is that permanent registration is possible only after two or three years of residence, and both the payment and document requirements are heavy. Costs and inequities would be greatly reduced if these requirements were lightened. A second option is to eliminate differences in service access between those with temporary and permanent registration. A third, suitable for the long term, is to replace *hộ khẩu* with a national identification card, with details held in a unified national database.

Gender Equity

Vietnam has made impressive achievements in gender equity. Differences in school enrollment and attainment by gender are minimal, and the gender wage gap is modest by global standards. In two areas, however, sharp differences still exist—in leadership and in the sex ratio at birth.

First, in business and particularly in government and political spheres, the leadership is overwhelmingly male. In the last decade and a half, the share of women in the National Assembly has been declining and is now at 24 percent (as of 2015). Few chairs of National Assembly committees are female. The civil service has a large share of women, but their representation in leadership positions is low, mostly at lower levels. There is a target that all ministries should have at least one female vice-minister, but the system for that is yet to be developed. Women's representation also remains low in key bodies of the Communist Party: the Politburo, the Central Committee, and the Secretariat. Women constitute only 18 percent of party leadership in communes, 14 percent in districts, and 11 percent in provinces.

Measures to boost women's leadership could focus on equalizing retirement ages in the labor code, using affirmative action as a short-term measure to ensure qualified women are fast-tracked to management positions, adopting a long-term program to identify potential women leaders early in their public career, and addressing gender stereotypes that limit women's career choices. This demands a long-term approach to update the education system and to promote healthier views of masculinity and gender roles in the media, and perhaps social media.

The second area of difference is the sex ratio at birth (SRB)—the number of male births per 100 female births. The much higher number of boys than girls born because of sex-selective abortion is gender discrimination and a threat to gender equity. The ratio was in the normal range of 105–106 in 1979 and 1989 (figure O.12). Since around 2005 it has risen rapidly, reaching nearly 114 in 2013, placing Vietnam—with India and China—among the countries with the highest SRBs. This imbalance will see a large number of surplus men starting in about 20 years, which may increase antisocial behavior, violence, and human trafficking.

FIGURE O.12 Total fertility rate has fallen over time, and the sex ratio at birth has increased sharply since 2005

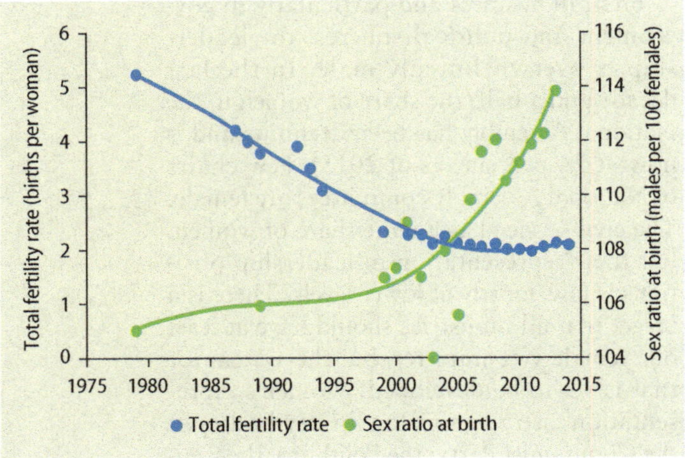

Sources: General Statistics of Vietnam.

The high SRB is a result of a combination of factors, including the high value placed by Vietnamese families on having sons, and the ready availability of ultrasound technology allowing sex identification. Families prefer sons in part because they traditionally have the roles of carrying on the family line and worshipping their ancestors. Another driver of the preference for sons is that they traditionally have the main responsibility for taking care of parents in old age. The population policy discouraging couples from having more than two children is a contributing factor. What would happen if that policy were loosened? Although the impact is highly uncertain, the slight increase in the total fertility rate in 2012–2014—possibly the result of a perceived policy shift—suggests that full elimination may well result in modestly higher fertility. The broader economic dynamics of fertility are probably more important determining factors: in a more prosperous country, the high opportunity cost of time and the wish to invest more in each child have reduced the desired family size.

It is likely that easing the two-child policy will help reduce the sex ratio at birth but not bring it down fully to normal levels. Government legislation to prohibit sex identification of fetuses to reduce sex-selective abortions has not proved effective. The imbalance in the SRB probably will change substantially only as parent preferences evolve. The government may be able to speed this evolution with, for example, public campaigns to emphasize the value of daughters, or by providing sufficient old-age support to lessen parents' concerns about not having a male offspring to support them in their later years.

The Emerging Agenda for the Rising Middle Class and the Aging Population

The second element of Vietnam's social-inclusion vision for 2035 is the emerging agenda of supporting the growing middle class to manage risks and pursue opportunities in a market economy. The country will also face a rapidly aging population, creating new challenges of elderly financial protection, health care provision, and long-term care.

Social policy should respond to the needs of an increasingly urban but also aging middle class whose needs are very different from those of the mass of rural poor that characterized Vietnam in the past. By 2035, Vietnam will be overwhelmingly a middle-class society, and the focus of social policy will have shifted from moving out of chronic poverty to helping the middle class achieve rising prosperity and manage the risks that could set back social and economic progress. While poverty will have been all but eliminated, in the middle-class society of 2035 there will still be a substantial group of poor and a larger population vulnerable to falling back into poverty. The growing share of elderly are likely to be at particular risk.

By 2035 more than half of Vietnam's population will be members of the "global middle class" ($15 or more per day consumption in 2011 PPP), with new expectations and challenges. They will expect that the state will provide a minimum standard of services, financial protection, and conditions for decent work, including affordable health care, quality education to at least senior-secondary completion (and often beyond), old-age financial protection and care services, and basic worker protections. They will also demand more voice, in independent-worker representation in the workplace, citizen oversight of public services, and broader civic participation. Middle classes globally have also tended to prefer avoiding high income inequality.

These changes will bring with them substantial new risks. For individuals, with aging and the rise of urban and sedentary lifestyles, health risks are shifting to noncommunicable diseases, which require more complex treatment regimens than the infectious diseases that previously dominated Vietnam's risk profile. The shift from family farming to wage jobs offers the promise of a better life but also exposes workers to new risks from economic volatility. These individual risks are mirrored by emerging societal risks: the demands of health care as well as social protection for an aging and middle-class population will create acute fiscal risks.

Ensuring High-Quality Basic Education for All

In Vietnam's increasingly market-oriented economy, the prospects for success in life are far greater for those with a high-quality education. Despite large gains over time in education attainment among Vietnamese at all incomes, the goalposts are constantly moving, and the country will require increasingly higher levels of educational attainment to meet its economic and social goals. The picture remains mixed, however, and suggests a need for continuing improvement. A child from a wealthy family in Hanoi or Ho Chi Minh City will typically receive high-quality instruction through upper-secondary school, supplemented by private tutoring, and go on to complete a university degree. In contrast, a child from a poor family in a rural area is unlikely to advance past lower secondary school (figure O.13).

Advances in education are also critical to Vietnam's overall economic success. High-income countries have workforces with high levels of advanced skills gained through education. These skills are essential to economic growth. The myriad specific skills combine in complementary ways with technology, and the educational foundations of the workforce allow individuals to change and adapt more quickly as the changes in technology and the demands of work accelerate.

The Vietnamese education system is inclusive, high-quality, and largely equitable through lower-secondary education. It then becomes exclusive, inequitable, and mediocre. It provides students with excellent foundations for success, but then fails to build on those foundations. Too many students fail to graduate from high school. Too few continue on to tertiary education; those who continue often do not receive a high-quality, relevant education.

A key policy priority will be ending the exam-based allocation of upper-secondary-school places and replacing it with universal secondary- school attendance. This is consistent with global experience—the Republic of Korea and other countries made high school completion universal as they grew richer (figure O.14). In Vietnam, this change will also mean that upper-secondary schools will have students with a greater range of abilities. Currently, students not admitted to academic senior-secondary school are usually offered a place in a technical and vocational high school, many of which suffer from low skill relevance, low graduation rates, and low student motivation. The fast pace of technological change and the increasing skill needs of industry will put even more pressure on the system. Consideration could be given to transforming the two separate subsystems (academic and technical/vocational upper-secondary schools) into a single system offering two tracks to a high school diploma.

A second priority is to continuously improve the quality and relevance of what students learn, allowing them to succeed

FIGURE O.13 A large gap in upper secondary school attendance remains between the poorest and richest 20 percent

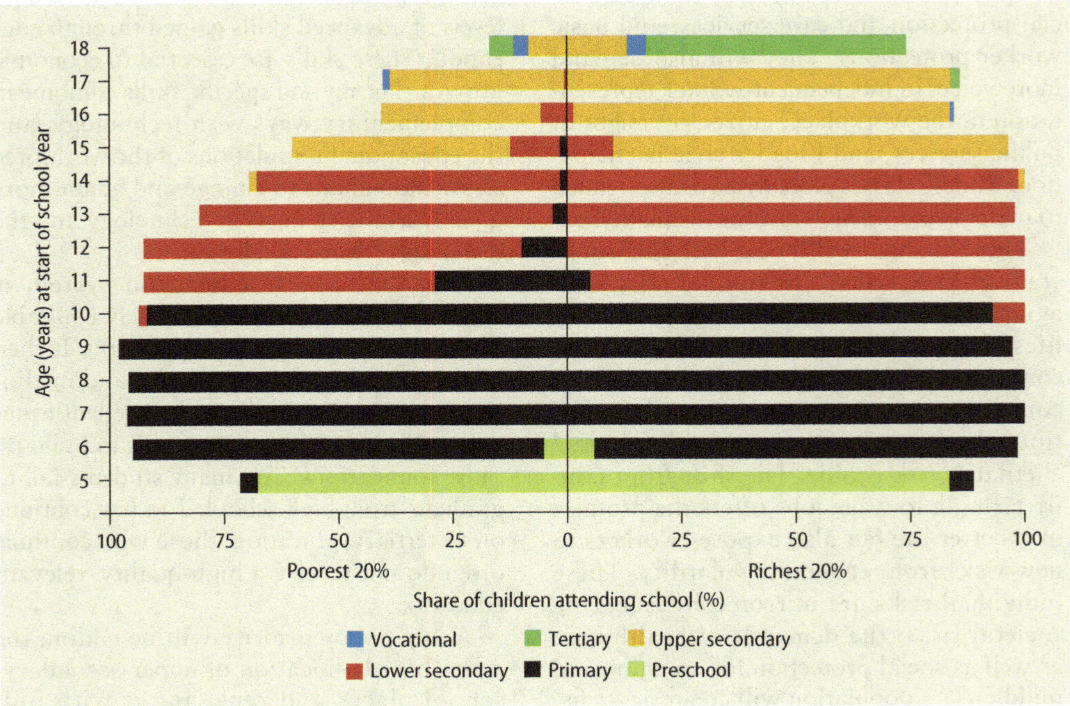

Source: General Statistics of Vietnam.

FIGURE O.14 Vietnam can follow the Republic of Korea's path in high school completion rates

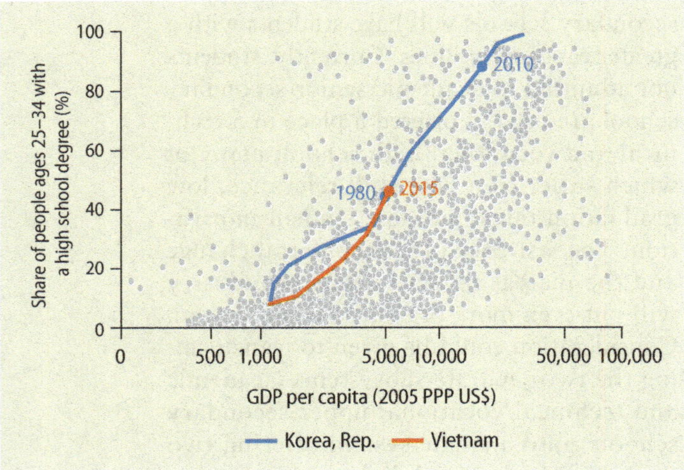

Sources: Barro-Lee Education Attainment Database 2010 and General Statistics of Vietnam.
Note: PPP = purchasing power parity.

in a more diverse and demanding tertiary-education system. Such gains would let them offer employers up-to-date skills and a high capacity to adapt to constant change in the workplace. The Vietnamese school system excels at accomplishing tasks that are more straightforward, but faces new challenges in developing noncognitive and complex problem-solving skills to prepare young adults for the labor market of a competitive upper-middle-income country.

Effective Labor-Market Institutions

To realize the full productivity benefits of a better-educated population, the Vietnamese labor market will need to encourage greater formality of employment while avoiding overly rigid regulation. This will depend in part on labor-market policies—and more specifically, on whether the country uses its current opportunity to address already-apparent weaknesses as it transitions from farms to factories and firms. Policy can help promote the growth of formal employment while ensuring that workers receive a fair share of the benefits of growth.

One concept that characterizes the policy goals toward which Vietnam might aim in its labor-market policies is "flexicurity." This involves striking a balance between flexible labor regulation that maximizes productivity growth and "creative destruction," and the needs of workers for decent, increasingly formal-sector employment that is equitably compensated. In other words, Vietnam can aim to protect workers rather than jobs as it deepens its structural transformation.

Improving industrial relations will be key, given the weakness of the current system, exemplified by the large number of wildcat strikes since 2006. In the medium term, Vietnam could consider more proactive measures to strengthen the system and promote harmony in the labor market. The Vietnam General Confederation of Labor and its affiliated unions could bar company executives and managers from key union positions (such as head of an enterprise union), following the example of other countries—such as Singapore, where company managers cannot hold principal union positions or sometimes even union membership. Vietnam could also continue to simplify regulations for resolving workplace disputes. And it could consider allowing firm-level worker councils or labor-management councils, as in many European countries and the Republic of Korea.

Finally, Vietnam could move more fundamentally toward an industrial-relations system suited to the needs of a mature market economy, where the interests of workers, employers, and the state are more properly represented in a true bargaining process by independent unions. Vietnam has already made strong commitments along those lines in the United States–Viet Nam Plan for the Enhancement of Trade and Labour Relations, a side agreement to the TPP. The main provision is as follows:

> Viet Nam shall ensure that its laws and regulations permit workers, without distinction, employed by an enterprise to form a grassroots labour union *(to chuc cua nguoi lao dong)* of their own choosing without prior authorization. . . . A grassroots labour union registered with the competent government body shall have the right autonomously to elect its representatives, adopt its constitution and rules, organize its administration, including managing its finances and assets, bargain collectively, and organize and lead strikes and other collective actions.

Vietnam further agreed that within five years, grassroots unions may form organizations "across enterprises and at the levels above the enterprise, including the sectoral and regional levels." If fully implemented, these measures will address many of the weaknesses in the current system, making for effective mediation of worker-employer conflicts.

A crucial element in determining productivity and labor market–equity outcomes is the minimum wage, which would be most effective if determined primarily with reference to productivity and competitiveness. Vietnam has so far taken a "living wage" approach, with a primary focus on the cost of living. Shifting to a "wage floor" approach that puts a primary emphasis on productivity and competitiveness as the drivers of minimum wage adjustments should be considered.

To achieve this shift, in the short term, the private sector would benefit from moderating the rate of minimum wage adjustments. In the medium term, existing plans to anchor minimum wage adjustments to real productivity growth could be put in place. (Many upper-middle- and most high-income countries exemplify the elements that Vietnam could incorporate in a minimum wage–setting mechanism.)

Vietnam would also benefit from streamlining regulations in employment protection to promote greater labor-market flexibility. It would benefit, first, from loosening regulation of labor-leasing enterprises and temporary and outsourcing contracts. To ensure that increased flexibility in the regulated labor market is accompanied by adequate worker security, Vietnam would ideally gradually expand its coverage of unemployment insurance and active labor market programs which, when well designed and implemented (such as public-employment services), can help enhance labor-market efficiency and worker welfare (World Bank 2014). Since such interventions tend to have important social-protection and fiscal implications, Vietnam should keep close track of the fiscal impacts of any expansion of unemployment insurance. It should also monitor the labor-tax wedge and explore options for financing a greater share of social insurance and active labor market programs out of general tax revenue.

Pensions and the Social Safety Net

As countries move up the development ladder, they typically expand their social protection systems to respond to the demands of a growing middle class. A key social protection challenge for Vietnam will be to expand pension coverage in a fiscally sustainable manner even as the ranks of the old-age population grow rapidly. This can be accomplished through diversifying the country's approach to pensions, reforming the existing public pension system, and gradually increasing pension spending. Separate from changes to pension policy, reforms are also needed to modernize and defragment the social safety net system. Additionally, as the old-age population expands, policy will need to address the growing need for aged and long-term care (ALTC).

Part of the social protection reform agenda is driven by the fact that Vietnam is at a demographic turning point, facing a slowdown in the growth of the labor force and a sharp expansion of the old-age population. The old-age dependency ratio—a common measure of the age structure of the population—has been roughly constant for decades in Vietnam but will climb from 10 to 22 between 2015 and 2035 and continue to rise in the following decades (figure O.15.) In other words, Vietnam will soon have many more old-age people to support for every person of working age.

Overall, contributory pension coverage in Vietnam is currently low, though not out of line with countries at similar levels of income (figure O.16). The pension system faces the common problem of middle-income countries of a "missing middle" in coverage: roughly the top 20 percent are in formal pension schemes, and a small bottom segment is covered by targeted social pensions, but the majority of the population do not have any pension at all until age 80 when they qualify for a social pension. Countries typically expand contributory pension coverage as they move toward upper-middle-income status, and Vietnam has set a goal of 50 percent coverage by 2020. Currently, however, it lacks a viable strategy to achieve this goal.

FIGURE O.15 The old-age dependency ratio will increase rapidly

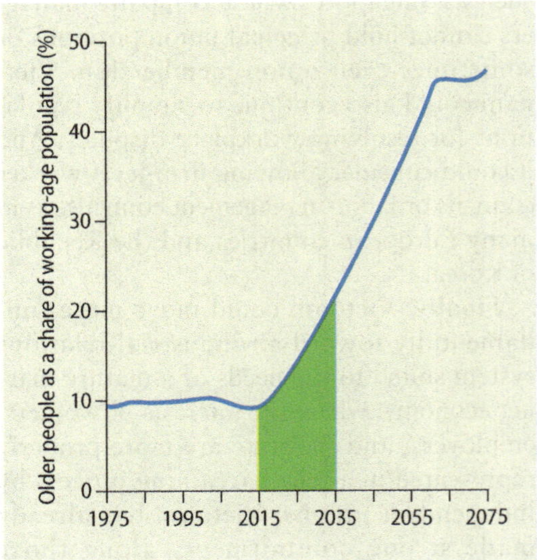

Source: UN World Population Prospects, the 2015 Revision (medium variant).

Scaling up pension coverage so dramatically will require a diversified approach, including subsidized coverage for informal-sector workers to incentivize their participation in contributory schemes, and phased lowering of the age for access to social pensions. Changes to the existing contributory pension system will also be needed. The formal-sector pension scheme is not financially sustainable, despite some reforms in 2014. It will begin to incur deficits from the 2020s and exhaust accumulated funds by around 2035. Even at current low coverage levels, the country cannot afford both the existing system and the contribution subsidies and wider social pensions that will be needed to expand coverage to informal workers. Needed reforms to the contributory system include raising the official retirement age, gradually eliminating the difference in retirement ages for men and women, removing incentives for early retirement, further reducing the annual accrual rate while broadening the base for collections to full compensation, and cutting the number of special categories of workers entitled to preferential early retirement.

Even with these cost-cutting measures, the combination of an aging population and ambitious pension coverage goals means that pension spending is likely to rise considerably. Countries with old-age dependency ratios equal to Vietnam's projected level in 2035 typically spend 8–9 percent of GDP on public pensions, well above the 2–3 percent that Vietnam has spent over the past decade. At the same time, average pension spending relative to country income and old-age dependency rates has generally been lower in East Asia than in other parts of the world. Projections for pension spending in Asia-Pacific Economic Cooperation countries suggest spending for lower-middle-income countries of around 6 percent of GDP by 2035. While these estimates need to be treated with caution, it seems reasonable to project pension spending by 2035 of 6–8 percent of GDP, a marked increase from current levels.

Changes will also be needed in the social safety net by 2035. Vietnam devotes

FIGURE O.16 As countries move to upper-middle-income status, pension coverage usually increases

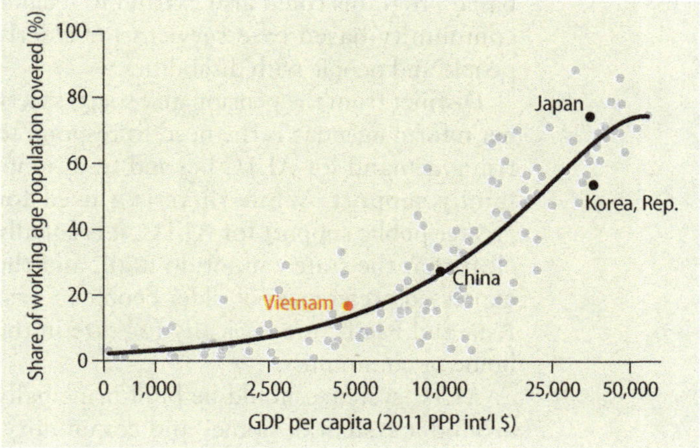

Source: World Bank, Pensions database.
Note: PPP = purchasing power parity.

considerable resources to its social safety net system, but fragmentation, poor targeting, and outdated delivery systems limit its effectiveness. Reforms are needed along four dimensions.

First, a more coherent policy approach is needed for social transfers to households, moving away from multiple fragmented programs with overlapping target populations and objectives. Fragmentation leads to high costs and poor program delivery.

Second, better systems for beneficiary identification and screening in targeted social-assistance programs will be needed to improve their poverty reduction impact. This would be built on improved integration of the proposed national ID system in social assistance program delivery, an improved poverty census to identify poor and vulnerable households, and more systematic enrollment procedures for social-assistance programs.

Third, modernization of the administrative machinery of the social-assistance system is needed. This will require significant investment in payment systems, management information systems, and improved client outreach and case-management mechanisms.

Fourth, the design of area-based antipoverty programs needs to be rethought to emphasize more diversified and community-driven income-generation approaches. Given Vietnam's rapidly aging population, these area-based programs could also expand to include community-based care services for elderly people and people with disabilities.

Distinct from the pension and social safety net reform agendas is the need to respond to rising demand for ALTC beyond traditional family support. While there is a need for greater public support for ALTC, it is equally clear that the state cannot do it all, and the expressed preferences of older people in East Asia and Pacific are typically for care in the home or community.

ALTC systems should be built principally around a system of home- and community-based care, though with an enhanced financing role for the state. The framework is the "continuum of care": the large majority of older people in need of care receive it in the home, those with somewhat higher needs access community-based care, and only a small and very frail portion require residential care. China's national policy, for example, is that around 90 percent of people should be cared for at home, 7 percent in the community, and 3 percent in residential care.

It is important to recognize that the government's role in financing ALTC can be distinct from the role of providing care. While the state may provide financing for ALTC (usually with copayment for all but the poor and people with disabilities), the private sector may have a substantial role in provision of care. But this, in turn, will place new demands on the state for standard-setting, human-resource development in the caring industry, and regulation of quality and the market rules of the game.

Universal Health Coverage and the Health System

The major policy challenge facing Vietnam's health system over the next 20 years will be to achieve universal health coverage—that is, to ensure that everyone has access to high-quality services without suffering financial hardship. The objective of universal health coverage is closely linked to Vietnam's overall equity agenda, both in ensuring access to services to promote social inclusion and in reducing poverty due to out-of-pocket payments for health care. Health-system performance will also become increasingly relevant for many of the broader trends facing Vietnam, including meeting the expectations of a growing middle class, addressing the challenges of an aging population, and pursuing economic growth. There is now strong evidence that conditions during early childhood—especially child nutrition—have a substantial impact on a wide range of economic and social indicators later in life, including schooling, learning, employment, and productivity. Ultimately this reality also has implications for economic growth. Increasingly the health of older adults will matter for economic performance, as Vietnam's aging population will pose new challenges to maintaining a healthy and productive workforce. Healthier older workers can help mitigate the impact of a rising dependency ratio.

Two big policy questions stand out for Vietnam's health system—on service delivery and health financing. On service delivery, will the health system maintain its current orientation, in which too many health care services are delivered at hospitals while too little is done at primary level facilities? Or will the system transition to focusing on primary care, with primary providers at the center of an integrated system? On health financing, how can the currently high level of total health expenditure be stabilized, with a concurrent reduction in reliance on out-of-pocket spending? An important question here is how the current pace of insurance enrollment can be accelerated, because by some estimates it may not be rapid enough to achieve 100 percent coverage by 2035 (from 70 percent today).

Service Delivery

The challenge is rooted in two interrelated problems: hospitals are doing too much, and primary care is doing too little. In addition, the different levels of the system are insufficiently coordinated. Vietnam has a hospital-centric system in which referrals and self-referrals to overcrowded facilities at the central and provincial levels are largely a result of low public confidence in the quality of primary-care health systems at the district level and below. The primary-care system is fragmented and ill prepared to address the challenge of noncommunicable diseases. There is a split between the preventive health system, which primarily implements independent disease control programs, and the curative system, which is largely responsible for treating illness, but not detecting or preventing it. For many patients the first point of contact is a private pharmacy, which is not connected to the public service delivery or health insurance system at all.

Strengthening service delivery for primary care is arguably the most important task facing health policy makers over the next 20 years. For quality and cost reasons, a strong primary-care function based on a continuous doctor-patient relationship is central to a modern, efficient health system. International evidence shows that a disease profile dominated by noncommunicable diseases requires more complex case management and coordination of care, and an integrated primary-care system is critical in the process.

To strengthen the primary-care system, a sustained program of reforms would include human-resource policies and development, more efficient resource allocation through reforms of provider payment mechanisms, improved gatekeeping modalities to ensure that people are treated at the appropriate level of care, coordination of care across levels of the health care delivery system, and quality-assurance mechanisms. This long-term agenda will require sustained commitment and investment. Strengthening primary care can also be supported by strong public health measures, especially related to tobacco control.

Strengthening hospitals can be done by balancing hospital autonomy granted under the "socialization" policy with greater accountability. Both the government and the public can play a role. For the government, a major factor will be to exert greater influence over hospitals through a more active role for a strategic purchasing agency (whether Vietnam Social Security or another agency) to promote quality and efficiency. This objective will require a shift from simply paying the bills submitted by providers to using information to ensure that patient care and cost-effectiveness are emphasized over hospital revenues. For the public, patients need recourse to grievance-redress mechanisms in case of clinical or financial wrongdoing.

Health Financing

The agenda over the next 20 years will be to stabilize the share of GDP spent on health near its current level and to shift the composition of spending to reduce reliance on out-of-pocket (OOP) expenditures. Vietnam now spends a larger share of its GDP on health—about 6 percent—than almost any other country in developing Asia, a burden on household budgets and the public purse. About 50 percent of total health expenditures are paid OOP. Most upper-middle- and high-income countries rely on OOP spending for less than one-third of the total. Some mix of government spending and insurance contributions will be needed to lower OOP spending.

Key to reducing reliance on OOP spending will be to expand insurance coverage to the roughly 30 percent uninsured population, but the current approach may not be adequate to achieve full coverage by 2035. Vietnam is relying on individual or household contributions and the gradual transition to a larger formal workforce. This process is slow and uncertain, and there will likely be a greater need for publicly financed contribution subsidies to encourage wider participation of nonpoor informal workers in health insurance.

The rebalancing of health expenditure between the state and citizens would require higher public spending on health care by 2035. A strong achievement would be for current health spending of around 6 percent of GDP to remain stable over the coming two decades, but with a gradual increase in the share of government spending from 2.5 percent of GDP to around 3.75 percent and a concomitant decline in OOP spending by individuals from 3 percent of GDP to around 1.75 percent. Donor and private insurance contributions are likely to remain modest. However, keeping overall health spending stable in the face of a rapidly aging population will require sustained efficiency improvements to control cost escalation.

Strengthening the efficiency of the health system will depend primarily on stronger provider-payment mechanisms for hospitals to discourage overtreatment and reforms to pharmaceutical procurement to control high costs. Hospitals purchase drugs at widely varying prices, and the high costs are passed on to the government or the population. Centralized procurement and better use of state purchasing power to negotiate prices under a framework contract with pharmaceutical companies would help control costs.

Public and Private Roles in Health

An important question for both service delivery and health financing is the role of the private sector. Around the world, governments are trying to achieve the right balance between public and private participation in all aspects of health-system reform. Global experience indicates that public financing will play a dominant role in paying for health care, but a significant role for private provision is more common.

There is no clear evidence from international experience that either public or private provision is "better." What matters most is strong accountability. Depending on organizational and financing arrangements, the public and private sectors may be equally prone to under- or overprovision, low quality, inefficiency, and other shortcomings. As with public providers, if private providers are to receive government funds, they should be held accountable for their activities. Accountability requires clearly delegating tasks, adequately financing service provision, collecting and analyzing information on what providers are doing, and enforcing the rules of the game. Regulatory and supervisory authorities can oversee public and private providers.

As Vietnam charts a path toward a stronger health system by 2035, a central challenge will be the difficult political economy of health reform. From tobacco lobbies to pharmaceutical companies to doctors, vested interests are likely to resist certain reforms. But Vietnam has made significant strides in the past decade—an important foundation for further progress.

Pillar 3 A Capable and Accountable State

Why Institutional Quality Matters for Growth and Development

Institutions—the formal and informal rules of the game for interactions in society—facilitate economic growth and development over the long term. They constrain or condition behavior by providing incentives to individuals and groups. These incentives determine whether and to what extent activities are fostered to create wealth, promote efficiency, and enhance welfare. For instance, an institutional framework that allows for easy and quick business registration provides greater incentives for new firms to enter the market, increasing competition, allocating resources more efficiently, and ultimately fueling economic growth. A rich literature documents the strong positive correlation between institutions and development—such as that between property-rights enforcement and economic growth and between the quality of educational institutions and educational attainment.

No country (barring some resource-rich ones) has risen to high-income status without strong economic and political institutions. While there is much country variation in political and economic organization, aggregate indicators such as the Worldwide Governance Indicators (WGI) show a robust correlation between high rankings on institutional quality and overall prosperity (figure O.17). Advanced economies have a system of highly evolved economic institutions that convey prices, define property rights, enforce contracts and competition policies, and close informational gaps between buyers and sellers (Commission on Growth and Development 2008). Almost as a rule, they also have highly developed political institutions—of voice and accountability. All the countries that have reached 50 percent of productivity of the United States are either 1s or 2s (the highest scores) on the Freedom House civil liberties index,[20] with one exception (Singapore) (Dollar 2015a).

There is also a surprising confluence in eastern and western thinking on institutions and even on their desired attributes (box O.3).

Not only are institutions important for economic and social development—a capable and accountable state is also desirable in and of itself. For a given level of income, it is safe to say that almost all societies would prefer a more accountable and less authoritarian state to a despotic one. The Vietnamese constitution describes the country as a "rule of law State of the People, by the People, and for the People," reflecting its people's desire to live as an open, democratic, and rule-based society.

Nevertheless, while global experience is clear on the long-term importance of good institutions, there is less clarity both about the specific institutions most important at various points in a country's development and about the precise path for institutional reform in different countries. The interplay between political institutions—to promote accountability, transparency, and inclusion in the political system—and income growth is especially complex and hard to determine. A strong positive link between political openness and the quality of economic institutions appears only at higher incomes (Dollar 2015b). In addition, the shape of political reform and how to bring it about are even harder to establish.

How Vietnam Performs on Institutional Quality

How should international experience be interpreted in light of Vietnam's positive record on growth and poverty reduction? Has the quality of its institutions kept pace with its economic and social progress, and can they support sustained progress in the future? These questions first require delving further into the various components of institutional quality and comparing Vietnam with other middle-income countries.

FIGURE O.17 The robust long-term correlation between prosperity and the quality of governance

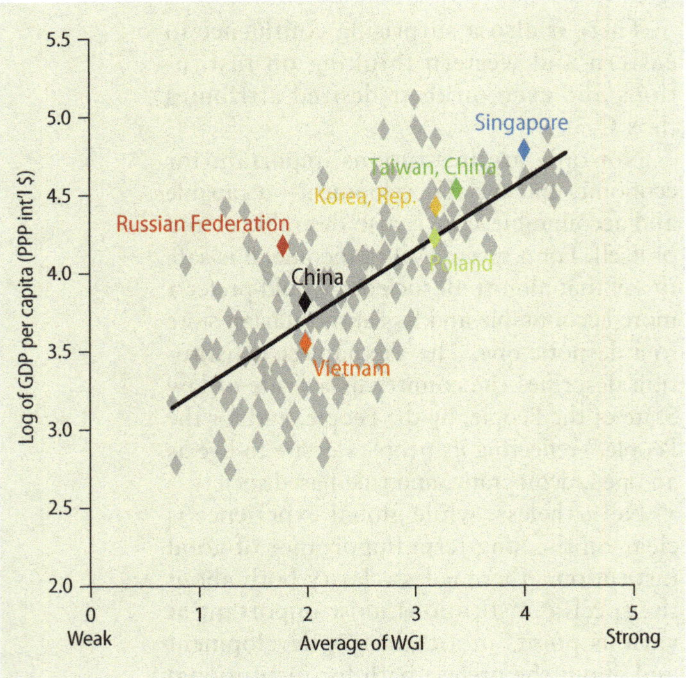

Sources: Kaufmann, Kraay, and Mastruzzi 2010; World Development Indicators, Worldwide Governance Indicators (WGI); and World Bank and the Ministry of Planning and Investment of Vietnam calculations.

Note: "GDP per capita (PPP US$)" is the average of GDP per capita in purchasing power parity in current U.S. dollars from 1996 to 2013. "Average of WGI" is the average of the six WGI Good Governance Indicators from 1996 to 2003. The scale of the WGI scores has been transformed from –2.5 (weak)/+2.5 (strong) into 0 (weak)/5(strong).

The WGI dataset provides one way to unbundle and measure different aspects of institutional quality (or governance). Since 1996 the WGI have measured six dimensions of institutional quality, and they now cover 215 economies.[21] Collectively, these indicators measure perceptions of "the process by which governments are selected, monitored and replaced; the capacity of the government to formulate and implement sound policies; and the respect of the citizens and the state for the institutions that govern the economic and social interactions between them."[22]

Among these dimensions, Vietnam does best on government effectiveness and on political stability (figure O.18). On both aspects, it is close to the average for all countries. It compares well with upper-middle-income countries and does better than other lower-middle-income countries. On government effectiveness, which measures perceptions related to the quality of public services and the government's commitment to sound policies in that regard, Vietnam has improved its relative performance in recent years.

But on two dimensions Vietnam does particularly poorly. First, on voice and accountability, it remains in the bottom tenth of all

BOX O.3 State effectiveness and development: Confluence of Eastern and Western thought

Economists who have studied in the Western tradition look to Adam Smith for the first definitive statement of the role of the state in economic development. For Smith, the proper realm of state action was limited to defense, justice, the rule of law, the establishment of public institutions, and the provision of public goods (Smith 1904). While often cited as an advocate for a limited state, Smith made it clear that state action included public education, control of monopolies, and other forms of business regulations. He understood the importance of an effective state to economic prosperity (Viner 1927).

Vietnamese economists have recourse to an older tradition, similar in many respects to the ideal state that Smith described. Confucian political philosophy is based on the creation and maintenance of a meritocratic bureaucracy, legal protection for property rights and contracts, military defense, and public works, especially water control. The aim of government was to protect the general welfare of people through mechanisms like stabilizing food prices, redistributing rice to the poor, and providing famine relief (Nolan 2004). The ideal monarch was expected to govern virtuously and to give equal emphasis to administration and moral guidance.

The characteristics of modern bureaucracy that Max Weber describes would not be unfamiliar to Chinese or Vietnamese officials under the *ancien*

(Box continues next page)

BOX O.3 (continued)

régime: fixed jurisdictions, hierarchical organization, meticulous record keeping, meritocracy, full-time employment (no moonlighting), and rule-based authority with all citizens subject to the same treatment (Weber 1946). Like the philosopher-officials of ancient China, Weber had in mind an ideal type of a properly functioning state, a model that governments in the real world may aspire to but rarely achieve. In the real world, rules, often unclear, are designed to serve special interests. Appointments are made on the basis of patronage rather than merit. Hierarchical structures are undermined by politics and clientelism. And overlapping responsibilities create confusion and lead to power struggles. The philosopher-kings of the Confucian ideal were challenged in practice by regional aristocrats and warlords in China, the Republic of Korea, and Vietnam.

Source: Pincus 2015.

countries, and its relative ranking across all countries has fallen since 1996. Second, it also compares poorly with middle-income countries on regulatory quality, which measures the perceptions of the capacity of the state to formulate and implement policies aimed at private-sector development; its ranking on this dimension has stagnated in the past 20 years.

On the other two dimensions—rule of law (which measures confidence in societal rules, including in contract enforcement and property rights) and control of corruption (which looks at perceptions of the extent to which public power is used for private gain and to which the state has been "captured")—Vietnam does worse than the average of upper-middle-income countries although it is roughly the same or better than other lower-middle-income countries. Its ranking has remained roughly the same on both aspects since 1996.

These comparisons indicate the aspects of institutional quality (or governance) that Vietnam might focus on in the coming years if it is to achieve the biggest development impact. As countries move up from lower to upper-middle-income status, their economies become more complex and diversified. The quality of government and particularly its ability to work with and regulate the private sector efficiently become even more

FIGURE O.18 Worldwide Governance Indicators, 2014

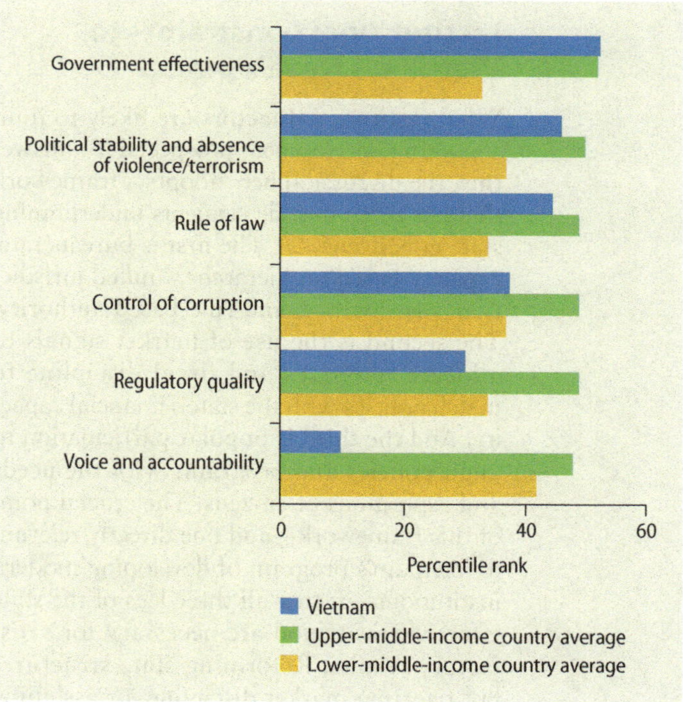

Source: Worldwide Governance Indicators, www.govindicators.org.
Note: The Worldwide Governance Indicators (WGI) are a research dataset summarizing the views on the quality of governance provided by a large number of enterprise, citizen, and expert survey respondents in industrial and developing countries. These data are gathered from a number of survey institutes, think tanks, nongovernmental organizations, international organizations, and private-sector firms. The WGI do not reflect the official views of the World Bank, its Executive Directors, or the countries they represent. The WGI are not used by the World Bank Group to allocate resources.

important. This can be seen in the large difference between lower-middle- and upper-middle-income countries in such indicators as regulatory quality, rule of law, and control of corruption. Voice and accountability in turn appear to become more important as countries make the transition to high-income status, even if the exact timing and nature of the relationship are hard to determine. In the long term, countries with more open and inclusive political institutions generate greater room for innovation and personal creativity, thus stimulating productivity improvements and higher standards of living (Acemoglu and Robinson 2013). For Vietnam, finding ways of building more open and accountable political institutions will eventually be essential.

Institutional Constraints to Vietnam's Development

What institutional factors are likely to limit Vietnam's development prospects? To answer this, the discussion here adopts a framework that has three specific elements underpinning state effectiveness.[23] The first is bureaucratic capacity based on hierarchy, unified jurisdiction, meritocracy, and rule-based authority. The second is the use of market signals to allocate resources and fiscal discipline to match policies with the state's financial capacity. And the third is popular participation to align policies and programs with the needs and aspirations of citizens. The crucial point of this framework—and one directly relevant to Vietnam's program of developing modern institutions—is that all three legs of the state effectiveness tripod are necessary for satisfactory results. Reforming state structures but rejecting market discipline, or assigning a larger role to the market mechanism while insulating government decision making from the community, is unlikely to generate positive outcomes.

Three mutually reinforcing factors dominate in explaining Vietnam's state effectiveness challenge: commercialization of state institutions, their excessive fragmentation, and few checks and balances within the government, along with limited voice and participation of citizens (Pincus 2015).

Commercialization of State Institutions

Commercialization of state institutions in Vietnam refers to emergence of an entrepreneurial business class within or closely connected to the state (rather than outside it). It also refers to the continuing strong engagement of the state in economic activity directly through SOEs, particularly through large state economic groups, and indirectly through close links between the state and an exclusive segment of the domestic private sector. Vietnam is not alone in having influential vested interests, but the degree to which relationships to the state are integral to economic success appears to be unusually high.

Commercialization of state institutions is not new, dating as far back as the beginning of central planning in the mid-1970s (immediately after Reunification). Pressure for reform started from below and grew from the cracks in central planning. With pervasive shortages and the economy on the brink of collapse shortly after central planning was instituted, individuals and entities with access to external aid began to trade outside the central planning system (Fforde and Paine 1987; Abrami 2002). Managers of state companies became adept at trading in scarce commodities, and local authorities tolerated cross-border smuggling to gain access to essential supplies in exchange for illegal levies, with part channeled into local government budgets to reduce deficits. Over time, growing tolerance toward these and other "fence-breaking" activities created underground markets for commodities and factors of production that gradually gained legitimacy and acceptance. The state increased the space for market transactions and, more important, was itself effectively marketized or commercialized (Cheshier 2010; Fforde 2007).

State commercialization has imposed efficiency costs on the economy and contributed to the stagnation in productivity (Pillar 1). One set of costs arises from the poor performance of SOEs, which have consistently been inefficient users of land and capital and which retain a dominant role in key sectors of the economy. Their presence is not unusual in many economies, especially in sectors that are natural monopolies (public utilities) or are capital intensive (large infrastructure), with competitive markets leaving plenty of room for the private sector to prosper. But in Vietnam, the SOE presence is almost across the board—from garment manufacturing to mobile telephone services and to banking—in activities where private players could do a better job.

And if the state decides to keep its extensive role in production, it needs to be neutral to private competition. This argues against state subsidies to SOEs, preferential tax treatment, and privileged access to land, finance, and government procurement contracts—all undermining the viability of domestic private firms. Crowding out a genuinely private commercial class independent of the state or its functionaries is the second cost of the commercialization of state institutions.

The blurred division between the state and the private sector imposes static inefficiencies on the economy as high-cost producers are rewarded at the expense of consumers and more efficient firms (box O.4). Dynamic inefficiencies also arise as potential investors are discouraged by regulatory risk and concerns that markets will be captured by connected firms. Beyond its costs to the economy, commercialization of state institutions weakens the effectiveness of the state itself. It creates powerful incentives for public officials to exploit their regulatory powers and allocations of property rights to lock in long-term benefits for themselves, their families, or their networks. Such abuses of public authority undermine the legitimacy of state institutions.

Excessive Fragmentation of the State

In tandem with commercialization of state institutions is their fragmentation—related and mutually reinforcing. State fragmentation refers to the lack of clear hierarchy and assignment of roles and responsibilities within the central government and between the center and the provinces—and to the inertia and inefficiencies this generates in formulating and implementing policy. Horizontal and vertical fragmentation of power has resulted in overlapping mandates, conflicting rules and decisions, and space for interagency bargaining in the bureaucracy. Apex

BOX O.4 Webs of state connections driving the pharmaceutical industry

The pharmaceutical industry has 170 companies, including 20 joint-venture foreign-invested firms, with the largest company controlling less than 5 percent of the market. SOEs have emerged in every province to supply generic medicines to local hospitals and clinics. Direct sales to hospitals account for about one-third of the market, and pharmacies the remainder.

Although the largest former SOEs have been equitized, they continue to prosper on the basis of close relationships with distributors and hospitals in their areas. Procurement is largely by individual hospitals, and bidding is open to corruption, with allegations of high markups for producers making payments to hospital administrators. Foreign enterprises, prohibited from distributing pharmaceutical products in Vietnam, rely on local distributors. Product registration, a responsibility of the Drug Administration of Vietnam, requires lengthy local trials and is conducted case by case, with the regulator retaining considerable discretion. Under these conditions, genuinely private and foreign firms are disadvantaged in market access, enabling small producers of generic drugs to survive in what on the surface looks like a highly competitive market.

Source: Pincus 2015.

institutions in central government include the Office of the Government, the Ministry of Finance, and the Ministry of Planning and Investment. These entities formulate policies, often deploying interministerial task forces to achieve consensus. Cohesion in planning is in theory provided by the guiding role of the Communist Party. However, in practice power within the state apparatus is fragmented across numerous agencies at every level, and between the center and provinces. The absence of a clear hierarchy and distribution of authority creates room for individual agencies to resist decisions they see as against their interests (box O.5). The result is often gridlock or decisions that are suboptimal from society's point of view.

The origins of state fragmentation, too, date back a few decades. The rejection of the planned economy that started with the *Đổi Mới* reforms shifted the balance of power from the central state to enterprises and local authorities in various ways. As output and prices were no longer centrally determined, the central government had fewer resources to allocate, so it became increasingly dependent on provinces for contributions to the treasury. Constraints on central budget funding meant that provinces were forced to rely on alternative sources of revenue, notably by creating and supporting local state enterprises to raise funds and implement infrastructure projects (Vu 2014). Foreign direct investment and international trade were no longer a monopoly of the central state units, and the high concentration of foreign participation in just a few provinces strengthened the hand of these localities immeasurably since the central government relied on them for the surplus needed for redistribution to poorer areas.

Vietnam is one of the most fiscally decentralized countries in East Asia, which has its benefits but also makes it more difficult for central institutions to set policy and to monitor and enforce delivery standards. The 1996 Law on the State Budget, revised in 2002 and in 2013, recognized the increasing role of local authorities and put in place a form of fiscal decentralization in the unitary state budget. Decentralization has included granting provinces powers over planning public investment, licensing foreign investment, and managing public-sector human resources.

BOX O.5 Narrow interests block a master plan

The development of the Ho Chi Minh City port system is a good example of institutional fragmentation. As a major producer of exported goods, Ho Chi Minh City and surrounding provinces need a modern port easily accessed from the main industrial zones. Ho Chi Minh City residents would like to move inner city ports to places where they will cause less traffic congestion—a change that would also free land for riverfront property development.

The prime minister approved a master plan in 2005 calling for four ports to relocate to the coastal province of Ba Ria–Vung Tau by 2010. Shortly afterward the Japan Bank for International Cooperation approved a loan of ¥36.4 billion ($328.6 million) for the Cai Mep–Thi Vai port complex. But each of the ports in Ho Chi Minh City is owned and operated by different companies or government agencies. Saigon Port is a subsidiary of Vinalines, the national shipping general corporation. Ben Nghe port is operated by a local state-owned company under the People's Committee of Ho Chi Minh City. The Vietnam International Container Terminal is a joint venture of the state-owned Southern Waterborne Transport Corporation, the NOL Group of Singapore, and Mitsui & Co. of Japan. Saigon New Port is owned by the navy.

In the end, the central government could not implement the master plan because the individual state agencies saw it as against their interests. Each agency used the regulatory powers and political influence at its disposal to advance a set of narrow financial interests.

Source: Nguyen and Pincus 2011.

Provinces have been granted increasing fiscal powers to raise revenues and broad provincial discretion in determining the composition of expenditures and transfers to lower-level governments. Subnational governments account for more than half the total public expenditures and more than 70 percent of public investments. This is accentuated by the numerous provincial-level governments—63 (58 provinces and 5 municipalities), a large number for a country of 90 million.

The growing diffusion of state power has created tensions between the attempts of central agencies to coordinate and rationalize policy and the efforts of subnational governments and subordinate units of central government to assert their autonomy. In addition, the lack of adequate incentives for regional coordination on investment decisions, despite the regional steering committees chaired by the deputy prime minister, has exacerbated the inefficiencies created by Vietnam's nested budgeting and planning systems. A prime example is excessive capital investment by subnational units. For example, almost all of Vietnam's coastal provinces have their own deep seaports. Similarly, there are about 260 industrial parks, in nearly every one of the 63 provinces, with plans to build 239 more by 2020. Yet the average occupancy of existing parks is well below half their capacity.

The absence of merit-based management of public servants exacerbates the adverse effect of commercialization and fragmentation of the Vietnamese state institutions on the quality of public administration. Developing meritocratic systems takes a long time and responds to particular political imperatives,[24] but some features of Vietnam's system present problems for efficiently recruiting and deploying public-sector staff. While low pay and difficulties in recruiting people with skills are challenges in most developing countries, three specific features impede a more strategic approach to the civil service in Vietnam.

First, though reforms were enacted to switch to a position-based system in 2008, they have not been implemented, and recruitment and promotion continue largely on seniority rather than merit. Second, civil service management remains incoherent, with human-resource functions carried out by three entities within the government plus the Central Committee Secretariat and Organization Commission. Third, duplication between party and government rules prevents deploying talent where it is most needed and limits the development of talent across the services. As a result, a highly professional public service has yet to emerge that can plan, design, and implement policies and strategies for an increasingly sophisticated economy and society (Phuc 2015).

Few Checks and Balances in Government—and Limited Citizen Voice and Participation

Vietnam's political system has adapted to create space for informed discussion of policy issues and assessment of government performance. The institutionalization of the National Assembly, provincial People's Councils, and "grassroots democracy" at the village level are examples. But Vietnam does not yet have a robust accountability system that can strengthen the state's effectiveness. Two constraints are fundamental.

The first is the absence of an effective system of checks and balances in the functioning of the different branches of the state. The National Assembly now engages in more meaningful discussion when passing legislation and is thus less of a rubber stamp for the executive's proposals. Indeed, in a few recent cases it has turned down proposals by the executive, such as rejecting the plan for a high-speed rail link from Hanoi to Ho Chi Minh City. But its role in formulating policy and supervising government remains weak. And while disseminating information and attracting public interest in political affairs, it is not yet a vehicle that can transform interest and opinion into accountability (Malesky, Schuler, and Tran 2012).

A key factor is a nomination process that limits competition and the resulting composition of the assembly. Membership is overwhelmingly part-time, with members in regular jobs in the executive at national or provincial levels. Quite a few are also leaders of SOEs, which creates conflicts of interest and a resulting bias to accepting whatever the executive proposes. Part-time membership and high rates of turnover between sessions (70 percent of deputies are new in the present convocation) also constrain the assembly's professionalization. People's councils, the equivalent of the National Assembly at the provincial, district, and commune levels of government, elect the members of the people's committees, which form the local executive.[25] But constraining their autonomy is an array of intersecting relationships and reporting requirements involving the Vietnam Fatherland Front, the council's party organization, the local people's committee, the standing committee of the National Assembly, and the central government. The supervisory function of the councils, limited to compliance with national policies and laws, does not touch on the performance of local government in implementing policies and programs (Vasavakul 2014).

The judiciary—the third branch of government—is also weak, with its impartiality undermined by heavy dependence on the executive. Appointing judges is subject to political and administrative pressures, while the hierarchical system of control in the judiciary undermines judges' independence in carrying out their duties. Many aspects of the executive's operations expressly do not fall under judicial supervision, while the courts are beholden to the executive for administering the court system. So, it is unsurprising that Vietnam's rankings on its judiciary's independence are below those of regional peers.

Nor is the judiciary an effective arbitrator of economic and social interests. Vietnam's formal legal framework has been augmented to meet the needs of a more complex market economy and to support its global integration. But the court system has not kept pace. The complexity of cases is increasing, given the growing sophistication of economic transactions and the body of law regulating them. The court system has remained effectively flat, with only a modest increase in the total number of courts and judges over the past 10 years. Underlining the weaknesses in the judicial system is the low public readiness to use the courts.

The second major constraint is the limited voice and participation of citizens. Vietnam has thousands of citizen organizations, and more than a third of the population is a member of one or more sociopolitical organizations.[26] The substantial increase in the number of business associations, credit groups, religious bodies, sports and cultural associations, and groups for the elderly is good. But they are not given the chance to participate in the same way as state-sanctioned organizations. So, the system is not inclusive enough, particularly as society becomes more complex and government-sanctioned mass organizations lose their relevance.

The government has only a few formal channels for consultations with citizen organizations on policy and planning. Grassroots democracy decrees have been put in place, beginning in 1998, to constrain the behavior of local officials. The decrees define or give a role to citizens in local decision making, including planning and managing locally funded projects, elaborating village codes, and handling some aspects of sanitation, village security, village boundary changes, development plans, and complaints. These decrees require holding more meetings between commune leadership and citizens, and making budget information available to the public (Fforde 2011). But the mode of citizen participation in local governance has not changed appreciably, and the ability to influence the decisions of commune governments remains limited. Decision-making power remains with the local people's committees.

Access to information, key to citizens exercising citizen voice to hold the state accountable, is still lacking. The country's governance practices have neither encouraged openness and transparency nor promoted public discussion of the state's actions. Information and data are difficult to acquire, even when public officials are required by law to provide them. Limits on the independence of the media constrain its ability in making information available to citizens. Vietnam's transformation since *Đổi Mới* has included more openness and transparency in governance and more space for citizens to discuss a range of sensitive issues publicly. But a culture of more open public debate on the state's performance will be required to achieve the country's long-term aspirations. As Vietnamese citizens become more prosperous, they will want to participate more effectively in governance to influence policy choices. They will also want the economic, social, and political freedoms that citizens enjoy in more advanced societies.

The Way Forward for the State

Modernizing the state will involve addressing all three pillars of state effectiveness: building a coherent and hierarchically organized state, applying the rationality of markets in economic policy making, and strengthening accountability through greater public involvement in decision making and stronger accountability mechanisms within the government. In 2035, the government will be less horizontally and vertically fragmented, with a clear separation between public and private interests and between the commercial and regulatory functions of the state. Economic regulations will be based on market principles, and the government will enforce clearly defined property rights. Greater separation between the executive, legislative, and judicial branches will enable each to perform the assigned roles without interference. Nonstate organizations, including social, religious, and professional organizations, will participate actively in public life, monitoring the performance of government and partnering with government agencies to implement activities and programs for the public good.

Building a Rationally Organized State with a Meritocratic Bureaucracy

The elimination of overlapping jurisdictions is essential for reducing vertical and horizontal fragmentation, and thereby decreasing the scope for bargaining and foot-dragging in the bureaucracy. A guiding principle should be to see that responsibility and authority for various public-sector functions are assigned to a single agency at the specified level of government. Delegation of tasks between and among levels of government would of course continue, but through clearly specified mechanisms and on the basis of objective performance targets.

Reforming Center–Local Relations

Addressing state fragmentation will require mechanisms for efficient center–local relations to clarify accountabilities and enable both tiers to work in consonance with clearly defined national goals. Reforming Vietnam's decentralization framework is key.

Vietnam needs a much clearer assignment of public-sector responsibilities and associated expenditures, especially between the central and provincial governments. To the extent possible, responsibility for planning, financing, and implementing public-sector functions would rest with a single level of government. Of course, this would not rule out delegating tasks between levels of government or dividing tasks within an area of public service—such as education, where personnel issues are handled centrally while delivery is local.

Three adjustments to the intergovernmental fiscal framework are also needed to match these changes. First, the nested budgeting system could be reformed to have financing more clearly follow functional responsibility. Such reforms in functional assignment and the corresponding systems for intergovernmental finance will likely improve accountability both upward to the central government and downward to citizens. Second, a closer match between functions and finances could inform capital investment plans, providing greater discipline in sectors where subnational governments spend, as well as making more explicit responsibility for recurrent costs when assets are built. Third, greater incentives to subnational governments to raise own-source revenues should accompany their increased accountability for financial management. In addition to providing greater authority with greater clarity in responsibilities for services, building a stronger direct link between subnational taxes and government outputs would strengthen accountability.

Strengthening the "Center of Government"

Given the scale and complexity of Vietnam's transformations in the next two decades, strengthening the center of government will be critical in addressing fragmented decision making. A stronger center will have several roles that cut across government agencies, managing strategy, coordinating policy, monitoring and reviewing performance, communicating results, and being accountable for implementation. Coordinating different agencies of government and aligning their objectives with the overall priorities of the government will be part of this role, as will monitoring the performance of different units of government, whether in different sectors or in the provinces. Communicating information to citizens about development outcomes can contribute to greater accountability.

Improving Public Administration

Reforming the civil service can reorient it in line with the changing role of the state from producer and owner to regulator, facilitator, and service provider. The capacity of the civil service could therefore be enhanced and its organization revamped, along three lines. First, merit can be a much greater factor in recruiting civil servants. Second, the profile of the civil service can be determined in line with the functions expected of it (rather than historical trends). Third, the compensation system for civil servants can be upgraded to attract and retain the required talent. One advantage in undertaking these reforms is that more than a fifth of civil servants will retire in the coming decade, increasing the freedom to reorient the age composition.

Applying Market Rationality to Economic Policy Making

Vietnam aspires to be a fully fledged market economy and to be recognized as such by international partners. The legal framework for a market economy has been put in place incrementally, from amending the Law on Enterprise in 1999, 2005, and 2014 to giving equal treatment of all economic sectors in the 2013 constitution. The government understands the need to level the playing field for all economic actors and clearly separate the regulatory and commercial activities it assigns to itself. This will involve providing for security of property rights, enforcing free and fair competition, and transforming the state from a producer to an effective regulator and facilitator. The government will also need to make sure that agencies directly or indirectly involved in economic regulation do not engage in business of any kind to avoid the appearance and reality of conflicts of interest.

Creating the space for a genuinely independent private sector will require political commitment at the highest levels of government and reduced state control over business and professional organizations, including the Vietnam Chamber of Commerce and Industry. Allowing these organizations to operate as authentic representatives of independent business interests would give voice to the domestic private sector and enable these groups to do more in monitoring government policy.

Enhancing the Security of Property Rights

The reform agenda would focus on transparency and on more stringent guidelines to reduce official discretion. The major challenge in the short to medium term is to reduce the opportunities for rents in valuing and converting land use.

First, publishing information on land transactions in auctions and (to the extent practical) in market sales of land-use rights needs to be enforced. All information in the property cadaster, including descriptions of each type of property, of rights held over the property, and of any restrictions on use, needs to be public. Any associated fees for access to this information could be minimized to reflect the actual costs of providing it. Land-use planning could be fully open to public consultation, and changes in land use, rather than ad hoc, could be planned with lead times for public review. Oversight mechanisms for procedural violations can be strengthened. And the rules for the government to expropriate land could be tightened to ensure a demonstrable public purpose and compensation could more closely match market terms.

In the longer term, the legal framework for property rights could include full fee-simple ownership rights. In addition, commercial investments could be made to obtain land through property markets, with voluntary participation of use-right owners, rather than state expropriation, which would be allowed only when there is a public- goods rationale such as building transport infrastructure.

Enforcing Competition

Vietnam needs a comprehensive competition policy framework to open markets to entry and competition and enforce effective competition policies. This policy and legal framework would apply equally to all firms (private or public). It would combat the most harmful anticompetitive practices, such as cartels. It would concentrate on deterring anticompetitive behavior and not on price control and regulation. It would be fair, transparent, rule-bound, and nondiscriminatory, and deviations from these principles would be rare, and only for meeting clearly defined national objectives applied fairly and transparently. The reform agenda associated with defining and implementing this framework (besides leveling the playing field between SOEs and private firms, which is discussed in the next section) includes the following:

- *Strengthen and give more autonomy to the Vietnam Competition Authority* (VCA). Lacking operational independence, at a significant productivity loss,[27] the VCA is a department directly under the Ministry of Industry and Trade, comprising ministerial representatives rather than independent technical experts. It lacks the basic authority to ask businesses for information to investigate competition cases. Remedying these anomalies would make the VCA more independent and more capable in its regulatory and enforcement functions.
- *Align the legal framework with consumer protection.* In addition to enhancing economic efficiency, improving consumer welfare is the other major objective of competition policy. The laws on competition and consumer protection and their enforcement accordingly need to be closely aligned to maximize the impact on consumer welfare. But a review of the consumer protection and competition laws shows that they are far from aligned. The VCA's mandate could be expanded over time to include aspects of consumer protection directly related to competition—following the example of the United States Federal Trade Commission, an independent federal agency that enforces both competition and consumer protection.
- *Rationalize exemptions to tackle cartels and other forms of concentration.* Addressing cartel behavior is an essential part of antitrust enforcement. Cartels have been associated with price increases of 10–45 percent in developing countries (Levenstein, Suslow, and Oswald 2003) and reductions in labor productivity and innovation (Broadberry and Crafts 2001; Evenett, Levenstein, and Suslow 2001; Symeonidis 2008). Hard-core cartels in Vietnam are exempt from anticompetitive enforcement if the market share of their participants is below 30 percent.[28] Even when

the shares are above 30 percent, several exemptions protect them. These and other exemptions in the Competition Law need a critical review to eliminate most of them, if not all. They create economic distortions, and in some cases they open the door to political interference. For instance, the decision on whether to grant an exemption goes to the minister of industry and trade if the failing-firm defense is used, and to the prime minister in some other defense such as contributions to exports.

Transforming the Role of the State in the Economy from a Producer to an Effective Regulator and Facilitator

Consistent with international good practice, the government could consider SOE ownership policy with clear ownership goals, focusing first on maximizing state capital. Globally, the best SOEs focus on financial performance. It may be useful to supplement this focus with explicit statements on supporting goals. Three fundamental and interrelated principles would drive this policy:

- *Adopt a commercial approach to state ownership.* This approach requires hard budget constraints and reliable and timely financial information, disclosing SOE financial statements for transparency, accountability, and fiscal discipline. Across-the-board improvements are also needed in accounting and financial disclosure practices. Vietnamese accounting standards could be made consistent with international financial reporting standards. In addition to internal audits, independent external audits of SOEs could be conducted in accord with International Standards on Auditing.

  Each SOE could have an appropriate dividend policy, approved by its board of directors. The state shareholder would not allow an SOE to retain or reinvest substantial cash surpluses without careful supervision by the SOE's board and the state shareholder. If an SOE cannot expect to earn an adequate risk- adjusted return on reinvested cash, the surplus cash could be returned to the Ministry of Finance as a regular or a special one-time dividend.

  Vietnam has too many SOEs, and the government could reduce its SOE portfolio to a manageable size. Many operate in manufacturing activities where there is no compelling rationale for state ownership. A central government target portfolio of about 20 "parent" SOEs seems reasonable for 2035, with a focus on strategic sectors, but even strategic SOEs should face competition.
- *Strengthen corporate governance.* Vietnam's SOEs need an active designated state shareholder. In the inappropriate current arrangement, the government is the state shareholder, many ministries or agencies exert ownership authority, and no specific government official is responsible for SOE performance. Taking Singapore as a model, the government could establish four or so state shareholding funds. To exercise ownership rights, these funds could review regular financial reports and disclosures and participate in annual and special shareholder meetings. They would vote the state shares in appointing directors to the board (and other matters for shareholder consideration). And they would help appoint an effective board at each SOE, appropriately staffed and organized. Except for normal matters relating to economic, environmental, and social regulation that affect all enterprises, government entities would have no authority or right to intervene in SOE affairs.

  The state shareholding funds could support efforts to further professionalize SOE management, providing market-based compensation, linking pay to performance, and controlling and disclosing related-party transactions. To act with authority, an SOE board will require members to act in the interest of the company, face no conflicts in doing so, and have relevant experience and expertise, including in the private sector. Selecting the SOE chief executive officer (CEO) and top management should follow good practice, which calls for empowering the board to appoint or remove the CEO. This power reinforces the board's key responsibility for overseeing management and ensures that the CEO is accountable to the board rather than to the government.

- *Level the playing field.* To complement stronger competition policies, the government needs to level the playing field between SOEs and private domestic or foreign firms. If an SOE is required to perform noncommercial work, the government could ensure that it receives adequate compensation. Relevant laws could be reviewed and amended to achieve greater consistency between the rules for SOEs and those for private firms. Vietnam's insolvency and creditor-debtor regime would also need to be consistent with international good practice and applied to SOEs. Finally, the government could seek greater alignment between public and private laws and regulations for labor and for procurement.

Strengthening State Accountability

By 2035, the Vietnamese state will have a well-functioning system of checks and balances between the different branches of the state, and citizens will have the ability to hold the state accountable. Both should also promote a stronger sense of individual responsibility and accountability among state officials.

Enhancing Checks and Balances

The state will need to provide for genuine checks and balances among the executive, legislature, and judiciary. Allocating power among the three branches will increase deliberations over government policy, and greater scrutiny of implementation should improve policy making and implementation.

The National Assembly could have its oversight span all the state's operations—reflecting all resources, assets, and liabilities in which the state has an interest. It could also be better equipped with full-time members, backed by trained staff. And measures could be put in place to address conflicts of interest that may diminish their oversight and to allow constituents to hold their legislators to account.

Vietnam needs a modern, independent and professional judiciary. Moves in this direction include increasing its transparency, disclosing more judgments and case records, and clarifying the roles of judges as arbiters rather than participants in cases. Selecting and promoting judges and other personnel could also be independent of executive influence. In exchange for heightened autonomy, rigorous laws and enforcement mechanisms could ensure ethical conduct and counter any conflicts of interest among judges.

Finally, specialized oversight agencies such as the State Audit of Vietnam, the Government Inspectorate, and ministerial and subnational Inspectorates, could be strengthened with greater autonomy, resources, and technical capacity.

Enhancing the Ability of Citizens to Hold the State Accountable

Vietnam has made some progress in creating conditions for citizens to participate in governance and demand accountability from government. Membership in nongovernment citizen organizations has grown rapidly—though not in all locations. The last several years have seen more public debate on development challenges, including corruption, the performance of ministers, and the weaknesses and poor management by SOEs. High Internet penetration now allows more use of social media for public debate. Three areas for reform could further increase accountability to citizens:

- *Relax limits on the space for people's social organizations.* Enabling citizen organizations to take part in decision making would give them a platform to take up issues and influence state action. A stronger legal framework would allow citizens to address their concerns and interests, and to have organizations with the administrative and fiscal capacity to pursue these interests. The draft Law on Associations, if enacted, would help autonomous people's social organizations develop.

- *Enhance citizen access to accurate and timely information.* Enacting the Law on Access to Information, under discussion for several years, and ensuring that the right to request information applies to all types of information (other than specific exclusions) and to all levels of government would be major gains. Greater transparency would strengthen people's social organizations and increase their ability to hold officials to account.
- *Provide greater independence for the media.* Separating media regulation from management and using civil (not criminal) remedies to improve the quality of reporting would allow the media to be more constructive.

Summary and Conclusions

Building on the nation's extraordinary record of success and energized by the aspirations of a rising middle-class society, contemporary Vietnamese leaders are charting a bold and ambitious future. Their ambition is emboldened by the opportunities that continue to unfold for Vietnam with greater regional and international integration, including through the ASEAN Economic Community and the TPP. In the 2035 vision, Vietnam will be at the higher reaches of upper-middle-income status. It will be a modern, creative, equitable, open, and democratic society with clear blue skies, clean water, and equal access to opportunities for all its citizens. This vision also foresees a state rooted in the rule of law with clear roles for the state, citizens, and the market; economic freedoms ensured by strong market institutions; and robust mechanisms to hold the government to account.

The Vietnamese people realize that achieving these aspirational goals will not be easy. Stagnation in productivity growth, inadequate attention to vulnerable groups, and growing environmental degradation are particular concerns. Current rates of labor-productivity growth, for instance, will yield per capita GDP growth in the range of 4.0–4.5 percent, well short of the aspirational 7 percent needed to take Vietnam to the higher reaches of upper-middle-income status by 2035. While a turnaround in productivity growth is yet possible, the reform agenda will be challenging. International experience on this front is also sobering, since only a handful of countries have mustered the necessary political will to carry out the needed reforms. The broader reform agenda will also be financially demanding. Given the state budget constraints, the needed investments will require much greater involvement of private investment together with ways to increase the efficiency of public spending so as to free up additional resources for investment, scale up revenue mobilization, and enhance access to domestic and external capital markets.

The country's aspirations and the supporting policy and institutional agenda stand on three pillars. The first one is balancing economic prosperity and environmental sustainability. The immediate emphasis has to be on ensuring more competitive and productive domestic enterprises, for which development of critical market institutions is important. Particular attention is needed to the institutions that protect private property rights and enforce competition policies. A stable, well- regulated, and inclusive financial sector and transparent and functioning land markets will also be crucial. And as the country embarks on an ambitious growth and economic modernization trajectory, its cities will need to better nurture private enterprise and innovation, support the growth of industrial clusters integrated with global value chains, and attract and agglomerate talent. Sustaining high growth over an extended period will also require an aggressive agenda to spur learning and innovation. An incentive-based national innovation system, focusing on the demand for and supply of innovation, can be very useful in this regard. Finally, Vietnam has to protect its natural resources, tap more clean energy sources and build climate resilience into economic planning, sectoral policies, and infrastructure investments so as to reduce the most severe risks posed by climate change.

The second pillar is promoting equity and social inclusion. The main elements of the middle-class and aging population agenda are expanding the pension system to cover a majority of the population, ensuring that nearly all children complete upper secondary school with job-relevant skills, establishing effective representation of workers through independent unions, and achieving universal health coverage. To reduce the barriers to inclusion for ethnic minorities, targeted initiatives in education, nutrition, and sanitation can close the large gaps in opportunities for ethnic minority children, along with giving them more voice. To make people with disabilities full participants in society, Vietnam can regularly monitor implementation of its strong commitments and create opportunities for people with disabilities and their families to be their own advocates through social organizations. Eliminating the link between the resident registration system and access to public services (currently affecting 5 million people) will improve urban migrants' access to schooling, health care, and administrative services. And minimizing gender discrimination in the retirement age and using affirmative action as a short-term measure will create more opportunities for women in public leadership roles.

The third pillar is bolstering the state's capacity and accountability. Today's stagnant productivity and weak environment for private-sector development are attributable to demonstrable gaps in state effectiveness. Vietnam's unique history has produced public-sector institutions that are commercialized and fragmented and that face insufficient scrutiny by citizens. Efforts to address these issues will build more coherent government structures and a stronger, more meritocratic bureaucracy. Market rationality can be applied more to economic policy making by clearly demarcating the public and private spheres, implementing conflict of interest provisions, enhancing the security of property rights (particularly around land issues), enforcing market competition, and streamlining state participation in the economy. And public accountability can be increased by allowing for genuine checks and balances among the three branches of government, providing a legal framework to promote the rights of citizens and improve their access to accurate and timely information, and assuring a stronger role for mass media.

Vietnam is at a turning point on its development path. There are tremendous opportunities on offer, as well as major challenges and difficulties. To achieve the 2035 vision, the only viable choice is for the country to carry out a bold program of reforms that is consistent with the three pillars. Without this, Vietnam will find it very hard to avoid the "middle-income trap" and will fall well short of its significant potential.

Current and future generations of Vietnamese people have the strong will, the spirit, and the capacity to implement the reform agenda successfully and move toward a prosperous, creative, equitable, and democratic Vietnam.

Notes

1. https://en.wikipedia.org/wiki/History_of_Vietnam.
2. Major steps included the decollectivization of agriculture in 1988, the creation of tradable land-use rights under the 1993 Land Law, the 1992 Law on Enterprises, the 1996 Foreign Investment Law, and liberalization of the trade regime, which paved the way for World Trade Organization membership in 2007.
3. Since 2008, the ratio of employment in the manufacturing sector to total employment has stagnated at about 14 percent.
4. The discussion on the four global megatrends draws on Centennial Asia Advisors 2015.
5. The three Asian economies are projected to contribute more than 40 percent of the increase in global GDP between 2014 and 2035, with their collective share in world GDP rising from 22 percent in 2014 to 29 percent in 2035.
6. This subsection draws on Centennial Asia Advisors 2015.
7. Intergovernmental Panel on Climate Change (IPCC) 2007 report, available from the General Statistics Office of Vietnam.
8. These projections do not take into account land subsidence, which further exacerbates the impacts of sea-level rise.
9. Today, the government registry comprises more than 650,000 domestic private enterprises, compared with only 40,000 in 1999 and virtually none in 1990.
10. Eighteen percent of Vietnamese adults have borrowed from a financial institution in 2015, up from 16 percent in 2011. In comparison, only about 7.5 percent of the population in the average lower-middle-income country has currently borrowed from a financial institution (World Bank's Global Findex database).
11. As per the Global Findex database, 31 percent of Vietnamese adults have accounts with financial institutions (the SBV estimates that 50 percent of adults have accounts), much less than the lower-middle-income country average of 43 percent. The gap is even worse for poor adults—19 percent in Vietnam compared with an average of 33 percent in lower-middle-income countries.
12. According to a report by Nhân Dân (The People), the official Communist Party news agency, the government received more than 1.2 million complaints and denunciations between 2003 and 2010, of which 70 percent were related to land. See http://www.nhandan.com.vn/mobile/_mobile_chinhtri/_mobile_tintucsukien/item/788102.html, accessed on October 19, 2015.
13. Changes in this realm typically involve a rising share of food distribution through modern supermarkets and out-of-home eating establishments, greater consumption of branded processed/convenient foods, a consolidation in agricultural collection and intermediate trading, the spread of cold-chain storage and logistical methods, and the application of increasingly stringent standards and sophisticated product traceability and quality management.
14. http://www.digitaltrends.com/mobile/iphone-cost-what-apple-is-paying/.
15. Customs procedures were evaluated before the 2014 rollout of Vietnam's web-based, single-window, e-customs system VNACCS/VCIS (Vietnam Automated Cargo and Port Consolidated System and Vietnam Customs

Information System). This system will almost certainly lead to improved customs performance.

16. Hai Phong port in the north has capacity shortfalls, while Cai Mep-Thi Vai port in the south has excess capacity.
17. There are more than 30 extrabudgetary funds at the central and subnational levels, such as the Vietnam Social Security Fund, the Enterprise Restructuring and Development Support Funds, and the Accumulation Fund for Foreign Debt Repayment. In addition, fully state-owned, quasi- fiscal, special-purpose vehicles—such as the Vietnam Development Bank—intermediate official development assistance disbursements like lending to SOEs.
18. In countries such as Japan and the Republic of Korea, the institutional mandates for land, infrastructure, transport, and water resources are vested in one line ministry, which enables better coordination of policies at the territorial and city levels.
19. Including the regional corridors of Hanoi–Hai Phong, Ho Chi Minh City–Cai Mep-Thi Vai, and Can Tho–Ho Chi Minh City and the interregional corridor between the Central Highlands and Ho Chi Minh City. A compelling economic case has yet to be made for a corridor linking Hanoi and Ho Chi Minh City. This corridor may emerge organically once the economic returns of the regional corridors become apparent.
20. The Freedom House civil liberties index captures freedom of speech, the press, association, and religion, on a scale from 1 (completely free) to 7 (unfree).
21. Voice and accountability; political stability and absence of violence/ terrorism; government effectiveness; regulatory quality; rule of law; and control of corruption.
22. See the World Bank's Worldwide Governance Indicators 2014.
23. This follows the "hybridity" model developed by Evans 2005.
24. For example, the introduction of meritocracy in Scandinavia emerged as the absolute kings had an incentive to establish a rule-based, capable, and independent—from anything but the absolute monarch—bureaucracy that could control the nobility and landed gentry. In the Republic of Korea, the legitimacy of the state depended on a capable and neutral public service when the meritocracy gained a foothold in the 1980s.
25. They are also responsible for monitoring local development plans and, since 2002, approving budget allocations for provinces, districts/wards, and communes/neighborhoods except for expenditures stipulated by central-government mandates.
26. According to the CIVICUS Vietnam assessment (2006) and the VUFO-NGO Resource Center's study of forms of engagement between civil society and state (2008). These citizen organizations include sociopolitical organizations under the Fatherland Front, professional organizations, local nongovernmental organizations, and community-based organizations.
27. De facto independence of the competition authority could translate into a 17 percentage-point reduction in the productivity gap with the United States (Voigt 2009).
28. Hard-core cartels include firms acting in collusion and engaging in price fixing, market partitioning, and bid rigging.

References

Abrami, Regina. 2002. "Self-Making, Class Struggle and Labor Autarky: The Political Origins of Private Entrepreneurship in Vietnam and China." PhD dissertation, University of California, Berkeley, CA.

Acemoglu, D., and J. Robinson. 2013. *Why Nations Fail*. New York: Crown Publishing Group.

Agénor, Pierre-Richard, Otaviano Canuto, and Michael Jelenic. 2012. "Avoiding Middle-Income Growth Traps." Economic Premise 98, World Bank, Washington, DC.

Arkadie, Brian Van, and Raymon Mallon. 2003. *Vietnam: A Transition Tiger*. Canberra, Australia: Asian Pacific Press at the Australian National University.

Barro-Lee Educational Attainment Dataset (database). http://www.barrolee.com/.

Bloom, Nicholas, and John Van Reenen. 2007. "Measuring and Explaining Management Practices across Firms and Countries." *The Quarterly Journal of Economics* 122 (4): 1351–1408.

Boly, Amadou. 2015. "On the Benefits of Formalization: Panel Evidence from Vietnam." UNU-WIDER Working Paper 2015/038, United Nations University, World Institute for Development Economics Research, Helsinki.

Brand, Claus. 2015. "Achieving and Sustaining Price Stability in Vietnam." Background paper for *Vietnam 2035*.

Broadberry, Stephen, and Nicholas F. R. Crafts. 2001. "Competition and Innovation in 1950s Britain." Business History, *Taylor & Francis Journals* 43 (1): 97–118.

Bunn, Christian, Peter Laderach, Oriana Ovalle Rivera, and Dieter Kirschke. 2015. "A Bitter Cup: Climate Change Profile of Global Production of Arabica and Robusta Coffee." *Climatic Change* 129: 89–101.

Centennial Asia Advisors. 2015. "Global Megatrends and Vietnam." Background paper for *Vietnam 2035*.

Cheshier, Scott. 2010. *The New Class in Vietnam*. London: Queen Mary University of London. https://qmro.qmul.ac.uk/jspui/handle/123456789/443.

CIVICUS. 2006. "The Emerging Civil Society: An Initial Assessment of Civil Society in Vietnam." Irene Norlund et al. (eds.) Hanoi: Civil Society Index Publications.

Coker, Richard J., Benjamin M. Hunter, James W. Rudge, Marco Liverani, and Piya Hanvoravongchai. 2011. "Emerging Infectious Diseases in Southeast Asia: Regional Challenges to Control." *Lancet* 377 (9765): 599–609. doi:10.1016/S0140–6736(10)62004–1.

Commission on Growth and Development. 2008. *The Growth Report 2008*. Washington, DC: Commission on Growth and Development.

Cung, Nguyen Dinh. 2015. "Reform of the Mindset and Removal of Institutional Bottlenecks for Transformation to a Full-Fledged Market Economy in Vietnam." Working Paper, Central Institute for Economic Management (CIEM), Hanoi.

Dollar, David. 2015a. "Some Lessons for Vietnam from Institutional Development in the Rapid Industrializers of East Asia." Background paper for *Vietnam 2035*.

———. 2015b. "Institutional Quality and Growth Traps." PAFTAD Working Paper Series YF37–07.

Eichengreen, Barry, Donghyun Park, and Kwanho Shin. 2011. "When Fast Growing Economies Slow Down: International Evidence and Implications for China." NBER Working Paper 16919, National Bureau of Economic Research, Cambridge, MA.

ERIA (Economic Research Institute for ASEAN and East Asia). 2012. *Mid-Term Review of the Implementation of AEC Blueprint: Executive Summary*. Jakarta: ERIA.

Evans, Peter. 2005. "Harnessing the State: Rebalancing Strategies for Monitoring and Motivation." In *States and Development: Historical Antecedents of Stagnation and Advance*, edited by Matthey

Lange and Dietrich Rueschemeyer, 26–47. Political Evolution and Institutional Change. New York: Palgrave Macmillan.

Evenett, S., M. Levenstein, and V. Suslow. 2001. "International Cartel Enforcement: Lessons from the 1990s." Policy Research Working Paper Series 2680, World Bank, Washington, DC.

Feenstra, Robert C., Robert Inklaar, and Marcel P. Timmer. 2015. "The Next Generation of the Penn World Table."*American Economic Review* 105 (10): 3150–82 https://www.ggdc.net/pwt.

Fforde, Adam, and Suzanne Paine. 1987. *The Limits of National Liberation: Problems of Economic Management in the Democratic Republic of Vietnam, with a Statistical Appendix*. London; New York: Croom Helm.

Fforde, Adam. 2007. *Vietnamese State Industry and the Political Economy of Commercial Renaissance: Dragon's Tooth or Curate's Egg?* Oxford: Chandos.

———. 2011. "Contemporary Vietnam: Political Opportunities, Conservative Formal Politics, and Patterns of Radical Change: Contemporary Vietnam." *Asian Politics & Policy* 3 (2): 165–84.

General Statistics Office of Vietnam (database). https://www.gso.gov.vn/Default_en.aspx?tabid=491.

Global Findex Database. http://datatopics.worldbank.org/financialinclusion/.

Investment and Trade Promotion Center (database). 2008. http://www.itpc.hochiminhcity.gov.vn/.

IPCC (Intergovernmental Panel on Climate Change). 2007. "Observations: Surface and Atmospheric Climate Change". In *Climate Change 2007: The Physical Science Basis*. Contribution of Working Group I to the Fourth Assessment Report of the Intergovernmental Panel on Climate Change. Cambridge, UK and New York, NY: Cambridge University Press.

Kaufmann, D., A. Kraay, and M. Mastruzzi. 2010. *The Worldwide Governance Indicators: Methodology and Analytical Issues*. www.govindicators.org.

Krugman, Paul. 1994. *The Age of Diminishing Expectations*. Cambridge, MA: The MIT Press.

Levenstein, Margaret, Valerie Suslow, and Lynda Oswald. 2003. *International Price-Fixing Cartels and Developing Countries: A Discussion of Effects and Policy Remedies*. NBER Working Paper 9511, National Bureau of Economic Research, Cambridge, MA.

Maddison Project (database). 2010. http://www.ggdc.net/maddison/maddison-project/home.htm.

Malesky, Edmund, and Markus Taussig. 2008. "Where is credit due? Legal institutions, connections, and the efficiency of bank lending in Vietnam." *Journal of Law, Economics, and Organization* 25 (2): 535–78.

———. 2009. "Out of the Gray: The Impact of Provincial Institutions on Business Formalization in Vietnam." *Journal of East Asian Studies* 9: 249–290.

Malesky, Edmund, Paul Schuler, and Anh Tran. 2012. "The Adverse Effects of Sunshine: A Field Experiment on Legislative Transparency in an Authoritarian Assembly." *American Political Science Review* 106 (04): 762–86.

Maloney, W. F., and Sarrias, M. 2014. "Convergence to the Managerial Frontier." Policy Research Working Paper 6822, World Bank, Washington, DC.

MICS (Multiple Indicator Cluster Surveys) (database). Various years. United Nations Children's Emergency Fund (UNICEF). http://mics.unicef.org/surveys.

MONRE (Ministry of Natural Resources and Environment). 2012. *Climate Change and Sea Level Rise Scenarios for Vietnam*. Hanoi, Vietnam: MONRE.

National Bureau of Statistics of China (database). The State Council, Beijing, China. http://www.stats.gov.cn/english/.

National Institute of Nutrition Surveys (database). http://viendinhduong.vn/products/en/28/p/Resource.aspx.

Nguyen, Cuong, and Quan Le. 2005. "Institutional Constraints and Private Sector Development: The Textile and Garment Industry in Vietnam." *ASEAN Economic Bulletin* 22 (3).

Nguyen, D.-Q., J. Renwick, and J. McGregor. 2013. "Variations of Surface Temperature and Rainfall in Vietnam from 1971 to 2010." *International Journal of Climatology* 34 (1): 249–64. doi:10.1002/joc.3684.

Nguyen, Xuan Thanh, and Jonathan Pincus. 2011. "Ho Chi Minh City Sea Port Relocation: A Case Study of Institutional Fragmentation." Fulbright Economics Teaching Program CE12-51-62.0. http://www.fetp.edu.vn/attachment.aspx?id=2002&Language=2.

Nolan, Peter. 2004. *China at the Crossroads*. Cambridge, UK; Malden, MA: Polity.

Penn World Table 8.0 (database). 2013. University of Groningen. http://www.rug.nl/research/ggdc/data/pwt/pwt-8.0.

Petri, Peter A., and Michael G. Plummer. 2014. "ASEAN Centrality and the ASEAN-US Economic Relationship." Policy Studies 69. Honolulu, HI: East-West Center.

Phuc, T. V. 2015. "Developing a Modern Civil Service Institution and Capacity of Civil Servants Based on the Actual Situation in Vietnam." Background paper for *Vietnam 2035*.

Pincus, Jonathan. 2015. "Vietnam: Building Capacity in a Fragmented, Commercialized State." Background paper for *Vietnam 2035*.

Rama, Martin. 2008. "Making Difficult Choices: Vietnam in Transition." Growth and Development Commission Working Paper 40, World Bank, Washington, DC.

———. 2014. "Vietnam." In *Handbook of Emerging Economies*, edited by Robert E. Looney. London: Routledge.

Rodrik, Dani. 2015. "Premature Deindustrialization." NBER Working Paper 20935, National Bureau of Economic Research, Cambridge, MA.

Smith, Adam. 1904. *An Inquiry Into Nature and Causes of the Wealth of Nations*. Edited by Edwin Cannan. London: Methuen and Company.

Steer, Lisbet, and Kunal Sen. 2010. "Formal and Informal Institutions in a Transition Economy: The Case of Vietnam." *World Development* 38 (11).

Symeonidis, G. 2008. "The Effect of Competition on Wages and Productivity: Evidence from the UK." *Review of Economics and Statistics* 90 (1).

Thanh, Vo Tri. 2015. "Vietnam's Perspectives on Regional Economic Integration." *Journal of Southeast Asian Economies* 32 (1).

Tran, Van Tho. 2015. "Vietnam Needs a Development-Oriented Market Economy: Review of 30 Years of Renovation and Looking Forward to the Future." Background paper for *Vietnam 2035*.

UN World Population Prospects (database). 2015. United Nations Department of Economic and Social Affairs, New York. https://esa.un.org/unpd/wpp/.

Van Thang, Nguyen, and Nick J. Freeman. 2009. "State-owned Enterprises in Vietnam: Are They 'Crowding Out' the Private Sector?" *Post-Communist Economies* 21 (June): 227–47. doi:10.1080/14631370902778674.

Vasavakul, Thaveeporn. 2014. "Authoritarianism Reconfigured." In *Politics in Contemporary Vietnam*, edited by Jonathan London. Palgrave Macmillan.

Viner, Jacob. 1927. "Adam Smith and Laissez-Faire." *Journal of Political Economy* 35 (2).

Voigt, S. 2009. "The Effects of Competition Policy on Development: Cross-Country Evidence Using Four New Indicators." *Journal of Development Studies* 45 (8).

Vu, Thanh Tu Anh. 2014. "The Political Economy of Industrial Development in Vietnam: Impact of State-business Relationship on Industrial Performance, 1986–2012". WIDER Working Paper 2014/158, United Nations University World Institute for Development Economics Research, Helsinki.

Vu, Thanh Tu Anh, David Dapice, Nguyen Xuan Thanh, and Do Thien Anh Tuan. 2015. "A Retrospective on the Past 30 Years of Development in Vietnam." Background paper for *Vietnam 2035*.

VUFO-NGO Resource Centre. 2008. *Forms of Engagement between State Agencies and Civil Society Organizations in Vietnam Study Report*. Hanoi: VUFO-NGO Resource Centre.

Wassmann, R. S. V. K. Jagadish, S. Heuer, A. Ismail, E. Redona, R. Serraj, R. K. Singh, G. Howell, H. Pathak, and K. Sumfleth. 2009. "Climate Change Affecting Rice Production: The Physiological and Agronomic Basis for Possible Adaptation Strategies." *Advances in Agronomy* 101 (08): 59–122. doi:10.1016/S0065–2113(08)00802-X.

Weber, Max. 1946. *From Max Weber: Essays in Sociology,* translated, edited, and with an introduction by H. H. Gerth and C. Wright Mills. Oxford, UK: Oxford University Press.

World Bank. 2009. *Country Social Analysis: Ethnicity and Development in Vietnam*. Social Development Unit, Sustainable Development Department, East Asia and Pacific Region. Washington, DC: Author.

———. 2012. Investing Across Borders indicators. Washington, DC: Author.

———. 2013. *Trade Facilitation, Value Creation, and Competitiveness: Policy Implications for Vietnam's Economic Growth*. Washington, DC: Author. http://wwwwds.worldbank.org/external/default/WDSContentServer/WDSP/IB/2013/09/26/000456286_20130926111227/Rendered/PDF/792350WP0v10EN00Box379821B00PUBLIC0.pdf.

———. 2014. *East Asia Pacific at work: employment, enterprise, and well-being*. Washington, DC: Author. http://documents.worldbank.org/curated/en/2014/01/19491819/east-asia-pacific-work-employment-enterprise-well-being.

World Bank and Ministry of Finance of Vietnam. 2015. "Vietnam Public Expenditures Review." Unpublished draft.

World Development Indicators (database). World Bank, Washington, DC. http://data.worldbank.org/data-catalog/world-development-indicators.

World Economic Outlook (database). International Monetary Fund, Washington, DC. https://www.imf.org/external/pubs/ft/weo/2015/02/weodata/index.aspx.

Worldwide Governance Indicators (database). World Bank, Washington, DC. http://info.worldbank.org/governance/wgi/index.aspx#home.

Part II

Background Chapters

1

Thirty Years of Renovation and Vietnam's Aspirations for 2035

Main Messages

The Sixth Party Congress formally endorsed the *Đổi Mới* (renovation) policy in 1986, after several years of policy experimentation aimed at improving economic incentives. *Đổi Mới* signaled a new direction in economic management, providing opportunities for all individuals and entities to contribute to, and garner the fruits of, economic development. It provided the basis for innovation and injected a new dynamism that greatly accelerated socioeconomic development.

Renovations in development thinking gradually introduced under *Đổi Mới* enabled four key transitions: from centrally planned and subsidized resource allocation to more market-based allocation; from a predominantly state-owned economy to a multi-actor economy with an increasingly dynamic private sector; from a closed economy to an increasingly open and internationally integrated economy; and from centralized to decentralized governance structures. Reforms gradually expanded economic rights, choices, and opportunities for Vietnamese people, especially in investment, production, and business activity. The role of the state is still evolving and being redefined as part of this reform process.

Đổi Mới has been difficult and complicated, requiring bold (and sometimes controversial) changes in perceptions and thinking. Key factors contributing to its success have included a pragmatic approach to the sequencing and pacing of reform—shock therapy was avoided, and reforms were implemented step by step after mobilizing broad-based public support (Rama 2008). Reforms built on the country's strengths, initially focusing on agricultural and labor-intensive sectors. Priority was given to human resource development. And international commitments were used to push through some difficult reforms.

Despite three decades of tremendous economic and social achievements, Vietnam still faces many development challenges. Average per capita income remains well below national aspirations; the rate of growth in productivity has declined in recent years; pressing social and environmental problems remain; many development programs have not been completed; inequities are beginning to widen, especially in the form of unequal access to opportunities for ethnic minorities and other marginalized groups; and the institutions of governance remain weak in critical areas. Vietnam must adapt more quickly to global opportunities and challenges if it is to avoid falling into the "middle-income trap" and lagging behind other more successful regional economies.

Future reform opportunities are considerable. Vietnam has learned valuable lessons from 30 years of *Đổi Mới*. There is a growing national consensus on the need for reform and renovation for the country's development. Participation in global economic integration trends and agreements provide additional opportunities for Vietnam to deepen its commitment to reform.

A key challenge is to change the mindsets of policy makers and the country's leaders, to catch up with the needs of a country that is transitioning from central planning to a socialist-oriented market economy. Part of it entails ending the conflicted attitude to what a socialist-oriented market economy is, and not allowing that to be used to justify preserving the state's dominance of the economy. The state would still have an important role in a functioning modern market-economy system (with the private sector at its core), by being an effective regulator and facilitator, correcting market failures, and providing a level playing field for all, on social and economic fronts.

Another revolution in mindsets would transform development rhetoric into practical actions backed by strong political will. This will be particularly important since the next stage of reform is more likely to adversely affect vested interests. Strong political determination and more systematic, evidence-led, and broader-based consultative approaches can help make difficult reforms happen.

Vietnam is aiming for a new development dynamism toward "prosperity, creativity, equity, and democracy" by 2035. It is moving toward realizing national aspirations for "a prosperous people, and a strong, democratic, equitable, and civilized country, in which all people enjoy an abundant, free, and happy life and are given conditions for their comprehensive development," as defined in the country's Constitution and in the "Credo for Country's Development in the Transition Period" of the Communist Party of Vietnam (CPV).

Achieving these objectives will require renewed reform efforts to manage six basic transformations or breakthroughs: enabling economic modernization and private sector development; building national innovation capacity; managing urbanization for greater economic efficiency; achieving sustainable and climate-resilient growth; promoting equity and social inclusion; and building modern institutions for an effective state. Each of these long-term transitions and their related set of reforms are discussed in depth in the following chapters.

Đổi Mới: Motivation, Process, and Results

Lead Up to *Đổi Mới*

After decades of colonization and devastating conflicts, Vietnam faced formidable development challenges after Reunification in 1975. Essential infrastructure had been destroyed, societal wounds from internal conflict were yet to heal, food and other basic commodities were in short supply, and millions of people had been left dead, maimed, or displaced (Rama 2008).

Facing this grim reality, the Fourth Party Congress of December 1976 adopted central planning as the reunified country's basic economic model. The choice was motivated by the victory of socialist forces in Vietnam, and the apparent economic successes of the Soviet central planning orthodoxy. Adopting a common economic model for the reunited country meant enforcing a socialist structure (including central planning) in the South, where parts of agriculture were collectivized, and a very large number of private enterprises were shut down, converted into cooperatives, or nationalized. Heavy industry—rather than agriculture and light manufacturing (which were more consistent with the country's comparative advantage)—became the focus of economic policy and heavy public subsidies (Arkadie and Mallon 2003). External economic assistance (largely from the former Soviet Union) helped bankroll centrally planned investment decisions (Rama 2008).

Central planning provided little information for economic actors and poor incentives (no market prices, ownership or profit incentives, or hard budget constraints). Weighed down by a distorted incentive structure, the economic system failed to reach the lofty targets of the 1976–80 Five-Year Plan. Economic stagnation and acute shortages of food and consumer goods worsened the living conditions of an already suffering population. Many undertook perilous journeys abroad in search of better opportunities (Rama 2008).

Partly in response to the poor outcomes from attempted central planning, experimentation with economic reforms began in the late 1970s (Arkadie and Mallon 2003). Socioeconomic targets were revised downward in 1979, and some barriers to private activity were unofficially relaxed. Some flexibility was introduced by moves to decentralize decisionmaking.

Despite early attempts to impose central planning, key elements of economic and political power were remarkably decentralized, and even fragmented horizontally and vertically (Pincus 2015). Central government budget resources were small in absolute terms and as a proportion of gross domestic product (GDP). A large share of the central committee members owed their positions to provincial power structures (Pincus 2015). With few central resources and limited central power to enforce central plans, subnational state agencies and enterprises faced strong incentives to be entrepreneurial to survive. Thus decentralization (unintentionally) facilitated and provided incentives for state entities to innovate and experiment with reform.

The stage was thus set for a series of localized "fence-breaking" policy experiments by enterprising local officials. These measures—introduced furtively and incrementally on a pilot basis outside the official system—injected elements of market mechanisms into some production and trading activities.

Focusing initially on agriculture, fence-breaking local officials allocated land to farmers and contracted them directly (rather than through cooperatives) to sell their output at near "market" prices that were well above official prices. Farmers responded to improved incentives, vastly raising their living conditions in a relatively short time (Rama 2008). Emboldened by early successes, some officials extended pilot reforms beyond agriculture, to state-owned enterprises (SOEs). Managers of selected SOEs were given some independence under a three-tier system in production and sales decisions (after meeting their central planning targets),[1] leading to increased production and growing trade outside official channels.

The growing tolerance for fence-breaking activities created "gray" markets for commodities and production inputs that gradually gained legitimacy and acceptance (Pincus 2015). Local authorities began tolerating cross-border smuggling to access essential supplies in exchange for unofficial levies, some of which were channeled to local government budgets. The Fifth Party Congress in Hanoi in March 1982 partially reoriented the planning focus from heavy industry to agriculture and light industry, with an export orientation (Arkadie and Mallon 2003).

The partial and opportunistic approach to pre–*Đổi Mới* reforms boosted agricultural and industrial production in some areas, stemming the decline in GDP in the early 1980s. But the reforms did not go far enough, and overall conditions for people were getting worse. Partial and semiformal reforms magnified business uncertainty, with policy fluctuating between deepening and relaxing central controls, and the emergence of dual (official and unofficial) markets for goods and assets.[2]

Macroeconomic stability was another casualty of partial reforms. Fiscal and external imbalances ballooned. Fiscal deficits and SOE subsidies were monetized, contributing to triple-digit inflation in the mid-1980s. The "price-salary-money" reform of 1985 (to decontrol output prices charged by SOEs and set by the State Price Committee, and to reduce state subsidies on consumer goods) failed to stabilize matters. Most of the population still lived in poverty in 1986, the majority far worse off than at Reunification.

Even so, the fence-breaking period proved to be an important phase of reform.

Spontaneous responses to localized reforms helped change mindsets of both the general population and some in the leadership. This helped lay the foundations for the subsequent, more comprehensive *Đổi Mới* reforms. And guiding the *Đổi Mới* reforms were some of the local leaders (subsequently elevated to national positions) who were at the center of the fence-breaking actions (Rama 2008). But fragmented power structures made it difficult to develop a more systematic and comprehensive approach to implementing more broad-based institutional reform.

Pressures for Change and Major *Đổi Mới* Reforms

The economic situation was dire on the eve of the formal launching of *Đổi Mới*. Annual inflation was running at more than 400 percent (Rama 2014), the real economy was stagnant and heavily dependent on foreign aid (Tran 2015), food was in short supply, the budget was chronically short of resources (Tu-Anh et al. 2015), and most people lived in poverty. A growing income gap with the rising East Asian economies (such as the Republic of Korea; Malaysia; Singapore; Taiwan, China; and Thailand) provided additional motivation for introspection and reform.

Facing a "social and economic crisis" (figure 1.1), Vietnam embarked on a path of economic renovation (*Đổi Mới*) in 1986 (box 1.1) (CPV 1991). *Đổi Mới* reflected a fundamental shift in the country's economic ideology, a recognition of the failures of central planning, and awareness that the fence-breaking market reforms of the previous decade were useful locally, but inadequate nationally to address the dire economic situation.

FIGURE 1.1 Vietnam: Reform, growth, and inflation, 1977–2015

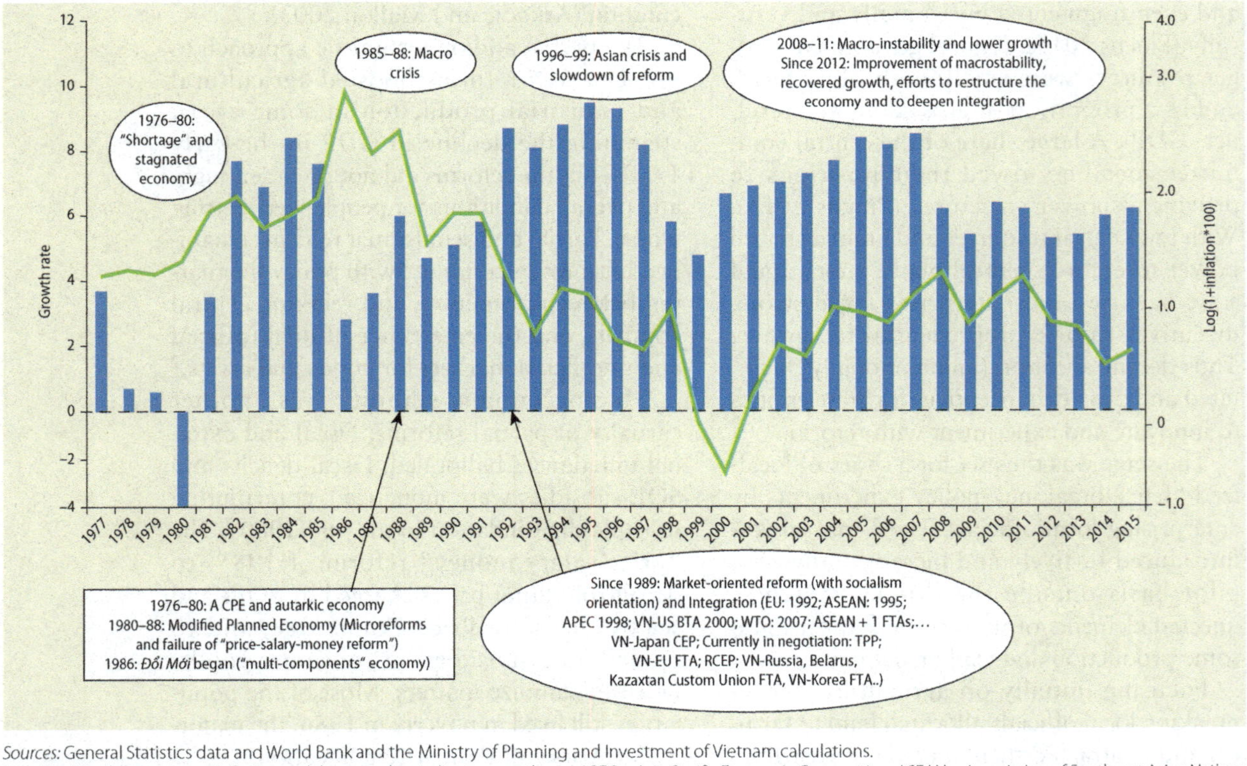

Sources: General Statistics data and World Bank and the Ministry of Planning and Investment of Vietnam calculations.
Note: The blue bars measures inflation, and the green line indicates growth rate. APEC = Asia-Pacific Economic Cooperation; ASEAN = Association of Southeast Asian Nations; BTA = bilateral trade agreement; CEP = comprehensive economic partnership; CPE = centrally planned economy; EU = European Union; FTA = free trade agreement; RCEP = Regional Comprehensive Economic Partnership; TPP = Trans-Pacific Partnership; VN = Vietnam; WTO = World Trade Organization.

BOX 1.1 A chronology of major market-oriented *Đổi Mới* reforms

1981: Directive 100 initiated output-contracting schemes to farmers, allowing them to keep output beyond a contracted amount.

1986: *Đổi Mới* was launched at the Sixth Party Congress, signaling a move from bureaucratic centralized management based on state subsidies, to a multisector, market-oriented economy, open to world markets.

1987: Rationing was abolished for many goods, and administered prices of several nonessential commodities were raised closer to market-clearing level. Domestic and external economic trade were liberalized, with domestic-trade checkpoints removed, and the Vietnamese dong was devalued. The Foreign Investment Law was approved (enacted in 1988).

1988: The Just 1988 Land Law provided for secure long-term land-use rights. Politburo Resolution 10 acknowledged households as autonomous agricultural production entities. Formal decollectivization started with households receiving a 15-year lease on their plots with the right to sell their produce at market prices.

1989: The Law on Export and Import Duties introduced custom tariffs. Most remaining price controls and subsidies were abolished. The state monopoly on foreign trade was relaxed: Private enterprises were allowed to engage in foreign trade. The Vietnamese dong was devalued, and the multiple exchange rate system was unified.

1990: The Company Law and the Law on Sole Proprietorships established the legal framework for private registered businesses and limited liability companies.

1990: The Ordinance for the State Bank of Vietnam (SBV) and the Ordinance for Commercial Banks, Credit Cooperatives, and Financial Companies were issued with commercial banking functions transferred out of the SBV, shifting the banking system from a single to two tiers. Private commercial banks were permitted.

1991: The first export processing zone was established near Ho Chi Minh City.

1991–94: There was a shift to market-based determination of the exchange rate, first with the establishment of two foreign exchange centers in Hanoi and Ho Chi Minh City, and later with the introduction of an interbank foreign exchange market. A pegged exchange rate regime was introduced.

1992: Vietnam signed a preferential trade agreement with the European Economic Community.

1993: The 1993 Land Law increased land tenure to 20 years (50 years for perennial crops) and gave households the right to exchange, transfer, lease, inherit, and mortgage land-use rights. Lending to rural households was encouraged. SOE equitization started.[a] Barriers to lending by the Asian Development Bank, International Monetary Fund, and World Bank to Vietnam were lifted.

1994: Economic Courts were established. The Labor Code was issued to protect rights of employees and employers, and to regulate contracts and social insurance. An arbitration mechanism was established.

1995: Vietnam joined the Association of Southeast Asian Nations (ASEAN).

1996: The State Budget Law defined tax and expenditure responsibilities of different levels of government.

1997–99: Value-added tax (VAT) and Corporate Income Tax were introduced.

1999: The Enterprise Law consolidated the Company Law and Law on Sole Proprietorships, and greatly simplified procedures to set up new enterprises.

2000. The U.S.–Vietnam Bilateral Trade Agreement (BTA) (effective December 2001) was concluded.

2000–02: The SBV introduced a base interest rate and abolished the ceiling on lending interest rates.

2001: Party Resolution 5 to accelerate SOE reform was passed. Thousands of SOEs were equitized, merged, or liquidated during the five-year plan period 2001–05.

2002: The 2002 State Budget Law (effective 2004) better defined intergovernmental fiscal relations and accelerated fiscal decentralization.

2003: A one-stop-shop system for administrative procedures was launched, including appraisal of

(Box continues next page)

BOX 1.1 (continued)

investment projects and issuance of business licenses and land-use right certificates.

2004: The institutional framework to promote competition was established: the Competition Law, the Vietnam Competition Administration Department, and the Vietnam Competition Council.

2005: The legal framework for all investors was unified with the promulgation of the Common Investment Law and Enterprise Law. Policies on state economic groups were launched.

2007: Vietnam officially became the 150th member of the World Trade Organization (WTO).

2013: The Master Plan on Economic Restructuring was launched, initially focusing on banks, SOEs, and public investment.

2014–15: The New Enterprise and Investment Law provided the foundations for business deregulation. The Program for Reviewing and Simplifying Administrative Procedures was launched.

2015: Vietnam completed negotiations on the Trans-Pacific Partnership (TPP) and the EU–Vietnam Free Trade Agreement (FTA).

2016: Implementation of ASEAN Economic Community.

a. The process can be carried out by one of the following methods: keeping the state shares intact and issuing new shares; selling part of the state's shares; detaching and then privatizing parts of an SOE; and (since June 1998) selling off all state shares to workers and private shareholders.

The *Đổi Mới* reforms, introduced in a staggered manner, focused on the following seven areas.

Price reforms

Rationing and administered prices were abolished for several nonessential commodities from 1987 (Arkadie and Mallon 2003). The dong was devalued in 1987 (and again in 1989)—to close the gap between the official and shadow-market exchange rates. Reforms were initially mostly partial, with the economy segmented between production within, and outside, the central planning system. More decisive and comprehensive price reform was introduced in 1989 and, by 1990, most official prices had been brought to near market-clearing levels, and most direct state subsidies had been eliminated (Leipziger 1992).

Agriculture sector reforms

Vietnam began *Đổi Mới* as an agriculture-dominated economy with a relatively small state-controlled industrial sector. With nearly 90 percent of the population living in rural areas and relying mainly on agriculture and natural resources, potential benefits from agricultural reform were considerable and unlikely to harm other segments of society. Measures to decollectivize production were introduced from 1988, and households began to replace cooperatives as the basic unit of production. The provision of long-term land-use rights to individuals (Land Law 1988), and later rights to trade, lease, inherit, and mortgage land-use rights (Land Law 1993), and a land titling program,[3] provided people with the confidence and incentive to make longer-term investments. With the lifting of official quotas and controls on domestic trade, the volume of agricultural goods traded in private markets began to soar. With more secure property rights, more market-based pricing (rice had been one-tenth of the market price in 1988) (Dollar and Litvack 1998), and stronger individual rights to make production, pricing, and trading decisions, sharp increases were recorded in agriculture productivity and output, and in rural incomes, thereby stimulating demand for other goods and services.

Sustained growth in agricultural output helped ensure food security, thus contributing to economic and social stability and in building support for broader reform.

Agriculture, forestry, and fishery output grew by a fairly stable 3.7 percent a year from 1986 to 2014, despite shocks. The value of agriculture, forestry, and fishery exports surged from about $0.5 billion in 1986 to $30.9 billion in 2014, an average annual growth rate of just over 17 percent. In contrast to the food shortages of the mid-1980s, Vietnam now ranks in the top five global exporters of coffee, tea, rice, pepper, cashews, cassava, rubber, and aquatic products.

Earlier agricultural reforms have largely run their course. The focus now needs to shift to modernizing and commercializing agricultural production, to upgrading processing and marketing systems, and to developing factor markets, with a more narrowly defined role for the government and an expanded role for the market (chapter 2).

Economic integration

While foreign trade—using gold and the U.S. dollar—occurred through informal channels even before *Đổi Mới*, the legal basis for goods and currency exchange was absent, and foreign private investment was virtually zero. A Foreign Investment Law was enacted in September 1988 and, combined with price, exchange rate, and property rights reforms, laid the foundations for sustained strong growth in foreign direct investment (FDI) inflows and FDI-led export growth. Removal of the state monopoly on foreign trade, eased restrictions on private sector involvement in trade, relaxation of export and import quotas, and reductions in trade taxes, coupled with the above exchange rate reform, further stimulated FDI and trade (Arkadie and Mallon 2003). Vietnam's merchandise exports amounted to $150 billion in 2014 (equivalent to 80 percent of GDP), three-quarters of which were manufactured goods. Most of these exports are powered by FDI, the stock of which now stands at more than $250 billion, sourced from more than 100 countries. Links to domestic private firms, however, are still weak (chapter 2).

Reforms linked to bilateral and multilateral free trade agreements (FTAs) have helped maintain the momentum for economic integration. Participation in the Association of Southeast Asian Nations (ASEAN) Free Trade Area (effective June 1996), the U.S.–Vietnam Bilateral Trade Agreement (BTA) (effective December 2001), and accession to the World Trade Organization (WTO) (effective January 2007) were important milestones. Several other bilateral trade agreements were signed. Vietnam has also recently agreed to the Trans-Pacific Partnership (TPP) and the European Union (EU)–Vietnam FTA, and is participating in negotiations for the Regional Comprehensive Economic Partnership between the ASEAN, Australia, China, India, Japan, Korea, and New Zealand.

Macroeconomic stabilization

The triple-digit inflation of the mid-1980s began to be contained from 1989 with tighter monetary policy, including higher interest rates and limits on credit growth (especially to SOEs), aided by strong supply responses to market-oriented economic reforms. Consumer price index inflation fell dramatically, from more than 400 percent in 1988 to 35 percent in 1989 (Leipziger 1992), and averaged about 30 percent in 1990–95 (Tu-Anh et al. 2015). It was then contained at single-digit rates until late 2007, when pressures spilled over from elevated global food and commodity prices and sustained rapid credit growth (annual credit growth averaged more than 30 percent per year between 1999 and 2010, much of it channeled into real estate). A cycle of moderate to high inflation followed, with a peak of 28 percent in August–September 2008, single-digit rates from April 2009 to October 2010, and another peak of 23 percent in August 2011.

Inflation has since been retamed (less than 1 percent in 2015) through a mix of tighter monetary policy, and global disinflationary trends (Brand 2015). The State Bank of Vietnam (SBV) needs to further strengthen monetary policy management to ward off future inflationary episodes: This will require it to focus its mandate more explicitly on price stability and to strengthen its operational and research capacity.

Fiscal deficits were reduced early in the *Đổi Mới* period, initially by eliminating export and production subsidies to SOEs, and later by focusing on revenue measures. From a low revenue base, reforms to broaden the tax base and strengthen tax administration resulted in revenue collections of 23–24 percent of GDP by 1996.[4] Remaining deficits were no longer monetized. Fiscal deficit and public debt have, however, risen sharply in recent years, as Vietnam sought to offset the weak private sector demand with countercyclical fiscal policy. With the need for fiscal consolidation now widely acknowledged, concrete measures are needed to boost revenue collection, improve the efficiency of spending, and strengthen debt management strategy and capacity.

Finance sector reforms—including the separation of commercial and central banking functions and the entry of joint-stock and foreign commercial banks—have been an important complement to macroeconomic stabilization, though a large part of the reform agenda remains (chapter 2).

Enterprise reforms

Key reforms centered on legalizing private enterprise, restructuring SOEs, introducing regulatory reforms to level the playing field for all enterprises, increasing competition among firms, and reducing compliance costs. The Law on Sole Proprietorships and the Company Law, both of 1990, established the legal basis for private enterprises and limited liability companies. Subsequent reforms to bring all enterprises under a single Enterprise Law helped accelerate private sector development. Ongoing regulatory reform initiatives (notably Government Resolution 19) have been critical in further reducing business startup and compliance costs, and in tackling emerging bottlenecks to the development of enterprises and of more competitive markets. Progress has been impeded, however, by vested interests within fragmented state power structures, and considerable barriers to domestic private sector growth remain (chapter 2).

The government also moved to increase SOE autonomy over production, pricing, and human resource decisions, aiming to make SOEs more profit oriented. Attempts to impose hard budget constraints, however, were undermined by SOEs' preferential access to land and credit from state-owned banks, and other forms of preferential treatment. Early SOE reforms in the 1990s focused on divestiture, mergers, and equitization of small and nonstrategic SOEs. Implementation of equitization has been patchy, accelerating somewhat in the early 2000s, but even then with mixed results (chapter 2). A strategic shift in 2005 to create state economic groups and benefit from their economies of scale and scope has not achieved intended outcomes—on the contrary, in some cases it has led to major financial losses.

Slow progress on enterprise—especially SOE—reform is indicative of the challenges in pursuing top-down reforms in a decentralized and fragmented power structure, especially when vested interests, including elements of the state apparatus, stand to lose from the reforms. Concentrated high-level political commitment is needed to secure reforms in such cases (chapter 7).

Decentralization

Despite a stated commitment to central planning, a legacy of prolonged internal conflict and limited central government resources contributed to a relatively decentralized power structure. Provincial leaders account for the largest share of central committee members, and it is the central committee that appoints national leaders. Fence-breaking was an early manifestation of the extent of decentralized power structures. Pressures for formal decentralization of fiscal and decision-making powers increased under *Đổi Mới*.[5]

The 2002 Budget Law (effective January 2004) with Resolution 08 (June 2004) helped accelerate fiscal decentralization, with more decentralized management of development investment, budget, land, and natural resources, and with greater SOE autonomy. This helped transform relationships within the state system, and between the state and business at the local level. Fiscal decentralization has had mixed results. For the dozen provinces that can balance their budgets (due to a strong business base or abundant natural resources), decentralization helped them expand their fiscal space considerably, and so they have become more independent from central government. In contrast, the central government has greater control over the remaining provinces that depend on net transfers from the national budget.

As discussed, the fragmentation of power associated with decentralization has made it harder for the national leaders to adopt reforms that have adverse impacts on local interest groups. Excessive fragmentation of investment decisions among provinces (which now account for almost 80 percent of total public investment) is another major concern (chapter 7).

Despite its challenges, decentralization has allowed local governments to be more proactive in improving the business environment and in meeting basic service delivery needs. The more proactive provinces have consistently performed well in Vietnam's Provincial Competitiveness Index (PCI).[6]

Social equity

Throughout the reform process, Vietnam has retained a strong emphasis on equity and social inclusion (chapter 6). The socioeconomic aspiration of developing a socialist-oriented market economy captures the balance in its preferences for equitable and market-led growth. Thus decades of rapid growth have not widened income inequality significantly. Equitable land distribution in the early years of *Đổi Mới*, driving a rapid increase in agricultural production, was important in laying the foundations for equitable growth. Equitable delivery of basic health and education services and provision of basic infrastructure (such as electricity and water), aided by public policy choices that equalized fiscal transfers across provinces with different levels of development, and a strong focus on facilitating small and medium enterprise development, further helped the country avoid the spike in inequality experienced in some other fast-growing economies.

Vietnam has always prioritized human resource development, achieving some equitable outcomes in basic literacy and numeracy. The approach to education changed with the launch of *Đổi Mới*, signified by a move from viewing education as part of the "ideology–culture revolution" and a form of welfare to seeing it as a necessary investment in development (box 1.2). Efforts to direct education now focus on specific solutions rather than general directions.

BOX 1.2 The education philosophy of Vietnam under *Đổi Mới*

1. The common principle: education and training is the top national priority.
2. The common mission of education and training: raising intellectual standards of the general population, training a skilled workforce, and developing talent.
3. The overall objective: the people are both the goal and the driving force of socioeconomic development.
4. Investment in education and training is considered an investment for development, equivalent to investment in infrastructure such as roads, electricity, the post, and so on.
5. The goal is to promote positive impacts (linking training with the needs of the labor market) while limiting the negative effects of the market mechanism on education and training: resisting the tendency toward commercialization.
6. Everybody provides education, and education is provided to everyone, promoting lifelong learning. Equity in education requires policies that bring education closer to the poor and support outstanding students to develop their talent.
7. The motto for education development: standardization, socialization, diversification, and democratization.

Despite good progress on maintaining social equity, significant challenges remain to provide equal access to opportunities for ethnic minorities and other marginalized groups, as noted in the next section.

Đổi Mới: An Overall Record of Strong Achievements with Emerging Challenges

Impressive growth on multiple fronts

Vietnam has recorded fast, stable, and inclusive economic growth in the three decades since the launch of *Đổi Mới*, emerging from being one of the poorest countries in the world to a dynamic middle-income country with key social indicators comparable to higher-income countries. Per capita GDP jumped from about $100 (current prices) in 1990 ($970 in purchasing power parity [PPP] terms) to about $2,200 in 2015 ($6,000 PPP). Real per capita GDP growth has averaged 5.5 percent a year since 1990 (figure 1.2). China is the only large economy to achieve a higher per capita GDP growth over this period.[7] Strong growth since 1990 places Vietnam well on the long-term income trajectory relative to global comparators (box 1.3).

While Vietnam's growth record overall has been positive, emerging concerns need to be resolved to ensure its long-term sustainability. Growth in labor productivity (output per worker) has been on a declining trend since the end of the 1990s (chapter 2), and is seen across most industrial subsectors, as well as in mining, finance, and real estate. In agriculture, labor productivity has grown robustly, but its level is still lower than in most of the region's middle-income countries. The reform agenda to reverse this declining productivity growth trend will be demanding, given that the decline has been broad based. Long-term investments in developing innovation capacities (chapter 3) and urban infrastructure (chapter 4) will be essential with an eye to sustaining strong, productivity-led growth over the next two decades and beyond.

Furthermore, growth has to a large extent come at the cost of the environment (chapter 5).

FIGURE 1.2 Per capita GDP growth, 1991–2014

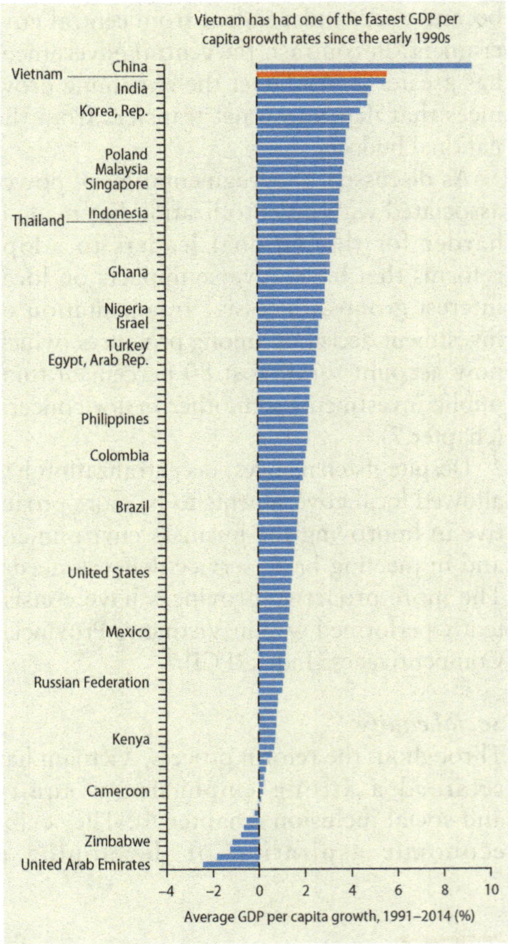

Sources: World Development Indicators; General Statistics Office data.

Vietnam's greenhouse gas emissions have grown the fastest in the region, while the environmental quality of its air, land, and water has deteriorated sharply. Water and air pollution have reached serious levels, especially near Hanoi and Ho Chi Minh City, posing major health risks. A large part of Vietnam's protective mangrove forests has been destroyed, while overfishing has seriously depleted the nearshore fisheries, posing threats to livelihoods. Removing natural forests in some upland areas has contributed to more frequent and severe flooding of lower-altitude farms and human settlements. Finally, Vietnam is one of the world's most vulnerable countries to climate change, with adaptation challenges accordingly

BOX 1.3 Vietnam's long-term growth trajectory relative to comparator countries

Vietnam's long-term income trajectory compares well against those of its global peers. A long-term comparison with China is striking on two counts. First, growth accelerations in both countries, although 13 years apart (starting around 1977 and 1990), begin at roughly the same per capita income of around $1,100 (2005 PPP). Second, 24 years into its growth acceleration (2014), Vietnam had kept up with China over the equivalent period (to 2001) (figure B1.3.1, left panel).

The story remains broadly similar against other successful economies (those with at least a 3.5 times increase in per capita income in the first 25 years of their growth acceleration) and over a 50-year period. The starting points for the growth accelerations were close, with Thailand at $835 (2005 PPP) at the lower end and Taiwan, China, at $1,365 at the upper end. About a quarter century into its growth acceleration, Vietnam's position is broadly at par with those successful economies (figure B1.3.1, right panel).

What happens from here on is critical. At roughly 25 years into their growth accelerations—where Vietnam is now—the economies that made it into the high-income ranks pulled ahead of the rest. The Republic of Korea and Taiwan, China, maintained their growth records for the first 25 years over the subsequent 25 years (years 25–50), but Brazil, Egypt, and Thailand started to see growth rates fall.

Vietnam is thus seemingly at a critical juncture. Decisions at this stage matter for meeting long-term income aspirations. If the country can carry out the reforms needed to pull up its GDP growth to its 7 percent per capita target, it would match the trajectory of China and, by 2035, stand a strong chance of reaching the incomes of Korea and Taiwan, China, in the early 2000s. At the upper reaches of upper-middle-income country status, it would be strongly positioned for the final ascent to high income. It would also have a stronger chance of catching up with, or even overtaking, its middle-income neighbors such as Indonesia and the Philippines. But if Vietnam's per capita growth slips to about 4 percent a year, its average income is only likely to move close to that of Brazil or Thailand, and its chances of catching up with the neighboring wealthier middle-income countries would be lower.

FIGURE B1.3.1 Vietnam has performed well on its long-term income trajectory

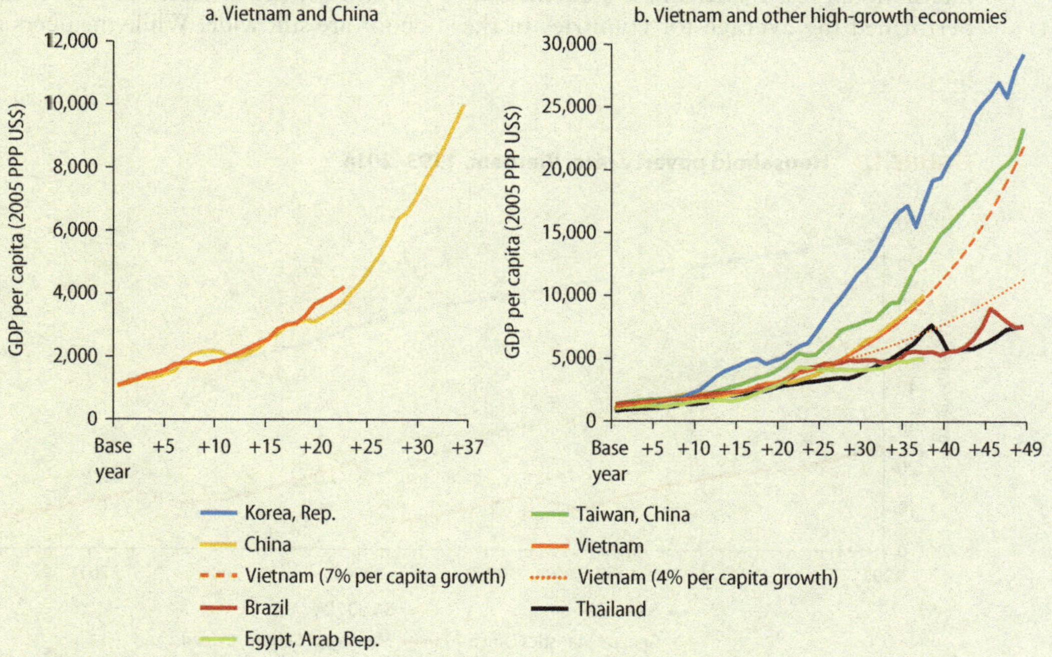

Source: Calculations based on data from University of Groningen (2013).
Note: Base years are 1951 for Taiwan, China and for Brazil; 1958 for Thailand; 1962 for the Republic of Korea; 1969 for the Arab Republic of Egypt; 1977 for China; and 1990 for Vietnam.

severe, especially in the Mekong Delta. With almost all large-scale hydropower potential tapped and with limited development of other renewable sources, greater reliance on coal is a growing threat to environmental sustainability and to energy security. The policy agenda involves protecting the quality of natural resources; building climate resilience into policies, planning, and investments; and finding ways to tap into more clean energy sources.

Poverty reduction and improvements in nonincome welfare measures

Social outcomes have improved remarkably since the launch of *Đổi Mới*. Based on a variety of international and national poverty lines, poverty has fallen rapidly (figure 1.3). The $1.90-a-day poverty rate fell from 50 percent in the early 1990s to 3 percent today. Using the General Statistic Office–World Bank standard, poverty incidence fell from about 58 percent to 13.5 percent over the same period.

Not only are incomes higher, but the Vietnamese population is better educated and has a higher life expectancy than most countries at a similar per capita income. In recent international tests, Vietnamese students outperformed the average for countries in the Organisation for Economic Co-operation and Development (OECD), with extremely little variation across income groups and urban–rural locations. The maternal mortality ratio has fallen below the upper-middle-income country average, while under-5 mortality has fallen by half, to a rate slightly above that average. Access to basic infrastructure has also improved sharply: electricity is now available to almost all households, up from less than half in 1993, and access to clean water and modern sanitation has risen from less than 50 percent of all households to more than 75 percent.

Reflecting the gains in per capita incomes and education and health outcomes, Vietnam's Human Development Index (HDI) has improved over the last 20 years. In 2014, its HDI score was 0.67 (figure 1.4), putting it at a global rank of 116 of 188 countries and in the category of "medium human development" countries. Progress has been uneven, however, and the rate of improvement is slowing (VASS and UNDP 2015).

Although Vietnam has avoided the sharp increases in inequality of other fast-growing countries, the differences between rich and poor are still wide. While members of ethnic

FIGURE 1.3 Household poverty rate, Vietnam, 1993–2014

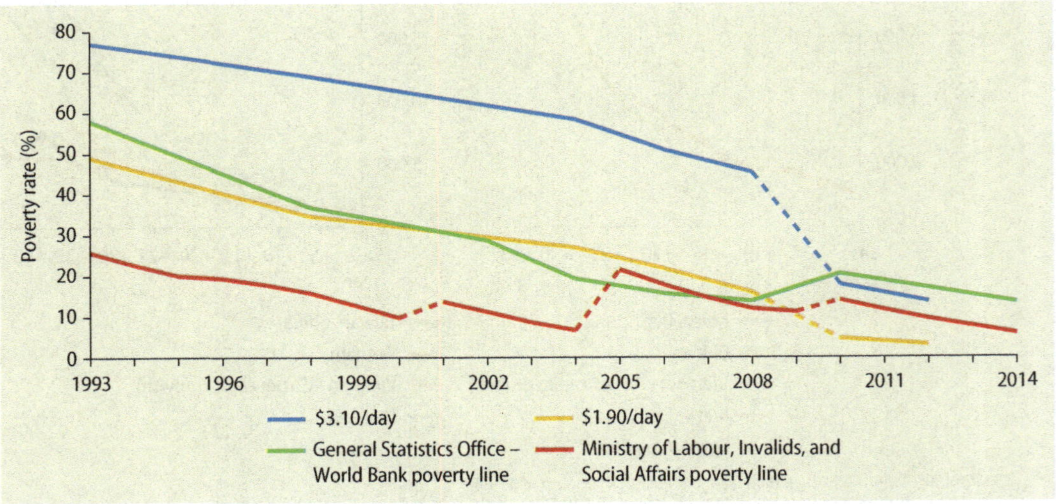

Sources: General Statistics Office data and World Bank and the Ministry of Planning and Investment of Vietnam calculations.
Note: Dotted lines indicate periods when substantial changes were made to poverty lines or methodologies.

minorities have experienced gains in welfare since the early 1990s, they face a growing gap relative to the majority population. With 14 percent of the population, they now make up almost 60 percent of the poor. Large numbers of urban migrants and those with disabilities find themselves similarly marginalized from the country's progress. Ensuring equality of opportunity remains an important agenda for Vietnam (chapter 6), and will become even more pressing as the forces of globalization, urbanization, and rising skill intensity of production deepen their impacts.

FIGURE 1.4 **The Human Development Index in selected countries, 1990–2012**

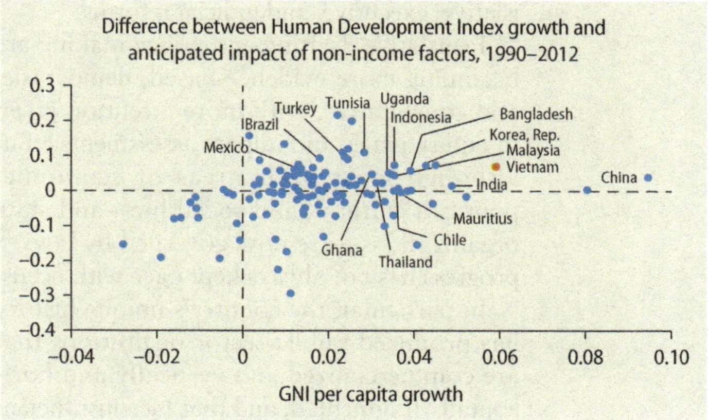

Source: United Nations Development Programme 2013.
Note: Based on a sample of 96 countries.

Emergence of a market economy with multiple types of ownership

The transition toward a socialist-oriented market economy has been gradually institutionalized. Since the launch of *Đổi Mới*, the National Assembly has revised the Constitution three times and promulgated and/or revised more than 150 codes and laws, and its Standing Committee has promulgated 70 ordinances. This has included a number of provisions that helped create a stronger legal basis for all firms, regardless of ownership, to enjoy the freedom to conduct business and compete on a more rules-based playing field. Many SOEs have been restructured and now operate under the unified Enterprise Law. The number of private businesses continues to expand rapidly, contributing substantially to employment creation and economic growth. An overwhelming majority, however, are small or medium enterprises and informal—and inadequately integrated with global supply chain opportunities, which prevents productivity gains through scale economies, specialization, and innovation (chapter 2).

Goods and services markets have been established and are being further developed and deepened, with growing links between domestic markets on the one hand and regional and world markets on the other. Prices of most goods and services are determined by market supply and demand. The labor market (in the formal economy) has also been increasingly active, although international economic agreements are likely to put severe pressure on more substantive change and reform. Financial and real estate markets are in place, albeit still in early stages of development.

But much more needs to be done to meet the institutional requirements of a truly competitive and transparent market economy (chapter 2). Reforms are needed to improve the "rules of the game" at all stages of the business cycle (protecting ownership rights, enforcing contracts, and ensuring market competition, participation, and exit); to develop factor markets (land, capital, labor, and technology); and to strengthen state mechanisms for economic management (with an emphasis on strengthening coordination, decentralization, professionalism, and accountability).

Public institutional reforms and the rule of law

Another pivotal change has been the transition to a state governed by law. The 1992 Constitution broadened the scope for reforming central state agencies.[8] With the introduction of the administrative reform policy in 1994, reforms to administrative procedures were launched to reduce burdens for businesses and citizens. Public administration reform master plans for 2001–10 and 2011–20 were introduced to modernize and improve the efficiency of the state's administrative capacity. The 2013 Constitution expanded the space for legislative, executive, and judicial reforms.

Legislative drafting and policy making are becoming more evidence-based, democratic, and consultative, with more attention given to equity issues and impact assessments.[9] But although most basic areas of economic, political, cultural, and social life—and state organizations—are now governed by laws,[10] progress has not always kept pace with needs.

In particular, the country's unique history has produced public sector institutions that are commercialized and vertically and horizontally fragmented, and that face insufficient scrutiny by citizens (chapter 7). Despite reforms, the state remains strongly engaged in economic activity—directly through SOEs and indirectly through close links with an exclusive segment of the domestic private sector. State fragmentation arises from the lack of a clear hierarchy or assignment of roles and responsibilities, both within the central government and between the center and the provinces. The absence of merit-based management of public servants exacerbates the weaknesses in public institutions. Election processes and mechanisms for engaging citizen organizations are still not robust enough to provide true citizen representation, and the country lacks a system of effective checks and balances among the three branches of government.

Why Has *Đổi Mới* Been Such a Success? Pointers for the Future

Vietnam has recorded considerable success in implementing *Đổi Mới* against difficult odds. In planning for 2035, it is instructive to identify the key factors that contributed to that success, while drawing lessons from the past approach to help guide the next generation of reforms—the core focus of the Vietnam 2035 report.

Overall, a pragmatic and flexible approach to reform that aimed to tap into the country's strengths was important to success, as was the early emphasis on human development, and a willingness to experiment and consider ideologically difficult suggestions. A focus on regional and international economic integration (and competition) also helped, with external commitments under trade agreements used to help lock in difficult reforms. Changes in mindsets over this period were partially reflected in the changing terminology, from questioning the merit of *the bureaucratic, subsidized, command economy* (mid-1980s) to accepting *the multi-actor commodity production economy* (late 1980s), to forming *a market-oriented economy with state management* (1990s), and finally to developing *a socialist-oriented market economy with socialism orientation* (since 2000).

Drilling more deeply, five aspects stand out. First, pragmatism replaced ideology as the primary basis of policy making from the onset of *Đổi Mới* (Pincus 2015). Vietnam has taken a step-by-step, evidence- and consensus-based approach to reform that put a premium on political and social stability, and avoided potentially destabilizing shock therapies (Rama 2008). *Đổi Mới* reforms were implemented at two levels: the Party provided broad direction to structural reforms, with implementation left to the provinces. Provinces often pushed the boundaries, providing opportunity for local experimentation, with the central structure drawing lessons from that (for example, with SOE reform). Efforts to avoid creating "losers in the political arena" helped ensure broad political acceptance (Rama 2014). Reforms where there would be clear losers, as with some elements of SOE reform and administrative simplification, proved much harder to implement.

Second, reforms were and remain homegrown, adding to their legitimacy and domestic appeal. External advice was welcomed, but judged on its merit, rather than just accepted as a condition for obtaining external assistance (which remained limited relative to the overall economy). Lessons from mistakes in the former Soviet Union and successes of neighboring China and the rest of East Asia were internalized, but only after adapting them to the Vietnamese context.

Third, Vietnam framed and sequenced the reforms to build on national strengths. The country's main endowments at the launch of

Đổi Mới were its underused fertile land and a literate workforce, although skill levels were still low and capital stock was in short supply. The early emphasis appropriately was on land reform and raising agricultural productivity in smallholder farming, where most people were employed. The focus then shifted to household business and labor-intensive manufacturing (for example, garments, footwear, and electronics) where most new jobs were being created. With Vietnam's advantageous location—close to countries such as China, Korea, Malaysia, Singapore, and Thailand, which were embedding themselves in global supply chains—regional integration also became an important focus of reform. The gradual discarding of policies that encouraged and subsidized inefficient heavy industry freed scarce capital for more productive investments.

Fourth, Vietnam committed early to build on its already relatively high and equitably distributed human capital. Literacy rates and life expectancy were already impressive for its income level at the onset of reform (Arkadie and Mallon 2003). Gender and rural–urban gaps were contained and further investments were made in human development under *Đổi Mới*: for example, the share of the public budget allocated to education has risen from about 5 percent in the late 1980s to about 20 percent now. The initial emphasis was on basic education: the net enrollment rate for primary and lower secondary school levels increased from 87 percent and 30 percent, respectively, in 1993 to 93 percent and 82 percent in 2010. More emphasis is now given to improving preschool coverage and higher education quality and standards, although the latter needs an even stronger reform push (chapter 3). A continuing strong emphasis on basic health care is reflected in relatively low child and maternal mortality rates, and relatively high life expectancy. The planning focus on human development has enhanced the returns from subsequent market-oriented reforms.

Fifth, where a domestic consensus was harder to forge, Vietnam used its commitments under external trade agreements to good effect, particularly to usher in some of the more complex enterprise and market institution reforms. Starting with the 1987 Law on Foreign Investment (enacted in September 1988), Vietnam has adjusted its legal framework not only to meet the basic regulatory requirements of its international agreements but also to enhance the benefits of integration. Plans to further boost global integration will require sustained changes in awareness, thinking, and the legal regulatory environment. Participation in the TPP, EU–Vietnam FTA, and other international agreements provides opportunities for Vietnam to implement reforms in sensitive areas such as the environment, labor relations, intellectual property rights, and government procurement.

Future Opportunities and Challenges

Domestic Factors

Vietnam's achievements under *Đổi Mới* are testament that, if reforms are carried out correctly, the rewards to society easily justify the effort. The gradual and pragmatic approach to reform, focusing on equitable outcomes, has helped minimize socioeconomic instability and ensure that reforms were both in the national interest and in the interests of the majority of individuals. This helped sustain popular demand for reform from a citizenry that associated a general improvement in well-being with economic renovation. Social consensus for market-oriented reforms is especially strong, but with clear signs that people's expectations are starting to outrun reform progress as they perceive it (box 1.4).

While pragmatism and flexibility facilitated reform, the lack of a comprehensive reform strategy has limited institutional development, undermining the prospects for efficient and sustained growth. There is growing awareness of the need for a renewed focus on improving the quality of growth during the next stage of reform.

The broad-based support for a market economy with private ownership provides a strong foundation for deeper reforms. But past approaches that worked well in the initial stages of reform (benefitting most segments of society)

BOX 1.4 Changing attitudes of Vietnamese society toward the market and the state

Vietnamese society would like to see a rapid transition to a market economy with private ownership, and is increasingly dissatisfied with the pace of change. This is borne out by the recent surveys (2011 and 2014) of people's Changing Attitudes to the Market and the State (CAMS) conducted by the Vietnam Chamber of Commerce and Industry (VCCI), with World Bank support. An overwhelming majority (89 percent) of respondents to the 2014 CAMS survey favored a market economy to a state-led one (figure B1.4.1). More than 70 percent preferred private ownership to state ownership, and the gap had intensified between 2011 and 2014.

Respondents acknowledged that the move toward a market economy was happening (with more than half agreeing in 2014 that Vietnam was primarily a market economy, against only one-quarter in 2011). But expectations for accelerated reforms are also rising. The share of respondents who felt in 2014 that the market-oriented reforms were taking place at a fast or very fast pace was significantly smaller than the share who thought that the pace was slow or very slow—in 2011 the latter group was shadowed by the former (figure B1.4.2). A similar result is seen on the question of whether or not the speed of transition from state to private ownership was fast or slow.

FIGURE B1.4.1 Perceptions about the preferred economic system

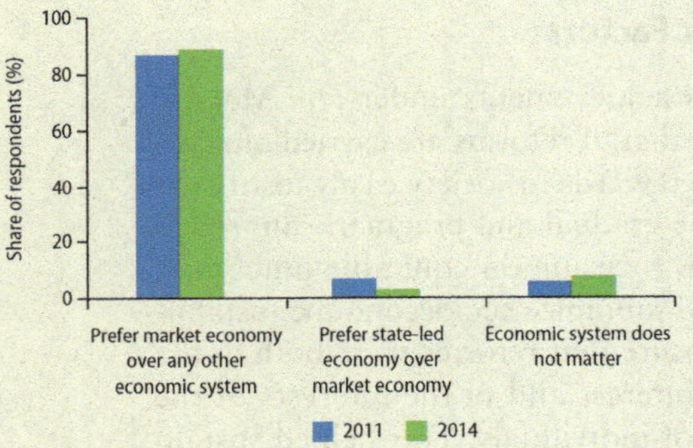

Source: VCCI and World Bank 2015.

FIGURE B1.4.2 Perceptions of the pace of transition

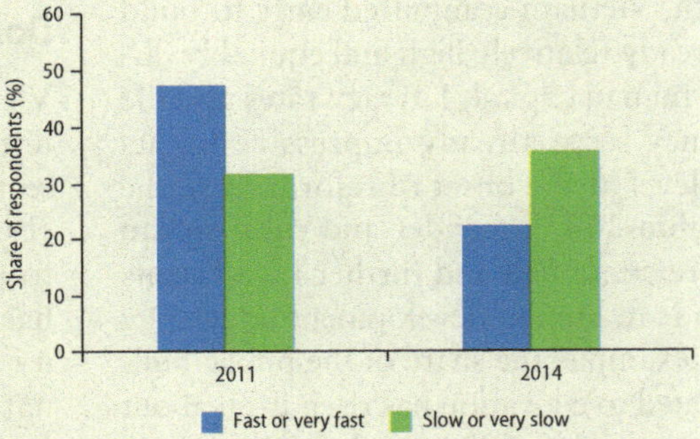

Source: VCCI and World Bank 2015.

will no longer be enough. Reforms from here on are likely to face greater resistance from interest groups that have evolved and gained considerable power since reforms began—and are likely have a lot to lose from some reforms. For the next generation of reforms, it will be even more important to consult widely, build the evidence base on the need for reform, and develop more medium-term strategies for formulating, marketing, and implementing reforms.

Vietnamese business leaders, researchers, and technocratic policy makers will need to continue playing a major role in guiding the reform process. This will require close, frank, and interactive channels for political leaders and policy makers to work with and enlist business leaders, technocrats, and researchers. This served policy making under *Đổi Mới* well and will be increasingly important for designing and implementing future policy.[11] The mass media and society at large, too, have to be involved in informing policy design, and in reviewing and monitoring progress and advocating a change in course when results are unfavorable.

Above all, the situation calls for more radical changes in the mindsets—of Party and government leaders, and of technocrats and policy makers. Despite the stated commitment to transitioning to a socialist-oriented market economy, consensus on the details of what that entails is still lacking. And the "socialist-oriented" part of the definition often gets used to justify preserving the state's dominance of the economy. An effective settlement of the debate would forcefully argue against this, while unambiguously endorsing the market's role in guiding resource allocation and the private sector's role in driving economic growth and job creation.

The state would be an equally important and equal partner as an effective regulator and facilitator, correcting market failures and providing a level playing field for all, on two important fronts. All firms—public and private, those with connections and those without, small and big, domestic and foreign—would face similar incentives and disincentives in the market. The government would provide equality of opportunity to succeed in life to all people, irrespective of predetermined circumstances such as gender, ethnicity, and location of birth or family origins.

There is a perception that "the dogma disease is still prevalent, there is still impartial thinking, irrationality, fear of renovation; renovation thinking is not resolute and strong" (Quy 2015). Prolonged debate about high-level ideological issues has slowed the economic transition and socioeconomic development. Strong leadership is now needed to provide a clear vision of the actions needed to build a truly competitive and equitable market economy.

Global Factors

Vietnam's location makes it a vital link between East, Southeast, and South Asia. Physical connections to Asia and maritime connections to the rest of the world have shaped Vietnam's history and will remain crucial. But the hyper-connectivity of the modern world (to which Vietnam is committed) overcomes many of the binds of geography. Future opportunities and risks are projected to be largely supra-regional, thus requiring geopolitical and economic outreach beyond the region.

The following categories of global megatrends will be important for Vietnam to consider in the next two decades.[12]

Geopolitics

The current shift in the world's economic and geopolitical axis from west to east and from north to south will define the coming decades. The rise of China is particularly significant. Geopolitical shifts will, however, be even more complex. Other regional powers—including developed economies such as Japan and Korea, and emerging powers such as Brazil, India, Mexico, the Russian Federation, and Turkey—are also likely to try to expand their spheres of influence.

The emergence of a multipolar world order gives rise to multiple possibilities, including more collaborations such as the Asian Infrastructure Investment Bank (AIIB) and the New Development Bank of the BRICS states (Brazil, Russia, India, China, and South Africa). There could be tensions, or even conflicts, between rising powers, or among rising and existing powers.

Cooperative relations with a rising China will remain essential. Vietnam is one of the signatories to and founding members of the AIIB. Its infrastructure financing needs over the next two decades will run into tens of billions of dollars a year. With most bilateral partners reducing their presence in Vietnam and private investors still reluctant to participate in infrastructure projects, the AIIB could cover some of the emerging financing gap.

Particularly acute for Vietnam are maritime issues with China. These go beyond just territorial concerns, as the maritime waters have considerable economic and strategic value, critical for shipping and communications and containing a wealth of fish stocks and energy and mineral reserves.

With the Middle East in turmoil, energy geopolitics will also have implications for Vietnam both as a producer and exporter of crude oil and as a rapidly growing consumer of petroleum products.

TABLE 1.1 Average annual growth in real GDP
Percent

	2016–20	2021–25	2026–30	2031–35	2016–35
United States	2.8	2.5	2.6	2.8	2.7
Europe	1.9	1.9	1.9	2.0	1.9
Japan	0.9	1.3	1.3	1.5	1.3
ASEAN	5.3	5.0	4.6	4.3	4.8
China	7.0	6.0	4.9	4.0	5.5
India	6.6	6.3	5.8	5.2	6.0
Rest of the world	3.5	3.4	3.1	2.9	3.2
World	3.5	3.3	3.2	3.0	3.2

Sources: Data and projections from Minor, Walmsley, and Strutt (2015) and World Bank and the Ministry of Planning and Investment of Vietnam calculations.
Note: ASEAN = Association of Southeast Asian Nations.

FIGURE 1.5 Regional shares of global GDP (baseline scenario)

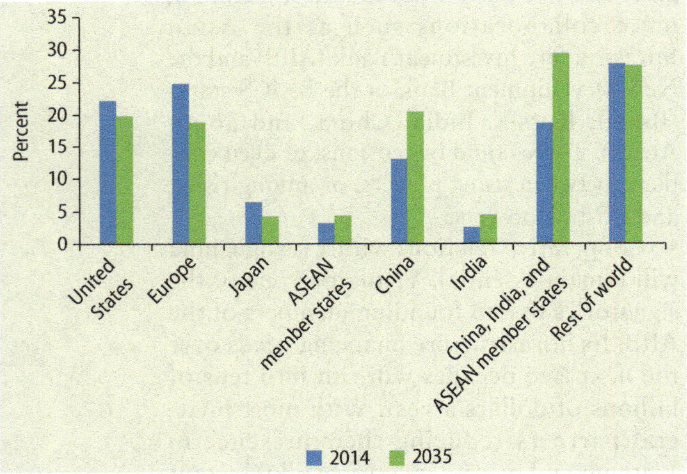

Sources: Data and projections from Minor, Walmsley, and Strutt (2015) and World Bank and the Ministry of Planning and Investment of Vietnam calculations.
Note: ASEAN member states = Brunei Darussalam, Cambodia, Indonesia, Lao PDR, Malaysia, Myanmar, Phillipines, Singapore, Thailand, and Vietnam.

In the midst of this fast-evolving world order, Vietnam will need to continue building its alliances judiciously with a clear eye on its long-term economic and political interests.

Global economics

The global economy is projected to grow at an average of 3.2 percent annually between 2015 and 2035 (table 1.1), with continuing advances in trade integration, urbanization, and technology the main drivers. The rise of China, India, and ASEAN member countries matched by the (relative) decline of the United States, Europe, and Japan is likely to be the most notable shift in the global economic structure in the coming decades (figure 1.5). The three Asian economies are projected to contribute more than 40 percent of the increase in global GDP to 2035, with their collective share in world GDP rising from 22 percent in 2014 to 29 percent in 2035.

China is the biggest part of this story. In this report's assessment, it is expected to overtake the United States as the world's largest economy (in market prices) in about 2032. It has been the world's largest exporter since 2009, and is the second-largest importer of goods. It is set to become an increasingly important source of investment financing for emerging economies, particularly regionally. China already accounts for 20 percent of Vietnam's trade, up from 10 percent in 2000. The large FDI inflows into Vietnam are linked, in part, to a shift in low-wage production from China. As real wages in China rise, producers will continue to seek opportunities for lower wage production bases—the "China+1 strategy." Vietnam's proximity to southern China—home to many production networks—gives it a competitive edge. Producers can benefit from its low wages and from being part of the Chinese supply network. The agglomeration of a nascent electronics–industrial cluster in the north–central parts of Vietnam (around Hanoi) is an early sign of these possibilities. Moreover, with a rapidly emerging middle class, the Chinese consumer market will be increasingly attractive for Vietnamese producers.

Global and Regional Economic Cooperation Agreements

Benefits of trade integration

Growth prospects in East Asia will also be underpinned by the ongoing shift toward multilateral (often regional) trade agreements. ASEAN integration—the ASEAN Economic Community (AEC) became a trading bloc in 2016—can generate considerable economic benefits. Estimates for Vietnam range from a 1–3 percent cumulative increase in national income.[13] But some obstacles need to be overcome. For example, slow progress has been made in dismantling trade barriers and ratifying ASEAN-wide agreements. Companies report that their ability to freely move goods, people, and capital across the ASEAN's political boundaries has not improved as much as expected. Data from the ASEAN Secretariat suggest that about 70 percent of AEC prerequisites have been adopted by ASEAN governments. The remaining tasks are the more difficult, and matter the most for investors.

Foreign investment is expected to increase in the AEC, with a boost to infrastructure development and manufacturing. The rise of the middle class in developing ASEAN countries will inject impetus into regional economic growth. ASEAN integration is also seen in Vietnam as a stepping stone to help lock in partnerships extending beyond the region (Thanh 2015)—especially the TPP (box 1.5) and the EU–Vietnam FTA—as well as the Free Trade Area of the Asia-Pacific (FTAAP) and the RCEP, which are still being negotiated.

The TPP countries account for 36 percent of world GDP and more than a quarter of all world trade. Vietnam is well placed to benefit: the TPP could add a cumulative 8 percent to Vietnam's GDP by 2030, with significant increases in exports and investment (table 1.2).[14] The main sources of these gains are likely to be tariff reductions (figure 1.6), especially on textiles and apparel, where U.S. tariffs are now more than 17 percent ad valorem. Reductions in nontariff measures for goods and services trade also promise to contribute heavily. Vietnam could also use TPP commitments to help lock in sensitive domestic policy reforms. The EU-Vietnam FTA offers similar potential gains in economic advancement and reform opportunity.

While Asia-Pacific Economic Cooperation (APEC)[15] has no mandate for conducting trade negotiations, the FTAAP provides an intriguing possibility for wider trade integration in the Asia-Pacific region.[16] If the

BOX 1.5 The Trans-Pacific Partnership

The TPP—comprising Australia, Brunei Darussalam, Canada, Chile, Japan, Malaysia, Mexico, New Zealand, Peru, Singapore, the United States, and Vietnam—has been billed as a 21st century trade agreement, or an ambitious, next-generation agreement. TPP agreements cover the following areas: cooperation and capacity building; services, including financial services, telecommunications, and temporary entry of service providers; customs; e-commerce; environment; government procurement; intellectual property; investment; labor; legal issues; market access for goods; rules of origin; sanitary and phytosanitary and technical barriers to trade measures; textiles and apparel; and trade remedies.

The TPP is also being tasked with addressing overlapping rules and regulations of existing trade agreements, in an attempt to bring some regulatory coherence to regional trade.

Sources: USTR and Minor, Walmsley, and Strutt 2015.

TABLE 1.2 Overview of the Trans-Pacific Partnership and Free Trade Area of the Asia-Pacific impacts on Vietnam, 2015–35

Cumulative percentage change relative to baseline growth, unless otherwise noted

	2020		2025		2030		2035	
	TPP	FTAAP	TPP	FTAAP	TPP	FTAAP	TPP	FTAAP
Real GDP	3.6	3.6	6.8	11.2	8.2	14.1	8.1	14.7
Real exports	5.0	5.4	13.4	14.4	16.8	20.3	17.1	23.7
Real imports	7.6	7.5	15.7	17.6	16.0	19.8	14.2	20.2
Real investment	13.6	12.9	21.3	32.2	15.0	27.0	6.3	17.8
Capital stock	3.1	2.9	9.3	11.2	12.9	18.8	11.9	20.1
Change in trade balance (USD million)	−4,941	−4,648	−9,148	−13,689	−6,051	−11,313	−169	−5,166

Source: Minor, Walmsley, and Strutt 2015.

FIGURE 1.6 Change in Vietnam's real GDP as a result of the Trans-Pacific Partnership, 2015–35

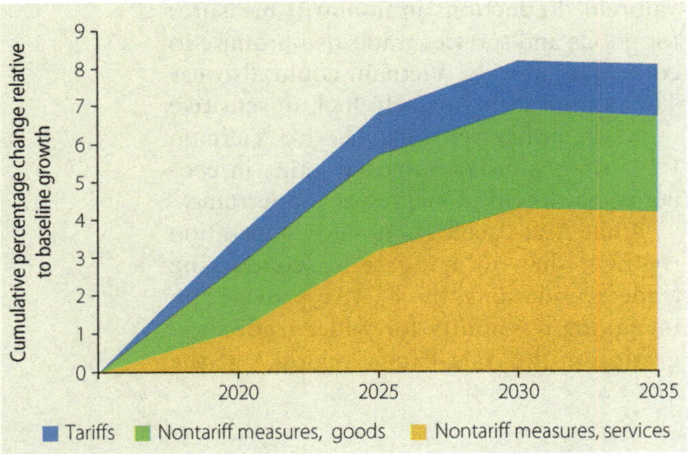

Source: Minor, Walmsley, and Strutt 2015.

FTAAP were also to be agreed and signed following the TPP agreement, it could well add another 6 percentage points to Vietnam's GDP by 2030 (in addition to the 8 percentage points from the TPP). In contrast to the TPP, the most significant source of economic gains from an FTAAP would be greater liberalization of nontariff measures. Investment in Vietnam, when the FTAAP is combined with the TPP, is projected to add a cumulative 32 percent to baseline investment projections by 2025.

Top-down multilateral trade integration is likely to be complemented by important subregional collaboration, including that within the Greater Mekong Subregion.

Water security and dwindling water supplies in the Mekong Delta

Dwindling and increasingly unpredictable water supplies, along with rising demand for water and energy, will require greater regional cooperation for energy and water security. The Mekong River flows through six countries (Cambodia, China, Lao People's Democratic Republic, Myanmar, Thailand, and Vietnam) with a watershed covering 795,000 square kilometers, about 6 percent of which is in Vietnam. Some 60 million people live in the watershed, including 21 million in Vietnam. The Mekong watershed has large hydropower potential, supports the world's largest inland fisheries, has the second-highest levels of aquatic biodiversity in the world, and provides water and nutrients to Vietnam's Mekong Delta.

The Mekong River offers challenges in transboundary water management. China became the first country to begin large development of its Mekong Basin hydropower resources in the mid-1990s. Other countries have built smaller projects, with larger developments planned. While investing in the

Mekong's hydropower potential is a financially attractive option for governments and private developers, it has many negative cross-border impacts. Hydropower dams, particularly those on the mainstream, can block migratory fish routes and reduce fish stocks. Hydropower reservoirs trap sediment that would otherwise flow downstream, providing nutrients to delta areas and the marine ecosystem that supports Vietnam's productive offshore fisheries. Mitigating these impacts presents a major challenge for the region and Vietnam.

Regional cooperation and energy security
Southeast Asia's energy demand is projected to increase by more than 80 percent between 2013 and 2035, to support a near tripling of the region's economy and a nearly 25 percent increase in population.[17] Regional countries will need to act together to ensure energy security.

Past policies are likely to increase reliance on imports of fossil fuels. Countries that used to be net energy exporters (such as Vietnam) are expected to become net importers. The share of coal in the energy mix is predicted to rise, contributing to an even higher carbon intensity and greater environmental costs. A more sustainable pathway is feasible, based on alternative policies supporting scale-up of energy efficiency, renewable energy, and application of modern low-carbon technologies. The distribution of energy resources among countries in the Greater Mekong Subregion is unbalanced, creating opportunities for cooperation and trade to the benefit of all the countries.

New Technical and Business Megatrends[18]

Technical innovations, fueled by the information revolution, will disrupt global production and trading patterns. Advances in digital technologies—including additive manufacturing (3D) printing, programmable microcontrollers, and second-generation computer numerical control milling and routing—make it easier and less expensive to manufacture customized, high-quality products. Major advances in renewable energy pose a growing challenge to conventional, and usually environmentally more damaging, energy sources. Next-generation genome sequencing and other biomedical advances are set to expand rapidly in the next decade, enhancing and extending human life. Advanced robots are being deployed on shop floors at a huge rate, boosting productivity and driving down costs.

The information revolution is also enabling disruptive innovations in business models. The Internet reduces many of the information advantages of colocation and cost-sharing. Raw materials and other inputs can be sourced on the Internet. Online platforms, such as Alibaba, Etsy, and Makers' Row, make it possible for manufacturers to search for customers without having to spend much on advertising and distribution. Crowdfunding sites such as Indiegogo and Kickstarter can help attract finance.

These trends bring mainly opportunities. But skill-intensive and labor-efficient technology may eliminate routine middle-income vocations. New technologies are already displacing handicraft producers in industries ranging from textiles to metalworking. Technical progress may increase inequality in labor productivity and wages, as those with technical skills earn more. Some argue that automation may contribute to premature deindustrialization in the developing world (Rodrik 2015). Vietnam needs to invest in upgrading the technical skills of its next generation and further improve the domestic business environment to maximize benefits from these opportunities—and mitigate possible risks.

Solar energy. Solar energy poses a growing challenge to conventional energy sources as costs decline. Its share of global electricity generation is expected to grow from 0.4 percent currently to 2.6 percent in 2035 (IEA 2013). With solar energy largely available all year, especially in southern and central Vietnam, potential opportunities to use solar panels and water-heating systems are tremendous.

Social mobility, analytics, and cloud services. These services present opportunities for

Vietnam to catch up with developed countries. The value of the cloud computing industry is projected to grow to $241 billion by 2020 (ICTC 2013). Such services could help reduce public service delivery costs. For example, the costs of chronic disease treatment could be reduced by 10–20 percent through better disease management (Manyika and Chui 2013). But close cooperation between scientists, enterprises, and the government is needed to maximize potential opportunities.

Genomics and life sciences (Battelle Technology Partnership Practice 2011; Drake 2011; Wadman 2013). Next-generation genome sequencing applications in health care, agriculture, and biofuels have the potential to boost economic output. Faster disease detection, more precise diagnoses, new drugs, and more customized disease treatments will extend and enhance lives. Improved understanding of the genetic makeup of plants and animals will accelerate the development of agricultural crops and animal breeds that are more nutritious, productive, and resistant to disease, insects, and drought. Genetically improved crops could help cut Vietnam's feed imports and the need for so many chemicals and other inputs. But environmental and consumer groups will also demand more information on the health risks, as well as improved regulatory systems to mitigate them.

E-commerce. E-commerce sales are growing rapidly in Vietnam, driven by rapid Internet uptake and even faster adoption of smart phones. A lack of apps for purchasing online, slow online payment growth, and concerns over the security of online purchases need to be rectified, however, and logistics services for traceable and timely shipping of small packages upgraded. Potential opportunities for domestic firms to cooperate with foreign partners in this area are manifold.

Additive manufacturing. 3D printer technology is set to challenge business models of mass production manufacturing by making mass customization possible at lower cost. While some labor-intensive activities might be at risk, it may also help broaden manufacturing opportunities for Vietnam. A risk is that, as the technology advances, manufacturing may move to smaller-scale, widely distributed, and customizable production. Some investors from developed economies may relocate production back to their home market.

Artificial intelligence. A recent survey of 170 artificial intelligence researchers found a significant consensus around a 90 percent probability that human-level machine intelligence will be attained by 2075, 50 percent probability by 2040, and 10 percent by 2022 (Bostrom 2014). As technology advances and costs are pushed down, industrial robots are becoming increasingly capable and affordable. The new generation of advanced robots is set to improve productivity gains and drive cost savings, replacing low-skilled jobs while requiring modern workers to be equipped with more sophisticated skill sets. Robots are likely to replace an increasing number of jobs in the automotive and electronics industries.

Advances in health care. An era of digitized medicine, where much routine medical care will take place at home, with hospitals and clinics mostly used for emergency treatments, is expected to emerge from about 2020 (Deloitte 2014). This would revolutionize health care productivity, as traveling and waiting times are reduced, medical prognoses become more accurate, and health care is made more affordable.

Global Climate Change

Climate change is potentially the most consequential global issue. The global mean temperature increased by 0.8°Celsius (°C) between 1880 and 2012 (IPCC 2013). Ten of the hottest years on record have occurred since 1990. The number of category 4 and 5 storms has risen sharply over the past 35 years. The surface area of the Arctic Sea's ice has shrunk to its lowest on record—with an accelerating rate of shrinking—and global sea levels have risen by about 10–20 centimeters in the past century. Rising sea levels increase the risk of storm surges and fluctuations in precipitation.

The recent Fifth Assessment Report (AR5) by the Intergovernmental Panel on Climate Change (IPCC)[19] shows that greenhouse gas emissions have continued to increase (IPCC 2014). These emissions are now on a path to a 3.5–4.0°C warmer planet by the end of the century (figure 1.7). The report warns that emissions need to go to zero in less than a century if there is to be any hope of limiting global warming to anywhere near 2–3°C.

Vietnam is among the five countries likely to be most affected by climate change. A high proportion of its population and economic assets are in coastal lowlands and deltas. Temperature increases in Vietnam have averaged about 0.26°C a decade since 1971 (Nguyen, Renwick, and McGregor 2013), twice the global average (Trenberth et al. 2007). On current trends, annual average temperatures will be 0.6–1.2°C higher by 2040 than in 1980–99 (ONRE 2012). Predictions show intensified heat and cold waves, and a 28–33 centimeter increase in sea levels on Vietnam's coast.[20] Seasonal variability in precipitation is projected to increase. Extreme flooding would also become more likely, particularly in the northern region, with increased risk of landslides in mountainous areas. The typhoon trajectory has shifted south in the past five decades. If this continues, Ho Chi Minh City will be at risk from typhoons. Coastal erosion and salinity intrusion are other accelerating risk factors.

Agriculture is projected to be hit hard, with the Mekong Delta likely to be the worst affected (Wassmann et al. 2009). Annual rice production could fall by 3 million–9 million tons by 2050, coffee plantations may become unsuitable (Bunn et al. 2015), and marine ecosystems will likely be severely affected. Climate change is also set to have adverse health consequences, including water- and vectorborne diseases and diarrheal illnesses (Coker et al. 2011). Flooding would compound the risks. The poor and elderly would be especially vulnerable to heat extremes.

FIGURE 1.7 Projections for surface air temperature increase

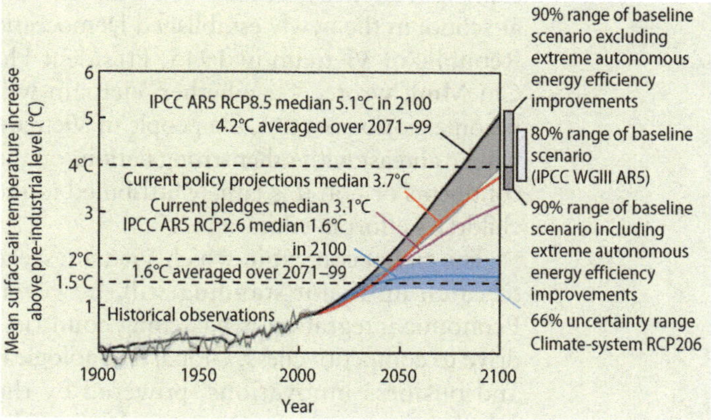

Source: World Bank 2014.
Note: RCP8.5, RCP2.6, and WGIII.

Vietnam's Aspirations for 2035

The motivations that fuel Vietnam's 2035 aspirations are internal and external. Internally, there is pride in a rich past—justifiable for a society with one of the world's longest continuous histories and civilizations. As recently as the early 19th century, Vietnam was a regional powerhouse, with an economy much larger than that of Malaysia, the Philippines, or Thailand (Maddison 2001). The period since has been one of a long, relative decline for Vietnam, with its per capita GDP growing by only about 0.4 percent a year between 1820 and 1960, and then falling into sharp decline for more than a decade on account of a devastating war (chapter 2). The world economy—many countries in the region included—expanded at an unprecedented pace, widening the gap with Vietnam.

Yet the post–*Đổi Mới* period has lifted Vietnam into the ranks of the world's middle-income countries, though the country is yet to close the gap with much of the rest of the world and regional economies, such as China, Korea, Malaysia, and Thailand, on per capita income.

A major part of Vietnam's aspirations for 2035 thus derives from its desire to *reclaim* its place among the community of nations—and not get left further behind regionally. That desire is not new, nor is the idea that the desired convergence with the world economy will not come without effort and investment in human capital. In a letter to students on their first day at school in the newly established Democratic Republic of Vietnam in 1945, President Ho Chi Minh wrote, "... whether Vietnam will become glorious or not, the people of Vietnam will be abreast with other strong nations on the continents or not, it is largely attributed to the children's effort in education...."

The global context in which Vietnam seeks to catch up is not standing still, however. Economic integration is hastening countries' drive to competitiveness. Global technological and business innovations, powered by the information revolution, are reshaping the world's economic, political, and social structures (Centennial Asia Advisors 2015), creating new opportunities and risks that have to be navigated judiciously. Building a skilled human resource base will remain a critical part of Vietnam's arsenal for the future.

In addition to catching up, Vietnamese aspirations also involve adopting modern institutional norms of OECD countries for living standards, rule of law, and creativity. These aspirations reflect an emphasis on clean water and clear blue skies; a healthy, secure, learned, and equitable society; and an effective state accountable for the material and social welfare of its citizens. Vietnam has also signed up to the United Nations Sustainable Development Goals, which set a comprehensive global development agenda for 2030 and will give more concrete shape to some of Vietnam's key long-term goals.

In sum, in this report's assessment, Vietnam's 2035 aspirations entail moving rapidly toward prosperity, creativity, equity, and democracy, as now described (and summarized in box 1.6).

A More Prosperous Society

By 2035, Vietnam seeks to be a moderately prosperous society, at the upper reaches of the upper-middle-income stratum. Its more mature market economy will be private sector–led, competitive, and closely integrated with the global economy. The domestic private sector will benefit from strong and modern market institutions that will ensure free and fair competition, security of all forms of private property rights, and competitive and transparent land and capital markets. The country's SOEs will be relatively few (preferably in the double digits), and run with a commercial approach that focuses on their financial performance and production efficiency. All corporations, private and public, will be subject to global good practice corporate governance regulations enforced without bias, and face a level playing field in all aspects.

Modern industries and a knowledge-based economy will thrive, housed in an efficient and well-connected network of modern cities, in which urban and rural policies are closely synchronized. Metropolises such as Hanoi and Ho Chi Minh City will interact with the global economy and provide the urban density and diversity that encourage learning, innovation, and new product development, connecting people and firms to the world. Cities such as Danang will allow producers to benefit from clustering, because they can choose workers and materials from a bigger pool, and to engage in beneficial competition. Towns such as Buon Ma Thuot in the Central Highlands, famous for its coffee, will let firms and farms exploit plant-level scale economies.

With this aspiration in mind, the 2011–2020 Socio-Economic Development Strategy sets out the objective "to become a basic industrialized country with the foundation of a modern and industrial country by 2020." However, despite broad acceptance, the precise definition of the term "modern and industrial" economy has not been announced (Tran 2015). While any definition would be arbitrary, this report lists five quantitative criteria for meeting that objective:

1. A GDP per capita of at least $18,000 (2011 PPP), roughly equivalent to Malaysia in 2010
2. A majority (more than 50 percent) of the Vietnamese population living in urban areas
3. A share of industry and services in GDP of more than 90 percent and in employment of more than 70 percent

BOX 1.6 Key features of aspirations for 2035

Key features of Vietnam's aspirations for 2035 may be broadly defined in the following ways:

- *A prosperous society* that will be at the upper reaches of upper middle income. Its market economy will be private sector-led, competitive, and intensively integrated with the global economy. Modern industries and a knowledge-based economy, housed in an efficient and well-connected network of modern cities, will drive growth.
- A *modern, creative,* and *democratic society* will be the driving force for future development. The emphasis will be on creating an open and free environment that promotes learning and innovation for all citizens, who will be guaranteed equal access to development opportunities and the freedom to pursue their vocations, while fulfilling their responsibilities without compromising national and communal interests.
- A *rule-of-law state* will be effective and accountable. It will clarify the relationship between the state and the citizenry and between state and market. It will perform its basic functions effectively, including developing and enforcing legislation; managing international relations; ensuring public safety and national security; and ensuring that markets function freely while addressing market failures. It will develop strong social institutions to ensure that the power belongs to the Vietnamese citizens and protect their right of pursuing creativity. It will develop clear lines of responsibilities between the legislative, judiciary, and executive branches for adequate checks and balances on the government.
- The *National Assembly* will comprise full-time deputies with the technical capacity and institutional autonomy to represent the sovereign people, exercise oversight over the executive, and pass quality legislation. The judiciary will similarly be suitably positioned, with autonomy and strong capacity to resolve disputes in a more diverse society and economy. The executive will be well integrated horizontally and vertically, with clear functions for central and subnational authorities.
- A *civilized society* will make every citizen and every political and social organization (the entire political system) equal before the law. Underpinning this will be robust, diverse people's social organizations that can exercise fundamental rights, including the people's direct democratic rights and the rights to information and association.
- A *responsible member of the global community of nations* will build global alliances and fulfill global responsibilities for peace and security while proactively seeking regional and global opportunities for economic integration.
- A *sustainable environment* will protect the quality of Vietnam's air, land, and water. It will build climate resilience into economic planning, social policy, and infrastructure investments to reduce the most severe risks posed by climate change. It will develop diverse, clean, and secure energy sources.

4. A private sector share in GDP of at least 80 percent
5. A score of at least 0.70 on the United Nations' HDI

How well is Vietnam positioned to become a modern, industrial economy by 2035? Its GDP per capita—$5,370 (2011 PPP) in 2014—would need to grow by at least 6 percent a year to reach the $18,000 mark by 2035 (figure 1.8). This would be significantly higher than the average per capita growth rate of 5.5 percent between 1990 and 2014—and well above the 3.8 percent average for all middle-income countries over that period. A lower and more feasible (but still ambitious) per capita growth rate of 5.0 percent (Vietnam's average in the last 10 years) would take its GDP per capita to just under $15,000 by 2035 and put the country on a par with Brazil in 2014, and thus well poised to reach $18,000 by 2040. A growth path of 7 percent (Vietnam's aspirational growth target) would take per capita GDP to $22,200, roughly the income of Korea's in 2002 or Malaysia's in 2013. This higher growth rate would also

FIGURE 1.8 Income per capita growth scenarios for Vietnam to 2035

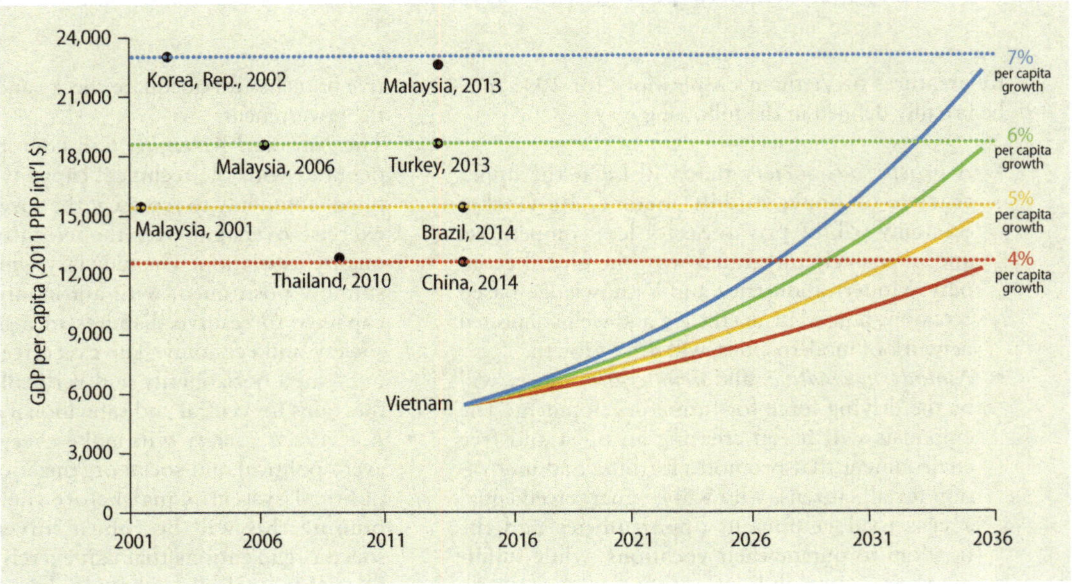

Sources: World Development Indicators and World Bank and the Ministry of Planning and Investment of Vietnam calculations.

enhance Vietnam's chances of catching up with Indonesia and the Philippines.

While seeking greater prosperity, Vietnam will work toward a *sustainable environment* by protecting the quality of its air, land, and water. It will build climate resilience into economic planning, social policy, and infrastructure investments to reduce the most severe risks presented by climate change. It will develop diverse, clean, and secure energy sources. And as a responsible member of the global community of nations, it will build global alliances and fulfill global responsibilities for peace and security while proactively seeking regional and global opportunities for economic integration.

A Creative Society

A modern, creative society will be the driving force for Vietnam's development. The emphasis will be on creating an open and free environment that promotes learning and innovation for all citizens, who will be guaranteed equal access to development opportunities and the freedom to pursue their vocations, while fulfilling their responsibilities without compromising national and communal interests. In some areas of science and technology, Vietnam will have moved up to the advanced level in the region and globally, sufficiently supporting the innovation needs of a dynamic, upper-middle-income country.

By 2035, it is foreseen that Vietnam will be host to globally and regionally recognized universities, attracting the best talent not just within the country but also regionally. More broadly, the higher education system (including a strong combination of universities, community colleges, and technical vocational institutes) will flourish in a competitive environment to enhance education and meet the growing learning needs of society. A student-centered approach will aim at sharpened self-learning and self-innovation capacity by students.

In addition to high-quality teaching and ample resources (enabled by autonomous structures), higher education institutions will serve as the centers for cutting-edge research and innovation of direct relevance to private companies. Complementing these institutions will be government research institutes, undertaking contracted applied research with industry while focusing on competitive fundamental research to serve the priorities of socioeconomic development. Research institutes of businesses, especially in large enterprises, will be formed, improving the private sector's innovation capacity. At the same time, a more dynamic domestic private sector, embedded in global supply chains, will create solid demand and absorb advanced knowledge for higher value-added goods and competitiveness, in both domestic and international markets.

An Equitable Society

Vietnam will continue to be a caring and equitable society, sensitive and responsive to the needs of its vulnerable members and providing a security blanket to those excluded on account of the vicissitudes of the market economy. The nation will be alert to the fact that sustaining the positive equity trends of the past is not something it can take for granted, especially as the forces of urbanization, globalization, and the rising skills intensity of production take firmer root.

By 2035, it is the nation's intention that all the country's people will have an equal opportunity to succeed in life, irrespective of their predetermined circumstances such as gender, ethnicity, and location of birth or family origins. The country's ethnic minorities will be seamlessly integrated with its social and economic fabric, having closed the gap with the majority population on most development indicators. Policy makers fully realize that that will require targeted interventions in education, nutrition, and sanitation, and providing greater voice for ethnic minorities. Vietnam will also redouble its efforts to fulfill its commitments to ensure inclusion of people with severe disabilities. It will also reform the *ho khau* system to ensure equal access to administrative and public services for urban migrants, which the current system prevents for the more than 5 million Vietnamese who lack permanent registration in their place of residence. Finally, on equality of opportunity, through reform in the population policy and an aggressive social campaign to raise awareness of the value of female children, Vietnam will eradicate the current practice of sex selection at birth.

The country is also aware that the future inclusion agenda will be shaped by two social megatrends: the rise of the middle class, which will also be increasingly urban and employed in the formal sector, and rapid population aging. It will therefore make great efforts along four policy dimensions. First, expand the pension system to cover most of the population, while ensuring the system's financial and fiscal sustainability. Second, ensure that nearly all of its children complete upper secondary school with job-relevant skills, with an emphasis on developing their noncognitive and complex problem-solving skills. Third, establish an industrial relations system suited to a mature market economy, where the interests of workers, employers, and the state are more properly represented in a true bargaining process. Fourth, make every effort to ensure citizens' access to good quality health services without imposing financial hardship on them. This will entail expanding and reforming the health insurance regime and shifting health care from its current focus on hospitals toward high-quality primary care at the center of an integrated system.

A Democratic Society

An effective and accountable *rule-of-law state* will be in place well before 2035. The country's governance structure will clarify the relationship between the state and the citizenry and between the state and market. The state will perform its basic functions effectively, through a well-organized government structure (both at the center and locally) and a strong, meritocratic bureaucracy. An effective state would perform well at developing and enforcing legislation; managing international relations; ensuring public safety and national security; and ensuring that markets function freely while addressing market failures.

An effective state will also apply market rationality to economic policy making. State–market relations will be characterized by a clearer division between the public and private spheres. Specifically, government agencies directly or indirectly involved in economic regulation would not engage in commercial business of any kind to avoid conflicts of interest. The state's role in the economy will be transformed from a producer to an effective regulator and facilitator, with the state focusing on providing a level playing field for the economy, while enforcing free and fair competition and more secure and transparent property rights, particularly on land issues.

The state will also develop strong social institutions, both to ensure that power belongs to citizens and to protect their right of pursuing creativity. It will develop clear lines of responsibility between the legislative, judiciary, and executive branches for adequate checks and balances among the three branches of government.

The National Assembly will comprise full-time deputies with the technical capacity and institutional autonomy to represent the sovereign people, exercise oversight over the executive, and pass quality legislation. The judiciary will similarly be suitably positioned, with autonomy and strong capacity to resolve disputes in a more diverse society and economy. The executive will be well integrated horizontally and vertically, with clear functions for central and subnational authorities.

A civilized society will make every citizen and every political and social organization (the entire political system) equal before the law. Underpinning this will be robust, diverse people's social organizations that can exercise fundamental rights, including the people's direct democratic rights and the rights to information and association, and a more robust and independent mass media.

* * *

Thirty years of *Đổi Mới* reforms have brought many successes. Vietnamese development aspirations for 2035 are bold, but the challenges are also huge. To achieve the aspirations, the following six transformations or breakthroughs will be essential, as examined in more detail in the following chapters:

1. Enabling economic modernization and private sector development (chapter 2)
2. Building national innovation capacity (chapter 3)
3. Managing urbanization for greater economic efficiency (chapter 4)
4. Achieving sustainable and climate-resilient growth (chapter 5)
5. Promoting equity and social inclusion (chapter 6)
6. Building modern institutions for an effective state (chapter 7)

Notes

1. State enterprises were allowed to keep 85 percent of the profits from activities beyond the targets, part of which could also be distributed to workers as a bonus. Provisions were also introduced for linking SOE workers' salaries to output.
2. Arkadie and Mallon (2003) argued, "Partial reform had left the economy in a difficult halfway house, with neither the constraints of a tight planning system, nor the policy instruments for managing a centralized economy, in place."
3. Benjamin and Brandt 2004. Half of all land had official title by 1997.
4. Estimates of revenue collection in 1991 vary from 7.6 percent of GDP (Leipziger 1992) to 13.6 percent (Arkadie and Mallon 2003).
5. This paragraph draws on Tu-Anh et al. 2015.
6. The PCI is a nongovernment initiative, jointly developed by the VCCI and the United States Agency for International Development, designed to assess the ease of doing business, quality of economic governance, and progress of administrative reform in all 63 provinces in Vietnam. The PCI is constructed using opinion data provided by domestic private businesses as well as published data on 10 dimensions of provincial economic governance: (1) entry costs for business startup; (2) access to land and security of business premises; (3) information transparency and equitability; (4) time requirements for bureaucratic procedures and inspections; (5) informal charges; (6) policy biases toward state, foreign, or connected firms; (7) proactivity of provincial leadership in solving problems for enterprises; (8) business support services; (9) labor and training policies; and (10) fair and effective legal procedures for business dispute resolution. Since the PCI was introduced in 2005, it has been used

by provincial governments to monitor and benchmark the competitiveness of their business environment. The PCI is, however, rarely used by the central government as an input to policy formulation. http://eng.pcivietnam.org.

7. This comparison excludes economies with a population of less than 1 million, and Bosnia and Herzegovina.
8. The number of focal point agencies of the government was reduced from 70 before *Đổi Mới* to 30 now (including 22 ministries and ministerial agencies, and eight government agencies).
9. These are well reflected in the Law on the Promulgation of Legal and Regulatory Documents in 2008 and 2015.
10. The number of laws and ordinances promulgated by the National Assembly and the Standing Committee of the National Assembly over 29 years of *Đổi Mới* (from January 1, 1987, to June 30, 2015) increased eightfold from the number of laws and ordinances issued in the 41 years before *Đổi Mới*. Notably, from September 2, 1945, to December 30, 1986, Vietnam promulgated 63 laws and ordinances, but from January 1, 1987, to June 30, 2015, 524.
11. Experience with the Enterprise Law is an example. The government established a Task Force (of technocrats and researchers) for Enterprise Law Enforcement, which accelerated implementation.
12. The discussion on the four global megatrends draws on Centennial Asia Advisors (2015).
13. ERIA 2012 and Thanh 2015.
14. Others have estimated double-digit gains for Vietnam, many times larger than for any other TPP country. Petri and Plummer 2014.
15. APEC members are Australia; Brunei Darussalam; Canada; Chile; China; Hong Kong SAR, China; Indonesia; Japan; the Republic of Korea; Malaysia; Mexico; New Zealand; Papua New Guinea; Peru; the Philippines; Russia; Singapore; Taiwan, China; Thailand; the United States; and Vietnam. The notable exception is India, which would be included in the RCEP.
16. It is notable that China announced its backing of an FTAAP at the APEC forum held in Beijing in November 2014, giving credibility to this track of negotiations.
17. In the International Energy Agency (IEA) baseline scenario (taking into account policy commitments and pledges made by governments), the region's oil demand would increase from 4.4 million barrels a day in 2013 to 6.8 million barrels a day in 2035, about 20 percent of projected world growth. Having grown at double-digit rates each year since 1990, coal demand is set to triple over 2011–35, with the increase accounting for nearly 30 percent of global growth. Natural gas demand is projected to increase by 80 percent to 250 billion cubic meters over the same period. The share of renewables in the primary energy mix is set to fall as rapidly increasing use of modern renewables, such as geothermal, hydropower, and wind, is offset by reduced use of traditional biomass for cooking. Southeast Asia's energy-related carbon dioxide emissions would almost double, reaching 2.3 gigatonnes in 2035.
18. This subsection draws on Centennial Asia Advisors (2015).
19. The IPCC is the leading body of global climate change assessments. It comprises hundreds of leading scientists worldwide and publishes regular assessment reports with the most recent scientific, technical, and socioeconomic information on climate change and its implications.
20. The projections do not take into account land subsidence, which further exacerbates the impacts of sea level rise.

References

Arkadie, Brian Van, and Raymond Mallon. 2003. *Vietnam: A Transition Tiger.* Canberra: Asian Pacific Press at the Australian National University.

Battelle Technology Partnership Practice. 2011. *Economic Impact of the Human Genome Project.* Columbus, OH: Battelle Technology Partnership Practice.

Benjamin, D., and L. Brandt. 2004. "Agriculture and Income Distribution in Rural Vietnam under Economic Reform: A Tale of Two Regions." In *Economic Growth, Poverty, and Household Welfare in Vietnam,* edited by D. Dollar, P. Glewwe, and N. Agrawal. Washington, DC: World Bank.

Bostrom, N. 2014. *Superintelligence: Paths, Dangers, Strategies.* Oxford: Oxford University Press.

Brand, Claus. 2015. "Achieving and Sustaining Price Stability in Vietnam." Background paper for Vietnam 2035.

Bunn, C., P. Laderach, O. Ovalle Rivera, and D. Kirshke. 2015. "A Bitter Cup: Climate Change Profile of Global Production of Arabica and Robusta Coffee." *Climatic Change* 129 (1–2): 89–101.

Centennial Asia Advisors. 2015. "Global Megatrends and Vietnam." Background paper for Vietnam 2035.

Coker, Richard J., Benjamin M. Hunter, James W. Rudge, Marco Liverani, and Piya Hanvoravongchai. 2011. "Emerging Infectious Diseases in Southeast Asia: Regional Challenges to Control." *Lancet* 377 (9765): 599–609. doi:10.1016/S0140-6736(10)62004-1.

CPV (Communist Party of Vietnam), Seventh National Congress. 1991. *Socio-Economic Stabilization and Development Strategy to the Year 2000*. Hanoi: National Political Publishing House.

Deloitte. 2014. *Healthcare and Life Sciences Predictions 2020: A Bold Future?* London: Deloitte.

Dollar, D., and J. Litvack. 1998. "Macroeconomic Reform and Poverty Reduction in Vietnam." In *Household Welfare and Vietnam's Transition*, edited by D. Dollar, P. Glewwe, and J. Litvack. Washington, DC: World Bank.

Drake, N. 2011. "What Is the Human Genome Worth?" *Nature News*, May 11.

ERIA (Economic Research Institute for ASEAN and East Asia). 2012. *Mid-Term Review of the Implementation of AEC Blueprint: Executive Summary*. Jakarta: ERIA.

General Statistics Office of Vietnam (database). https://www.gso.gov.vn/Default_en.aspx?tabid=491.

ICTC (Information and Communications Technology Council). 2013. *Canada's Cloud Imperative: Improving Business Opportunities through Enabling Services*. Ottawa: ICTC.

IEA (International Energy Agency). 2013. *World Energy Outlook 2013*. Paris: Organisation for Economic Co-operation and Development (OECD)/IEA.

IPCC (Intergovernmental Panel on Climate Change). 2013. "Summary for Policymakers." In *Climate Change 2013: The Physical Science Basis. Contribution of Working Group I to the Fifth Assessment Report of the Intergovernmental Panel on Climate Change*, edited by T. F. Stocker, D. Qin, G.-K. Plattner, M. Tignor, S. K. Allen, J. Boschung, A. Nauels, Y. Xia, V. Bex, and P. M. Midgley. Cambridge, U.K.: Cambridge University Press.

———. 2014. "Summary for Policymakers." In *Climate Change 2014: Mitigation of Climate Change. Contribution of Working Group III to the Fifth Assessment Report of the Intergovernmental Panel on Climate Change*, edited by O. Edenhofer, R. Pichs-Madruga, Y. Sokona, E. Farahani, S. Kadner, K. Seyboth, A. Adler, I. Baum, S. Brunner, P. Eickemeier, B. Kriemann, J. Savolainen, S. Schlömer, C. von Stechow, T. Zwickel, and J. C. Minx. Cambridge, U.K.: Cambridge University Press.

Leipziger, Danny M. 1992. "Awakening the Market: Vietnam's Economic Transition." Discussion Paper 157, World Bank, Washington, DC.

Maddison, A. 2001. *The World Economy: A Millennial Perspective*. Paris: OECD Development Centre.

Manyika, James, and Michael Chui. 2013. "All Things Online." *Foreign Affairs* (September).

Minor, P., T. Walmsley, and A. Strutt. 2015. "The Vietnamese Economy through 2035: Alternative Baseline Growth, State-Owned Enterprise Reform, a Trans-Pacific Partnership, and a Free Trade Area of Asia and the Pacific." Working Paper, World Bank, Washington, DC.

MONRE (Ministry of Natural Resources and Environment). 2012. *Climate Change and Sea Level Rise Scenarios for Vietnam*. Hanoi: MONRE.

Nguyen, D.-Q., J. Renwick, and J. McGregor. 2013. "Variations of Surface Temperature and Rainfall in Vietnam from 1971 to 2010." *International Journal of Climatology* 34 (1): 249–64. doi:10.1002/joc.3684.

Petri, Peter A., and Michael G. Plummer. 2014. "ASEAN Centrality and the ASEAN–US Economic Relationship." Policy Studies 69, East-West Center, Honolulu, HI.

Pincus, Jonathan. 2015. "Vietnam: Building Capacity in a Fragmented, Commercialized State." Background paper for Vietnam 2035.

Quy, Luong Xuan. 2015. "New Thinking on Socio-Economic Development of Vietnam in the New Context." National Political Publishing House, Hanoi.

Rama, Martin. 2008. "Making Difficult Choices: Vietnam in Transition." Commission on Growth and Development Working Paper 40, World Bank, Washington, DC.

———. 2014. "Vietnam." In *Handbook of Emerging Economies*, edited by Robert E. Looney. London: Routledge.

Rodrik, Dani. 2015. "Premature Deindustrialization." Working Paper 20935, National Bureau of Economic Research, Cambridge, MA.

Thanh, Vo Tri. 2015. "Vietnam's Perspectives on Regional Economic Integration." *Journal of Southeast Asian Economies* 32 (1): 106–24.

Tran, Van Tho. 2015. "Vietnam Needs a Development-Oriented Market Economy: Review of 30 Years of Renovation and Looking Forward to the Future." Background paper for Vietnam 2035.

Trenberth, K., P. Jones, P. Ambenje, R. Bojariu, D. Easterling, A. Klein Tank, D. Parker, F. Rahimzadeh, J. A. Renwick, M. Rusticucci, B. Soden, and P. Zhai. 2007. "Observations: Surface and Atmospheric Climate Change." In *Climate Change 2007: The Physical Science Basis. Contribution of Working Group I to the Fourth Assessment Report of the Intergovernmental Panel on Climate Change*, edited by S. Solomon, D. Qin, M. Manning, Z. Chen, M. Marquis, K. B. Averyt, M. Tignor, and H. L. Miller. Cambridge, U.K.: Cambridge University Press.

Tu-Anh, Vu-Thanh, David Dapice, Nguyen Xuan Thanh, and Do Thien Anh Tuan. 2015. "A Retrospective on the Past 30 Years of Development in Vietnam." Background paper for Vietnam 2035.

UNDP (United Nations Development Programme). 2013. *Human Development Report 2013—The Rise of the South: Human Progress in a Diverse World.* New York: UNDP.

University of Groningen. 2013. Penn World Table 8.0 (database). http://www.rug.nl/research/ggdc/data/pwt/pwt-8.0.

USTR (Office of the United States Trade Representative). "Outlines of TPP." USTR, Washington, DC. https://ustr.gov/tpp/outlines-of-TPP.

VASS (Vietnam Academy of Social Sciences) and UNDP. 2015. *Viet Nam Human Development Report 2015: Growth that Works for All.* Hanoi: Social Sciences Publishing House.

VCCI (Vietnam Chamber of Commerce and Industry) and World Bank. 2015. *Vietnam in Transition—Changing Attitudes to the Market and the State 2014.* Hanoi: VCCI.

Wadman, M. 2013. "Economic Return from Human Genome Project Grows." *Nature News* June 12.

Wassmann, R., S. V. K. Jagadish, S. Heuer, A. Ismail, E. Redona, and R. Serraj, R. K. Singh, G. Howell, H. Pathak, and K. Sumfleth. 2009. "Climate Change Affecting Rice Production: The Physiological and Agronomic Basis for Possible Adaptation Strategies." *Advances in Agronomy* 101 (08): 59–122. doi:10.1016/S0065-2113(08)00802-X.

World Bank. World Development Indicators (database). http://data.worldbank.org/data-catalog/world-development-indicators.

———. 2014. *Turn Down the Heat: Confronting the New Climate Normal.* Washington, DC: World Bank.

2

Enabling Economic Modernization and Private Sector Development

Main Messages

The world around Vietnam presents unprecedented possibilities as well as risks and development traps that can cause prolonged economic stagnation. Vietnam has done well in exploiting its opportunities and managing the risks and pitfalls coming its way. Since 1990, it has been among the world's fastest growing economies, steadily narrowing the income gap with more developed parts of the world. Even more remarkably perhaps, the country has achieved growth *with* equity rather than *at the cost* of it, unlike many other fast-growing economies. Vietnam still has a lot to learn from the world as it ascends the development ladder. But the global community, in its search for broader development solutions, could also learn from Vietnam's many successes.

Yet Vietnam's development story is far from over. Its gross domestic product (GDP) per capita in 2013 was less than 40 percent of the world average in purchasing power parity (PPP) terms (figure 2.1) and less than 20 percent in market prices. Vietnam could reach parity with world average income by 2035 if it could raise the rate of per capita growth to 6.0–6.5 percent a year (from the current 5.0–5.5 percent a year). It would have to remain alert to future development traps that could result in several decades of economic stagnation—a pitfall that many developing countries can attest to—in a global context that is no longer as hospitable as before the global financial crisis.

Development traps invariably are about productivity stagnation, and this is where Vietnam's growth record gives cause for concern. Growth of labor productivity (output per worker) has been declining since the late 1990s, explained by a sharp decline in total factor productivity (TFP) growth. Moreover, the decline in labor productivity growth has been seen across most sectors, but especially in mining, construction, public utilities, and finance and real estate, where state-owned enterprises (SOEs) have retained their dominant role. Thus far it has been easy to overlook these trends. GDP growth since the early 2000s has been led by forces that compensated for weak and declining productivity growth but are now reaching their natural limits. Rapid labor force growth made up for low and declining economy-wide labor productivity growth. Large-scale structural transformations offset the low and declining labor productivity growth at the sectoral level. And an acceleration in capital accumulation counterbalanced the low and declining TFP growth.

FIGURE 2.1 Strong growth has enabled Vietnam to narrow the income gap with the world average

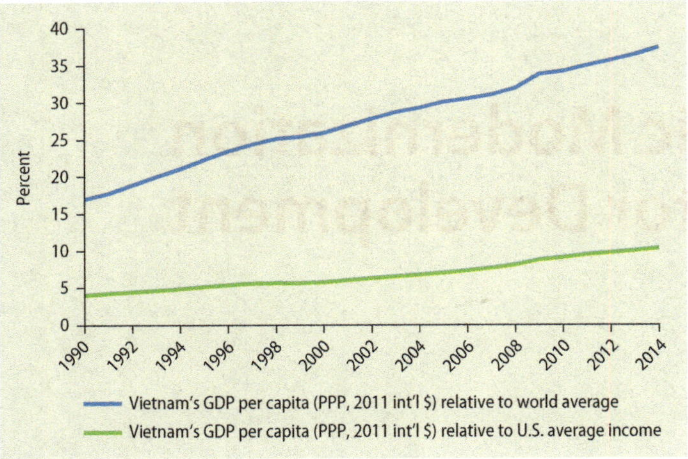

Source: Calculations based on the World Development Indicators.

But in the next development phase, each of these factors is expected to weaken sufficiently to expose economic growth to weaknesses in underlying productivity trends.

Several factors explain the weak productivity growth. The public sector's presence in production and control over factor markets remain pervasive, with the state still making up about a third of GDP. Public investment is not as efficient as it should be because of the uncoordinated and often incoherent investment decisions of a fragmented state (chapter 7). Further more, SOEs—driven by distorted incentives and by multiple objectives that rarely include profit—are nearly all inefficient producers. Widespread inefficiencies in state investment thus perpetuate the economy-wide productivity weakness. But they do not explain the worsening productivity growth. Their performance, though still weak, has been stable because of a series of restructuring measures.

The main reason for the drop in productivity growth is especially worrisome. Steady erosion of the productivity growth of the domestic private sector—universally viewed as the main engine of future growth—has ensured that it is now just as inefficient on average as the state sector. Why?

Domestic private firms are overwhelmingly small, which prevents productivity gains from scale economies, specialization, and innovation—ingredients for sustained long-term growth (World Bank 2007). Moreover, small firms have become increasingly capital-intensive, which—without scale economies—has led to a sharp decline in their capital productivity. The few large domestic firms are usually even more unproductive than the smaller ones. This reflects their short-term view on investment and profits and their rising concentration of land and capital assets in construction, real estate, and banking and finance—sectors that have shown some of the country's lowest levels and growth of productivity. Foreign-invested firms have grown their presence in Vietnam and led the country's rapid growth in manufacturing and exports. But links with domestic firms have been lacking in key sectors, impeding productivity-enhancing transfers of technology and management practices. There is an emerging concern about a "Mexican phenomenon."[1]

Reviving productivity growth is imperative if Vietnam is to meet its ambitious income objectives for 2035. The reform agenda will be demanding, given that the productivity growth decline is widespread. An immediate focus is needed on four fronts.

First, Vietnam needs to create an enabling environment for a more productive and competitive domestic private sector. This will require the microeconomic foundations of the market economy to be strengthened, with emphasis on protecting property rights and enforcing competition policies. Correcting distortions in the factor markets—capital and land markets primarily—will also be important. (Factor markets are restrictive, underdeveloped, and overly controlled and managed by the state.)

The second reform priority is a comprehensive overhaul of the SOE sector. Increased attention is needed to reduce the number of enterprises under majority state control, from more than 3,000 now to fewer than 100 later. The government could also issue a clear SOE ownership policy that focuses on raising the value of state capital (barring exceptional cases), enforced by obligating the SOEs to face direct market competition pressures and hard budget constraints. They should also be required to uphold global standards for reporting requirements and be insulated from any bureaucratic interference. The policy could also delineate and streamline ownership and regulatory responsibilities within the government. And staffing the SOEs with competent professional managers and board members is also needed.

Equal treatment of all enterprises is critical for success on both these reform priorities. Notably, equal tax and dividend policies and access to land, capital, and government procurement contracts for all enterprises are crucial. Firms with all-important connections—SOEs, most foreign-invested firms, and some large domestic private firms—have an unfair advantage over the domestic private sector (which does not have them). The problem with this model is that the connected firms are not necessarily the most productive. This undermines the quality of the enterprise sector and carries larger costs for innovation, productivity, and economic growth.

The third reform priority reorients agriculture toward a market-driven, commercially oriented system, with far less state interference. Just under half the Vietnamese labor force is engaged in this sector. And even though this ratio could shrink by half in the next two decades, agriculture's performance will have a major impact on economywide labor productivity. Two major sets of changes are needed. The first—agricultural transformation—involves mechanization, land consolidation, organized farm services, and flexible and market-determined land-use patterns (with less administratively imposed focus on rice). The second is centered on modernizing and commercializing the entire agro-food system, from procurement at farm gate to processing and distributing commercially valued food products and enforcing safety standards. To promote the two transformations, the state should invest more selectively and efficiently, focusing on basic public goods and services, while facilitating greater investment by farmers and the private sector.

The fourth reform priority is to improve the links between more productive exporting firms and local suppliers, enabling domestic firms to increase productivity. Reviving the domestic private sector is a prerequisite for success. But reform extends to removing barriers to profitably participating in global value chains (GVCs) in key sectors. Reform also covers addressing the cross-cutting issues of strengthening the modern services sector, an important input for manufacturing production, and improving the connection of supply chain centers within Vietnam and between the country and its trading partners.

Beyond these "more immediate payoff" reforms, the government will also need to complete those that take longer, preempting bottlenecks to growth a decade or so from now. These reforms would seek to create more robust learning and innovation structures, promote urban agglomeration, and ensure environmental sustainability—topics addressed in depth in their own chapters.

Vietnam's Growth and Economic Modernization Record

Đổi Mới and Economic Growth

In less than three decades since the launch of *Đổi Mới* (economic renovation), Vietnam has built an impressive record of fast, stable, and inclusive economic growth. First, GDP growth per capita has averaged 5.5 percent a year since 1990 (figure 2.2a), yielding a three-and-a-half-fold increase in average income. Worldwide, only China recorded faster rates of per capita growth over this period.[2] Second, growth has been remarkably stable, with volatility declining markedly (figure 2.2b) and becoming among the lowest in the world.[3] Had Vietnam's growth been as volatile as Thailand's, it would have been 1 percentage point lower each year.[4] Third, growth has been highly inclusive. Per capita income of the bottom 40 percent has grown by 9 percent annually since the early 1990s, outpacing income growth of the top 60 percent, thereby ensuring shared prosperity and significant reductions in poverty.

FIGURE 2.2 Vietnam has had 25 years of fast, stable, and equitable economic growth

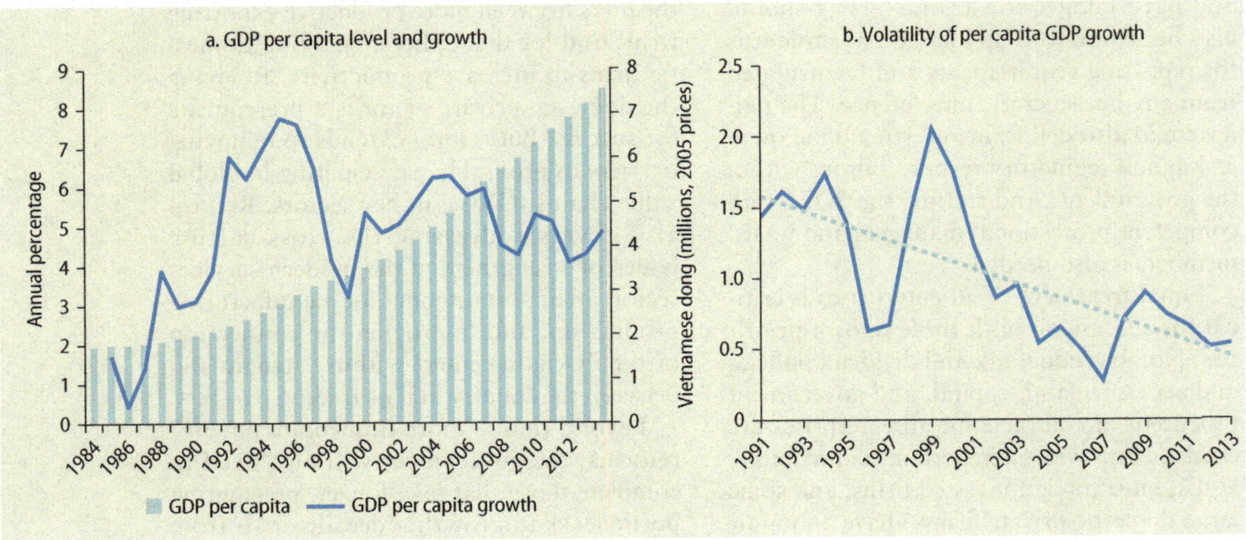

Source: Calculations based on the General Statistics Office of Vietnam.
Note: Volatility in year *x* is measured as the standard deviation of annual per capita growth over five consecutive years—year *x* and the four years preceding year *x*.

The strong growth record has been underpinned by rapid accumulation of factors of production, with the labor force almost doubling in size and the capital stock growing sixfold in real terms since 1990. Growth has also been reinforced by impressive gains in human capital and a strong initial burst of TFP growth.[5] The rapid increase in the labor force reflects favorable demographics. The share of the working-age population (15–60 years) in the total population has shot up from 53 percent in 1985 to close to 68 percent. This demographic dividend coincided with economic liberalization and a rising demand for labor, enabling productive absorption of the labor force increase. That translated into higher GDP growth. The reduction in the dependency ratio also helped increase the national savings rate—from 3 percent in 1990 to more than 30 percent now—which, in turn, helped finance a major surge in investment expenditure.

Economic growth has brought economic transformations and modernization, manifest in four mutually reinforcing ways.

1. Structural transformation have shifted resources from agriculture to manufacturing and services.
2. Outward orientation of the economy has lodged Vietnam more deeply in GVCs.
3. Transition from a centrally planned and state-dominated economy to a market-oriented system has allowed the private sector taking an increasing role.
4. Spatial transformation has shifted population from rural to urban areas.

Spatial transformation is discussed in chapter 4. The other three are briefly described below.

Growth and economic transformations were rooted in a sequence of reforms after the onset of *Đổi Mới* (chapter 1) to remove market distortions, stabilize macroeconomic conditions, leverage the forces of global integration better, and deepen human capital development.

Accelerated Structural Transformation

As national incomes rise, the employment and GDP shares of agriculture fall and those of industry and services grow. These trends have been seen with empirical regularity in developing countries and are grounded in sound economic theory (Lewis 1954; Fei and

Ranis 1964; Chenery 1979). This pattern has characterized East Asia, including Vietnam, especially well.[6,7] As in the rest of the region, structural transformation in Vietnam has been an outcome and a facilitator of economic growth. While responding to the different opportunities generated by economic development and modernization across sectors, the process has reinforced economic growth by reallocating resources from the more traditional, less productive sectors (such as crop cultivation and informal trading activity) to the more productive sectors (such as modern manufacturing and services).

Large-scale sectoral shifts have been at play in Vietnam since at least 1990 (figure 2.3). The shift out of agriculture has been dramatic, with the sector's share in GDP falling from more than 40 percent in the late 1980s to less than 20 percent in recent years. That decline has been mirrored by a rise in services and industry shares. These sectoral GDP trends have been broadly matched by sectoral trends in employment.

Structural transformation trends in Vietnam have been broadly consistent with global patterns. Compared with the Republic of Korea in particular, Vietnam has, however, retained a far larger share of employment in agriculture relative to its income (figure 2.4). The share of agriculture in GDP has been more in a "normal" range, highlighting Vietnam's lower labor productivity in that sector. The reverse is true for industrialization. While the share of employment in Vietnam's industry sector has been in a normal range, the share of GDP in the sector has been significantly higher than in the average country. This reflects higher labor productivity, likely because of greater capital intensity in the sector. Vietnam's transformation to services has been characterized by a steeper increase in the employment share than in the GDP share. This move reflects slow growth in services' labor productivity. Vietnam's structural transformation patterns have been broadly similar to China's, after adjusting for differences in income.

Consistent again with global patterns, the sectoral shifts have been accompanied

FIGURE 2.3 Large-scale sectoral shifts have been at play in Vietnam for at least 25 years

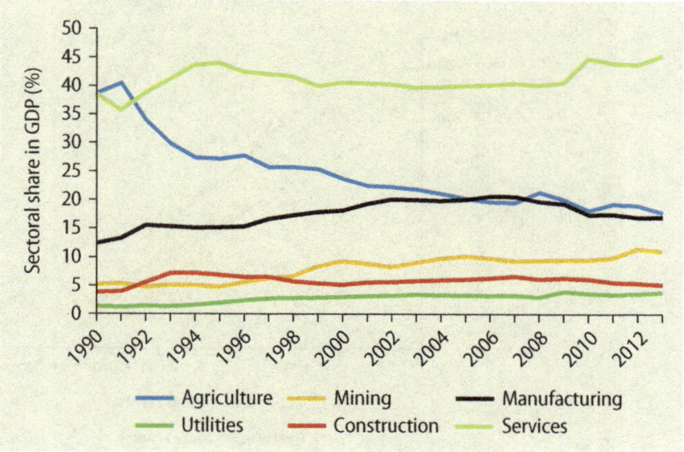

Source: Calculations based on General Statistics Office of Vietnam.

by structural changes within agriculture and the rural economy. These include consolidation of landholdings, increasing commercialization of agricultural production, reduced labor and increased mechanization and use of purchased inputs for production, and shifts in land-use patterns. They also include changes in the commodity composition of agricultural GDP and a growing importance of nonfarm employment and other income sources within rural areas (Dawe 2015).

The pace of these rural structural changes has been uneven. For example, the consolidation of commercial agricultural production and the movement of labor from farm to nonfarm activity has happened quickly. But agricultural-land consolidation remains at an early phase (figure 2.5).[8] Shifts in land-use patterns have also been relatively slow, and crop diversification is still at an early stage. A comparison with China reflects the historical importance and the policy and investment attention given to rice production—despite rapidly shifting food consumption and expenditure patterns within Vietnam (figure 2.6).[9] Even with these constraints, an increasing share of agricultural output comes from the faster growing noncrop subsectors, mainly livestock and aquaculture (figure 2.7).

The most significant change is the rapid rise of wage employment—even if

FIGURE 2.4 Vietnam's structural changes are broadly consistent with global patterns

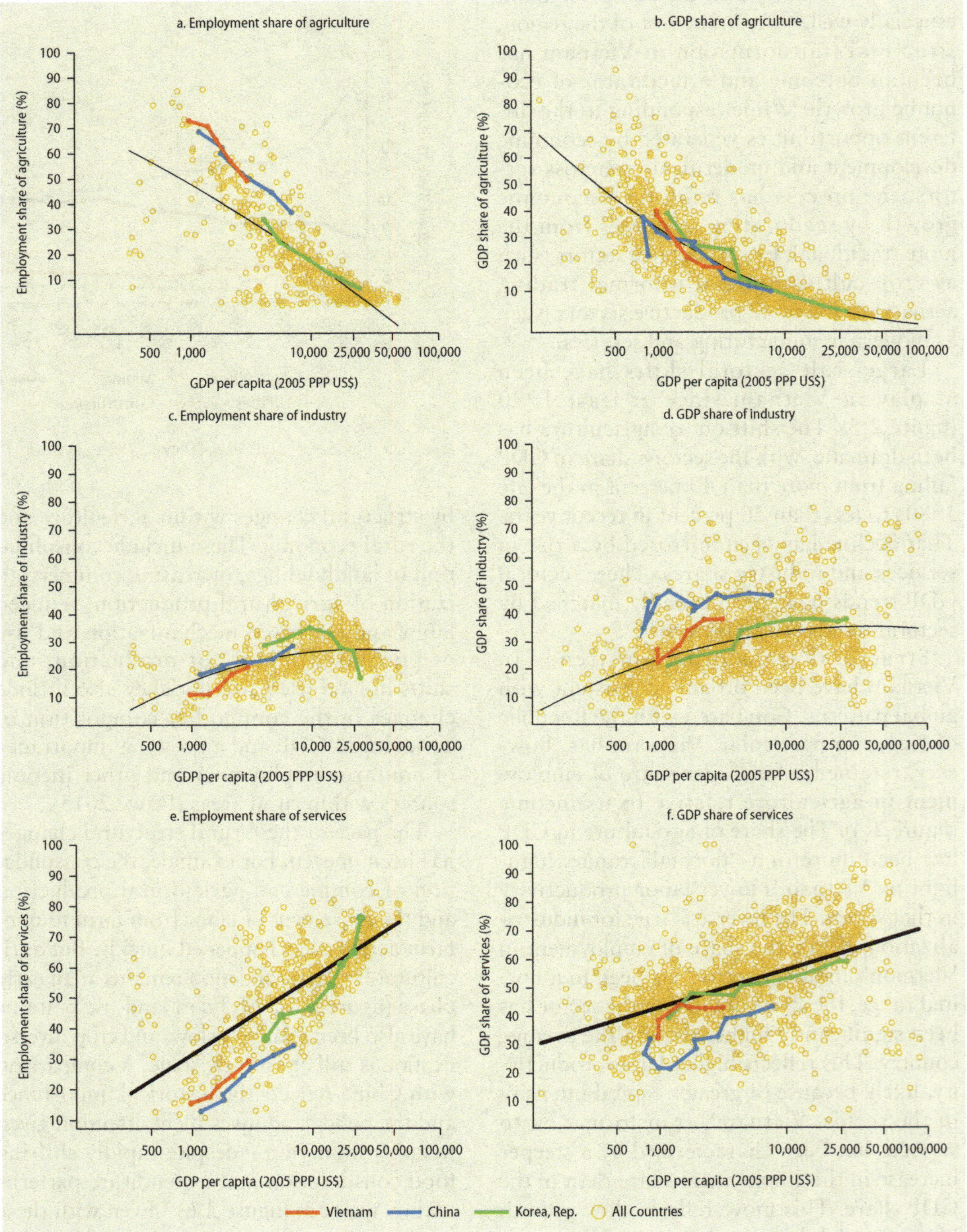

Sources: Calculations based on the General Statistics Office of Vietnam (for Vietnam) and World Development Indicators (for all other countries) for sectoral shares of GDP and employment; http://www.rug.nl/research/ggdc/data/pwt/ for GDP per capita.

FIGURE 2.5 Consolidation of agricultural land has happened at a slow pace

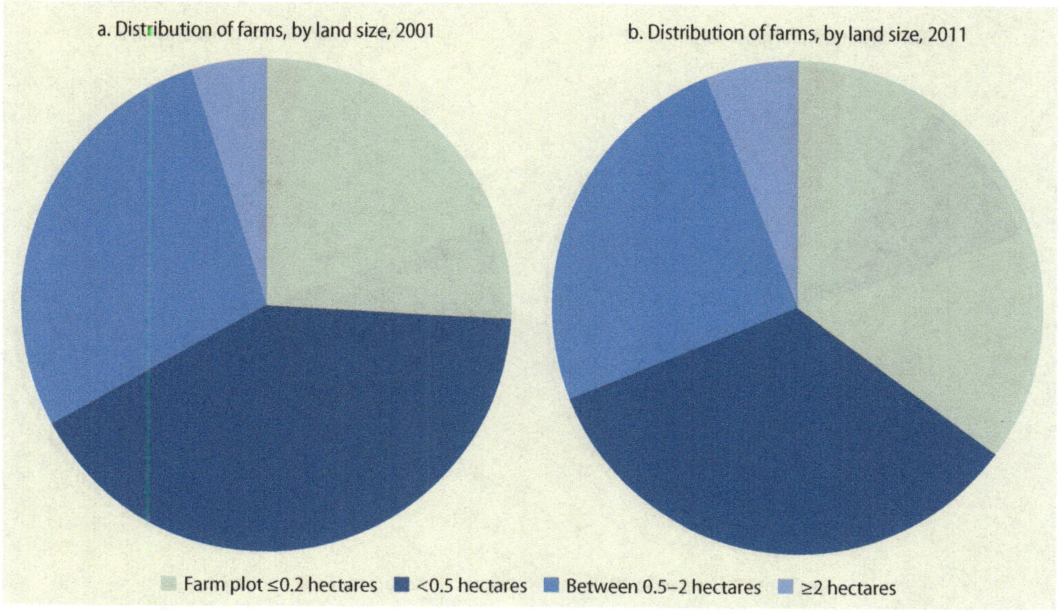

Source: Calculations based on the General Statistics Office of Vietnam.

FIGURE 2.6 In comparison with China, Vietnam has given heavy policy and investment attention to rice production—despite food consumption and expenditure patterns rapidly shifting away from rice

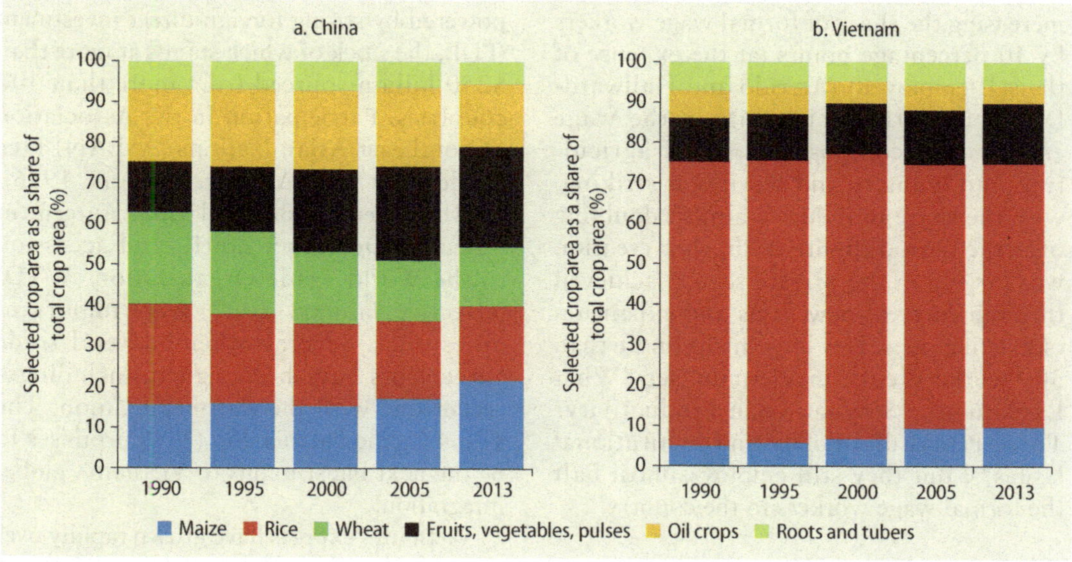

Source: Calculations based on the General Statistics Office of Vietnam.

FIGURE 2.7 Livestock and aquaculture production is gaining share in agriculture

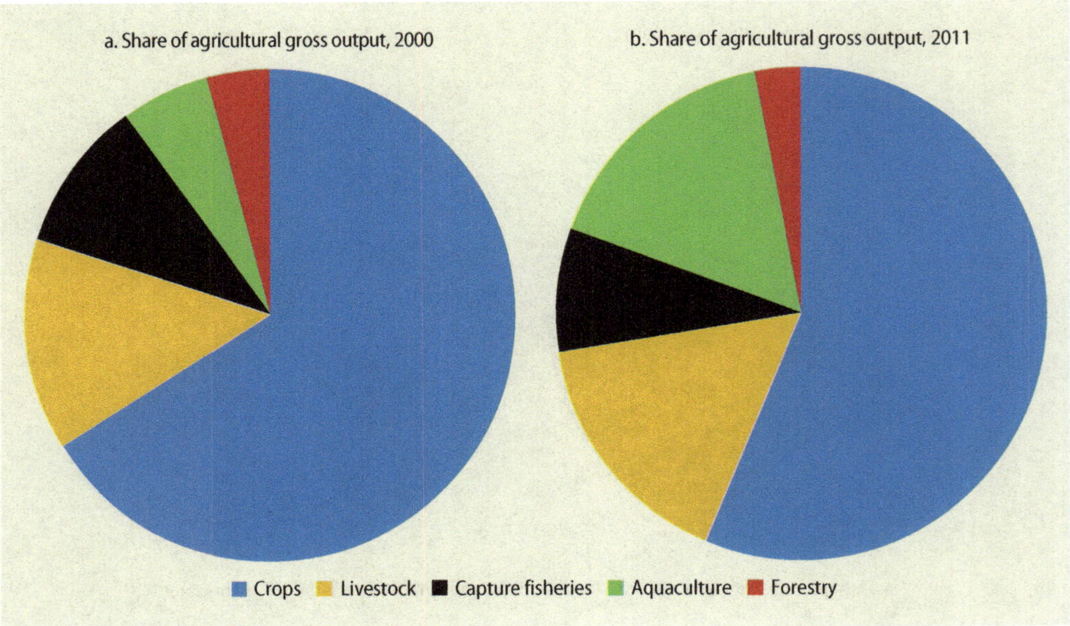

Source: Calculations based on the General Statistics Office of Vietnam.

self-employment still dominates (figure 2.8a). Vietnam created 5.6 million net new formal wage jobs between 2004 and 2012, increasing the share of formal wage workers by 10 percentage points (at the expense of the self-employed) (Aterido and Hallward-Driemeier 2015). The shift in the wage employment composition out of agriculture into industry and services is striking, with the share in industry almost doubling over the period (figure 2.8b). Job creation was largely in the private sector, achieved through entry of new firms and expansion of existing ones. Few large firms (more than 300 workers) exist in Vietnam (see "What Explains the Stagnation in Productivity? Three Primordial Policy and Institutional Issues"). But they still employ almost half the formal wage workers in the country.

Rapid Outward Orientation Integration

Vietnam has done extremely well in deepening its integration with the global economy and leveraging the opportunities presented. Measured by the ratio of total trade to GDP (figure 2.12a), Vietnam is one of the world's most open economies. Most of its trade is powered by strong foreign direct investment (FDI), the stock of which stands at more than $250 billion sourced from more than 100 countries. Participation in the Association of Southeast Asian Nations (ASEAN) Free Trade Area (AFTA) (effective June 1996), the U.S.–Vietnam Bilateral Trade Agreement (effective December 2001), and accession to the World Trade Organization (WTO) (effective January 2007) were important milestones. Several other bilateral trade agreements have been signed, including a recent one with the European Union. The Trans-Pacific Partnership (TPP) promises to be the next big stimulus to Vietnam's global integration.

Vietnam's exports have grown rapidly over the past decade and a half (figure 2.9a)—significantly faster than global and regional averages. Manufacturing exports have led the export boom. Having grown at more than 20 percent a year on average—in

FIGURE 2.8 Rise of wage employment and its sectoral shifts, 2004 and 2012

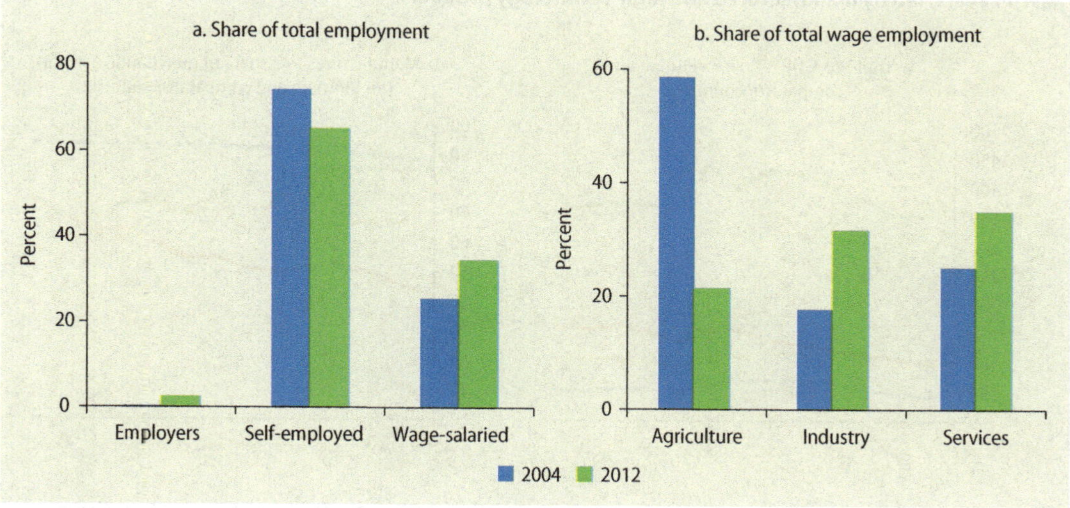

Source: Aterido and Hallward-Driemeier 2015.

nominal dollars—since the early 2000s, they were recorded at more than $100 billion in 2014. Their share of total merchandise exports increased from 43 percent in 2000 to more than 75 percent (figure 2.9b). Not only much bigger, Vietnam's export basket is also much more diversified than in the early 2000s.[10] It partly reflects a successful transition from exporting primary commodities (such as crude oil and rice) first toward low- and medium-tech manufactured goods (such as apparel and footwear) and later more sophisticated products (such as machinery and electronics) (figure 2.9c). Service exports, however, have remained lackluster (figure 2.9d).

Trade and investment liberalization has allowed industrial clusters to emerge with the presence of local private and foreign-invested firms (figure 2.10). The concentration of labor-intensive garment companies is high in the southeast region in Ho Chi Minh City and the provinces of Dong Nai and Binh Duong. That region also attracts local investment in plastics, rubber, and chemicals, and foreign investment in electrical equipment and machinery. Outdoor furniture products and animal feed are concentrated along the south-central coast. An export-oriented food processing cluster is growing fast in the Mekong Delta. Large investments by Intel in Ho Chi Minh City—and by Samsung and Canon in the northern provinces around Hanoi—are beginning to attract other investors in support and related industries. This signals the rise of electronics and information technology (IT) clusters. Tourism in several coastal regions still has a great growth potential.

Uneven Pace of Transition to a Market Economy

Vietnam is an economy in transition, transforming from a state-dominated, centrally planned system into one increasingly driven by market forces and owned by the private sector. This third major economic transformation is also happening on a large scale, although its pace has been more uneven than the first two transformations, generating important imbalances along the way.

Product markets have been largely liberalized. Before *Đổi Mới*, product prices were set by the state with little regard to market demand–supply conditions; not that prices had much meaning for enterprises that

FIGURE 2.9 Vietnam's exports have consistently grown faster than global and regional averages for the past 15 years, led by manufactured and high-technology products

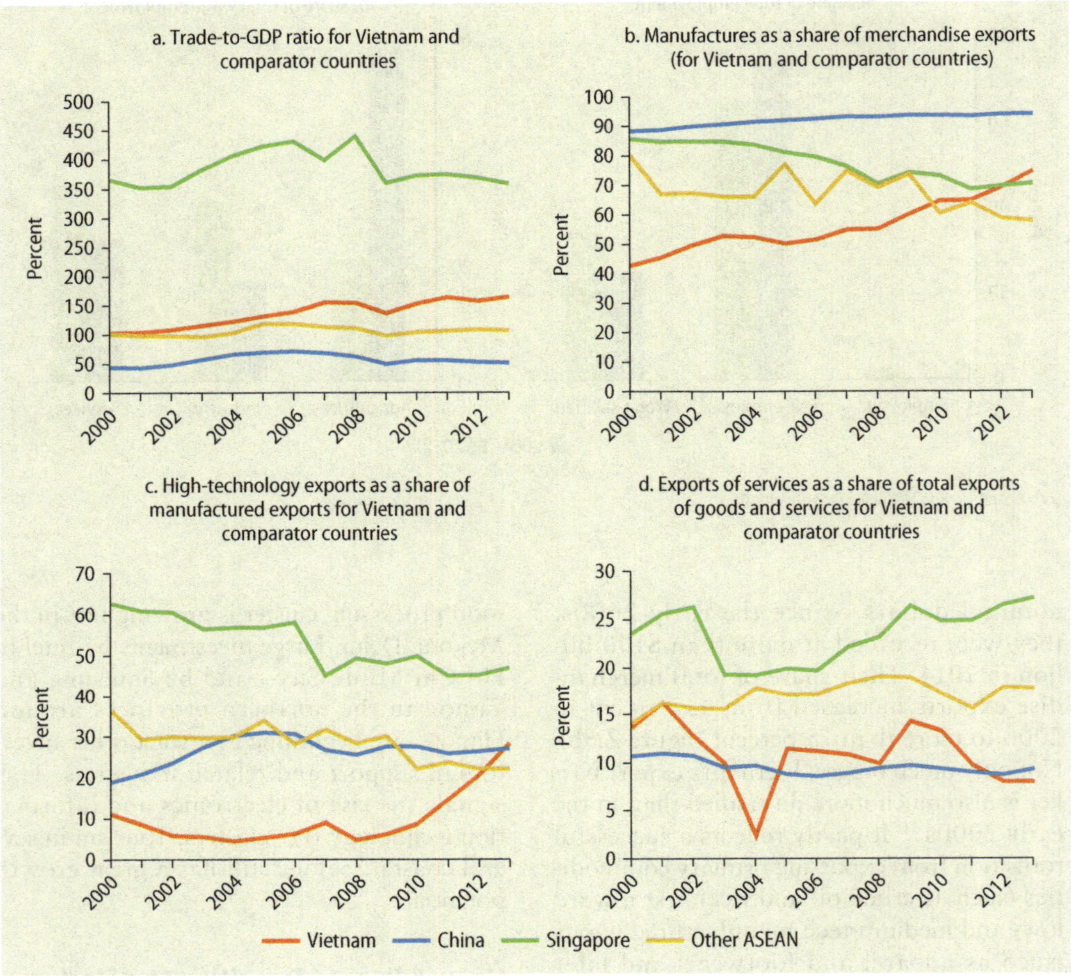

Source: Calculations based on World Development Indicators.
Note: Service exports are calculated as the difference between total goods and services exports and merchandise exports. ASEAN refers to the Association of Sotheast Asian Nations (Indonesia, Malaysia, the Philippines, Singapore, and Thailand).

needed to respond mainly to state-imposed production quotas. Now only a handful of prices in product markets are administered, and state-determined production quotas are a thing of the past.[11] Trade and foreign exchange controls were lifted early in the *Đổi Mới* process. This allowed domestic product prices to align with global prices and effectively ended the system of multiple exchange rates. Factor markets have also been liberalized, though at a notably slower and more uneven pace than product markets. Land and capital markets in particular remain underdeveloped and distorted, weighed down by heavy state involvement.

The state's withdrawal from direct production has been substantial, if fitful. The number of enterprises fully owned by the state fell from a little more than 12,000 in 1989 to less than 750 in 2014. The scale and scope of SOE equitization have, however, not always been uniform. They have gone through several phases from the closure and merger of several thousand small loss-incurring SOEs in the early 1990s—often accompanied by large-scale layoffs—to more gradual progress later in the decade. Another acceleration cycle was in the early 2000s, followed by a slowdown that started in 2008. In Vietnam's case, equitization does not mean privatization. An enterprise is considered equitized if the state holds anything less than 100 percent of its capital. Indeed, the state still holds a majority stake in more than 3,000 SOEs, more than 2,000 of them equitized. Even so, the share of SOEs in output and various factor inputs has declined sharply since the early 2000s (figure 2.11).

But the state's participation as an owner of productive assets is more encompassing than just the SOEs. It has a heavy—and growing—presence in activities such as government services, public administration, and security and defense. The share of the state in GDP is therefore still high at around one-third, less than its 40 percent share in 1995 but the same as in 1990. The state's share in total employment and investment has not changed notably. And the state has retained a virtual monopoly or oligopoly in sectors such as coal, banking, construction, fertilizer, utilities, and rubber and plastics (figure 2.12) (World Bank 2011).

The decline in importance of SOEs is mirrored by expansion of the domestic and foreign private sectors. Driven by a sequence of reforms to legalize first household and then nonhousehold enterprises (box 2.1), the private sector has grown at an exponential pace since the early 1990s. The government registry lists more than 650,000 domestic private enterprises, a dramatic rise from just 40,000 in 1999 and virtually none in 1990. Millions more household enterprises are unregistered.[12] The 2000 Enterprise Law proved to be a major turning point, catalyzing a more than 15-fold increase in registered private firms (figure 2.13). The domestic private sector made up only 12 percent of assets in the enterprise sector in 2001, a share that increased to half in 2013, while the sector's share in employment rose from 33 to 61 percent over this period. Concurrently, the share of foreign firms in employment increased from 12 to 26 percent, though the sector became less

FIGURE 2.10 Trade and investment liberalization has allowed industrial clusters to emerge with both local private and foreign-invested firms

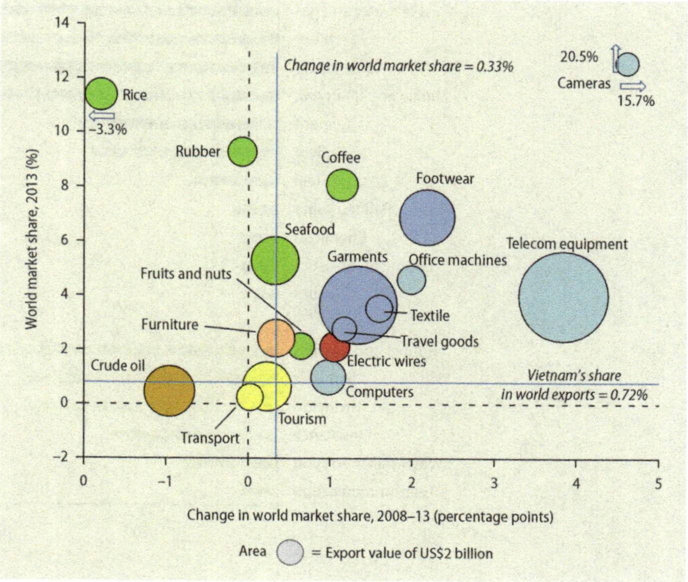

Source: Tu Anh et al. 2015.

FIGURE 2.11 State-owned enterprises have seen a declining role in the economy since the early 2000s

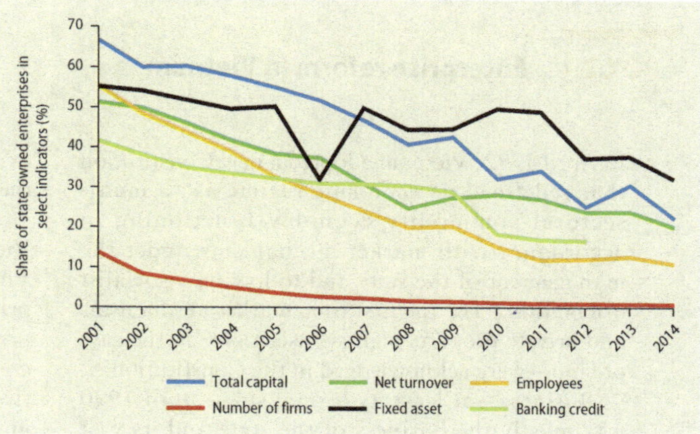

Source: Calculations based on the General Statistics Office of Vietnam and the State Bank of Vietnam.

capital-intensive and saw its share in assets fall from 22 to 20 percent.

Opportunities, Risks, and Challenges for Future Growth

Vietnam's success heavily reflects the catch-up growth that has produced extraordinary

FIGURE 2.12 The state has retained a virtual monopoly or oligopoly in several sectors

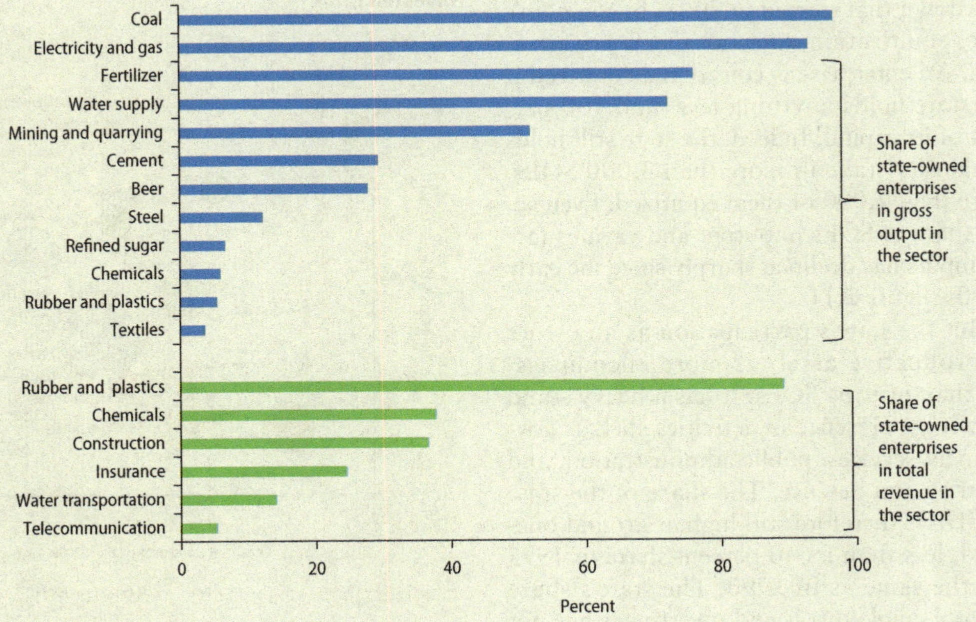

Source: Calculations based on the General Statistics Office of Vietnam.

BOX 2.1 Enterprise reform in Vietnam

In April 1992, Vietnam adopted a new Constitution that redefined its economic regime as "a multi-sectoral commodity economy functioning in accordance with market mechanisms under the management of the state and following a socialist orientation." For the first time market mechanisms and private property rights—user rights in the case of land—were acknowledged in the Constitution.

Business—at least its formal side—until 1990 was mostly the business of the state and its vast network of SOEs, which made up about half of industry and services sector output in 1989 and employed about half of the nonagricultural work-force (Dodsworth et al. 1996). The banking sector had only four state-owned banks, whose credit flowed only to the public finances and SOEs. Private business was not yet legal. Whatever private activity existed was illegal and informal, though still under the watchful eye of the state.

Even so, private business has a long history in Vietnam. At the height of central planning, most Vietnamese workers were engaged in the informal private sector. The state was aware of the illegal private activity but also recognized its usefulness in creating jobs. It largely turned a blind eye in a practice called "fence-breaking." This history of and mixed attitude toward private business still marks the state of mind of Vietnam's entrepreneurs, who place a heavy premium on having political connections to do well—if not to survive,—in business (Malesky and Taussig 2009).

The cost of suppressing private enterprise was recognized early in the reform process. One of the reform actions (under Decree 27/ND and Decree 29 in 1988)

(Box continues next page)

BOX 2.1 (continued)

was therefore to legalize private business and establish a registration process for household enterprises.

The turning point in the state's formal acceptance of a market-based approach and adoption of a more tolerant view of private owned and managed commercial activity came in the early 1990s, first by way of the 1990 Company Law on Sole Proprietorship. This law gave legal recognition to the right of the domestic private sector to operate in stipulated areas. Then in April 1992 Vietnam adopted a new Constitution, Article 15 of which redefined its economic regime (see above). "Market economy," however, was still considered an inappropriate term. It took another 10 years—until the Ninth Party Congress of April 2001—for the system to accept the "socialist-oriented market economy" as the official way to describe its economic system.

In the 1990s private enterprises were still the subject of "socialist rehabilitation" and were only allowed to do business in areas stipulated by law. And starting and operating a formal private business was not made easy. To establish a business, private entrepreneurs needed to acquire a license from the provincial planning committee, after securing approval from the provincial people's committee. During this process entrepreneurs also had to obtain many sublicenses from different government agencies with authorities at several government levels having excessive discretionary power. Compared with the state sector, private businesses also faced unfavorable treatment on credit, trading rights, access to land, and tax applications. This bias continues to dog private enterprise development.

The 2000 Enterprise Law made it easier for private enterprises to register and enter sectors that were earlier reserved for SOEs. It also encouraged more existing businesses to register.

The 2005 Enterprise Law marked another milestone. For the first time, the regulatory framework for different ownership categories of enterprises was unified. Differentiated legal treatments of SOEs, foreign direct investment (FDI), and domestic private enterprises were essentially removed. This action paved the way for Vietnam's accession to the World Trade Organization (WTO) in 2007. Protection of the rights and freedom to do business also improved with the 2005 Enterprise Law, which nullified all licenses and business conditions that were not specified in laws, ordinances, or decrees as of September 1, 2008.

The 2005 Enterprise Law was recently replaced by the 2014 Enterprise Law, which removed the overlaps between the 2005 Enterprise Law and the 2005 Investment Law. The new law further simplified business licenses, introduced online business registration, and moved regulations on corporate governance closer to international practice.

expansion in East Asia and elsewhere since the end of the Second World War (box 2.2). Some economies—such as Japan, Singapore, Korea, and Taiwan, China—sustained high growth for some five decades and were propelled to high-income status. Others—such as Brazil, Indonesia, Mexico, Thailand, and the Arab Republic of Egypt—showed promise for two or three decades, but then became mired in the middle-income trap. China's ascent, though incomplete, is on a trajectory similar to that of the first group. Grasping the catch-up opportunities, Vietnam is well positioned on its long-term income trajectory relative to its global comparators.

A strong growth record has led to ambitious goals for the future. Noted in chapter 1,

FIGURE 2.13 The number of newly registered domestic private companies has risen sharply since the 2000 Enterprise Law

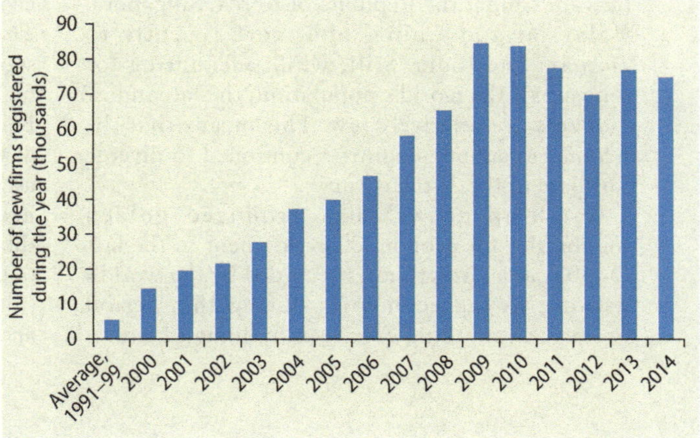

Source: Tu Anh et al. 2015.

BOX 2.2 Global context: A golden period of growth?

A rapid rise from impoverishment to modernity, or from agrarianism to industrialization, is a recent artifact of economic history. Global living standards did not change at a perceptible pace in the preindustrial world but have since surged remarkably (figure B2.2.1). While income per person in the West nearly doubled between 1 CE and 1820, it has since grown by more than 20 times (Jones 2015). In 1820, the per capita income gap between the richest and the poorest nations stood at roughly a 5:1 ratio.[a] Based on sustained growth in some countries and relatively flat incomes in others, the difference is now 300:1.[b]

Two major phenomena explain why living standards have taken off in the last two centuries. The first is technological growth. Remaining at nearly zero through the end of the 18th century, technological growth accelerated by way of the industrial revolution. It gathered pace in the 19th century, first in the United Kingdom and then in the rest of Western Europe, the United States, and a few other countries (Commission on Growth and Development 2008). Still, the "magic potion" of industrialization was imbibed by only a handful of nations, resulting in massive divergence between their productivity and living standards and those in the rest of the world (Pritchett 1997).

The second phenomenon is rapid catch-up growth of the late industrializers. During catch-up growth, latecomers benefit from investment flows and the transfer of technology and know-how from richer economies. This phenomenon was enabled by a surge of globalization and hyperconnectivity, starting with Japan and extending to Taiwan, China; the Republic of Korea; Singapore; Malaysia; and China, and more recently to Vietnam and India. Still, while accounting for almost half the world's population, the late industrializers are relatively few. This means that the income gap among countries continued to diverge until late in the 20th century.

Catch-up growth has produced golden possibilities for economic development in the last 50–60 years. Growth rates recorded by the world's fastest-growing economies during this period far surpass anything ever seen in human history. In Korea, the world's fastest growing economy since 1960, GDP has risen at an average annual 8 percent, increasing by a factor of almost 30 over the period. Taiwan, China, the world's second fastest growing economy, has expanded at an average 7 percent since 1960. In comparison, over 1870–1960, the two fastest growing economies were República Bolivariana de Venezuela (3.2 percent growth) and Sweden (2.1 percent).[c]

But simply being present in the golden period of growth has not guaranteed enrichment. The promise of faster growth and rapid convergence with industrialized nations has proved elusive for all but a handful of emerging economies that were able to show the necessary resolve. The report of the 2008 Commission for Growth and Development found that only 13 economies—nine in East Asia—grew at an average 7 percent or more over at least a 30-year stretch between 1950 and 2006. If the report were written in 2015, it would likely have included Vietnam and India among the successful economies—a possibility that the 2008 report foresaw.

What were the main elements of high-growth economies' resolve? The Growth Commission identified five:

1. They fully exploited the world economy.
2. They maintained macroeconomic stability.
3. They mustered high saving and investment rates.
4. They let markets allocate resources.
5. They had committed, credible, and capable governments.

But even 30 years of unimpeded rapid growth is not enough to close the gap with high-income economies. The Growth Commission identified only six of the 13 successful economies (five in East Asia) that achieved high-income status. Of the remaining seven, four—Brazil, Indonesia, Malaysia, and Thailand—are struggling in the middle-income trap. The story of China's ascent to high-income status is still being penned. Economists have blamed stagnant productivity on the inability of countries—not just the fast-growing ones—to break out of their middle-income status (Eichengreen, Park, and Shin 2011; Agenor, Canuto, and Jelenic 2012).

(Box continues next page)

BOX 2.2 (continued)

FIGURE B2.2.1 Global living standards took off after the eighteenth century

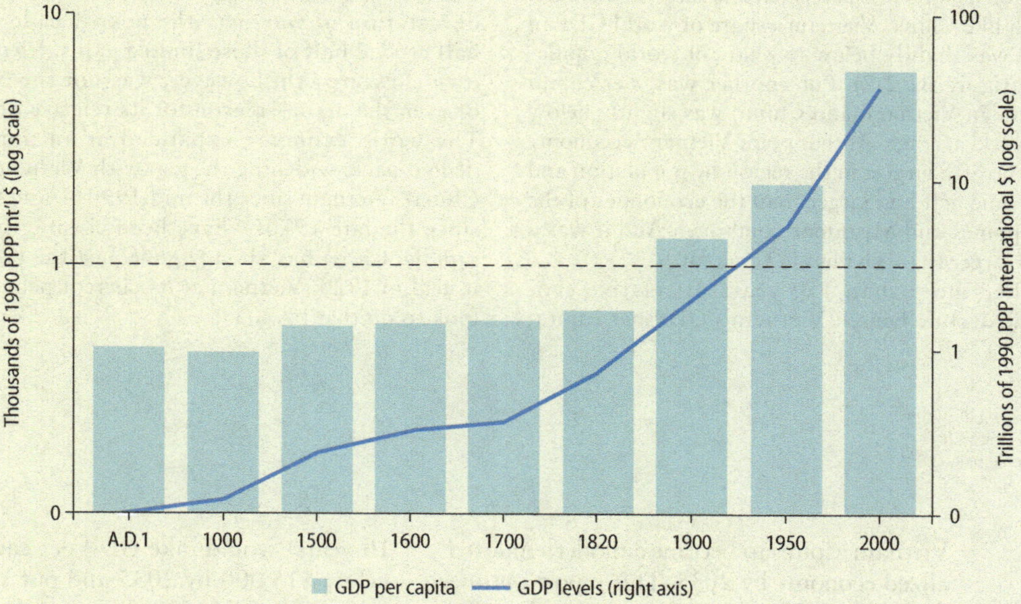

Source: Commission on Growth and Development 2008.

FIGURE B2.2.2 Vietnam's share of global GDP relative to its share of global population has been recovering since the late 1980s

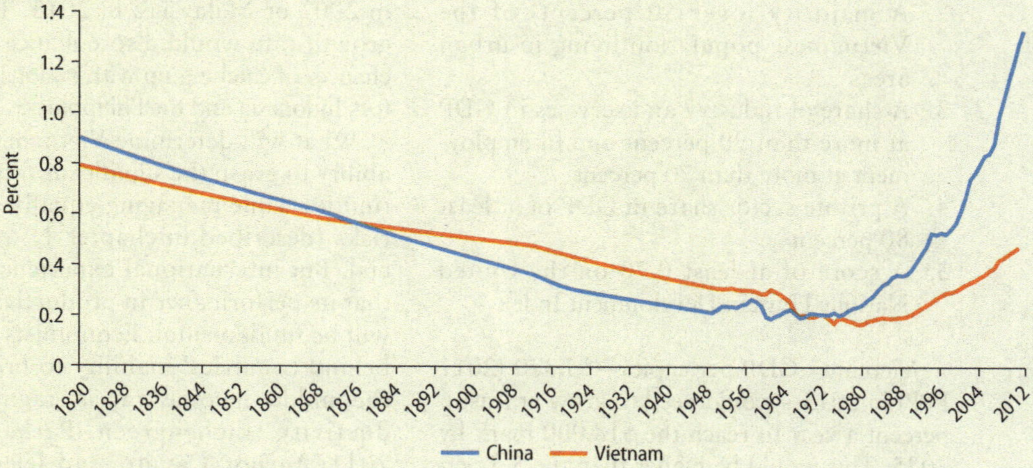

Source: Calculations based on The Maddison-Project.

(Box continues next page)

BOX 2.2 (continued)

Vietnam's own development trajectory reflects the global shifts just described and internal changes. Much like China, Vietnam's share of world GDP in 1820 was slightly below its share of world population (figure B2.2.2). Put another way, per capita income in Vietnam (and China) was slightly below the world average. At that point Vietnam's economy was the fifth largest in the region by population and economic heft and larger than the economies of the Philippines and Myanmar combined. And it was a third larger than Thailand's economy.

Then more than 150 years of relative economic decline began. Vietnam's GDP per capita, growing at some 0.4 percent a year, increased by close to 80 percent between 1820 and 1960. The devastation of war over the next decade and a half eroded half of those limited gains. Vietnam's own slow growth, however, was not the only—or even the main—reason for its relative decline. The world economy expanded at an unprecedented pace, widening the gap with Vietnam (and China). Vietnam since the mid-1990s—and China since the late 1970s—have been closing the gap rapidly. China has already gone past the position it held in 1820. Vietnam at its current pace could look to do that by 2035.

a. The Maddison Project 2013.
b. Penn World Tables 8.0.
c. The Maddison Project 2013.

Vietnam aspires to become a modern industrialized economy by 2035. This report outlines five quantitative criteria for meeting that goal.

1. A GDP per capita of at least $18,000 (in 2011 PPP), roughly equivalent to Malaysia in 2010
2. A majority (over 50 percent) of the Vietnamese population living in urban areas
3. A share of industry and services in GDP at more than 90 percent and in employment at more than 70 percent
4. A private sector share in GDP of at least 80 percent
5. A score of at least 0.70 on the United Nations Human Development Index

Vietnam's GDP per capita—$5,370 (2011 PPP) in 2013—would need to grow at least 6 percent a year to reach the $18,000 mark by 2035. This would be higher than the 5.5 percent average per capita growth rate between 1990 and 2014, and well above the 3.7 percent average for all middle-income countries over the same period. A lower and more feasible—but still ambitious—5.0 percent per capita growth rate (Vietnam's average over the last 10 years) would take GDP per capita to just below $15,000 by 2035 and put Vietnam on par with Brazil in 2014 (figure 1.8). The country would be well poised to reach $18,000 by 2040. A 7 percent growth path (Vietnam's aspirational growth target) would take per capita GDP to $22,200, roughly Korea's income in 2002 or Malaysia's in 2013. This higher growth rate would also enhance Vietnam's chances of catching up with regional comparators Indonesia and the Philippines.

What will determine Vietnam's path? Its ability to grasp the significant future opportunities while managing equally significant risks (described in chapter 1) will be crucial. But international experience suggests that its performance in productivity growth will be fundamental. Economists agree that behind countries' inability to break out of the middle-income trap is stagnating productivity (Eichengreen, Park, and Shin 2011; Agénor, Canuto, and Jelenic 2012). The trap is countries' inability to move beyond an economic model that generates growth mainly from factor accumulation and structural transformation. These forces have finite lives and weaken well before the economy is close to moving beyond middle-income status, resulting in a future of economic stagnation.

The significance of productivity performance is not just a lesson of global experience. Vietnam's future growth scenarios bear it out. At least 90 percent of future growth will have to come from labor productivity in any realistic scenario. The contribution of labor force growth will shrink to less than 10 percent because of projected demographic changes. Moreover, TFP growth would need to be revived to make a meaningful contribution. Underlying these outcomes, sectoral productivity performance would also need to increase sharply (box 2.3).

Long-term patterns of Vietnam's productivity growth have been deteriorating. For example, labor productivity growth has been on a downward trend since the late 1990s (figure 2.14). Other measures of Vietnam's productivity performance give similar results. The rest of this section unbundles the productivity challenge further.

Vietnam's Productivity Challenge: A Tale of Two Growth Episodes

> Productivity isn't everything, but in the long run it is almost everything. A country's ability to improve its standard of living over time depends almost entirely on its ability to raise its output per worker (Krugman 1994).

A breakdown of economic growth trends since 1990 shows two starkly different growth models: one in the 1990s, and the other in the "long" 2000s (table 2.1).[13] GDP growth in the 2000s (6.6 percent) was a full percentage point lower than in the 1990s. The decline was because of the slowdown in labor productivity growth, which was only partly offset by higher labor force growth.

The most striking difference in the two periods, however, is not the decline in labor productivity growth but the shift in its determinants.

BOX 2.3 A baseline scenario for income growth up to 2035

An average GDP growth of around 6 percent (or around 5 percent per capita) will take Vietnam's GDP per capita to just below $15,000 (2011 PPP) by 2035. Such change will put Vietnam on par with Brazil in 2014 or Malaysia in 2001. Tables B2.3.1 and B2.3.2 describe how the demand- and supply-side structures would evolve.

On the supply side, agriculture's share of employment would fall to 25 percent—roughly the same as China in 2015, Turkey in 2012, and Mexico in the late 1990s—while rising to 37–38 percent for industry (including mining) and for services. The share of GDP in agriculture would fall to under 10 percent—similar to China in 2010—while increasing in industry and services. These structural changes would be matched by an increase in the urbanization rate, from 33 percent to more than 50 percent by 2035.

On the demand side, the investment rate would remain strong at just over 30 percent until 2025, before tapering to 27 percent over the next decade. This decrease reflects a gradual decline in domestic savings and a rising role of domestic consumption, which would account for three-quarters of demand-side GDP by 2035. Export and import shares in GDP would each gradually taper toward 80 percent, lower than today but still representing significant outward orientation compared with peer countries. The current account would move from a small surplus in 2015 to a balanced account in 2016–17. It would then gradually slip into a slight deficit of around 1 percent of GDP, funded mostly by sustained FDI inflows and rising portfolio inflows. This would happen sometime after 2025, once the domestic financial sector has been sufficiently developed and the capital account liberalized.

What would be the main implications of this baseline scenario for labor-productivity growth and its determinants?

(Box continues next page)

BOX 2.3 (continued)

First, this scenario would require 5.6 percent average annual labor productivity growth. Between 2013 and 2035, 92 percent of GDP growth would result from such growth. This marks a large shift from 2000–13, when it accounted for 55 percent of GDP growth.

Second, the scenario would need a significant increase in labor productivity growth across all major economic sectors (table 2.2). Productivity growth within sectors will need to account for close to 80 percent of future labor productivity growth, as the contribution of structural transformation is expected to stabilize at around 20 percent.

Third, TFP growth would need to account for close to half the labor productivity growth. Capital deepening will still retain an important role (though less than before), contributing about one-quarter to the labor productivity increase. The rest would come from growth in human capital. This, again, would be an uphill task considering how different the relative contributions have been in the past decade and a half.

TABLE B2.3.1 Structure of the economy, supply side
Percent

	Share of total employment			Share of GDP		
	Agriculture	Industry and mining	Services	Agriculture	Industry and mining	Services
1990	73	11	16	34.6	23.2	42.2
2000	68	12	20	24.8	34.8	40.4
2013	49	23	28	17.6	38.6	43.9
2025	32	31	37	12	40	48
2035	25	37	38	9	41	50

Source: Calculations and projections based on the General Statistics Office of Vietnam.

TABLE B2.3.2 Structure of the economy, demand side
Percent

	Consumption	Investment	Exports	Imports	Gross national savings	Current account balance
1990	93.5	15.9	23.7	33.4	0.0	
2000	73.3	30.5	50.0	53.7	0.0	3.4
2013	71.1	30.5	90.0	91.5	31.0	5.6
2025	72.3	30.1	82.7	83.7	29.2	−1.0
2035	74.6	27.1	79.7	80.5	26.4	−0.8

Source: Calculations and projections based on the General Statistics Office of Vietnam.

First, more than 70 percent of Vietnam's labor productivity growth in the 1990s can be explained by TFP growth (annex 2B). The rest came from improvements in human capital (measured by returns to rising years of schooling). Capital deepening (measured by the capital-output ratio) made a negligibly negative contribution. In the 2000s, the contribution of capital deepening rose to almost 60 percent, reflecting a sharp increase in the investment rate from 26 percent in the 1990s to 33 percent over 2000–13. In the later period, TFP stagnated, making no contribution to labor productivity or GDP growth. Human capital accelerated its pace of growth because of rising education among workers.

Second, labor productivity growth in the 1990s stemmed from productivity growth within sectors, with structural transformation playing a negligible role (table 2.1). The situation reversed in the 2000s as labor productivity growth declined sharply in a majority of economic sectors (table 2.2). But the pace of structural transformation increased with an acceleration in the movement of labor from agriculture to services and industry (see table B2.3.1). In the four sectors dominated by the public sector—mining, construction, public utilities, and finance and real estate—labor productivity growth was negative in the latter period. The scenario in table 2.2 also makes clear the sharp turnaround in labor productivity growth needed in each sector if Vietnam is to achieve 6 percent average growth (5 percent per capita growth) in the next two decades. For higher growth trajectories, the turnaround needed in labor productivity growth at the sector level is even more spectacular.

What Explains the Stagnation in Productivity in Vietnam? Three Primordial Policy and Institutional Issues

Despite its seemingly robust economy, Vietnam faces a serious problem of low (and falling) productivity growth. This could stymie its 2035 income aspirations. What explains these trends? And why do they differ between the 1990s and 2000s?

Initial productivity gains in the earlier period reflected the country's move toward a market economy and removal of many distortions imposed under central planning. These included production quotas, multiple price controls, collectivized agriculture, trade and investment restrictions, and a ban on formal private enterprise. Most of these restrictions were lifted in the initial phases of *Đổi Mới*. Systems more friendly to the market and the private sector were in place by the early 1990s. These early steps gave a big boost to productivity across the economy. But by the end of the 1990s, their induced benefits had been exhausted. More fundamental policy and institutional issues become more binding.

FIGURE 2.14 Labor productivity growth has been on a declining trend since the late 1990s

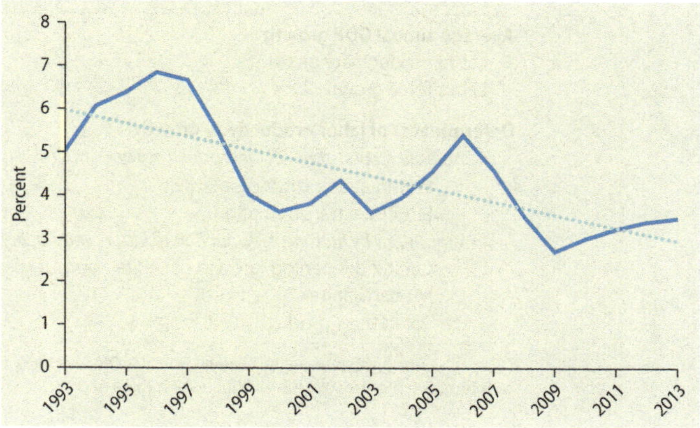

Source: Calculations based on the General Statistics Office of Vietnam.
Note: Three-year moving average.

These issues included inefficient SOEs, weak and worsening domestic private sector performance, and fragmented, smallholder-dominated agriculture with heavy state involvement.

SOE inefficiencies have widespread effects

Vietnam's state sector has a long history of inefficient resource use, dating to the days of central planning when all formal productive activity was in the public sector's hands. Accounting for 40 percent of total investment, the sector contributes just 30 percent of GDP growth. It reflects the weak performance of the SOEs as captured by the low, firm-level asset (capital and land) and labor productivity measures throughout the 2000s (figures 2.15a and b). Inefficient resource use by the SOEs is glaring but not surprising. SOEs have little incentive to be at their productive best. They are sheltered by protected markets and from stringent reporting requirements. They benefit from preferential access to land, capital, government contracts, and other tacit and explicit privileges. And they are laden with unclear social and political objectives. Yet under growing pressure to restructure, they have at least sought to ensure that their feeble productivity does not deteriorate further.

TABLE 2.1 Sources of growth in Vietnam, 1990–2013
Percent

	1991–2000	2001–13
Average annual GDP growth	7.6	6.6
Labor productivity growth	5.2	3.8
Labor force growth	2.2	2.7
Determinants of labor productivity growth		
Contributions of within-sector productivity and structural transformation		
Within-sector labor productivity	99.8	37
Structural transformation	0.2	63
Contributions by factors of production to labor productivity[a]		
Capital deepening (growth of capital–output ratio)	−3	59
Human capital	30	40
Total factor productivity	72	0

Source: Calculations based on the General Statistics Office of Vietnam.
a. Annex 2B, using the scenario with increasing value of α.

TABLE 2.2 Sectoral GDP and productivity growth, 1990–2035
Percent

Period	Agriculture	Mining	Manufacturing	Public utilities	Construction	Wholesale and retail trade	Finance and real estate	Other services	Aggregate
GDP growth									
1990–2000	3.9	7.6	10.3	11.1	8.9	7.4	6.8	4.5	7.6
2000–13	3.5	2.3	9.9	10.6	8.1	7.8	5.7	10.4	6.6
2013–35 (projected)	2.9	2.7	7.9	3.0	6.8	7.0	6.4	6.5	6.1
Labor force growth									
1990–2000	1.5	−1.9	3.4	0.6	3.4	6.7	3.9	2.9	2.2
2000–13	0.1	2.7	6.9	15.9	10.4	5.5	10.0	5.6	2.7
2013–35 (projected)	−2.6	0.5	2.9	−1.1	3.0	2.1	2.2	1.3	0.4
Labor productivity growth									
1990–2000	2.7	17.1	7.1	11.0	6.3	0.1	4.1	1.6	5.2
2000–13	3.4	−0.4	2.8	−4.6	−2.1	2.1	−4.0	4.6	3.8
2013–35 (projected)	5.6	2.3	4.9	4.1	3.7	4.8	4.3	5.1	5.6

Source: Calculations and projections based on the General Statistics Office of Vietnam.

The performance of domestic private enterprises gives even more cause for concern

Driven by a sequence of reforms to first legalize and then facilitate private enterprise, the private sector grew exponentially after the late 1980s. The sector's growing presence, however, has been marked by worsening productivity since the early 2000s (figure 2.15) to such a degree that there is little daylight between labor and asset productivity in the private and SOE sectors. A comparison with asset productivity of nonpublic firms in China is revealing. Vietnamese nonpublic firms, on average, were using their assets more productively than their Chinese counterparts in the early 2000s. But by 2014, their asset productivity had fallen to less than half that of Chinese nonpublic firms.

Given its hesitant emergence, Vietnam's much lower entrepreneurial confidence than many of its developing-country peers is hardly surprising (box 2.4).

A comparison across firm sizes and sectors throws further light on the weak productivity performance of Vietnamese private enterprises.[14] Domestic private firms are overwhelmingly small (figure 2.16) and informal, which prevents productivity gains through scale economies, specialization, and innovation. Of those registered, 94 percent had 50 or fewer employees in 2013, up from 89 percent in 2001. Millions of nonregistered (informal)

FIGURE 2.15 Low firm-level asset (capital and land) and labor productivity measures reflect Vietnam's long-inefficient state sector and worsening performance of private enterprises

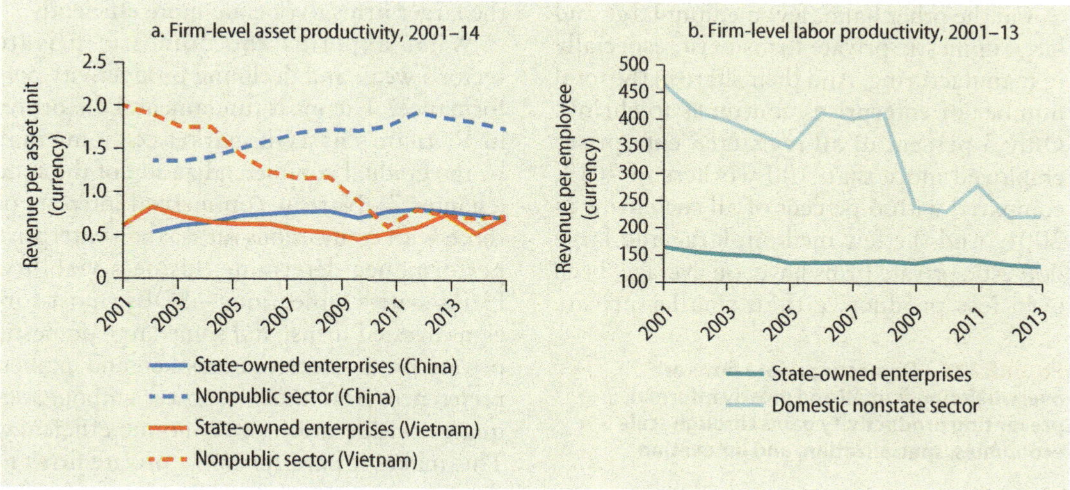

Source: a. Calculations based on the General Statistics Office of Vietnam, and the National Bureau of Statistics of China.
b. Calculations based on the General Statistics Office of Vietnam.
Note: Revenue per employee is estimated after controlling for the effects of the asset-to-labor ratio and total assets.

BOX 2.4 Low entrepreneurial confidence in Vietnam

While propensity and aptitude for entrepreneurship have increased in Vietnam, they remain lower than in regional comparator countries. Of Vietnamese adults surveyed in 2013, 37 percent perceived an opportunity to start a new business, and 24 percent showed an intention to start a business. This compared with respective averages of 61 percent and 45 percent in countries at similar development. Some 49 percent felt that they had the required entrepreneurial capabilities, compared with 69 percent in the comparator group.

On all these scores, Vietnam trails Thailand, Indonesia, and the Philippines by a fair margin. On the flip side, 57 percent of Vietnamese adults feared failure, almost double the average of 31 percent in comparator countries. This lack of confidence in their abilities and in the business environment around them belies their desire to become entrepreneurs. Of surveyed adults, 63 percent wanted to become entrepreneurs (75 percent for the comparator group) while 82 percent saw entrepreneurship as socially prestigious (80 percent for the comparator group).

Source: Global Entrepreneurship Monitor 2013.

household enterprises operate at even lower scales. Household firms can raise their labor productivity and profits from entering the formal sector and becoming growth oriented (Boly 2015). Many have taken that path, but millions more choose not to. They are reluctant to endure bureaucratic scrutiny and withstand rent and regulatory problems. These regulatory issues are reflected in Vietnam's modest ranking of 90 (of 189) in the World Bank's Doing Business Indicators. Performances are strikingly low on the subcategories: paying taxes (rank 168), ease of starting a business (119), access to electricity (108), dealing with business insolvency (123), and protection of minority investors (122).

Over time smaller firms have also been building capital intensity (proxied by the asset-to-revenue ratio, which grew fourfold over 2001–13). Given their lack of scale economies, capital investment is not a comparative advantage of small firms. This factor was evident in their sharply declining asset and labor productivity (figures 2.17a and b).

On the other hand, few medium-large and large domestic private firms exist, especially in manufacturing. And their share in the total number of enterprises continues to shrink. Only 3 percent of all registered enterprises employed more than 100 workers in 2013, compared with 6 percent of all such firms in 2001. And the few medium-large and large domestic private firms have, on average, been even less productive than smaller private firms (figure 2.17). This is contrary to expectations because scale economies should allow the larger firms to operate more efficiently.

What explains the domestic private sector's weak and declining productivity performance? The most fundamental distortion in Vietnam's nascent market economy may be the gradual commercialization of the state (chapter 7). Narrow commercial interests of those with connections rather than enterprise performance determine business viability. Firms with connections—SOEs, most foreign-invested firms, and some large domestic private firms—receive unspoken and explicit preferences from those in power without adequate consideration of economic efficiency. This makes it hard for many private firms to thrive, even if they are productive.

Benefitting from the relatively safe and welcoming environment in Vietnam as well as the many mentioned preferences, foreign-invested firms have grown their presence in Vietnam, leading the country's rapid growth in manufacturing and exports. By 2015, the FDI sector was contributing over half of manufacturing output in over 70 percent of export turnover in Vietnam. But links with domestic firms have been lacking in key sectors, impeding productivity-enhancing

FIGURE 2.16 Domestic private firms are overwhelmingly small and mostly informal, preventing productivity gains through scale economies, specialization, and innovation

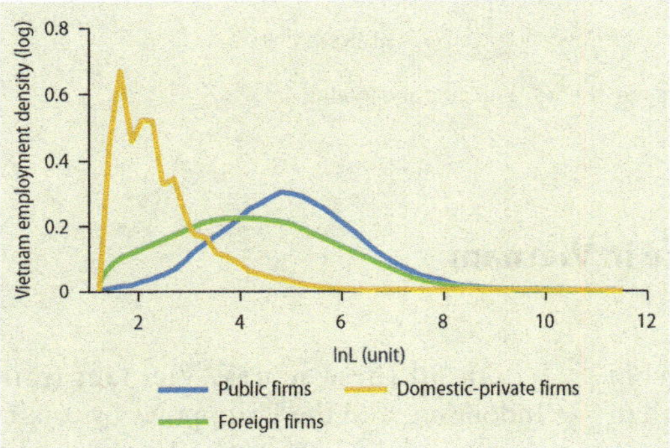

Source: Aterido and Hallward-Driemeier 2015.

FIGURE 2.17 Large domestic private firms have, on average, been less productive than smaller private firms

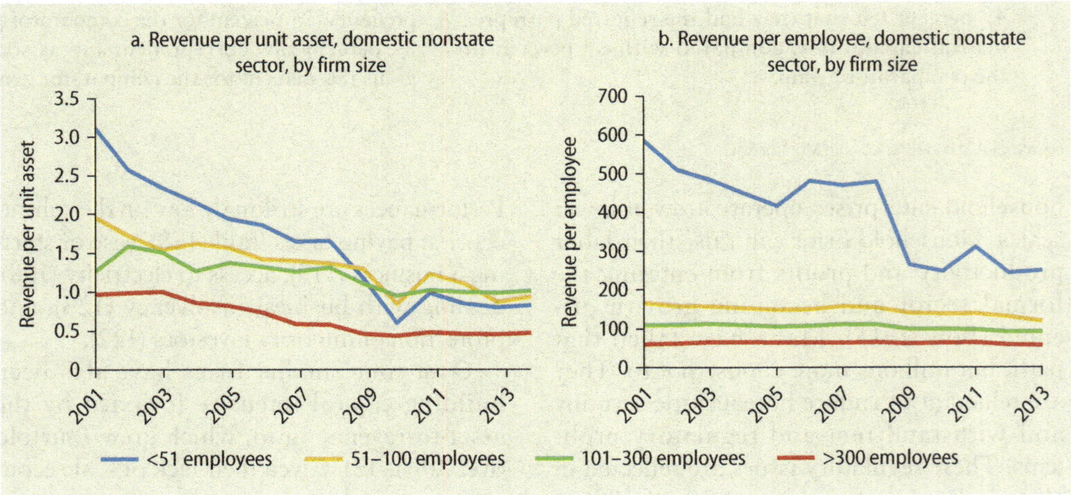

Source: Calculations based on the General Statistics Office of Vietnam.
Note: Revenue per employee is estimated after controlling for the effects of the asset-to-labor ratio and total assets.

transfers of technology and management practices. There are few joint ventures (around 80 percent of FDI in Vietnam is in 100-percent foreign invested companies), and the vertical link between FDI and local companies is weak (only about a quarter of inputs in FDI are purchased in Vietnam, of which a significant proportion is from other foreign-invested companies). Hampered by limited capabilities in both the SOEs and domestic private enterprises, the internal business forces in Vietnam are proving too weak to effectively take advantage of external forces.[15] The situation raises concerns of a possible "Mexican phenomenon"—which warns of overreliance on FDI and a few large companies leading to an outcome of "two economies in one country."[16]

The state's commercialization has produced an uneven and partial approach to market reforms, leading to two imbalances. First, embracing markets as the mechanism for allocating resources coincides with a more cautious and ambiguous approach to giving up state control of production and to accepting domestic private ownership of productive assets. This has led to a growing entrepreneurial business class within rather than outside the state. It has also resulted in a continued heavy SOE presence in many economic sectors.

Second, embracing markets has been uneven. Progress has been impressive in opening product markets and integrating them with the global economy under international trade agreements. But this progress has been accompanied by a more subdued and muddled approach to developing and relaxing factor markets, evident in inefficient land and capital allocation. For example, significant land and capital assets were accumulated in the construction, real estate, and banking and finance sectors between 2001 and 2013. But these sectors were among the least productive (figure 2.18). Allocations are likely influenced by arbitrary administrative decisions and connections, at onerous economic cost and as substantiated by a considerable literature. A 2008 study, for example, finds that the allocation of bank credit relates to the presence or absence of connections (Malesky and Taussig 2008). The most profitable private firms do not even attempt to get bank loans. Updating the analysis to 2013, this report finds that the results still hold (annex 2A). Many provinces with a high density of SOEs provide less credit

FIGURE 2.18 Land and capital assets have been accumulated in sectors that have made the least productive use of them

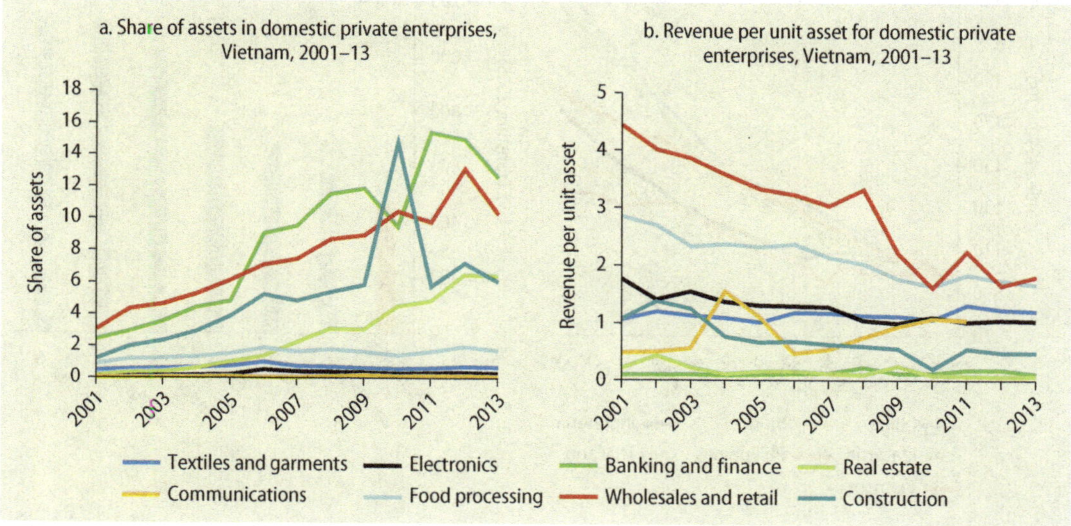

Source: Calculations based on the General Statistics Office of Vietnam.

to private firms and require more time to issue land-use rights certificates than other provinces (Freeman and Nguyen 2006, for example). Easier access of the SOEs to credit, land, and export quotas in the garment and textile sector reduces private firms' profitability and viability (Nguyen and Le 2005). These impediments require vigorous efforts to develop and ease competitive markets for land and capital, as per the reform agenda described below in "Liberalizing factor markets."

Neglect of essential market institutions has also hurt productivity. The greatest weaknesses are in the institutions responsible for protecting private property rights and for ensuring free and fair competition. These institutional weaknesses have impeded the emergence of large, competitive private firms and have further discouraged small household firms from entering the formal sector (Malesky and Taussig 2009). This occurred even though switching from informal to formal activity can raise firms' productivity and profitability (Boly 2015). (The reform agenda to develop these market institutions is discussed in the next section.)

Under prevailing market conditions, use of social and political capital—and not necessarily talent—explains private firms' entry and profitability (Malesky and Taussig 2009; Kinghan and Newman 2015). The adverse impact of these factors on domestic private firms' performance should not surprise anyone. In the presence of noncompetitive and state-controlled factor markets and inadequately developed formal market institutions, firms turn to informal institutions and networks. In these environments, they often find illegitimate means to enter the market, grow, and become more profitable (Steer and Sen 2010). Those more adept at garnering political capital or exploiting connections, however, are not necessarily better at running a business.

Agricultural labor productivity remains low

Agriculture has made enormous progress since the late 1990s, but emerging concerns about the quality and sustainability of its growth model require urgent policy attention. Sectoral labor productivity remains low against comparator countries despite rapid gains since 1990 (figure 2.19). This is

FIGURE 2.19 Labor productivity in agriculture remains low, even after growing strongly since 1990

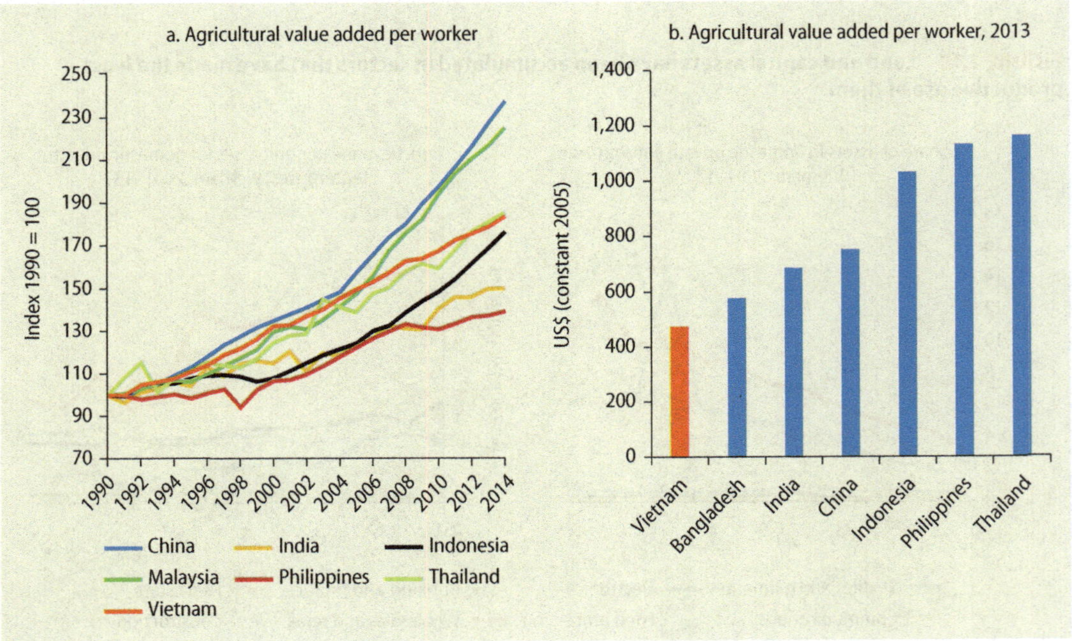

Source: Calculations based on the General Statistics Office of Vietnam and World Development Indicators.

mainly because of fragmentation of agricultural land ownership and the dominance of rice in the use of the best land and much of the country's irrigation capacity. Productivity of agricultural land—measured by value added per hectare—is higher in Vietnam than most regional peers, including China, Indonesia, the Philippines, and Thailand. This is because of intensive farming practices, involving high concentration of workers and heavy use of chemicals, fertilizers, water, and other inputs. But the growth of land productivity has slowed—and has been slower than most regional peers since 1990—because returns from intensive land use have reached their limits. And water resource management from rivers originating from other countries is becoming increasingly challenging.[17] Important issues facing the sector include low value-added, uncertain food safety, and low smallholder profitability. Issues also include price-discounted commodities in international markets, little technological or institutional innovation, and considerable underemployment among agricultural workers.

Promoting Economic Modernization and Enhancing Competitiveness of the Private Sector

The imperative to improve productivity growth to meet Vietnam's income aspirations for 2035 is clear and strong. GDP growth since the early 2000s has been led by forces that compensated for weak and declining productivity growth but are now reaching their natural limits. Rapid labor force growth made up for low and declining labor productivity growth across the economy. Large-scale structural transformations offset low and declining labor productivity growth at the sectoral level. And accelerated capital accumulation counterbalanced low and declining TFP growth. In the next phase of development, each of these compensatory factors will have a sharply diminished impact, exposing economic growth to weak productivity trends.

Vietnam has one key advantage. It is early enough in its development stage to reignite productivity growth without compromising the 2035 income objectives. At a similar development stage in the early 1980s, Korea saw a major acceleration in its labor productivity growth. This suggests that a turnaround in such growth is still possible (box 2.5). But it also highlights how demanding the institutional reform agenda is.

A demanding reform agenda can, however, easily overwhelm and immobilize the government's technical and capacity elements and its financial capabilities. It is therefore crucial to apply a prioritizing filter to sequence the reforms. In Vietnam's case, the priority must be to revive the domestic enterprise sector's productivity. Reforming the SOE sector is important for this. It will correct the widespread inefficiency in resource allocation by the SOEs. It will also consolidate their presence in a few strategic areas while freeing space for the private sector. The current environment, however, does not support the emergence of productive domestic private firms. SOE reforms, then, must be matched by urgent measures to improve the enabling conditions for the private sector. Emphasis must be on strengthening market institutions and liberalizing factor markets. These foundational reforms will run alongside two other broad policy actions. One is to modernize and commercialize agriculture, which engages almost half the workforce in a country almost 70 percent rural. The other is to strengthen participation in GVCs, given the heavy and likely increasing reliance on external markets.

These pillars broadly constitute the reform program to revive Vietnam's productivity growth in the short to medium term, with their impact likely to be most acutely felt over the next 10 years or so. The country's 2035 income aspirations need, however, to take account of constraints that are farther down in time and require reforms with long-term gestation. These reforms include building an innovation-led economy, developing modern

BOX 2.5 Labor productivity growth in Vietnam, China, and the Republic of Korea

Vietnam seeks to emulate the growth experiences of the Republic of Korea and perhaps even China. Therefore, we compare the sectoral labor productivity performances of the three countries at similar development stages. China's labor-productivity growth in the period leading up to 2000 (when its GDP per capita was similar to Vietnam's in 2013) was far stronger than in Vietnam in the 2000s (table B2.5.1). The difference was particularly noticeable in the industry and service sectors. China had the momentum to support the strong productivity growth that has followed since.

Comparison with Korea is instructive in a different way. Its aggregate labor productivity growth in the 1970s was almost the same as Vietnam's in the 2000s: Korea's productivity growth was higher in industry and services and lower in agriculture. Strong labor force growth was thus a crucial part of that country's GDP growth in the 1970s. After 1980, however, its labor productivity growth increased sharply, especially in industry and agriculture. This occurred on the back of a series of stabilization and structural reforms. Some reforms launched in the late 1970s and early 1980s immediately helped improve productivity growth. These included agricultural modernization, macroeconomic stabilization, and greater emphasis on competition and market deregulation. Other reforms—such as those related to urbanization, higher education, and research and development (R&D)—operated with a significant lag, having begun many years earlier.

TABLE B2.5.1 Labor productivity growth in Vietnam, China, and the Republic of Korea

	Vietnam		China			Korea, Rep.	
	1990–2000	2000–13	1978–90	1990–2000	2000–13	1970–80	1980–95
Aggregate	5.2	3.8	5.4	8.5	9.4	3.5	5.4
Agriculture	2.7	3.4	2.8	3.7	7.5	2.0	7.5
Industry (including mining)	9.0	−0.6	3.6	11.1	7.8	3.1	9.1
Services	2.1	1.9	6.1	5.0	7.2	2.6	1.3

Sources: General Statistics Office of Vietnam; Economic Statistics System of the Bank of Korea and Korean Statistical Information Service; National Bureau of Statistics of China and Ministry of Human Resources and Social Security of China.

and efficient urban structures to promote economic agglomeration, and ensuring environmentally sustainable development.

Restructuring SOEs: Creating a Level Playing Field

Despite past contributions and reforms, Vietnam's SOEs are faltering. They use labor, land, and capital inefficiently. Some State Economic Groups have destroyed state capital through imprudent expansion, diversification, and debt financing. Vietnam will need a thorough reform of its SOE sector to become an advanced market economy by 2035. Through well-structured reforms—and under certain conditions—the SOEs can even contribute to national development objectives.

Consistent with international good practice, the government could issue an SOE ownership policy that includes clear goals.[18] The policy would focus, first, on maximizing state capital.[19] The best SOEs in the world focus on financial performance.[20] It may be useful for the government to supplement this policy with explicit statements on supporting goals. For example, New Zealand's SOEs have been directed to be good employers, as profitable and efficient as comparable private sector businesses, and socially responsible by responding to local communities' needs and interests.

Further contribution from Vietnam's SOEs will depend on three aspects of reform measures: take a focused commercial approach to state ownership, apply good corporate governance practices, and ensure that all enterprises—public or private, foreign or domestic—play by the same rules.

Commercial Approach to State Ownership

A commercial focus requires hard budget constraints and reliable and timely financial information. A hard budget constraint will imply, in most cases, no soft financing from the state budget or implicit or explicit guarantees of SOE commercial debt. Exceptions would be few and based on well-defined and transparent criteria. Each SOE would have an appropriate dividend policy, approved by its board of directors. The state shareholder would not allow an SOE to retain or reinvest substantial cash surpluses without careful supervision by the SOE's board and the state shareholder. If an SOE cannot expect to earn an adequate risk-adjusted return on reinvested cash, this surplus cash should be returned to the Ministry of Finance as a regular or a special one-time dividend. Cash requirements will vary depending on whether an SOE is in a growth, cyclical, or stable business. These should factor into the dividend policy recommended by each SOE's management to its board of directors.

SOE financial statements will need to be disclosed, for transparency, accountability, and fiscal discipline. Across-the-board improvements in Vietnam's accounting and financial disclosure practices are needed. Vietnamese Accounting Standards will need to be consistent with International Financial Reporting Standards (World Bank 2014). In addition to internal audits, independent external audits of SOEs would be conducted in accordance with International Audit Standards. It will be important to upgrade professional training for the state shareholder and SOE accountants and auditors.

The government will need to reduce its SOE portfolio to a manageable size. Vietnam has too many SOEs. Many (especially the General Corporations) operate in manufacturing activities, such as beer, chemicals, food processing, and textiles and garments. No compelling rationale for state ownership exists in these areas. A central government 2035 target portfolio of about 20 parent SOEs seems reasonable. Most of these parent corporations would be holding companies with subsidiaries in related businesses and proper arrangements for corporate governance at the holding company and subsidiary levels. The target of 20 or so parent SOEs is a compromise between China and advanced social-market economies.[21] These parent SOEs could include many of Vietnam's existing State Economic Groups. A final decision on the size of Vietnam's SOE portfolio would require detailed analysis and government deliberation.

The government's majority SOE holdings could focus on strategic sectors, though even strategic SOEs should face competition. These sectors could include steel, cement, mining, oil production, power generation, water and air transport, and certain telecommunications subsectors.

The government would benefit from selling shares in most of the 20 SOE parent companies down to about a 36 percent ownership stake. Vietnam's Company Law could allow a 36 percent owner the power to block extraordinary corporate events that require 65 percent shareholder approval.[22] This blocking minority approach—followed in Austria by Österreichische Industrieholding (the Austrian industry administration)—would establish market values for these companies and facilitate follow-on access to capital market financing. The sale of majority (not absolute) control to private investors would increase proceeds from share sales and attract serious qualified—and possibly foreign—investors.[23]

Corporate governance

The SOEs need an active designated state shareholder. The current arrangement is inappropriate. The "government" is designated as the state shareholder. And many ministries or agencies exert ownership authority to review financial statements, approve investment plans, and hire CEOs, for example. This occurs without any specific government official being responsible for SOEs' performance. Taking Singapore as a model, the government could establish four or so State Shareholding Funds (SSFs) to act as the state shareholder in SOEs, with portfolio responsibilities as follows:

- *Financial Services Fund*—This fund could include state-owned commercial banking, development banks, and insurance companies and any other nonbank financial institutions.
- *Network Services Fund*—This fund could include road, air transport, rail transport, inland water transport, and post and telecommunications SOEs.
- *Energy Fund*—This fund could include mining, petroleum, and electricity SOEs.
- *Industry Fund*—This fund could initially include heavy and light industry SOEs and SOEs engaged in agriculture and agroprocessing.

The government should avoid any bureaucratic interventions in SOEs on the basis of ownership. To exercise its ownership rights, the designated state shareholder—an SSF, for example—could review regular financial reports and disclosures. The designated state shareholder could participate in annual and special shareholder meetings. It could vote state shares in selecting board directors and handle other matters for shareholder consideration. This entity could also help establish an effective board of directors (appropriately staffed and organized) for each SOE. Except for routine economic, environmental, and social regulation matters that affect all enterprises, government entities would have no authority or right to intervene in SOEs' affairs.

The Ministry of Finance would hold a majority—likely 100 percent—of the shares in each SSF. Little can be gained by distributing SSF shares to other ministries. Other ministerial interests could be recognized through intragovernment consultations and director appointments. It would be important for state shareholders to support efforts to raise the quality of SOE management. This would include providing market-based—rather than civil service–based—compensation, and linking it to performance in fixed-term management contracts. This effort also would include controlling and disclosing related-party transactions. SOE managers should regard SOE management as a desirable career choice, not simply as a means for promotion within the government or the Party.

Boards of directors play a central function in SOE governance. The board carries ultimate responsibility for SOE preservation and performance, and thus preserves or maximizes state capital. An effective board must comprise highly qualified directors capable of exercising objective, independent judgment to guide strategy development and monitor management. To act with authority, a modern SOE board requires members who act in the interest of the company, face no conflicts in doing so, and possess relevant experience and expertise, including from the private sector. To establish strong SOE boards, the government needs a strong policy and procedural framework for director nominations. Key elements of such a framework include standards for board objectivity, professional criteria for director selection and removal, and a structured nomination process that includes timely appointment and disclosure of results.

Selection of each SOE's chief executive officer (CEO) and top management should follow good practice. This increasingly calls for empowering the board to appoint and—subject to clear criteria—remove the CEO. This reinforces the board's key duty for overseeing management. It also ensures that the CEO is accountable to the board rather than to the government.

The SSFs' authority to use cash balances and to borrow would need to be strictly controlled, at least initially. Experiences from advanced countries are a sharp warning about giving state investment funds too much flexibility to borrow and to initiate investment projects. SSFs would be free to sell and trade existing SOE shares and assets. But the government, as SSF shareholder, could prohibit or limit SSF borrowing and require each SSF to forward cash proceeds from dividends and share/asset sales to the Ministry of Finance. Each SSF could retain a portion of cash proceeds to cover its operating expenses, as agreed with the fund's shareholder.

Level playing field

The government should provide a level playing field between SOEs and private domestic or foreign firms. First, if an SOE is required to perform noncommercial work, the government would ensure that the SOE receives adequate compensation. Second, the government would further eliminate any preferential treatment for SOEs, including. subsidies, favorable antitrust or tax treatment, or favored access to land, credit, or public procurement opportunities. Third, the government would also review and amend laws to achieve greater consistency between the rules for SOEs and those for private firms. Fourth, the government would ensure that the insolvency and creditor/debtor regime is consistent with international good practice and that it applies to SOEs. Fifth, the government would seek greater alignment between public and private law/regulation on labor and on procurement.

Strengthening Microeconomic Foundations to Enhance Competitiveness of the Private Sector

> With insecure property rights, poorly enforced laws, barriers to entry, and monopolistic restrictions, the profit maximizing firms will tend to have short time horizons and little fixed capital, and will tend to be small scale. The most profitable businesses may be in trade, redistributive activity, or the black market. Large firms with substantial fixed capital will exist only under the umbrella of government protection with substantial subsidies, tariff protection, and payoff to the polity—a mixture hardly conducive to productive efficiency. (North 1990)

This section focuses on the microeconomic market economy foundations for creating better enabling conditions for private sector development. They involve well-functioning institutions for enforcing free and fair competition and protecting property rights and competitive factor markets, discussed in the next two subsections.

Efficient markets also require stable and predictable price signals and sustainable macroeconomic balances, which call for resilient and credible macroeconomic institutions to manage monetary and fiscal policies. This reform agenda is covered in the report's Overview.

Strengthening market institutions

The evidence is compelling that functioning markets require well-defined rules of the game, enforced transparently and predictably. The agenda calls for strong market institutions whose role is especially important in the early phases when markets are underdeveloped and small distortions can have amplified effects. In Vietnam, the emphasis must be on enforcing competition and ensuring the security of property rights.

Institutions for free and fair competition

Effective competition is essential for private sector development and economic competitiveness.[24] Firms typically acquire many of their inputs—transport, energy, financial services, telecommunications—in local markets. If these upstream markets lack competition, goods and services for production are not priced competitively. New domestic firms may then find it difficult to enter. Existing firms may become less competitive than their foreign and SOE rivals. Reforms that open markets and remove anticompetitive regulation thereby lead to significant productivity gains.

Well-functioning markets have shown positive results across the world. In transition economies, firms facing more competition have seen faster sales growth (Carlin, Schaffer, and Seabright 2004). In Africa, the entry of an additional mobile phone operator, for example, was found to increase subscriptions by 57 percent (Gebreab 2002). Higher markups reduced productivity growth in Jordan and Morocco (Sekkat 2009).

Weak competition in telecommunications alone cost the Mexican economy around $129.2 billion in 2005–09 (OECD 2012a). Healthy competition in domestic markets also enhances export growth (Goodwin and Pierola Castro 2015). Further, weak competition can be more harmful to the poor than to the rich, as found in Mexico (Urzua 2009).

Despite a decline in market concentration since the early 2000s (Aterido and Hallward-Driemeier 2015), Vietnam still ranks in the middle ranges of cross-country comparisons of competitiveness in domestic markets. For example, it ranks 65th in the world on Intensity of Local Competition and 69th on Extent of Market Dominance (World Economic Forum 2014). In the region, Vietnam ranks behind China, Indonesia, Malaysia, Thailand, Singapore, and in certain cases the Philippines. Comparisons show concerns not just with the quality of competition-related institutions but also enforcement. On this measure, the country ranks 87th in the world and 12th in the region.

The dominant position of SOEs in many markets is a major constraint on competition. Their presence is not unusual in many economies, especially in sectors that are natural monopolies (public utilities) or are capital intensive (large infrastructure), with competitive markets leaving plenty of room for the private sector to prosper. In Vietnam, however, SOE presence is almost across the board, including sectors such as garment manufacturing, mobile telephone services, and banking, where private players can do a better job. And if the state does keep its extensive role in production, at the very least that role needs to be neutral to private competition. This argues against the privileges extended to Vietnam's SOEs, which undermine the viability of domestic private firms.

Regulations in key network services—especially electricity and transport—further thwart private competition. For example, Vietnam Electricity's position as the sole purchaser of wholesale electricity, combined with price regulation, creates an unviable environment for private firms. In transport, Vietnam and Cambodia have signed agreements to allow for back-hauling services. But the quota of 500 Vietnamese trucks is not assigned competitively. At airports, the slot allocation policy is not competitive. State-owned Vietnam Airlines has grandfathered rights on international routes, while charter flight rights on domestic routes are granted case by case.

Vietnam needs a comprehensive competition policy framework to open markets to entry and competition, and then to enforce competition policies. This framework would reflect four key principles:

1. Apply policies equally to all firms (private or public, domestic or foreign).
2. Combat the most harmful anticompetitive practices, such as cartels.
3. Concentrate on deterring anticompetitive behavior rather than on price control and regulation.
4. Operate in a fair, transparent, rule-bound, and nondiscriminatory manner.

Deviations from these principles should be rare and only for meeting national objectives that are clearly defined and applied fairly and transparently. The reform agenda that defines and implements this framework includes the following:

- *Strengthen and give more autonomy to the Vietnam Competition Authority* (VCA). The VCA lacks operational independence, which causes a great productivity loss for the economy.[25] It is a department-level entity directly under the Ministry of Industry and Trade and composed of ministerial representatives rather than independent experts selected on technical criteria. These representatives are not protected by immunity against dismissal for legitimate exercise of their functions. The VCA lacks basic authority to ask businesses for information to investigate competition-related cases.
- *Align the legal framework with consumer protection.* Besides enhancing economic efficiency, the other major objective of competition policy is improving consumer

welfare. The laws on competition and consumer protection—and their enforcement—thus need to be closely aligned. A review shows that this is not the case. VCA's mandate could be expanded over time—after strengthening its autonomy and capacity—to include aspects of consumer protection that directly relate to competition. This follows the example of the United States Federal Trade Commission, an independent federal agency that enforces competition and consumer protection.

- *Rationalize exemptions to tackle cartels and other forms of concentration.* Addressing cartel behavior is an essential part of antitrust enforcement. Cartels have been associated with price increases of 10–45 percent in developing countries (Levenstein, Suslow, and Oswald 2003) and lower labor productivity and innovation (Broadberry and Crafts 2001; Evenett, Levenstein, and Suslow 2001; Symeonidis 2008). In Vietnam hard-core cartels are exempt from anticompetitive enforcement if participants' market share is below 30 percent (article 9).[26] Even when the shares are above 30 percent, several exemptions protect them (article 10). These and other exemptions in the Competition Law need a critical review to eliminate them. Not only do these exemptions create economic distortions, in some cases they also open the door to political interference. For example, the decision on whether to grant an exemption goes to the Minister of Industry and Trade if the failing firm defense is used. The decision goes to the Prime Minister in other forms of defense, such as contribution to exports (article 25).
- *Consider market contestability in establishing market dominance.* The Competition Law establishes market dominance based on market shares but not market contestability (article 11). This needs to be revised to consider entry, exit, and expansion barriers; the company's financial power; and the duration of market power in establishing market dominance.
- *Increase the threshold for intervention in merger control.* Effective merger control policy is important for preserving market competition, and has been found to result in major savings for a number of countries.[27] The merger control framework in the Competition Law in Vietnam diffuses authorities' attention too thinly, not allowing them to focus on—potentially—the most harmful transactions. Merger prenotification thresholds are based on market shares (article 20), and participants in even minor transactions must be notified if transactions result in more than 30 percent of market share, while concentrations that achieve a joint market share of more than 50 percent are prohibited (article 18). A notification threshold based on market share is more uncertain for the private sector than objective thresholds such as turnover.
- *Ensure a level playing field for all firms, public and private, foreign and domestic.* For reforms to level the playing field between private firms and SOEs, see the section below on "Restructuring the SOEs." To level the playing field between domestic private and foreign firms, policies will have to equalize tax and other incentives given to the two groups and level their access to land.

Institutions for security of property rights and contract enforcement

For a well-functioning market economy, participants need to have confidence that their transactions and property rights will be enforced. The Rule of Law Index in the World wide Governance Indicators is a good measure of these microinstitutions. The index "captures perceptions of the extent to which agents have confidence in and abide by the rules of society, and in particular the quality of contract enforcement, property rights, the police, and the courts, as well as the likelihood of crime and violence."[28] Its earliest year is 1996, when Vietnam had good rule of law for its income level and relative to its peers. This may be why it has seen strong growth (figure 2.20a).

Institutional development needs, however, to keep pace with economic change. Vietnam

FIGURE 2.20 Vietnam's ranking on the rule of law measure has declined since 1996, while its per capita GDP has increased sharply

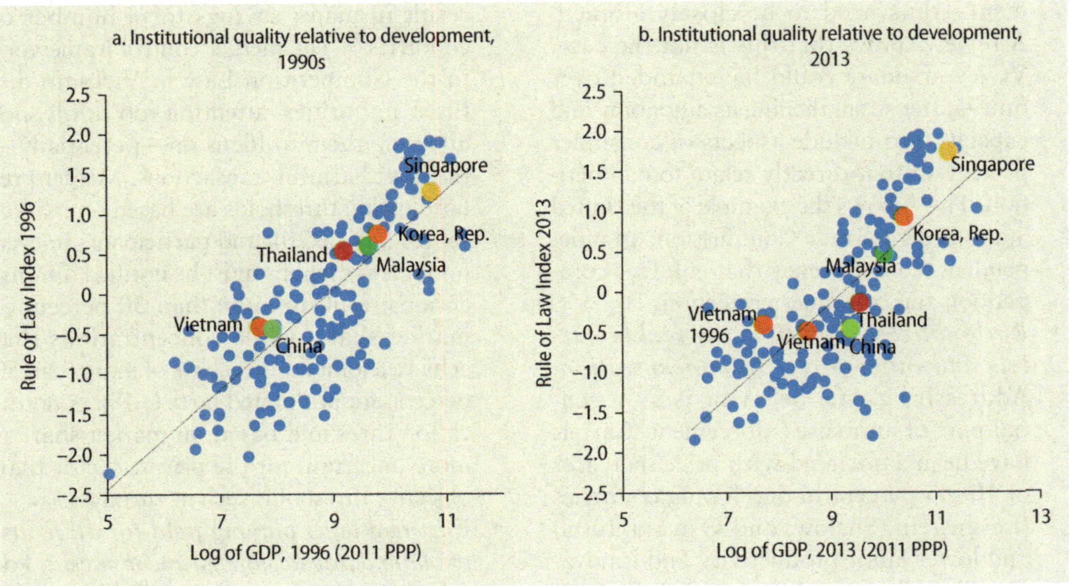

Source: Calculations based on the Worldwide Governance Indicators and World Development Indicators.

FIGURE 2.21 Vietnam's performance on rule of law seems to be especially lagging on property rights

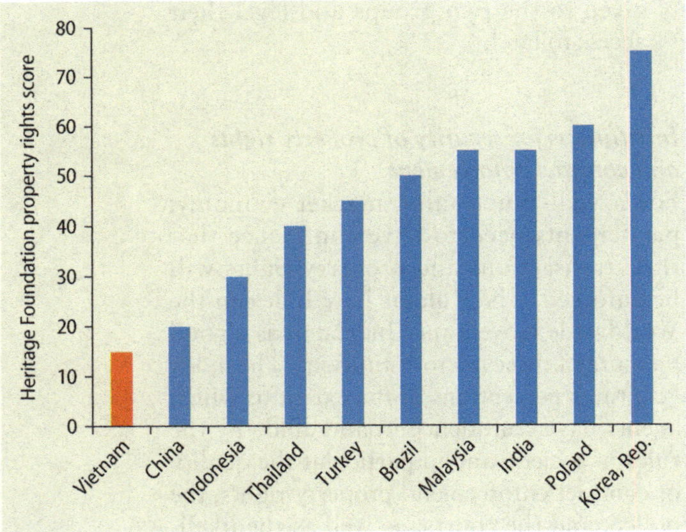

Source: Heritage Foundation 2015.

is now competing with more developed peers, but it does not have especially good institutions among that group. Vietnam's ranking on the rule of law measure has declined since 1996, while its per capita GDP has increased sharply (figure 2.20b). Korea and Singapore are excellent examples of economies that continue to get richer while improving the rule of law. They are growing well for their cohort.

On the rule of law, Vietnam is especially lagging on property rights, according to the Heritage Foundation (figure 2.21). It ranks a more creditable 74 of 189 countries on the Contract Enforcement measure of the World Bank Group's Doing Business Indicators, but still trails China, Malaysia, and Thailand among the region's middle-income countries.

Vietnam's main property rights challenge relates to security and tradability of land-use rights, which disproportionately—and in different ways—affect domestic private firms (box 2.6). The state's power to take back land from private users under broadly defined "public interest" weakens confidence of the holders of land-use rights. Recourse mechanisms to challenge the state's decision, however arbitrary it may be, are largely absent. Security of property rights, a precondition for private enterprise development, is a casualty in the end.

BOX 2.6 Secure access to land in Vietnam remains a binding constraint to firm growth

Secure access to land has consistently been a major barrier to private enterprise growth in Vietnam. The Provincial Competitiveness Index (PCI) series—introduced in 2006 and based on an annual survey of about 7,000 domestic private firms—highlights the problem. In 2014, about a third of all surveyed firms expressed concern about land appropriation by government. This figure while high was a sharp improvement from earlier years, when more than half the surveyed firms expressed similar fears (figure B2.6.1). The 2013 Land Law made a difference in perceptions. Proper implementation, however, still has some way to go. The law has added some unnecessary complications, as shown in Case 2 below. In contrast, land tenure is more secure for foreign-invested firms, only 18 percent of which expressed such a concern in 2014. Concern among SOEs is by all accounts even less widespread, putting domestic private firms at a disadvantage.

Land rentals in industrial parks offer domestic private firms a solution. But even these places mitigate the problem only up to a point. In the following cases of companies A and B, each is performing strongly in an industrial park but is unable to expand because of issues with access to or security of land use.

Case 1: Company A is a domestic private steel producer with an investment plan to build additional production capacity of about 4,000 tons a day. In 2006, it submitted the plan—together with its application—for a large parcel of land in an industrial park managed by the Provincial People's Committee (PPC) of a province near Ho Chi Minh City. Its application was rejected because land parcels of the size needed were not available in the park. Most had been allocated to foreign-invested firms. Company A received a parcel that was only large enough for a plant half of its planned capacity.

In 2009, the company decided to implement the second phase of its plan. But land was still unavailable. It had to buy the rental rights of a second parcel from another domestic company to build a second steel plant in the same industrial park, about 1 kilometer from the first plant. Company A now must incur additional overhead costs and between-plant transportation costs. Its direct competitor, a foreign-invested firm with similar capacity and products, faced little trouble acquiring a large piece of land in the same industrial park. The foreign-invested firm has even secured its own seaport in the park.

Case 2: One of Vietnam's leading paper producers, Company B has faced a different land-use rights security issue. In the early 2000s it moved to an industrial park near Ho Chi Minh City, renting two large land parcels and paying the rental fee for 50 years. The upfront payment made the company eligible to borrow from commercial banks, using its long-term land rental as collateral. This allowed rapid production expansion, with an increase of several hundred times in charter capital since the company was established. It also allowed the company to reach export markets in more than 20 countries. But the 2013 Land Law, for all its benefits, also brought an unexpected twist for Company B and others like it. A common interpretation of the law is that industrial park tenants can only use their land-use right certificates ("red books") as collateral if the park's developers have paid the land-use fees in full to the state. Many park developers (including the one for Company B) are unable to pay. This adversely affects hundreds of private enterprises such as Company B, curtailing their ability to use their factory land as collateral, again putting them at a disadvantage against foreign-invested firms.

FIGURE B2.6.1 Share of firms perceiving a low risk of land appropriation

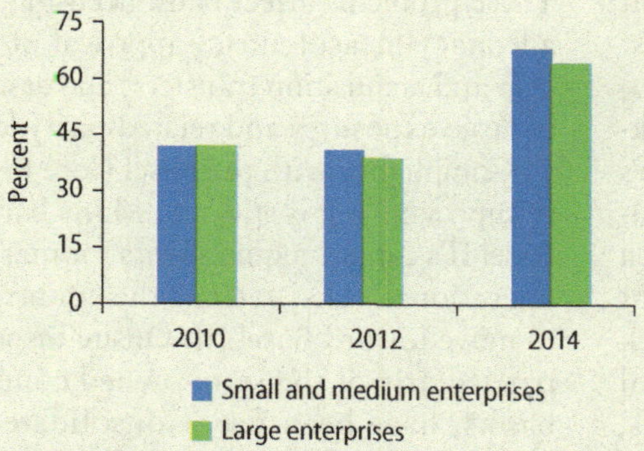

Sources: Calculations based Provincial Competitiveness Index 2010, 2012, and 2014.

Liberalizing factor markets

Vietnam's financial sector remains relatively underdeveloped, with the banking sector saddled with deep-seated structural problems and capital markets still in their infancy. Land markets are even less developed. Moreover, state influence on credit and land-allocation decisions is excessive, leading to widespread and steep economic inefficiencies. Labor market regulations are less onerous, but even those are not free of policy concerns (chapter 6).

Building financial markets

The financial sector has expanded rapidly, coinciding with rapid GDP growth since the early 1990s.[29] Assets are now large for a lower-middle-income country (LMIC). But commercial banks continue to dominate the financial sector. Their assets are larger than Vietnam's GDP, and the average ratio of assets to GDP is much larger for Vietnam than for most other low- and middle-income countries. And state-owned commercial banks continue to play an oversized role in the banking sector.

Following an expansion period, domestic private banks have experienced a reduction of their share in total assets since 2011. This reflects mergers, reforms (including higher capital requirements), and limits on short-term deposit rates to prevent weak banks from bidding for deposits. The government has allowed entry of more foreign banks. Their number climbed from 38 in 2007 to 62 in 2014, but their overall share in banking assets has not increased much. Vietnam's capital markets and nonbank financial institutions have also evolved. They represent a potential source of funding for investment in the next couple of decades. The two stock markets in Ho Chi Minh City and Hanoi have a combined listing of around 700 firms, a high figure compared with other LMICs. Market capitalization, however, is low for the number of firms. This reflects the small size of listed firms and the sales of only small portions of SOEs' equity capital.

Significant scope exists for the financial sector to play an even stronger role in Vietnam's economic development. The sector has done a reasonably good job of mobilizing savings. But it has fallen short in allocating credit to its most productive use and in providing an inclusive payment system. Much of the lending—especially by state-owned commercial banks—has gone to SOEs or, increasingly, to private companies with connections. This often crowds out lending to productive domestic private sector segments. Financial inclusion has increased since the early 1990s but remains an issue for less well-off Vietnamese, especially those in rural areas. A healthier domestic financial sector will be necessary also for effectively conducting monetary policy and liberalizing the capital account in the future.

Banks are struggling after taking a hit when the global financial crisis toppled the real estate market (where banks had heavy exposure). Their average return on assets fell by more than 1 percentage point after the crisis (from 1.8 percent in 2007 to 0.5 percent in 2012). Their reported nonperforming loans (NPLs) have risen and are generally considered understated. And their provisions are lower than middle-income peer countries in East Asia. Many of the NPLs and restructured loans are related to SOEs. Cross-ownership of private banks by each other and by enterprises (including SOEs) remains high. Moreover, the legal definition of related parties is narrow and information on it is limited. These problems affect bank licensing, capital adequacy measurement, approval of ownership and acquisition transfers, and assessment of large exposures and related-party lending.

Compliance with the Basel Core Principles is improving but is still low. Many banks lack Basel II's capital requirements for market and operational risks, even as the country looks to move toward Basel III. Onsite inspections, particularly of the state-owned commercial banks, have been few. Consolidated bank supervision (of banks and their associated business groups) is lacking. And offsite monitoring also needs to improve.

The government has taken steps to deal with these banking sector problems and reduce the risk of crisis. These actions have tightened risk classification of loans

BOX 2.7 Deposit Insurance of Vietnam

Founded in 1999 Deposit Insurance of Vietnam (DIV) is a potentially important part of the safety net for banking. But it needs to strengthen its finances and its resolution policies for weak banks. It covers individual deposits of up to D 50 million (about US$2,500).[a] It is a pay-box system, with each insured institution paying a premium of 0.15 percent of its average insured deposit balance. DIV's financial balance is less than 1 percent of bank deposits. Over the next 20 years this basic approach is reasonable. But as the GDP per capita and deposit size grow, decisions will need to be made on increasing DIV's financial base and on increasing covered deposits.

Although DIV has existed for over 16 years, it has never been used to resolve NPLs or liquidate insolvent banks. It has mainly helped with People's Credit Funds. The DIV policy has been to merge institutions to address problems, as is done by the U.S. Federal Deposit Insurance Corporation. The current approach may reflect government concern that closure and pay-off of a weak bank's depositors might trigger more general bank runs. It may also reflect DIV's limited funds, which are too small to liquidate even two medium-size Vietnamese banks.

Moreover, DIV's resources have been invested in its member banks, which pose a risk to DIV's capacity to insure bank deposits. It may even intensify the liquidity problem if these members face a liquidity or solvency crisis. The 2012 Law on Deposit Insurance allows DIV to invest in government bonds and structured investment vehicle bills and deposits. But it is unclear how much DIV's investment policy has changed. DIV also does not have the capacity to take over and run an institution. (Many deposit insurance institutions in other countries also lack this capacity.) The Credit Institution Law complicates DIV capacity to merge institutions, take over an institution, or even assume collateral on bank loans.

DIV could be strengthened in three ways. First, its funds could be transferred into government bonds. Structured investment vehicle bills and deposits in the SBV could be transferred within a reasonable time, following the 2012 Law on Deposit Insurance. The transfer should not, however, be done so rapidly that it creates liquidity problems. Second, if more funds are necessary for systemic support, the DIV should have access to government funds in a well-defined manner from SBV, for example, as in Peru. Third, the Credit Institution Law and the DIV Law need to be strengthened to give DIV capacity to purchase and assume assets, and then to sell them.

a. The maximum deposit insured is about 50 percent larger than GDP per capita.

and other financial assets. They have also strengthened bank regulation and supervision, government institutions to help clean up the problems, and financial reporting and capital adequacy requirements. It would be beneficial to deepen implementation of these and other actions and to adopt international accounting standards.

Four key items are on the reform agenda for the financial system over the next 20 years:

Reducing the risk of major financial crisis. Vietnam's response to potential financial crisis could be accelerated if the government strengthens the National Monetary Advisory Council. The council could meet regularly, supported by a technical team to provide daily reports, drafts of notifications, and instructions to banks. Information on the financial system could be improved by better offsite data and supervision from the State Bank of Vietnam (SBV). Crisis response to liquidity problems could be strengthened by firming the resources of the Deposit Insurance of Vietnam (DIV). This measure would require a gradual shift in the DIV's funds from banks to government debt. The measure would also require legal changes that permit the government to borrow from SBV on behalf of the DIV in large crises, under well-defined conditions (box 2.7).

Stabilizing and developing the banking sector. The immediate priority is to resolve the large NPL overhang in banks while

BOX 2.8 Vietnam Asset Management Company

The Vietnam Asset Management Company (VAMC) was established in 2013 with a capital of D 500 billion (about US$25 million),[a] which increased to D 2 trillion in April 2015. The VAMC can buy bad loans from banks at book value or market prices, making purchases with VAMC special zero-interest bonds. A bank can use these bonds to access liquidity from SBV or to refinance loans through SBV. The bonds must involve annual provisions of 20 percent by the bank on the refinanced loan. If a bank with high NPLs refuses to sell bad debt to the VAMC, SBV can carry out a special inspection or hire an independent auditor to assess the quality of the bank's assets.

The VAMC approach holds promise but needs to be greatly strengthened to reduce the banks' NPLs significantly, in four areas. First, the VAMC's capital remains small relative to the amount of the NPLs. Second, substantial legal reforms are needed to improve workouts and claim enforcement by the VAMC, for example, to manage the collateral well and to sell it. Third, the management capacity needs improvement. The NPLs sold to VAMC will lose value unless they are managed well and sold. Fourth, the VAMC's restructuring capacity requires changes in legislation to improve its capacity to support state-owned commercial banks. This is mainly true of their SOE NPLs, which could be better handled by the government under a new system backed by the necessary laws. The ability of the government to deal with these NPLs may, however, be complicated by the new relations between the state-owned commercial banks and the SBV.

VAMC likely needs yet more resources beyond those it received when the government quadrupled its capital to D 2 trillion in Decree 34. It also requires greater flexibility, with its operating capacity and activities widened beyond the current use of the liquidity support approach and supported by changes in laws and regulations. In particular, substantial changes in the legal framework will be needed to strengthen claims enforcement, ease obstacles to voluntary workouts, and increase sales of collateral on the NPLs. Changes in the legal framework will also improve VAMC's operations (including management of its holdings of assets) and improve its management of collateral on weak bank loans extended to the SOEs.

The experience of Indonesia and the Republic of Korea in dealing with weak banks after the Asian crisis may interest Vietnam. Indonesia established an agency similar to VAMC to handle weak banks and manage collateral on the NPLs. But once the agency got going, it was effective in handling the bad debts and their collateral and in selling the collateral and the banks that were taken over (Enoch 2000, 2001). Indonesia's experience suggests the need to improve VAMC and the treatment of weak banks promptly. Korea's response involved not only improving bank management but also closing many "merchant" banks, which focused on loans to industrial corporations. That country's experience suggests that some bank closures may eventually be necessary in Vietnam, undertaken with caution.

a. A centralized asset management company (DATC) was created in 2003 to reduce the NPLs in the system, but has had limited impact.

steadily increasing their capital. A good starting point would include confidential (including operational) audits by international firms and strong application of prudential norms, without regulatory forbearance. These early measures can be effective in cleaning up NPLs, as shown in Korea and Indonesia after the Asian crisis in the late 1990s. They would be especially desirable for state-owned commercial banks.

For private banks deemed sound by the audits, NPL resolution would involve direct sales of collateral related to the NPLs and transfers of the remaining NPLs and related collateral, under a more robust legal framework, to a strengthened Vietnam Asset Management Company for their management, recovery, and sale (box 2.8). Private banks deemed insolvent would need to be closed, merged with viable banks, or sold (either directly or through the company), with an injection of capital from the owners, new owners, DIV, or (in exceptional cases) the government.

The state-owned commercial banks, particularly Agribank, need additional new capital and extensive treatment of their NPLs to clean them up and allow an increase in their lending, based on relevant legal revisions. The treatment of state-owned banks' NPLs and the collateral on their NPLs, both of which may involve SOEs, are likely to need special legal amendments, especially since at least some of the collateral sales may involve sales to the private sector. At a minimum, the treatment of their NPLs is likely to involve a special administrative track for SOEs' NPLs to the state-owned banks. This may be handled by setting up a program within the government, with qualified staff to resolve bad loans.

For undercapitalized state-owned banks, the government could put in capital, as has been done in India, for example, and some capital could be raised from sales through additional equitization. The second option would depend on expectations of better profitability and returns on these banks' shares, especially because the role of private investors in state-owned banks' management is likely to remain light.

Beyond resolving NPLs, banking sector reforms would also include steps to improve performance and higher capital requirements for the banks. This will depend on better enforcing improved regulations. It will also depend on supervising risks taken by banks (especially state-owned banks) and by other assets sellers, such as insurance and pension firms. One major improvement would be to apply macroprudential supervision and better offsite supervision. Another improvement would be a gradual shift to international regulatory and accounting standards. Moving toward Basel III would mean higher requirements for capital—including capital for market and operational risks—and fewer incentives for excessive risk-taking by bank owners (as noted, in a context where some banks are struggling to meet even Basel II requirements). A third improvement would be greater information on business groups, which would enable consolidated supervision of bank groups while helping reduce connected lending and cross-ownerships across financial and nonfinancial institutions.

Consolidating the shift from state- to private-owned banks needs to continue. Foreign—especially regional East Asian—banks have an important role. Regional banks have increased their presence worldwide, and the pattern is reflected in East Asia, including Vietnam. The trend is likely to continue, at least in the near future, which suggests that foreign banks' increased presence in Vietnam is likely to come from within the region. This trend may get a boost from the government's recent decision to allow foreign ownership of more than 30 percent of domestic bank capital, on the prime minister's approval. Such increases, however, have not yet been made. Regional banks' rising role also suggests a need for greater information exchange between SBV and other regional bank supervisors to reduce risks of spillovers of bank problems from one country to another.

Developing a larger, more diverse financial sector. Deepening the capital markets (starting with the market for government debt) will be important, which will also need changes to the legal and accounting frameworks to bring them into line with international standards. Three important measures (carried out successfully in Peru, for example) would be the government's maintenance of a predictable pattern of its debt offers, further development of a benchmark rate index on government debt, and the development of new types of government or private debt instruments. For example, legal changes could permit government or private firms to sell new bonds—such as infrastructure bonds—under well-defined conditions.

Other capital-market reforms should focus on the medium term and the need for more foreign investment in the equity market to support investment and growth. Cooperation and coordination between the various agencies responsible for financial supervision—SBV (for banks), the Ministry of Finance (for insurance), and the State Securities Commission—could be strengthened, with the supervisory institutions of Peru as a good example.[30] Accounting rules that more closely follow international accounting standards would make such investment more attractive. As in most developing countries, development of contractual savings institutions (such as insurance companies) has only begun in Vietnam. But their role will increase over the next 20 years as the economy modernizes. Generating investor interest in insurance companies will depend on improved clarity of company accounts, tighter compliance with international standards, and a strengthened Insurance Supervisory Agency. That agency could be improved by developing a self-financed supervisory system, which considers governance, valuations, market conduct, internal controls, and insurance companies' involvement in business groups.

Increasing financial inclusion. Among LMICs, Vietnam has done relatively well in lending to individuals, but not as well in taking deposits and remittances.[31,32] This likely reflects Vietnam's fewer bank branches per capita and limited use of mobile phones and money-transfer operators for remittances. More branches—particularly in rural areas—would support more remittances, but they would be costly. Banks lack funds for such a large expansion of branches.

Alternative uses of mobile phones for remittances and deposits could be done at low cost, although Vietnam would need major changes in regulation—for finance and mobile telephony—to take advantage of the country's large number of mobile phone subscriptions. A good international example is Kenya's M-Shwari, which by end-2014 had added 9 million accounts since its launch in 2012. It also had total deposits of $45 million and outstanding loans of nearly $18 million. Its deposit holders can apply for short-term loans. Legal changes are required to allow remittances through mobile phones and provide security for the remitter through related trust accounts at banks.[33]

Going to the next step, additional laws would be necessary to allow phone companies to link to banks for opening small bank deposits based on the information used for mobile phone purchases (to satisfy the Know-Your-Customer regulations). Still later, linked banks could offer small, short-term loans, as in Kenya. Legislation would also require that bank deposits related to mobile phone activities be invested only in safe assets in trust funds, which would be easier to implement if the government bond market were improved. Bank deposits would also be eligible for deposit insurance, for which fees would be paid.

Higher-quality credit information on borrowers is needed. All lenders could be required to submit credit information on their borrowers to a central registry. Information on potential borrowers should also include their payments to public utilities, which is useful for first-time loan applicants. The borrower must be uniquely identified through a system that, for example, creates a unique, easily accessible, computerized number linked to a photo that cannot be easily forged.[34] The link between remittances, mobile phone activities, and an account/loan application can also be used to provide information on the loan applicant's activities.

Developing land markets

Land, according to the Vietnamese constitution and law, is owned by the public and managed on its behalf by the state. Land-use rights for specified periods are issued to private individuals, who have the right to transfer these rights to other individuals. The state may take back the land and annul the rights in the national interest, based on compensation according to law.

The legal framework for individual rights to land use is subject to the interpretation of numerous, overlapping laws. And its implementation is equally riddled with a plethora of implementing regulations and overlapping mandates. This is just at the national level. Provincial and municipal administrations issue their own instructions on land use and transfer.

The markets for trading land-use rights are, in effect, missing (Cung 2015). There are virtually no functioning primary markets for land. The role of the markets is played by state agencies often using ill-defined administrative procedures. And the price at which land-use rights are issued bears little semblance to what the true market-determined price would be.

Secondary land markets are more prevalent, but they operate under multiple constraints. Market mechanisms are rarely deployed in cases involving reclassification of land use from agricultural to nonagricultural land. In such cases, land-use planning decisions by local administrations—and not demand-supply conditions or local preferences—determine the reclassified purpose of land use. Moreover, the "seller"—or the private individual (often a farmer) giving up a land-use right—is unlikely to receive fair compensation. The benefit goes mostly to the local government and the "buyer," who often receives the land allocation at prices below what a functioning secondary land market would produce.

The missing land markets are problematic from several angles. For one, their absence—with weak property rights—fosters a patronage-based business model.[35] This model allocates land to those with connections or access to the state and state officials rather than to the most productive or innovative firms. Their lack undermines efficiency in other ways, too. A land-use right holder who wants to change land-use purpose for a more rewarding economic activity will find administrative costs high, often prohibitively, and the processes time consuming. Missing land markets also create distortions in urbanization patterns. The development of functioning and transparent land markets, therefore, is an important and urgent policy priority.

Modernizing and commercializing the agriculture sector

Agricultural growth and development over the past decade was based on highly intensive use of production inputs and of human and natural resources. In the future, a unifying motto for the sector should be "achieving more from less." The sector will need to yield greater producer, consumer, ecosystem, and economic benefits with less intensive use of land, labor, water, environmentally harmful inputs, and other natural resources. This will require greater efficiency in land and water use, a shift toward more knowledge and skill-based agricultural practices, better realized economies of scale and scope within value chains, and marked shifts in the functions—and performance of those functions—by government.

Many of the challenges Vietnamese agriculture faces as it transitions to an efficiency-based and higher value-added sector cannot be addressed through changes in agricultural policies alone. Addressing the sector's longer-term transitional challenges of competitiveness and sustainability requires broader economic reforms, especially for land (ownership/tenure and use rights), the role and operating conditions of the SOEs and banks, policies, and institutions including those associated with science and technology, and approaches to government decentralization and coordination. (The policy agendas for these matters are covered in this and other chapters.)

Beyond these broader changes the following sector-specific policy shifts will be essential. The state should:

- *Lead less and facilitate more.* To help modernize agriculture, the government will need to narrow its focus to providing core public goods and services while enabling much greater investment by farmers and the private sector.[36] On food safety and environmental standards it may need to cautiously calibrate the regulatory side, allowing firms to adopt practices incrementally rather than introducing abrupt measures that demand immediate compliance. Effective government programs will involve targeted subsidies, technology transfer programs, and capacity-building interventions. All are preferable to simply de-licensing or otherwise penalizing lagging firms.
- *Facilitate more efficient use of agricultural land.* Land consolidation in various forms will be crucial for more efficient agricultural land use, which will require a better-functioning land market. This would make

land allocation more efficient and achieve greater security of land tenure, encouraging farmers to undertake fixed investments while offering them flexibility to lease their land to more productive users. Land consolidation will also allow increased mechanization, increasingly important as labor costs rise. Flexibility is needed partly because the paddy land designation policy has led Vietnam to far overshoot its food security objectives. This has generated a massive exportable surplus that produces only modest incomes for farmers and net returns to the country. The government has set goals for converting some paddy land and—with Decree 35—has established rules that should provide farmers and local leaders with greater scope to convert land to other agricultural uses or introduce rotations between seasons. The revised policy still restricts farmers from converting paddy land for more permanent purposes, such as planting tree crops. This restriction should be reconsidered after the impacts of the current reform are observed.

- *Facilitate more efficient and sustainable use of irrigation water.* Irrigated agriculture needs to increase factor productivity and better account for its water use. In 2014, an irrigation restructuring scheme was announced, adopting sustainable development objectives and pointing toward a combination of technical advances and institutional reforms. It also called for upgrading and modernizing the existing irrigation schemes and for fully decentralizing their management to the provinces. As the subsector fully decentralizes, the focus of change and modernization practice will be among the provinces. They are responsible for irrigation investment planning, implementing government investments on irrigation, and operation and maintenance. Yet the Ministry of Agriculture and Rural Development, working with provincial and user agencies, will need to facilitate a more service-oriented approach. Reforming the subsector will be a long-term effort with measures to resolve the long-term financing of irrigation and drainage management companies. Measures are needed to improve the ministry's accountability and oversight and its incentives to deliver requested and reliable irrigation services. Measures are also needed to strengthen the relationships between these companies and water-user organizations.
- *Foster knowledge-based agriculture through a radical reform of extension services.* Shifting from resource-intensive to knowledge-based agriculture will require major changes in the ways farmers learn and gain access to technical and commercial information. Government and public extension services will still be important, but less as the main provider of centralized advisory services and more as a broker, mobilizer, and funder of services others provide. For many extension agencies, moving into these roles will require them to embrace structural and cultural changes. They can accomplish this by building new skill sets, reframing their mission, and modifying staff incentives by changing performance-measuring criteria. Other countries are adopting an "extension-plus" concept, which policy makers could consider for Vietnam. The approach centers more on brokering relationships and facilitating reciprocal knowledge flows than on providing direct, one-way information and technology (as from knowledge institutions to end users).
- *Strengthen systems and capacities for managing emerging food safety risks.* The ongoing shifts in consumer diets toward animal products and other high-value and processed foods have increased consumers' exposure to food safety risks. This has led to demands for higher food safety standards. The government has responded by streamlining institutions, revamping its food safety regulations, and investing in laboratories. It also plans to task agencies previously in charge of export food safety to take more responsibility for the domestic area. The government, however, has yet to identify new financial and human resources, which in the meantime put severe pressure on regulatory agencies. It also needs to do more to encourage firms to actively use the issued quality standards

that apply to their goods and supplies, and facilitate their efforts in this regard.

- *Manage climate change risks to agriculture.* Domestic agriculture is expected to be heavily affected by climate change through sea-level rise, saltwater intrusion, higher temperatures, modified rainfall patterns, and heightened storm intensity. Such risks require land-use changes, improved early-warning systems, more flexible and resilient infrastructure, and—perhaps most important—improved capacities of farmers for adaptive management. Faced with similar risks, more countries have embraced "climate-smart" agriculture, a concept that integrates or mainstreams adaptation and mitigation objectives into sector development efforts.
- *Foster collective action.* Common types of collective action organizations—including cooperatives and industry associations—have often served political rather than technical or commercial functions. Yet in recent years, the government has recognized the importance of institutional collaboration for fostering innovation and improving industry performance. The Agricultural Restructuring Plan advocates a broader application of public–private partnerships and contract-farming models. The government can also support producer and industry organizations in two broad ways: it can invest in institutional strengthening, and it can use its legal and regulatory authority to create a supportive environment.
- *Strengthen green agriculture policies and implementation capacities.* Several promotion policies conflict with environmental protection goals. Examples include efforts to conserve fisheries while promoting fishery resources, with comanagement in the same locations as where fuel or boat-building subsidies are offered to expand local fish-processing capacity. Similarly, efforts to restrict farmers from cutting trees and cultivating steep slopes may be undermined by promoting new investments in nearby ethanol plants with large feedstock requirements. And government waivers and subsidies for water and irrigation service fees temporarily increase farmer incomes but contribute to improper water management, often in ways that increase greenhouse gas emissions. Through incentives and information—whether from procurement, R&D, extension, quality management systems, or environmental service payment schemes—the government can enable and encourage private sector investment and action in environmental protection. It can directly invest in environmentally protective infrastructure, or help others mobilize such resources. What is suitable and feasible depends on the type and scale of the environmental problem and the prevailing institutional context within the location or value chain.

Leveraging External Trade Opportunities for Growth

Vietnam's participation in GVCs has been highly rewarding. Given that trends in global production and trade networks are always unfolding (box 2.9), the country has much room to enhance its role in GVCs. Moreover, its export production for many key products is mainly at final assembly stage, as in electronics GVCs. That is to be expected in the early stages of participating in GVCs. It will likely remain important given Vietnam's large pool of unskilled labor still waiting to move into manufacturing (and services). However, since only 64 percent of Vietnam's export value added comes from domestic inputs (down from 79 percent in 1996)—a figure that is much lower in sectors such as electronics—it has ample scope to develop upstream industries.

While retaining the niche for assembly production (at least in the medium term), Vietnam could also profitably expand into production of supplies. This will require promoting and establishing competitive private firms (see above for that policy agenda) that can implement production links with foreign-invested firms and supply them with intermediate products for assembly. Eventually, as Vietnamese firms get savvier and globally more competitive (through scale economies and technological upgrading), the country should look for the emergence of some domestic lead firms at the head of their GVCs. This

BOX 2.9 Trends in global production and trade networks

In today's industrial era, business systems are being formed in detailed and rapidly evolving global and regional labor divisions, generally referred to as GVCs. It has become more common for value to be added to a product in two or more countries before final use (Feenstra 1998). This boosts trade in intermediate goods and services and the share of imports in exports ("import intensity") for countries deeply engaged in GVCs. It also means that countries can specialize in narrow business functions in the chain, such as innovation or manufacturing.

Lead firms in specific industries are driving economic integration. Faced with slow growth at home, large lead firms from developed countries are likely to continue establishing operations in large emerging economies, such as China, India, Brazil, and Vietnam. These economies have a huge potential consumer base and competitive labor markets. Another trend is the growing importance of large suppliers and services providers. GVC actors that can operate in multiple locations absorb risk for lead firms and increase capacity use in facilities that can produce for multiple buyers. In the 1990s, the most successful United States and European suppliers—such as Siemens, Valeo, and Flextronics—quickly became major global players with facilities around the world. A handful of elite East Asian suppliers—such as Pao Chen, Quanta, and Foxconn—and trading companies—Li & Fung, for example—also took on more tasks for multinational affiliates and global buyers. These global suppliers are expanding production not only in China but in other Asian countries and more recently in Africa, Eastern Europe, and Latin America. As resources in the global supply base improve, more lead firms are gaining the confidence to embrace the twin strategies—often intertwined—of outsourcing and offshoring.

Industrial policy in Vietnam, as elsewhere, will thus need to fit into strategic decisions by lead firms and global suppliers on how to organize global production, which business functions could be hived off and offshored and outsourced, and which locations make sense. Decisions on outsourcing and offshoring are strategic, but corporate boards and bosses do not make them in a vacuum. Country policies and international agreements set the background to these decisions. The form and effects of industrial policy have evolved along with changes to GVCs' business networks. As GVCs continue to grow rapidly, it will take time for the underlying business systems to mature. In recent years, retailers and branded manufacturers in wealthy countries have gained experience in international sourcing. Developing countries have acquired the infrastructure and capabilities needed to sustain larger operations. And their suppliers have upgraded their capabilities in response to larger orders for more complex goods.

GVCs can drive rapid development, but they can also wall off domestic companies that specialize in assembly from innovation, new industry creation, and high profits. They can also become an obstacle for workers seeking highly paid, technologically sophisticated, intellectually satisfying work. Successful development will depend on how quickly and how well entrepreneurs and policy makers understand these emerging dynamics, grasp opportunities in promising niches, take advantage of inputs and capabilities from outside the country, and develop innovative corporate strategies and policy solutions in concert with a wide range of actors, domestic and foreign.

will mark the end of the chain where returns are multiple times higher. Think of Apple (the United States), which retains more than 45 percent of the wholesale price of a new iPhone as gross profit.[37] Samsung (Korea), Huawei (China), and Tata Group (India) are other names to keep an eye on.

How can Vietnam deepen its participation in GVCs? The characteristics of GVC activity, including the potential for future growth and barriers to growth, are different in different sectors. Key features of GVCs relevant to Vietnam must, therefore, be identified separately to provide meaningful policy recommendations. This final section highlights the reform agenda through four important GVCs for Vietnam. Within these four GVCs, growth in value added in exports has been strong (figure 2.22). They will remain important export generators for the country. The section also considers two cross-cutting GVC-related themes that affect all sectors.

FIGURE 2.22 Four global value chains—agribusiness, textiles and apparel, transport equipment, and electronics/ICT equipment—will continue to be export generators for Vietnam

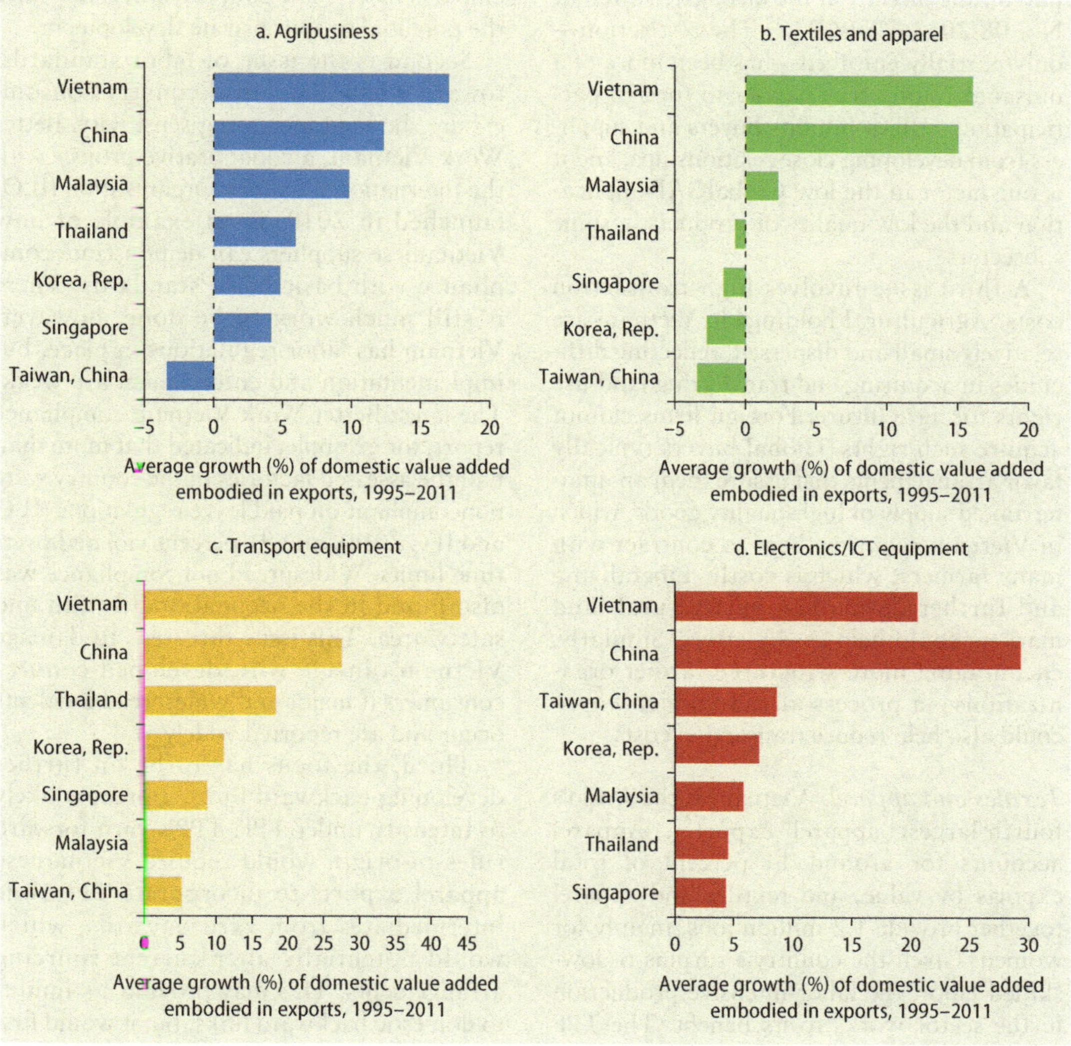

Source: Calculations based on OECD/WTO Trade in Value-Added database.

Opportunities in four key GVCs

Agribusiness. Domestic value added embodied in Vietnam's agricultural exports has been expanding rapidly (figure 2.22a). As global agribusiness GVC activity intensifies over the next two decades, Vietnamese farmers and businesses will have openings to upgrade production into higher value-added activities, especially in some half-dozen sectors (table 2A.2). Foreign investment will often be important.

Strengthening Vietnam's position in agribusiness GVCs raises important policy issues, however. First, institutional gaps in quality and food safety standards disadvantage the country. Domestic standards—for example, Vietnam Good Agricultural Practices (VietGAP)—are typically below those required by global players, which usually follow Global Good Agricultural Practices (GlobalGAP). This is reflected in lower unit prices for Vietnamese producers (table 2A.3).

A second hurdle arises from a recent legal regulation banning foreign-owned firms from purchasing directly at the farm gate (Circular No. 08/2013/TT-BCT).[38] The restriction—only partially enforced—has been more of a nuisance than a true barrier to foreign participation. Still, it inhibits buyers and suppliers from developing close relationships, and it is one factor in the low GlobalGAP application and the low quality of products in some subsectors.

A third issue involves high transaction costs. Agricultural holdings in Vietnam are relatively small and dispersed, reflecting difficulties in acquiring and transferring land-use rights for agriculture. Foreign firms cannot acquire such rights. Global buyers typically favor arrangements that assure them an uninterrupted supply of high-quality goods, which in Vietnam requires them to contract with many farmers, which is costly. Liberalizing and further developing agricultural land markets could help ease matters. Similarly, encouraging more structured farmer organizations—a process already under way—could also help reduce transaction costs.

Textiles and apparel. Vietnam is the world's fourth-largest apparel exporter. Apparel accounts for around 14 percent of total exports by value, and textiles and apparel together provide 1.2 million jobs, mainly for women. Given the country's surplus of low-skilled labor, the labor-intensive production in the sector works to its benefit. The TPP agreement will add to this advantage, as Vietnam gains duty-free access to the United States, Japan, and other TPP markets.

Outstanding issues remain, however. Vietnam specializes in low value-added activities, in line with the "cut, make, trim" model, aiming more at basic market segments rather than the upper end where margins are greater.

Four reforms are forthcoming for upgrading in garment GVCs. First, the SOEs still retain a prominent role in the sector. Distortions that create space for the SOEs may be crowding out the domestic private sector, including in upstream subsectors that could potentially have higher added value. Moves toward greater equitization—including that of the market leader Vinatex, which employs more than 200,000 workers—have the potential to spur private development.

Second is the issue of labor standards, toward which developed-country consumers are showing increasing sensitivity. Better Work Vietnam, a collaborative project with the International Labour Organization (ILO) launched in 2010, is an example of how Vietnamese suppliers can demonstrate compliance with basic labor standards. There is still much work to be done, however. Vietnam has labor regulations in place, but implementation and enforcement are weak. The latest Better Work Vietnam compliance report, for example, indicated that more than half the assessed factories in the country were noncompliant on paid leave regulations (ILO and IFC 2014), and 91 percent violated overtime limits. Widespread noncompliance was also found in the occupational health and safety area. This issue threatens to damage Vietnam's image with developed country consumers if major and widespread incidents occur and are reported widely.

Third, the focus has to be on further developing backward links, a process likely to intensify under TPP. TPP's yarn forward rules-of-origin would require Vietnamese apparel exports to incorporate TPP-zone intermediates from yarn onwards, which would potentially alter current sourcing arrangements. This may provide a stimulus to domestic backward links, but it would first require upstream investments. The environmental costs associated with textile production will also need to be factored in.

The fourth area is functional upgrading—or developing service industries linked to apparel—including sourcing, supply chain management, design, product development, marketing, and branding. For this, local human capital needs to be enhanced. Upstream firms can become more productive only if they have access to a pool of skilled engineers and technical workers with industry-specific skills. Such workers are in short supply, in part because the strategy of lead foreign firms has been to undertake higher value-added activities at their headquarters.

Transport equipment. Transport equipment exports have been growing well. Strong domestic demand for motorcycles provides the basis for high-volume production, high local content, and growing exports.[39] Vietnam is becoming an export platform for motorcycles and motorcycle parts. Motorcycle exports have grown at 10–20 percent annually in recent years. The expansion of the motorcycle market—and of the local supply base to support it—is reflected in the product focus of the largest motor vehicle suppliers in the country (table 2A.4). Aside from a large cluster of wire harness producers, Vietnam has several important suppliers of motorcycle parts (including tires, ignition switches, and clutches).

Passenger vehicle production, by contrast, suffers from excessive fragmentation, overcapacity, and lack of supporting industries. This leads to high costs, excess capacity, low-volume production, and low profitability at most facilities. In 2013, total passenger vehicle production capacity in Vietnam's 14 assembly plants was about 60 percent of the capacity of a typical plant in a large market such as the United States (Berger 2014). Even so, average capacity use for passenger vehicle assembly in Vietnam is estimated at around 40 percent. Moreover, most parts are imported from high-volume facilities abroad. Because auto parts constitute about 90 percent of the value of finished vehicles, Vietnam's passenger vehicle industry is unlikely to pick up strongly as long as the market suffers low domestic demand and negligible exports.

The roots of Vietnam's poorly performing passenger vehicle industry can be traced to 1996, when investment licenses were issued excessively. Steps to rationalize the passenger vehicle manufacturing sector are needed, mainly by discouraging the continued operation of low-volume producers. Such producers contribute to extreme fragmentation and eliminate any chance of developing a healthy supporting parts industry. Assembly of these brands could possibly be shifted to contract manufacturers to increase volumes at these plants and ensure that domestic customers have access to a variety of products. But as vehicle models share few common parts, this will not stimulate supporting industries. Production should be concentrated in those assembly plants with the highest volume and largest domestic supply base.

Information and communications technology. Vietnam has emerged as a major hardware assembly hub in information and communications technology (ICT) GVCs, with rapid export growth since 2009. By 2013, 80 percent of ICT hardware production was for export, and ICT-related products now account for more than 30 percent of the country's exports. Vietnam is well integrated into regional value chains, with most intermediate goods imported from regional countries. Most final goods are exported to advanced markets—such as the United States, Japan, and Europe—though export destinations are not as concentrated as sources of intermediate goods imports. The top 10 destinations account for roughly 60 percent of final ICT goods exports.

In recent years, Vietnam's ICT hardware export growth has depended heavily on imported components, more than in comparator countries (figure 2.23). A large share of its hardware exports can be linked to foreign investors. Production consists mainly of imported intermediate inputs assembly.

The challenge now is to move up the GVCs in ICT. Higher value-added activities—particularly design, R&D, and component production—are attractive over the

FIGURE 2.23 High import content of electronics exports

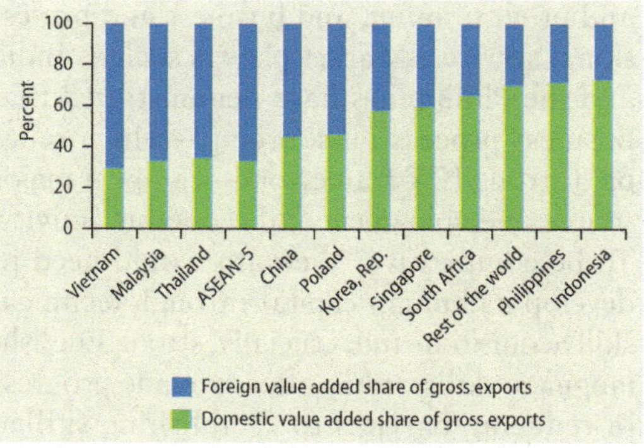

Source: Calculations based on OECD/WTO Trade in Value-Added database.
Note: ASEAN-5 refers to a subgroup of five members of the Association of Southeast Asian Nations (Indonesia, Malaysia, the Philippines, Singapore, and Thailand).

long run. A strong case exists for promoting greater R&D. But ICT is not the only sector where R&D activities can have positive spillovers. Thus, measures such as tax credits should be applied generally to avoid unduly favoring ICT or any other sector. Upgrading participation in the GVCs would also mean incorporating more and higher value-added services in the chain. This progress toward "servicification" is needed in the existing domestic electronic manufacturing industry and in its nascent ICT-enabled business services, which hold considerable promise.

Cross-cutting themes important for all GVC sectors

Developing a strong modern service sector. Vietnam needs a robust modern service sector for continued success in leveraging external opportunities. This is one area where it lags behind its competitor countries. Services account for about 43 percent of all economic activity, a figure essentially unchanged since 2000. This share is similar to that in China and other ASEAN countries but much lower than in most middle- and high-income countries.

Modern services such as finance, insurance, telecommunications, and transport and logistics are critical inputs for manufacturing exports. Also, direct service exports offer the opportunity to diversify exports. If Vietnam can develop its human capital with its ICT infrastructure and connectivity, it can become competitive in ICT-enabled sectors. These include design services, software and programming, and business and professional services. Market players such as India and the Philippines have demonstrated that business process outsourcing—which relies on a strong ICT framework—can be a major source of employment and economic activity. To be competitive, Vietnam would need to develop its human capital through technical skill acquisition and, crucially, strong English-language skills. It has already made progress in reducing barriers to establishing skilled personnel and individual services. And the ASEAN Mutual Recognition Arrangements for professional services, for example, will help facilitate the movement of talent into the country. As in goods sectors, services are outsourced based on sophisticated contractual arrangements. This means that areas such as contract enforcement and the rule of law are again important foundational areas.

An effective innovation startup ecosystem needs to be established to exploit opportunities in ICT-enabled services. Vietnamese innovative startups will need reliable access to risk capital from launch through the growth phases. Infrastructure is another deficiency in the technology startup ecosystem. The country now has some 20 accelerators and incubators, but they do not have much of a track record. These efforts need to be expanded with assistance from partners who understand local and global markets.

This area would benefit from connections with the diaspora community, an influence that was important in developing advanced services in India, Singapore, and Taiwan, China, among many other economies. Many of some 4 million overseas Vietnamese have settled in the United States. The technology professionals among them can bring connections to foreign capital, markets, management teams, and other tools that would help local entrepreneurs build and grow their companies. While some have returned to start firms, they have generally found support difficult to come by (box 2.10).

The foreign investment regime recognizes three categories of sectors. Some are unconditionally open to foreign investment, while others are either prohibited or conditionally open. Conditionally open means that screening procedures are in place. A wide variety of service sector investments fall under the conditional category (table 2A.5). It will be important to rationalize this list to provide a level playing field for all investors, domestic and foreign.

Dispute resolution is an important issue. Investors, wary of the legal system, often specify dispute settlement by arbitration in other jurisdictions, such as Singapore. The increasing complexity of services sector transactions and links to manufacturing make it important to reinforce the rule of law and contract enforcement. The GVCs are based on complex webs of contracts among participating firms. So contract enforcement

BOX 2.10 Vietnamese successes in ICT services industries

Although the environment for Vietnam's ICT-related businesses is challenging, some success stories provide models for emulation. One is Mobivi, which started as a mobile payment platform designed by an overseas Vietnamese entrepreneur. But given low margins in that market, however, the company changed tack in 2011 to develop iCare, an employee benefits company focused on the market segment of workers making $200–$250 a month. It facilitates purchase of consumer goods by factory workers using interest-free installment plans. It relies heavily on ICT, including through SMS and website-based purchasing. Mobivi's business model is to sell at the retail price and purchase at the wholesale price, which allows for a wide margin (20–30 percent). Success at home has provided the basis for moving into other markets including Cambodia, India, Indonesia, and the Lao People's Democratic Republic.

Other successes include VNG Corporation, which began in game development and recently shifted into social networking. Appota began by licensing games from China and has now created its own mobile platform for digital content.

The list of such stories is not, however, as long as it could or has to be given Vietnam's ambitious development plans. The technical talent exists, but managerial skills are harder to find. Similarly, some venture capital firms from the United States and Japan are in Vietnam. But the network is not strong enough to support the potential volume of activity. Nor are exit strategies obvious: the only ICT firms on the stock exchange are large SOEs.

is important for joining—and especially moving up—higher value-added chains.

Vietnam could also leverage its membership in ASEAN to push services-related reforms regionally. ASEAN remains restrictive on services trade: the average Services Trade Restrictions Index (STRI) for the region is 60 percent higher than the global average. Vietnam's STRI scores fall below (better than) the ASEAN average in all subsectors, which reflects healthy progress on related regulations (figure 2.24). Given the importance of the sector to growth prospects, Vietnam has much to gain from giving more impetus to broad-based service trade facilitation within ASEAN. Although ASEAN is committed to liberalizing service trade, the focus has been on formal barriers. But even then implementation has been mixed. Attention will need to turn from clear restrictions to more challenging issues, such as harmonizing regulations.

FIGURE 2.24 Vietnam's Services Trade Restrictions Index scores are better than the Association of Southeast Asian Nations' average in all subsectors, reflecting progress on related regulations, 2012

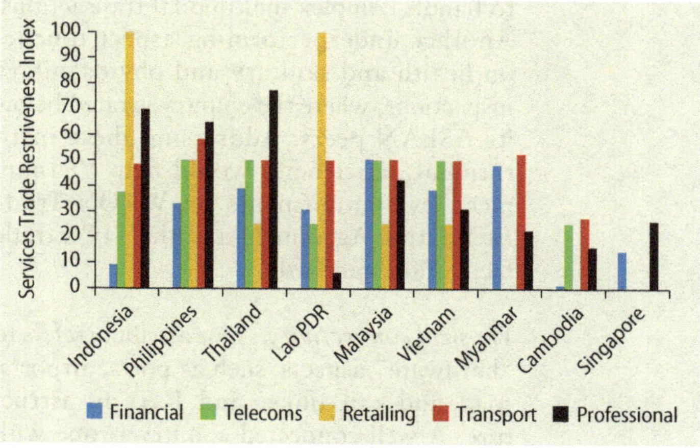

Source: Gootiiz and Mattoo 2015.
Note: STRI = Services Trade Restrictions Index.

Improving connectivity for trade

As Vietnam integrates more fully and profitably with GVCs, it must also boost its connectivity. Firms in value chains need to be able to move goods within Vietnam and across its borders cost-effectively and reliably. This will keep inventory carrying costs low and comply with the strict requirements of lead firms for on-time delivery. Connectivity has three key attributes, all requiring policy attention.

Institutional connectivity. This is the "software" side of things and includes trade facilitation, structural and regulatory reforms, and transport and logistics facilitation. Vietnam performs relatively well on the World Bank's Logistics Performance Index

(LPI), ranking 48th of 160 countries on the overall rating. It is also the highest among the lower-middle-income countries, although still lagging regional upper-middle-income countries such as China, Thailand, and Malaysia. Its rankings have improved since 2007 across the board, except for customs procedures (table 2.3).

Some areas of weakness remain. The critical bottleneck relates to hundreds of complicated noncustoms regulations permitting trade activities across the border. These activities are managed and granted by a raft of state management agencies.[40] The overall regulatory approach is piecemeal, at times overlapping and contradictory. Despite the recent progress in customs reform and the implementation of the National and ASEAN Single Window, compliance costs in time and money for goods clearance on and behind the border remain high. And development of the trade logistics sector—a core part of the connectivity agenda—still has no national action plan. Local logistics service suppliers, while numerous, do not always have the capacity to handle complex multimodal transactions. Another underperforming aspect touches on health and sanitary and phytosanitary inspections, where the country is rated below its ASEAN peers. Addressing these institutional deficiencies would help Vietnam meet its commitments on WTO's Trade Facilitation Agreement and the TPP's trade facilitation standards.

Physical connectivity. This attribute refers to "hardware" aspects, such as ports, airports, road and rail links, and ICT infrastructure. A well-connected country is one with abundant and high-quality physical infrastructure, especially international gateways and multimodal interfaces. It also includes energy, which is vital to the continued success of manufacturing firms and can be effectively traded among neighboring countries.

While Vietnam comes out well on the infrastructure component of the LPI (ranking 44th in the world), many aspects of the transport infrastructure require attention to keep pace with rapidly rising demand. Current modes are overloaded in and around the major economic clusters and these do not connect well to each other or to major trade gateways. This reflects lack of coordination to develop economic zones and transport corridors. Key issues include poor road conditions and grossly underdeveloped freight-rail and inland-waterway infrastructure. Another key issue includes supply–demand mismatches in deepwater maritime port infrastructure. Lingering shortcomings in connective infrastructure explain why the country faces elevated logistics costs—roughly 21 percent of GDP, against an estimated 15 percent in Thailand and 19 percent in China. They also explain why global investors consider Vietnam-based supply chains unreliable. From a trade competitiveness angle, freight and logistics are not yet key drivers of direct investment, whether foreign or domestic.

Though Vietnam's expressways require further investment, transport expenditures need to be rebalanced from roads (the costliest form of domestic freight transport) to multimodal facilities (for handling and storing goods in high-capacity warehousing). This will be needed to take advantage of more cost-effective transport modes, such as

TABLE 2.3 Logistics Performance Index rankings

	Overall LPI	Customs	Infrastructure	International shipments	Logistics quality and competence	Tracking and tracing	Timeliness
Vietnam 2007	53	37	60	47	56	53	65
Vietnam 2014	48	61	44	42	49	48	56
China 2014	25	27	26	10	32	23	31
Malaysia 2014	28	38	23	22	35	29	36
Thailand 2014	35	36	30	39	38	33	29

Source: Calculations based on World Bank Logistics Performance Index.

inland waterways and rail. Rebalancing will also be needed from capital spending to transport assets maintenance. Some 80 percent of public spending on transport goes primarily to expanding and then preserving the road network alone. Simultaneously, government departments meet only about 50–60 percent of maintenance spending needs for waterways nationally. As a result, the average size of barges plying Vietnam's vast waterway network in the Mekong and Red River deltas—estimated at 100 deadweight tons at year-end 2010—is well below the internationally recognized minimum threshold for economic efficiency of 1,000 deadweight tons. This reduces the cost efficiency, reliability, and environmental advantage of waterways against roads.

A push to mainstream integrated planning for transport and logistics across modes, locations, and public sector functions should be near the top of the government's agenda.

People-to-people connectivity. The third attribute refers to ease of movement of people across borders (for service provision, education, and tourism). Vietnam has abolished caps on the number of foreign workers that foreign firms can hire. It has also introduced new procedures for obtaining work permits for them. Managers, executives, and specialists who enter the country as intracorporate transferees are allowed to stay for an initial three years, subject to extension. But there is still wide scope to better meet global businesses' needs to bring in specialist international staff, since any restrictions affect Vietnam's attractiveness as a production destination. Improving proficiency in English, especially in the study of technical topics, and narrowing the skills gap of Vietnamese workers with international and regional standards will further improve opportunities for the country. Vietnamese workers and businesses could also be encouraged to seek better opportunities abroad, especially in markets with strong commercial links with Vietnam. As shown by India and other globally integrating developing countries, this can be an effective path to learn and absorb technology, foreign cultures, and good practices—and improve capabilities to work in a global environment. Finally, Vietnam could make easier the visa procedures for foreign tourists to better exploit its immense tourism potential.

Annex 2A Empirical Relationship among Political Connection, Firms' Access to Credit, and Profitability

The purpose of this research note is to estimate the relationships among political connection, access to credit, and firm performance in Vietnam. It does so by updating the results of an earlier published paper by Malesky and Taussig that pursued a similar line of inquiry (Malesky and Taussig 2008). Using a two-stage empirical approach, Malesky and Taussig found statistically significant evidence that connections influenced banks' credit allocation decisions in Vietnam (see table 2A.1). Updating the Malesky and Taussig analysis with more data, this note gets even stronger results of how connections influence credit access.

Specifically, the current analysis confirms a strong, statistically significant relationship between political connection and credit access. Results show that, while a firm with no connections has a 51 percent chance of receiving a loan, a firm with one connection to the provincial government has a 58 percent chance. Those with two and three connections, however, have chances of 67 percent and 71 percent, respectively. Firms with better credit access are found not to be more profitable. The current analysis supports Malesky and Taussig's conclusion that the most profitable investors in Vietnam have forgone the formal banking system, preferring to finance their activities out of reinvested earnings or informal loans.

TABLE 2A.1 Main results

Key variables	Malesky and Taussig	Current note
Political connections variables (instruments)		
Share of firms with connection with local authorities	0.320	0.287
Share of firms with 1 connection	0.316	0.274
Share of firms with 2 connections	0.004	0.012
Share of firms with 3 connections	0.000	0.001
Share of firms with credit*independent variable)	0.512	0.546
Firm performance (outcome variables)		
Net profit or losses after taxes and operating expenditure (8-point scale in 2006 but 5-point scale in 2009–14)	4.37	3.50
Employment size (8 categories)	2.98	2.69
Capital size (8 categories)	2.87	3.09
Empirical strategy		
Other firm control variables	Having land-user-right certificate, firm age, equitized, share owned by the government, sector	
Other province control variables	PCI, SOE share of credits, firm distribution	Province fixed effects
Method used to address selection of credit	Heckman selection	Instrumental variable
Period observed	2006	2009–14
Number of observations	6,319	36,089
Impact of political connection on credit (first-stage estimates)		
Connection (dummy)	0.034**	0.054***
Connection (scale variable)	0.036**	0.044***
Impact of political connection on profitability (reduced form estimates)	0.0431	0.006
Impact of credit on profitability (second-stage estimates)	0.046	0.308
Impact of credit on investment growth (between year t and t–1) (second-stage estimates)	0.0894***	0.112***

*$p < 0.05$, **$p < 0.01$, ***$p < 0.001$.
Note: PCI = Provincial Competitiveness Index; SOE = state-owned enterprise.

Data

The note uses data from 2009–14 Provincial Competitive Index Surveys of the domestic private enterprises. The data are representative at the provincial level. The final repeated cross-sectional dataset includes 36,089 observations covering the five-year period.[41]

Political connection is defined based on information about employment history of a business owner before the firm is established. It contains (i) whether the owner was a government or military officer, (ii) whether the owner was working as a manager in an SOE enterprise, or (iii) whether the owner was working as an employee in an SOE enterprise. The variable, therefore, is either a dummy indicating whether a firm has one of these characteristics or a categorical variable indicating whether a firm has none, one, or all three characteristics.

Access to credit is defined as having a loan from a formal bank (whether a state-owned or private commercial bank).

Outcome variables include: profitability (scale from 1–5), growth in investment, or growth in number of employees.

Empirical Method

The empirical strategy is a two-stage instrumental variable (henceforth IV) estimation.[42]

Correlation estimation

Reduced form. Relationship among political connection, credit access, and a firm's performance—ordinary least square estimation.

Causal estimation (addressing the selection bias of credit access)

First stage. The impact of political connection on a firm's credit access—political connection is an instrument for a firm's credit access.

Second stage. The impact of whether firms having loans (predicted from the first stage) on the firm's performance.

All estimates control for province-fixed effects (which reflect the difference in the Provincial Competitiveness Index, the nature of loan market, and development) and time-fixed effects (which account for inflation and economic cycles).[43] The standard errors are adjusted for heteroskedasticity and within-cluster correlation (clustered by province).

Empirical Results

Political connections have a strong and statistically significant effect on a firm's credit access. In the ordinary least squares estimation with full-scale measure of connection—holding other things constant—having one connection to the provincial government increases the probability of a loan by about 4.4 percent.[44] Whereas a firm with no connections has a 51 percent probability of receiving a loan, a firm with one connection to the provincial government has a 58 percent probability. Those firms with two or three connections have 67 percent and 71 percent probabilities, respectively, of receiving loans.[45] Though the magnitude of the impact decreases—as low as 3.0 percent—if we account for provincial fixed effects, the coefficient on political connections remains highly significant.

The reduced form regressions find that neither access to bank credit nor a firm's "connectedness" correlates with profitability. The IV estimation, which accounts for the selection bias, reveals no causal impacts of credit access on profitability.

Other important determinants of profitability, according to the ordinary least squares reduced form, are sector (manufacturing and agriculture are less profitable than services), land-user-right certificate, and especially employment size. Unlike the Malesky and Taussig analysis, higher capital (measured as total asset) is not associated with being more profitable.

Potential Limitations

Selection bias is the main source of concern for this type of analysis. More profitable firms are likely to have more retained surplus to reinvest, potentially offsetting their desire to seek bank credit. This note has sought to address the reverse causality by using the IV technique mentioned above.

TABLE 2A.2 Selected agribusiness sectors and upgrading potential in Vietnam

Sector	Key reasons for selection
Specialty rice mills	• Little need for investment in general rice mills because local investors continue to expand mills and have access to requisite capital, technology, and skills • Sufficient general rice grades from local mills for current buyers • Investors are keen to build specialty rice mills (fragrant, glutinous, etc.), if local authorities and farmer groups are ready to work with them to organize farmers to grow these rice varieties • Investors see rising demand and prices and want to secure supply • For Vietnam, these investments offer potential to increase higher-value rice exports, raise farmer incomes, and reduce costs (since investors will want to work with farmers to introduce new varieties, minimize fertilizer and pesticide usage, and improve agronomy)
Rice-product manufacturing	• Growing demand for gluten-free products is raising global demand for rice-based products • Lead firms or investors with the latest gluten-free technologies and market-intelligence can assist in tapping into this market • The usual limitations on shipping bulky or fragile items may limit some opportunities. But for global food companies seeking to tap into this growth trend, Vietnam could be a natural choice

(Table continued next page)

TABLE 2A.2 Selected agribusiness sectors and upgrading potential in Vietnam *Continued*

Sector	Key reasons for selection
Specialty (arabica) coffee mills	• Investors see little value in investing in Robusta processing mills. Professional wet or dry milling does not add sufficient value to beans over standard farmer-processed beans • Investors are interested in building mills for arabica in suitable area if local authorities and farmer groups are ready to work with them to organize farmers to grow more arabica • Investments offer potential to increase higher-value coffee exports, raise farmer incomes, and reduce costs (with improved varieties, fertilizer and pesticide usage, and agronomy) • Suitable arabica areas are in remote parts of the Central and Northern Highlands, where farmers have fewer income opportunities
Fruit, vegetable, and flower farms—storage, grading, and packing	• Compared with other agri-export leaders, Vietnam currently exports limited volumes of fresh fruit, vegetables, and flowers • Even for the domestic market, modern chilled warehousing, transport, and packing operations are surprisingly underdeveloped • Attracting lead firms to help establish state-of-the-art, fresh-produce handling centers near Hanoi and Ho Chi Minh City airports—for domestic and export markets—would create increased income opportunities for Vietnam's fruit, vegetable, and flower farmers
Fruit and vegetable—secondary processing	• Similarly, development of fruit and vegetable processing facilities (juicing/drying/canning/ freezing) will assist in expanding exports and enable farmers to generate revenues beyond fresh sales during harvest season
Aquaculture—primary processing	• Numerous local firms already doing well and expanding fast • Sector could benefit from new investment in latest technologies, market access, brands, etc. • Particular opportunity in new areas where Vietnam has not yet developed significant expertise, such as marine and seaweed farming
Aquaculture—secondary processing	• Significant opportunity to attract investors with technology and know-how to tap into underdeveloped high-value segments, such as smoked fish • Opportunity to attract investors with technology and know-how to develop improved fish-oil and fish-meal processing facilities • Despite volumes, feed producers complain that current fish-meal quality in Vietnam is inferior and they still need to import fish-meal

Source: McKenna 2015 based on International Finance Corporation.

TABLE 2A.3 Vietnamese unit prices for key export crops compared with world averages

	Average export revenues (US$ per ton)			
			Value gap	
Major export products	**World**	**Vietnam**	**n**	**%**
Rice	639	514	125	20
Aquaculture products	2,100	1,967	133	6
Rubber	5,307	4,189	1,118	21
Coffee	4,037	2,191	1,846	46
Tea	3,333	1,594	1,739	52

Source: McKenna 2015 based on IFC (FAOSTAT, FAO Fisheries & Aquaculture Statistics Yearbook 2012, UNCTAD/ITC Trade Map).

TABLE 2A.4 Main global motor vehicle parts suppliers in Vietnam

Company	Product(s)	Nationality	Year of major investment(s)
Sumitomo, various companies including Sumiden VN Automotive Wire; Sumi-Hanel Wiring Systems; SEWS Components	Wire harnesses and wiring components	Japan	Various years
Yazaki,	Wire harnesses and wiring components	Japan	2001

(Table continued next page)

TABLE 2A.4 Main global motor vehicle parts suppliers in Vietnam *Continued*

Company	Product(s)	Nationality	Year of major investment(s)
Hitachi Cable	Wire harnesses	Japan	2008
Denso San Pham	Various engine parts, gas pedal assemblies, etc.	Japan	2001
Bridgestone	Tires for passenger vehicles	Japan	2014
Yokohama	Tires for motorcycles, light trucks, and industrial vehicles	Japan	1997
IRC	Tires for motorcycles	Japan	1997
Kumho Tires	Tires for passenger vehicles	Korea, Rep.	2008
Hyundai Kefico	Sensors and actuators for vehicles	Japan	2010
Toyota Boshoku	Seats and interior parts; side curtain airbags	Japan	1996 and 2004
Robert Bosch	Pushbelts used for continuously variable transmission (CVT) in automobiles. Embedded software and mechanical design, as well as IT and IT-enabled services for local and regional customers.	Germany	2008: Gasoline Systems Division 2011: Engineering and Business Solutions Division
Asahi Denso	Ignition switches and locks for motorcycles	Japan	2006
Exedy	Clutches for motorcycles	Japan	2006
Kyocera Vietnam	Ceramic components and connectors	Japan	2014
Toyoda Gosei	Bags for airbag modules	Japan	2005

TABLE 2A.5 Classification of sectors for investment

Prohibited for all investors	Conditional for all investors	Conditional for foreign investors
• Projects detrimental to national defense, security, and public interest	• Sectors impacting national defense, security, and social order	• Radio and television broadcasting
• Projects detrimental to historical and cultural traditions and ethics	• Banking and finance	• Production, publishing, and cultural products distribution
• Projects detrimental to people's health or that destroy natural resources and the environment	• Sectors impacting public health	• Mining and minerals processing
• Projects for treatment of imported toxic wastes	• Culture, information, press, and publishing	• Telecommunications and Internet services
• Other projects banned by law	• Entertainment services	• Public postal networks, postal and delivery services
	• Real estate	• Construction and ports and airports operation
	• Mining and natural resources exploitation	• Goods and passengers transport
	• Education and training	• Fishing
	• Other sectors in accordance with law	• Tobacco production
		• Real estate
		• Import, export, and distribution
		• Education and training
		• Hospitals and clinics
		• Other sectors as per international treaties

Source: Molinuevo 2015, based on the United Nations Conference on Trade and Development (UNCTAD) 2008.

Annex 2B Growth Accounting to Identify Sources of Growth

This annex develops a growth accounting framework to estimate the contributions of capital (physical and human), labor, and total factor productivity (TFP) to long-term GDP and labor productivity growth.

The starting point is the standard neoclassical constant-returns-to-scale Cobb-Douglas production function to describe overall production:

$$(2A.1) \quad Y_t = A_t K_t^{\alpha} (L_t H_t)^{(1-\alpha)}$$

where Y symbolizes real GDP, K is the physical capital stock, A is the Solow residual that represents TFP, α is the share of capital stock in output under perfect competition, L is the employed labor force, and H a measure of human capital based on education stock and returns on education. (A more accurate proxy for human capital would also include learning-by-doing, but lack of data precludes this here.) L*H therefore may be viewed as *effective labor.*

Following Klenow and Rodriguez-Clare (1997), H is further defined as $= e^{0.rS}$, S is the average number of years of schooling per worker, and r is the rate of return on a unit increase in S.

The initial stock of capital in Vietnam in 1989 is assumed to be twice the size of GDP. The capital stock data are then extended through 2013 using the perpetual inventory method.

(2A.2) K_t = *(1–geometric depreciation rate)* K_{t-1} + *Gross Fixed Capital Formation (t–1).*

Dividing both sides of (2A.1) by Y_t^{α} and solving for Y_t gives

(2A.3) $Y_t = (K_t/Y_t)^{\alpha/(1-\alpha)}(L_tH_t)Z_t$

Where $Z_t = A_t^{1/(1-\alpha)}$ is total factor productivity measured in labor-augmenting units.

Divide both sides of (2A.3) by L to get

(2A.4) $Y_t/L_t = (K_t/Y_t)^{\alpha/(1-\alpha)}H_tZ_t$

The left hand side of (2A.4) is output per worker or *labor productivity.*

All data except for S are from the General Statistics Office of Vietnam. The data on S, the average years of school attainment by population aged 15 years or more, are from the updated Barro and Lee (2013) database on education attainment. The frequency of the Barro-Lee database is every five years and their data extend until 2010. The annual data within each five-year period is filled using the assumption of a constant geometric growth rate within that period.

Assume r = 0.1, which is the general assumption in the literature.

From (2A.4), the growth rate of labor productivity may be written as

TABLE 2B.1 Sources of GDP growth in Vietnam

	1990–2000 (%)	2000–2013 (%)	2013–2035 (%)
Labor productivity (GDP per worker) growth	5.2	3.8	5.6
Human capital growth	1.6	1.5	1.3
a = 0.4			
TFP growth	4.2	0.1	3.6
*a/(1–a)**Capital-output ratio growth	–0.5	2.2	0.5
Contribution of TFP growth to labor productivity growth	79.8	1.7	65.2
Contribution of capital deepening	–10.2	57.3	9.2
Contribution of human capital growth	29.8	40.1	24.2
a = 0.33			
TFP growth	4.0	0.6	3.8
*a/(1–a)**Capital-output ratio growth	–0.4	1.6	0.4
Contribution of TFP growth to labor productivity	77.0	16.5	67.7
Contribution of capital deepening	–7.6	42.2	6.8
Contribution of human capital growth	29.8	40.1	24.2
a = 0.33 in 1990 gradually increasing to 0.38 in 2014 and 0.42 in 2035*			
TFP growth	3.8	0.0	3.1
*a/(1–a)**Capital-output ratio growth	–0.5	2.2	0.5
Contribution of TFP growth to labor productivity	72.1	0.1	55.0
Contribution of capital deepening	–2.9	58.8	19.2
Contribution of human capital growth	29.8	40.1	24.2

Note: (1) r = 0.1, a standard assumption in the literature for Mincerian return to education. (2) Average annual GDP growth for 2015–35 assumed at 6.1 percent. (3) Average annual capital stock growth for 2015–35 assumed at 6.9 percent (compared with 8.5 percent for 1990–2015). (4) Average annual human capital growth for 2015–35 = 1.4 percent (compared with 1 percent for 1990–2015). (5) Average annual labor force growth for 2015–35 = 0.5 percent (compared with 2 percent for 1990–2015).
**a* gradually increases as the production function become increasingly more capital intensive with the changing structure of the economy from farming to industry and services.

(2A.5) *Labor productivity growth = TFP growth + $\alpha/(1-\alpha)$*capital-output ratio growth + human capital growth*

Applying (2A.5) and assuming 6.1 average percent GDP growth between 2015–2035 gives the results shown in table 2B.1.

Notes

1. The "Mexican phenomenon" refers to the formation of "two economies in one country," with a modern high-productivity economy led by multinational companies, and an outdated low-productivity economy created by a mass of small domestic businesses. The overall economy still grows, even though long-term growth is not sustainable.
2. This comparison excludes economies with a population less than 1 million and Bosnia and Herzegovina.
3. The standard deviation of Vietnam's annual per capita growth over 1991–2013 was 1.21. Across the world, out of a sample of 175 economies that had comparable data, only Guatemala and Swaziland's growth had a lower standard deviation than Vietnam's. In other words, growth in 172 out of the 174 comparator economies countries was more volatile than in Vietnam.
4. A substantial literature has established a negative causal effect of volatility on growth (for example, Ramey and Ramey 1995; Hnatkovska and Loayza 2004). In estimating the impact on growth if Vietnam had Thailand's growth volatility, we use coefficients estimated in Hnatkovska and Loayza (2004).
5. TFP growth reflects a combination of improved resource allocation, innovation, technological upgradation, institutional reforms, and a whole host of other factors that growth in factors of production leaves unexplained.
6. McMillan and Rodrik (2011) show a positive impact of structural transformation on labor productivity in East Asia but a negative impact in Latin America and in Africa.
7. McCullough (2015) also challenges this finding that agriculture is marked by lower productivity. Once the hours worked are controlled for, agriculture is as productive on average as manufacturing or services. The issue is that agricultural hours are concentrated in certain periods, with substantial periods when few hours of work are needed, leading to fewer overall hours worked in agriculture. Thus value added per person remains lower, even if value added per hour worked is the same.
8. The share of rural household income derived from primary agriculture fell from 43 percent in 2002 to 32 percent in 2012 as the number of agricultural households fell from 10 million to 9 million, reflecting farm to nonfarm movement.
9. An explicit policy bias toward growing rice to meet national security needs explains the inertia in crop diversification. For example, much of the irrigated lowland areas have been designated as rice lands, while the expansion of irrigation and a high proportion of public research and advisory service resources have also been geared toward meeting national or provincial rice production goals.
10. In 2010, Vietnam exported 2,580 products to 141 countries, more than twice as many products as a decade earlier (1,264), which were exported to 109 countries.
11. The ones that remain cover the sale of gasoline, diesel, and other fuels; electricity; liquid petroleum gas (LPG—cooking gas); chemical fertilizer (UREA and NPK); plant and vegetable insecticides; vaccination for husbandry; eating salt; milk for children under 6 years old; sugar (white and refined); paddy and ordinary rice; and preventive and treatment medicine for humans (defined on the list of basic and essential medicines).
12. The number of household businesses—registered and unregistered—grew rapidly, from 1 million in 1992 to close to 4 million by 2010 (Malesky and Taussig 2009).
13. Although productivity performance started to deteriorate after 1997 (likely triggered by the Asian crisis), we choose 2000 as the break point to separate the cyclical effects from the long-term trend effects.
14. This chapter defines large enterprises as those employing over 300 workers, medium-large 101–300, medium-small 51–100, and small 50 or fewer.
15. Tran Van Tho and Nguyen Thi Tue Anh, Background paper for Vietnam 2035 Report.
16. In 2009, labor productivity in small and medium-sized enterprises in Mexico was 8 percent of that of large enterprises (most of them multinationals), down from 28 percent in 1999, even as Mexico became the

5th largest carmaker in the world by reaping the benefits of the American Free Trade Agreement (NAFTA). This was an important factor in the low productivity growth (0.8 percent per year) of the country as a whole in the period 1999–2012 (Bolio et al 2014).

17. The two largest rivers in Vietnam—the Mekong and Red Rivers—originate from China. The Mekong flows through Myanmar, Thailand, Lao PDR, and Cambodia before flowing into Vietnam. The dozens of large hydropower projects built upstream, especially in China and Lao PDR, have had a huge impact on water resources and ecosystems in the Mekong Delta, exacerbating the effects of climate change in this region. Besides the comprehensive and long-term measures in managing water resources and living conditions in the Mekong Delta, Vietnam also needs to promote regional cooperation and argue for the role of international organizations to improve responsibilities and coordination between the countries in the basin and ensure a system that is fair for all.
18. Ownership policy should also define the state's role in the corporate governance of SOEs and how the government will implement its ownership policy. OECD 2005 Guidelines, p. 13.
19. There will be special situations where the focus of an SOE is not amenable to maximization of state capital. This could include SOEs involved in, for example, armaments production or cultural preservation. In such cases, it may be appropriate for the state shareholder to focus on productivity and technical efficiency measures as well as qualitative indicators of administrative, service, and corporate social responsibility performance, as SOE monitoring systems in the Republic of Korea and New Zealand have done.
20. For example, in Sweden, each SOE is expected to provide "economic value added" by earning more than the cost of its debt and equity capital. In Singapore, the Temasek state shareholding fund expects its government-linked corporations to maximize their financial performance on economic value added, return on assets, and return on equity.
21. China now has 0.1 centrally owned SOE for every million population. Advanced social-market jurisdictions range from 14.2 (Norway) to 0.4 (Netherlands) SOEs per million population, with a median of about 2.2. Low ratios are also found in Switzerland (1.0), Singapore (2.0), and Sweden (2.0). Applying these parameters to Vietnam's population of 93 million suggests a target portfolio of anywhere from nine to 214 centrally owned SOE parents. Twenty would allow for Vietnam's current state economic groups and some important SOEs beyond those.
22. These may include change in the controlling shareholder, relocation, major asset sales, merger, liquidation, or equity dilution.
23. Not every SOE parent/subsidiary will be appropriate for mixed private–public ownership. Exceptions may include SOEs involved in defense production or those of little or no interest to private investors.
24. This section draws on a background note prepared by Martha Martinez Licetti, Georgiana Pop, Tanja Goodwin, and Tuvshee Bold.
25. De facto independence of the competition authority could translate into a 17 percentage-point reduction in the productivity gap with the United States (Voigt 2009).
26. Hard-core cartels include firms acting in collusion and engaging in price fixing, market partitioning, and bid rigging.
27. For example, the consumer saving from merger control was estimated to be at least £640 million in 2000–05 (OECD 2012b), while in the United States, the Department of Justice reported consumer savings of about $1 billion for fiscal year 2009.
28. http://info.worldbank.org/governance/wgi/index.aspx#doc
29. This subsection on capital market reforms draws on Hanson (2015).
30. In Peru, the supervisory agencies are physically grouped together, and in addition to separate agencies for banks, insurance, and equity markets, a separate agency is included for systemically important institutions.
31. Eighteen percent of Vietnam's population borrowed from a financial institution in 2015, up from 16 percent in 2011. By comparison, in the average lower-middle-income country, only about 7.5 percent of the population has current borrowings from a financial institution (Global Financial Development Database).
32. Per the Global Financial Development Database, 31 percent of Vietnamese adults have accounts with financial institutions (although SBV puts that figure at 50 percent), much less than the average of 43 percent in lower-middle-income countries. The gap is even worse for poor adults—19 percent versus 33 percent.

33. While the remittance or the transfer to a deposit is being completed, typically within one day, the funds should be invested in a well-defined, trust account, as is best practice in countries that have developed remittances through mobile phones.
34. India, for example, is undertaking a countrywide provision of computerized personal identification.
35. According to a report by Nhân Dân (The People), the official Communist Party news agency, government bodies at all levels received more than 1.2 million complaints and denunciations between 2003 and 2010, of which 70 percent were related to land. http://www.nhandan.com.vn/mobile/_mobile_chinhtri/_mobile_tintucsukien/item/788102.html accessed October 19, 2015.
36. Including nonagricultural investment to enhance the rural institutional environment and improve human well-being; such investments relate to education, sanitation and clean water supply, and health care.
37. See http://www.digitaltrends.com/mobile/iphone-cost-what-apple-is-paying/.
38. This, according to the government, was in response to the perception that foreign firms were overpaying at the farm gate, while failing to invest in farm-extension services, as required by law. Domestic enterprises, which had supposedly invested more in extension services, were unable to match the foreign firms' higher purchasing prices. This encouraged farmers to break contracts with domestic firms (that is, they benefitted from the extension services but then failed to honor the terms of sale).
39. Some 40 million units were registered in 2014 for a population of 90 million, making Vietnam the fourth-largest two-wheeler market in the world after China, India, and Indonesia.
40. Nearly 300 trade-related procedures are regulated and required through a complex set of legislative documents and regulations for releasing export and imports, in addition to customs rules. These licenses are managed and granted by multiple state management agencies, including the Ministry of Industry and Trade (MOIT), the Ministry of Agriculture and Rural Development, the Ministry of Transport (MOT), the Ministry of Planning and Investment (MPI), the Ministry of Resources and Environment (MONRE), the Ministry of Health (MOH), the Border Defense Force of the Ministry of Defense (MOD), the Economic Police of the Ministry of Public Security (MPS), the Ministry of Science Technology and Environment (MOSTE), the Ministry of Culture, Sports, and Tourism (MCST), the Ministry of Construction (MOC), and the State Bank of Vietnam (SBV).
41. The PCI surveys started back in 2006 but the question about performance of an enterprise was changed in 2009, which makes it inconsistent to pool together the data of the whole period.
42. The Malesky and Taussig paper uses Heckman selection model (maximum likelihood estimation), which relies heavily on the nonlinearity assumption without identifying the exclusion restriction.
43. The Malesky and Taussig paper includes a series of province-specific variables but does not report the province-fixed effects. Since we are mainly interested in the impact of political connection other than local variables, we adopt the fixed-effect model which absorbs such province differentials.
44. The marginal effect in the Malesky and Taussig paper is 3.6 percent.
45. For ease of estimation, we employ a linear model for all estimates. In fact, the probit model indicates a nonlinear relationship with the marginal effects decreasing across political connection levels.

References

Agénor, Pierre-Richard, Otaviano Canuto, and Michael Jelenic. 2012. "Avoiding Middle-Income Growth Traps." Economic Premise 98, World Bank, Washington, DC.

Aterido, Reyes, and Mary Hallward-Driemeier. 2015. "Enterprise Dynamics and Job Flows in Vietnam 2004–12: Implications for Continued Dynamism for 2035." Background paper for Vietnam 2035 Report.

Barro, R., and J-W. Lee. 2013. "A New Data Set of Educational Attainment in the World, 1950–2010." *Journal of Development Economics* 104 (1): 184–98.

Berger, Roland. 2014. "Automotive Value Chain: Global Outlook (Study on Future Automotive Growth Markets)." Report for the World Bank Group with Redseer Consulting, World Bank, Washington, DC.

Bolio, Eduardo, Jaana Remes, Tomás Lajous, James Manyika, Morten Rossé, Eugenia

Ramirez. 2014. *A Tale of Two Mexicos: Growth and Prosperity in a Two-Speed Economy*. McKinsey Global Institute.

Boly, Amadou. 2015. "On the Benefits of Formalization: Panel Evidence from Vietnam." WIDER Working Paper 2015/038, United Nations University World-Institute for Development Economics Research (UNU-WIDER), Helsinki.

Broadberry, Stephen, and Nicholas Crafts. 2001. "Competition and Innovation in 1950s Britain." *Business History* 43 (1): 97–118.

Carlin, Wendy, Mark Schaffer, and Paul Seabright. 2004. "A Minimum of Rivalry: Evidence from Transition Economies on the Importance of Competition for Innovation and Growth." *Contributions to Economic Analysis and Policy* 3 (1): Article 17.

Chenery, Hollis. 1979. *Structural Change and Development Policy*. New York: Oxford University Press.

Commission on Growth and Development. 2008. *The Growth Report: Strategies for Sustained Growth and Inclusive Development*. Washington, DC: World Bank.

Cung, Nguyen Dinh. 2015. "Reform of the Mindset and Removal of Institutional Bottlenecks for Transformation to a Full-Fledged Market Economy in Vietnam." Working Paper, Central Institute for Economic Management (CIEM), Hanoi.

Dawe, David. 2015. "Agricultural Transformation of Middle-Income Asian Economies: Diversification, Farm Size and Mechanization." ESA Working Paper 15-04, Food and Agriculture Organization of the United Nations Agricultural Development Economics Division, Rome.

Dodsworth, John, Erich Spitäller, Michael Braulke, Keon Hyok Lee, Kenneth Miranda, Kenneth, Christian Mulder, Hisanobu Shishido, and Krishna Srinivasan. 1996. "Vietnam: Transition to a Market Economy." Occasional Paper 135, International Monetary Fund, Washington, DC.

Economic Statistics System (database). The Bank of Korea, Seoul. http://ecos.bok.or.kr/EIndex_en.jsp.

Eichengreen, Barry, Donghyun Park, and Kwanho Shin. 2011. "When Fast Growing Economies Slow Down: International Evidence and Implications for China." Working Paper 16919, National Bureau of Economic Research, Cambridge, MA.

Enoch, Charles. 2000. "Interventions in Banks during Banking Crises: The Experience of Indonesia." Policy Discussion Paper 00/02, International Monetary Fund, Washington, DC.

———. 2001. "Indonesia Banking Crisis: Two Years of Living Dangerously 1997–1999." Working Paper 01/52, International Monetary Fund, Washington, DC.

Evenett, Simon, Margaret Levenstein, and Valerie Suslow. 2001. "International Cartel Enforcement: Lessons from the 1990s." *The World Economy* 24 (9): 1221–45.

Feenstra, Robert. 1998. "Integration of Trade and Disintegration of Production in the Global Economy." *The Journal of Economic Perspectives* 12 (4): 31–50.

Fei, J. C. H., and G. Ranis. 1964. *Development of the Labor Surplus Economy: Theory and Policy*. Homewood, IL: Richard D. Irwin for the Economic Growth Center, Yale University.

Freeman, Nick, and Nguyen Van Lan. 2006. "Corporate Governance in Vietnam: The Beginning of a Long Journey." Private Sector Discussion 22, International Finance Corporation–Mekong Private Sector Development Facility, Washington, DC.

Gebreab, Frew Amare. 2002. "Getting Connected: Competition and Diffusion in African Mobile Telecommunications Markets." Policy Research Working Paper 2863, World Bank, Washington, DC.

General Statistics Office of Vietnam (database). Hanoi. https://www.gso.gov.vn/Default_en.aspx?tabid=491.

Global Entrepreneurship Monitor. 2013. *Viet Nam Report 2013*. Global Entrepreneurship Research Association, London Business School, London.

Goodwin, Tanja, and Martha Pierola Castro. 2015. "Export Competitiveness: Why Domestic Market Competition Matters." Public Policy for the Private Sector Note 348, World Bank, Washington, DC.

Gootiiz, Batshur, and Aaditya Mattoo. 2015. "Regionalism in Services: A Study of ASEAN." Policy Research Working Paper 7498, World Bank, Washington, DC.

Hanson, James. 2015. "Vietnam's Financial Sector and Its Development." Background paper for Vietnam 2035 Report.

Heritage Foundation (database). 2015. Washington, DC. http://www.heritage.org/index/explore.

Hnatkovska, V., and N. Loayza. 2004. "Volatility and Growth." In: *Managing Economic Volatility and Crises*, edited by J. Aizenmann and B. Pinto. Cambridge, UK: Cambridge University Press.

ILO (International Labour Organisation) and IFC (International Finance Corporation). 2014. "Better Work Vietnam: Garment Industry 7th Compliance Synthesis Report." Geneva: ILO.

Jones, Charles. 2015. "The Facts of Economic Growth." Working Paper 21142, NBER, Cambridge, MA.

Klenow, P., and A. Rodriguez-Clare. 1997. "The Neoclassical Revival in Growth Economics: Has It Gone Too Far?" *NBER Macroeconomics Annual* 12: 73–103.

Kinghan, Christina, and Carol Newman. 2015. "Social Capital, Political Connections, and Household Enterprises: Evidence from Vietnam." Working Paper 2015/001, World Institute for Development Economics Research (WIDER), United Nations University, Helsinki.

Korean Statistical Information System (KOSIS) (database). Statistics Korea. Daejeon, South Korea. http://kosis.kr/eng/.

Krugman. 1994. The Age of Diminished Expectations. Cambridge, MA: MIT Press.

Levenstein, Margaret, Valerie Suslow, and Lynda Oswald. 2003. "International Price-Fixing Cartels and Developing Countries: A Discussion of Effects and Policy Remedies." Working Paper 9511, National Bureau of Economic Research, Cambridge, MA.

Lewis, W. Arthur. 1954. "Economic Development with Unlimited Supplies of Labour." *The Manchester School* 22 (2): 139–91.

The Maddison-Project (database). 2013. Groningen, Netherlands. http://www.ggdc.net/maddison/maddison-project/home.htm.

Malesky, Edmund, and Markus Taussig. 2008. "Where Is Credit Due? Legal Institutions, Connections, and the Efficiency of Bank Lending in Vietnam." *Journal of Law, Economics, and Organization* 25 (2): 535–78.

———. 2009. "Out of the Gray: The Impact of Provincial Institutions on Business Formalization in Vietnam." *Journal of East Asian Studies* 9 (1): 249–90.

McCullough, Ellen. 2015. "Labor Productivity and Employment Gaps in Sub-Saharan Africa." Policy Research Paper 7234, World Bank, Washington, DC.

McKenna, Jonathan M. 2015. "Vietnam 2035: A Global Value Chain Perspective on Agribusiness." Background paper for Vietnam 2035 Report.

McMillan, Margaret, and Dani Rodrik. 2011. "Globalization, Structural Change and Productivity Growth." Working Paper 17143, National Bureau of Economic Research, Cambridge, MA.

Ministry of Human Resources and Social Security (MOHRSS) of the People's Republic of China (data). Beijing: MOHRSS. http://english.gov.cn/archive/statistics/.

Molinuevo, Martin. 2015. "The role of regulation in Vietnam's Services Sector." Background paper for Vietnam 2035 Report.

National Bureau of Statistics of China (NBSC) (database). Beijing: The State Council. http://www.stats.gov.cn/english/.

Nguyen, Cuong, and Quan Le. 2005. "Institutional Constraints and Private Sector Development: The Textile and Garment Industry in Vietnam." *ASEAN Economic Bulletin* 22 (3): 297–313.

North, Douglass C. 1990. *Institutions, Institutional Change, and Economic Performance*. Cambridge, UK: Cambridge University Press.

OECD (Organization for Economic Cooperation and Development). 2005. OECD *Guidelines on Corporate Governance of State-Owned Enterprises*. Paris: OECD.

———. 2012a. *OECD Review of Telecommunication Policy and Regulation in Mexico*. Paris: OECD.

———. 2012b. "Stock Taking on Evaluation." Working Party 2 on Competition and Regulation, Directorate for Financial and Enterprise Affairs, Competition Committee, OECD, Paris.

OECD/WTO Trade in Value (TiVA) database. Organisation for Economic Co-operation and Development–World Trade Organisation joint initiative, Paris. http://www.oecd.org/trade/valueadded.

Provincial Competitive Index (data), various years. Vietnam Chamber of Commerce and Industry (VCCI) and United States Agency for International Development, Hanoi. Available at: english/pcivietnam.org.

Pritchett, Lant. 1997. "Divergence, Big Time." *The Journal of Economic Perspectives* 11 (3): 3–17.

Ramey, Garey, and Valerie Ramey. 1995. "Cross-Country Evidence on the Link between Volatility and Growth." *The American Economic Review* 85 (5): 1138–51.

Sekkat, Khalid. 2009. "Does Competition Improve Productivity in Developing Countries?" *Journal of Economic Policy Reform* 12 (2): 145–62.

Steer, Liesbet, and Kunal Sen. 2010. "Formal and Informal Institutions in a Transition Economy: The Case of Vietnam." *World Development* 38 (11): 1603–15.

Symeonidis, George. 2008. "The Effect of Competition on Wages and Productivity: Evidence from the United Kingdom." *The Review of Economics and Statistics* 90 (1): 134–46.

Tu Anh, Vu Thanh, David Dapice, Nguyen Xuan Thanh, and Do Thien Anh Tuan. 2015. "A Retrospective on the Past 30 Years of Development in Vietnam." Background paper for Vietnam 2035 Report.

UNCTAD, Investment Policy Review Viet Nam, United Nations. 2008. New York and Geneva.

Urzua, Carlos. 2009. "Distributive and Regional Effects of Monopoly Power." Working Paper 2009–04, EGAP and Tecnológico de Monterrey, Mexico City.

Voigt, Stefan. 2009. "The Effects of Competition Policy on Development: Cross-Country Evidence Using Four New Indicators." *Journal of Development Studies* 45 (8): 1225–48.

World Bank. 2007. *An East Asian Renaissance: Ideas for Economic Growth*. Washington, DC: World Bank.

———. 2011. *Vietnam Development Report 2012: Market Economy for a Middle-Income Vietnam*. Washington, DC: World Bank.

———. 2014. "Vietnam: Financial Sector Assessment." Washington, DC: World Bank. http://documents.worldbank.org/curated/en/2014/06/20375067/vietnam-financial-sector-assessment.

———. n.d. Global Financial Development Database. World Bank, Washington, DC. http://data.worldbank.org/data-catalog/global-financial-development.

———. n.d. Logistics Performance Index (LPI). World Bank, Washington, DC. http://lpi.worldbank.org/.

———. n.d. Services Trade Restriction Index. World Bank, Washington, DC. http://iresearch.worldbank.org/servicetrade/.

———. n.d. World Development Indicators (database). World Bank, Washington, DC. http://data.worldbank.org/data-catalog/world-development-indicators.

World Economic Forum. 2014. *Global Competitiveness Report 2014–2015*. Geneva: World Economic Forum.

3

Building National Innovation Capacity

Main Messages

Vietnam's economic aspirations require it to raise its growth rate. As the previous chapter showed, the majority of new gross domestic product (GDP) will need to come from higher labor productivity. Most of that, in turn, will have to come from resuming total factor productivity (TFP) growth—from growth in new and better ways of combining labor and capital. Since 1990, Vietnam has grown mainly by expanding the labor force and both foreign direct investment (FDI) and domestic capital. But demographic shifts and limit of capital mobilization are now closing that option. Future growth will have to come from a labor force that works smarter with higher quality capital resources.

How will Vietnam achieve this? Following the path outlined in the previous chapter, improved policies, removal of distortions, better allocation of production factors, and a level playing field can provide the initial impetus for sustained, higher growth. These alone, however, cannot be the basis for long-term, sustained improvements in productivity and growth. They need to be complemented by widespread, intensive learning by workers in firms and on farms and by researchers, faculty, and students at research institutes, universities, and colleges. They need to bring new knowledge to bear on production. It will require employees possessing the knowledge and skills to produce goods and services that are several times more valuable than what they produce for each hour they work today. This process requires the support of institutions that allow continual updating of knowledge and skills.

In an innovation-led economy, new knowledge is used in most economic sectors and by most firms. Some firms conduct classic research and development (R&D). Others occasionally upgrade technology through capital investments or labor reorganization. Some added value will come from increased output volumes—making more with less. Some will come from increased quality—making products and services better than they are now. Firms will make products that did not exist before, and will use production techniques previously untried. The reiterative process of seeking new technologies to improve production is at the heart of an innovation-led economy, where success is marked by TFP gains.

Such learning requires firms—the demand side for innovation—to show greater urgency in pressing for new technologies and in raising their ability to absorb and use them.

Some gains come from putting firms under greater pressure to compete (Foundation I, box 3.1). Gains also come from helping them identify, adapt, and use knowledge and technology (Foundation II), including ensuring a sound, enabling environment. On the supply side, some gains entail raising R&D quality and relevance. Other enhancements involve improving the advanced human capital training system (Foundation III), such as the tertiary education system (Foundation IV). Success also includes ensuring that the demand and supply sides are appropriately linked.

In its most basic sense the national innovation system (NIS) encompasses organizations and policies that allow firms and workers to produce in new and better ways, continuously adding knowledge to products. At first much of the new knowledge will exist elsewhere in the world but will be new to Vietnam. Later more and more of it will be new to the world (frontier knowledge). Some of that new knowledge will be produced in Vietnam through R&D in its firms and universities.

Making this system function well is a decades-long process. Vietnam's NIS is weak and contributes little to output or growth. The good news is that if improvements begin now, the system can be strong as need grows. Few firms are held back by lack of indigenous R&D capacity. Failure to capitalize on spillovers from existing knowledge investments is a more binding constraint. As firms gradually become more knowledge-intensive, R&D will play a more decisive role in productivity and competitiveness. Vietnam needs to strengthen its NIS right away.

The proliferation of trade agreements, such as the Trans-Pacific Partnership, will affect knowledge production in Vietnam. It will deregulate labor markets and allow firms to import skills. But for the country to avoid being only a low-wage, low-skill labor provider in the Association of Southeast Asian Nations (ASEAN), it must recommit to

BOX 3.1 Four foundations of an innovation-led economy

The path to such an economy would build on four foundations:

Foundation I: Raising the demand for knowledge in firms, mainly by increasing the competitive pressure under which they operate. Many noneconomic factors—political connections, bureaucratic inefficiency, lack of competitive pressure—mean that firms that are not the best producers can survive, sometimes comfortably. Labor productivity does not have to grow to ensure a firm's survival, so productivity has stagnated. Raising competitive pressures will force firms to seek knowledge to stay in business.

Foundation II: Helping firms improve their capacity for "technology learning." This gradual process educates Vietnamese firms in the process and production technologies used elsewhere. It gives an advantage to the fastest-learning firms and prepares them to seek "frontier knowledge"—information that is new to the world.

Foundation III: Raising knowledge production, advanced human capital training, and R&D quantity, quality, and relevance. The tertiary education[a] and research sector would expand and improve quality while creating and deepening connections to the rest of the world. Vietnam's government research institutes (GRIs) and tertiary education institutions would achieve a new dynamism of responding to the need for relevant knowledge and skills.

Foundation IV: Continuously improving the quality and relevance of labor force skills through increased responsiveness and dynamism in tertiary education. The average worker raises his or her skills and human capital by completing more and better education in a wider range of economically useful disciplines. These workers enter firms not only with current skills, but as lifelong learners who update their knowledge and skills to stay current with leaders in their sectors and industries.

a. Throughout the chapter "tertiary education" will be used to refer to all formal postsecondary education leading to a recognized credential. Tertiary education institutions include universities, colleges, and postsecondary technical, and vocational institutions, among others. The term is used to emphasize that universities and university-level education should not be the sole focus of policy in this educational subsector.

developing a successful NIS. This would help it close the gap in technology and knowledge with the world's fast-growing and prosperous economies, one that threatens to widen rather than shrink. The next 20 years will see unprecedented challenges. Vietnam's response to climate change and environmental and energy concerns requires it to draw on the best (and continuously advancing) global knowledge.

The acceleration of information technology, robotics, and artificial intelligence will pose challenges and opportunities for domestic manufacturing and communications. Vietnam is an increasingly open economy, enmeshed in international markets and competition. Disruptive technological breakthroughs anywhere will affect it, but a modern NIS will prepare it to maximize the opportunities while managing the challenges.

Faster productivity growth that underlies continuing prosperity gains will require an unambiguous commitment to a dynamic private sector. Fundamental reforms to the tertiary education systems that produce higher-order human capital require the same clear commitment. Vietnam also needs to guarantee a business and education climate that values openness to new ideas and risk-taking. These elements were critical to the rapid growth in reference economies, such as the Republic of Korea, Singapore (with China, Vietnam's role models—box 3.2), and Taiwan, China. The Vietnamese government has, however, been a weak and inconstant partner to firms. And it has not sufficiently implemented reforms in the tertiary education and research systems. Both arenas need far greater dynamism to meet the challenges of the next 20 years.

This chapter reviews the state of the innovation system and proposes an agenda for improving it. It begins by assessing where Vietnam now stands in innovation capacity. It next looks at the demand side and examines how the need for knowledge and the absorptive capacity of firms can be improved. It then considers how the supply of knowledge and skills from higher education and research can be at its best. The last part of this chapter proposes a three-stage approach for developing national innovation capacity, with the goal of creating an innovation-led economy.

BOX 3.2 Who are Vietnam's role models?

East Asia's economies can offer lessons to Vietnam. The Republic of Korea and Singapore, for instance, proved successful in transitioning across sectors and promoting sectors of high value added. China is following a similar path.

Korea. With a population of 50.2 million, Korea seems closer to Vietnam in scale than Singapore or China. A key difference is that Korea relied little on FDI and developed its national champions from scratch. The Korean government had independence and disciplinary capacity to enforce a system of firms' access to government support based on their export performance. This helped create the Korean miracle. Vietnam's experience with state-owned enterprises suggests that its government does not have such independence or capacity.

Singapore. With a large multinational company (MNC) presence and a well-documented ability to move up the value chain, Singapore potentially offers many lessons in how to integrate into global value chains (GVCs) and develop the service sector. With a population of 5.4 million, it is perhaps a model for the large urban areas of Hanoi and Ho Chi Minh City. As with Japan and Korea, Singapore put tremendous emphasis on upgrading its private sector by improving productivity and quality.

China. China, like Vietnam, faces great challenges in developing an autonomous, high-quality innovation system to support local firms. Also like Vietnam, China's development model has relied heavily on FDI. But unlike Vietnam, China's population of 1.4 billion gives it bargaining leverage with MNCs in transferring technology and developing backward links.

Innovation Capacity: Where Is Vietnam Today?

Vietnam's performance on innovation is weak on both the demand and the supply sides of the innovation equation.

Foundation I: Demand for Knowledge in Firms

Current demand for knowledge by firms is negligible, manifest in a slowdown in productivity growth, aggregate competitiveness that lags regional comparators, and negligible firm demand for and production of R&D.

Productivity

Labor productivity grew in the 1990s, led by sharp increases in TFP. After 2000, TFP halted and stayed flat, and the labor productivity increases that followed the *Đổi Mới* slowed down significantly. Firms have added more workers and machinery. But because they are not improving their knowledge or technology, growth in output per hour worked is slowing down. Vietnam will be unable to close productivity gaps with the region's more advanced economies unless it raises its innovation performance.

Competitiveness

Crude measures of Vietnam's innovation capacity—its ability to identify, adapt, or invent technologies to become more productive and diversify into new goods—point to mixed performance. The Global Competitiveness Report 2015–16 ranks Vietnam 56th out of 140 countries on overall competitiveness (a massive improvement over a ranking of 68 in the previous year), while coming in 95th on higher education and training, 92nd on technological readiness, and 88th on innovation and business sophistication. This places it broadly in the same realm as India and Mexico but far below Chile, China, Korea, Malaysia, Thailand, and Taiwan, China (table 3.1).

R&D

Vietnam does not publish reliable, internationally comparable statistics on gross expenditure for research and development (GERD) or subcomponents—itself a policy gap to be closed. The best estimates of comparable GERD figures put spending at about 0.3 percent of GDP.[1] This is low and inadequate, worsened because the majority of spending is for staff salaries at government research institutes (GRIs). Perhaps three-fourths of these staff members may not be directly involved in research. This means that Vietnam is only spending about $1 per person a year on science and technology (S&T). Advanced Organisation for Economic Co-operation and Development (OECD) countries may spend closer to $1,000 per person.

TABLE 3.1 Vietnam's ability to identify, adapt, and invent new technologies and to become more productive and diversify into new goods is weak

Country	GCI 2015–16 rank (of 140)	Score (1–7)	GCI 2014–15 rank (of 148)
United States	3	5.61	3
Taiwan, China	14	5.28	14
Malaysia	18	5.23	20
Korea, Rep.	26	4.99	26
China	28	4.89	28
Thailand	32	4.64	31
Chile	35	4.58	33
Vietnam	**56**	**4.30**	**68**
Mexico	57	4.29	61
Brazil	75	4.08	57
India	55	4.31	71

Source: World Economic Forum 2015.
Note: GCI = Global Competitiveness Index.

The government's target to spend 1.5 percent of GDP on research and exploration (R&E) by 2015 and 2 percent by 2020—outlined in the Strategy for Science and Technology Development 2011–20—cannot be achieved by a massive government R&D push alone. The quality of spending—and the policies that define it—will be at least as important as the quantity. In advanced countries, private companies conduct the majority of R&D. Firms translate new knowledge into value-added productivity and growth. GERD tends to rise with development, reflecting that firms' decisions to invest in knowledge and R&D cannot be separated from decisions to accumulate physical capital (figure 3.1).[2]

The figure suggests, first, that Vietnam is below the average for R&D spending as a share of GDP against countries at similar levels of development. It is worth noting that China's and India's unusually high GERD and patenting rates (table 3.2) are caused by the vast R&D and patenting activities of multinational corporations and cannot be compared to Vietnam's (Branstetter, Li, and Veloso 2013). Second, the figure suggests that raising GERD productively accompanies a rise in national income and removal of barriers to investment in physical and knowledge capital. Reflecting in part the low levels and quality of R&D activity, Vietnam is far behind comparator countries in patenting activity, with 0.01 patents per 100,000 people (table 3.2).

FIGURE 3.1 Countries' research and development expenditure tends to rise with overall development level

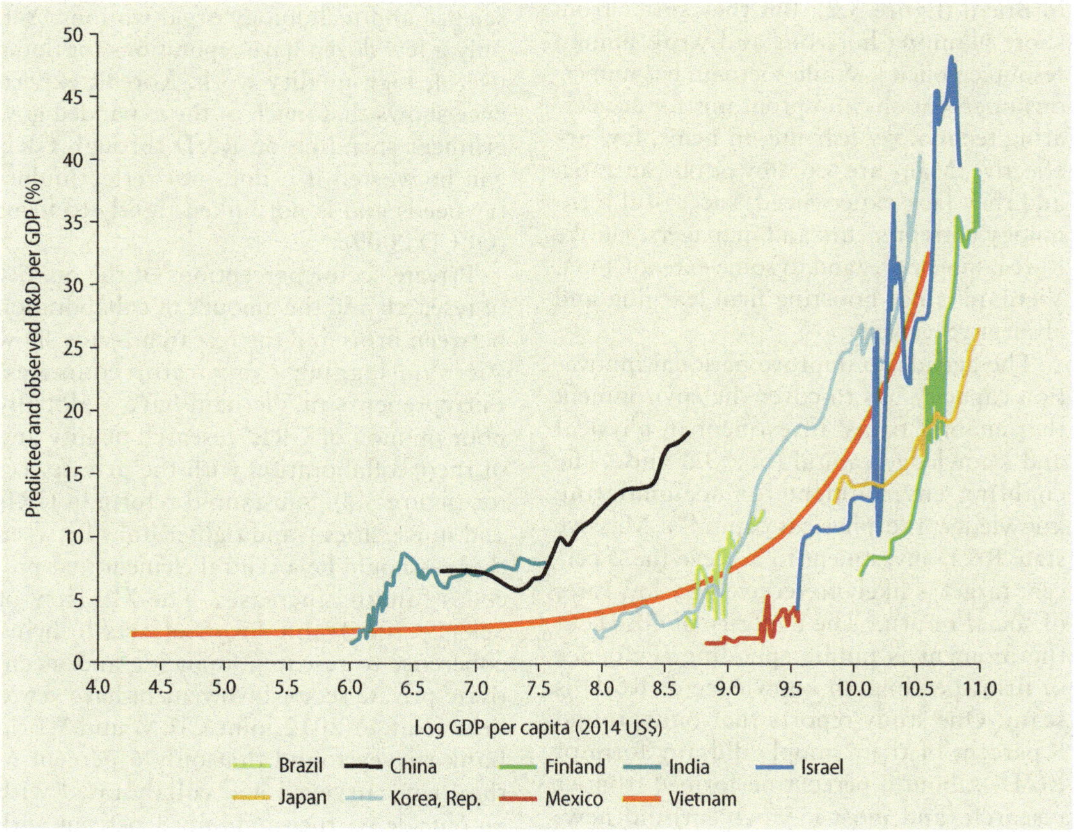

Source: Goni and Maloney 2014.

TABLE 3.2 Vietnam is far behind comparator countries in patenting activity, reflecting weak research and development activity

	Patents	
	Total	Per 100,000 population
United States	277,835	88.52
Korea, Rep.	14,548	29.09
China	5,928	0.44
India	2,424	0.19
Brazil	254	0.13
Mexico	155	0.13
Thailand	77	0.12
Chile	54	0.31
Vietnam	**5**	**0.01**

Source: U.S. Patent and Trademark Office Database (http://www.uspto.gov/learning-and-resources/open-data-and-mobility).

Foundation II—Firms' Capacity for Technology Learning

Vietnamese firms are better managed than expected, considering the country's level of development. They rank between firms in India and China and about equal to those in Brazil (figure 3.2). But they suffer from short planning horizons and weak human resource policies. While Vietnam has numerous interventions and programs for accelerating technology learning in firms, few are effective. Many are too slow or bureaucratic, and they lack experienced, successful technology entrepreneurs and managers. Unlike Korea, Singapore, and to some extent China, Vietnam is not boosting firm learning and absorptive capacity.

The agenda to improve national innovation capacity has to cover the environment that enables firms' investment in physical and knowledge capital (box 3.3 and "The enabling environment for accumulating knowledge and physical capital"). Massive state R&D investment to achieve the 2 percent target is likely to receive very low rates of social return.[3] The majority of GERD at the moment is public spending. Evidence of firm spending on knowledge or R&D is scant. One study reports that only around 8 percent of their sample did any form of R&D—about 3 percent performed frontier research, and most (55 percent) did new-to-the-firm research (Rand and Tarp 2012). A 2012 World Bank and Central Institute for Economic Management survey of 352 employers showed that only 10 percent had a dedicated R&D unit with modest average spending. Even this seems high, given aggregate spending measured (OECD–World Bank 2014). Both studies draw samples of firms that represent the formal private sector or state-owned enterprises (SOEs). But the two types of firms employ only 7.4 million workers, 15 percent of Vietnam's labor force of 52.6 million. Demand for and production of R&D in the rest of the firms (most of them in the informal sector) is likely to be miniscule.

Foundation III—The Quantity, Quality, and Relevance of High-Order Knowledge Production

R&D is conducted almost exclusively in the public sector, within a system of many small GRIs. Official statistics list more than 600 GRIs and more than 2,000 registered science and technology organizations. Yet, only a few dozen have reputations for doing useful, high-quality work. Korea's experience shows that much of the expanded government spending on R&D through GRIs can be wasted if it does not reflect industry needs and is not linked tightly to firms (OECD 2009).

Private sector perceptions of the quality of research and the amount of collaboration between firms and the research sector show Vietnam lagging comparator countries. Entrepreneurs in Vietnam have a globally poor opinion of GRIs' research quality and of their collaboration with the private sector (figure 3.3). Substantial reform in GRIs and universities—and tighter links between them—should be a central element that precedes funding increases. The Ministry of Science and Technology's efforts to bring coherence to research financing and incentivize private sector involvement have yet to bear fruit. A 2012 joint CIEM and World Bank survey found that only 6 percent of the firms surveyed had collaborated with an outside partner and only 1 percent with a university or GRI (OECD–World Bank 2014, 118).

Research productivity is also low for the country's income. In 2011, researchers in Vietnam published only 432 articles in journals included in the Science Citation Index and Social Sciences Citation Index.[4] This puts Vietnam ahead of Indonesia and the Philippines but comes to less than one article a year for each GRI, which should concern policy makers. Low- and middle-income countries—such as Jordan, Kenya, and Morocco—are around the same absolute output, despite populations several times smaller than Vietnam's. Vietnam's publications nearly doubled between 2006 and 2011, but in any given year tiny Singapore still publishes 10 times more articles.

Domestic graduate education and advanced training of human capital are also weak, although a bright spot is appearing as the government sends qualified students abroad for PhD training. But Vietnam maintains separate systems for conducting

FIGURE 3.2 Vietnam performs better than expected on management practices, given its income level

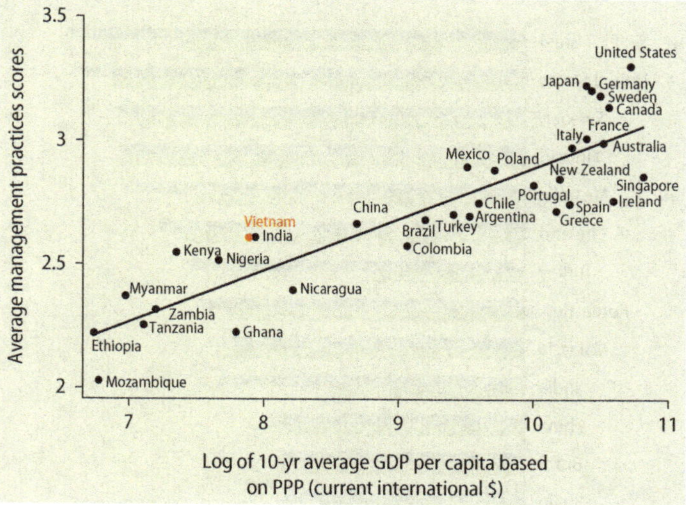

Source: Bloom et al. 2015.
Notes: April 2013, World Economic Outlook (IMF); PPP = purchasing power parity.

BOX 3.3 How a sound national innovation system promotes firm learning

In a well-developed national innovation system, R&D is not an end in itself. It is the way firms constantly improve the quality of their products, lower prices, and gain advantage over their competitors. Businesses become "learning firms" not because they want to, but because they must to stay in business. If they stop learning and improving, their competitors will offer better products at better prices, taking away market share, revenues, and profits.

The product cycle for smart phones shows how concretely firm learning is tied to these three fundamental aspects of firm health. Converting research into the powerful computing and communications technologies of smart phones, leading firms such as Apple and Samsung expect to keep improving. Samsung steals Apple's customers with its larger display screen, and Apple steals them back with a fingerprint recognition lock. A relentless drive to incorporate more knowledge into their products puts these two firms at the forefront of innovation—not because they find R&D interesting but because they need its results to survive.

An NIS is healthy and effective when it supports the highest number and quality of competitions among firms to see which can commercialize knowledge best. Under pressure to improve, firms seek knowledge through R&D and capable employees. And they spend time and energy to make sure they can use it well. Early in this process governments can often selectively accelerate firm learning by providing technological consulting services, tax breaks for R&D, and intellectual property right protection. They can also accelerate firm learning by linking knowledge suppliers in universities and government research institutes.

An effective NIS allocates funding to basic research for the next generation of advances. Simultaneously, it exploits the commercial potential of current knowledge—balancing long- and short-term goals. Policies fund the most productive researchers and ensure continuous review of the quality and relevance of research results. Career advancement for researchers should depend on the extent to which they meet these goals and make knowledge ready for firms to use.

Human capital, some representing specialized research skills, is as important as R&D. The growing ranks of complementary skills—such as management, marketing, and logistics—are equally important. They help the firm synergize everything into a knowledge-intensive product designed to impress customers.

FIGURE 3.3 Vietnamese entrepreneurs view scientific institutions and university–private sector collaboration as lagging

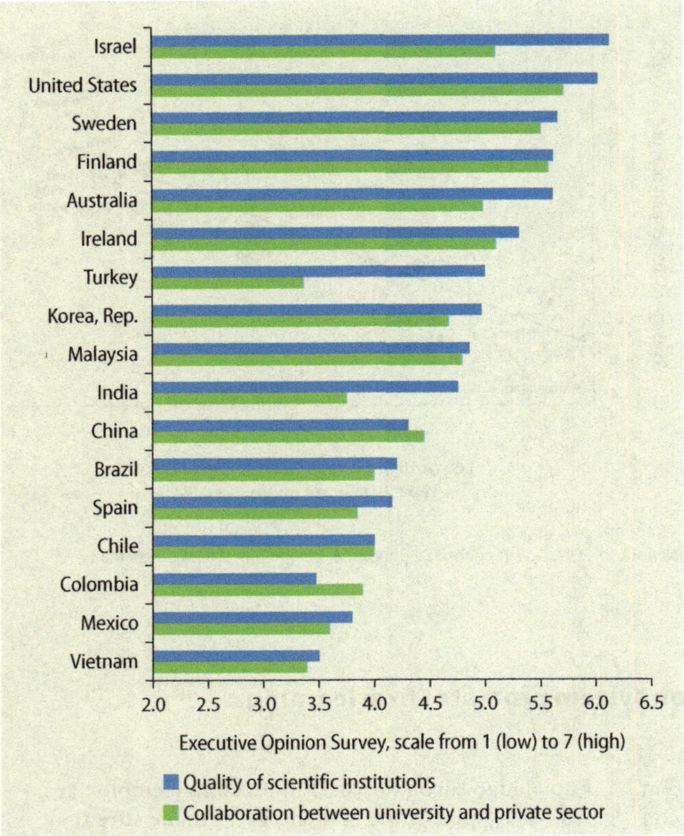

Source: World Economic Forum 2010.

research (mostly in GRIs) and for training researchers and advanced human capital (through the graduate education system). This raises the costs of both systems while lowering effectiveness.

Foundation IV—The Quality and Relevance of Skills in the Labor Force

The quality of workforce skills suffers from structural deficiencies in Vietnam's tertiary education system. Total undergraduate enrollment increased by 57 percent between 2005 and 2012. But the country barely kept pace with its competitors in G20 and OECD countries (table 3.3). Students' choice on whether to attend—plus what and where to study—continues to be hampered by various bureaucratic and regulatory obstacles.

Recent reforms have sought to create more autonomous and responsive tertiary education institutions, but intentions have run ahead of accomplishments. Policies to increase institutional autonomy have devolved some decisions, but far too many institutional decisions are still subject to governmental review or approval. Even the most independent tertiary education institutions operate within narrow confines

TABLE 3.3 Workforce skills suffer from structural deficiencies in the tertiary education system

	2005	2010	2011	2012	Growth (%)
Population (18–24 years old)	9,168,000	9,245,400	8,465,200	7,887,800	
Share of tertiary enrollment (%)	15.1	23.4	26.1	27.6	
Undergraduate					
Total enrollments	1,387,107	2,162,106	2,204,313	2,177,299	57
Colleges	299,294	726,219	756,292	724,232	142
Universities	1,087,813	1,435,887	1,448,021	1,453,067	34
Total graduates	210,944	318,345	402,277	425,208	102
Colleges	67,927	130,966	169,400	176,917	160
Universities	143,017	187,379	232,877	248,291	74
Postgraduate					
Total enrollments	34,982	67,388	85,504	72,731	108
Doctoral	3,430	4,683	6,233	5,958	74
Master	31,552	62,705	79,271	66,773	112
Total graduates	5,780	15,630	18,834	17,204	198
Doctoral	359	504	549	343	−4
Master	5,421	15,126	18,285	16,861	211

Source: Ministry of Education and Training 2013.

for spending, generating revenue, and establishing salary and enrollment policies. The burdens of bureaucratic oversight make it almost impossible to accomplish the primary task: give students the skills employers need. That means giving students good jobs and providing employers with a way to raise productivity. Accelerating technological change means that this problem will worsen unless bolder and quicker reforms are adopted. The government's effort to create new model universities in partnership with economically advanced countries is a step in the right direction. This experiment should be replicated and rapidly scaled up throughout the system.

The central argument of this chapter is that improving the NIS requires a broad approach that covers demand for innovation by firms and supply of high-quality human capital, knowledge, and R&D. The demand and supply aspects of innovation capacity are discussed next.

Innovation: The Demand (or Firm) Side

The private sector generates wealth and must be at the center of the policy focus over the medium term for strengthening innovation capacity. Vietnam has made progress in many of the factors that encourage firms to innovate. *Đổi Mới* reforms have exposed firms to external ideas and competition and created myriad opportunities at home and abroad. The FDI sector makes up more than one-third of all formal private sector employment. And export growth has consistently been an important driver of growth in the past two decades. These foundational steps have to be capitalized on.

Dynamizing a Critical Mass of Firms

The main priority is to develop a critical mass of dynamic and innovative firms that provide the demand side for innovation. Otherwise all efforts on the S&T side will be supply-push and, in the worst case, costly and worthless high-tech ventures. Signals from the government, however, do not yet reflect awareness of this. Domestic private firms feel the government's lack of response to their needs.

These challenges vary by firm type. For each—SOEs, foreign firms, and domestic enterprises—Vietnam needs to remove the barriers to productivity growth and government support.

SOEs

The SOE sector is large but lacks dynamism. It needs more competitive pressure if it is to be a growth driver. Some argue that these firms could be the basis for national champions—similar to *chaebols,* Korea's large family-owned conglomerates. But despite their huge government subsidies and support, they have failed to show sustained or aggressive export growth. An ongoing government program for increasing productivity and upgrading quality would guarantee strong demand for technological knowledge and innovation. But the codependent relationship between the government and SOEs—exchanging protected markets for shared profits—is no formula for driving dynamic, competitive growth.

Foreign firms

Vietnam's substantial FDI, which has fueled growth and provided millions of jobs, offers the potential for domestic firms to integrate into global value chains (GVCs). The competition implicit in these firms' export orientation remains a constant incentive to productivity growth and innovation, although not always at home. Vietnam's position in the value chain is in assembly work. Such work limits technological spillovers for the country's domestic firms. An emerging applied research/programming industry in Ho Chi Minh City and Da Nang may lead to the type of R&D established in China and India. But although these firms provide job opportunities for those with an information technology education, the spillovers are not automatic.

Foreign enterprises enjoy established communication channels with the government, and their weight in the economy guarantees a certain regulatory response. But as Singapore's experience shows, domestic firms seeking to integrate into the supply chain require—at least at first—a support system to raise their ability to meet the price, quality, and timeliness requirements multinational companies (MNCs). Domestic firms also need a well-developed NIS to move beyond assembly tasks into activities that contribute more value.

Domestic enterprises

Roughly 96 percent of Vietnamese firms are small and medium enterprises (SMEs). Vietnam's domestic private firms—established SMEs and burgeoning high-tech outfits—face challenges in exports, management, and the business climate. But entrepreneurs claim that government does not take the enterprising and nurturing approach of the Asian miracle economies. Rather it acts like a paper tiger (box 3.4). The plethora of laws on finance, tax rebates, intellectual property rights (IPR), and property grants to high-tech firms are on paper only. When firms or new entrepreneurs try to take advantage of the laws, they find officials who are unfamiliar with them or who obstruct the businesses' efforts. Countries such as Korea and Singapore at similar stages of development were more consistent, targeted, and effective in their support. Some firms—usually SOEs and MNCs—are large enough to communicate their concerns about the business environment or government policy. But the fragmented SME sector lacks direct connections or business associations to lobby the government.

Vietnamese Firms' Capacity to Innovate

Increasing firm capacity is essential to adopt technologies from abroad or from MNCs, and to ensure that government-sponsored research is effective. This involves developing firms' capacity for technology adoption and, eventually, invention (Rand and Tarp 2012).

Vietnamese firms' capacity to innovate is weak. Responding to a survey on research diffusion, 42 percent of GRI and university personnel report that firms lack the technological capacity to use research (Oh 1997). Many respondents felt the private sector was uninterested in using their research and stressed

BOX 3.4 Many policies exist only on paper

Vietnamese law offers numerous measures to support the private sector. Entrepreneurs in a cross section of firms, however, consistently respond that these measures exist only on paper.

For example, high-tech start-ups—in theory—are guaranteed property-tax exemptions and access to credit. But in reality they consistently report that none of these benefits exist. Worse, they hesitate to file for patent protection because they often see their ideas stolen rather than protected. Approval processes for new products are wearingly long.

For example, the Vietnam National University, Ho Chi Minh City, may lose the opportunity to commercialize "bio X-ray film." Vietnamese hospitals successfully piloted this newly developed product, which costs roughly a fifth of the imported product. It shows promise in becoming a profitable product in export and domestic markets. But scaling up has been hampered by weak marketing skills, scant access to credit, slow approval processes, and unresponsive government support. Despite the product's huge price advantage, a preference for imported technologies and an inability to scale up rapidly mean its future is uncertain.

The contrast with the more successful Asian tigers is stark. In the Korean economy's high-growth phase, the government guaranteed credit lines to firms that met export targets. And the Korea Trade Investment Promotion Agency offered strong export-network support to young small firms.

BOX 3.5 Firm upgrading in an MNC-dominated economy: Singapore

Singapore has relied to a great extent on large inflows of foreign multinational companies (MNCs) rather than on indigenous companies. In the 1990s, about 75 percent of its manufacturing output and 80 percent of its exports came from foreign MNCs. Large parts of the service sector even today are foreign-owned, especially hotels, transport, and financial services.

In response, the Economic Development Board (EDB) successfully cultivated foreign MNC links and spillovers, working closely with the firms represented on its advisory board. This gave the EDB direct information on MNC preferences, obstacles, and desired policy changes.

Realizing in the 1980s that spillovers from MNCs to domestic SMEs were weak, the Singapore government launched a nationwide campaign to promote awareness of the importance of productivity growth. It contracted with the Japanese Productivity Center to help establish what would eventually become an extensive system of SME support services: the Singapore Standards, Productivity, and Innovation Board (SPRING).

The EDB introduced the Local Industry Upgrading Program in the early 1980s to leverage MNCs. Under the program it selected a few local supply industries essential for upgrading activities in the foreign MNC. It also paid for MNC experts to work in local firms.

The EDB also worked with MNCs to establish training centers for skills that could be used across many industries, thus ensuring interindustry spillovers. The government financed the project but left training to MNCs rather than institute its own training centers and schools.

Among several financial and technical assistance schemes, the Local Industry Finance Scheme extended loans to buy machinery and equipment. The Local Enterprise Technical Assistance Scheme gave grants to external experts to upgrade operations and management. The Skills Development Fund shared the costs of investing in upgrading workforce skills.

The government also identified and supported 14 clusters, many of them cross-cutting. They included finance, shipping, tourism, construction, electronics, insurance, commodity trading, precision engineering, heavy engineering, information technology, general support industries, and petroleum and petrochemicals. Each cluster was tested for efficiency and competitiveness. And each had some common core comparative advantage, whether natural, created, or in industry structure. These clusters provided high-end tasks while assembly work progressively went to other countries.

The Agency for Science, Technology, and Research sponsored 12 research institutes to undertake R&D projects related to industry needs.

Source: Blomström, Kokko, and Sjoholm 2002; Maloney and Sarrias 2014; Toh 2005; Wong 2008.

the lack of firms' absorptive capacity, illustrating the critical need for firm upgrading in an NIS. And domestic firms lack production and knowledge links with FDI firms.

Ensuring that FDI firms do not simply constitute an enclave but actually "pull" the domestic private sector requires a strong domestic SME sector and the right skills mix. It is also vital to use GVCs because, for some time yet, Vietnam may rely on MNCs as private sector leaders—a precedent seen in Singapore in the 1980s (box 3.5). At that time, the Singaporean government realized that, despite a massive MNC presence, local firms were not benefitting or upgrading and put in place some effective programs. Similarly, in Korea, SMEs did not enjoy many spillovers from the *chaebols* that dominated the economy. Recognizing that spillovers are greater with more domestic firm capacity,[5] that country employed firm-upgrading programs that showed positive results.

The same problem is now apparent in Vietnam. Most spillovers are from providers of goods sold in the Vietnamese market. But only a few come from providers to local producers for export, even though this is a major economic activity (Newman et al. 2014). For example, Samsung Vietnam found that—among the 200 prospective SME suppliers responding to a call for interest—none could generate the combination of price, quality, and timeliness needed to be part of the supply chain. Important lessons may be learned from the Singaporean and Korean examples in this regard.

A proxy for measuring Vietnamese firms' capacity to innovate: management quality

Measures of domestic firms' capacity to innovate are scarce and hard to compare internationally. To rectify this, the London School of Economics and Stanford University conducted the World Management Survey. Researchers interviewed Vietnamese firms using a methodology the two institutions have used around the world. This permits comparisons with other countries and a deeper diagnostic of limitations.

First, the exercise reveals a broad positive relationship between managerial quality and GDP (figure 3.3). (The academic literature increasingly supports this finding.) Second, Vietnam is substantially below the world average but better than expected, given its income level. It is about the same as Brazil, Chile, China, India, and even Greece. Third, weak results for India and China are consistent with the view that their high R&D and patenting numbers are driven by MNCs, and their true innovation capacity is far below that suggested by these indicators.

Breaking down these management scores, figure 3.4 suggests that Vietnam is strong on monitoring. But the country is weak on setting long-term targets, introducing new technologies and best practices in operations, and developing human resource policies. Interviews with firms reveal that many managers meet their targets all the time. Anything less than 100 percent target achievement is unacceptable for senior management. But regardless of forward-thinking and strategic policies, Vietnamese managers emphasize that their principal objective is profit. The focus is always on the short term (Bloom et al. 2015).

This is consistent with the report that 84 percent of firms surveyed had no technology adaptation or R&D programs (Rand and Tarp 2012). A longer time horizon expressing a vision of long-term firm and product upgrading is largely absent, as are the human resources for innovation. For example, developing talent is expensive and often unnecessary because it is perceived to be easy to replace workers and even managers. This creates a gap as active innovation requires a dominance of best practice and a multiyear strategy for the firm.

Management quality thus becomes an important complement to stimulating R&D.

FIGURE 3.4 Managers in Vietnamese firms are strong on monitoring but weak on setting long-term targets, introducing new technologies, and reforming human resource policies

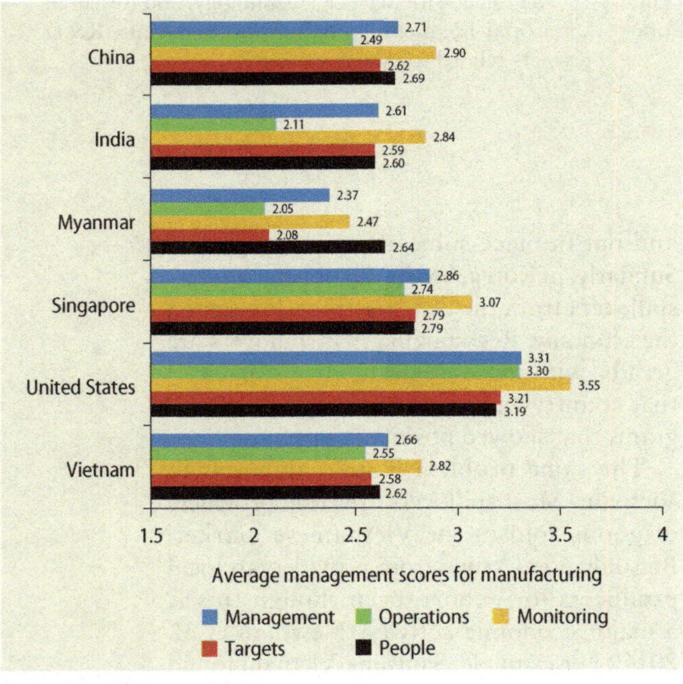

Source: Bloom et al. 2015.

What drives management quality?

As with most developing countries, Vietnam lags across the firm spectrum. Even its best—top 10 percent—firms lag behind the average firm in the United States, the frontier benchmark (figure 3.5). Two critical factors in average management quality have been identified. One is the level of competition in that it both trims the left tail, and nudges the rest of the distribution to be better. The other is the ownership structure (Bloom and Van Reenen 2007). Human capital and management training quality is important across the distribution, though mainly at the bottom.[6] This finding underlines the need for a variety of high-quality skills—as for Foundation IV—beyond research and technical skills promoted under Foundation III.

Technological extension services

Vietnam faces important firm-capacity constraints. Innovation cannot develop without a sophistication threshold among its firms and farmers, beginning with the basics. Throughout the advanced world, governments have employed extension services to facilitate technological transfer to firms and farms. These programs are important for upgrading firm capabilities. They are also useful in identifying high-growth gazelles—the small group of firms responsible for most employment growth. In the United Kingdom, these firms were termed "the vital 6 percent," which accounted for more than half of all jobs created.[7] It may be obvious that these firms should be supported, ensuring access to credit and improving their organizational capabilities. But it is extremely difficult to identify these firms beforehand, since there is no typical high-growth firm. Their heterogeneity spans sectors, business models, ownership structures, and trajectories.[8] A broad system of firm extension paired with private sector organizations—such as chambers of commerce and banks working across the private sector, as in Japan and Singapore—can help identify potential gazelles that may merit support.

The Vietnamese government recognizes the need to raise quality and productivity in such firms. Doing this involves some programs that are similar to those in Japan, Singapore, and elsewhere, including those of the Vietnam Productivity Institute (VPI). Interviews with the VPI, however, point to room for design and staffing improvements. The Japanese, Korean, Colombian, and Singaporean systems rely heavily on "extensionists" with ample private sector experience. The VPI is staffed almost entirely by Hanoi Business School graduates with little real-world experience. Most of the Colombian extensionists, by contrast, had worked in MNCs or large national firms, often in high positions. Only this kind of expertise will promote private sector demand for these services. Without large government subsidies, the VPI's survival is questionable.

FIGURE 3.5 Even the best firms in Vietnam fall below the average firm on the frontier benchmark

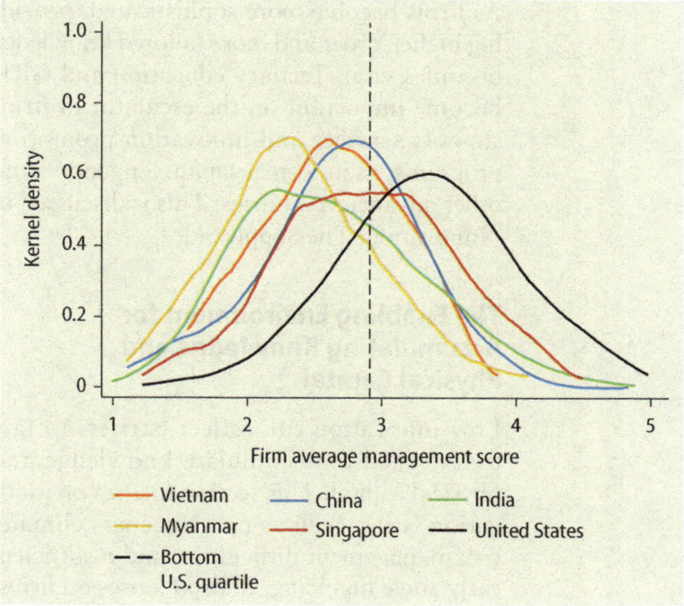

Source: Bloom et al. 2015.
Note: Sixty-four percent of Vietnamese firms score within the range of the bottom quartile of U.S. firms.

Japan helped develop Singapore's formidable firm-support services (see box 3.5). The Japan International Cooperation Agency undertook an evaluation of the VPI and recommended possible reforms. A firm-support system review at different sophistication levels is proper. In Japan, Korea, and Singapore, such "5S/*Kaizen*"-type programs, which stress continuous and gradual improvements, have been crucial to upgrading.[9]

Higher-order support to upgrading and innovation

As firms become more sophisticated, providing higher-order and more tailored knowledge becomes vital. Tertiary education and GRIs become important on the escalator of firm-support services and innovation-promotion programs, as in Korea, Japan, Singapore, and other advanced countries. This is discussed in "Innovation: The Supply Side."

The Enabling Environment for Accumulating Knowledge and Physical Capital

Low innovation can reflect barriers to factors needed to accumulate knowledge and physical capital. This section focuses on innovation issues such as poor business climate, risk-management difficulties, and insufficient early-stage financing. It also focuses on firms' ineffectual investment readiness, poorly run government financial support programs, and weak IPRs protection.

Managing risks

Development is a process of placing wagers, as any investment has risks. Investments in accumulating knowledge capital are no different. And invention risks can be even higher because the distribution of returns is unlikely to be well understood. Institutions and skills that ease risk management are essential (box 3.6).

For instance, it is important to reduce risks for adopting agricultural technologies (Foster and Rosenzweig 2010). The rate of quality upgrading—a crucial innovative activity—is close to the variance in quality growth rate. And rich countries are undertaking the riskiest—and thus highest-return—investments in quality upgrading.[10] Therefore investment in knowledge for quality (or productivity growth) appears facilitated to the extent that firms and countries can manage this risk (Acemoglu and Zilibotti 1997).

To enable risk-taking, Vietnam needs to work on the following three areas:

1. Improve entrepreneurs' ability to evaluate and manage risks through the types of programs discussed earlier.
2. Reduce risks in the system by assuring consistent and supportive rules over the long term.[11]

BOX 3.6 Efficiency and risk management in rice: An Giang Plant Protection Company in the Mekong Delta

Established in 1993, the An Giang Plant Protection Company creates a value chain for rice export. It includes providing input services, transferring the cultivation-control process, and supporting harvesting. The value chain also includes drying and transporting rice, grinding, free storage, and marketing. The company integrates 25,000 paddy fields into large fields that make up 2.5 percent of the Mekong Delta. But it expects to more than double that amount by 2018. Integration in this value chain increased smallholder household income by 50 percent in one year.

An Giang addresses three key innovation and production issues.

It reduces transaction and information costs and risks. An Giang reduces farmers' information costs through researching and choosing seed and fertilizer. It also manages transport. Managing the input and marketing process—thus providing better technical assistance—further reduces the costs and risks farmers face.

It alleviates credit constraints. The company lends to farms for input purchases.

It resolves market failures in research and innovation. The Vietnam Academy of Agricultural Sciences reports that new technologies have allowed the farmers in the Mekong Delta to increase from one to three crops per year. Productivity is rising through new seed types and more, but it is hitting limits. An Giang's agricultural research center collaborates with the government-supported Omon Rice Institute to develop new seeds and fertilizers.

There is substantial room for scale-up and the government could promote it. Nineteen more similar firms could cover 40 percent of the Delta by 2020, with expected impacts on productivity.

3. Assist in managing risks through institutions or approaches that help diversify them. Such assistance includes supporting tertiary education and GRIs, developing a modern financial sector, and aiding information collection. Assistance also includes help offsetting appropriation externalities, such as export-support agencies and innovation support funds.

Improving the business climate

Doing Business indicators capture some dimension of the enabling environment and how it aids investment in physical and knowledge capital. Table 3.4 shows that Vietnam ranks better than Brazil overall, but lags far behind regional middle- and high-income economies, as well as Mexico and Chile in Latin America. It is weak in entrepreneurs' ability to start a business, protect investors, pay taxes, and resolve insolvency—all essential to doing business. Only 3 percent of Vietnamese firms reported no barrier to upgrading processes and technology: financing constraints, technological know-how, and basic infrastructure proved important issues, but not communication infrastructure (Rand and Tarp 2012).

Innovation and start-up finance

Entry opportunities—mainly for innovative young firms—diminish without a developed system to support early-stage financing. Such firms require a spectrum of financing sources as they move from the proof-of-concept phase to being established and listed publicly. Vietnam has tentative representation in most lifecycle phases, but it is miniscule. Interviews with start-up personnel suggest that domestic intermediaries have weak capacity to evaluate risk.

Government programs to mitigate market failures and provide financing over the innovation life cycle are fragmented, deficient in coverage, and poorly coordinated. Private capital markets require greater public support to meet the needs of SMEs and highly innovative start-ups. Such support mainly includes providing technical assistance and developing an exit strategy for private equity funds. (Technical assistance, when delivered with private equity, can unlock more investment commitments. But Vietnam's small private equity funds limit the government's ability to provide technical assistance.) Such twinning is the rule in venture capital in the United States, where managerial resources are often scarce in young, growing firms. The most innovative entrepreneurs are not necessarily endowed with managerial talent. A major role of venture capital is to field good managers (De Carvalho, Calomiris, and Matos 2008). Government programs that simply provide risk financing without experienced managers are missing an important part of the equation. The Malaysian government purchased part of a U.S.-based venture capital firm to secure finance *and* expertise. Brazilian success in developing venture capital is largely because

TABLE 3.4 Vietnam is weak in ease of paying taxes and starting a business, protecting investors, and resolving insolvency—all essential to doing business
Ranking

Economy	Ease of doing business	Starting a business	Dealing with construction permits	Getting electricity	Registering property	Getting credit	Protecting taxes	Paying taxes	Trading across borders	Enforcing contracts	Resolving insolvency
Korea, Rep.	4	23	28	1	40	42	8	29	31	2	4
Taiwan, China	11	22	6	2	18	59	25	39	65	16	21
Malaysia	18	14	15	13	38	28	4	31	49	44	45
Mexico	38	65	67	72	106	5	57	92	59	41	28
Chile	48	62	24	51	56	79	36	33	63	56	58
Thailand	49	96	39	11	57	97	36	70	56	57	49
China	84	136	176	92	43	79	134	132	96	7	55
Vietnam	90	119	12	108	58	28	122	168	99	74	123
Brazil	116	174	169	22	130	97	29	178	145	45	62

Source: World Bank 2015.
Note: These are global rankings based on Doing Business 2016 scores.

of *Novo Mercado* and *Bovespa Mais*, which provide an exit strategy to private equity investors by taking companies public (box 3.7). Vietnam should consider similar exit opportunities.

Investment readiness

Established SMEs and start-ups need to overcome an important hurdle: they must present a solid business case to financial intermediaries. Many entrepreneurs lack the most basic financial statements. They do not understand what banks and other financial intermediaries are looking for. And they may not understand how financial instruments—such as angel or venture capital—function. Issues cut across all sectors of the economy. Many start-ups lack the collateral and track record that financial entities need to make investment decisions.

New investment-readiness programs, sponsored by a government or by financial intermediaries, redress the demand side of the financing problem (see Mason and Kwok 2010). These programs may take a year or more to be effective. They require important business diagnostics and come at, possibly, high costs to the public purse. They may be considered part of the entire package of firm-support programs linked to technological extension programs and incubators and accelerators. For example, Vietnam Silicon Valley, a start-up accelerator mentors other start-ups to structure and prepare them to pitch their proposals to potential investors.

Government financial support programs to firms

The government can provide financial support to firms through indirect and direct channels. For indirect support, it can ease the collection of information that financial institutions require before giving a loan, thereby lowering the cost of borrowing for qualifying firms. For example, collateral laws and registries help firms leverage their assets for loans, and credit information systems can document young firms' creditworthiness. Few start-ups, however, have much of a track record. The government can help through direct subsidies (taking on risk) or tools that identify potential success (based on personal characteristics, for example). A well-developed system of firm support combined with business associations can greatly increase an entrepreneur's or a firm's information (see World Bank 2014).

Direct support to firms for innovation is also justified, mainly on the grounds of market failure arising from the appropriability externality. For example, a firm may invent a technology—or invest in identifying and adopting an existing technology—and then be copied by its competition. This eliminates much of the intended profit of investing in knowledge. Financial incentives from the government can raise the private return to equal the social return, taking the form of direct subsidies, tax write-offs, matching grants, and patents.

Tax Write-Offs. Many countries allow firms to deduct R&D or related expenses from their

BOX 3.7 Capital market development and exit facilitation: Brazil's *Novo Mercado*

Private equity eventually needs an exit. Brazil has radically increased flows for initial public offerings through *Novo Mercado*, a premium listing tier that requires firms to adopt governance standards that are stronger than legally demanded. Increased transparency is important to stimulate the venture capital and private equity market. In 2007, *Novo Mercado* celebrated its 100th company, hosting 81 of Brazil's 113 initial public offerings since its founding.

Bovespa Mais, which broadly holds to *Novo Mercado* standards, targets small and mid-cap firms. It hosts companies with a gradual strategy of access to capital markets. It helps them with transparency, shareholder-base growth, and liquidity. *Novo Mercado* and *Bovespa Mais* are crucial to developing the venture capital/private equity market in Brazil.

income taxes. Vietnam's Law on Technology Transfer (2006) permits tax write-offs for S&T development and technology transfer. But such write-offs often lead to firms merely reclassifying activities and workers. In Korea, for example, such measures were only marginally helpful in stimulating innovation activities. Nor do they help build links among NIS actors. Finland abandoned its tax write-offs in favor of matching grants to create incentives for collaboration among private firms and research bodies.

Matching Grants. Evaluations reveal mixed results for developing countries with modest take-up by firms. Vietnam's system has little funding. Interviews at the National University in Ho Chi Minh City in 2015 showed that excessive paperwork is a great problem. And even for those that qualify, disbursement tranches are small.

Matching grants also require sophisticated actors on both sides of the match. Without vibrant firms, even the best research entities can have no partner. And in the end the firm is looking for a research body that can add value.

Collaboration between firms and research institutes is low in Vietnam. At an earlier point in its development, Korea found that its private sector believed that tertiary education and GRIs did not produce the necessary knowledge. SMEs, on their part, lacked the ability to use knowledge generated by research bodies. Korea's Science and Technology Policy Institute concluded that the best approach was direct technology transfers from GRIs and tertiary education. Rotating personnel from the research sector into firms or having masters and doctoral students work in firms were sound forms of technology transfer. In Finland, rotating masters and PhD students through firms created the highest ranked university–firm interactions.

Incubators and Accelerators. Many startups have marketable ideas but lack experience in organizing a firm, training managers, accessing credit, and developing a long-term vision. Incubators such as Vietnam Silicon Valley can combine mentoring, business plan preparation, and links to potential finance in a common environment. This encourages networking and mutual learning. Shorter-term accelerator programs may help in the adolescence phase where technical issues are consolidated, but strategic guidance is in demand.

Three caveats for incubators are in order. First, gazelles often are targeted to the high-tech sector, but the sector itself is not necessarily a good predictor of these fast-growing companies. In the United States, incubators often pair with small-business development centers. These centers serve firms from any sector and provide a one-stop shop for *all* new firms. Half the funds for these centers come from the Small Business Administration. The other half comes from such entities as state legislatures, private sector foundations, and state and local chambers of commerce. The Singapore Standards, Productivity and Innovation Board developed the Incubator Development Programme, which provides up to 70 percent grant support to incubators and accelerators. Vietnam might consider expanding beyond the sectors served by Vietnam Silicon Valley, a start-up accelerator. A matching grants system, for example, could leverage emerging areas of expertise.

Second, the easiest part of such programs is to provide real estate, but the services and, more profoundly, the quality of the professionals offering them are what make the programs effective.

Third, incubator services cannot replace the broader business framework the government sets. A weak financial framework will inhibit the emergence of angel investors or venture capital providers. It will also constrain the more mainstream financial services that incubators may match with entrepreneurs.

Intellectual property rights

Vietnam needs to strengthen its IPR procedure and adapt it to the needs of entrepreneurs, mainly its SMEs. A well-enforced method is crucial in fostering innovation—through patents, trademarks, copyrights, and geographic indications. Firmly protected

IPRs are a must for MNCs to share their technologies with local firms and undertake higher-order R&D in Vietnam. High-tech companies are explicit about not taking their cutting-edge technologies to China, which lacks IPR protection and a trustworthy judiciary to enforce the rights. U.S. multinationals respond to changes in reforming countries' IPR regimes by increasing technology transfers to them (Branstetter, Fisman, and Foley 2006).

Enforcement of IPRs has always played an important role in the intellectual property system. Countries may use civil, administrative or criminal measures, depending on the nature and seriousness of the infringements. In many nations, the laws do not stipulate the application of administrative measures to deal with IPR infringements. However, in Vietnam today, IPR infringements are mainly resolved by administrative measures, leading to inadequately compensated damages of IPR holders (box 3.8).

Establishing this transparency and reliability is essential for Vietnam to be a full partner in the global knowledge market. But this is not the case. Interviews with Vietnamese start-ups reveal that inventors find their patents are not enforced. They are wary of applying for patents because ideas may be stolen. Thus, the patent office now does the reverse of what is expected: securing property rights for the inventor while disseminating new knowledge. Once the patent office is functioning well, an independent judiciary will be needed to resolve IPR disputes.

It is unclear how benefits from commercializing new ideas should be divided. Cash-strapped research programs and low-paid academics should benefit from accessing a share of returns to products they develop. For example, the consensus is that they get nothing from the farmers' use of their new rice varieties. The Law on Science and Technology (2000) and the Intellectual Property Law (2005) that govern ownership of research outputs and copyright are only occasionally useful.

Innovation: The Supply Side

Dynamic firms require access to the best global knowledge through research, smart capable workers, and product or process technologies. Fast-growing and high-income

BOX 3.8 Vietnam should strengthen staff capacity and promote the resolution of IPR infringements by civil measures

In Vietnam, most IPR enforcement is through administrative agencies. Courts play a small role. Between 2006 (the IP Law came into effect in 2005) and 2013, the courts handled 200 IPR cases, just 1 percent of the administrative agencies' cases. Meanwhile, in 2013 and 2014, the inspectors handled 32,474 cases nationwide with D 139 billion worth of fines. Administrative sanctions, where the highest fine is D 500 million (around US$22,000) for organizations and D 250 million for individuals, are insufficient to deter repeated violations.

Administrative measures of IPR infringement are intended solely to deter and prevent future violations, not to pay damages to IPR holders. The administrative fines are paid into the state budget.

The infringements have become more sophisticated in many fields, such as patents, trade secrets, copyrights, trademarks, and unfair competition. Meanwhile, the staff allocated to IPR enforcement has been inadequate. Only 7.7 percent of IPR enforcement officers have received training in this field.

Jurisdiction over IPR infringement has been given to many different agencies—Inspectorates, Market Management, Customs, and the Police and People's Committees at all levels. But there is a lack of close coordination among them, diluting accountability.

Protecting one's intellectual property is a civil right. Vietnam should promote the resolution of IPR infringements by civil measures rather than administrative ones.

Source: Electronic Nhan Dan Newspaper, April 25, 2015 (http://en.nhandan.com.vn/).

economies continuously demand more and better knowledge and skills. This drove a near-doubling of global expenditure on R&D from about $750 billion in 2001 to more than $1.4 trillion in 2011.[12] China, for one, has gone from conducting little R&D a generation ago to becoming the world's second-largest research funder. It is increasingly recognized for its ability to exceed international quality standards. Despite massive increases in tertiary education worldwide, returns to higher education are rising in dynamic economies. Demand for educated workers continues to grow faster than supply (Carnoy et al. 2013).

An NIS supply side provides firms with most of the highest-quality, firm-relevant knowledge. When Foundation III is strong,[13] GRIs and research universities produce the knowledge and advanced human capital needed (such as PhD scientists and researchers). They are linked tightly enough to firms to allow them to be routinely transferred. When Foundation IV is strong,[14] the tertiary education system imparts relevant, high-quality skills to a broad range of young people before they join the workforce.

Making the supply side work requires coordinated efforts across policy subareas, directed primarily down two main paths. First, invest more while concentrating resources on the nation's best and most productive researchers. Second, deregulate tertiary education so that more providers—including more private providers—can compete to serve students' needs.

Countries that have improved their NIS supply side have charted a multidecadal course through policy formulation and implementation. In its science, technology, and innovation (STI) development, Vietnam is not far behind where these successful countries were at Vietnam's current income per capita. Similar to basic education indicators, many of Vietnam's key STI indicators are now where successful countries were 20 or 30 years ago. Building STI research capacity and excellent tertiary education institutes is a decades-long process. Countries such as Brazil, China, Korea, and Singapore have made the deepest sustained commitments to these policy goals and have reaped the largest rewards. If Vietnam can learn from and imitate the most successful countries' policies, it could be recognized as a leading country for human capital and research by 2035. Achieving this will, however, require changes to the trajectories of several policies.

Investing More While Concentrating Resources on the Nation's Best and Most Productive Researchers

Vietnam has made great efforts to improve the framework for its S&T research system. It now includes the Ministry of Science and Technology and the National Foundation for Science and Technology Development (NAFOSTED). It also includes agencies such as the National Agency for Science and Technology Information and policy plans such as the Strategy for Science and Technology Development 2011–2020. Yet these efforts have not smoothed the path to stronger S&T capacity, which includes many of the elements other countries have used.

Investing more in research, knowledge, and advanced human capital

Vietnam's GERD is low (about 0.3 percent of GDP), with most going to GRI staff salaries. Korea was investing significantly more on R&D at Vietnam's per capita income. Its R&D expenditure went up from 0.25 percent of GDP in 1963 to 2.8 percent in the early 1980s, and investment quality improved enormously (KOICA Vietnam Office 2015). Many contemporary economies in East and South Asia have similarly committed to creating innovation-led economies through sustained investments in S&T research. In 2001, China, India, Japan, Korea, Malaysia, Singapore, Thailand, and Taiwan, China, made up 25 percent of global R&D spending. By 2011 their share had grown to 34 percent.[15] Vietnam will not become an innovation-led economy unless it invests more while improving spending quality. It risks losing more ground to global and regional competitors.

Concentrating resources and rewarding the best through merit-based allocation

Extreme fragmentation is a serious challenge for the research system. Vietnam has 642 officially recognized GRIs and more than 2,000 S&T organizations. Dispersing resources and talent makes conducting high-quality research difficult. The GRIs managed by the Vietnam Academy of Science and Technology have the best infrastructure and highest prestige, yet only 7 percent of personnel hold PhDs (OECD–World Bank 2014).

Creating the National Foundation for Science and Technology Development is a positive step toward removing the GRIs' monopoly. It can place research resources under competitive, peer-reviewed, and merit-based allocation. It can also promote evaluation and accountability measures for research funding. And it can break down barriers between tertiary education– and GRI-based researchers. Its main drawbacks are its small funding allocations and research grants.

New policies should ensure that future funding is provided only to GRIs with good records on output and research impacts. GRI performance should be evaluated routinely.

Korea and Singapore fund and manage GRIs more efficiently in two ways. First, they concentrate on a few high-quality institutions. Korea has far fewer government-related research institutes (along with a small number of high-quality science and engineering research centers tied to tertiary education).[16] Singapore's research strategy places biomedicine as the priority. The country lists about a dozen GRIs in this field and half as many in engineering and physical sciences managed by the Science and Engineering Research Council. Policies in both countries ensure a critical mass of qualified infrastructure and research staff.

Second, they seek to match the key GRIs with their most pressing economic and social challenges. To assimilate foreign technologies rapidly, Korea designed and managed the Korean Institute for Science and Technology, the Korean Institute of Machinery and Metals, and the Electronics and Telecommunications Research Institute.

Part of improving the funding system is reducing the bureaucratic burden on researchers. Time spent managing grants subtracts from research time. Many researchers in Vietnam feel that the government micromanages grant funding, and not constructively. The head of researchers at the Van Neuman Institute in Ho Chi Minh City reports that for a $10,000 grant, he must report a product for every $1,000. So the institute does not work with the government. In other instances, new funding mechanisms have been created but suffer debilitating implementation delays. As early as the 1990s, leading research agencies from the developing world—such as the Research Foundation of the State of São Paulo—were measuring themselves against the world's best research funding agencies and working to eliminate red tape. Vietnam should imitate these efforts.

Evaluating the quality and relevance of research output and activities

Vietnam's research outputs are modest. In 2011, it published less than one article per GRI on the Science Citation Index and in the Social Sciences Citation Index. More important is the near-total absence of research output and impact evaluation. GRIs are funded largely for proposed tasks. It is unclear whether there is any systematic quality and impact measurement, creating debilitating negative incentives when GRI funding does not reflect productivity. The United Kingdom provides a model for Vietnam to consider (box 3.9).

Balancing funding for basic and thematic research

The best research funding allocation should promote measurable progress on key thematic challenges of national importance. It is unclear whether Vietnam's funding does this. All countries must decide how to balance spending on basic research relative to thematic research, promoting excellence through open competition and funding special projects and programs. Successful countries achieved this balance by ensuring the following: Funds are allocated to solve key

BOX 3.9 The United Kingdom research output and impact: Systematically evaluated under the Research Excellence Framework

The United Kingdom's three Higher Education Funding Councils allocate more than £2 billion annually for research. To calculate the resulting value, the Research Excellence Framework undertakes continuous and consequential assessments of its quality and impact. In a three-year exercise, large samples of research are examined in detail. The results are fed back into the allocation process, helping to ensure future resource allocations go to the best and most productive researchers.

The 2011–14 assessment had four main panels with 36 subpanels to review almost 200,000 items of research output from more than 50,000 researchers at over 150 universities. The panels relied heavily on international members and used uniform criteria to ensure that their judgments were valid across disciplines and from year to year. The assessment was comprehensive, combining analysis of research outputs, impacts, and environment into an index of overall quality.

The assessment found that in 2014, 30 percent of U.K. research was world-leading, with 46 percent "internationally excellent," 20 percent "internationally recognized," and 3 percent "nationally recognized."

Perhaps the most important aspect of the exercise concerns the incentives it creates for researchers, whether as individuals, or in teams, departments, or tertiary education. They know their work will be reviewed and measured against their peers, and their scores are likely to influence future funding success and career directions. Not least, U.K. citizens have information on the value of their tax investments in research.

problems, not support institutions. GRIs do not have a monopoly on funding; any qualified researcher or research group can compete (box 3.10). Line ministries cooperate with S&T ministries to ensure that they use peer-reviewed, merit-based allocation procedures and that researchers are accountable for outputs. Resources are sufficient and not fragmented among many small grants. Research and advanced training (chiefly PhD training) can be linked.

Without systematic evaluation in Vietnam, it is difficult to link GRIs' research funding and performance to the main national priorities in, for example, economic development, agriculture, or the environment. A comprehensive international review of STI policy in 2014 found that planning still follows the algorithms of central planning. Research is ostensibly connected to socioeconomic goals, as expressed in 5-year development plans or 10-year development strategies. But planning labors under four constraints:

1. It is conducted by bureaucrats and administrators who lack subject-area expertise.
2. It suffers multiple overlaps at national, departmental, and local levels (with high administrative costs at each level).
3. It is tied to centrally allocated budgets that are not subject to competition or accountability for outputs.
4. It fails to coalesce around important research themes or to be cross-disciplinary.

Uniting the research and university-based graduate education systems

Developing countries face a dilemma: they must expand the number of researchers while improving research quality. Most countries concentrate resources among the most productive researchers, getting a double payoff when the best researchers generate research productively and train the next generation through graduate education.

Vietnam's research and university-based graduate education systems are separate, which increases costs while often lowering quality and productivity. The biggest downside, though, is the failure to leverage research resources to increase the number of high-quality researchers through domestic

BOX 3.10 Using research funds to promote progress on key thematic challenges of national importance: Mexico's *fondos sectoriales*

In 2002, a new S&T law gave Mexico's National Council for Science and Technology (CONACYT)—equal to a ministry of science and technology—responsibility for coordinating S&T activities and budgets for federal agencies. The law stressed applied research linking scientific activities to national problems and directing science into areas of social value.

It created sector funds (*fondos sectoriales*)—operated with federal agencies—to finance projects that addressed, for example, health needs, agriculture, and the environment. The *fondos* operated with matching funds from CONACYT and the different federal agencies. Any researcher or research group—in a GRI or based at a tertiary educational institute—could compete for the funds. The *fondos* removed existing monopolies on funding sources. In doing so, they raised quality and relevance while increasing advanced research training. Many institutional weaknesses in the S&T system hampered implementation. But creating these funds and performance contracts with GRIs was an important step in overcoming traditional inertia and monopolies on research funding.

Sources: OECD 2009 and Gonzalez-Brambila, Veloso, and Lever 2007.

PhD programs. As Vietnam moves toward 2035, the country should unite its research and graduate education systems. Simultaneously, it should cut the number of less effective GRIs and promote strong, research-linked doctoral programs.

Merging the two systems will help reach the ideal number of qualified staff for the expanding tertiary education system and—more broadly—for firms and the labor market. Countries with successful NISs have achieved the desired number for these two groups. Researchers and professors fill faculty positions in tertiary education institutions, raising the share of PhD holders and the quality of teaching. Average graduates from first-degree tertiary programs receive better teaching and can bring more knowledge and relevant skills to their firms.

Improving the quality of human capital in these groups is necessary to drive productivity and add production value. Advanced-knowledge workers cannot make firms more productive without a base of qualified and capable employees. Some analytic traditions in STI policy note a ratio of 1:10:100 researchers to engineers to employees with good skills in finance, accounting, management, marketing, and human resources. But these ratios vary greatly across industries and among firms, even in the same industries. Whatever the ratio, a critical mass of human capital in an NIS is not limited to research talent or to the higher education research subsector. Policies must promote success in research and even broader success in higher education, based on a strong domestic graduate education system.

Building high-quality domestic graduate programs and research universities

Vietnam is building its links to the best global knowledge, which will allow it to train more advanced human capital domestically. It will also help solve problems of low research quality and low qualifications among higher education faculty. Converting international links into domestic quality requires upgrading the number and quality of graduate programs domestically and promoting high-quality research at home. Vietnam has not done well in this area.

Doctoral enrollments have grown but graduate numbers have not kept pace, suggesting weaknesses in doctoral programs. Master's degrees, though, have been a bright spot, with enrollment and graduates more than doubling over 2005–12 (see table 3.3). Evaluation of specific programs has confirmed the positive impact on higher education quality of more master's degrees among teaching and research faculty (Vietnam Education Foundation 2014).

Brazil and Mexico, countries with relatively few doctoral students abroad, have upgraded their own graduate education programs. Brazil has gone from producing fewer than 1,000 PhDs domestically in the late 1990s to more than 10,000 a year, while maintaining attention to quality. Coordination for the Improvement of Higher Education Personnel (CAPES), Brazil's quality assurance agency for graduate programs, has built a reputation for consequential evaluation. It assesses all masters and doctoral programs on a seven-point scale using such criteria as faculty qualifications and research output and quality. High-scoring programs are allocated more scholarships, but low-scoring ones risk losing access to government funding. Tying funding to performance has paid off handsomely for Brazil.

Vietnam's quality assurance systems, however, have been slow to develop, focusing on undergraduate programs and based at institutions tied to the two flagship universities. Experience from Uruguay suggests that quality-assurance agencies should be fully independent of any given tertiary education institution to be neutral in judging quality of their peers (who are also their competitors).

Vietnam could adopt the Brazilian model of CAPES for improving its quality in graduate education. The quantity and quality of Vietnamese domestic graduate education are below the corresponding benchmarks for Brazil some 20 years ago (CAPES began evaluating graduate programs in 1998). But if Vietnam institutes and follows a rigorous evaluation regime that guides expanded funding, it can imitate Brazil's success in achieving a critical mass of human capital produced in its own universities.

Accessing the global knowledge frontier through international links

A strong domestic research and graduate education system thrives when it is connected to global knowledge networks, mainly the frontier. Accessing it is a long-term, continuous process that creates research networks through sending national PhD students to work with the world's best researchers. The process promotes research excellence at home in tertiary education institutes and GRIs. And it produces attractive career conditions at home for researchers and knowledge workers.

China is the leading country to reach the global knowledge frontier by sending citizens to study with top researchers abroad. For more than 25 years, Chinese students have dominated the ranks of foreign graduate students in PhD programs at top- and middle-tier universities worldwide. The government has borne much of the costs of sending these students, even though fewer than one in five may return home within 10 years. But it believes the web of knowledge ties gained from creating a pool of international Chinese research talent more than justifies the costs of the investment.

Vietnam fares well in accessing global knowledge, with government-supported programs to send students abroad for PhDs. Its doctoral students are an increasing presence in high-quality graduate education programs in Australia, Europe, Japan, Korea, and the United States. Numbers earning doctorates at the United States' research universities, however, are far behind those of Asian competitors (table 3.5).

TABLE 3.5 Vietnam's doctoral students are an increasing presence in the United States, but their numbers fall short of Asian competitors

	Earned doctorates in the United States, 2013	
Country	**Number**	**Per million population**
Korea, Rep.	1,381	27.54
Singapore	91	16.85
China	4,789	3.53
India	2,205	1.76
Vietnam	**141**	**1.57**
Mexico	154	1.26
Brazil	142	0.71

Source: Calculations based on U.S. NSF data and World Development Indicators.

Deregulating Tertiary Education so that More Providers Can Compete to Serve the Needs of Students

Some areas of progress

The evolution of Vietnam's tertiary education system over the past 10 years is partly successful in expanding access. Enrollments increased 57 percent between 2005 and 2012 (see table 3.3), when the share of the age group enrolled rose from 15 percent to more than 25 percent. Coverage in Vietnam grew faster between 2001 and 2011 than in eight other regional countries (table 3.6).

Two major legislative reforms were passed: the Higher Education Reform Agenda in 2005 (box 3.11) and the Higher Education Law in 2012.[17] They set ambitious targets for raising quantity and quality. They also grant increasing amounts of autonomy to higher education institutions in areas such as curriculum, resource use, staff hiring, admissions and enrollment policy, revenue generation and tuition fees, and other administrative procedures. The reforms created a quality assurance system. And institutions have undertaken self-assessment, reporting regularly to the government. An academic credit system has been launched to lower the number of required contact hours and allow greater flexibility in teaching. Public higher education institutions have received a new governance structure that creates university councils for institutions and transfers decisions to them. The Ministry of Education and Training (MOET) and other ministries formerly made such decisions. Faculty qualifications at universities have improved: between 2005 and 2012 faculty members with PhDs grew by 54 percent, and those with master's degrees by 134 percent (table 3.7). One in six university faculty now has a PhD, and more than half the faculty have at least a master's degree.

More progress needed

The quality, relevance, and efficiency of tertiary education remain low, however. Policies prevent some aspiring students from accessing tertiary education, paying tuitions at levels consistent with willingness- and ability-to-pay, and studying what and where they want. The number of providers is limited, and the pace of change is slow. While the rest of the developing world has been experiencing a sea change in tertiary education—with vastly expanded enrollments and hugely increased private provision—Vietnam's system is widely criticized for being stagnant.

To earn a living, faculty must often teach long hours of badly planned classes. An increasingly complex array of fees and payments for special classes is emerging to allow institutions to raise revenue while tuition stays capped. These special classes absorb professors' time and attention, further lowering quality for the average student. The effect of current policies is to remove incentives for positive change and fail to reward innovative behavior. Shaped by these policies, the institutions are unsuited to play a positive role in an innovation-led economy.

TABLE 3.6 The share of the age cohort attending tertiary education has grown in many national systems (gross enrollment rate as a percentage of the relevant age cohort)

Country	2001	2002	2005	2007	2010	2011	Compound annual growth rate, 2001–11
Cambodia	2.37	2.45	3.33	7.25	14.07	15.83	13.5
Brunei Darussalam	14.25	14.53	17.69	17.95	17.60	19.72	5.5
Indonesia	14.36	15.01	17.74	18.40	24.89	27.20	12.8
Lao PDR	3.09	4.15	7.79	11.40	16.09	17.09	14.0
Malaysia*	25.05	27.41	27.92	30.25	37.13	35.97	10.9
Myanmar	10.33	–	–	10.14	–	13.81	3.5
Thailand	39.23	40.04	44.18	48.11	50.03	52.58	0.34
Timor-Leste*	–	8.57	–	–	17.74	–	9.17
Vietnam	**9.38**	**9.63**	**15.88**	**18.17**	**22.39**	**24.43**	**15.0**

Source: UNESCO Education Statistics Databases.
Note: *The growth is computed based on available data for given years. – = not available.

BOX 3.11 The Higher Education Reform Agenda, 2006–20

The Higher Education Reform Agenda outlines government strategy for higher education and research through 2020. The main objectives are the following: First, increase capacity to allow a higher participation rate in tertiary institutions. This requires large investments in infrastructure and in training new lecturers and faculty. Second, increase the system's quality and efficiency. Third, introduce or reinforce research in tertiary education facilities to train new teachers better, enrich and upgrade teachers' skills, and upgrade the quality and international visibility of Vietnamese universities. Fourth, improve governance of the higher education and research system nationally and regionally, including universities.

Quality and efficiency goals include lowering teacher–student ratios, revising entrance exams, training teachers better, and improving teaching methods. They also include developing research at universities that broaden teachers' scholarship, transforming selected institutions into teaching and research institutions, and improving curriculum frameworks and assessment of learning outcomes. Goals address greater curriculum flexibility and student mobility via a credit-accumulation system. They also address developing a high-quality culture within institutions, including an accreditation system for all institutions (public and nonpublic) at national level.

These goals imply greater freedom for individual institutions and measures that create a climate of competition among and within institutions. The government set the following targets for education: Increase revenue from S&T activities to 15 percent of total university revenue by 2010 and to 25 percent by 2020. Increase the proportion of university teaching staff with a master's degree to 40 percent by 2010 and to 60 percent by 2020. Increase the share of university teaching staff with a doctoral degree to 25 percent by 2010 and to 35 percent by 2020. Reduce the ratio of university students to teaching staff to 20:1 by 2020.

TABLE 3.7 University faculty have improved qualifications, with one in six faculty now having a doctorate and more than half a master's degree (number of faculty by qualification)

	2005	2010	2011	2012
Colleges	**13,972**	**23,622**	**24,437**	**25,643**
Doctor	293	586	633	693
Master	3,422	7509	8766	10015
University/college degrees	57	14939	14696	14714
Other qualifications	10,200	588	342	221
Universities	**34,294**	**50,951**	**59,672**	**61,674**
Doctor	5,744	7,338	8,519	8,869
Master	12,609	23,299	28,037	29,476
University/college degrees	15,732	20,059	22,547	23,002
Other qualifications	209	255	569	327
Total	**48,266**	**74,573**	**84,109**	**87,317**

Source: Ministry of Education and Training 2013.

Defenders of the system cite increases in coverage as progress. But increases in coverage only prevent Vietnam from falling further behind growth of coverage among its G20 and OECD competitors. Many high-school diploma holders who want a higher education cannot find a satisfactory institution. Figures from 2013 indicate that only 40 percent of those seeking tertiary education were offered admission. Perceived levels of instruction are low. Faculty salaries are inadequate and compel staff to take multiple teaching jobs, often at different institutions. Students must adapt their preferences for degree programs and careers to what higher education institutions offer. Required contact hours are often unjustifiably long but remain mandatory. Required patriotic and political curriculum reduce time devoted to a student's main academic focus. The government manages enrollments based on existing space and partial and speculative projections of future labor market conditions. Too few faculty members have PhDs. And career advancement still favors seniority.

Many of the quantitative targets in the Higher Education Reform Agenda 2006–2020 remain unmet. Most important, the higher education system is not innovative. An unclear and contradictory regulatory environment prevents institutions from making key decisions on quality and relevance. They lack incentives and freedom to improve the education they offer. The regulatory environment also discourages new providers from entering, mainly the more dynamic private providers.

De facto autonomy for higher education institutions is limited. Tertiary education institutions may propose enrollment targets to MOET but must calculate them according to the traditional norms for "capacity." MOET must also approve them and is willing to continue managing student numbers by limiting enrollments in certain disciplines. Faculty salaries are still tightly regulated for public institutions. In theory, private institutions set tuition as they see fit—but in practice, they find numerous limits on their ability to expand (World Bank 2016).

Many of the current policies fail to serve their intended purposes. Worse, they have negative consequences.

- Tuition caps were meant to make university affordable for poor families, but no reliable data exist on how effective the tuition limits are in allowing poor students to attend. Since a student from a poor family has only a 10 percent chance of entering university compared with a student from a rich family, tuition levels are structurally below the willingness and ability to pay. This results in a negative outcome: institutions lack funds while students and families who *could* pay more pay only nominal tuition. A web of fees and other payments has evolved in response to tuition caps, further distorting revenue and incentives.
- Entrance exam policy was meant to ensure that those who attend have the academic ability to succeed. It now functions mainly to allocate students to existing spaces created by institutions. The priority is to fill these spaces, leaving many students to study for degrees that do not interest them and that have no labor market link.
- Enrollment limitations are meant to be based on quality but they use metrics such as spaces and faculty qualifications. These are not quality indicators except in the most serious abuses. They slow change and force students into only the available places.
- Bureaucracy keeps down the number of private tertiary education providers, limiting student choice, retarding innovation, and favoring the status quo.

These de facto policies weigh heavily on any moves to improve quality, relevance, and coverage of the Vietnamese higher education system. The government should consider new policies on deregulating tertiary education in the following five areas.

Removing restrictions on revenue created by tuition caps

Earlier reforms changed the higher education system from one that was fully funded with public money. Now public and private institutions charge tuition, and private institutions depend almost completely on tuition revenue. But the amount they can charge is limited and low internationally. Policy seeks to limit what higher education institutions can charge, on public institutions through the tuition framework and on the private side indirectly.[18]

Revenue restrictions highlight a major challenge for the system. The country cannot afford to publicly finance the combination of coverage, quality, and relevance it requires. Public spending for higher education is 3.5 percent of government spending. It was 158 percent higher in real terms in 2012 than in 2008 (Tran and Crawford 2015). Revenue shortages prevent institutions from developing true full-time, highly qualified faculty and hamper professors' commitment to institutions and students. They also limit the amount and quality of physical facilities.

Yet the main avenue for raising revenue—private student contributions—is underused. The government's rationale for restrictions is to keep higher education affordable for poor families. It prioritizes affordability for the poor over revenues that drive innovation, quality, and relevance. But it does so without evidence that the policy helps the poor receive a higher education. Thus, poor people are unlikely to pursue higher education. The unintended consequences of this policy are to make higher education affordable for students and families who have the means—and likely the willingness—to pay more.

A system allowing institutions—public and private—to have de facto full autonomy in setting tuition rates should be a main feature. It requires robust financial aid arrangements to measure the true financial needs of poor students and to provide assistance. Creating such a system poses technical challenges, but the experience of many other countries provides options to overcome them. Limiting revenues across the board can only continue to stifle incentives for systemwide improvement.

Current government proposals to raise the private contribution of social services beneficiaries create an opportunity to reform tertiary education tuition policies. These policies should have three goals: require private beneficiaries (students and families) to pay as much of the cost as possible, raise revenues to reflect beneficiaries' willingness to pay and the costs of providing the service, and ensure that qualified but financially needy aspiring students receive financial assistance. A system that meets these goals would eliminate tuition caps and would focus government spending on financial aid.

Eliminating restrictions on enrollment

Enrollment goals in the Higher Education Reform Agenda—particularly for enrolling in private higher education—have not been met. The pace of expansion has been controlled by MOET out of concern that quality could suffer if expansion is too quick.

The widening gap between demand for university places and approved admissions attest to unmet demand by students aspiring to university degrees. The national university entrance exam, while slowly decreasing in importance, still determines university admission. Government influence in determining admission cut-off points and enrollment quotas remains strong.

This policy of slowing or repressing demand prioritizes a "consumer protection" role that the government exercises on behalf of aspiring students. It rests on a two-pronged rationale. First, it is better to deny aspiring students access to tertiary education than to allow them to enroll in programs that do not meet government-determined quality standards. Second, the government's means for assessing quality are adequate and better than those of aspiring students. In reality, the government's instruments for judging quality (for example, physical space and faculty credentials) are no better than the judgments students and families can make about the relative value of programs. The distorting effect of the government's policies is to lower the quality of programs by removing institutions' incentives to heed student demand or improve. By protecting students from enrolling in a few bad degree programs, the government stifles the dynamism that comes from having institutions compete to offer students the best programs. Many countries achieve both goals with much lighter government regulation of institutions and by assuring that institutions compete to provide students with the best choice of educational options. The cost of eliminating perceived "fraudulently substandard" programs is to lower the quality of all programs.

Promoting unmet demand for enrollment also exacerbates revenue deficits created by tuition caps. Every aspiring student who fails to enroll also fails to pay revenue into the system.

With this policy, Vietnam stands in opposition to other fast-growing developing countries that have allowed student demand to determine the rate of enrollment growth (box 3.12). Vietnam's main comparators have

BOX 3.12 Rapid expansion of private higher education satisfies demand for skills in India

Over the last two decades, a rapidly growing Indian economy has led to great demand for an educated and skilled labor force. To meet the needs of a dynamic economy, private enterprises have sprouted to complement public educational institutions, which are plagued by capacity constraints. Over the past few decades, the private sector has driven capacity creation in higher education.

The policy environment for private higher education improved starting in the mid-1990s, coinciding with falling investment by the federal government and the states. In 2001, when private unaided institutes made up 42.6 percent of all higher education institutions, 32.8 percent of Indian students studied there. By 2006, the share of private institutes had risen to 63.2 percent and their student share to 51.5 percent.

Source: Sudarshan and Subramanian 2013.

prioritized meeting demand for higher education over promoting administrative mechanisms for ensuring quality. They have made this choice believing that aspiring students and their families can judge the quality of the programs they seek, not perfectly but at least as well as government bureaucrats. This is especially true when governments provide information to students about higher education institutions to allow informed decision making.

Instruments available to measure quality, such as faculty credentials, square footage of available physical space, and numbers of library books are crude proxies for true measures of quality. Some countries, such as Colombia, have introduced tests that assess changes to student learning to have more reliable quality measures. Most governments, however, rely increasingly on labor market success of graduates and institutional completion rates as the best among crude proxy measures.

Allowing institutions to expand to meet student demand may threaten quality in the short run. But it initiates competition for students among institutions, which ultimately drives quality improvements.

Some countries have also embraced open enrollment because it promotes a value-added approach to tertiary education. Traditional thinking views higher education as a scarce and precious resource that must be directed to only the best and brightest. Modern policies foster the belief that any student can benefit—not just the brightest—and that raising the skills of poor and mediocre students is as important as raising the skills of the brightest. This means promoting strength and encouraging enrollment in universities and nonuniversity tertiary institutions such as colleges.

Permitting students to enroll in the degree program of their choice

Higher education's central-control legacy still influences the way aspiring students are allocated into degree programs. The system is supply driven: Students fit their career plans to available spaces. In more dynamic systems, institutions adapt their degree programs to the demands of aspiring students. This arrangement obliges the student to assess the future labor market value of the intended degree program. The back-and-forth between what students seek and what institutions offer—while imperfect—is the best way to drive programs toward quality and relevance.

When a higher education system successfully develops, students become the most reliable judges of future labor market needs. They want a good return on the investment in their own human capital. They have the most at stake and therefore should be informed and trusted with the decision.

Most also pay substantial tuition. When a system becomes student-centered, institutions pay attention to students' demands, offering high-quality programs according to what aspiring students seek.

Vietnam can create the responsiveness and dynamism it needs by loosening policy to increase revenue in the system. It should allow enrollments to be determined by student demand and create a larger role for private sector providers. It should also have institutions adapt to students (not vice versa). The country's traditional practices prevent the tertiary education system from reaching its full potential.

Expanding the number of providers to diversify student choice on where and what to study

By 2035 Vietnam's higher education system will need to double and greatly improve. The skill demands of the workplace will likely continue to accelerate. Secondary school graduation rates will increase, and the return to tertiary education will likely remain high. Both outcomes will raise demand for higher education.

Vietnam permits private higher education, but policies are suboptimal in two important ways. First, enrollment restrictions discourage the best potential providers. Second, processes for obtaining permission to operate a private tertiary education institution are slow and not transparent. Such discouragement of additional providers harms students' interests.

A system without restrictions on enrollment, tuition, or degree choice attracts potential tertiary education providers. When their numbers increase, they can compete against each other to offer students the best education at the best combination of price and quality. Policy elements then combine to produce a dynamic and responsive tertiary education system.

Making information for aspiring students a cornerstone of quality assurance

The government's main efforts in quality assurance focus on accreditation of degree programs rather than of institutions. The accreditation agencies are called independent because they do not report directly to the government. But two of the three accreditation centers are agencies within public universities. Therefore, they do not match the accepted international definition of "independent."

Quality promotion should involve providing students with information about where and what to study, but this instrument is underused. Such information has a strong secondary value and would provide elements now missing from policy making. These measures of degree program relevance directly relate to employment success and graduate salaries. Policy should promote shaping the type of graduates required by the labor market. But empirical measures do not exist to judge whether—and to what extent—this is happening. Providing information to students could improve decision making—for them and for policy makers—by informing decisions based on empirical evidence.

Vietnam has taken initial steps in this area but has not yet achieved a strong and reliable information system to enable students to make the best choice. Such a system gains value as student choice becomes more important in policy. As students assume the main role in choosing how to invest in themselves, they will require more detailed information, including the following:

- Graduate employment success
- Average salaries of graduates by degree program
- Faculty qualifications, accomplishments, and ratios of faculty to student
- Test scores and academic qualifications of students by degree program
- Graduation and dropout rates and the average time to graduation (by degree program)
- Student satisfaction of subject measures

For this system to be effective, nearly all tertiary education institutions must provide complete and comparable information.

Indicators of Success: Toward a System with World-Class Universities

Foundations III and IV form the basis of a strong research system connected to a robust graduate and undergraduate education system. When these foundations are solid, a few apex institutions—world-class universities—sit atop a pyramid made strong by supportive policies. Vietnam has no universities in the top 500 in either of the two best-known ranking systems.[19] More spending alone cannot change this. Improved policies are as important as increased resources if Vietnam is to establish itself among countries with world-class universities.

Policies that promote apex institutions are also beneficial to the tertiary education system. In Vietnam, the tertiary education system is intellectually uninspiring and an unattractive career option for the most talented students. As the country moves toward 2035, vigorous pursuit of the policies discussed stands to change that. The best success indicator will be when Vietnam's universities attract the best national and international talent as sought-after places to study and work.

By Way of Conclusion: Moving Toward an Innovation-Led Economy

The developed economies have gone from a factor-driven economy (phase 1) to an efficiency-driven economy (phase 2) to an innovation-driven economy (phase 3), with transitions between the phases. Vietnam was named by the World Economic Forum in 2015–16 among 16 countries that are in the transition from phase 1 to phase 2.[20]

As chapter 1 noted, Vietnam aspires to the higher reaches of upper-middle-income country status by 2035. Then, Vietnam will be at the end of phase 2, or even at an early point in the transition to phase 3 (like Malaysia in 2012–2013). To get there, it must reach phase 2 by 2025.

The growth of a factor-driven economy is mainly based on the increase of unskilled labor, physical capital, and natural resources. As a country moves into phase 2, higher labor productivity results from learning and applying available technology through higher education and training. In phase 3, increased productivity and economic growth come mainly from innovation and the application of advanced technology, more sophisticated manufacturing processes, and a high-quality workforce.

To achieve its 2035 objectives, Vietnam will need to build and develop innovation capacity appropriate to each stage of development.

How can Vietnam do that? First, science, technology, and higher education must reach a more advanced level, capable of providing knowledge and high-quality human resources to the business sector. At the same time, domestic private firms will experience strong and dynamic growth. The NIS can then grow in a competitive and efficiency- and incentive-driven environment and contribute significantly to productivity. The TFP growth should account for more than 40 percent of GDP growth.

A more dynamic domestic private sector can create solid demand and absorb advanced knowledge for higher value-added goods and competitiveness in both domestic and international markets. It is also important to enhance the firms' capacity to upgrade and adopt the latest technologies, by upgrading human capital of managers, deploying more effective technological extension services, and creating an enabling environment for accumulating physical and (risky) knowledge capital. Enterprises can then participate more effectively in the GVCs, playing the leading role for domestic value chains and industry clusters.

Vietnam must develop a system of research institutes that are dynamic, effective, and linked with private firms and the global knowledge network. Public research institutions can be restructured toward higher autonomy to fit the market economy, undertaking contract-applied research with industry while focusing on competitive fundamental research to serve the priorities of socio-economic development. Research institutes of businesses, especially in large enterprises, will also be formed, improving the innovation capacity of the private sector. In some areas of science and technology, Vietnam will move up to the advanced level in the region and globally, sufficiently supporting innovation in economic sectors and enterprises for more effective competition.

Higher education must be comprehensively reformed to satisfy the labor needs of a market economy. Research and postgraduate education should be integrated, and public universities should become autonomous. Private and nonprofit universities will flourish in a competitive environment to enhance education quality and meet the growing learning needs of society. A student-centered approach would aim at sharpened self-learning and self-innovation capacity by students. Qualified and high-quality human resources can then be provided appropriately to satisfy social needs as the core force for innovation.

These objectives cannot be realized without intensive and comprehensive reforms of the regulatory and policy environment. The recommendations in this chapter should be translated into specific agendas and programs, appropriately designed for each development phase. This will be a huge challenge for Vietnam, but it is the logical path given the development histories of successful nations.

Notes

1. The National Agency for Science and Technology Information has published estimates of GERD as high as 0.5 percent of GDP, but by its own admission, these are not calculated using standard, internationally accepted methodologies. Hence we choose 0.3 percent as probably a more comparable figure.
2. See, for instance, Klenow and Rodriguez-Clare (2004) and Maloney and Rodriguez-Clare (2007).
3. Goni and Maloney (2014) show that returns appear to follow an inverted U. Initially, countries farther from the frontier achieve higher rates of return as the potential for adopting new technologies rises—Schumpeterian catch-up. However, as countries move further from the frontier, the quality of entrepreneurs, the business climate, and human capital also worsen, making R&D less effective in promoting growth. This lack of complementarities offsets distance from the frontier.
4. National Science Board 2014. Comparable article counts are normed to include the corresponding fractions of articles with multiple authors, to allow for accurate international comparisons. Article counts where full credit for the article is given to each of the multiple authors lead to higher totals. For Vietnam, nationals are coauthors on some 1,400 articles a year.
5. Blomström and Kokko 1998. This is the case even in countries where intellectual property rights are weak. First, interviews with multinational corporations reveal how careful they are about taking their frontier technologies to countries where the technologies are not protected. Hence, the degree to which multinationals do very high-level research is likely to depend on the quality of the IPR regime. Second, Zhao (2006) shows that, consistent with the previous section, firms can protect their intellectual property due to the absence of key complementarities needed for exploiting it, such as marketing networks, expertise, or firm capacity. Again, benefiting from R&D and S&T spending requires close attention to these complements.
6. Maloney and Sarrias (2014) find less of an effect of competition and, like Bloom et al. (2015), find the level of human capital and training of management is critical across the distribution.
7. High-growth firms are defined in OECD (2009) as "enterprises with average annualized growth in employees of turnover greater than 20 percent per annum, over a three-year period, and with more than 10 employees in the beginning of the observation period."
8. Brown et al. (2014) argue that they are not necessarily young. In the United States, the average age of the firm was 25 and in the United Kingdom 70 percent were at least five years old. Second, in the United Kingdom fewer than 15 percent of United Kingdom firms emanate from high-tech sectors. Third, universities suggest that very few high-growth firms have their roots in universities. Fourth, most are not backed by venture capital or other sources of entrepreneurial finance. Fifth, the growth of high-growth firms is extremely uneven, undergoing longer periods of low or no growth punctuated by short "bursts" of

rapid growth. Hence rapid growth is rarely sustained in the longer term and today's high-growth firms will not be tomorrow's. That is, while a particular firm may generate employment-growth rates of 20 percent this year, its subsequent performance may not justify supporting it over a steady, but substantially more modest, grower.

9. According to interviews, there are not separate words for innovation and invention. It is important to stress that, for instance, the key concept of *kaizen* in Japan is a gradual increase in productivity through incremental improvements rather than great leaps forward. Firms are unlikely to implement large inventions that are not well run and that have not passed through a gradualist phase of improvements. Again, in the medium term, the policy needs to focus as much on strengthening firm capacity as fomenting large innovation leaps in the S&T apparatus.
10. Krishna, Levchenko, and Maloney 2015. Quality as measured by export unit values to the United States.
11. Recently, instability in the regulations surrounding the high-tech sector and the Internet have been cited as a potential barrier to the further development of the sector (Ives 2015).
12. National Science Board 2014. www.nsf.gov/statistics/.
13. Raising the quantity, quality, and relevance of R&D, knowledge production, and advanced human capital training.
14. Continuously improving the quality and relevance of skills in the labor force, through increased responsiveness and dynamism in tertiary education.
15. National Science Board 2014. Note that increased funding may be from a variety of sources, including multinational corporations operating in the country.
16. A list of Korean Research Institutes is available at: http://people.duke.edu/~myhan/c_blri.html.
17. The Higher Education Law 2012 attempts to deal with some critical aspects, such as autonomy of institutions, university councils, multitiered higher education, private higher education, accreditation, and quality assurance.
18. In the literature, the most frequently cited ways of limiting tuition in private institutions are regulations that do not allow tuition to exceed 5 percent of median family income in a given region and restrictions on property ownership by private institutions combined with requirements to show enough physical space for expanded enrollment. The first limits revenue per student, and the second limits marginal revenue by limiting the growth of enrollment.
19. *Times Higher Education Supplement* and Shanghai Jiao Tong University.
20. World Economic Forum's Report in 2015–16 (table 2) ranked Vietnam among 16 economies in the *transition phase* from phase 1 (factor driven) into phase 2 (efficiency driven); Vietnam was in phase 1 in 2014–2015 (factor driven) (World Economic Forum 2015).

References

Acemoglu, Daron, and Fabrizio Zilibotti. 1997. "Was Prometheus Unbound by Chance? Risk, Diversification, and Growth." *Journal of Political Economy* 105 (4): 709–51.

Blomström, Magnus, and Ari Kokko. 1998. "Multinational Corporations and Spillovers." *Journal of Economic Surveys* 12 (3): 247–77.

Blomström, Magnus, Ari Kokko, and Fredrik Sjöholm. 2002. "Growth and Innovation Policies for a Knowledge Economy: Experiences from Finland, Sweden, and Singapore." Background report for the LAC Flagship Report, World Bank, Washington, DC.

Bloom, Nicholas, and John Van Reenen. 2007. "Measuring and Explaining Management Practices across Firms and Countries." *The Quarterly Journal of Economics* 122 (4): 1351–408.

Bloom, Nicholas, Raissa Ebner, Kerenssa Kay, Renata Lemos, Raffaella Sadun, Daniela Scur, and John Van Reenen. 2015. "Management Practices in Vietnam." Background paper for Vietnam 2035 Report.

Branstetter, Lee, Guangwei Li, and Francisco Veloso. 2013. "The Globalization of R&D: China, India, and the Rise of International Co-Invention." Draft report, World Bank, Washington, DC.

Branstetter, Lee, Raymond Fisman, and C. Fritz Foley. 2006. "Do Stronger Intellectual Property Rights Increase International Technology Transfer? Empirical Evidence from U. S. Firm-Level Panel Data." *The Quarterly Journal of Economics* 121 (1): 321–49.

Brown, Ross, Colin Mason, and Suzanne Mawson. 2014. "Increasing 'the Vital 6 Percent': Designing effective public policy to support high growth firms." Nesta Working Paper

14/01. England: Nesta. http://www.nesta.org.uk/publications/increasing-vital-6-percent-designing-effective-public-policy-support-high-growth-firms

Carnoy, Martin, Prashant Loyalka, Gregory Androushchak, and Anna Proudnikova. 2013. "The Economic Returns to Higher Education in BRIC Countries and Their Implications for Higher Education Expansion." Working Paper 253, Rural Education Action Project, Stanford University, Palo Alto, CA.

De Carvalho, Antonio Gledson, Charles Calomiris, and João A. Matos. 2008. "Venture Capital as Human Resources Management." *Journal of Economics and Business* 60 (1): 223–55.

Electronic Nhan Dan Newspaper, April 25, 2015. http://en.nhandan.com.vn/

Foster, Andrew, and Mark Rosenzweig. 2010. "Microeconomics of Technology Adoption." *Annual Review of Economics* 2 (1): 395–424.

Goni, Edwin, and William Maloney. 2014. "Why Don't Poor Countries Do R&D?" Policy Research Working Paper 6811, World Bank, Washington, DC.

Gonzalez-Brambila, Claudia, Francisco Veloso, and Jose Lever. 2007. "Mexico's Innovation Cha-Cha." *Issues in Science and Technology* 24 (1): 1–64.

Ives, Mike. 2015. "As Technology Entrepreneurs Multiply in Vietnam, So Do Regulations." *New York Times*, February 8.

Klenow, Peter, and Andrew Rodriguez-Clare. 2004. "Externalities and Growth." In *Handbook of Economic Growth*, edited by Philippe Aghion, and Steven Durlauf. Amsterdam: Elsevier.

KOICA Vietnam Office. 2015. "Korea's Experiences on Innovation, Science, and Technology." KOICA Vietnam Office, Hanoi.

Krishna, Pravin, Andrei Levchenko, and William Maloney. 2015. "Growth and Risk: The View from International Trade." Unpublished manuscript, World Bank, Washington, DC.

Maloney, William, and Andrés Rodríguez-Clare. 2007. "Innovation shortfalls." *Review of Development Economics* 11 (4): 665–84.

Maloney, William, and Mauricio Sarrias. 2014. "Convergence to the Managerial Frontier." Policy Research Working Paper 6822, World Bank, Washington, DC.

Mason, Colin, and Jennifer Kwok. 2010. "Discussion Paper on Investment Readiness Programmes." Organisation for Economic Co-operation and Development, Paris.

MOET (Ministry of Education and Training, Socialist Republic of Vietnam). 2013. *Statistical Yearbook 2013*. Hanoi: MOET.

Murphy, Kevin, Andrei Shleifer, and Robert W. Vishny. 1991. "The Allocation of Talent: Implications for Growth." *The Quarterly Journal of Economics* 106 (2): 503–30.

National Science Board. 2014. "Research and Development: National Trends and International Comparisons." In *Science and Engineering Indicators 2014*. Arlington, VA: National Science Foundation. https://www.nsf.gov/statistics/seind14/index.cfm/chapter-4.

Newman, Carol, John Rand, Theodore Purdendu Talbot, and Finn Tarp. 2014. "Technology Transfers, Foreign Investment and Productivity Spillovers: Evidence from Vietnam." IIIS Discussion Paper 440, Institute for International Integration Studies, Trinity College, Dublin.

OECD (Organisation for Economic Co-operation and Development). 2009. "OECD Reviews of Innovation Policy: Mexico." OECD, Paris.

OECD–World Bank. 2014. *Science, Technology, and Innovation in Viet Nam*. Paris: OECD Publishing.

Oh, Chai Kon. 1997. "A Study on the Promotion of the Effective Diffusion of National R&D Results." Science and Technology Policy Institute, Seoul.

Rand, John, and Finn Tarp. 2012. "Characteristics of the Vietnamese Business Environment: Evidence from a SME Survey in 2011." Central Institute for Economic Management, Hanoi.

Sudarshan, Anand, and Sandhya Subramanian. 2013. "The Private Sector's Role in Indian Higher Education." In *India Infrastructure Report 2012: Private Sector in Education*, edited by Infrastructure Development Finance Company, 178–184. Oxford: Routledge.

Toh, Mun-Heng. 2015. "Singapore's Participation in Global Value Chains: Perspectives of Trade in Value-Added (No. DP-2015-50)." Economic Research Institute for ASEAN and East Asia, Jakarta, Indonesia.

Tran, Carolyn, and Michael Crawford. 2015. "The Vietnamese Higher Education System: Characteristics and Challenges." Under review.

U.S. Patent and Trademark Office. USTPO Database. http://www.uspto.gov/learning-and-resources/open-data-and-mobility

Vietnam Education Foundation. 2014. "Observations on the Current Status of Higher Education in Agricultural Sciences, Civil Engineering, Computer Science at Selected Universities in

Vietnam." Vietnam Education Foundation, Arlington, VA.

William Maloney, and Andrés Rodríguez-Clare. 2007. "Innovation Shortfalls." *Review of Development Economics* 11 (4): 665–84.

Wong, Kok-Seng. 2008. "Using Foreign Direct Investment and MNCs to Upgrade Domestic Labour and Firms: Singapore's Experience." Presentation, Economic Development Board, Singapore.

World Bank. 2014. *Global Financial Development Report 2014: Financial Inclusion*. Washington, DC: World Bank.

———. 2015. *Doing Business 2016: Measuring Regulatory Quality and Efficiency*. Washington, DC: World Bank.

———. 2016. "Financial and Academic Efficiencies of the Vietnamese Public Higher Education Institutions: A Dynamic Network Data Envelopment Analysis Approach." Under review.

World Development Indicators (database). Washington, DC: World Bank. http://data.worldbank.org/data-catalog/world-development-indicators.

World Economic Forum. 2010. *Global Competitiveness Report, 2010–11*. Geneva: World Economic Forum.

———. 2015. *Global Competitiveness Report, 2015–16*. Geneva: World Economic Forum.

Zhao, Minyuan. 2006. "Conducting R&D in Countries with Weak Intellectual Property Rights Protection." *Management Sciences* 52 (8): 1185–99.

4

Managing Urbanization for Greater Economic Efficiency

Main Messages

Urbanization—increasing the densities of people and production in cities and towns—is one of the most striking features of economic development. Incomes tend to rise, especially when accompanied by increases in the contribution of industry and services to economic activity and jobs. Indeed, Vietnam's extensive urban transformation over the past three decades has levered its economic development. In 1986, the country had fewer than 12 million urban residents; now it has more than 30 million, and urban areas contribute more than half the gross domestic product (GDP).

In the midst of urbanization and rising economic density, Vietnam has kept regional and rural–urban disparities in check—mainly through central transfers aimed at poorer areas to expand basic services and infrastructure across the country. Even within cities, slums and urban segregation appear less of a challenge than in many other developing economies.

As Vietnam embarks on an even more ambitious growth trajectory over the next 20 years, cities will need to do more to nurture a burgeoning domestic private sector, to support the growth of firm clusters that can integrate into global value chains (GVCs), and to nurture and agglomerate talent. This role will require reshaping policies and investments to tackle three emerging constraints: low and stagnant density, rising distance, and persistent divisions.

Such reshaping is important since the current urbanization model is constraining economic transformation. The first constraint—stagnant density—comes from the land conversion–based urban development model, with industrial zones developed ahead of demand in recent years, and the proliferation of small-scale, fragmented urban areas. As a result, the density of urban population has remained unchanged since 2000, forgoing the potential boost to productivity growth that higher density could have provided.

The second constraint—lengthening economic distance—comes from limited connectivity between cities and markets and from unreliable supply chains and high logistics costs. In metropolitan areas, gridlock and bottlenecks weigh heavily on economic efficiency and make cities less attractive places to live and conduct business. And weak regional connections are lengthening economic distance, with Vietnam's provinces and cities more like independent oases than parts of an integrated marketplace, even across short distances. As a result, urban spatial development in Vietnam is concentrated only in the Hanoi and Ho Chi Minh City metropolitan areas. And although the urban–rural gaps in incomes and access to infrastructure and social services have narrowed, the urban–rural connectivity remains weak and fragmented.

The third constraint—rising social division—relates to migrants to urban areas receiving lower wages and having far less access to urban services. Without permanent residence under the household registration system (*hộ khẩu*), migrants face numerous difficulties in many daily aspects of urban living, such as applying for a job, trying to get a loan, registering a business (or motorbike), buying or renting a house, and signing up for medical insurance. These make it far harder for them to invest in their human capital and durable assets, cutting the longer-term potential for agglomeration economies.

There are five main causes that restrict the positive impacts of urbanization in Vietnam: (i) *unsuitable land policies* have distorted land transfer, transactions, and effective land-use, promoting excessive conversion of agricultural land to industrial land; (ii) *the city classification system* encourages localities to expand the size of their urban areas and make excessive investments, without considering critical indicators such as population density and links to push growth; (iii) *lack of coordination* in mass transit infrastructure development and core urban area development is coupled with institutional fragmentation in large cities, with limited consideration paid to transit-oriented development and land use in public transit projects; (iv) *lack of attention to rural–urban links* has mostly served livelihoods rather than modern agribusiness, which has comparative advantages in Vietnam; and (v) *the household registration system* creates discrimination against migrants in the labor market and restricts their access to social services.

The signals are clear that the current urbanization model is constraining economic transformation and social inclusion. Vietnam will have to amplify economic density around large metropolitan areas and secondary cities with demonstrated potential. It will have to shorten the economic distance to large markets to enable specialization. And it will have to dissipate social division in access to services between migrants and urban residents to encourage human capital development for greater agglomeration economies. This will require a mindset change about urbanization, the benefit will be agglomeration economies across a vibrant portfolio of towns and cities performing complementary functions:

- Metropolises such as Hanoi and Ho Chi Minh City will interact with the global economy and provide the urban diversity that encourages learning, innovation, and new product development, connecting people and firms to the world.
- Cities such as Haiphong, Da Nang, and Can Tho will allow producers both to benefit from clustering because they can choose workers and materials from a bigger pool and to engage in beneficial competition. These cities will be aggregators for the hinterland economy and be part of GVCs.
- Towns such as Buon Ma Thuot in the Central Highlands, which is famous for its coffee, will let firms and farms exploit plant-level scale economies by providing roads (for inputs and outputs) and schools and other amenities (for workers' families).

Two main sets of policies need to be honed for Vietnamese cities to better support economic growth: upgrading institutions and expanding connective infrastructure.

Upgrading Institutions

Enable land markets. The core of urban policy reform is letting land markets emerge and flourish. Reforming land institutions—including strengthening land registration and adopting market-based land valuation—are priorities to reduce excessive and fragmented urban land conversion. Increasing the transparency of land pricing by setting up mechanisms to regularly publicize land values obtained in auctions and individual land sales could be a good starting point. Linked closely to land policy is the supply of land for affordable housing for low-income households. These efforts need to be tied to local government fiscal reforms that promote broader use of land and property taxes as an alternative to land conversion fees for local revenues.

Enhance planning coordination. Local governments are rewarded for business expansion within their boundaries, undermining potential clustered development or scale economies in infrastructure investment. The City Classification System encourages infrastructure development at a very local level, fragmenting urban development. There is need to strengthen institutions for integrated urban planning—within and across sectors (land use and transport) and contiguous urban areas—to encourage scale economies at corridor, metropolitan area/conurbation, or regional level. In Japan and the Republic of Korea, for example, the institutional mandates for land, infrastructure, transport, and water resources are vested under one line ministry, helping better coordinate policies at the territorial and city levels. This step requires a "whole of government" approach, which would require the central government to carefully review the mandates of line ministries and align them to international best practices.

Strengthen urban planning. Urban planning departments need to strengthen their capabilities urgently. Master plans and other physical plans need to be linked to the budget process; if plans cannot be supported by key investments, their credibility will suffer. Coordination mechanisms that can align provincial and city plans are essential, especially since socioeconomic development plans, urban master plans, and sector infrastructure plans are prepared by different departments, often run on different schedules, and use inconsistent data and projections for planning. The timing of planning needs to be synchronized, and the number of plans that govern within a territorial space needs to be rationalized. Vietnam also needs a professional cadre of urban planners who can plan and manage cities. Emphasis on this discipline needs to be greater in university education and in the talent hired within the ministries and provinces.

Policies and institutions need to be reformed to better facilitate rural–urban migration. *Hộ khẩu*–based management needs to be amended to provide easier access to urban services for migrants. In addition, fundamental reforms should be required in vocational training and job creation for migrants to equip them with skills to readily meet the demand of firms and urban residents. Basic social infrastructure and services to support migrants—such as housing, schools, medical services, and health insurance—should be assured. And associations that support and protect the rights of migrants should be developed.

Expanding Connective Infrastructure

Mainstream integrated transport and logistics platform. The government should focus on mainstreaming integrated planning for transport and logistics spatially across modes. Roads to big ports, including Haiphong, and Ho Chi Minh City, need to be rebuilt so that cargo can reach the ports easily. The focus should be on key road corridors and expressways to tackle issues in supply chains and reduce the burden of road transport costs on the economy. Accompanying it, attention should also be paid to the development of transport infrastructure to connect regional-level cities located in key agricultural zones such as the Mekong River Delta and Central Highlands to increase connectivity and best leverage the strengths of Vietnam's agriculture sector. It is prerequisite to attract private investments in rural areas and support the formation of urban cores and industry-service clusters in the key agricultural zones.

Expand the volume and quality of urban transport services. These are closely tied to refinements in urban planning.

Develop inter regional transport system to connect the strategic commercial agricultural production areas in the Mekong River Delta and Central Highlands. This is the prerequisite for attracting investment into rural areas, developing urban centers and agro-industry clusters in these regions.

In addition, there is a need to synchronize policies for rural and urban development—policies now developed in isolation. Not only inefficient, this also feeds the perception that rural and urban areas are in competition—as for water resources—and that urban development has come at the expense of rural development. It is important to see rural–urban relations as the venue for the structural transformation of the economy. And a symbiotic relationship between rural areas and a hierarchy of urban areas will likely determine how inclusive Vietnam's future urbanization will be.

In implementing these policies and supporting investments, Vietnamese authorities may want to recalibrate the roles of the state and the market in managing how the country urbanizes. In particular, they could usefully:

- Refocus the role of the state and improve its capabilities in areas that only the government can manage. These include strengthening capacities and increasing coordination for urban planning (including information and land use), public finances, and social services, as well as increasing investment in infrastructure to support urban plans.
- Redistribute responsibilities, with powers and resources, among national, local, and metropolitan governments to ensure that issues to be addressed at a regional scale are not undermined by local interests.
- Relax the state's control and involvement in activities that are managed more efficiently by markets, particularly the factor markets—such as those for land—where state control has produced costly distortions. Here the solution is not new regulations but fewer restrictions and enhanced use of market mechanisms to allocate factors of production.

Urbanization and Economic Transformation in Vietnam

Well-managed cities are critical for Vietnam's transformation into a modern industrialized economy. Evidence from today's developed countries and rapidly emerging economies shows that urbanization is a source of dynamism that can enhance productivity—in fact, no country in the industrial age has ever achieved sustained increases in national income without urbanizing. Urbanization propels the necessary spatial transformation that accompanies the structural transformation from agriculture to manufacturing and services.

These spatial and structural shifts are clearly unfolding in Vietnam, with the share of employment in agriculture rapidly declining as the country urbanizes (figure 4.1). The country's experience between 1996 and 2012 mirrors China's in the 1980s and the 1990s. And as Vietnam has grown and urbanized faster over the past two decades, the relationship between urbanization and incomes has been consistent with that of other countries (figure 4.2).

Cities Are Important for Economic Growth

By generating agglomeration economies, cities can enhance productivity and spur innovation and economic diversification nationally. The underlying reason is density. The most basic agglomeration economy is reduced transport costs for goods. In the early 1900s, New York and London were manufacturing powerhouses, places where factories located to be close to customers and transport infrastructure. Toward the end of that century, four-fifths of Chicago's jobs were compactly contained within four miles of State and Madison Streets, close to people's housing and to infrastructure (Grover and Lall 2015). Many of these benefits increase with scale: towns and small cities cannot reap the same benefits as larger cities do. International evidence suggests that the elasticity of income per capita to city population is 3–8 percent.[1] Each doubling of city size raises its productivity by 5 percent on average.

The density and size of cities can also create a market for specialized services, including logistics, advertising, legal support, and management consulting. These services are critical for allowing young firms to focus on their

FIGURE 4.1 Urbanization goes hand in hand with structural transformation

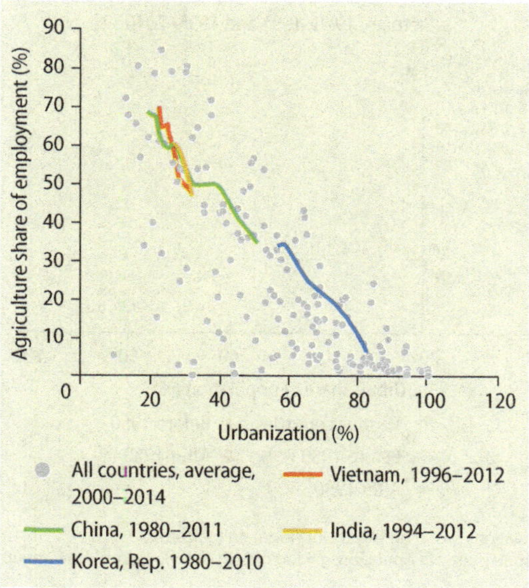

Source: Calculations based on World Development Indicators data.

FIGURE 4.2 Urbanization trends in Vietnam appear as strong as in the Republic of Korea and in China

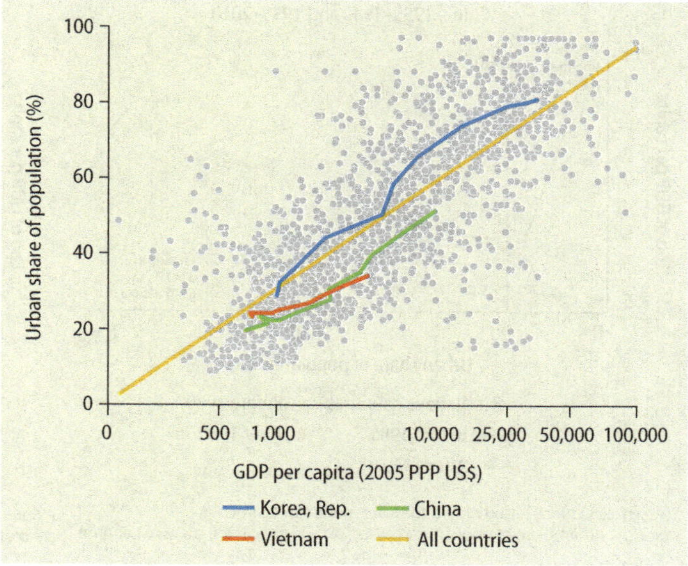

Source: Calculations based on World Development Indicators data.
Note: PPP = purchasing power parity.

"big idea" or core competences, without having to worry about supporting functions. The larger the cluster, the more specialized the service providers can be. Think of New York City, where a young fashion designer does not need an in-house lawyer to manage incorporation and intellectual property. She can also link to logistics firms to connect with merchandisers in Hong Kong SAR, China, and to production houses near Colombo, Sri Lanka.

Cities are also instrumental in matching skills with job opportunities, and density allows for an integrated, "thick" labor market. Skill matching will become more important by 2035 since the current generation of Vietnamese children will be better educated than their parents and will look for jobs that more fully reward their skills. Just as many Indian children growing up to become software engineers in the 1990s lined up to move to India's software hub of Bangalore, getting cities such as Ho Chi Minh City to flourish can help Vietnamese children find the firm that really wants them and will pay for their skill set. Research in the United States shows that workers in cities where the number of college graduates increases faster also have faster salary gains than workers who live in cities where the number of college graduates stagnates (Moretti 2004). This relationship is particularly strong for workers in high-tech jobs.

Given the economic benefits that cities can provide, it is unsurprising that urbanization and economic growth go hand in hand. Countries that are more developed have more urbanization, and countries that switch from slow to rapid economic development also switch from slow to rapid urbanization (China in figure 4.3), a generalizable fact that also describes Vietnam's experience (figure 4.4).

Vietnam has paid special attention to urbanization and urban development. In 2009, the prime minister approved the Master Plan for Development of Vietnam's Urban System to 2025 with a Vision to 2050. Under the plan, the urban population will reach 52 million by 2025, or more than half the country's people. This goal implies an annual increase in urbanization of 1.5 percentage points over 2010–25, up from 0.5 percentage points over 1993–2013. Based on the urban population's growth in the plan, the average annual growth rate in the coming decade will be up to 5.3 percent. Under this plan the

FIGURE 4.3 Urbanization and the transition from slow to fast growth in China

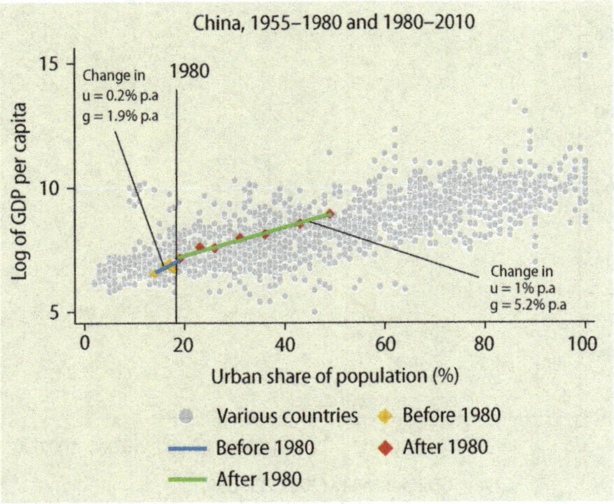

Source: Calculations based on World Development Indicators.
Notes: u = urban share of population; g = log of GDP per capita; p.a. = per annum.

FIGURE 4.4 Urbanization and the transition from slow to fast growth in Vietnam

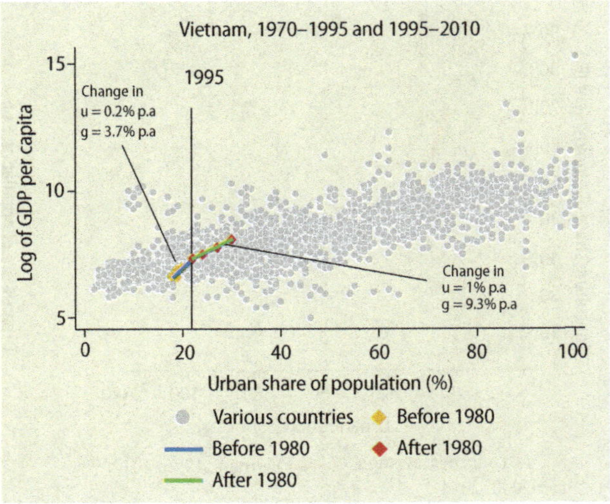

Source: Calculations based on World Development Indicators.
Notes: u = urban share of population; g = log of GDP per capita; p.a. = per annum.

portfolio of towns and cities in Vietnam would be larger and more sophisticated, and major cities, especially Hanoi and Ho Chi Minh City, would become highly competitive global economic centers.

A Fast Road for Vietnam, but Bumps Ahead to Be Smoothed

Other emerging economies have much to learn from Vietnam's (positive and negative) experiences. Over the past three decades, the country has undergone an extensive urban transformation. Since the *Đổi Mới* policy was launched in 1986, the urban population has grown 3.4 percent a year—from fewer than 12 million urban residents to more than 30 million. Urban areas now contribute more than half of GDP.

Vietnam's institutions for service provision have evolved to support rapid urbanization. The state of slums, urban segregation, and congestion in the cities is less problematic than in most other developing countries, and market-led urban development followed by moderate government interventions has created an urban fabric where different income groups are largely integrated (Huynh 2012). Vietnam has also achieved nearly universal electricity coverage in rural and urban areas and has largely removed regional disparities in coverage. Access to water has surged from 20 percent in 2002 to 99 percent in 2015.[2] Telecommunication has developed strongly with 133 million subscribers over the population of 90 million by end-2015.[3]

Vietnam's urban achievements along its journey to middle-income status are impressive, but the challenges in its transition to becoming an upper-middle-income economy are considerable. The urban challenges are further analyzed through the intuitive framework in the 2009 *World Development Report*, which is based on three spatial dimensions (density, distance, and division), three market forces (scale economies, labor mobility, and low transport and communication costs), and three policy constructs (institutions, infrastructure, and interventions) that address policy challenges.

The three factors need to act together to influence three spatial transformations:

1. Agglomeration, driven by *density*
2. Specialization, driven by reduced economic *distance*
3. Migration driven by dissipating *division*

Although urbanization in Vietnam has helped achieve rapid growth, three sets of constraints are emerging:

1. *Low and stagnant population density* alongside fragmented urban development, particularly outside the cores of Hanoi and Ho Chi Minh City
2. *Increasing economic distance* (in the quality and costs of transport and logistics), with limited connectivity between cities and markets, unreliability across the supply chain, and high logistics costs, new urban expansion—particularly in peri-urban areas—unconnected to transport infrastructure, and limited connectivity between urban and rural areas
3. *Persistent migrant–resident division* (who have or do not have *hộ khẩu*), as migrants have limited access to basic services in urban areas and job opportunities in urban areas

Vietnam's Urbanization in 3D: Density, Distance, and Division

Low and Stagnant Urban Density and Fragmented Urban Development

Low-density urban development

Between 1991 and 2014, Vietnam's official urban population doubled from 14 million to 30 million, and the proportion of the urban population in the total population increased by one-third, with an annual rate of urban population increase well above the global average (figure 4.5).

Alongside the urbanization of people, the urbanization of land has been just as rapid, contributing to urban population densities stagnating at relatively low levels. Between 2000 and 2015 Vietnam added 652,144 hectares of urban land, while its urban population increased by 10.2 million. Density remained stagnant at 18.9 urban residents per hectare (table 4.1). As an illustration of the emerging patterns of people and land urbanizations, consider New York's Manhattan Island as a metric. Manhattan is home to 1.6 million people living on 8,746 hectares of land. Although Vietnam's urban population increased by eight "Manhattans" between 2000 and 2015, the country's urban land area increased by 75 Manhattans. This stagnation in urban population density accompanied the slowdown of GDP growth in the 2000s, driven by the slowdown in growth of labor productivity (chapter 2).

In fact, land has been converted to "urban" commercial, residential, and industrial uses so rapidly that Vietnam has exceeded its urban land expansion goals (table 4.1). The area of urban residential land in 2010 was almost twice that in 2000, reaching 134,000 hectares, some 20 percent higher than the target set by the National Assembly (111,000 hectares). Urban built land area per capita in 2010 was 185 square meters, 1.5 times higher than the planned target.

Of Vietnam's land area, 0.9 percent is part of urban agglomerations (similar to China's despite far lower levels of urbanization, and higher than in Indonesia and the Philippines). In fact, the land area under plan is much higher than actual built-up land area, greatly affecting the efficiency of resource use.

Low and stagnant urban densities with limited infrastructure impede agglomeration economies. Evidence from around the world shows that the benefits from urban growth come from encouraging economic densification through the substitution between land and nonland inputs. At the city level, economic density can be increased by investing more capital on the same piece of land (increasing the height or floor space) alongside coordinated investments in transport that enable movements of people and products. These dynamics are not happening yet on a sufficient scale in Vietnam.

Consider the Ho Chi Minh City metropolitan area—Vietnam's economic powerhouse, where the urban land expansion has been the fastest in Vietnam at 4 percent a year, among the fastest in East Asia. Population density in its urban core is 44,000 persons/km^2 and drops to 26,000 for places within an hour's drive and to 15,000 for places at the outskirts of the urban area, two hours' drive from the core. Population densities in other major

FIGURE 4.5 Vietnam's urban population growth in the global picture

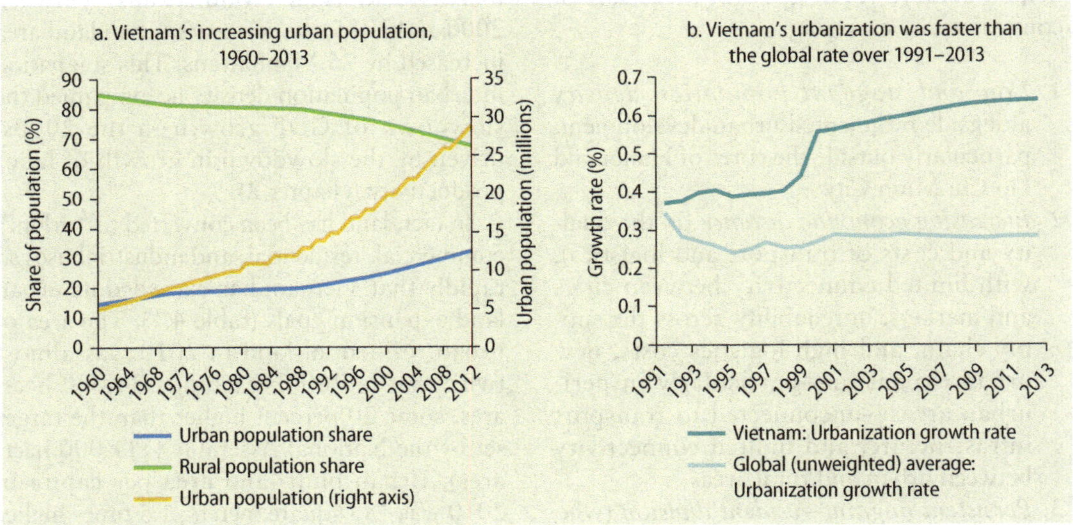

Source: Calculations based on World Development Indicators.

TABLE 4.1 Urbanization of land and people, 1995–2015

Year	Total number of urban areas	Total area of urban land (hectares)	Urban percentage of total land area	Total urban population (millions)	Urban share of the population (%)	Urban density (urban residents per hectare)
1995	420	836,117	2.53	14.9	20.8	17.9
2000	629	990,276	2.99	18.7	24.1	18.9
2005	675	1,153,549	3.48	22.3	27.1	19.4
2010	752	1,372,038	4.14	25.4	29.6	18.6
2015	775	1,642,420	4.96	31.0	34.3	18.9

Source: Vo and Van Thang 2013 (p. 33) and General Statistics Office of Vietnam.

FIGURE 4.6 Low-density spatial expansion can dampen agglomeration economies

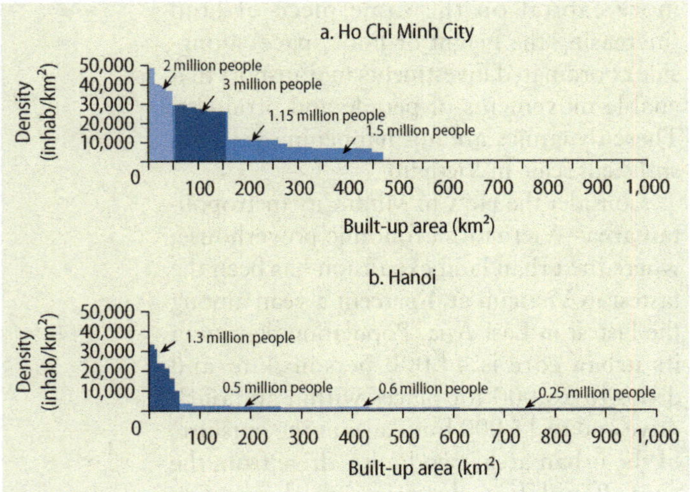

Source: Salat 2013.

urban centers around the world are far higher: downtown Singapore, 1 million persons/km^2; downtown Hong Kong SAR, China, more than 6 million; and Manhattan, 3.7 million.[4]

Much of the development in the metropolitan areas of Ho Chi Minh City and Hanoi is in peri-urban areas beyond the urban core (figure 4.6). Featuring low-density development with weak regional connections, Vietnam's urban areas are like fragmented oases that do not function like economically and physically integrated metropolitan regions. For example, on an ordinary day, and even at off-peak hours, it takes nearly two hours to travel from the central business district of Ho Chi Minh City to the center of Binh Duong New City, a distance of only 40 kilometers. If such patterns persist,

Vietnam's cities will be overwhelmed by traffic congestion and emissions.

Two factors exacerbate low-density and fragmented urban expansion: government decisions in locating industrial zones in peri-urban areas and the City Classification System, which encourages fragmented urban expansion (map 4.1).

Limited efficiency of peri-urban industrial zones

Industrial zones have had a big part in Vietnam's success. According to official statistics of the Ministry of Planning and Investment, there were 299 industrial zones in September 2015, of which 212 were operating with an occupancy rate of 66 percent. They were home to 5,964 foreign-invested projects with total registered capital of $96 billion and to 5,647 domestic-invested projects with a total registered capital of around D 568 trillion (around $26 billion). Their gross output accounted for one-quarter of GDP. In July 2014, industrial zones employed more than 2.2 million workers and indirectly created jobs for about 2 million other workers.[5] Productivity in the zones is higher than in neighboring cities (figure 4.7).

Urbanization benefits economies by increasing total factor productivity (TFP) through agglomeration, clustering, and economies of scale. In Vietnam, TFP growth has resulted from clustering and industrial zone development (Howard et al. 2014), but clustering has slowed as a result of economic dispersion.

While the number of industrial zones in recent years has rapidly expanded, the government has sited them in peri-urban locations with little uptake. Industrial zones and clusters covered 23,000 hectares in 2000, increasing to 100,000 hectares in 2010 (equal to 39 percent of nonagricultural production land)

MAP 4.1 Urban expansion in the Ho Chi Minh City agglomeration

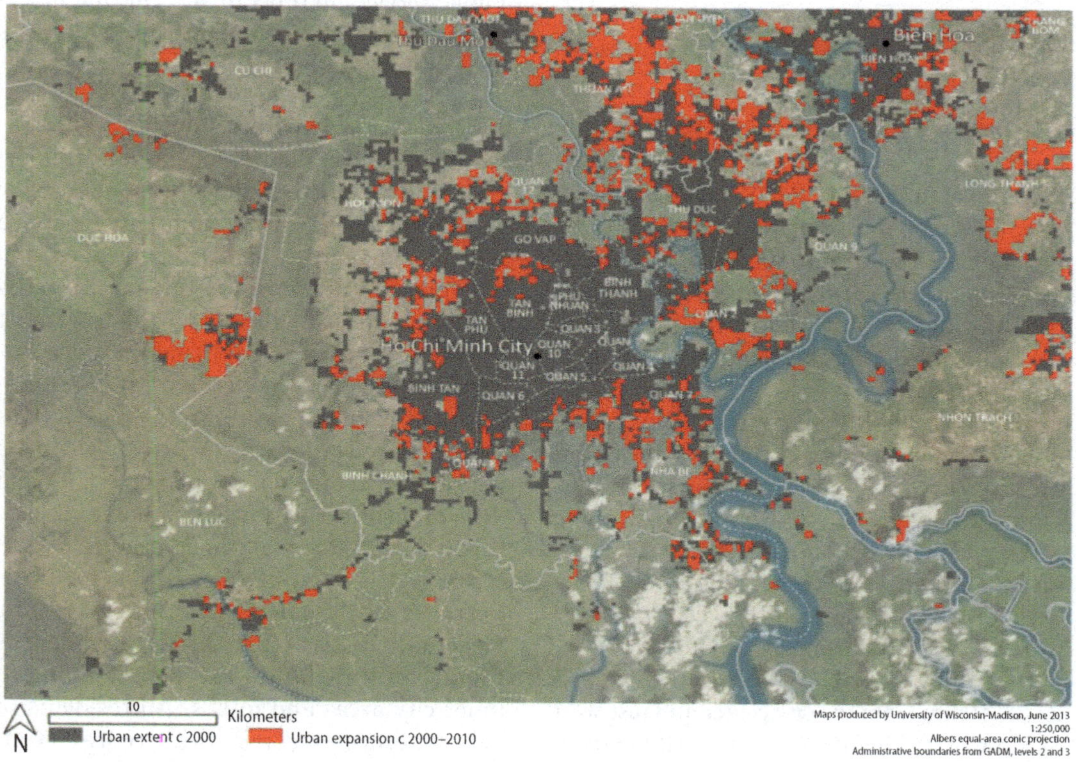

Source: World Bank 2015a.

FIGURE 4.7 Productivity is higher in industrial zones than in neighboring cities

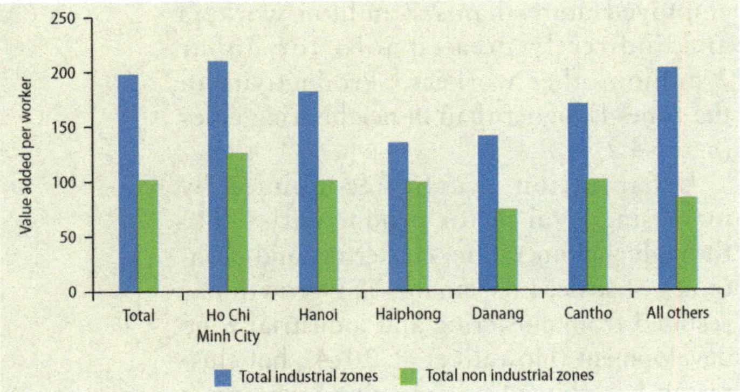

Source: World Bank spatial analysis by geo-referencing firm-level data for 2011.

TABLE 4.2 Occupancy rates of industrial zones with comparable zoning and boundary definitions

City	Occupancy rate of industrial zones (%)	Year	Source
Ho Chi Minh City	56.4	2013	Government
Hanoi	44.7	2013	Government
Da Nang	49.6	2013	Government
Metro Manila	90.2	2014	Colliers International
Shanghai	89.8	2014	Colliers International
Beijing	99.0	2012	Beijing Business News
Los Angeles	97.6	2013	Colliers International
Long Island, New York	94.6	2013	Colliers International

(Vo and Van Thang 2013). By 2010, however, the share of used area in industrial zones had fallen to less than 50 percent (Nguyen 2012), much lower than in global comparators, raising concerns that diversifying such zones in less developed regions was a poor idea (table 4.2).

In the Ho Chi Minh City and Hanoi metropolitan regions, industrial zones farther from the city center have lower occupancy rates, especially beyond 10 km from the city center, where many peripheral zones have occupancy rates less than 10 percent (figure 4.8). (The exception is the 46-hectare Xa Mat Border Gate Export Processing Zone on the border with Cambodia.) The Tan Binh Industrial Zone, 10 km from the city center and just west of Ho Chi Minh City Airport, is 100 percent occupied, as is the Vinh Loc Industrial Zone, 13 km from the city center. But the Tan Phu Trung industrial zone in Cu Chi District was completely unoccupied in 2014; it is 24 km from the city center. Similarly, the Dau Giay industrial zone in Dong Nai Province, 50 km from the center of Ho Chi Minh City, has an occupancy rate of 2.5 percent (map 4.2). Patterns are similar in Hanoi.

Urban expansion and development of industrial zones led by administrative directive rather than demand is thus unlikely to spur economic growth. That view is buttressed by using nightlights as a proxy for economic growth: urban expansion over 2000–10 was not a leading indicator for subsequent economic growth in 2011–12.

The massive construction of industrial zones that have high vacancy rates has major fiscal implications and resource allocation tradeoffs. Assuming that all industrial zones are serviced with roads and infrastructure, the 70,810 hectares of vacant industrial land in Hanoi, Ho Chi Minh City, and Da Nang represent a capital investment of more than $20 billion, which could have been invested in public services in other areas. This misallocation is expected to continue if proper policies are not in place (box 4.1).

Fragmented urban expansion

Another issue is the fragmentation of industrial and residential development outside these zones. If Ho Chi Minh City's pattern holds in other cities, up to 70 percent of land occupied by industries is outside formally approved industrial zones. This scattered development of industrial land reflects a systemic problem with Vietnam's urban planning and development controls. Master plans are prepared and approved by local and national governments, but planning laws and development regulations are ignored in peri-urban districts to an alarming degree.

Official statistics rarely pick up these patterns of "stealth" urbanization. The General Statistics Office of Vietnam defines the urban population as "people living in inner city areas and towns. All residents of other administrative units (rural communes) are regarded as [belonging to the]

FIGURE 4.8 Industrial zone occupancy rates are lower, the farther from the center, in the Ho Chi Minh City region

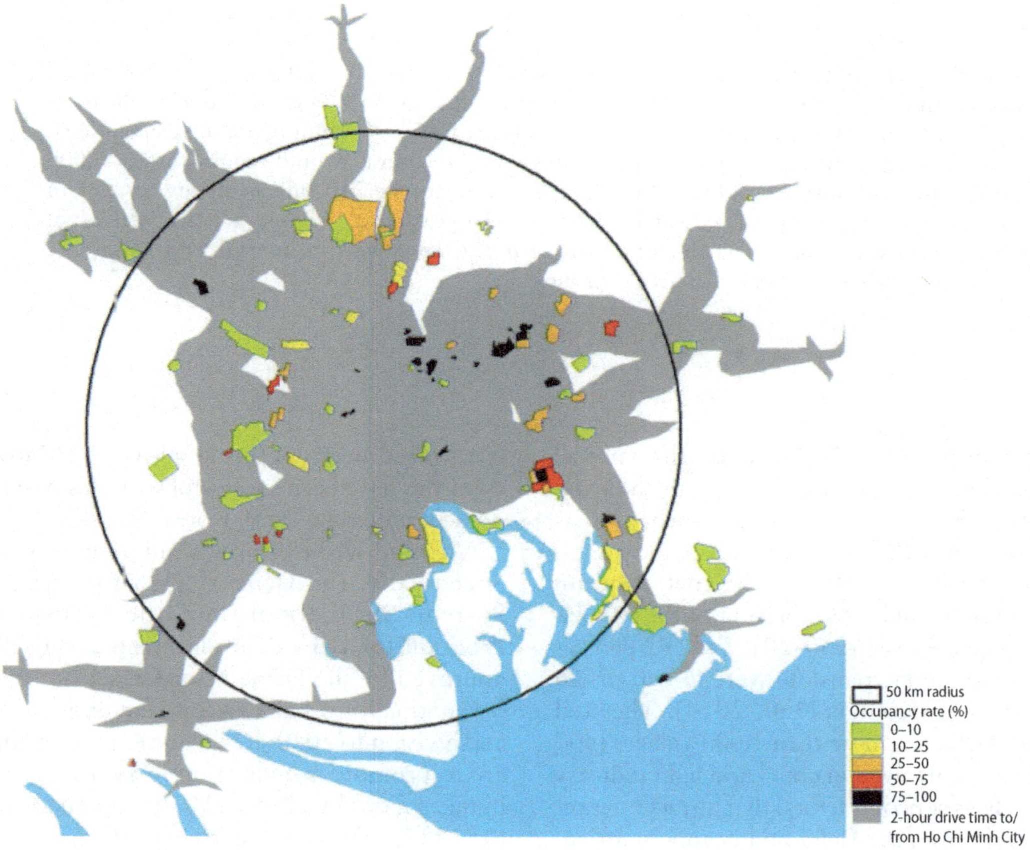

Source: Chreod 2015.

MAP 4.2 Many industrial zones are empty in the periphery of Ho Chi Minh City metropolitan region

Tan Phu Trung IZ, Cu Chi District, HCMC
est: 2013
occupancy rate: 0.0%
kms. to city center: 24

Dau Giay IZ, Thong Nhat District, Dong Nai Province
est: 2008
occupancy rate: 2.5%
kms. to city center: 50

Source: Chreod 2015
Note: IZ = industrial zone.

BOX 4.1 Underused industrial parks proliferate despite high costs

The problem of underused industrial zones will worsen if all the ones in the master plan are built. Despite the low use rate of current zones, nearly 239 more, on 54,882 hectares of land, have been approved for implementation during 2011–20. In addition, the approved master plans of national and local governments include construction of three national economic zones on a combined area of 265,000 hectares and 1,643 provincial-level industrial clusters on a land area of 73,000 hectares. The Ministry of Planning and Investment estimates that the country would require, at $300,000 per hectare, nearly $40 billion in investment in the next 10 years just to construct the infrastructure for the approved industrial and economic zones.

Source: World Bank 2011.

rural population." But with the spatial expansion and growth of cities, much development has taken place in peri-urban areas beyond the officially defined urban core.

In the Ho Chi Minh City metropolitan area, for example, 48.5 percent of the population increase over 1990–2012, and 62 percent of urban land expansion, were in peri-urban communes (Kontgis et al. 2014). The Red River Delta has more than 1,000 villages (400 in Hanoi) involved in crafts and light industry (largely as subcontractors) that attract migrant workers from the Delta and beyond, particularly the Northeast (Fanchette 2012). These trends are more pronounced around the major urban agglomerations of Ho Chi Minh City (figure 4.9) and Hanoi, which are more urbanized than reported by the General Statistics Office. These areas have not been planned and serviced to "urban" standards, limiting their ability to support the dense development of housing, industry, and commerce that can enable scale and agglomeration economies.

Increasing Distance

Limited development of secondary cities

Harmonious development and appropriate definitions of functions among various types of urban areas are of great importance. For example, large cities should provide a diverse range of services and connect to external areas, to achieve international competitiveness, while secondary cities should focus on specialized manufacturing activities. Many countries have been successful with this development pattern, as with Korea (box 4.2).

Vietnam wishes to see similar successes. Specifically, the General Plan for Urban Systems in Vietnam and the National Program for Urban Development 2011–20 approved by the Prime Minister, set out the orientation for urban development until 2025 and a vision to 2050. Key features of the plan are to promote urbanization in priority economic regions by 2015 and in urbanized areas by 2025, creating a network of cities by 2050.[6]

But the record up until now is one of spatial concentration of output and population in the two growth poles of Hanoi and Ho Chi Minh City, with only limited emergence of secondary cities. The Hanoi and Ho Chi Minh City regions (including provinces within a two-hour drive from the center of the city) produced 84 percent of Vietnam's industrial output value in 2013. Densities of output per km^2 are by far the highest in these two regions (map 4.3). The core municipality's share of the country's output value declined in both regions between 2005 and 2013, while shares of adjacent and nearby provinces increased quite significantly, as industries located (or relocated) to lower-cost peri-urban areas, in a normal pattern of industrial spatial change in large metropolitan regions.

Hanoi and Ho Chi Minh City core areas account for more than 10 percent of Vietnam's

FIGURE 4.9 Fragmented and stealth urbanization in Ho Chi Minh City metropolitan region

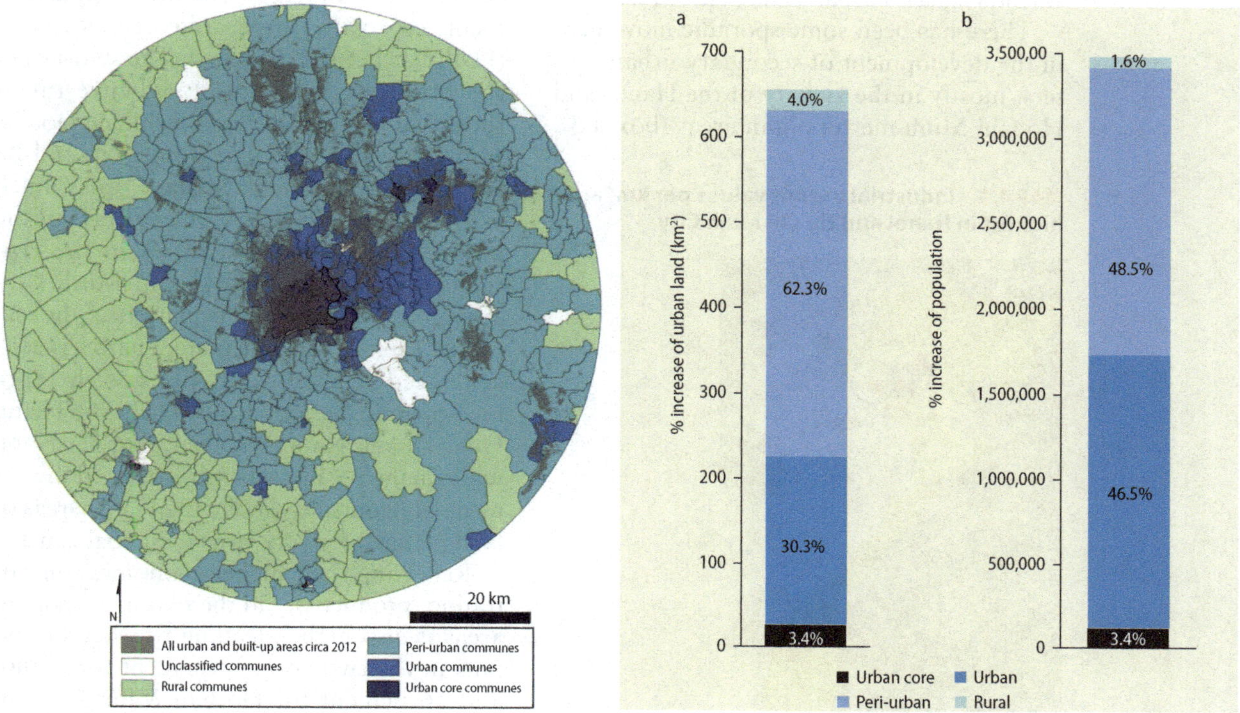

Source: Reprinted from *Applied Geography* Volume 53, Caitlin Kontgis, Annemarie Schneider, Jefferson Fox, Sumeet Saksena, James H. Spencer, and Miguel Castrence. "Monitoring peri-urbanization in the greater Ho Chi Minh City metropolitan area," 377–388, 2014, with permission from Elsevier.

BOX 4.2 The Republic of Korea's secondary cities are important for manufacturing jobs

Secondary cities in Korea have grown as employment centers, particularly for manufacturing, and become more important as the national economy developed. For example, as rural–urban migration accelerated over 1983–93, the share of national manufacturing employment in Seoul, Pusan, and Taegu fell from 44 percent to 28 percent, while rising in small cities and rural areas from 26 percent to 42 percent. Rising labor and land costs drove labor- and land-intensive manufacturing industries out of central Seoul—reducing manufacturing's share in employment for Seoul from 32 percent in 1980 to 11 percent in 2010, as the share of services rose from 58 percent to 81 percent.

Source: Lee 1998.

population, with 30 smaller statutory cities holding 9.2 percent (figure 4.10). The shares of the two metropolitan regions increased by 5.6 percent, compared with a 1.9 percent gain for the four cities ranging in population from 500,000 to 2 million (one is Da Nang), a loss of 0.1 percent in cities ranging from 200,000 to 500,000, and a small gain of 0.7 percent in 17 cities ranging from 100,000 to 200,000 (figure 4.11). There has also been an extensive hollowing out of the southern portion of the Red River Delta and much of the Mekong Delta. Such population concentrations in large metropolitan regions are not unique to Vietnam. Agglomeration effects have increased in metropolitan regions' population share in, for example, the Philippines, Korea, and, to less extent, China's Sichuan Plain (Chreod 2015).

There has been some sporadic movement in the development of secondary urban centers, mostly in the vicinity of the Hanoi and Ho Chi Minh metropolitan areas (box 4.3).

MAP 4.3 Industrial output values per km² are highest in Hanoi and Ho Chi Minh City

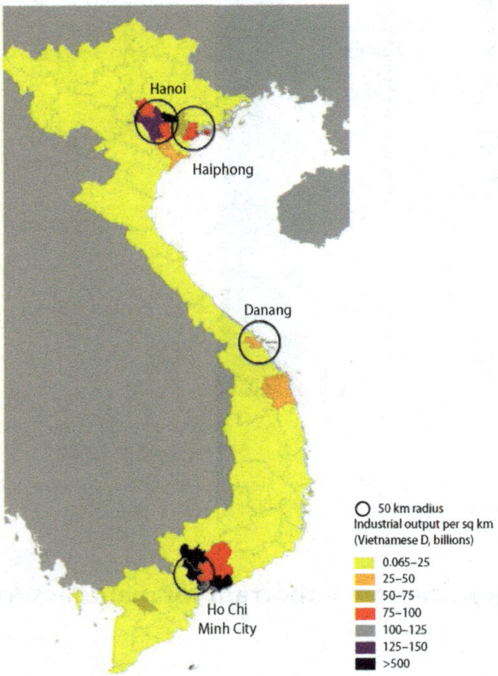

Source: General Statistics Office of Vietnam.

For other localities and for secondary urban centers far from these two, attracting investment, especially foreign direct investment (FDI), has been very limited. The statistics of the Ministry of Planning and Investment show that the four localities including Ho Chi Minh City, Binh Duong, Dong Nai, and Ba Ria Vung Tau alone have made up as much as 41 percent of total registered FDI in the past three decades; localities in the two regions of Hanoi and Ho Chi Minh City accounted for about three-quarters of the registered capital. The remaining quarter is concentrated in a few localities with large investment projects, such as Ha Tinh, Thanh Hoa, Quang Nam, Phu Yen, and Da Nang while many localities barely attracted investment from outside, despite their large areas of land planned for very large industrial zones.

Reflecting their higher economic concentration, productivity in the two metropolitan areas is also higher, leading to wage premiums in the two cores (9 percent for Hanoi and 16 percent for Ho Chi Minh City) in addition to the 8 percent general wage premium for urban areas over rural areas, controlling for job, sector, education, gender, and age (Demombynes 2015). These wage premiums reflect higher labor productivity in the two cities (figure 4.12). These figures together with evidence from many other countries indicate that stagnation in urban density will

FIGURE 4.10 Share of Vietnam's population, by city size, 2009

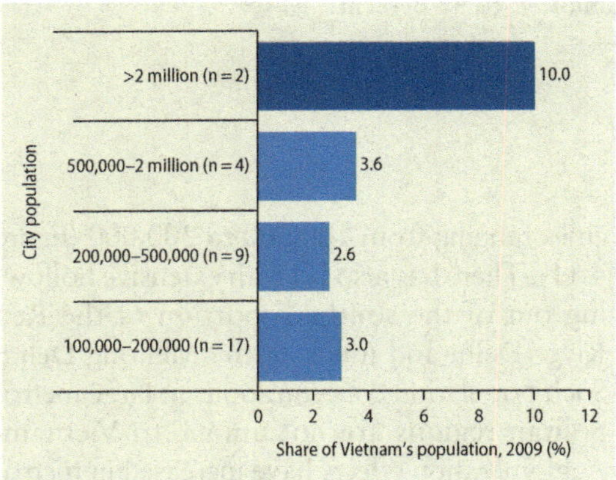

Source: General Statistics Office of Vietnam.

FIGURE 4.11 Change in share of Vietnam's population, by city size, 1989–2009

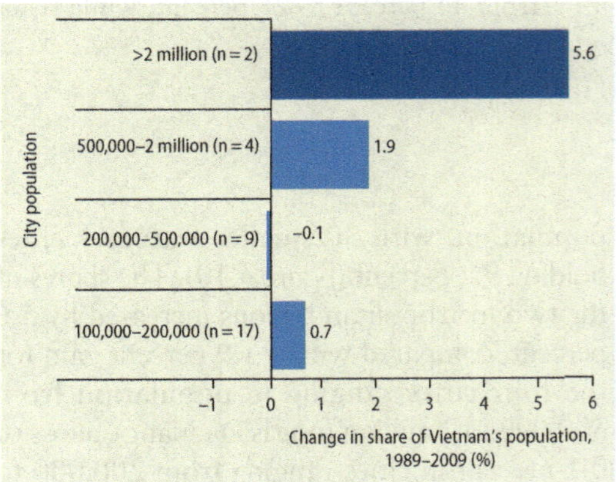

Source: General Statistics Office of Vietnam.

BOX 4.3 Some urban centers near the two metropolitan areas have been successful in attracting investment

In the North, Bac Ninh Province, to the southeast of Hanoi, has attracted a large Samsung mobile telephone assembly plant and a large Foxconn plant for assembly of Internet-protocol phones, routers, and modems. Samsung manufacturing complexes in Bac Ninh and Thai Nguyen provinces have led to investments by nearly 100 suppliers from the Republic of Korea.[a] In the South the Dong Nai provincial government has granted 1,479 investment certificates with a total value of $27 billion.[b] In Binh Duong province to the northeast of Ho Chi Minh City, more than $20 billion had been invested by foreign firms and $550 million by domestic firms by end-2014.

Source: http://www.sggpnews.org.vn/Business/2014/12/111928/.
a. http://www.saigon-gpdaily.com.vn/Business/2015/5/113693/.
b. http://en.baomoi.com/Info/Dong-Nai-ranks-first-in-FDI-attraction/3/544581.epi.

FIGURE 4.12 Urban wage premiums are small outside Hanoi and Ho Chi Minh City

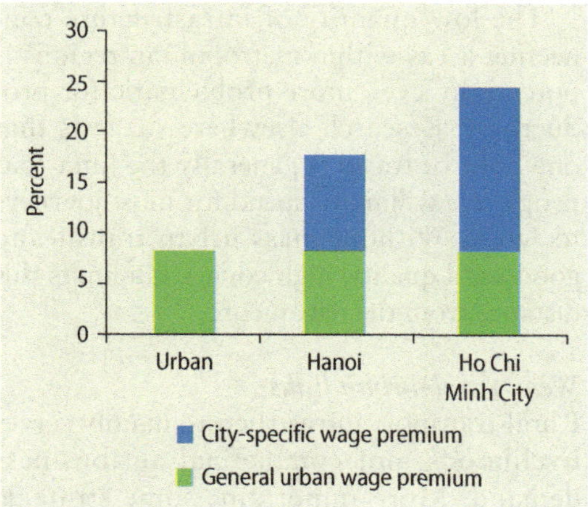

Source: Demombynes 2015.

not be conducive to enhancing agglomeration economies of scale and scope.

Although metropolitan concentration has supported productivity and economic efficiency, policy makers are concerned about the implications of such patterns for spatial equity. Some are anxious that the Ho Chi Minh metropolitan area has become too big and that policies are needed to limit its growth and that of other large cities—and to divert economic and population growth to secondary cities in lagging areas farther in the hinterland. Vietnam's rising economic integration presents an opportunity toward this objective.

In the GVCs that Vietnam is part of, its contribution has been mostly at the final-assembly end; backward links with the local economy have not yet developed. That is normal at early stages of entering GVCs. But as the domestic content of Vietnam's export value added rises, there will be opportunities to develop backward links by clustering firms in related industries—stirring demand for secondary cities. Intermediate-size secondary cities can support "localization economies," which come from the spatial clustering of buyers and suppliers in the same industry.

An important point is that secondary cities and metropolitan areas are not substitutes, they are complements. Each type and size of urban settlement has its own unique functions, which tend to broadly complement each other. The alternative to a large city is another large city, not a small town. The kind of economic activities that give rise to a big city—high-end manufacturing and services, transportation nodes, government centers, and financial centers (generating agglomeration economies)—if displaced will merely give rise to other big cities, not a large number of small towns. Activities in small towns are related more to demand from the agriculture hinterland and rely more on scale economies at the level of the plant.

Costly logistics and poor transport infrastructure constrain urban development

Vietnam's investment in connective infrastructure has shortened many economic distances.

In manufacturing and agriculture, trade costs are much lower than expected for the economy's stage of development, and these costs have fallen sharply, particularly in manufacturing (Shepherd and Balijepalli 2015), from higher to lower than China's (whose costs also declined). Similarly, on the Logistics Performance Index, Vietnam stands out as an "overperformer"—its score is much higher than expected based on its income alone.

These very successes, however, throw into relief the major bottlenecks of economic distance. Logistics costs are high and interregional transport quality is low, preventing secondary cities from connecting to markets, and intrametropolitan transport is congested and lacks mass transit. A country of 90 million people, Vietnam has not developed a railway system with speeds of 100 kilometers an hour. It has only 700 kilometers of operational international-standard expressways. This is not only low in its own right but low relative to Vietnam's targets of 2,639 kilometers by 2020 and 3,114 kilometers by 2030. Congested and unsafe two-lane roads carry most truck shipments, at an average truck speed on the intercity highway network of roughly 40–50 kilometers an hour. Amid low barriers to entry in the cutthroat trucking market, truck overloading is rampant, service quality is low, and empty backhauls average 30 percent.

High transport costs hold back the development of urban areas outside Hanoi and Ho Chi Minh City, although many are part of the metropolitan regions. High congestion costs hurt the attractiveness and productivity of locations beyond the urban periphery, given that short-distance freight trips of less than 200 km account for 87 percent of all freight movement in Vietnam, that 98 percent of all inland waterway movements are less than 200 km, and that 73 percent of road journeys are less than 100 kilometers (World Bank 2011). Further, 60 percent of the freight movement of the economic centers is intraregional. And intraregional costs of connectivity are very high. Moving freight within Vietnam's metropolitan areas costs $0.20 per ton-kilometer, twice the cost of the equivalent trips in India.

Lingering shortcomings in domestic and international connectivity are a root cause of Vietnam's elevated logistics costs of 21 percent of GDP, against an estimated 19 percent in China and 15 percent in Thailand.[7] They are driven by unreliability and unpredictability in Vietnam-based supply chains, which suggests that, from a trade-competitiveness angle, freight and logistics are not—yet—a key driver of direct manufacturing investment, whether foreign or domestic. The primary drivers of such investment appear to be political and economic stability, reliable and cost-effective access to electricity and other basic utilities, proximity to the supply chains in Southern China, and comparatively low-cost labor.

The low quantity of infrastructure connecting areas within metropolitan regions is potentially even more problematic for productivity. Research elsewhere suggests that one hour of travel is generally the limit that people are willing to spend for most journeys to work. Without mass urban transit and good road quality, high congestion limits this distance from the urban core.

Weak rural–urban links

Rural transport infrastructure mainly serves livelihoods, not commercial agribusiness demand. More important, some strategic interregional transport corridors, such as railway and highway systems, have not been developed to connect the Central Highlands and Mekong River Delta, the two areas with large-scale agricultural production, or to connect poor regions such as the Northwest to major markets, ports, and border gates.

Lacking electricity for agricultural production is common in the highlands, remote areas, and ethnic minority areas. In agricultural production areas, such as the Southeast and Mekong River Delta, the demand for electricity for agricultural production, especially for irrigation, has not been matched by supply. Information and media about agricultural science and technology and markets and policies for agriculture and rural areas remain underdeveloped.

Weak infrastructure and poor connectivity between rural and urban areas are major obstacles to attracting enterprises' investment to rural areas and agriculture production. Only 1 percent of registered enterprises are in the agriculture sector, and agricultural enterprises are usually small or medium-size, constituting about 96.5 percent of the total number of agricultural enterprises. Compared with the great potential of Vietnam's agriculture, supporting industry for agriculture is very weak. Most of plant protection medicine, veterinary medicine, agricultural machinery, and so on, except for urea, have been imported. The processing industry has not fully developed clusters associated with material zones and had low added value. Besides, the weakness in warehouse, loading, shipping, and payment have pushed up production costs, reducing the competitiveness of agricultural products. The number of processing enterprises—especially deep processing with high-quality service providers or those classified as "science and technology" enterprises in agriculture—has been very low.

Moreover, very few enterprises sign contracts with farmers for distributing products, providing input services, investing in material zones, and sharing outcomes and risks. Agricultural land of households in Vietnam averages about 0.5 hectares per household and is usually divided into four or five pieces. More than 80 percent of Vietnamese farmers have less than 1.0 hectares. The very small production scale of farmers causes difficulties in applying new technologies, raises the process management cost, and increases transaction cost between enterprises and farmers.

Because the allocated land is so small and fragmented, farmers lack motivation for investing in production and applying technology. Much labor in agriculture is underemployed, and income from agriculture accounts for only 30 percent of the total income of farm households. The majority of farmers have to seek income from nonagricultural sectors, so they abandon their land. But the ability of rural areas to generate income and employment, particularly in industry and in agricultural support services, has remained weak. That is why the last resort for farmers who lack land and have low incomes is to move to urban areas.

But their migration to urban areas is uncoordinated, spontaneous, and temporary, having historically been weighed down by the *hộ khẩu* (the household registration system) (see "Persistent Division"). Most rural migrants working in urban areas only do simple jobs such as construction worker, taxi driver, porter, assistant, without labor contracts, insurance, or accommodation. So they continue to hold farmland as a hedge, transforming it from "production" to "hedging." Land remains fallow in many areas, while capable farmers face difficulties in accumulating land, which they need to apply technology in agricultural production.

Persistent Division

Vietnam has made impressive inroads in reducing economic division. Poverty has declined dramatically in both rural and urban areas (figure 4.13). Although urban poverty rates are much lower than rural poverty rates, the rural–urban divide is much less than in other countries that grew rapidly. International experience suggests that a convergence of living standards generally precedes a convergence of incomes, so urban–rural disparities often increase during

FIGURE 4.13 Urban and rural poverty headcount rates are falling

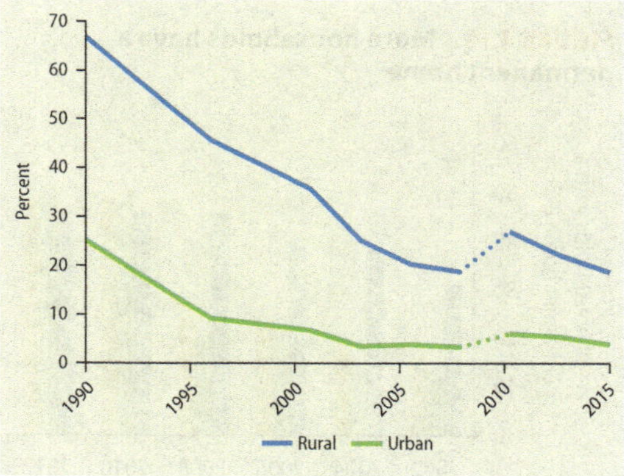

Source: General Statistics Office of Vietnam 2005, 2013, and 2015.
Note: Figures are based on the World Bank-GSO poverty line. Dotted lines indicate a period during which the survey and poverty measurement methodology were changed substantially.

early stages of development (World Bank 2009). But Vietnam has avoided a large divergence between rural and urban incomes. Indeed, it is already seeing rural–urban incomes converge. According to the General Statistics Office of Vietnam. income per capita in rural areas was only 36.9 percent of that in urban areas in 1995, but 52.8 percent in 2014.

Rural and urban areas have also converged on some measures of noneconomic welfare. In 2010–12, the number of households in rural areas having permanent dwellings was higher than in urban areas (figure 4.14). By 2015, 99.8 percent of villages and 98.7 percent of rural households nationwide had access to electricity. So almost all Vietnamese households have it, impressive in relation to many other countries with similar or higher incomes. Indonesia, with a much higher GDP per capita, has a rate of only 64 percent.

But rural areas still lag significantly behind on the shares of households using hygienic latrines, hygienic water, and trained workers in total employment (table 4.3). In 2012, the share of the population aged 15 with no certificate or who had never gone to school was 23.1 percent in rural areas, twice the share in the urban areas. The share of people who had college or university degrees in rural areas was 3.4 percent, 4.6 times lower than in the urban areas.

In short, people in urban areas have more education and better access to health, but rural areas have improved relatively and absolutely. Compared with other countries at similar incomes, Vietnam has gone a very long way toward closing the rural–urban education gap.

Much of Vietnam's success in rural–urban and regional convergence is attributable to public investment (as a percentage of GDP). Although expenditure per capita is still much higher in wealthier areas, central transfers are highly progressive (they are higher as a share of regional GDP) and became more so over 2007–11. In addition, transfers or support from family members or relatives contributed considerably to reducing rural–urban income and living standard gaps.

The biggest problem of division is the restriction on rural–urban migration. Institutionalized in *hộ khẩu* (the household registration system), it has created a second-class citizenship. The migrant population has less access to social insurance, affordable housing, and urban health care systems, often pays more for water and electricity, and faces barriers to education for children. Controlling for education, migrant income is 21 percent lower than that of nonmigrants (General Statistics Office 2005). Even controlling for household and individual characteristics (including per capita income), children aged 11–18 are 40 percent less likely to be in school if they do not have permanent *hộ khẩu*. This helps to explain why rural–urban migrants are mostly in the informal sector and hesitate transferring their agricultural land-use rights to other farm households in the countryside.

FIGURE 4.14 More households have a permanent home

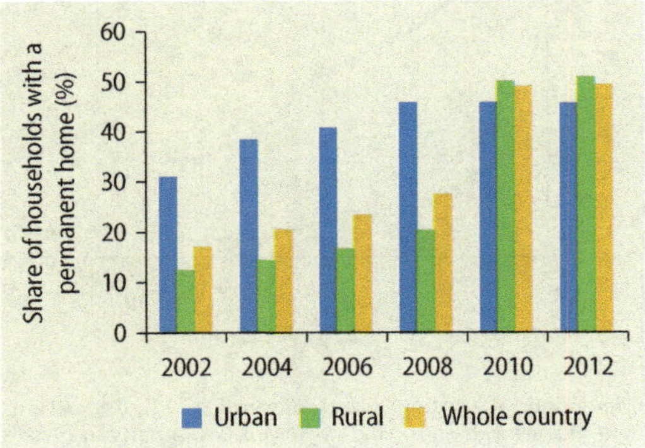

Source: General Statistics Office of Vietnam 2013.

TABLE 4.3 Access to services is converging for urban and rural residents
Percent

Indicator	Urban	Rural
Share of literate labor in the labor force	98.4	93.4
Share of trained workers in employment	33.7	11.2
Share of households using hygienic water	98.1	87.9
Share of households using hygienic latrines	93.7	70.0
Share of households using electricity	99.8	96.6

Source: General Statistics Office of Vietnam (2014) for 2013 and General Statistics Office of Vietnam (2013) for 2012.
Note: Data are for 2012 or 2013. Trained workers completed three-month-equivalent (or longer) training courses.

Causes of Low and Stagnant Density, Rising Distance, and Persistent Division

Low and stagnant urban density, rising distance, and persistent division have five main causes: inappropriate land policy, inappropriate city classification and planning policies, fragmentation and lack of coordination in infrastructure development and irrational metropolitan development, a lack of attention to effective rural–urban connectivity, and the residence policy for inhabitants.

Inappropriate Land Policy

Distorted land conversions and transactions
A lack of market-driven land pricing leads to artificially cheap industrial land and expensive urban-residential land, impeding the urbanization of people and jobs while encouraging that of land. Using land conversions to attract industry leads to land urbanization, not to economic growth that stimulates greater demand for urban land. Land-use misallocations are connected to land transfers in the public sector and to the proliferation and underuse of industry-zoned urban land.

Land markets in Vietnam also reflect the deeper issues of land management and governance. The huge discrepancies between the set price for land and its market price (often 10 times higher) cause large distortions and bottlenecks in the land market. This two-price system transfers huge benefits and values to developers and speculators while causing losses to individuals (mainly farmers) who are forced to transfer land. Because land allocations and deals related to taxes, concessions, and permissions for developers and investors are based on artificially deflated land values, the state is forfeiting considerable public benefit by undervaluing one of its most valuable assets. Moreover, artificially low-priced land stimulates land sales that contribute to widespread and fragmented urban development with great infrastructure inefficiencies (and the associated capital costs).

Zonal-land prices often correspond little with market prices, especially for desirable properties. The provinces approve and make available land-price tables. They routinely use set prices to transfer land, creating a dual land market in which industrial uses acquire land well below its true market value. This has distorted investment projects, leading to speculative land acquisition in expansive industrial parks, inefficient use of scarce land, and discontented land owners who feel they were inadequately compensated. The actual value of land in Vietnam has been put at more than $200 billion (Ho and McPherson 2010).

Weak land registration
Policy makers have exerted enormous efforts and put in place well-staffed provincial and district offices to issue land-use certificates for private land and to establish a comprehensive cadaster of privately owned land. But shortcomings remain. There are no provisions for communal land—creating obstacles to mining and industrial investment in areas with communal rights or inciting conflict. And with land-use leases nearing their end, the lack of clarity for renewals creates uncertainty that impedes investment. The Ministry of Natural Resources and Environment is responsible for the national land database—containing all legal documents, cadastral records, master plans, land prices, land statistics and inventories, land cases handled by the inspectorate and the courts, and dispute-settlement records. But the requirements have not been specified for common standards and interoperability. The focus has been on first-time issuance of land-use certificates rather than on a sustainable system that generates fee income to independently sustain its operation in the long term.

Provinces have their own systems, with different levels of development of cadastral and spatial records, and with textual and spatial records often not linked. This has led to many informal transactions (at underreported prices), which threaten the integrity of records and open the door to fraudulent transactions. Integration with banks, courts, local tax maps, and land-use plans was not envisaged, so many of the gains of a modern multipurpose land administration system could not be exploited.

The 2013 Land Law aims to address these issues. It sets mechanisms to recognize communal land and clarifies contractual terms. Land rights can be exchanged, transferred, leased, mortgaged, and contributed as capital to ventures. Land ownership limits encourage investment (two-thirds hectares of rice land but 10–30 hectares for perennials in delta or midland and mountainous regions) and lengthen the standard contract period for agricultural land to 50 years, commercial investment to 70 years, and residential land "for a long and stable term." Automatic renewal upon expiry is established as a default, and a limited land fund at the community level (up to five years) can be established.

The 2013 law makes land registration compulsory and requires certificates, including cadastral maps, for each parcel and for attached assets. Provincial people's committees are responsible for this and for conducting first-time registrations (jointly to husband and wife for married couples) in a way that is sustainable and that provides avenues for online access. National funding is to be made available for the Ministry of Natural Resources and Environment to provide the technical specifications for such an exercise and to produce a yearly report, including the extent to which legal provisions (for example, on consultation) were followed. With a new legal framework, Vietnam needs to implement concrete actions in land registration and management.

Unsustainable revenues from land distort incentives

Land-based financing models are unsustainable. The 2013 decentralization marked a sharp increase in local transfers of land to investors in return for one-off land-use fees. This financing model now contributes 20–30 percent to local government revenue. Overreliance on it, as China illustrates, prompts local governments to acquire bad debts backed by unrealistic prospects of future land acquisition.

Land taxes account for merely 0.07 percent of GDP, around one-tenth the developing country average and about one-thirtieth the Organisation for Economic Co-operation and Development (OECD) average. The lack of a coherent land- and property-taxation system prevents local authorities from tapping a stable and recurring revenue source and creates distortions by overtaxing investment (Ho and McPherson 2010).

The potential of land taxes to more sustainably generate revenue for local governments has been underrealized for three reasons. The tax base is incomplete due to the lack of a comprehensive cadaster. Land prices are undervalued because of insufficient independent data. And local governments do not systematically collect revenue. Unlike many other developing and middle-income countries, Vietnam is forgoing an important source of revenue at the expense of not creating public goods.

The 2013 law establishes an independent valuation profession. The provincial people's committees must seek advice from the profession in setting land-price tables, which are restricted to land-use levies, taxes, fees, and fines, among others. The law mandates case-specific independent valuations to lease land and to compensate land-use rights, and it mandates public auctions to transfer land for residential, industrial, or infrastructure investment. The only exemptions are for land allocated for agriculture, low-income housing, residential land for the landless or for public purposes, and mining. Purchasers can decide whether to pay a lump sum or annual installments.

The law also requires local governments to implement a land-use levy and annual installments, while creating more options to tax land, and to use such instruments as betterment levies to capture increases in the value of land from infrastructure investment. Although the levy is based on the land-price tables, the land-rental fees depend on lease terms and the auction price. Clear regulations need to be established.

The success of land acquisition motivated by public interest and for economic development has led to its further use as an alternative to market-based transfers to foreign-invested enterprises. Compensation is mainly based on land-price tables known to differ vastly from market prices, distorting investment decisions, including those by companies with marginally viable or totally ineffective business plans, and eliciting more than 10,000 complaints and denunciations.

Inappropriate City Classification and Planning Policies

The city classification and category upgrading distort motivations

The city classification and category upgrading encourage localities to expand the size of their urban areas and make excessive investments. The City Classification System was developed in 1990 by the Ministry of Construction and amended in 2001 and 2009, creating incentives to rapidly convert land along lines that are inimical to development and to urbanization. Its original goal was to spur the development of cities using indicators set by the central government to determine budget transfer allocations, thus influencing local choices and investment allocations.

This link to the central transfers rather than to strategic planning encourages unplanned urban expansion. To qualify for one of the six urban categories, cities have to reach at least 70 of a maximum 100 points. Most points target infrastructure, population, and GDP growth. Urban density's 5-point maximum is similar to the nonfarm labor indicator's maximum and far lower than that of all other indicators—urban infrastructure (55), urban population size (10), urban function (15), architecture of urban landscape (10). A city can easily reach 70 by constructing additional infrastructure, expanding cadastral boundaries to increase population, and exaggerating their local GDPs (which may be a reason for local GDP growth rates to usually be 1.5 times higher than the national average) while ignoring more substantive criteria such as population density.

This policy leads local governments to pursue a one-dimensional approach to urban development, focused on increasing inputs. The disassociation of quantity and location prevents the central and local governments from assessing where and how to invest and what the geographic priorities for budget allocation should be. Global experience shows that Latin American countries have paid very high prices for poor urban planning and massive urban development (box 4.4).

Local authorities benefit from an expansion of business within their boundaries, undermining the potential agglomeration-based development and the economies of scale in infrastructure investment. The urban classification system encourages local infrastructure development, leading to massive and fragmented urban development. At the end of 2014, Vietnam had 775 urban areas, including 49 urban districts under 5 municipalities, 64 provincial cities, 47 district-level towns, and 615 commune-level towns (General Statistics Office 2014). The system creates incentives to reclassify land, particularly at the fringes of consolidated urban areas, and produces urban sprawl. Low-density development in peri-urban areas is a profitable venture for developers, since land can be acquired cheaply from farmers. The conversion of peri-urban land without a

BOX 4.4 Unplanned growth has been expensive in Latin America

The rural–urban migration of the 1960s and 1970s demanded serviced land much faster than the speed the planning and development system was delivering it. Lacking a framework for growth, this demand led to informal land dealers and others developing land in cities in an unplanned manner, creating structural conditions for traffic congestion, inequality, and low productivity. The cost to improve these unplanned urbanized areas was three to five times what it would have cost to urbanize the land originally with better planning.

spatial planning structure means that any classified agriculture land, even far from the consolidated urban areas, can be developed.

The higher the ranking, the more power cities have to issue land-use certificates and to allocate land for and to lease land to households and individuals (Urban Solutions 2011). After the upgrade of Thai Nguyen (metropolitan Hanoi) to Class I, central transfers remained stable while local receipts—fueled by a spike in land sales and use rights—markedly increased (figure 4.15).

There are coordination issues between the Ministry of Home Affairs (MOHA), which is responsible for defining the administrative boundary of urban areas, and the Ministry of Construction, which runs the City Classification System (CCS) and is the leading agency of urban planning and management. For example, the merging of the provinces within Hanoi has led to the absorption of rural populations in the Hanoi agglomeration. Similarly, the indicators for cities upgraded to Class I reveal deviation from targets related to density, highlighting the sprawling growth in peri-urban areas. Between 2009 and 2011, seven cities attained Class I status. Of these, only one (Nha Trang) met minimum density standards (table 4.4).

Having cities compete for the same objectives and governments allocate funding to individual cities hampers the opportunity to create clusters. The current CCS awards a maximum of 2 points for public transport and 1 for education facilities. There are no mechanisms for cross-jurisdictional cooperation. Indeed, in large cities, districts compete to attract population and investors, often inconsistent with the city's master plan. Entrepreneurial local governments and pressure from property developers contribute to extensive peri-urban development. And in unplanned residential areas on the fringe of consolidated urban cores, urban infrastructure networks are mostly provided only after urban development. As a consequence, three-fourths of new urban housing units lack sufficient services (UN-HABITAT, forthcoming).

FIGURE 4.15 After receiving Class I status in 2009, Thai Nguyen's local receipts nearly doubled

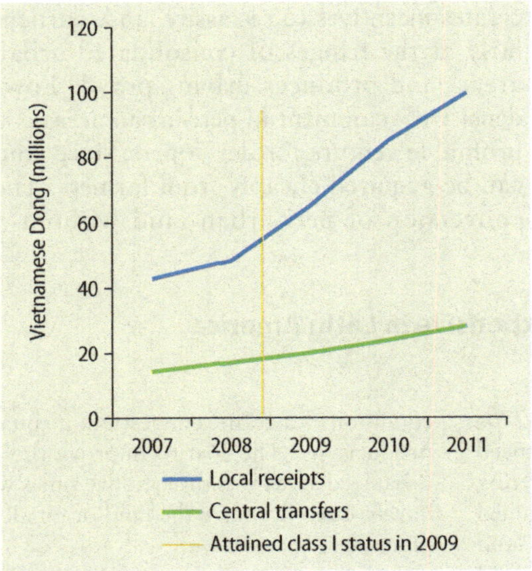

Source: Ministry of Finance data and World Bank and Ministry of Planning and Investment calculations.

Ineffective planning

Vietnam has five different kinds of plans that govern the system (table 4.5).

Socioeconomic development plans are one of the most important and are the responsibility of the Ministry of Planning and Investment. They are usually developed every five years, with the latest being the Ninth Five-Year Plan (2011–15). They set goals and detailed production and investment targets across regions and productive sectors of the economy and combine (often without prioritizing) sector-plan proposals. They are

TABLE 4.4 Criteria assessment of cities upgraded from Class II to Class I

City	Year upgraded	Population	Density (average)
Can Tho	2008	1,199,817	856/km^2
Da Lat	2007	n.a.	n.a.
Nha Trang	2007	397,563	30,000/km^2 (city center)
Nam Dinh	2010	352,108	5,290/km^2
Tay Nguyen	2009	279,689	1,474/km^2
Viet Tri	2011	188,564	4,561/km^2
Vinh	2007	305,609	2,911/km^2

Source: UN-HABITAT City Profiles.
Note: Bold indicates that the target was met; n.a. = not applicable.

TABLE 4.5 Types of master plans and plans in Vietnam

Type of master plan/plan	Scope
Orientation	National general policy
Regional master plan for economic zones	Multiprovince or multicity
Master	Province or city
Zoning	Development control in cities or towns
Detailed area	District, ward, industrial zone, or project

prepared with limited economic and financial analysis, without full consideration of prospective resources. They are therefore lists of projects essentially driven by production targets. Potential social and environmental impacts are overlooked. At the provincial level, the Departments of Planning and Investment screen proposals submitted by local governments before passing them on to the Ministry of Planning and Investment.

Spatial or physical plans are generally referred to as master plans, construction plans, or detailed area plans for specific projects. This planning retains the practices of an era when the state was in charge of all construction projects. Master plans propose spatial arrangements of land uses, building footprints, and infrastructure for a province, city, district, or development site in progressively greater detail. The plans are prepared by the Ministry of Construction or subordinate departments of construction at the province and city level. Most are prepared by the National Institute of Urban and Rural Planning, which became the Vietnam Institute of Architecture, Urban, and Rural Planning in 2008. Its functions are research, physical planning, capacity building, international cooperation, and consultancy activities.

Preparation is also a top-down process that determines production outputs by sector rather than by cross-sector inputs and coordination. The widely dispersed responsibilities and unclear procedures make it difficult to bring sector agendas together, resulting in inefficient planning and ineffective implementation producing delays, higher costs, and undesirable environmental impacts. The limited information shared among authorities and sectors and the uncoordinated development of different sectors need revisions to follow actual development. There is also a lack of high-level private-sector involvement in preparing and implementing plans.

In reality, the master plans, by design, cannot be implemented. Their objectives, rarely linked to a budgeting process, often describe an ideal set of conditions that a city would achieve after flawless implementation of the plan. The influence of "external" conditions, such as demand and the availability of resources, is barely considered. This process leads to a mismatch between demand and supply, as most of the infrastructure identified in the master plan may not materialize during the implementation. A lack of priories also contributes to asymmetric decision making. In fact, the plans seem to serve only as a tool for bargaining among government authorities at different levels on resource allocation, mobilizing resources from various external organizations and encouraging the private sector's involvement in the construction and operation of cities through the changes in the master plans (Huynh 2015).

Functional planning across various government departments creates bottlenecks in this process. In Vietnam, the socioeconomic development plans, urban master plans, and sector infrastructure plans are prepared by different departments at the provincial level. The coordination between these departments is limited, as with city administrations. Poor coordination in sequencing is exacerbated by a silo approach to plan making, in which planning institutes tend to overlook economic and social dimensions and, conversely, socioeconomic planners tend to overlook the spatial dimensions. The various plans often run on different schedules and use inconsistent data and projections. For example, the period of a master plan for a centrally run city is between 20 and 25 years, with a vision for 50 years (for a township, 10–15 years), but socioeconomic plans are drafted every five years. The intended sequence of spatial planning consistent with socioeconomic and sector plans does not always happen. And since land-use plans are developed independent of sectoral plans, there are no true systemic spatial considerations that focus on planning infrastructure investments.

Fragmentation and Lack of Coordination in Infrastructure Development and Metropolitan Management

Fragmentation and lack of coordination in infrastructure development

One primary reason that transport modes are misaligned not only with supply and demand but also relative to each other is that they are planned individually and on a largely decentralized, separated, and fragmented basis. The limited capacity of bridges and roads as well as the overall condition of transport infrastructure increase costs. The loose decentralization and lack of coordination in developing regional infrastructure, economic corridors, and metropolises undermines the efficiency of existing infrastructure. For example, the oversupply of container-handling capacity at Cai Mep–Thi Vai coexists with fully used facilities in Ho Chi Minh City only 80 kilometers away—and therefore part of the same freight corridor. The Cai Mep–Thi Vai port uses less than 30 percent of its capacity because of the continued operation of inner-city river ports in Ho Chi Minh City.

Comparing the main ports—such as Ho Chi Minh City region, Haiphong, and Da Nang—with Tanjung Pelapas in Malaysia shows that berth lengths are not adapted to the maximum vessel size and storage capacity. Of the 18 dry ports in Vietnam, only one is connected by rail to the national railway network. Haiphong port is missing a direct access road and a railway connection to ease container movements (refer to annex 4A). This indicates a lack of sufficiently coordinated market and connectivity analysis for freight across modes, creating misalignments and inefficiencies.

Irrationalities in metropolitan development

The organic features of Vietnam's cities—mixed land-use neighborhoods, shophouses with people living above or behind their stores, and motorcycles as the primary means of transport—have historically produced relatively good urban mobility (World Bank 2011). Average commuting times in cities in Vietnam are correspondingly short: 15 minutes in Da Nang, 18 minutes in Hanoi, and 20 minutes in Ho Chi Minh City.[8] The urban structure and the infrastructure in the two largest cities, Hanoi and Ho Chi Minh City, are inappropriate for cars as the major means of transportation.

In the central business district of Hanoi, only 9 percent of the area is devoted to street space, and in Ho Chi Minh City less than 8 percent, similar to Bangkok, which is notorious for traffic congestion, and much lower than New York's Midtown Manhattan (32 percent) or Seoul's Jung District (14 percent) (map 4.4). In addition, both New York and Seoul have extensive underground transit networks, which reduce the need for surface transportation.[9] Their public transportation systems are also very good, capable of accommodating considerable numbers of daily commuters.

An increase of car ownership to 250 passenger cars per 1,000 people would provoke total gridlock in central Hanoi, where the density is 400 people per hectare (World Bank 2011). The car-owning population grew at an average annual rate of 15.2 percent during 2008–14. The risk of gridlock is not due to excessive human or built density, but to irrationalities in the road system and the absence of efficient public transport. Most districts in Paris's *intramuros* (central district) are comparable in human density to Hanoi's or Ho Chi Minh City's densest districts, which have three to four times more surface area per inhabitant. The remaining Parisian districts are two to three times denser in surface area than Hanoi's, with car ownership of 330 per 1,000 people but no gridlock. In the Hanoi and Ho Chi Minh City core centers, there are not enough medium-scale streets connecting the local network of 4-meter-wide lanes to the 40-meter-wide roads.

A tenfold difference in the width between small lanes and wide roads is not ideal.

MAP 4.4 Hanoi's street space is ill suited for urban transport

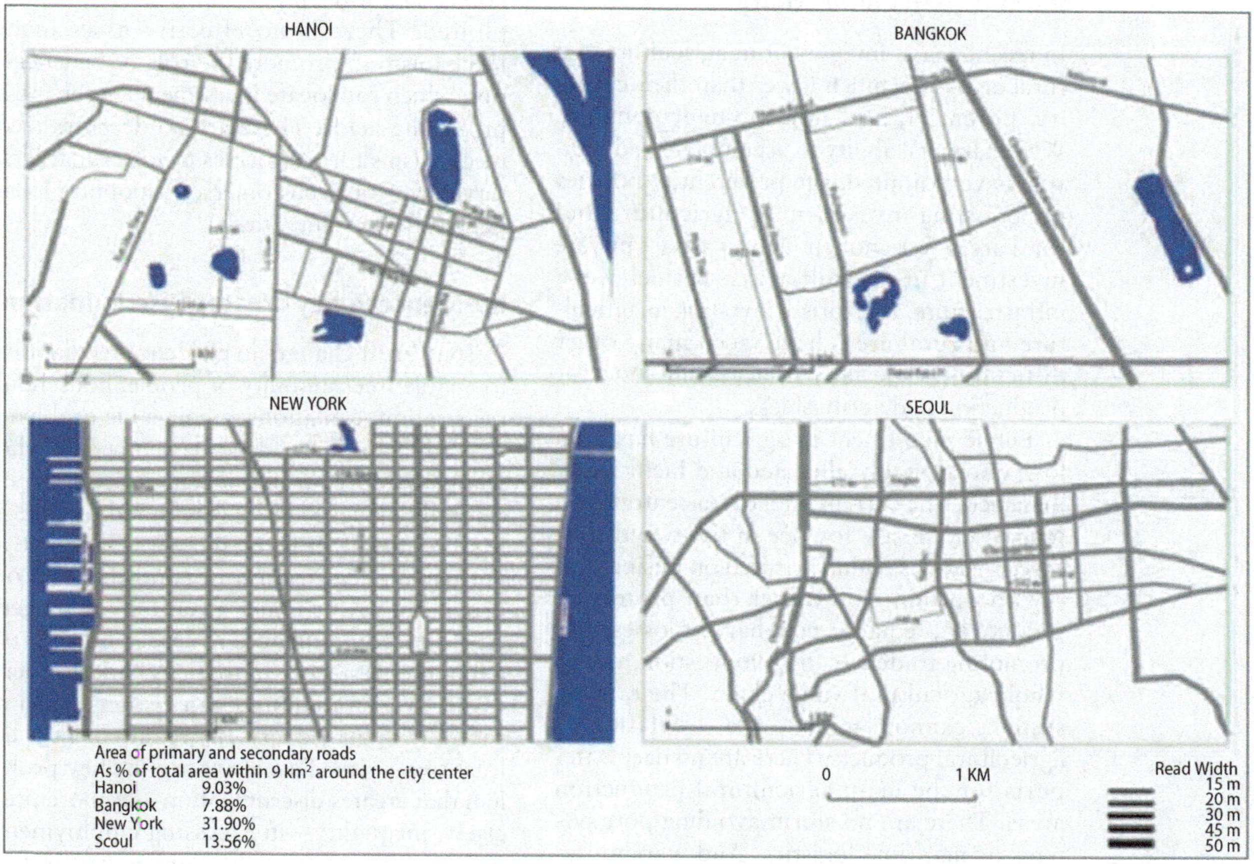

Source: World Bank 2011.

Sixty percent of the Parisian streets are less than 12 meters wide. And Parisian boulevards are like the avenues and streets in Manhattan—20 meters wide in most cases and 30 meters wide for the rest. Further studies are necessary, with a robust methodology on the street patterns of Vietnamese cities, their connectivity, and the percentage of streets in each size category. Such studies could measure the local and global imbalances at various scales and orient investments in street infrastructure.

Experience from other countries shows that urban compression and large capacity transport systems are closely related, especially when urban development is based on public transport. Hong Kong SAR, China; New York; Seoul; Singapore; and Tokyo are good examples. Given the very high density of population and employment in Singapore and in Hong Kong SAR, China, public transport systems are extremely efficient. So to address traffic congestion, especially in Hanoi and Ho Chi Minh City, Vietnamese policy makers should take advantage of the organic relationship between urban compression and the public transport systems. But the development plans for the center of Hanoi and Ho Chi Minh City show that it may not be possible due to the conflicting policies. On the one hand are the tens-of-billions-of-dollar plans to build a large-capacity public transport system based on metro, trams, and express buses (Clement and Charles 2015). On the other hand is the view associated with policies on restricting density and height in the central areas, which could create numerous small congestion points that will ultimately spread out in these big cities.

Lack of Attention to Develop Effective Rural–Urban Connectivity

In recent years, investment in agriculture and rural areas was much lower than their capacity, potential, and development demand. While farmers' ability to accumulate and reinvest is very limited, the preferential policies for boosting investment in agriculture and rural areas were not enough to attract private investment in difficult areas. Besides weak infrastructure, enterprises investing in agriculture and rural areas have faced many other difficulties, especially in accessing land for production and agribusiness.

Public investment in agriculture has been low, unreasonably allocated and inefficiently managed. The current budget concentrates on irrigation, mostly for rice in the two deltas. Investment has mainly focused on raising supply and production rather than protecting production, reducing post-harvest losses, and promoting trade, creating congestion for the whole agricultural value chain. The railway systems cannot facilitate the circulation of agricultural products. There are no deepwater ports for the main agricultural production areas. There are no storm-avoiding port systems or maritime logistics. And warehouses and processing facilities are poor.

Investment has paid attention only to quantity rather than quality and efficiency. Even in irrigation, maintaining, preserving, and improving water use efficiency have not been attended to. Irrigation systems reach only 78 percent of their designed capacity. Only 43 percent of the area of new vegetable crops and industrial crops has been irrigated initially. Irrigation for fisheries, salt industry, and industrial plants has been very limited. Electricity supply for rural areas has been regularly cut off, causing difficulties for livestock production and intensive aquaculture. This is a general problem for rural infrastructure and social services such as health, education, culture, and communication. This undermines the competitiveness of rural businesses and discourages business investment in rural areas.

Investment in agriculture and rural areas has relied heavily on the state budget; policies to mobilize private investment, government bonds, and foreign loans have been underexploited. There is no effective assessment mechanism to promote the role of beneficiaries, which can locate investments in the most promising fields. There are no decentralized mechanisms for authorities to foster markets, serve farmers as customers, or mobilize local people and communities.

Residence Policy Creates Discrimination

Despite great changes in residence regulations to enable freer mobility of people, household registration regulations remain a big problem. According to the residence law, a person who wants to apply for permanent registration in centrally managed cities is required to have a legal residence. If he or she wishes to have a permanent registration in rural districts or provincial towns under a centrally managed city, the requirement is at least one year of temporary residence in that city. And for permanent registration in urban districts under a centrally managed city, the requirement is at least two years. This is exactly the key problem that creates discrimination—or more precisely, inequality—in accessing employment opportunities (especially in the public sector when permanent resident status is a binding requirement) and other basic services, such as education and health care.

Because of these risks, rural–urban migrants mostly participate in the informal sector, and lack instruments to protect their rights, such as labor contracts, social security, and education.

Institutions and Infrastructure: Cities to Lead Vietnam's Transformation into a Modern Industrialized Nation

Over the next two decades, policy makers should focus on enabling cities to reach their potential and enhance the pace of national economic development. Lessons from the urban development experience of countries such as Japan can be particularly useful given similarities in land area and population (box 4.5). The lessons are that policies that strengthen urban institutions can promote urban development at scale, and better connective infrastructure can expand market access to foster economic specialization. In this way, Vietnam will benefit more from agglomeration economies across a vibrant portfolio of towns and cities.

The system of cities will have complementary functions. Metropolises such as Ho Chi Minh City will interact with the global economy and provide the urban diversity that encourages learning, innovation, and new product development, connecting people and firms to the world. Regional cities such as Haiphong, Da Nang, and Can Tho will allow producers both to benefit from clustering because they can choose workers and materials from a bigger pool and to engage in beneficial competition so as to promote development. These cities will be aggregators for the hinterland economy and be part of GVCs. Towns such as Buon Ma Thuot in the Central Highlands, famous for its coffee, will let firms and farms exploit plant-level scale economies by providing roads (for inputs and outputs) and schools and other amenities (for workers' families). Service clusters with infrastructure and basic business-supporting services should serve specialized cultivated areas in rural districts. But it is difficult to predict the mix of metropolises, cities, and towns—or the size of these settlements (box 4.6).

BOX 4.5 Some advanced regional economies have adopted efficient systems of developing their cities

Japan has developed its cities in a highly efficient way, by creating a well-integrated and well-connected spatial hierarchy of subcenters, linked by the most developed subway network in the world. Rather than rely on excessive rural-to-urban land conversion and then suffer from detrimental urban sprawl, Japan based its urban growth on internal intensification through well-balanced spatial-planning policies and a balance between microprocesses and large-scale structuring interventions. Also very useful for Vietnam are the lessons from urban development in the Republic of Korea and Taiwan, China—with large-scale peri-urban areas surrounding Seoul or Taipei—and from the development of compact cities based on public transport in Hong Kong SAR, China, and in Singapore.

BOX 4.6 A portfolio of modern and livable cities

Vietnam is still in the incipient stage of urbanization. The path that it follows in the next 20 years will determine the spatial development of cities. If land development continues in the business-as-usual approach of low-density development, Vietnam will face increased congestion, illiquid land markets with increasing housing costs, catching up to mass transit needs in the metropolitan context, stretching out public services and externalities like air pollution and environmental deterioration.

But if Vietnam chooses a low carbon path, policy makers will have to switch from a quantity to a quality approach. They will have to fine-tune the urban planning and City Classification System to meet the demands of the market and society. In some areas, the state will have to play a key role in regulation and policy setting. In others, it will facilitate a greater role for the private sector, as in land redevelopment, mass transit, solid waste, water supply, sanitation, and, to some extent, social services. The other key principle will be to have a level playing field for the public and private sectors.

The path followed will require strong leadership at the central and local levels to promote the vision of modern and livable cities with efficient and affordable public services and a conducive environment for domestic and international businesses.

That depends on how families and businesses "pick" different types of Vietnamese cities as places to live and do business, and how the state corrects market imperfections.

In preparing for the transition to upper-middle-income status and a modern industrialized nation, authorities could enhance the economic efficiency of their cities. This is critical for higher productivity, greater innovation, and the development of a vibrant urban middle class—markers of high-income economies with vibrant cities. The focus should be on upgrading institutions and expanding connective infrastructure.

Upgrading Institutions to Support Urban Development

Enable land markets

At the core of urban policy reform is letting land markets emerge and flourish. Reforming land institutions—such as strengthening land registration and bringing in market land valuation—is a priority to reduce excessive and fragmented urban land conversion. Increasing the transparency of land pricing by establishing mechanisms to regularly publicize land values obtained in auctions and individual land sales could be a good starting point. These efforts need to be tied to local government fiscal reforms that promote broader use of land and property taxes as an alternative to land-conversion fees for revenues.

The supply of land for affordable housing for low-income households needs to be in close accordance with land policy. Going forward, the priority should be to make information available in the public domain to help establish common knowledge and inform the decisions of investors.

To enable land markets, the following issues should be considered:

- Increase the transparency of land pricing by establishing mechanisms to regularly publicize land values obtained in auctions and individual land sales (for example, by cross-checking with buyers to deal with undervaluation) and to check these against the land price tables.
- Link cadaster to tax maps documenting potential revenue, based on different valuation formulas, to promote broader use of land taxation to generate revenue for local governments. Use this link to develop and disseminate draft regulations for land taxation required in the law.
- Under the 2013 Land Law, expedite forming an independent valuation profession, and use land information to make the transition toward parcel-specific valuations.

Rationalize and make more transparent the land-acquisition processes

The success of land acquisition for public interest and for economic development has led to its widespread use as an alternative to developing land markets. Levels of compensation are largely based on land-price tables known to be vastly different from market prices, leading to distorted investment decisions (including by companies with marginally viable or totally ineffective business plans) and a large number of complaints and denunciations (more than 10,000 a year).

The conditions for public land acquisition have been tightened in the 2013 Land Law.

- Foreign-invested enterprises can no longer benefit from land acquisition.
- Investors must demonstrate financial capacity for implementing a project and make a deposit in accord with the investment law.
- Investors are not eligible for any compensation if the land they received is taken back due to noncompliance with investment plans (a 24-month delay).
- Although reference to land-price tables can be made, an independent land valuation must be conducted for each land acquisition project. Compensation must be for land and for other livelihood-relevant activities and possessions (job training, relocation, and plants and livestock) as specified in a resettlement plan that must incorporate input from the affected population.

The content of urban land-use plans specifies public goods and topics that may be subject to externalities. Plans must be prepared in a public process, with detailed procedural instructions written in law (such as conducting meetings to discuss district-level plans and issuing reports summarizing all responses received and how they have been addressed). Independent appraisal boards should be established to provide technical support and verification of plans at all levels. Detailed requirements for publicizing plans are also laid out in the law.

Create stable revenues from land

Revenues from land currently make up a huge share in local government budget revenues. But given that most of these revenues are one-time revenues from transforming land-use rights, they are neither stable nor sustainable. This creates difficulties for local governments when the real estate market becomes stagnant, as in Da Nang recently.[10] International experience shows that real estate taxes can be a stable source of revenues. Vietnam should therefore consider promulgating a real estate tax and a property tax. Since such taxes are highly progressive, they would likely promote better equality.

Make land available for affordable housing

An estimated 11,500 hectares of urban land is needed each year for affordable housing (World Bank 2015b). But the formal supply is failing to keep pace with demand, forcing up prices and reducing affordability, partly because the existing land administration framework is complex and inefficient. Key challenges are in delivering serviced land in mobilizing vacant or underdeveloped land in cities, tracking and enforcing the requisite 20-percent land contribution (Decree 188), using land-value capture tools to extract value from new development, and integrating land-use planning and coordination between the relevant ministries—Construction, Home Affairs, Natural Resources, Public Investment, and Transportation.

The 2013 Land Law and the 2015 Housing Law recommit the government to ensuring that low-income Vietnamese are not excluded from the market and to supporting their access to affordable and adequate housing. The Housing Law has reoriented the housing policy toward urban areas, particularly self-built housing and affordable rentals.

Update and refine the City Classification System

Key recommendations here include:

- *Develop a new set of urban indicators to shape a strategic approach to urbanization.* This project is being undertaken by the Ministry of Construction, which is conducting studies focused on criteria to be included in a new decree (Government of Vietnam 2015). See box 4.7 for Shanghai's use of urban indicators to guide strategic decisions.
- *Collect reliable and open data on urban indicators.* Data at metropolitan levels are scarce. Indicators based on administrative jurisdictions fail to reflect the changing dynamics in peri-urban areas, where most development takes place in cities under pressure to urbanize rapidly. But cities are not islands, so their success is related to the planning and management of the space around them. The activities of cities go well beyond any local government's administrative boundaries to include peri-urban areas and the corridors that connect them with other centers of activity.
- *Create a spatial-development framework closely associated with the economic development strategy.* The government is considering regional planning as an approach for a more efficient use of land and resources. In 2009, Prime Minister Nguyen Tan Dung approved the Adjustment of the Master Plan Orientation for Vietnamese Urban System Development up to 2025 with a Vision toward 2050. The plan identifies key economic zones targeted to accelerate socioeconomic development. These positive steps should be further developed in combination with a reform of the classification system that establishes economic and social goals. These goals would form the basis for a strategic spatial structure supported at the local planning level (Kim 2014).

BOX 4.7 Shanghai moving away from GDP as a driving indicator of urbanization policy

Shanghai has become the first major city or province in China to abandon GDP metrics for 2015 as government policy shifts toward growth's quality over quantity. Analysts say an excessive focus on GDP contributed to urban sprawl and environmental degradation as officials encouraged the reclassification of agricultural land to build housing developments. Growth in GDP has long been a key metric to evaluate the performance of local officials, helping to determine whether they were promoted. Officials in these cities have built successful careers on GDP-based evaluations, making it difficult to adjust their policy focus.

More than 70 Chinese smaller cities and counties and at least two municipal districts in Shanghai had previously canceled GDP targets, but the decision by Shanghai confirms a shift from the pursuit of economic growth at all costs toward measures that address unequal income distribution, problems with the social welfare system, and environmental cost and in general encourage better quality of life.

Source: Financial Times 2015, January 26. http://www.ft.com/intl/cms/s/0/2c822efc-a51d-11e4-bf11-00144feab7de.html?siteedition=uk#axzz3UeGtfHwM.

- *Generate a mechanism for metropolitan coordination.* A clear framework for decentralization needs to be in place for a metropolitan or regional approach. This entails delegating decision-making powers at the regional level as well as creating management entities that enable the coordination of policies and budgets between local governments within the region. The role of provincial government and other subregional administrative divisions would have to be analyzed to avoid duplication of administrative procedures and an extra tier of bureaucracy. A culture of planning at the central level and functional silos also needs to be revised. This requires a shift from command-and-control planning systems to articulating a common regional direction, aligned with those of other regions, and establishing practical guidelines that can be implemented at the subregional level. See Poland's experience in box 4.8, where the emphasis has shifted from a centralized to a local planning approach. To attract investment, transparency and accountability must be firmly established at the local level to attract investment. Localities need to develop capacity to prepare and enforce detailed plans.
- *Implement regional plans for economic and territorial development.* This process will require a dedicated management entity at a regional level. Political synchronization over the long term with provincial and local leaders (who have mandates of five years) will demand significant institutional innovation away from the current status quo. The influence of the regional entity on the policies of the various subregional localities may be stronger if they are tied to resource allocations from the local government. The legal status of the regional entity must be clearly designed, as must its mandate over provinces and local governments. Laws should define regional-planning competencies, tax-collection structures, and resource-allocation responsibilities—and the policies to ensure participation, transparency, and accountability.

Strengthen urban planning

There is also a need to strengthen institutions for integrated urban planning—within and across sectors (land use and transport for example)—based on harnessing scale economies at the corridor, metropolitan, and regional levels. In countries such as Japan and Korea, the institutional mandates for land, infrastructure, transport, and water resources are vested under one-line ministries. Such arrangement encourages better coordination of policies at the national and city levels. This integration calls for a "whole of government"

BOX 4.8 Poland's spatial planning transition

During the years of central planning in Poland, which lasted until the late 1980s, urban planning was a top-down exercise. It was based on theoretical models and standards, with limited relation to economic reality and the possibilities of the state's budget. These "good wishes" plans focused on zoning land for housing and industry, as well as roads and other infrastructure needs, which were estimated centrally. The central government also established urban standards that allocated land for education, recreation, health, culture, retail, and other functions. Allocations were generous, as land could be purchased (or expropriated) as through eminent domain at very low costs. The central government and its regional and local branches were the main stakeholders in the processes, while urban planners and state-owned contractors (the word *developer* was not known then) simply followed their instructions. The planners' task was reduced to observing regulations emanating from the central government, which resulted in generations of risk-averse technical cadres.

The first wave of reforms in the 1990s discontinued urban standards, because the state was not able to fulfill its own ambitious projections, even though land was allocated by master plans at nearly no cost. Reforms also focused on altering planning structures from a top-down, arbitrary tool of central authorities to a function assigned to elected local governments. These reforms ended the illusion of freely available land donated by an omnipotent state/public investor/developer. However, reforms were not accompanied by compulsory property taxes, even though private property was restored to its original owners. In addition, replacing the old spatial plans within five to nine years with new planning tools was too radical and perhaps naïve, as spatial planning was made mandatory even with low capacity. The majority of the municipalities could not perform their obligations effectively.

The Land Use Planning and Management Act of 2003 brought a second stage of reform. It was a complex effort to improve planning regulations and instruments to adjust them, step by step, to come to terms with a free-market environment. Local planning became more substantial and linked to an emerging strategic-planning practice, as well as to the dynamics of the real estate market. But some measures required further attention. Supplementary planning instruments, introduced to accelerate the master planning process, ended in many cases through the substitution of local plans. Development inconsistent with local spatial policies was in many cases approved. Developers became the main players, sometimes at the cost of public interest. A key lesson is that spatial planning should not be a rigid dogma and that binding local plans should ensure a spatial order that benefits society as a whole. Furthermore, spatial-planning reforms should be part of a broad package of state reforms in the transition from a centrally planned economy to a market economy.

Source: Buczek 2013.

approach, which would require the central government to carefully review and align the line ministries' mandates to international best practices.

Urban planning departments need to strengthen their capabilities urgently to integrate socioeconomic realities when developing physical plans. Master plans and other physical plans need to be linked to the budget process, for if plans cannot be supported by key investments, their credibility will suffer. In addition, coordination mechanisms can align provincial and city plans, especially since socioeconomic development plans, urban master plans, and sector infrastructure plans are prepared by different departments, often run on different schedules, and use inconsistent data and projections for planning. The timing of planning needs to be synchronized, and the number of plans that govern territorial space needs to be cut heavily (ideally to two or three). Vietnam also needs to create a professional cadre of urban planners who can plan and manage cities.

As Vietnam urbanizes, planning must be linked to economic strategies at the metropolitan level. Key to metropolitan and regional planning is assessing the extent to which spatial strategies emanate from economic strategies. The economic influence of cities is not confined to administrative boundaries but spreads to a greatly enlarged metropolitan area encompassing peri-urban areas and rural hinterlands. Connected with functional corridors to other urban centers and subcenters of activity, they can attain a regional scale. To reap the advantages of agglomeration, urban centers would need to become part of an economically and spatially defined system of cities.

The following principles can contribute to it:

- *The economic strategy can be a tool for coordinating metropolitan and regional plans.* There is a critical need to leverage regional plans by developing associated management structures and investment incentives for cities in the region to work together.
- *Investment must focus on successful agglomeration, concentrating it in clearly defined clusters.* The current radial structure around Ho Chi Minh City might fail to encompass the productivity in growth areas outside the core area, which must be supported through integrating land-use, transport, and infrastructure planning to optimize market demand, value chains, population projections, and goals for social and economic development.
- *Not all cities can thrive on the same industry.* For example, it would be unrealistic to encourage every city in the region to attract investment as an information technology (IT) industry center. The region would benefit from complementary industries financed by investments in spatially efficient infrastructure. Enabling collaboration within a system of cities requires mechanisms for coordinating resource mobilization, allocation, and service delivery.
- *Management units must be created consistent with the most efficient methods of formulating an economic strategy.* The spatial development system must not limit management options to fixed administrative boundaries. Nor should it create an additional layer of planning bureaucracy. Instead, it should bring together planning and financial instruments with management, which can range from simple coordination, information exchange, and capacity sharing between local governments to a full merger of authorities.

Reform residence policy

Policies and institutions need to be changed to further enable rural–urban migration. The household registration policy should change to enable migrants' easy access to services in urban areas. In addition, fundamental renovations of vocational training and employment for migrants should equip them with skills to meet the needs of businesses and urban populations. Infrastructure and basic social services should support migrants, including housing, schooling, health care, health insurance, and social insurance. And associations should be formed to support and protect the rights of migrants.

Connective Infrastructure to Better Link Cities and Neighborhoods

Vietnam's connectivity challenges are attributable to both the transport of goods across regions and congestion within urban areas. Institutional reforms will be essential to coordinate investment in cross-province infrastructure and to improve the quality of intrametropolitan connectivity. Improvements to roads, rail, and seaports will all be necessary to lower internal transport costs and connect Vietnam to other regional markets (box 4.9).

Mainstream integrated transport and logistics platforms

The government should push to mainstream integrated planning for transport and logistics across modes, geographies, and public sector functions. The focus should be on key road corridors and expressways to tackle issues in supply chains and reduce the burden of road transport costs on the economy. Integrated planning that is less decentralized—for example, at the corridor level, metropolitan area, conurbation, or even regional

BOX 4.9 Potential for high-speed rail

Evidence from the literature suggests that high-speed rail (HSR) links were developed to increase accessibility and connectivity between core cities in the range of 400–600 kilometers (Vickerman 2012). The direct causality of the HSR and its economic benefits (given the high costs of investments) for agglomeration and economic concentration are difficult to establish because the experience has been mixed (Cervero and Murakami 2012). China, France, Japan, the Republic of Korea, and the United States have developed HSR from a different perspective, some focusing on connectivity from a travel passenger demand perspective (Japan, United States) and others focusing on facilitating better access across key economic cities (China, France, Korea, and the United States).

Promoting HSR requires careful planning and strategic vision to promote corridor development and is often part of a deliberate policy to promote growth and development, which is often resource-intensive. Other factors also play an important role like optimal distances between cities, differentiated production centers along the corridor, facilitation of logistics and people, and interjurisdictional coordination.

Vietnam, given its long coastline (close to 2,000 kilometers), needs to sequence interventions to improve connectivity from Hanoi and Ho Chi Minh City from a public investment perspective. In the next 10 years, policies should focus on strengthening of agglomeration around Ho Chi Minh City and Hanoi, with an emphasis on improving the connectivity of the secondary cities around these large cities, such as Hanoi–Haiphong or Ho Chi Minh City–Can Tho–Binh Duong. Once these agglomerations are well established, the focus could shift to connecting Ho Chi Minh City to Central Vietnam and Hanoi to Central Vietnam. This can be done by improving the road network, but also by improving the existing rail network to facilitate logistics. Finally, with economic benefits and available private long-term financing, it is possible for HSR to link the major agglomerations (Hanoi–Ho Chi Minh City).

Source: Report team.

level—would result in better-integrated solutions. Such an approach might have prevented, for example, the oversupply of container-handling capacity at Cai Mep–Thi Vai coexisting with fully used facilities in Ho Chi Minh City only 80 km away—and therefore part of the same freight corridor. Integrated planning that is less fragmented, with fewer agencies, may not only help to simplify the planning process but also strengthen accountability, since responsibility is more clearly assigned to parties that are best able to manage the planning and associated execution. The current utilization rate of the Cai Mep–Thi Vai port is less than 30 percent, because its supply–demand balance is hindered by the continued operations of inner-city river ports in Ho Chi Minh City.

A national strategy would also increase collaboration across government agencies, including the Ministries of Transport, Finance, Planning and Investment, and Industry and Trade. This strategy would also be supported by strong fiscal discipline through adequate auditing and reporting mechanisms because the gap between fiscal space for transport, investment plans, and the actual budget is shrinking. That offers a tremendous opportunity to improve the ability to leverage public resources for private investment and financing through public-private partnerships for large transport infrastructures.

Integrated planning can help the government agencies conceive, design, and implement individual connectivity-enhancing projects. In addition, a national strategy for logistics and transport could provide goals, approaches, and policy direction to pursue at the national, provincial, and local levels. The joint Port Authority of New York and New Jersey in the United States better aligns the interests and plans of an entire region. The Port Cluster Management Authority No. 5 in the Ho Chi Minh City region, for example, can be a good first pilot to adopt the U.S. experience.

Expand metropolitan transport solutions

Traffic congestion will increase even with increased construction of roads for individual means of transportation. And no super city can address traffic congestion without a large-capacity public transport system. The increased use of cars and changes in housing types require multimodal solutions. The logistics infrastructure of the two largest cities, Hanoi and Ho Chi Minh City, cannot sustain cars as the major means of transportation. Of similar size to such European cities as Paris and Amsterdam, Vietnamese cities can develop integrated multimodal transport systems by basing the projects on their successful counterparts in Europe. The fine grain of Vietnam's urban fabric and street patterns is advantageous when businesses and services are rebuilt at walking distances from each other and a dense and efficient public transport network courses through their periphery.

As Vietnam enters a crucial phase of urbanization—shifting from 30 to 50 percent of its land area—policy makers need to plan modes of transportation that will best enhance urban mobility. The 30–50 percent urbanization process in China has been carried out through a massive transformation of rural land into urban land and the development of large-scale infrastructure. But this urbanization has led to massive urban sprawl and a huge dependence on cars. Japan, by contrast, has maintained and—if anything—increased its connectivity and diversity while limiting rural land conversion. The result: a vibrant urban economy and social integration through myriad microprocesses.

Lessons from China: Avoid locking in to a "large scale" mindset

In China's early stages of urbanization, the massive and accelerated conversion of rural land into urban land brought in large amounts of capital, further fueling the process. The resulting economic growth led to large-scale industrialization and social transformation. Further, as mentioned previously, at this stage China suffers from severe urban sprawl based on giant infrastructure and isolated buildings, a marked contrast to the much finer grain of Chinese historical spatial forms. This new stage of development for Chinese cities has severed the traditional links between family generations and between neighborhoods. Spatial zoning and large-scale separation of activities have greatly increased mobility and imposed strict separations between economic classes and the time for work and for leisure.

The diversity among Chinese cities, with their different local climates and cultures on a semicontinent spanning many latitudes, has been reduced to a single uniform category of modern city, which consumes massive amounts of energy and will be locked into car dependency far into the future. This urbanization model is not only environmentally unsustainable—it also jeopardizes the future of China's transition toward a more mature society less dependent on low-cost labor. The goal was more innovation as a research-based engine of economic growth.

China has so far built its intra- and interurban networks at a much larger grain than other countries. The result has been an exponential collapse in the total number of possible links and paths between urban elements, compared with cities and city systems in Europe and the United States. This lack of medium- and small-scale street networks has a big impact on managing traffic flows.

That rules out the deployment of a variety of transport choices—walking, cycling, buses with short distances between stops, tramways, dense subways, regional trains. People cannot efficiently time their daily commute. Everyone has only two choices: the large-scale mass transit system or the urban highway. The lack of short-range local diversity and choice creates inefficiency. The whole system has peaks that could be better dissipated by a variety of modal choices in a large "space of paths," fitting the distances to travel in a finer grain, and a better-structured city organized around a variety of scales. To avoid congestion, the large scales are overdimensioned and segregated from the smaller scales, which prevents intermediary and small scales connected to the large scale. This reinforces large scales against intermediary and small scales and eventually locks cities into large-scale dependence.

Japanese Successful Organization Based on Fine Grain

In many respects Vietnam's spontaneous urban dynamics are closer to Japan's, whose narrow and elongated shape is similar to Vietnam's, and its population is roughly the same. Japan increased its rate of urbanization from 25 percent in 1950 to 65 percent in 1980, while rising over 30 years of sustained growth from poverty after the destructiveness of World War II to become the third-largest world economy, just after the United States and China. Japan developed the largest city in the world, Tokyo, with 38 million inhabitants, in a highly efficient way. Myriad microprocesses created a highly complex, well-integrated, and well-connected spatial hierarchy of subcenters, linked by the world's most developed subway network. Rather than rely on excessive rural to urban land conversion and then suffer from detrimental urban sprawl, Japan based its urban growth on internal intensification through well-balanced spatial-planning policies and myriad microprocesses for larger-scale structuring interventions.

By preserving and reinforcing fine-grain and local connectivity, Japan has avoided the destruction wrought by the collapse of the centuries-old social structure in China. Japanese society supports both social resilience and vibrant economic activity. By providing an appropriate framework for investment at the district, city, and national scales, Japan has produced well-balanced cities with high degrees of connectivity—also at the district, city, and national scales. The numerous medium-scale projects and investments, in comparison with the very large-scale projects in China, have avoided the large-scale dependence that China suffers from—and have instead contributed to the emergence of livable, low-carbon, and successful cities.

There also is much to learn from other Southeast Asian countries whose development level is not greatly higher, such as Indonesia, the Philippines, and Thailand. But some urban areas in the region still face many problems. For example, to different extents, Bangkok, Jakarta, and Manila have to deal with extremely difficult issues that reduce their competitiveness. Hanoi and Ho Chi Minh City certainly do not want to fall into the similar situation in the future. So, it will be very difficult for Vietnamese urban areas to avoid troubles if the country relies on the experiences of countries with just a little higher level of development.

In contrast, Hong Kong SAR, China; Korea; Singapore; and Taiwan, China, are success stories, attributable to reasonable policies. This is the destination that Vietnam wants to emulate. The urban development lessons from Korea and Taiwan, China, with large urban areas around Seoul and Taipei and their urban management experience, especially the urban compression development based on public transport in Hong Kong SAR, China and Singapore, are of great value for Vietnam.

Strengthen rural–urban connectivity

The rural–urban relationship needs to change from competitive to complementary to create synergy. Rural areas can be the supplier and market for urban areas. Peri-urban areas can be greenbelts, providing leisure for residents of big cities.

Balanced spatial development between urban and rural areas can ease the excessive concentration of people, reduce congestion and social problems in major cities, and promote agglomeration and scale economies in urban centers. When the rural–urban gap is narrowed, migration will be based on people's preferences rather than pushed by poverty.

The core of Vietnam's economic success is rapid growth while keeping inequality in check. But continuing this success requires knowing how to integrate rural areas into urban engines. Improving rural–urban connection is the key to tackling this challenge.

Infrastructure is an important element of rural–urban connection. The development of a three-tier urban system, as mentioned above, will facilitate the integration of regions and remote areas. For urban centers in key agricultural areas—such as the Red River Delta, Central Highlands, Southeast, and Mekong River Delta—the state should prioritize investments to create systems of transportation, warehouses, and vehicles appropriated to agro-ecological zones. It also needs to form systems of railways, ports, and specialized road or air transport for the major agricultural products. In addition, synchronous service systems, especially agricultural science centers, can tie research to training and extension.

Industrial service clusters should be developed at district level, linking specialized production regions with main markets for agricultural products. Attracting enterprise investment is necessary to connect farmers to markets, mobilize local labor, and reduce the residential concentration that overloads infrastructure in the short term in large urban areas. Removing obstacles to fulfilling procedures, leasing land, registering businesses, and providing tax-free and fee-free incentives can encourage professional farmers and household businesses to register as enterprises to expand production. Procedures and costs related to business registration should be reduced as much as possible. Enterprises that hire local labor, sign long-term contracts, or offer vocational training for employees after recruitment should receive incentives and special support (such as land and credit). Service enterprise groups that organize agricultural production, agribusiness, and high-tech processing enterprises and create added value from sub-sectors' byproducts should be given priority. In addition, the quality of labor and labor markets should be improved in rural areas. Sharing vocational training expenses with enterprises that employ local labor would also be helpful.

Annex 4A Haiphong City: The Challenges and Promises of a Gateway in Transition

Haiphong, Vietnam's third-largest city and the most important international gateway to the northern region, illustrates the challenges facing Vietnam as it manages its dual transition from lower to higher urbanization and from limited to wider connectivity. According to the 2009 population and housing census, Haiphong has an urban population of 847,000, although the broader province of Haiphong has about 1.9 million people. It is located approximately 105 km from Hanoi on National Highway 5 (NH5).

NH5 is the main artery linking Hanoi with Haiphong port, a cluster of container, bulk, and break-bulk terminals along the Cam River. A limited-capacity road, it is heavily exposed to congestion, particularly because it passes through Haiphong's city center, contributing to inner-city congestion and increasing emissions. It also undermines safety due to the mix of motorbikes, light vehicles, and heavy vehicles traveling to and from Haiphong port.

Despite being Hanoi's gateway to the world, Haiphong has thus far been developed as a river port. As a result, the container terminals currently serving Haiphong port, including Hoang Dieu, Chua Ve, and Dinh Vu, are limited in draft, able to receive vessels of up to only 2,000 TEUs (twenty-foot equivalents) in capacity. This increases the cost of transport per landed container and reduces the efficiency of port operations, which are fragmented across multiple small vessels. Unsurprisingly, terminals at Haiphong port are nearly full, most with utilization rates of at least 70 percent.

Recognizing this pressing supply–demand mismatch, the government has embarked on large-scale infrastructure projects. First, an international-standard expressway has been under construction over the past six years to link Hanoi and Haiphong. This 105 kilometer, $2 billion facility will bypass Haiphong city center and connect Hanoi directly with Haiphong port. With these features, the Hanoi–Haiphong expressway will become a game changer, providing hinterland connectivity for Vietnam's northern region.

Second, the deep-water port of Lach Huyen is being developed on Cat Hai Island, to the east of Haiphong City. In Phase 1, expected to be operational in late 2017, it will have annual handling capacity of 1 million TEUs, with a draft of 13 million, able to handle vessels of up to 6,000 TEUs in capacity initially and up to 8,000 TEUs or more after further channel dredging. Lach Huyen will be directly connected to the mainland via what will become Vietnam's longest sea bridge, with a total length of 15.6 km. The bridge will connect Lach Huyen with the Dinh Vu industrial park and the Hanoi–Haiphong expressway. By bringing large mother vessels for the first time to northern Vietnam, Lach Huyen, like the Hanoi–Haiphong expressway, promises to be a connectivity game changer for the northern region.

Lach Huyen can be expected to bring benefits to container shipping lines (and their customers) by allowing them to deploy larger ships with lower costs per container unit (World Bank 2013). The calling of mother vessels at Lach Huyen may result in savings of about $74 million a year through the elimination of feeder vessels now transshipping containers to foreign ports. Shippers and, by extension, end customers in Vietnam's export products will ultimately benefit from having access to more direct routing choices to more markets at lower logistics costs than today.

Typical of network-based infrastructure and services, initial investments to develop network density attract further development. For Haiphong, the Lach Huyen port and the Hanoi–Haiphong expressway have attracted complementary facilities and services, such as modern international-standard warehousing and cargo-handling facilities; container-freight stations; consolidation and deconsolidation centers; and a privately operated "logistics zone" for handling, staging, storing, and repairing containers. In other words, an integrated ecosystem of infrastructure and service provision is developing in Haiphong thanks to a critical mass of connectivity improvements.

Haiphong is the only rail-enabled port in Vietnam (connected all the way to Kunming, China) with direct access to the Red River Delta inland waterway network and to an international airport (Cat Bi). So further investments in and improvements to rail, air, and inland waterway infrastructure provision and service delivery could expand the multimodal connectivity of Haiphong and the broader Hanoi and northern region even further. For example, in January 2015 Cat Bi Airport launched a $70 million expansion of its passenger terminal, which will modernize the airport facilities and bring passenger capacity from 800,000 to 4 million travelers a year. The new terminal is expected to become operational by the end of 2016.

With simultaneous improvements to air, land, and maritime connectivity, Haiphong sets an unprecedented example of the successful development of a major regional gateway. But the sustainability of these investments, which run into billions of dollars, will depend on how the facilities are planned and managed going forward. Making full use of the newly available capacity in a way that truly enhances connectivity will require multimodal coordination, which is not generally promoted under Vietnam's current institutional framework. And if current demand expectations materialize, Lach Huyen will by 2022 find itself at capacity and need to deliver Phase 2 of its development plan. Government authorities and all relevant stakeholders (terminal operators, connecting road operators, shippers) should undertake integrated planning for Phase 2, well in advance of the point when the capacity is already reached and demand and supply have again fallen into mismatch.

Lessons can be learned from developing Phase 1, which had delays of about two years due to financing, technical, and implementation constraints (such as delays in land acquisition and resettlement compensation). It is also necessary to ensure that the quality and standard of all connecting infrastructure—across local roads, expressways, waterways, and railways—remain adequate to handle the expected higher volumes facilitated by Lach Huyen and the other Haiphong terminals.

Despite its scale, the current development drive in Haiphong suffers from the modal planning and delivery imbalances that have affected much of the past development of Vietnam's transport infrastructure. It has largely neglected rail (primarily) and inland waterway (secondarily) connectivity improvements. As the only rail-enabled port in the country, and as a link between the Chinese and Vietnamese rail networks, Haiphong and the northern region have substantial opportunities for rail intermodal connectivity. The nature, scale, and implications of this opportunity should be considered, measured, and integrated into the planning for regional connectivity in the future.

Finally, the urban fabric of Haiphong as a city should not be neglected. Although Haiphong as a port city has an economic impact that goes well beyond its city limits, the multimodal infrastructure that makes it a gateway should be planned in the context of the city itself to ensure that urban transport can coexist with gateway transport. This represents yet another dimension of integrated planning—integration across modes for both freight and passenger transport. The experience of Ho Chi Minh City offers many potential lessons for Haiphong. Ho Chi Minh City's inner-city ports have created congestion that has resulted in significant economic costs to commuters, tourists, and other users of the transport network. As an "early intervention," with only a fraction of the population and complexity of Ho Chi Minh City, Haiphong is well positioned to act early to prevent some of the congestion and environmental impacts that affected Ho Chi Minh City as a fellow gateway city.

Source: Blancas Mendivil 2015.

Notes

1. After controlling for skill level of the labor force. See Rosenthal and Strange 2003.
2. See http://www.evn.com.vn/News/Tin-tuc-Hoat-dong/Dau-tu-Xay-dung/998-so-xa-nong-thon-tren-ca-nuoc-co-dien201618.aspx.
3. See http://www.baomoi.com/Nam-2015-Viet-Nam-co-120-6-trieu-thue-bao-di-dong/c/18268774.epi.
4. See http://densityatlas.org/casestudies/.
5. See http://khucongnghiep.com.vn/tinhoatdong/tabid/63/articleType/ArticleView/articleId/1113/Default.aspx.
6. The planning framework for urban development in Vietnam follows the orientation specified in the General Plan for Urban System in Vietnam (Decision 445/QD-TTg dated 07/4/2009).
7. This is an estimate by the World Bank; the lack of data in transport and logistics is a serious impediment to policy reform and modernization of this sector.
8. These data are taken from the substantial household surveys undertaken by ALMEC in 2008 for Da Nang, 2004 for Hanoi, and 2002 for Ho Chi Minh City.
9. The possible development of surface public transport in Vietnam is also severely limited by the lack of road space: 2.5 percent in Ho Chi Minh City (only 14 percent with a gauge greater than 12 meters, which allows the passage of large buses); 35 percent usable only by two-wheelers; and 7 percent in Hanoi compared with 25 percent in Paris, for example.
10. See http://vietnamnet.vn/vn/kinh-doanh/284910/giac-mo-da-nang-con-gi-sau-con-sot-dat.html.

References

Blancas Mendivil, Luis. 2015. *Engaging the Private Sector in Transport and Logistics Planning and Policy Making: Options for Vietnam*. Washington, DC: World Bank.

Buczek, Grzegorz. 2013. *The Spatial Planning System: The Transition from a Centrally Planned to a Market Economy in Poland, 1989–2013*. Washington, DC: World Bank.

Cervero, Robert and Jin Murakami. 2012. *High-Speed Rail and Economic Development: Business Agglomerations and Policy Implications*. Berkeley, CA: University of California Transportation Center. http://www.uctc.net/research/papers/UCTC-FR-2012-10.pdf.

Chreod, Ltd. 2015. "Spatial Implications of Urbanization in Vietnam." Background paper for Vietnam 2035 Report.

Clement, Musil, and Simon Charles. 2015. "Building an Ambitious Public Transport System in Ho Chi Minh City." Working paper, PADDI, Ho Chi Minh City. http://paddi.vn/wp-content/uploads/WP_PADDI_01_ENG_high-quality.pdf.

Demombynes, Gabriel. 2015. "Analysis of 2014 Labour Force Survey by World Bank Staff." Background paper for Vietnam 2035 Report.

Fanchette, Sylvie. 2012. "Periurban Craft Villages in the Storm of Hanoi Expansion." In *Trends of Urbanization and Suburbanization in Southeast Asia*, edited by T. N. Q. Tran, N. Quertamp, C. de Miras, N. Quand Vinh, L. Van Nam, and T. Hoang Truong, 231–56. Ho Chi Minh City: CEFURDS, LPED.

General Statistics Office of Vietnam. 2005. *Statistical Yearbook of Vietnam 2005*. Hanoi: General Statistics Office of Vietnam.

———. 2013. *Statistical Yearbook of Vietnam 2013*. Hanoi: General Statistics Office of Vietnam.

———. 2014. *Statistical Yearbook of Vietnam 2014*. Hanoi: General Statistics Office of Vietnam.

———. 2015. *Statistical Yearbook of Vietnam 2015*. Hanoi: General Statistics Office of Vietnam.

Goswami, Arti Grover, and Somik Lall. 2015. "Jobs and Land Use within Cities. A Survey of Theory, Evidence, and Policy." Policy Research Working Paper 7453, World Bank, Washington, DC.

Government of Vietnam. 2015. *Overview of the Grading System for Urban Areas in Viet Nam*. Hanoi: Urban Development Agency.

Ho, Dang, and Malcolm McPherson. 2010. *Land Policy for Socioeconomic Development in Vietnam*. Cambridge, MA: Harvard Kennedy School Ash Center for Democratic Governance and Innovation. http://ash.harvard.edu/links/land-policy-socioeconomic-development-vietnam.

Howard, Emma, Carol Newman, John Rand, and Finn Tarp. 2014. "Productivity-Enhancing Manufacturing Clusters: Evidence from Vietnam." Learning to Compete Working Paper 14, Brookings Institute, Washington, DC.

Huynh, Du. 2012. *The Transformation in Ho Chi Minh City: Issues in Managing Growth*. Doctor of Design Dissertation. Cambridge, MA: Harvard Graduate School of Design.

———. 2015. "The Misuse of Urban Planning in Ho Chi Minh City." *Habitat International* 48 (1): 11–19.

Kim, Boram. 2014. "Initial Assessment of the Viet Nam Indicator Systems Relevant to Urban Development." Working paper, UN-HABITAT, Hanoi.

Kontgis, Caitlin, Annemarie Schneider, Jefferson Fox, Sumeet Saksena, James Spencer, and Miguel Castrence. 2014. "Monitoring Peri-urbanization in the Greater Ho Chi Minh City Metropolitan Area." *Applied Geography* 53 (1): 377–88.

Lee, B. 1998. "Land Use Regulations and Efficiency of Seoul's Economy." *International Journal of Urban Sciences* 2 (1): 48–72.

Moretti, Enrico. 2004. "Human Capital Externalities in Cities." In *Handbook of Regional and Urban Economics*, edited by G. J. Duranton, V. Henderson, and W. Strange. Amsterdam: North Holland-Elsevier.

Nguyen, Binh Giang. 2012. *Social Regional Impacts of Industrial Zones in Vietnam*. Hanoi: Social Sciences Publishing House.

Rosenthal, S. S., and W. C. Strange. 2003. "Geography, Industrial Organization, and Agglomeration." *Review of Economics and Statistics* 85 (2): 377–93.

Salat, Serge. 2013. *Low-Carbon Urban Spatial Planning: Issues and Options for Vietnam*. Urban Morphology Institute.

Shepherd, Simon, and Chandra Balijepalli. 2015. "A Game of Two Cities: A Toll Setting Game with Experimental Results." *Transport Policy* 38 (1): 95–109.

UN-HABITAT (United Nations Human Settlements Programme). Forthcoming. *Vietnam City Profiles*. Hanoi: United Nations Human Settlements Programme (UN-HABITAT).

Urban Solutions. 2011. *Urban Planning, Land and Housing—Vietnam Urbanization Review*. Report prepared as background paper for the Vietnam Urbanization Review, World Bank, Washington, DC.

Vickerman, Roger. 2012. "High-Speed Rail: The European Experience." In *Territorial Implications of High-Speed Rail: A Spanish Perspective*, edited by J. de Ureña, 17–33. London: Ashgate.

Vo, Dang Hung, and Nguyen Van Thang. 2013. *Improving Land Sector Governance in Vietnam: Implementation of Land Governance Assessment Framework (LGAF)*. Washington, DC: World Bank.

World Bank. 2009. *Reshaping Economic Geography: World Development Report 2009*. Washington, DC: World Bank.

———. 2011. *Vietnam Development Report 2012: Market Economy for a Middle-Income Vietnam.* Washington, DC: World Bank.

———. 2011. *Vietnam Urbanization Review.* Washington, DC: World Bank.

———. 2013. *Taking Stock: An Update on Vietnam's Recent Economic Developments.* Washington, DC: World Bank.

———. 2015a. *Summary Report.* Washington, DC: World Bank. http://documents.worldbank.org/curated/en/2016/03/26012370/making-whole-greater-sum-parts-review-fiscal-decentralization-vietnam.

———. 2015b. *East Asia's Changing Urban Landscape: Measuring a Decade of Spatial Growth.* Washington, DC: World Bank.

5

Achieving Sustainable and Climate-Resilient Growth

Main Messages

Vietnam is a long narrow country with nearly 3,260 kilometers of coastline, two major river deltas, and mountains on its western and northeastern borders. It depends on natural resources to a much larger extent than other middle-income countries in the region. The nonagriculture sector has grown at twice the pace of agriculture since 1990, and rural villagers have migrated to cities and craft villages to seek jobs in industry and services. But strong economic growth since the early 1990s and the ongoing economic and spatial transformations have brought with them severe stresses on the environment.

The sustainability of Vietnam's current economic growth model is threatened by the degradation of land-based assets and air and water pollution. The country's income aspirations for the next 20 years will require its economy to rapidly industrialize and urbanize. Achieving the rapid growth needed to meet these aspirations by conducting business as usual will further degrade the country's natural assets and lower productivity growth between now and 2035. And economic growth may be more severely compromised beyond that.

Strengthening the management of natural assets is critical in transforming several productive sectors, including agriculture, fisheries, forestry, tourism, and food and beverages. Improving water and air quality is also important for sustainable economic growth and for quality of life. Achieving these goals will require the country to make more productive and sustainable use of its natural resources and to be innovative in addressing environmental constraints to growth. Inaction will impose a drag on growth and otherwise worsen living conditions, as in other countries such as China where air pollution is calculated to contribute to 1.6 million deaths a year, roughly 17 percent of all deaths in that country (Rohde and Muller 2015).

Compounding the problem, Vietnam is vulnerable to climate change and weather variability. Climate change threatens development, with more than half the workforce dependent on natural resources and the majority of the population living in coastal areas and low-lying deltas. Models predict that the mean temperature increase will be 0.6–1.2°C by 2040 and 1.1–3.6°C by 2100. A 2°C warming scenario projects heat extremes covering nearly 60–70 percent of the land and a higher frequency of intense storms and associated extreme rainfall.

Social costs of environmental and natural resource degradation stem from the inequitable distribution of these economic costs. The poor in rural areas are mainly in the Northern Mountains and Central Highlands or in some of the coastal provinces, areas vulnerable to climate change. Unsustainable resource use often blights fishing communities and ethnic minorities, who are reliant on surrounding natural assets for their livelihoods and well-being. Similarly, vulnerable children and elderly among the urban poor are more likely to bear the costs of air and water pollution.

These environment-related outcomes have several underlying causes. Public investment decisions are neither well-coordinated nor generally efficient while public institutions to enforce environmental regulations lack adequate capacity and resources. Market imperfections and pricing distortions undercut private sector investment. Similarly, the state-owned enterprises (SOEs), such as those in forestry, hinder productivity gains and generate limited public benefits, while contributing to degradation of the resource base. Poor coordination among key ministries with overlapping mandates in implementing climate change action plans—for which financial resources are limited (World Bank 2015)—also complicates matters.

To achieve sustainable growth, Vietnam will have to do the following:

- Improve governance through strong institutions that are better coordinated at implementing and enforcing policies, plans, and investments.
- Develop incentives for private and public investments that are innovative, reduce environmental pollution, and increase income and nonincome measures of welfare.
- Ensure that information is credible and publicly accessible, informs decision-making, improves monitoring, and enhances accountability.

The importance of these three action areas may be seen in the solutions for the major environmental challenges that Vietnam faces. Reversing land degradation will require changes in agricultural practices and greater investments in preserving ecosystem services. These shifts will require coordination within government and between the public and private sectors, and developing accessible and user-friendly data and knowledge that can be used in decision making. They will also require a functioning land market, accelerated restructuring of SOEs engaged in natural resources, and incentives to mobilize private investments. Local governments will require incentives to address land degradation and to adopt environmental policies that may result in short-term costs but guarantee long-term gains. As interventions are pushed through, oversight must ensure that they do not harm vulnerable communities.

For reducing air and water pollution, the government will need to enhance governance by tightening coordination among the numerous ministries involved (such as agriculture, energy, industry, and transport) and remove policies that maintain artificially low tariffs, such as unpriced irrigation water. Equally important will be enforcing standards for good practice and imposing penalties and fines for violating regulations. The responsible public institutions will need support to strengthen their capacity to coordinate among themselves and to monitor and enforce compliance. This approach will be especially important in meeting the growing demand for energy, shaping not only the impact of the country's energy mix on air and water quality but also its footprint from greenhouse gas (GHG) emissions.

Adapting to climate change will require better governance through coordination among multiple agencies and levels of government on strategic regional plans. Efforts to reduce the exposure of different cities in a region to climate change will need to be coordinated. It will be similarly important to coordinate among line agencies and levels of government in watersheds, where the impact of changes in surface water availability will need to be addressed jointly to reduce disproportionate negative impacts downstream. Public and private investment in enhancing resilience to climate change will be essential for a sustainable growth path because of the country's vulnerability to climate-related disasters such as flooding and drought, and its exposure to sea-level rise. Another fundamental need is to build the data and evidence base for taking decisions using monitoring systems like Hydromet.

Vietnam is well placed to rethink its growth path and embark on a sustainable, inclusive, and resilient growth trajectory to 2035. It has approved several strategies (for example, Climate Change Strategy), signed on to various international treaties, and launched market-based instruments to improve resource use (for example, payments for forest environmental services). Further developing its current approach and adopting additional measures would minimize the costs of degradation on growth, augment resilience to climate change, and meet national commitments the government has made in, for example, its Socio-Economic Development Strategy (2011–2020), which calls for better policies and mechanisms to improve the collective economy, farm-based economy, and craft villages in achieving sustainable development.

Worldwide experience indicates that sustainable growth requires policies that deal with political economy realities, such as vested interests and entrenched behaviors. It also requires incentives to internalize externalities and innovative financing instruments to support long-term investments. Sustainable growth should thus be based on strategies that do not bind the country to a path with irreversible adverse impacts but that maximize local and immediate benefits without generating negative externalities. Policies should promote and incentivize smart decision-making and innovative investments by the public-private sector, and facilitate financing of the upfront costs for sustainable growth.

Shifting Vietnam to a more environmentally sustainable path for economic growth will have trade-offs. The main one is to bear upfront the costs of new technologies and policy measures for sustainable growth. These will yield long-term benefits and leave open options for new types of growth, such as nature-based and cultural tourism. They will also help retain uncontaminated water resources for fish production. The net cost of sustainable growth is usually modest.

Environmental Sustainability: A Key to Growth and Development

Vietnam, a major development success story, is aspiring to industrialization, greater modernity, and a higher quality of life. As part of this aspiration, the country is aiming for an annual growth rate of 7 percent per capita. Yet if it pursues these goals following business as usual, environmental stresses from income growth, urbanization, and industrialization are likely to increase significantly between now and 2035. Without changes in policies and practices, growth will place unsustainable pressures on land, water, and energy resources. Put simply, real growth that takes account of a depleting resource base will be lower than measured growth, and so undermine health, productivity, and development potential. The environmental quality of water and air is important not only for ecosystem health and the quality of life but also for economic growth and development.

Climate change poses a major threat to development in Vietnam, where more than 50 percent of the workforce and income depends on climate-sensitive natural resources. The majority of the population lives in coastal or low-lying deltas. Without considering potential changes in temperature, rainfall, and other climatic variables, old and inefficient infrastructure and current social development paths could increase economic vulnerability.

How Vietnam handles this transition over the next two decades will determine whether the country can maintain its economic growth and move into the higher reaches of upper-middle-income status—or whether it gets mired in an expanding cycle of dirty industries, degraded natural resources, and polluted land, air, and water. Many countries have grown at the expense of environmental quality and natural resource degradation, and they have come to regret it. The "grow now, pay later" strategy is often counterproductive, since the damage is either irreversible or costs more to correct. From a natural capital perspective, the real income of these countries did not grow as fast as traditional measures of national income suggest.

Improving environmental quality is critical for Vietnam to transform itself in several productive sectors, including agriculture, fisheries, food, beverages, forestry, and tourism. It must also minimize the costs that poor households bear in vulnerable regions (Central Highlands, Northern Mountains, and coastal areas). A Harvard University study estimates that each year Vietnam has about 4,000 premature deaths related to generating coal-fired power.

Taking early action to improve the environment can reduce the risk of investments leading to hidden costs—such as those for health—and exceeding the country's ecological carrying capacity. In China, for example, environmental degradation cost 9 percent of gross national income in 2008. In 2014, 60 percent of groundwater samples from 200 Chinese cities showed poor groundwater quality, while 16 percent of the samples were extremely poor. Contamination in and around industrial sites and arable land in China also poses threats for urban expansion and food safety. Pollution has become a leading cause of human illness and water stress in China.

Vietnam faces environmental concerns that require dedicated attention from policy makers to address the main challenges to optimizing sustainable use of natural assets and improving productivity—land degradation, air and water pollution, and limited adaptation to climate change. Policy makers will need to direct growth to a sustainable path that

- Recovers and maintains land resources;
- Builds climate resilience into economic planning and infrastructure development; and
- Restores and preserves the environmental quality of water, air, and land resources by ensuring a continued clean, affordable, and sustainable energy sector that provides sufficient energy to a growing economy while minimizing environmental and social impacts.

Countries such as Germany, Japan, Morocco, and the Republic of Korea have sought to limit the drag of poor environmental performance on growth and to improve the quality of life. These development paths include some of the necessary conditions for sustainable, inclusive, and resilient economic growth (box 5.1).[1] The conditions include the following:

- Get the prices right.
- Institute policies that complement pricing (or substitute for them when prices are ineffective or unchangeable).
- Make needed financing available.
- Manage the transition so that changes do not disadvantage the poor (Fay et al. 2015; World Bank 2012).

For Vietnam and other countries aiming for more sustainable development, this means three main actions across such key sectors as energy, industry, urban, water, land, agriculture, fisheries, and forestry:

1. Improve governance and strengthen institutions to coordinate, monitor, and enforce plans, policies, and regulations for sustainable natural resource and environmental management.
2. Institute innovative incentives for public-private investment that benefit the environment and the poor by getting prices right, creating an enabling regulatory

BOX 5.1 Gains from sustainable, inclusive, and resilient growth

A wide range of countries have adopted practices to engender green growth. Such policies in Germany, for example, have enabled an internationally competitive environmental goods and services sector to burgeon, focusing on renewable energy. Under the German model of promoting wind and solar power, the government needed to create strong financial incentives for the industry. In Costa Rica, performance-based payments for green practices have amounted to $230 million since their launch. Funds come from a fuel tax and a water tariff. In the Republic of Korea, investment in green infrastructure generated—after two years—a quarter of the investment value through job creation.

Some benefits of a green growth path are improved management of water, land and soil, atmospheric assets, and sustainable fish and timber stocks. Economic benefits include the resilience of assets to natural hazards and exogenous shocks and upgraded adjusted net savings. Social benefits include improved health, preservation of cultural heritage, and improved and stable governance institutions. Quantifying some of these benefits is difficult. For Vietnam, a benefit of such a growth path includes reductions in the cost of climate change adaptation, such as lowering the total cost of adaptation in aquaculture (estimated at $130 million a year over 2010–50). It would also reduce the cost of wastewater management, which, if unaddressed, could range from $12.4 million to $18.6 million a day in 2030.

Policies that promote sustainable growth can do more than improve environmental management. They can lead to a growth path that includes investments with low greenhouse gas (GHG) emissions and notable economic and public health gains. For example, clean transport is associated with substantial fuel savings and reduced air-quality-related complications and deaths from respiratory illnesses. At the household level, funds that would otherwise be spent on filling the tanks of cars with gasoline could be used to purchase other goods and services. Improved energy efficiency can enhance the competitiveness of industry by reducing production costs. Benefits from measures to reduce GHG emissions can also be incorporated in agriculture, by—for example—avoiding excessive and inappropriately timed application of fertilizers, notably nitrous oxide. This measure could lower farmers' production costs and prevent yield-reducing soil pollution.

A sustainable growth path is also important for Vietnam to meet national commitments. Its Socio-Economic Development Strategy 2011–20 includes several environmental targets, including increasing forest cover to 45 percent. These targets ensure that most urban and rural residents have access to clean water and sanitation. They guarantee that all new production facilities and businesses apply clean technology or are equipped with pollution reduction or waste disposal devices. They also make certain that more than 80 percent of existing businesses achieve business environmental standards. In 2012, Vietnam also adopted a green growth strategy that aims to achieve a low-carbon economy to enrich natural capital and become the principal direction in sustainable economic development. The National Environmental Protection Strategy has been in place since 2004 and commits Vietnam till 2020 to continue to improve living-environment quality. The country will also enhance proactive adaptation capacity to climate change. It has also committed to controlling and limiting environmental pollution, degradation of natural resources, and biodiversity deterioration.

Building on several of these national commitments, Vietnam has put forth its Nationally Determined Contribution (NDC) to mitigate climate change. This NDC presents the country's GHG reduction path for 2021–30, which includes reducing domestic GHG emissions in 2030 by 8 percent versus business as usual. With international support, Vietnam commits to reducing emissions by up to 25 percent. The NDC also describes the adaptation gaps in financing, technology, institutions, policies, and human resources, as well as the priority adaptation measures for 2021–30.

environment, and increasing access to long-term financing.

3. Improve public access to and use of information for decision making, monitoring, and accountability.

Environmental Challenges in Vietnam Today and in the Future

Growth over the past 25 years has imposed significant environmental costs in Vietnam, such as rapid depletion and degradation of natural resources and environmental pollution from urban and industrial wastewater. While urban water and air pollution are beginning to pose serious health hazards, exacerbating the risks is rapidly growing energy consumption, which is increasingly reliant on coal-powered electricity generation. Vietnam also is one of the countries most vulnerable to climate change, with settlements and economic activity in the Mekong Delta at especially heightened risk. In recent years, Vietnam's increase in GHG emissions has been one of the world's fastest.

Natural Resource Degradation

Land degradation and soil erosion

Land is a relatively scarce resource in Vietnam, with acute stresses on its quality. With just 0.11 hectares per capita, one-sixth of the world average, Vietnam ranks 159th in the world in per capita land resources. Pressures are exacerbated by the fact that 9.3 million hectares (representing about 28 percent of total land area) are considered uncultivable, of which 7.5 million hectares have been affected by desertification. About 5.1 million hectares are unused land, 2 million are used although the land is seriously eroded, and another 2 million are at risk (with reduced soil fertility or severely degraded land) (Nguyen 2013). Agriculture and forestry are especially constrained by soil degradation, which affects the productivity of land and downstream systems.

Soil erosion is a serious concern, given the topography (three-quarters of the country is covered by hills and mountains) and the change in soil features, vegetation, rainfall patterns, and climatic conditions in some parts (Bao and Laituri 2011). The total erosion-prone area amounts to 13 million hectares, or 40 percent of natural areas (Nguyen 2010).

Unsustainable agricultural practices loom large in accelerating land degradation as well as other environmental concerns (box 5.2). Despite the conversion of an estimated 700,000 hectares from agricultural to nonagricultural uses, the total area under agriculture has grown nearly 15 percent (from 8.9 million to 10.2 million hectares) since 2000. Most of this expansion took place at the expense of upland or mangrove forests. The 1990s' growth of coffee and aquaculture production also occurred largely at a cost to forests.[2] Expansion continues through increased use of steeply sloped land for cassava production in upland areas and a surge in rubber plantation areas on the back of recent price increases.

Agricultural land is also being cultivated more intensively. While the area under paddy has changed little, the total harvested area grew by an average of 1.7 percent a year during the 2000s. This reflects a shift toward double and triple cropping. But expansion of the third rice crop in the Mekong Delta has had severe environmental effects. Disruption of natural flooding processes has restricted the transfer of nutrients and normal cleansing effects, leading farmers to use more fertilizers and pesticides, often at the cost of soil quality. In upland areas, the fallow periods of shifting cultivation have been shortened to the point of almost continuous cultivation, degrading the soil.

Since the early 1990s, cultivation of upland rice, maize, soybean, cassava, and forest crops has seriously eroded the Northern Mountains and the Central Highlands (Siem and Phien 1999). In the uplands, expanding coffee cultivation has deforested and degraded land. Coffee monoculture contributes to soil erosion, especially when the crop is planted on steep slopes. Some 74 percent of coffee planted in Dak Lak Province grows on

BOX 5.2 Agricultural growth has a growing environmental footprint

Agricultural growth in Vietnam has been encouraged by domestic policy reforms, international trade agreements, and public investments, especially in agricultural research, irrigation, and other rural infrastructure (see chapter 2 "Enabling Economic Modernization and Private Sector Development" for details). Growth has also been heavily based on expanded and intensified agricultural land use and an intensive use of material inputs, especially fertilizers and pesticides. The downside is a large and extensive environmental footprint: agriculture is a major cause of deforestation, land degradation, excessive water use, greenhouse gas emissions, biodiversity loss, and water and air pollution. Table B5.2.1 presents the agro-environmental hotspots for seven commodities.

Recent agricultural changes include intensive use of fertilizers, pesticides, and water for crops. Antibiotics use in aquaculture is also notable. Fertilizer application grew rapidly during the 1990s but has more or less stabilized since the early 2000s. Still, at nearly 300 kilograms per hectare, the rate is about twice that in other Southeast Asian countries. Farmers rarely have the soil tested and seldom apply fertilizer with the optimal composition or at the best time. And poor water management practices see a large proportion of fertilizer run-off into streams or groundwater or emitted as nitrous oxide.[a] Vietnam needs to avoid the serious land degradation and water pollution effects of heavy fertilizer use that China has suffered.

Despite a range of programs over the years to promote integrated pest management, Vietnam uses pesticides heavily. The use of newer, less toxic products has grown, along with the use of less expensive generic (and sometimes inaccurately labeled) products. Some of the latter are no longer permitted for use in many of the Vietnam's agricultural export markets. Pesticide use appears to have increased sharply since the mid-2000s, perhaps because of increased pest pressure from more intensive production and the development of pesticide resistance. Frequent and late-season chemical spraying has contributed to growing concerns about pesticide residues in rice, tea, and fruits and vegetables, although systematic data are not available on the extent and seriousness of the problem. On the basis of past violations, Vietnamese products entering the European Union are subject to more frequent sampling and testing (EU Food and Veterinary Office 2014). Relatively strong national legislation is in place, yet the capacities to advise on and monitor agrochemical use is patchy within government and among food distribution and trading companies.[b]

As Vietnam transitions from an agricultural economy, the sector's decline in importance could be gradual (similar to the Philippines and Thailand), given the large rural population and the reliance on agriculture and fisheries for jobs. Greater inequality in income will also cause poor rural households to become more reliant on agriculture and increase their use of inorganic inputs or convert land to augment their incomes.

TABLE B5.2.1 The downside of agricultural growth is a large and extensive environmental footprint

Commodity	Location	Soil degradation	Water/air pollution	Water scarcity and salinization	Deforestation and loss of biodiversity	Greenhouse gas emissions
Rice	Mekong River Delta	High	High	High	Medium	High
Coffee	Central Highlands	Medium	Medium	High	High	High
Corn	Northern Mountains	High	Low	Medium	High	Medium
Cassava	Northern Mountains and Central Highlands	High	Low	Medium	High	High
Pork	Red River Delta and Southeast	High	Medium	Low	Nonimpact	Medium
Shrimp	Mekong River Delta	Medium	High	Low	High	Medium
Catfish	Mekong River Delta	Medium	High	Low	Medium	Nonimpact

High Medium Low Nonimpact

Source: Khoi et al. 2015.

a. The Food and Agriculture Organization of the United States estimates that some 80 percent of the nitrous oxide emissions in Vietnam derive from agriculture.
b. Perhaps even more serious have been the health risks to farmers and others drawing water from streams collecting pesticide run-off. One study (Dasgupta et al. 2005) found that among surveyed Mekong Delta rice farmers who were medically tested, 35 percent had signs of poisoning—from organophosphates and carbamates, with 21 percent having symptoms of chronic poisoning.

unsuitable, sloping land (>15 degrees), with production causing soil erosion of more than 100 tons per hectare a year.

Water

The risks of water resource degradation and depletion from climate change and increasing water exploitation—within and outside Vietnam—raise concerns over water availability in the future. Until recently some 80 percent of total freshwater withdrawals in the country came from agriculture (figure 5.1). Since the mid-1970s, some $6 billion (present value) has been invested in irrigation, about 80 percent of the government's capital investment in the sector. Although irrigation coverage is high with most suitable areas equipped, the irrigation systems were designed primarily for rice (World Bank 2013a). But irrigation has helped diversify agricultural production, including in coffee, horticulture, and aquaculture (World Bank 2013a).

Several factors impede increased water productivity. From the design perspective, irrigation schemes do not typically have structures for accurate flow measurement and control. Low canal density results in high dependency on field-to-field conveyance. This makes it difficult to deliver water flexibly and reliably. Fields are also inadequately equipped for field and storm drainage, constraining the timing of harvesting. Further, most of the irrigation schemes were developed 30–40 years ago, with high levels of deferred maintenance. Incomplete structures and water losses during operations have many schemes operating at only 60–70 percent of capacity. This means that irrigated land is not achieving the expected yield increases of 35–65 percent during the dry season and 20 percent during the wet season.

FIGURE 5.1 Making water available in the future means addressing today's water exploitations

Water usage by different sectors (share of total water use)

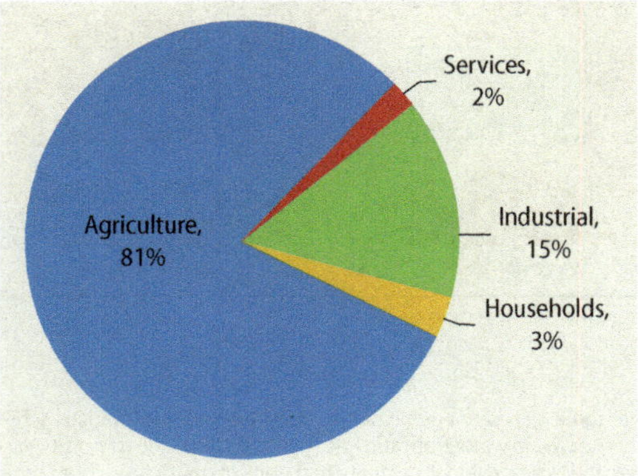

Source: General Department of Irrigation 2013.

In addition, financial incentives to improve water-use efficiency do not exist. Obtaining a license to use water for irrigation is costly. But the irrigation-water tariff ceases once the irrigation system is established. This applies to more than 100 different types of irrigation systems (at different scales) in Vietnam, including canals, dykes, and water storage.

The reengineered Red and Mekong River Deltas have also altered the natural ecosystem's equilibrium. Changed surface water flows in the Mekong River Delta are causing inland movement of saline water. This affects soil fertility and saline balance and poses risks to aquatic and terrestrial habitats. In addition, countries upstream of the Mekong River have built hydraulic works (dams and reservoirs), reducing the water flows into Vietnam and making them more variable.

Forests, biodiversity, and ecosystem services

Forests. Although the surface area of Vietnam's forests has increased from 29 percent of total surface area in 1990 to 45 percent in 2013 (after having fallen from 72 percent in 1909), degradation has continued. Over the past 20 years, primary forests have decreased by 79 percent. The area under mangroves has declined by 70 percent in nearly five decades due to toxic chemicals in the earlier years and shrimp farming practices more recently (MONRE 2005). Only 8 percent of land area is covered by resource-rich tropical rainforests, compared with 50 percent in other Southeast Asian countries (Trương Quang Học 2012).

Forests are primarily in the north and the Central Highlands (figure 5.2), which have high levels of poverty. Timber production is concentrated in the Central Highlands (34 percent), the North-Central Region (23 percent), and the South-Central Region (17.4 percent).

FIGURE 5.2 Vietnam has lost an alarming percentage of "primary" forest over the past 20 years, although its overall forest cover is around 40 percent

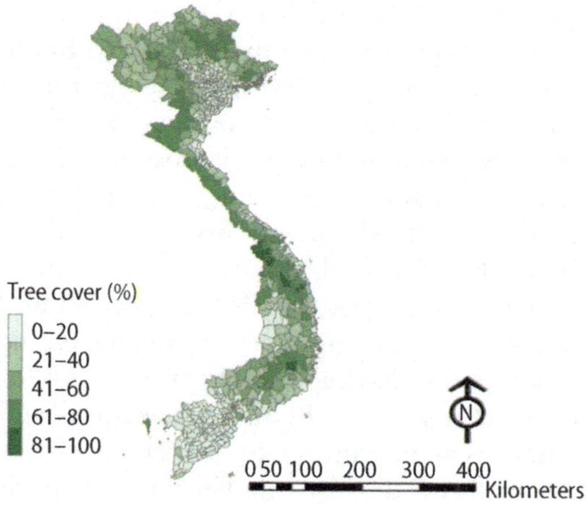

Since the late 1980s Vietnam's state forestry has moved to sustainable management and social participation (Dang et al. 2012). Following the poor outcome of a logging ban in the 1990s and the collapse of centralized forest management (MARD 2001), recent reforms have improved the rights and benefits of nonstate actors. Under current regulations, nonstate actors can become production-forest plantation owners with limited autonomy over the forest they manage (Dang et al. 2012).

SOEs and a number of private small and medium enterprises are involved in timber production and harvesting, including high-value commodities such as rubber. The economic rents from forests have been declining since the mid-1990s, as the sector's share in gross domestic product (GDP) fell from 5 percent to 1.4 percent. Even so, forests are important for providing employment, income generation, and ecosystem services. While not all countries report their forest employment numbers, Vietnam seemingly has the most significant full-time employment in the forest sector in the East Asia region. But even these numbers are underestimated; they do not reflect subsistence and other informal forest use. Although the Northern Mountains' ethnic minorities have experienced welfare gains since the early 1990s, they are facing a growing welfare gap in comparison with the ethnic majority (see chapter 6 "Promoting Equity and Social Inclusion"). These minorities rely on forests to meet their subsistence needs and to generate income.

Deforestation and forest degradation are heavy in the northwest and the south. The drivers include mainly illegal logging and conversion to agricultural land for food crops in the deltas.[3] They also include perennial crops in the Central Highlands and shrimp farms and other forms of aquaculture in the Mekong Delta (UN-REDD 2009). Along the coast, mangrove areas declined by 62 percent between 1943 and 1999. More recently, shrimp production has destroyed more than half the remaining mangrove forest area.

The wood industry is a major timber consumer and deforestation contributor. Underlying causes are poor commercial logging practices and harvesting of timber by rural households. Legal exploitation results in logging degradation. Such exploitation occurs when government-licensed and large commercial logging operations harvest plantations for timber exports and paper production. Degradation also happens when smaller operators act without government permission or licenses. With the population growing and becoming wealthier, the demand for land, paper, and timber is expected to compete with traditional fuelwood production. This is even more likely if more modern fuels are unavailable for rural households. Projected regional demand for wood chips and global industrial demand for wood are likely to extend the pressure on the forest sector.

Biodiversity. Vietnam is ranked as the 16th most biodiverse country, with 59 "important bird areas," (BirdLife International 2013) for example. In 2006, it was home to 128 protected areas (now known as "special use forests"). These protected areas include 30 national parks, 48 nature reserves, 11 species or habitat conservation areas, and 39 landscape protection areas, constituting 7.6 percent of the country's natural area. They shelter important forest ecosystems, and endangered, rare, and endemic fauna and flora and their habitats. But degradation of biodiversity is a growing challenge in Vietnam.

Vietnam now ranks in the world's top 15 countries suffering from declining mammal species, top 20 for declining bird species, and top 30 for declining plant and amphibian species. Over the past few decades Vietnam has contributed to the loss of regional and global biodiversity through three channels. First, endangered species are illegally traded, often for food and medicinal purposes. Second, tropical timber is imported from neighboring countries to support its own wood-processing industry. Third, live animals and plant products from threatened species are consumed (USAID 2013). Conversion of its forests (including mangroves) has negative implications for terrestrial and aquatic species for which forests are important habitat.

Of Vietnam's aquatic creatures, 236 are listed as endangered, precious, or rare. And the number of endangered wildlife species was 882, including 418 animal and 464 plant species (Ministry of Science and Technology and Vietnamese Academy of Science and Technology 2007). Nine species classified as endangered in 1992–1996 were classified extinct in the wild in 2007. The number of aquatic species, especially shrimp and fish of high economic value, has also declined.

Beyond losses caused by habitat conversion, Vietnam is also losing biodiversity owing to illegal trade in animal and plant products (USAID 2013). For example, of 53 species hunted or collected at Bac Huong Hoa Nature Reserve, 14 are globally threatened and 36 are nationally protected (USAID 2013). The rising purchasing power of Asian consumers is expected to increase demand for what are considered luxury and status products.[4] High profits, poor law enforcement, and well-established trafficking networks make it difficult to clamp down on illegal activities.

Vietnam is a transit and destination country for traded wildlife. On compliance with and enforcement of CITES (Decisions and Resolution) for three target species[5] (tigers, elephants, and rhinos) in China, the Arab Republic of Egypt, Thailand, and Vietnam, only Vietnam shows little progress for trade in tigers and in rhino parts. For elephants, key aspects of compliance and enforcement need strengthening (WWF 2012).

Ecosystem services. In addition to biodiversity and timber, forests provide other environmental and ecosystem services. Vietnam's contribution to reducing soil erosion and sedimentation and to enhancing soil-protection ability in watersheds with hydropower dams is widely recognized.[6]

The government has issued decrees and made a strong commitment to implementing schemes for sharing benefits and paying for ecosystem services (PES). These actions will compensate provinces and districts that manage lands for downstream benefits. The institutional setting for PES relies heavily on establishing forest protection and development funds at central and provincial levels. The institutional arrangements for PES at the provincial level are in place, and between 2009 and 2012, the arrangements generated $85 million, 98 percent of which was from hydropower plants and water supply companies (Pham et al. 2013).

Fisheries and aquaculture

Marine resources are central for employment, subsistence, and revenue generation. Between 2000 and 2010, the sector grew by 13.6 percent a year in volume and 10.4 percent in value. Fisheries production in 2010 was estimated at 5.2 million tons, including 2.5 million tons from capture fisheries and 2.7 million tons from aquaculture. In 2012 the sector accounted for about 4 percent of GDP (similar to the garment and textile industry) and 8 percent of merchandise exports. Nearly 8 million people—9 percent of the population—rely on fisheries-related activities for a major source of their income. While aquatic exports have grown and now exceed $5 billion a year, more than two-thirds of the volume of fish caught or produced is consumed domestically. Such consumption is growing rapidly, with an estimated 50 percent of Vietnamese obtaining their dietary protein from aquatic products.

Marine fisheries productivity has been falling for a long time, seemingly more steeply in recent years. More than 100,000 small fishing vessels are operating in nearshore areas (within six miles of the coastline), and the vast majority of these have a horsepower below 49. The quality of marine fisheries has also been declining. The share of the catch comprising "trash fish" and small fish has risen. Trash fish now account for an estimated 60 percent of the total marine catch, most of which is consumed locally or used in producing fish sauce or fish feed for aquaculture.

Overfishing is especially evident in the nearshore areas, which are the fishing grounds for some 85 percent of the country's fishing fleet and the primary source of livelihood for poor or near-poor coastal communities.

Although the exact fisheries stock is unknown, fishers continue to catch more than the allowed limits, hurting regeneration and restoration. Some fishers adopt destructive practices in prohibited areas and during times of spawning. The de facto, open-access nature of fisheries in Vietnam, and the scarce data, poor zone enforcement, and inconsistent communication across scales need to be reversed to convert capture fisheries into a source of green revenue.

Unlike coastal fisheries, aquaculture growth has been phenomenal (figure 5.3). In 2008, Vietnam accounted for almost 5 percent of global output, more than triple its share from a decade earlier and third globally behind China and India. In 2005, shrimp were produced in brackish-water aquaculture systems, accounting for 98 percent of production volume. Fish accounted for 99 percent of freshwater aquaculture production. In 2009, southern provinces from Da Nang to Ca Mau accounted for 79 percent of the country's total aquaculture area and 80 percent of the total aquaculture output.[7] The pond culture of brackish-water shrimp dominates in farmed area (71 percent of the aquaculture area). Freshwater catfish farming accounts for 47 percent of aquaculture production by weight.[8]

The Ministry of Agriculture and Rural Development (MARD) and its provincial departments manage the development of aquaculture. MARD has six regional centers responsible for food safety and quality control, and they regularly conduct inspections

FIGURE 5.3 The prominence of aquaculture in Vietnam's economy requires close coordination, biosecurity investments, and efforts to stem water pollution and water use in fisheries

Fisheries production

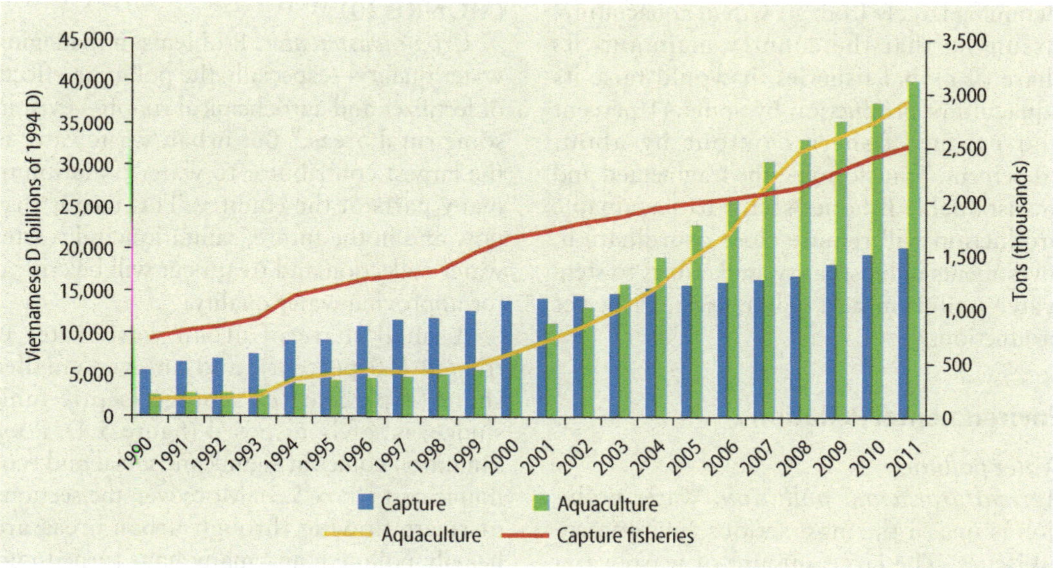

Source: Calculations using General Statistics Office of Vietnam data.

for harmful substances. The Vietnam Association of Seafood Exporters and Producers and the Vietnam Fisheries Society also promote the industry.

No system is in place to certify sources of quality seed and to ensure that adequate biosecurity measures are taken at the farm level. Each year diseases affect some 30–70 percent of the total production area, reducing yields and leading many growers to fail entirely. In shrimp farming, low-quality and infected seed or shrimp fry are the main causes of diseases. But intensive farming has required greater use of antibiotics. Similarly, intensive catfish cultivation has led to high frequency of disease, increasing need for treatments.

Antibiotics and chemicals have affected Vietnam's reputation in international seafood markets. The catfish industry, for example, has attracted strong criticism based on alleged environmental and food safety issues. And while evidence is mixed on the use of treatments for diseases, local eutrophication impacts are evident (FAO 2014). Operators can afford the treatment costs; in shrimp aquaculture, the profits from clearing mangroves to expand production are particularly high.

Global forecasts to 2030 for fisheries production in Vietnam, including aquaculture and capture fisheries, point to an increase stemming largely from growth in aquaculture. Assuming that the country maintains its share of global fisheries, it would raise its aquaculture production by some 41 percent and capture fisheries output by about 10 percent. Transforming the fragmented and unsustainable fisheries sector to sustainable production will require close coordination, investments in biosecurity, and efforts to stem water pollution and water use in fisheries production.

Environmental Pollution

Water pollution

Agricultural water pollution. Water pollution is one of the most serious environmental issues. The large amount of wastewater from aquaculture production in the south threatens water quality in the Mekong Delta. Vietnamese shrimp farms have polluted surrounding waters and themselves been hurt by poor water quality. In intensive shrimp production systems, farmers often use large amounts of chemicals and antibiotics to keep the overcrowded shrimp healthy. Effluents from these ponds, which also contain large quantities of organic waste, contaminate surrounding freshwater and coastal waters. Studies indicate that common water pollution indicators—such as biochemical oxygen demand, chemical oxygen demand, and total suspended solids—increase over the growing period and with the age of the ponds.

There have been several recent episodes of large-scale shrimp loss in many provinces of the Mekong Delta due to water pollution. For example, the shrimp loss was spreading in more than 500 hectares of Soc Trang Province, with 30 percent of prawn output lost in February and March 2012. Also in 2012, almost all shrimp died in 600 hectares of the total 6,000 hectare farming area in Tra Vinh Province within one month due to disease. In Ca Mau Province, more than 20 percent of the total 3,500 hectare aquaculture farming was diseased. In Phu Tan and Dam Doi districts, the shrimp died in 50 percent of the farming area (MONRE 2012).

Urban wastewater. Problems in managing water quality—especially the polluting effects of fertilizer and agrochemical runoff—exist in some rural areas.[9] But urban wastewater is the largest contributor to water pollution in many parts of the country. This means that now and in the future, sanitation and wastewater collection and treatment will be critical for improving water quality.

A small share of urban wastewater is treated (10 percent), and an even smaller share (4 percent) of septage (septic tank sludge) is safely disposed (figure 5.4). Poor sanitation comes at significant social and economic costs (box 5.3). Moreover, the sections of rivers flowing through urban areas are heavily polluted, and many have turned into sewage or dead rivers.

Changing regulations and standards since the first standard was issued in 1995 have created uncertainty among local governments for designing and implementing wastewater projects. Selecting high-cost treatment technology—much of it financed with official development assistance—while overlooking lower-cost technologies has further affected standards. For example, many sewerage systems have focused on wastewater treatment facilities alone, while sewage collection has been neglected. Only in Hai Phong are septic tanks regularly emptied. Fewer than half the hospitals in Vietnam have proper wastewater treatment systems.

Low tariffs (which limit public-private partnerships and self-financing by water and wastewater utilities) have resulted in the private sector being minimally involved in wastewater. The absence of an effective regulatory system for private investments has the same outcome.

Industrial water pollution. Industrial zones discharge an estimated 1 million cubic meters of untreated wastewater a day directly into receiving water bodies. That equals about 70 percent of the country's total industrial effluent discharges. High pollution levels have severe implications for human health and natural ecosystems. They are also constraining urban development and the sustainability and future growth of industry and agriculture.

FIGURE 5.4 Wastewater treatment needs low-cost solutions, regulatory certainty, and market incentives

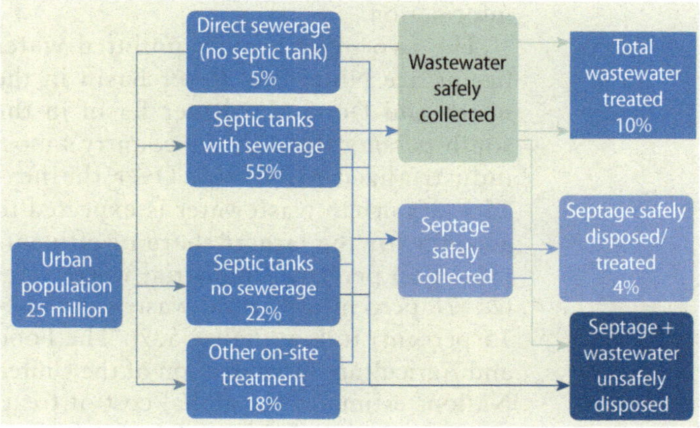

Source: World Bank and Australian Aid 2013.

BOX 5.3 Costs of poor sanitation

Diarrhea is the sanitation-related disease with the most cases, at 7.05 million a year, and significant economic costs (table B5.3.1) (World Bank 2008). The economic cost of treating patients can be estimated using an average cost of $4.50 per case of waterborne illness, for a total cost of $31.7 million.

Diarrhea is also the main cause of death from poor sanitation and hygiene, accounting for around 4,600 deaths a year. Malnutrition-related diseases, such as lower respiratory infections, account for an estimated further 1,500 deaths a year and are attributed to poor sanitation. Malaria follows with 600 deaths a year.

TABLE B5.3.1 The estimated cost of poor sanitation-related impacts is US$780 million

Aspect	Cost (US$ million)
Impact of poor sanitation	780
Water-related diseases	262
Impact on water sources	287
Land use	119
Other welfare losses	43
Tourism	69

Source: World Bank and the Ministry of Planning and Investment of Vietnam calculations, drawing from different sources.

Among the shortcomings of Vietnam's regulatory system are policies that promote industrial growth without considering environmental pollution. Another deficiency is limited resources—personnel and funding—for environmental monitoring. Failings are evident in insufficient enforcement because of corruption and inadequate resources. Other shortcomings are low penalties for noncompliance and little public disclosure of industrial pollution information.

The two most heavily polluted water basins are Nhue-Day River Basin in the north and Dong Nai River Basin in the south passing through the country's most industrialized provinces. Over the next 15 years urban wastewater is expected to account for the largest share of effluents (about 60 percent). Industrial wastewater (25–28 percent) and rural wastewater (12–15 percent) follow (figure 5.5). The Food and Agriculture Organization of the United Nations estimates the global cost of treating water to range from $1 to $1.5 per cubic meter. This implies costs for Vietnam of $12.4–18.6 million a day by 2030 if treatment measures are only put in place then. In Vietnam's southern key economic zones, the cost estimate for 2010 was $867 million.

FIGURE 5.5 The economic implications of Vietnam's wastewater cleanup gives pause

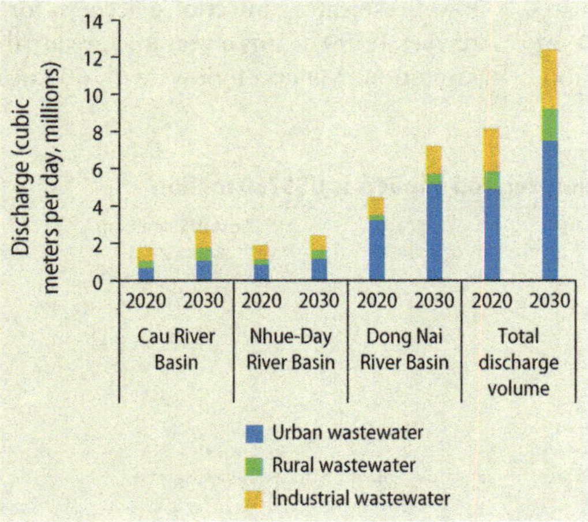

Source: Thang 2015.

Air pollution

The growth of fossil fuel energy consumption by industry and coal-fired power plants in northern Vietnam (discussed in more detail below) is increasing air pollution. Satellite images show high levels of average fine particulate matter (PM2.5) around Hanoi, approaching levels in China and several times higher than safe levels recommended by the World Health Organization. Some pockets of very high concentrations in urban and industrial zones are also shown (figure 5.6). Major sources of PM2.5 pollution include industrial fuel combustion, resuspension of road dust, coal and biomass emissions (such as rice husks for cooking and heating), and—during harvest season—residues from burning fields.

Cross-border environmental issues

Many of Vietnam's 2,360 rivers with a length of 10 kilometers or more flow from neighboring upstream nations, adding an extra transnational/cross-border layer of complexity to managing the associated environmental challenges. The challenges include polluted transboundary rivers, transmission of air pollution across borders, and water pollution from oil spills, marine litters, transportation of hazardous materials, demolition of old ships, and invasive alien marine life species.

Every year, the coastal waters of Ba Lat River (Nam Dinh Province) receive 37.3 billion m^3 wastewater from the Red River, containing 232,000 tons of BOD, 353,000 tons of COD, 31,000 tons of nitrogen, 7,000 tons of phosphorus, 29 million tons of suspended solids (organic waste), 4,000 tons of heavy metals, 210 tons of pesticides, 343 tons of chemical fertilizers, and more than 13,000 tons of oil. The waste comes not only from manufacturing establishments, agricultural production, and trading and cities in Vietnam, but also from watersheds of other countries.

A series of oil spills in the Gulf of Tonkin *(Vịnh Bắc Bộ)* are also a major source of concern in preventing and controlling cross-border environmental pollution. There were 89 oil spills in the gulf during 1987–1997 and another 50 during 1997–2010 (Center for Global Change Research 2015).

FIGURE 5.6 Fine particulate matter, driven by industry and coal-fired power plants in the north, is approaching Chinese levels

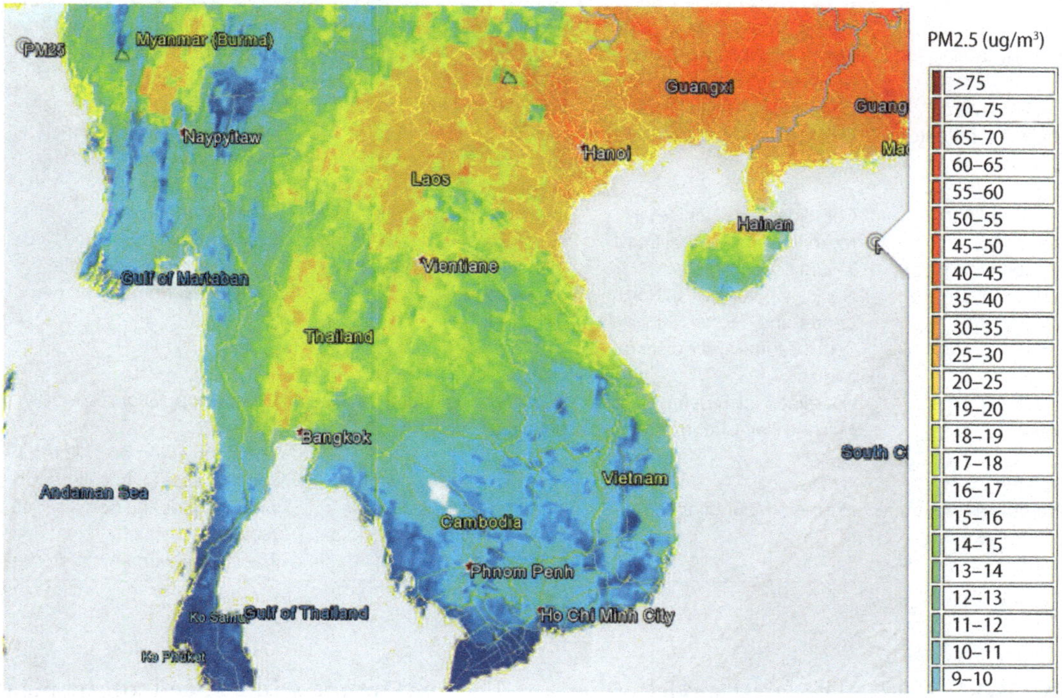

Source: World Bank and the Ministry and Planning of Vietnam calculations using available data.
Note: PM2.5 = particulate matter that are 2.5 micrometers or less in size; μg/m³ = micrograms per cubic meter of air.

The situation calls for Vietnam to strengthen the cooperation with regional countries and international organizations to better manage the transnational environmental issues.

Vulnerability to Climate Change

Vietnam has a high and increasing exposure to gradual-onset impacts associated with rising sea levels, ocean warming, and growing acidification, alongside sudden-onset impacts linked to tropical cyclones and fast-rising heat extremes (World Bank 2013b). Evidence is increasing that climate change is already occurring in Vietnam and will intensify over the coming decades (table 5.1).

Highly unusual and unprecedented heat extremes[10] are projected to escalate with extreme temperature events, frequently exceeding past temperature ranges. Trends show a mean temperature increase in Vietnam of about 0.26°C a decade since 1971 (Nguyen, Renwick, and McGregor 2013), which is more than twice the global average rate of about 0.13°C a decade for 1956–2005 (Trenberth et al. 2007). The Ministry of Natural Resources and Environment (MONRE) projects that the global annual mean temperature will increase by 0.6–1.2°C by 2040 (depending on location) relative to the average during 1980–99 and by 1.1–1.9°C to 2.1–3.6°C by 2100 (MONRE 2012). Under the latter scenario, heat extremes virtually absent now will cover nearly 60–70 percent of the total land area in summer. Unprecedented heat extremes will affect up to 30–40 percent of the land area in the northern-hemisphere summer.

An increase in the frequency of intense storms and associated extreme rainfall is projected in Vietnam. Changes in observed annual rainfall were not significant over 1958–2007, with variations across regions. Annual rainfall decreased in northern Vietnam but increased in southern areas

TABLE 5.1 Vietnam has a high and increasing exposure to gradual-onset impacts of climate change

Expected climate changes	Vulnerable region	Main consequence	Vulnerable community
Temperature rise of 2.3°C by 2100	Mountainous regions: Northeast, Northwest, and North Central Red River Delta	Reduced integrity of natural ecosystems; some agriculture subsectors will be affected	Poor farmers Ethnic minorities, the elderly, women, children
Sea-level rise of about 3 centimeters a decade	Coastline: Red River Delta, Mekong Delta, Central Coast Islands	Salinization, loss of land, impacts on agriculture, worsening of extreme weather events (storm surges)	Coastal population, especially poor farmers and fishermen The elderly, women, children
More marked seasonality of precipitation: wetter wet seasons and drier dry seasons	Coastline: Red River Delta, Mekong Delta, Central Coast Mountainous regions: Northeast, Northwest, North Central and Central Highlands, South Central and Northern Midlands	Impacts on agriculture; greater challenges for water resources management (particularly in dry seasons)	Coastal population Residents in mountainous areas, especially ethnic minorities The elderly, women, children
Increase in total rainfall	Coastline: North Delta, Mekong Delta, Central Coast	Impacts on agriculture, urban drainage	Coastal population, especially fishermen The elderly, women, children
Extreme weather events more common or more extreme	Central Coast Northern Mountains and Midlands	Potentially more economic impacts (particularly for vulnerable groups) and loss of life	Farmers, especially in Northern mountainous and Central regions The elderly, women, children

Source: World Bank 2010.

(MONRE 2012). The latest model projections show a substantial and rising increase in both magnitude and frequency of heavy precipitation events (World Bank 2013b). MONRE scenarios project total annual rainfall increasing from 0.5 percent in the Central Highlands and 0.6 percent in the southern region to above 3 percent in the north-central and north delta regions by 2040 (MONRE 2012). Seasonal variability is projected to increase: the wet season is forecast to see a rise in precipitation of 5–14 percent in southern Vietnam.

For Southeast Asia, the maximum number of consecutive dry days (a measure for drought) is also expected to increase, indicating that minimum and maximum precipitation extremes are likely to be amplified.

The intensity and maximum wind speed of tropical cyclones making landfall in Vietnam are projected to increase significantly. Maximum surface wind speed during tropical cyclones is forecast to rise by 7–18 percent for a warming of around 3.5°C above preindustrial levels for the western North Pacific Basin. But the center of activity is projected to shift north and east (Murakami et al. 2012). The maximum wind speed of tropical cyclones making landfall is projected to increase by 6 percent for mainland Southeast Asia, though combined with a decrease of 35 percent in the number of land-falling cyclones (Murakami et al. 2012). As sea-surface temperatures rise, tropical cyclone-related rainfall is expected to increase by up to a third, indicating a higher flood risk in low-lying and coastal regions.

Projections show that a significant sea-level rise over the coming decades in Vietnam will exacerbate the impacts on currently affected communities. For instance, the South Hai Thinh commune in the Red River Delta experienced a 34 percent increase in the erosion rate over 1965–95 (and a subsequent 12 percent increase over 1995–2005), attributed to the direct effect of sea-level rise (Duc, Nhuan, and Van Ngoi 2012). By mid-century, the sea level is likely to be 28–33 centimeters above 1980–99 levels (MONRE 2012). Close to the equator, sea-level rise along the coastline relative to 1986–2005 is forecast to be 10–15 percent higher than the global mean by the end of the 21st century.

Natural processes put the delta regions at risk of land subsidence. Human activities such as drainage and groundwater extraction greatly exacerbate subsidence, increasing coastal flooding. In the Mekong Delta, man-made subsidence is 6 millimeters a year (Syvitski et al. 2009). The projected loss of mangrove forests from sea-level rise and human activities—which increase coastal erosion—is a deep concern and likely to accelerate coastal erosion.

Climate change will sharply increase salinity intrusion in coastal areas. As described in the Mekong Delta Plan (see figure 5.8 in "Adaptation to Climate Change"), salinity intrusion is already occurring during the dry season, hurting crop yields appreciably. With an unfixed saline-brackish border, the Delta is particularly vulnerable to increased salinity intrusion associated with sea-level rise. The total area affected by such intrusion in the Mekong River Delta, with concentrations higher than 4 grams per liter, will increase from 1,303,000 hectares to 1,723,000 hectares if the sea rises by 30 centimeters (World Bank 2010).

Potential impacts on key sectors and regions

Given the multiple channels for climate change to affect Vietnam, the economic and social impacts are likely to be significant and widespread, with some vulnerable groups especially at risk (see table 5.1).

Agriculture. Climate change is expected to affect agriculture in several ways. For instance, land for rice will be cut steeply. Much attention has focused on the potential impact of changes in temperature on rice yields. Any assessment of climate change on agriculture must consider changes in land use caused by salinization and flooding. But not all outcomes will be negative. Higher temperatures and changes in rainfall may permit cultivation of some crops in areas where they previously were not viable.

Climate change and sea-level rise will affect yields and production of key crops, such as rice, maize, cassava, sugarcane, and coffee (table 5.2). For rice, the worst yield reductions are about 12 percent in the Mekong River Delta and about 24 percent in the Red River Delta. In the Mekong River Delta a 30 centimeter sea-level rise by 2050 would result in a loss of 193,000 hectares of rice area due to inundation. Some 294,000 hectares will be lost due to salinity intrusion, without adaptation in both cases. The lost rice area would reduce rice production by about 2.6 million tons a year, based on current yields.

Aquaculture. In the Mekong River Delta, aquaculture is particularly important for employment and rural income. Higher temperatures, greater storm frequencies, increasing sea levels, and other effects of climate change are likely to affect fish physiology, ecology, and aquaculture operations. Some fish species, such as catfish, may increase more rapidly with higher temperatures. But they may also be more vulnerable to disease. The main effects of climate change on aquaculture are likely from increased flooding and salinity. Moderate and major shrimp producers may pay more for pumping water to maintain water and salinity levels. The industry is capital intensive and growing rapidly, so adaptation is likely to be autonomous, with the costs borne by operators. The total cost of adaptation is estimated at $130 million a year over 2010–50, or equivalent to 2.4 percent of total costs (figure 5.7).

Fisheries, particularly coral reef fisheries, are expected to be affected by the impacts of sea-level rise, warmer oceans, and ocean acidification. Maximum catch potential in Vietnam's waters is projected to decrease 16 percent (Cheung et al. 2010). Given a 100 centimeter sea-level rise, Vietnam is expected to lose 8,533 square kilometers of freshwater marsh (a 65 percent loss) (Blankespoor, Dasgupta, and Laplante 2012). These marshlands support human well-being by:

- Supplying timber, fuelwood, and charcoal;
- Regulating floods, storms, erosion, and saltwater intrusion;
- Providing biodiversity and habitat for commercial fish species to breed and spawn; and
- Supporting culture for recreational and aesthetic pleasure.

TABLE 5.2 Climate change and sea-level rise will affect yields and production of key crops

Agroecological zone/river basin	Potential impacts of climate change without adaptation
North-West	Rice yield declines by 11.1 percent to 28.2 percent; yields of other crops decline by 5.9 percent to 23.5 percent. Generally the Dry scenario results in more yield reduction than the Wet scenario. MONRE scenario has the least yield reduction.
North-East	Rice yield declines by 4.4 percent to 39.6 percent; yields of other crops decline by 2.7 percent to 38.3 percent. The largest yield reduction can be with either the Dry or Wet scenarios, depending on crops. MONRE scenario has the least yield reduction.
Red River Delta	Rice yield declines by 7.2 percent to 32.6 percent; yields of other crops decline by 4.1 percent to 32.9 percent. The largest yield reduction can be with either the Dry or Wet scenarios, depending on crops. MONRE scenario has the least yield reduction.
North-Central Coast	Rice yield declines by 7.2 percent to 32.6 percent; yields of other crops decline by 4.1 percent to 32.9 percent. The largest yield reduction can be with either the Dry or Wet scenarios, depending on crops. MONRE scenario has the least yield reduction.
South-Central Coast	Rice yield declines by 8.4 percent to 27.0 percent; yields of other crops decline by 4.0 percent to 20.9 percent. Generally the Dry scenario results in more yield reduction than the Wet scenario. MONRE scenario has the least yield reduction.
Central Highlands	Rice yield declines by 11.1 percent to 42.0 percent; yields of other crops decline by 7.5 percent to 45.8 percent. The largest yield reduction can be with either the Dry or Wet scenarios, depending on crops. MONRE scenario has the least yield reduction.
South-East	Rice yield increases by 4.3 percent in the dry scenario, remains the same in the wet scenario, and declines by 8.8 in the MONRE scenario. Yields of other crops decline by 3.0 percent to 22.7 percent. The largest yield reduction can be with any of the three scenarios, depending on crops.
Mekong River Delta	Rice yield declines by 6.3 percent to 12.0 percent; yields of other crops decline by 3.4 percent to 26.5 percent. The largest yield reduction can take place under any of the three scenarios, depending on crops,

Source: World Bank 2010.
Note: Taking into account differences in projections generated by different global climate models (GCMs), a selection of climate scenarios was based on the ranking of GCMs with sufficient geographical detail by the climate moisture index (CMI) for the IPCC SRES A2 emission scenarios. There were 14 GCMs that met the criteria for consideration. The driest (IPSL-CM4) and wettest (GISS-ER) scenarios were used as the Dry and Wet scenarios. In addition, MONRE's climate projection for the medium emission scenario was included to represent the middle of the distribution of GCMs in terms of the CMI.

FIGURE 5.7 Projected reduction in aquaculture income as a result of impacts of climate change without adaptation

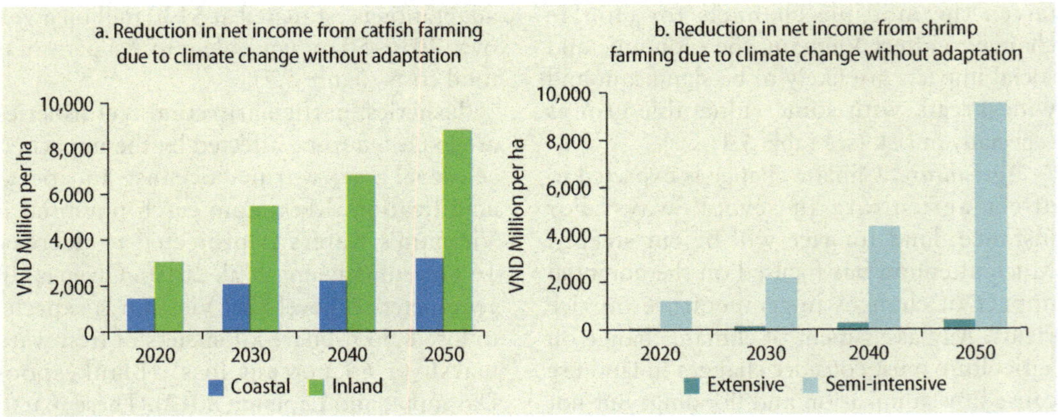

Source: World Bank 2010.
Note: "Extensive" takes place in large coastal ponds relying on tidal water exchange but stocked from hatcheries with the use of fertilizers to promote the growth of natural organisms to feed the shrimp. "Semi-intensive" uses smaller ponds and higher stocking rates, relying on water pumps and aeration to maintain water quality as well as a variety of formulated feedstuffs. It also includes additional costs of water pumping to maintain water and salinity levels.

Cities. Increased tropical cyclone intensity, sea-level rise, and coastal flooding are projected to affect coastal cities, where increasingly large populations and assets are exposed to climate change risks. High urban growth rates, combined with inadequate urban housing, lead to expanding informal settlements. Ho Chi Minh City is expected to be particularly exposed. A study that quantified its current and future citywide flood risks projects that up to 60 percent of developed area will be affected by a 100 centimeter sea-level rise.[11] Without adaptation, the planned urban development for 2025 increases Ho Chi Minh City's exposure to sea-level rise by 17 percent. Floods associated with sea-level rise and storm surges carry great risks in informal settlements, where 41 percent of the urban population lived in 2005 (UN-HABITAT 2007). Lack of drainage and damage to sanitation and water facilities accompany the health threats in these settlements.

Health. Negative human health impacts include waterborne and vector-borne diseases (such as malaria, dengue, and encephalitis) and diarrheal illnesses—and are especially pronounced in the less developed, densely populated, and poorer areas (Coker et al. 2011). Flooding compounds the risk and is associated with immediate risks, such as drowning and the disruption of sanitation and health services resulting from damaged infrastructure (Schatz 2008). In cities the effects of heat extremes are pronounced. High temperatures could result in high human morbidity and mortality, especially among the growing numbers of elderly people. Coastal aquifers provide people living in coastal areas with water resources, and drinking salt-contaminated water can have detrimental health impacts (Vineis, Chan, and Khan 2011). Potential health problems include hypertension and other conditions linked to increased salinity exposure through bathing, drinking, and cooking. These include miscarriage (Khan et al. 2011), skin disease, acute respiratory infection, and diarrheal disease (Caritas Development Institute 2005).

Infrastructure. Climate change—especially sea-level rise, temperature increase, climatic variability, and intensified natural disasters—will put at risk some of Vietnam's critical infrastructure assets, especially transportation networks and power plants and equipment near the coasts, since these were not designed with climate change factors in mind.

Greenhouse Gas Emissions

From 2000 to 2010, Vietnam had the fastest growth in GHG emissions in the region (figure 5.8). Its total and per capita emissions almost tripled, while the carbon intensity of GDP rose by 48 percent. On all three measures, Vietnam's growth was one of the fastest in the world. It ranked much higher than other countries in the region, including Cambodia, China, Indonesia, Malaysia, the Philippines, and Thailand. Given the growth of its economy and the high and increasing trends in energy (and carbon) intensity of its GDP, Vietnam should consider smarter energy and transport choices that will help bend the GHG emission of this trajectory down to less risky ranges.

High and rapidly growing energy intensity

Energy use in Vietnam is rising faster than in any other country in the region, led by oil and electric power. With current trends and policies, the share of coal for power will rise from 23 percent in 2013 to nearly 60 percent by 2030. The country will remain a net energy exporter for the next few years. But by 2020, it is expected to be a net importer of coal, largely to fuel the power sector. Between

FIGURE 5.8 In only one decade, the three measures of carbon dioxide emissions—greenhouse gas emissions, per capita emissions, and carbon intensity of GDP—increased by 50 percent

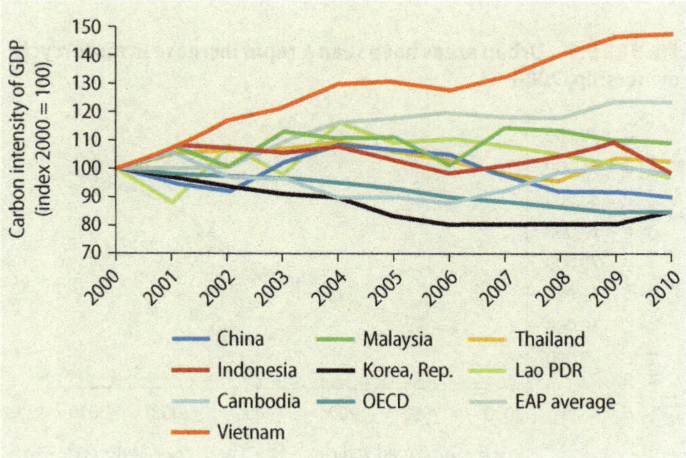

Source: Calculations based on World Development Indicators.
Note: EAP = East Asia and Pacific; OECD = Organisation for Economic Co-operation and Development.

2000 and 2010, electricity demand grew by about 14 percent a year. But per capita electricity consumption is still relatively low (one-third that of China). Electricity demand will continue to grow at about 10 percent a year over the next decade. Energy policy in the coming years—involving energy efficiency, renewable energy, and natural gas—will have to balance both Vietnam's energy security and containing air pollution and GHG emissions.

At 237 kilograms, Vietnam already has the highest energy intensity—the ratio of energy use in kilograms of oil equivalent per constant 2005 $1,000 of GDP—in East Asia. This is also higher than the world average of 208 kg. Electricity intensity (kilowatt-hour per US$ of GDP in constant 2000 US$) is around 1.5, nearly twice the world average of 0.8 (World Bank 2013c). Energy intensity has been increasing in large part because of the growth of industrial energy use, accounting for about one-third of national energy consumption.

Vietnam's iron and steel plants use twice the energy per unit of output as the global average, largely because they use old technology. Getting the price right could improve power-generation technology and could cut carbon dioxide emissions over the next 15 years (World Bank 2015). The country also has a conservative plan to increase the share of electricity produced from wind, biomass, and solar between 2010 and 2030. But to move to a more ambitious path, it must complete resource-potential studies for these three sources, plus small hydro. It must move forward with utility planning and operational capabilities to fully integrate renewables. It is important to draw on lessons from developing utility-scale renewable energy projects to design attractive feed-in tariffs for wind, biomass, and solar to provide incentives for private development and scaling up.

Growth of transport

Fossil fuel consumption has been increasing in transport. Motorcycles have seen the fastest rise over a decade, dominating growth in vehicle ownership (figure 5.9). In Hanoi, public transportation provides only about 7 percent of passenger trips, and in Ho Chi Minh City around 5 percent. The largest share of motorcycles nationwide is in cities, with 15 percent in Ho Chi Minh City and 8.5 percent in Hanoi in 2010 (MONRE and MOT 2012). Vehicles in Ho Chi Minh City accounted for one-third of total registered vehicles in Vietnam in 2012 (MONRE 2012).

Judging from international experience, automobile ownership will increase as incomes rise. But motorization rates (the number of automobiles per 1,000 persons) remain below those in other countries at similar income levels, reflecting higher acquisition costs for automobiles, including import duties and other taxes that are likely to fall with Association of Southeast Asian Nations (ASEAN) integration.

FIGURE 5.9 Urban areas have seen a rapid increase in motorcycle ownership, 2000–11

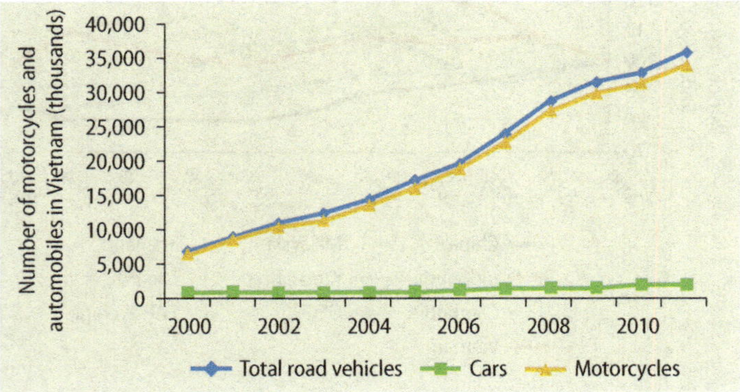

Source: Ministry of Natural Resources and Environment and Ministry of Transport 2012.

Underlying Causes and Priority Challenges

Vietnam must tackle the environmental challenges stemming from the current growth pattern to sustainably achieve upper-middle-income status and reduce the inequitable cost distribution of environmental degradation. To manage this task, it will need to set priorities for determining the degree of irreversibility (for example, if a large commitment of the resource makes a change in use or nonuse thereafter unlikely), the scale of impact (for example, the number of people affected), and whether taking corrective action is viable.

These criteria (based on evidence and expert opinion) generate four immediate environmental concerns: preserving natural resources, especially by reversing land degradation, reducing air pollution, decreasing water pollution, and adapting to climate change (discussed in more detail in "Growing Sustainably toward 2035: The Road Forward").

Vietnam needs to also preemptively and proactively attack the three main underlying causes of these four challenges to achieve more sustainable growth and to avoid the increasing burden of health costs, resource degradation, and low productivity.

Weak Institutional Capacity to Coordinate, Monitor, and Enforce Sustainable Practices

Limited coordination among institutions results in contradictory policies, poor planning, and ineffective and incoherent investments. For example, it is not feasible to expand local fish processing or boat building in the same locations where fishery conservation is under way. Institutional fragmentation discussed in chapter 7 "Building Modern Institutions for an Effective State" is a big part of the problem.

Poor coordination among institutions is notable in the deltas where vulnerability to climate change is high. The institutional landscape in the Mekong Delta is complicated, with planning and implementation roles unclearly spread across several ministries, agencies, and provinces. This format makes it challenging to plan for and build resiliency. The government faces huge challenges in coordinating the activities and investments of central and local agencies in the water, environment, transportation, and agriculture sectors. This creates negative implications for how cities in the delta are buffered against climate change.

The environmental challenges of air and water pollution underscore the need to augment institutional capacity to guide, monitor, and enforce sustainable practices. Too few trained monitors, weak penalties for lack of compliance, and little publicly accessible information allow water and air pollution to persist. Those guiding agriculture—which is now heavily based on intense land use and material inputs—have yet to identify ways to enforce pollution regulations. The small production scale and nonpoint source pollution present heavy transaction costs. And the highly fragmented production system across many small producers and over wide geographic areas can be difficult and expensive for monitoring staff to reach.

Effective regulations and monitoring and enforcement systems need to be in place if the country is to grow in a sustainable manner, especially in sectors that generate negative externalities. These include energy, agriculture, and industry. Many techniques from varied settings worldwide mitigate the environmental effects of agriculture (Liniger and Critchley 2007). A subset of them is already being piloted or applied widely in Vietnam, though generally not on a scale that will have much impact. As a result, Vietnam remains ineffective in managing increasing threats to agroindustries, ranging from pests to excessive inputs.

As noted, excessive antibiotic use in aquaculture is contaminating freshwater bodies, threatening the national reputation in key export markets. The country is one of the lowest ranked in complying with European Union (EU) standards and suffers from a high rejection rate. This is another upshot of the shortfalls in guidance from public institutions. Standards for food safety and for sustainable production are inadequately enforced in agriculture, fisheries, and forestry. These measures will be effective only when carried out in conjunction with incentives for sustainable investments.

Price Distortions and Minimal Incentives for Engaging the Private Sector

The impact of price distortions is evident in the environmental challenges in water and energy. The lack of irrigation water pricing means there are hardly any incentives to cut water use or adopt technologies to that end. Overuse of water for growing coffee and increased droughts are raising concerns about groundwater use in the Central Highlands. A coffee tree needs on average 350–400 liters of water per application (Khoi et al. 2015), carried out every 20–25 days during the dry season (Hagger and Scheep 2012). Many farmers in the Central Highlands use up to 800 liters.

Low coal and electricity prices, partly responsible for high energy intensity, crimp incentives for investments in energy efficiency. Although Vietnam increased average tariffs by 53 percent between 2010 and 2015, cumulative inflation was 57 percent over the period, taking real electricity prices down a shade to among the lowest in the region (table 5.3). Another impact of low tariffs is on the capacity of utilities to finance investment, operations, and maintenance or to attract private investment. Without the latter, Vietnam will find it hard to finance the large power infrastructure it needs or to move to newer and lower carbon-intensity fuels, such as natural gas, wind, and solar. An estimated $5 billion in annual investments will be needed to match the requirements in the power sector up to 2030, for which private participation will be essential. Low tariffs will also hinder efforts to increase regional power trade, especially from the large undeveloped hydropower potential in the Lao People's Democratic Republic.

Vietnam uses many fossil fuel subsidies. Vietnam Electricity Group (EVN) enjoys domestic coal and gas input prices well below world market prices. In 2012, coal was sold to electricity producers at about 60 percent of the export price and 70 percent of the production cost. In 2013, the price covered coal output costs but was still below world market prices. This keeps the average cost of electricity production from fossil fuels artificially low, which is why a large and increasing share of electricity generation comes from coal and gas.[12] Such subsidies slow the pace of modifying the energy mix to less-polluting and renewable sources.

The subsidization of the energy sector is not all through fiscal transfers. It also includes preferential treatment of SOEs, especially for access to land and to finance (see chapter 2). SOEs dominate the energy market and have wasteful practices that make them operationally inefficient. The monopoly of SOEs and slow reforms of energy SOEs are also barriers to building a competitive energy supply market. In 2012, the total debt of the three main energy corporations was around $15 billion, roughly a quarter of the debt owed by all SOEs in the country (UNDP 2014).

Systemic changes in incentives and behavior are needed not only at site level but also at community, landscape, and national levels. Incentives that engage the private sector are necessary for ideas to become action. The public sector cannot be the sole investor, and the private sector should play a greater role in providing environmental services and in managing natural resources. In sectors such as agriculture (including fisheries and forestry), the expanded role of public institutions is holding back investments in innovation and stifling competitiveness. The public sector, usually budget-constrained, should target its spending toward areas that leverage private investments or that are purely public goods, such as cleaning contaminated sites.

TABLE 5.3 Cumulative inflation surpassed tariffs and percentage increase show that real electricity prices are among the lowest in the region

	3/2009	3/2010	3/2011	12/2011	6/2012	12/2012	8/2013	3/2015
Electricity tariffs (VND/kWH)	948.5	1,058	1,242	1,304	1,369	1,467	1,508.85	1,622.01
Electricity tariffs (US cents/kWH)	4.7	5.3	6.2	6.5	6.8	7.0	7.1	7.6
Increase (%) in VND tariffs	–	11.5	17.4	5.0	5.0	5.0	5.0	7.0

Source: Electricity Regulatory Authority of Vietnam.
Note: kwH = kilowatt hour; VND = Vietnamese dong.

This approach not only offers incentives and leverages private resources—it also uses government funds more efficiently.

Inadequate Information

Evidence-based decisions and public support are integral to managing natural resources efficiently. Both require good scientific information. For example, anecdotal information based on fish-catch surveys suggests that Vietnam's $1.5 billion–2.5 billion[13] coastal fisheries industry is facing serious issues over fish stocks, but no credible analysis of the stocks and their supporting ecosystems has been made to allow them to be managed sustainably. Without scientific evidence, policy makers and the general public are unlikely to make good long-term decisions. Evidence from the U.S. East Coast cod fishery shows how fisheries can suddenly collapse—and fail to recover—with dire consequences for those depending on them. Vietnam's fishing industry could be at similar risk. But without data, no one can tell.

In Vietnam, data on ambient air pollution, emissions levels, and source structures are also scarce. Some transportation data exist, but few data are available for other sectors. Understanding is also lacking on how much some sectors contribute to urban air pollution. This information gap must be plugged to understand PM2.5 formation and its impact—and to augment the environmental and economic effects that have focused on total suspended particles and PM10. The urgency is underscored by plans for expanding coal-fired power generation. Potential air pollution must inform decisions today.

Policy makers require more knowledge of other countries' experiences to adopt a more ambitious renewable energy path before 2035. They need resource-potential studies for biomass, wind, solar energy, and additional run-of-river hydro. They must also draw on lessons in developing utility-scale renewable energy projects to design dynamic tariff systems that attract the private sector.

Vietnam will need to adopt current technology and systems to generate, validate, and allow public access to information. The information needs are wide ranging. Data and information that determine natural resource management and improve resource governance in subsectors must be stronger. Available information should be accessible in a user-friendly format, downscaled and sector specific. Coordinating how information is used should also be enhanced to improve planning, particularly among agencies working together at the central and subnational levels.

This would ensure that information is understandable and accessible to the public, under access-to-information laws. Integrated platforms that convert data to user-friendly outputs and inform planning and management exist in Vietnam, but they need to be harmonized across sectors and government levels.

Growing Sustainably Toward 2035: The Road Forward

By 2035, Vietnam envisions a solid foundation for sustainable and efficient growth. This will involve a proactive approach to protecting natural resources and the environment, making efficient energy choices, and shielding the country from the worst effects of global climate change. Vietnam under this scenario would meet most, if not all, of its international commitments to lower greenhouse gas emission, achieve green growth, and maintain ecological balance. Vietnam's vision sees achievement of environmental targets that are equivalent to the current levels of regional developed industrial countries.

Global experiences point to how sustainable growth requires good policies adapted to the national political economy and to entrenched behavior. Vietnam is well placed to avoid becoming one of the countries wrestling with irreversible environmental degradation and onerous remediation costs. In line with the evolving global agenda on sustainable development (as articulated in the UN Agenda 2030 for Sustainable Development, which includes the Sustainable Development Goals) and addressing climate change

BOX 5.4 Sustainable Development Goals related to environmental issues

1. Ensure availability and sustainable management of water and sanitation for all.
2. Ensure access to affordable, reliable, sustainable, and modern energy for all.
3. Build resilient infrastructure, promote inclusive and sustainable industrialization, and foster innovation.
4. Make cities and human settlements inclusive, safe, resilient, and sustainable.
5. Take urgent action to combat climate change and its impacts.
6. Conserve and sustainably use the oceans, seas, and marine resources for sustainable development.
7. Protect, restore, and promote sustainable use of terrestrial ecosystems, sustainably manage forests, combat desertification, halt and reverse land degradation, and halt biodiversity loss.

(box 5.4), Vietnam has issued a series of strategies and action plans (United Nations General Assembly 2015).

Vietnam can transition to a sustainable growth path if it translates its various strategies and action plans into practice—and addresses the main environmental challenges by implementing three key action areas: improving governance through strong institutions that are well coordinated and effective in monitoring and enforcing policies; incentivizing private sector investments; and providing relevant and robust information that is publically accessible.

This section presents actions the government could take in strengthening institutions, incentives, and information to address the four main environmental challenges identified above: preserving natural resources (including land), reducing air pollution, reducing water pollution, and adapting to climate change.

Address Land Degradation while Modernizing Agriculture, Aquaculture, Forestry, and Fisheries

The share of primary agriculture is expected to decline by about half a percentage point a year, so that by the early 2030s it accounts for about 8 percent of GDP (see chapter 2). But agroindustry, with food distribution and logistics—and other services—could account for twice this share, implying that the agro-food complex will account for between one-fifth and one-fourth of GDP (World Bank 2016). This will require mitigating agriculture's role in land degradation and producing more from less—transforming the sector.

Land management systems need to be installed on sloping lands to reduce land degradation. This requires spatially coordinated approaches between districts and provinces to optimize different land uses and employ systems similar to payments for environmental services (PES). Coordination of technical services is also important for diversifying land use on farms and across the landscape. In Ca Mau province local policy makers identified the environmental and commercial benefits of diversified land use through the concept of an "organic coast" that maintains less input-intensive shrimp–mangrove aquaculture. Similar approaches could be adopted elsewhere.

In addition, improving the sustainability of offshore and nearshore fishing will need different approaches. Offshore fishing requires proactive management and restrictions prior to the depletion of fisheries, including through strict zoning enforcement, limiting the number of fishing boat permits, and close coordination among governments at all levels. The adoption of marine spatial planning strategies could be useful for determining the feasible offshore fishing locations and volumes. This approach can also be important for conserving marine ecosystems and coastal areas, protecting endangered species, and restoring or protecting marine fish stocks. Co-management in fisheries is crucial to the effort to conserve, manage, and extract fish stocks effectively in Vietnam (box 5.5).

Vietnam will need to modify agricultural policies—such as those promoting fish processing, biofuel production, and irrigation—that contradict environmental protection goals. It will also have to enable and encourage private actors to invest in environmental protection through incentives and information. Drawing on international experience, Vietnam could promote agro-environmental strategies that anticipate and prevent degradation in the first place (World Bank 2016). In addition, public revenue could co-finance private land manager investments (by subsidizing landowner restoration of riparian areas, for instance). Public revenue could pay producers or communities for ecosystem stewardship that benefits the public. Such revenue could also provide financial incentives (through preferential credit to producers who use sustainable practices, for example). Incentives to internalize positive externalities from landscape restoration (for example, payments for water services resulting from watershed management) and sustainable resource management can also promote stewardship. In Dak Lak, the government is sharing the cost coffee farmers incur to adopt water-saving technologies. The government is also providing credit—on preferential terms—to farmers who replant coffee bushes while improving soil and water management practices.

To make agricultural practices more sustainable, the government will also need to shift its role to a facilitator of agricultural modernization, as did governments in Brazil, Chile, Mexico, and Thailand. The shift should see the government focusing on core public goods and services. This involvement should encourage and enable farmers and the private sector to make a greater investment in agricultural practices. It should also promote greater value added rather than a higher volume of low-quality products. The shift should emphasize coordination to achieve food safety in the supply chain from farm to fork. In Thailand, the government has facilitated the application of Code of Conduct and Good Aquaculture Practice—which contains standards for food safety and quality, environmental protection, social responsibility, health and welfare of animals, and data collection and traceability. The Vietnam government could propose incentives to get domestic producers to adopt certification systems of environmental and biosafety standards.

Institutions, incentives, and information would also be key as Vietnam looks to generate higher and more sustainable income from forest production and environmental services.

BOX 5.5 Co-management is crucial for sustaining marine fisheries

Co-management in marine fisheries means building a partnership between the local stakeholders and the government to manage natural resources. The co-management approach has been strongly supported in the Vietnam Law of Fisheries. In addition, the local democracy policies of the government strongly advocate this co-management approach, by robustly empowering communes in planning, developing, and managing resources. But the approach has not been widely applied and needs to facilitate formalization of fisheries groups so they can fully benefit from the arrangement.

The application of co-management on a large scale will require effective consultation with stakeholders and adequate justification for the change (including social and economic justifications). The effective application of co-management will also require more enforcement and rising productivity (for justifying transaction costs). Globally competitive manufacturers such as Peru and Chile have adopted co-management. Thailand has also applied the approach. In Chile, it has resulted in resource sustainability as well as benefits for fishermen.

Vietnam will also need to strengthen institutional capacity at both the central and local levels. This will not only strengthen enforcement of regulations and ease operating conditions for enterprises (through speedier issuance of permits and land use rights, for example). It will also ensure better collection of data and information on forest boundaries, inventory of species, soil conditions, forest management practices, and market opportunities. Vietnam will also need to restructure its timber processing industry to lower production costs—for instance, in 2011, the paper production costs in Vietnam were 10–30 percent higher than in other ASEAN countries. Consolidating the domestic processing industry will be important to have fewer wood chip and paper manufacturers operating on greater scale. Other complementary measures include accelerating SOE equitization in forestry, strengthening spatial planning for locating high-yield plantations, institutionalizing the value of ecosystem services and natural capital, and assisting local communities, through mechanisms that ensure their participation in forestry-related value chains and return to them a fair share of the profits.

Vietnam, among the early adopters of the program of PES, has benefitted from its economic returns, as discussed earlier. Following the example of other developing countries, it can now look to expand the program, while keeping an eye on maintaining positive economic returns (box 5.6). Two additional financial resources for ecosystem services from forests are carbon markets and tourism. First, Vietnam can generate sizable revenues in the international carbon market from carbon sequestration by its forests (CIFOR 2009, 2012). Second, tourism can create revenues that can be reinvested to maintain ecosystem services. Vietnam's mountains and coastal landscapes make it an attractive tourism destination, a potential that is far from fully tapped.

BOX 5.6 Payments for ecosystem services: A market-based approach to environmental management

Payments for ecosystem services (PES) are a market-based approach to environmental management, including direct compensation to land managers for maintaining specific ecosystem services, often through conservation and recovery activities. PES transactions are voluntary and dependent on the continuation of an identified ecosystem service (or a form of land use to secure the service) (Wunder 2007). The payments can be made directly in cash, or other forms of compensation, and can be used, for example, to encourage landowners to plant trees for carbon absorption, restore forests for water purification, preserve scenic beauty for cultural values and aesthetics, or sustain biodiversity for less fertilizer and pesticide needs. In agriculture, PES is often used for farmers to fallow, or conserve production systems or contribute to ecosystem services.

Over the past decade, the PES programs have expanded rapidly, thanks to the increasing involvement of the private sector as buyers and the maturing market for ecosystem services such as carbon, water, and biodiversity. Although private conservation groups and companies are important actors in PES programs, public bodies are still the key buyers of ecosystem services (UNEP 2012).

Government-financed payments for ecosystem services appear to be more common in many countries. Some of the biggest PES programs—in Mexico, Costa Rica, Colombia, and China, have been largely or entirely financed by domestic resources, such as tax revenues or water and power user fees (Milder, Scherr, and Bracer 2010). The Grain for Green Program in China and the Conservation Reserve Program in the United States are two PES programs funded by the government and deployed on a large scale to restore more suitable land cover to agricultural land, to minimize environmental degradation from agriculture.

Vietnam could also allow modern land markets, since they are critical in improving environmental quality. Many industries or other high-polluting activities are in fast-growing urban areas. The traditional market solution to rising urban land values is to displace lower-valued industrial sites, but not in Vietnam. Finding alternative revenue sources for local governments—such as revenue from property, sales, or income taxes (see chapter 4)—would help remove highly polluting industries from densely populated areas. The industrial relocation from Dalian, China, shows how transforming land markets can benefit the environment.

SOE equitization needs to be accelerated, for economic efficiency and environmental sustainability. SOEs are inefficient producers (see chapter 2), dominating the energy sector (and active in some natural resource sectors, such as forestry). Accelerating their restructuring and equitization to bring in private capital and innovation would improve productivity and reduce their environmental impacts. To foster competition, equitization will need to be backed by measures to get prices right and clarify tenure and property rights. Such complementary actions will build private sector confidence to invest in Vietnam and also help "pull up" the viable small and medium enterprises that are investing in sustainable activities. Equitizing SOEs would also reduce the state's conflict of interest when it acts as producer of resources and enforcer of environmental standards.

The government can generate and make publicly available information on land, ownership, sector investments, and climate change. It is already pursuing the e-government program, which puts in place a mechanism for increasing government productivity and efficiency and enables services catering to citizens' needs. Countries in Europe have launched spatial data infrastructure activities, some national and others subnational. A European Commission–financed effort to assess the socioeconomic impact of spatial data infrastructure around 2007 found that, in Catalonia, the spatial data infrastructure was financially justified and the numbers for one year showed that it generated internal savings of about 2 million euros. One of the major sociopolitical benefits is that the infrastructure has reduced the digital divide between larger and smaller municipalities. It also has enabled smaller municipalities to provide services that previously were not feasible. In addition, five years after its inception, many public organizations are interested in publishing their geodata and making it available through the single platform (Almiral et al. 2008).

In Vietnam, the National Spatial Data Infrastructure—which will be one of the core data platforms for sharing, accessing, and managing natural and artificial objects by geographic location—will enhance efficiency in local and central government policy making. MONRE has been assigned to prepare a plan to set up a National Committee on Geographical Names and Spatial Data Infrastructure. It should be supported to do so in an expeditious manner. The government could also promote affordable information and communications technology, including publicly accessible spatial data apps to collect and share real-time information on environmental and demographic variables.

It is also important to build capacity and coordination among research organizations, public agencies, and think tanks to analyze the resultant data from the above initiatives. This action will ensure that these bodies prioritize approaches and improve public agencies' use of data (including data monitoring and enforcement). It will also ensure that approaches are developed for using data to inform decision making.

Generating and disseminating information will also be crucial for revising the fisheries sector in a sustainable way. For both offshore and coastal/nearshore fishing, information on fish stocks is crucial but lacking. For nearshore fisheries, the tradeoffs with flood prevention measures in agriculture need to be better understood—how physical structures that manage water flows (such as floodgates, dams, causeways, and weirs) can disrupt the reproductive environment for fish by impeding their free passage along the waterways, which is essential for their survival. Reversing this lack of information can improve the management of fisheries resources.

Reduce Air Pollution while Meeting Growing Demand for Energy and Greater Urbanization

The uncertainty over the contribution of different sectors to air pollution underscores the need to promote coordination and planning across institutions and sectors. Vietnam could benefit from cities and urban clusters that develop multipollutant air quality management implementation plans. The country needs to develop and adopt regulations on vehicle emissions standards and on fuel quality. The government could also initiate industrial permits to control air emissions from the relevant industrial sectors. For air pollution, adopting the National Action Plan on Air Quality Management deserves immediate attention.[14]

In the energy sector, it would be valuable to enforce the law on energy efficiency and conservation and the decree on sanctions for violations on energy efficiency. Energy-efficiency building codes are mandatory for all new investments into building projects. Implementation could be bolstered by addressing government authorities' inadequate code monitoring and enforcement. Mandatory standards, such as those for widely used energy-efficiency equipment, are also important. These standards can help reduce energy consumption (and energy imports), saving consumers large amounts of money.

The government needs to be the regulator of operations in the energy sector by setting and enforcing environmental standards. Vietnam could reduce its air pollution by improving energy efficiency in the industrial sector. It could benefit from putting in place mandatory performance-based targets combined with financial incentives for industry and provinces. Standards could also be used to improve energy efficiency among end users, particularly iron and steel plants. Investing in their energy-efficiency measures is expected to reduce energy consumption by about 45,000 gigawatt-hours (GWh) between 2015 and 2030.

China has developed comprehensive national and local building codes. The national code covers design, construction, and operation (variations of the urban residential code for different climate zones). In addition, each province can develop its own more stringent commercial and residential building codes. Some provinces, such as Beijing and Tianjin, have implemented standards that are roughly 10–15 percent more efficient than national codes. Compliance with the energy-efficiency codes for new buildings are supervised and enforced through regular inspections of new construction and random inspections of completed projects. Regular inspections for new construction follow a "loop system" with four phases of administrative review and licensing. Finished projects that violate the standards are considered illegal construction that cannot be sold or occupied until violations are rectified. The government has other noncompliance penalties, such as imposing fines, revoking licenses, and requiring that noncompliant buildings or their components be corrected (Feng et al. 2015).

An immediate policy measure is to phase out energy subsidies and increase electricity tariffs (while maintaining protections for low-income consumers). This will encourage private investment to meet future energy demand and enable energy suppliers to cover their investment and their operation and maintenance spending. Raising energy prices would also promote incentives for energy-efficiency investments, particularly in the industrial sector where financial returns are directly related to electricity tariffs or other fuel costs. It would also allow electric utilities to meet the costs of new investment and operational expenses. The increase in prices may also motivate upgrading and rehabilitating the aging coal-fired power plants. This action could substantially contribute to increasing efficiency, reducing GHG emissions[15] and air pollution, and developing incentives for investments in new power generation. Higher energy prices would also facilitate competition and the workings of the wholesale electricity market.

The government needs to promote more aggressively wind, solar, and natural gas development and regional power trade, especially hydropower from the Lao PDR. Vietnam's heavy reliance on generating coal-fired power to meet future electricity demand conflicts with its GHG emissions reduction targets. The country needs to continue developing attractive feed-in tariffs for wind, solar, and biomass or other financing mechanisms (such as auctions). These provide incentives for developing nonhydropower and reduce transaction costs associated with renewable energy. The government is conducting a comprehensive renewable energy mapping project collecting and managing all data on hydropower, biomass, wind, and solar resources. This information should be a basis for future policy decision making.

India, for example, provides private investors with a tax incentive to invest in renewable energy. It enables businesses to take—as a tax deduction—100 percent of the capital costs of renewable energy projects. The idea is that tax deductions linked to the amount of investment can provide valuable benefits for producers. In Bulgaria, the government provides nontax incentives. It offers a 20 percent grant and an 80 percent loan-support mechanism for new hydropower plants smaller than 10 megawatts. This incentive also includes biomass heating, wind power parks under 5 megawatts, and solar, biogas, and small geothermal generators.

The value of combining tax and nontax incentives is also recognized in Spain's energy sector, one of the world leaders in renewable energy. Spain has the second-largest capacity for solar thermal electricity, the third-largest for small hydroelectric, and the fourth-largest for wind power. The sector employs 200,000 people and includes more than 400 companies. Although Spain has taken back some of these subsidies because of fiscal costs, the economy has derived major benefits from the incentives regime, including installation of 3.9 GW of renewable energy capacity between 2000 and 2010, which augmented annual solar photovoltaic electricity generation from 18 GWh in 2000 to around 6.4 terawatt-hours (TWh) in 2010 (Bridle and Beaton 2012).

The transport sector should coordinate new development with mass transit to create connected communities, strategic development corridors, and other efficient transport options. Transitioning to electric vehicles could reduce transport-related pollution.

Reduce Water Pollution from Urban, Industrial, and Rural Areas

Vietnam needs to bolster the capacity of its public institutions to better monitor and enforce programs and policies that aim to reduce the environmental impacts of industry. Cleaner production has been used to reduce waste and lower resource consumption in industry while improving its performance. Sectors such as textiles, food processing, and leather estimate an average savings potential of 30 percent for water without major investments in infrastructure. Based on government surveys, only 11 percent of industrial facilities in Vietnam were using cleaner production techniques to reduce their energy, fuel, and materials consumption in 2010, pointing to much room for improvement.

The Green Credit Trust Fund promotes long-term investments by Vietnam's small and medium enterprises in production technology that have a positive impact on the environment. This is achieved thanks to a partial reimbursement of the credit offered by the trust fund depending on the environmental impact resulting from the investment. For example, if an investment made using credit from the fund reduces negative environmental impact by 30 percent (such as reducing wastewater), the trust fund will reimburse 15 percent of the credit. Similarly, an environmental improvement of 50 percent from the original conditions would result in 25 percent of the credit being reimbursed.

The country also faces an urgent need to achieve universal access to sanitation in urban and rural areas, for environmental and health reasons. Municipal wastewater is predicted to be the largest source of wastewater over the coming decades. Sewage treatment levels need to be raised substantially from the 10 percent of recent years.

The government has already set a fee on effluents with the aim of reducing water pollution and helping public wastewater utilities cover investment and operation and maintenance expenses. This fee must be enforced and reviewed to check whether it is high enough to change behavior.

Based on international experience in developed countries, private sector investment in sustainable technologies often exceeds public investment. Furthermore, government regulation of environmental protection standards requires the private sector to invest in environmental protection. Private firms can contribute to improving sanitation and wastewater treatment by financing environmental infrastructure. With properly designed policies (including intellectual property rights protection), the private sector can introduce sustainable treatment technologies and innovations, mitigating environmental pollution. Acquiring better technologies and management processes should be a goal of domestic and foreign private investment. The government can help ensure that this happens by encouraging private sector involvement in a fair, efficient, and safe regulatory environment.

Tax incentives or direct subsidies for environmental investments further encourage private sector involvement. To reduce pollution, Vietnam should provide incentives for the private sector to operate within green industrial zones. In recent years, Korea has transformed 12 of its industrial parks to green zones, yielding economic benefits of some $44 million and reducing GHG emissions by nearly 200,000 tons a year. Industrial symbiosis within an economic zone is another novel concept that provides simple but cost-effective solutions to achieve efficiency and reduce waste through an exchange of energy, waste, and material resources between firms. The waste of one enterprise becomes the input to another's production activities. One example is creating a company-to-company network through a waste-heat-recovery steam generator. Another focuses on a solid waste collection, segregation, and recycling network. A wastewater reclamation and reuse network involves installing microfiltration and purification equipment. The Kalundborg eco-industrial park in Denmark and the Ulsan eco-industrial park in Korea apply this process.

Vietnam will also need to tackle pollution challenges linked to its craft villages. More than 2,500 in number and distributed mainly in the Red River Delta, they tend to engage in economic activity that often includes metal recycling and leather tanning and involves plastic and lead, causing serious environmental pollution. Water pollution is a leading problem, affecting not only the craft villages but also downstream villages. The formulation of appropriate policies and measures for an environmentally sustainable operation in craft villages has encountered local customs and practices. In addition to the broader solutions involving enforcement of pollution control–related regulations and investment in wastewater treatment infrastructure, it is necessary to develop a master plan to address the special needs of craft villages.

In agriculture, Vietnam needs to remove support policies that work counter to the environment, such as waiving water-use fees. But it will have to make such changes while maintaining measures to protect the rural poor from their impact. It also needs to improve public access to information on water consumption and pollution and to galvanize broad public support for government measures. Publicly accessible information will help identify laggards in adopting improved wastewater treatment.

Adapt to Climate Change

Cities in the Mekong Delta that are vulnerable to climate change could have considered a broad set of adaptation measures. They could have "worked with nature" by emphasizing coastal resource management, for example, or by protecting mangrove and natural reef ecosystems. They could have climate-proofed infrastructure by improving storm-drainage systems and water supply and treatment plants. And they could have protected or relocated energy or solid waste management facilities. But the region remains highly exposed to sea-level rise, with informal settlements at particular risk. Greater coordination among national and subnational institutions is needed to enhance resilience to climate change.

Greater coordination should be facilitated by developing a single, coordinated, multisectoral plan for each of the regions most vulnerable to climate change. These include the Deltas, Central Highlands, and Northern Mountains. Similar to the Mekong Delta Plan (see figure 5.10), the single plan should develop a long-term strategic and sustainable vision for each region and include policy recommendations. The plan should also guide the government in coordinated development planning and future investments.

In the medium term, Vietnam needs to augment its subnational capacity to conduct risk and uncertainty analyses (related to socioeconomic, investment, and climate models) and use a decision-support framework to determine suitable investments. Efforts to build capacity and mainstream climate risks in development policies should enable the provinces to improve integrated spatial planning across sectors. They should also ensure that land and water resources are managed, taking into account the long-term perspective (and potential climate and development impacts). The aim is to increase local government participation in defining the plans and boosting their willingness to engage in implementation.

Vietnam can augment the sustainability of its natural resources through appropriate coordination and implementation of sector-specific adaptation measures that blend ecosystem-based and infrastructure-based approaches. For water resources, Vietnam will need to continue to invest in flood control, fresh water supplies during the dry season, monitoring of saltwater intrusion, regulation and management of water for aquaculture, coastal protection, and so on at large scale (including regionally). In addition to these solutions is the need for a

FIGURE 5.10 Developing in each region a single coordinated multisectoral plan, similar to the Mekong Delta Plan, will facilitate better coordination with the center

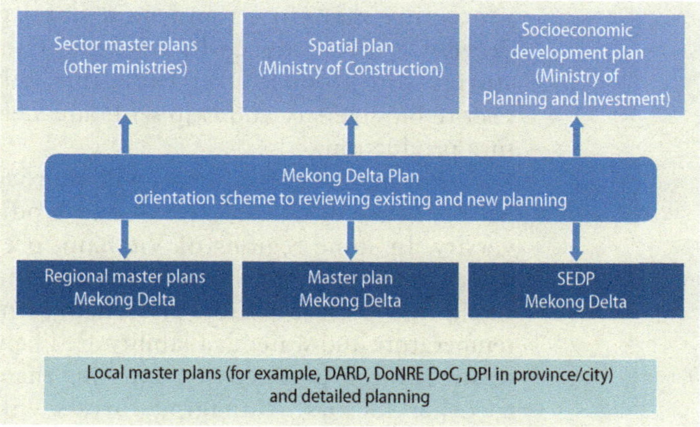

Source: Royal HaskoningDHV 2013.
Note: DARD = Department of Agriculture and Rural Development; DoC = Department of Construction; DPI = Department of Planning and Investment; MoC = Master Plan of Mekong Delta; MPI = Ministry of Planning and Investment; MPI DoNRE = Department of Natural Resource Environment.

fundamental shift in the approach to moving water supply from groundwater to surface water to prevent land subsidence. Such a shift will require investing in water conservation and measures to reduce reliance on groundwater extraction; restructuring, rehabilitating, and upgrading irrigation systems; constructing more multipurpose reservoirs; and developing watershed management mechanisms.

Measures in agriculture will need to be climate smart and market savvy. Augmenting the resilience of the agricultural production system could entail promoting agricultural land use changes that both mitigate climate-related risks and respond to emerging market signals, funding research and extension to develop and diffuse new crop and animal varieties tolerant to changing conditions, achieving water savings in irrigation systems by rehabilitating infrastructure and through better management practices and incentives (water charges), and increasing the availability of timely weather information and seasonal climate forecasts, with the knowledge to best use this information.

Smart measures in aquaculture will need to blend the development or use of climate-resilient varieties with investments in dyke upgrading that can help reduce flooding and salinization. For estuaries where conditions have not completely compromised the ecosystem, an option is replanting and protecting mangroves and mud flats to prevent erosion caused by sea-level rise, storms, and floods. Over time, this will restore biodiversity and help with aquaculture production.

Restoring mangrove forests will improve the resilience of coastal areas—and biodiversity. In some regions of Vietnam, predicted changes in climate will increase the likelihood of forest fires, and changes in temperature and water availability are likely to stress forest productivity, exposing them to other factors. Managing forests will enhance their resilience to these changes. Expanding the area under forests with more diverse species can also help adapt these natural systems.

Measures to adapt to climate change should not be limited to the natural resource sectors. They will need to extend to health sectors and to industry. Many of the necessary investments can be beneficial independent of climate change, as they entail augmenting resilience to unexpected shocks.

Vietnam also needs to improve the information base it uses to inform plans and investments for climate resilience. This requires mechanisms for monitoring and collecting additional data—such as Hydromet and survey data—and for developing a comprehensive, publicly accessible, and user-friendly knowledge base. Improving the information base will improve the government's ability to reexamine sectoral policies on agriculture (triple rice cropping, for example), urban development (including nature and spatial development), and water resource management (such as choice of infrastructure or nonstructural measures to control floods and saline intrusion) to adjust land use to changing water regimes (between fresh, saline, and brackish waters). This would enable the government—at multiple levels—to internalize natural resource conditions and trends. It could capture the influence of climate change, natural processes, and human actions. The government could also enhance opportunities for restoration and conservation.

Measures in Common

The Vietnamese government will also need to push through with actions important for all priority environmental issues. It should build the human capital to engage in sustainable management practices by training workers and building a technical cadre of graduates. As it invests in improving its education system, it should ensure that the curriculum for graduates interested in environmental fields is suffused with the latest ideas and best practice for sustainable growth.

The government also needs to invest in transitioning low-skilled labor from sectors such as aquaculture and agriculture to low-carbon and sustainable industries (potentially in the same sector). The EU's approach to addressing some of the challenges facing fisheries-dependent communities could be noted. Twenty-one EU member states helped form local multi-actor partnerships, known as fisheries local action groups, which could then access the European Fisheries Fund to promote local development. These groups must create new opportunities for jobs and growth by launching alternative or complementary activities. A wide range of local promoters—businesses, civil society organizations, local governments, and fishers themselves—implemented fund-financed projects. They aimed to revitalize communities heavily reliant on dwindling fisheries without increasing extractive fishery activities.

The central government should provide local governments with incentives to implement environmental policy by devising alternative revenue-raising or budget-funding strategies. Local governments need to raise revenue and create jobs in order to maintain their development trajectories. But their fear of chasing away industry or losing public revenue—from selling or taxing natural resources—may impede them from conducting environmental policies. China provided cash transfers and enabled local governments to tax chemical inputs, thus allowing local governments to adapt national agro-environmental strategies.

Vietnam will benefit from benchmarking local governments with explicit performance indicators of sustainable growth. These indicators would track performance and offer rewards and promotions to lower officials who have fostered environmental programs and improved environmental quality in their jurisdictions. Such benchmarking can create incentives for behavioral change among local governments. For example, Brazil transfers additional tax revenue to municipalities that perform well on environmental indicators. In China, local government officials' performance is evaluated on environmental indicators and economic growth indicators.

For many households and smallholder enterprises, natural assets are the only option for generating revenue. To avoid severe economic impacts from conservation policies, it is important for private investments to generate gains to welfare that extend beyond broad economic growth. This can be achieved by creating jobs or reducing poverty through shared benefits. The latter could cover monetary and nonmonetary benefits, such as preferential access to skill-upgrading for youth in forest-dependent households. Similarly, fishing communities should receive safety nets and training until fisheries recover and assistance in moving workers to other fields.

Policy makers could raise resource pricing—such as for electricity and water—with knowledge of the potential impacts on the poor. For electricity, government protection programs have limited the large impacts of tariff adjustments on the poor. For example, the social tariff for households consuming up to 50 kWh a month helps insulate poor households from price increases. Similar policies should be used when other resource prices are increased.

Trade-Offs Associated with Sustainable, Inclusive, and Resilient Growth

Evidence from other countries—including Brazil, Costa Rica, Malaysia, and the Philippines—shows that measures for sustainable growth can offer short- and long-term benefits. In the short term, most benefits are local. They stem from improvements in accessing energy, managing water and waste, and controlling pollution, most frequently in agriculture and urban sectors. While urgent to prevent locking in irreversible decisions, investments in reducing deforestation and improving land management generate medium- to long-term benefits. These benefits include reduced soil erosion and fewer emissions-related payments.

Trade-offs in policy measures vary, depending on the scale and type of economy and how measures are implemented. Short-term gains can be tied to costs from price increases, for example, or changes in access and short-term setbacks in competitiveness. Measures to reduce pollution can include enforcing certification standards. Firms can meet lower pollution targets by investing in new technology. Other pollution-reducing measures can include property rights, changes in access to public resources, and charges for resource use (such as water fees). Trade-offs between intertemporal benefits and local and global benefits of sustainable growth measures should be balanced with the urgency required for the measures. This helps to avoid locking in irreversible actions that do not consider the environment or climate change. Table 5.4 provides a generalized representation for developing countries.

In Vietnam, where natural-input use in industry is heavy, policies for sustainable growth can raise the rate of return as they improve resource use, reduce waste, and cut inefficiencies and lost output. Sustainable growth policies can also reallocate time and money from polluting practices to beneficial activities such as education. Strengthened environmental policies can potentially slow capital accumulation and growth in the short term. But if it includes investing in innovation, the trade-offs are less pronounced. Moreover, welfare—not reflected in measures such as GDP—is improved.[16] Investment of revenue generation from sustainable agriculture, fisheries, and forestry can also help to improve competitiveness.

TABLE 5.4 Trade-offs should be balanced with the urgency required for the measures

	Local and immediate benefits	
	LOWER (Trade-offs exist between short- and long-term or local and global benefits)	**HIGHER (Policies provide local and immediate benefits)**
Inertia and/or risk of lock-in and irreversibility		
LOWER (action is less urgent)	• Lower-carbon, higher-cost energy supply • Carbon pricing • Stricter wastewater regulation	• Drinking water and sanitation, solid waste management • Lower-carbon, lower-cost energy supply • Loss reduction in electricity supply • Energy demand management • Small-scale multipurpose water reservoirs
HIGHER (action is urgent)	• Reduced deforestation • Coastal zone and natural area protection • Fisheries catch management	• Land use planning • Public urban transport • Family planning • Sustainable intensification in agriculture • Large-scale multipurpose water reservoirs

Source: World Bank 2012.

In summary, policy, financial, and intertemporal trade-offs associated with measures for green, inclusive, and resilient growth depend on how they are implemented. Vietnam can adapt experiences of countries that have successfully adopted measures for such growth. It will need to design green and climate-resilient policies that stimulate innovation and are augmented with targeted, socially complementary policies. In the long term, these measures will pay for themselves.

Vietnam has a unique opportunity to take advantage of its natural assets and redirect its growth path to one that is sustainable, inclusive, and resilient. Strengthening public institutions, engaging the private sector, introducing needed financial support, and using existing technologies and information can engender change. In following a sustainable growth path, the country should also consider accessing public financing sources—such as the Green Climate Fund—to facilitate needed investments in the short term.

Notes

1. This term growth is taken as synonymous with green growth that is inclusive and resilient to climate change.
2. Nearly half the mangrove forests in the Mekong Delta were destroyed by shrimp aquaculture expansion.
3. General Statistics Office of Vietnam data that were available up to 2013.
4. Traffic, as cited in USAID 2013.
5. The World Wide Fund for Nature (WWF) has a scorecard of how well the countries are using the resources they have available to them to handle CITES compliance.
6. A questionnaire was developed and administered to stakeholders on the importance of valued ecosystem components and found that forest and forest products (especially from primary forests) were seen as important, followed by soil and erosion control.
7. VASEP 2010 and http://pubs.iclarm.net/resource_centre/WF_2776.pdf (viewed May 2015).
8. See http://pubs.iclarm.net/resource_centre/WF_2776.pdf (viewed May 2015).
9. The larger irrigation schemes are managed by state-owned irrigation and drainage management companies (IDMCs), whose operating revenues come from a combination of public subsidies and water use charges to industry and municipalities. Since 2008, most farmers have been exempt from paying fees for services provided by the IDMCs. This measure was adopted to improve farmer welfare, but has weakened IDMCs' accountability to local water user organizations.
10. Defined using thresholds based on the historical variability of the current local climate. Unusual heat extremes are defined as three-sigma events. Unprecedented heat extremes are defined as five-sigma events.
11. Excluding the impact of subsidence, due to lack of data; Storch and Downes 2011.
12. The fossil fuel subsidies on electricity and petroleum products include price controls,

grants to (electricity) consumers, low-interest and preferential loans, government loan guarantees, tax and tariffs credit, and exemptions.

13. Estimation using 2013 General Statistics Office of Vietnam data on fish catch and price.
14. The Plan includes a broad range of activities organized under seven focus areas—regulation, organizational strengthening, emissions reduction and prevention, investments and financial incentives, international cooperation, monitoring and inspection, and dissemination and public awareness. Implementation requires coordination among MONRE, Ministry of Home Affairs, Ministry of Transport, Ministry of Industry and Technology, Ministry of Construction, Ministry of Housing, along with provinces and cities.
15. We could save 15–20 GW by aggressively promoting solar and wind, implementing demand-side energy efficiency, and taking full advantage of regional trade. Using current emissions factor information for the whole energy system and existing and new power plants, and the emissions reduction from avoiding 15–20 GW of imported coal, it is estimated that emissions reductions from saving 15–20 GW are between 161,753,400 and 215,671,200 tonnes of carbon dioxide equivalent a year.
16. See http://www.oxcarre.ox.ac.uk/files/OxCarreRP2014135(2).pdf.

References

Almiral, Pilar Garcia, Montse Moix Bergadà, Pau Queraltó Ros. 2008. *The Socioeconomic Impact of the Spatial Data Infrastructure of Catalonia*. JRC Scientific and Technical Reports. Brussels, Belgium: European Commission. http://inspire.ec.europa.eu/reports/Study_reports/catalonia_impact_study_report.pdf.

Bao, Tran Quang, and Melinda Laituri. 2011. "Defining Required Forest Area for Protection Soil from Erosion in Vietnam: A GIS-based Application." *VNU Journal of Science, Earth Sciences* 27 (1): 63–76.

BirdLife International. 2013. *Country Profile: Vietnam*. Cambridge, UK: BirdLife International. http://www.birdlife.org/datazone/country/vietnam.

Blankespoor, B., S. Dasgupta, and B. Laplante. 2012. *Sea-Level Rise and Coastal Wetlands Impacts and Costs*. Washington, DC: World Bank.

Bridle, Richard, and Christopher Beaton. 2012. *Assessing the Cost-Effectiveness of Renewable Energy Deployment Subsidies: Solar PV in Germany and Spain*. Winnipeg, Canada: Global Subsidies Initiative. https://www.iisd.org/gsi/sites/default/files/rens_cba_solar_germany_spain.pdf.

Caritas Development Institute. 2005. *Base Line Survey of Brackish Water Resources and Environmental Situation in Shyamnagar, Satkhira*. Dhaka, Bangladesh: Caritas Development Institute.

Center for Global Change Research. 2015. *Cross-Border Environmental Issues in Southeast Asia in the Context of Regional Integration*.

Cheung, William W., V. Lam, J. Sarmiento, K. Kearney, R. Watson, D. Zeller, and D. Pauly. 2010. "Large-Scale Redistribution of Maximum Fisheries Catch Potential in the Global Ocean under Climate Change." *Global Change Biology* 16 (1): 24–35.

CIFOR (Center for International Forestry Research). 2009. *Can Payments for Environmental Services Reduce Deforestation and Forest Degradation?* Bogor, Indonesia: CIFOR.

———. 2012. "The Context of REDD+ in Vietnam: Drivers, Agents and Institutions." Occasional Paper 75, CIFOR, Bogor, Indonesia.

Coker, R., B. Hunter, J. Rudge, M. Liverani, and P. Hanvoravongchai. 2011. "Emerging Infectious Diseases in Southeast Asia: Regional Challenges to Control. *Lancet* 377 (9765): 599–609.

Dang, Thi Kim Phung, Esther Turnhout, and Bas Arts. 2012. "Changing Forestry Discourses in Vietnam in the Past 20 Years." *Forest Policy and Economics* 25 (1): 31–41.

Dasgupta, Susmita, Craig Meisner, David Wheeler, Nhan Thi Lam, and Khuc Xuyen. 2005. "Pesticide Poisoning of Farm Workers: Implications of Blood Test Results from Vietnam." Policy Research Working Paper 3624, World Bank, Washington, DC.

Duc, D., M. Nhuan, and C. Van Ngoi. 2012. "An Analysis of Coastal Erosion in the Tropical Rapid Accretion Delta of the Red River, Vietnam." *Journal of Asian Earth Sciences* 43 (1): 98–109.

Electricity Regulatory Authority of Vietnam. 2016. Ministry of Industry and Trade.

EU Food and Veterinary Office. 2014. Final Report of an Audit Carried Out in Viet Nam from 18 to 27 February 2014 to Evaluate Controls of Pesticides in Food of Plant Origin Intended for Export to the EU. DG (SANCO) 2014-2177-MR Final. Ref. Ares(2014)1935555-13/06/2014.

FAO (Food and Agriculture Organization of the United Nations). 2014. *The State of World Fisheries and Aquaculture: Opportunities and Challenges*. Rome: FAO.

Fay, Marianne, Stephane Hallegatte, Adrien Vogt-Schilb, Julie Rozenberg, Ulf Narloch, and Tom Kerr. 2015. *Decarbonizing Development: Three Steps to a Zero-Carbon Future*. Washington, DC: World Bank.

Feng, Wei, Nan Zhou, Stephane de la Rue du Can, Michael Bendewald, and Ellen Franconi. 2015. *Building Energy Codes in China: Recommendations for Development and Enforcement*. Chicago, IL: Paulson Institute. http://www.paulsoninstitute.org/wp-content/uploads/2015/10/Building-Code-Roadmap-Oct-2015_vfinal_EN.pdf.

Hagger, Jeremy, and Kathleen Scheep. 2012. "Coffee and Climate Change. Impacts and Options for Adaptation in Brazil, Guatemala, Tanzania and Vietnam." Working Paper Series 4, Natural Resources Institute, Chatham, UK. http://www.nri.org/images/documents/promotional_material/D5930-11_NRI_Coffee_Climate_Change_WEB.pdf.

Khan, A., X. Xun, H. Ahsan, and P. Vineis. 2011. "Climate Change, Sea-Level Rise, & Health Impacts in Bangladesh." *Environment: Science and Policy for Sustainable Development* 53 (5): 37–41.

Khoi, Dang, Chinh Kim, Nhung Nguyen, My Bui, Thinh Pham, Trang Le, Dao Nguyen, and Oanh Pham. 2015. *Vietnam's "Green Agriculture" Strategies and Policies: Closing the Gap between Aspirations and Application*. Hanoi: Center for Agricultural Policy.

Liniger, H., and W. Critchley. 2007. *Where the Land Is Greener: Case Studies and Analysis of Soil and Water Conservation Initiatives Worldwide*. Berne, Switzerland: World Overview of Conservation Approaches and Technologies.

Milder, J. C., S. J. Scherr, and C. Bracer. 2010. "Trends and Future Potential of Payment for Ecosystem Services to Alleviate Rural Poverty in Developing Countries." *Ecology and Society* 15 (2): 4.

Ministry of Science and Technology and Vietnamese Academy of Science and Technology. 2007. *Vietnam Red Data Book Part I and II*. Hanoi: Ministry of Science and Technology and Vietnamese Academy of Science and Technology.

MONRE (Ministry of Natural Resources and Environment). 2005. Vietnam State of Environment Report: Biodiversity. Hanoi: MONRE.

MONRE. 2012. *Climate Change and Sea Level Rise Scenarios for Vietnam*. Hanoi: MONRE.

MONRE and MOT (Ministry of Transport). 2012. *Towards Development of Strategic Directions for Promotion of Environmentally Sustainable Transport in Vietnam by 2020*. Hanoi: MONRE and MOT.

Murakami, H., Y. Wang, H. Yoshimura, R. Mizuta, M. Sugi, E. Shindo, Y. Adachi, S. Yukimoto, M. Hosaka, S. Kusunoki, T. Ose, and A. Kitoh. 2012. "Future Changes in Tropical Cyclone Activity Projected by the New High-Resolution MRIAGCM." *Journal of Climate* 25 (9): 3237–60.

Nguyen Anh Hoanh. 2010. "Comprehensively Studying Geographical Arising and Land Degradation Aiming the Purpose of Reasonably Using Land Resource and Preventing Disaster in Binh-Tri-Thien Region." Doctor of Philosophy Dissertation, Hanoi.

Nguyen, D., J. Renwick, and J. McGregor. 2013. "Variations of Surface Temperature and Rainfall in Vietnam from 1971 to 2010." *International Journal of Climatology* 34 (1): 249–64.

Nguyen, Quang Thuan. 2013. *Vietnam's Environment in Development Process Current Status and Policy*. Hanoi: Vietnam Academy of Social Sciences. http://en.vssr.vass.gov.vn/UserControls/News/pFormPrint.aspx?UrlListProcess=/noidung/tintuc/Lists/chinhtrikinhte&ListId=d9bc5411-997a-47e6-804b-a359a1dd92d2&SiteId=37596567-bc8d-47de-878d-a9d5b872324b&ItemID=222&SiteRootID=2b7991c6-6eaa-456f-96d1-5ad217b4db46.

Pham T., K. Bennet, T. Vu, J. Brunner, N. Le, and D. Nguyen. 2013. "Payments for Forest Environmental Services in Vietnam: From Policy to Practice." Occasional Paper 93, CIFOR, Bogor, Indonesia.

Rohde, Robert, and Richard Muller. 2015. *Air Pollution in China: Mapping of Concentrations and Sources*. Berkeley, CA: Berkeley Earth.

Royal HaskoningDHV. 2013. *Mekong Delta Plan (Under the Vietnam-Netherlands Partnership Arrangement on Water Resources Management and Climate Change)*. Ho Chi Minh City: Royal HaskoningDHV. www.mekongdeltaplan.com.

Schatz, J. J. 2008. "Floods Hamper Health-Care Delivery in Southern Africa." *Lancet* 371 (9615): 799–800.

Siem, Nguyen Tu, and Thai Phien. 1999. *Upland Soils in Vietnam: Degradation and Rehabilitation.* Hanoi: Agriculture Publishing House.

Storch, H., and N. Downes. 2011. "A Scenario-based Approach to Assess Ho Chi Minh City's Urban Development Strategies against the Impact of Climate Change. *Cities* 28 (6): 517–26. doi:10.1016/j.cities.2011.07.002.

Syvitski, J., A. Kettner, I. Overeem, E. Hutton, M. Hannon, G. Brakenridge, J. Day, C. Vörösmarty, Y. Saito, L. Giosan, and R. J. Nicholls. 2009. "Sinking Deltas due to Human Activities." *Nature Geoscience* 2 (10): 681–86.

Thang, P. 2015. "Inputs to Viet Nam 2035: Chapter 6. Sustainable Development." Draft in May 2015. Hanoi.

Thang, P., H. Tuan, N. Hang, and G. Hutton. 2008. "Economic Impacts of Sanitation in Vietnam." Technical Paper, World Bank Water and Sanitation Program, Jakarta.

Trenberth, K., P. Jones, P. Ambenje, R. Bojariu, D. Easterling, A. Klein Tank, D. Parker, F. Rahimzadeh, J. Renwick, M. Rusticucci, B. Soden, and P. Zhai. 2007. "Observations: Surface and Atmospheric Climate Change." In *Climate Change 2007: The Physical Science Basis*, edited by S. Solomon, D. Qin, M. Manning, Z. Chen, M. Marquis, K. Averyt, M. Tignor, and H. Miller, 235–336. Cambridge, UK: Cambridge University Press.

Trương Quang Học. 2012. "Vietnam: Nature, Environment and Sustainable Development." Hanoi: Science and Technology Publishing House.

UNDP (United Nations Development Programme). 2014. *Green Growth and Fossil Fuel Fiscal Policies in Viet Nam.* Hanoi: UNDP.

UN-HABITAT (United Nations Human Settlements Programme). 2007. *State of the World's Cities in 2006/7.* Nairobi, Kenya: UN-HABITAT.

United Nations General Assembly. 2015. "Transforming Our World: The 2030 Agenda for Sustainable Development." Resolution adopted by the General Assembly on 25 September 2015, United Nations General Assembly, New York.

UN-REDD (United Nations Collaborative Programme on Reducing Emissions from Deforestation and Forest Degradation in Developing Countries). 2009. *Detailed Program Outline of UN-REDD Program.* Hanoi: UN-REDD.

USAID (United States Agency for International Development). 2013. *Vietnam's Tropical Forest and Biodiversity Assessment.* USA Foreign Assistance Act, Section 118/119 Report. Washington, DC: USAID.

VASEP (Vietnam Association of Seafood Exporters and Producers). 2010. *Sustainable Aquaculture Development in Southern Provinces.* Ho Chi Minh City: VASEP. http://seafood.vasep.com.vn/seafood/50_3120/sustainable-aquaculture-development-in-southern-provinces.htm.

Vineis, P., Q. Chan, and A. Khan. 2011. "Climate Change Impacts on Water Salinity and Health." *Journal of Epidemiology and Global Health* 1 (1): 5–10.

World Bank. 2008. *Economics of Sanitation in Vietnam, Water and Sanitation Program.* Washington, DC: World Bank.

———. 2010. *Economics of Adaptation to Climate Change: Vietnam Country Study.* Washington, DC: World Bank.

———. 2012. *Inclusive Green Growth: The Pathway to Sustainable Development.* Washington, DC: World Bank.

———. 2013a. *Vietnam Irrigated Agriculture Improvement Project.* Washington, DC: World Bank. http://documents.worldbank.org/curated/en/2013/12/18713829/vietnam-credit-irrigated-agriculture-improvement-project.

———. 2013b. *Turn Down the Heat: Climate Extremes, Regional Impacts, and the Case for Resilience.* Washington, DC: World Bank. http://documents.worldbank.org/curated/en/2013/06/17862361/turn-down-heat-climate-extremes-regional-impacts-case-resilience-full-report.

———. 2015. *Financing Vietnam's Response to Climate Change: Building a Sustainable Future—Key Findings and Recommendations of the Climate Public Expenditures and Investment Review.* Washington, DC: World Bank.

———. 2016. *Transforming Vietnamese Agriculture: Gaining More from Less. Vietnam Development Report.* Washington, DC: World Bank.

World Bank and Australian Aid. 2013. "East Asia Pacific Region Urban Sanitation Review: A Call for Action." http://www.worldbank.org/content/dam/Worldbank/document/EAP/region/eap-urban-sanitation-review-full-report.pdf

World Development Indicators. http://wdi.worldbank.org/tables.

Wunder, S. 2007. "The Efficiency of Payments for Environmental Services in Tropical Conservation." *Conservation Biology* 21 (1): 48–58.

WWF (Worldwide Fund for Nature). 2012. *Wildlife Crime Scorecard: Assessing Compliance with and Enforcement of CITES Commitments for Tigers, Rhinos and Elephants*. Wildlife Crime Scorecard. Geneva: WWF.

6

Promoting Equity and Social Inclusion

Main Messages

Vietnam has made tremendous achievements in human development and social inclusion since the launch of *Đổi Mới* in 1986. It has sustained rapid growth without large increases in inequality, a feat few countries have managed at any level of development. It has made impressive gains in health, with sharp gains in life expectancy, steep reductions in infant and maternal mortality, as well as communicable disease incidence, and rapid expansion of health insurance coverage. The vast majority of children are now in school, and their results on international tests surpass those of many much wealthier nations. The country has also put in place a nascent pension and social safety net system and eased restrictions on the movement of people nationally. These accomplishments have contributed to remarkable progress as Vietnam has launched itself out of the ranks of low-income countries.

The question for Vietnam today is how social policy and institutions can play a role in achieving the country's aspirations over the next 20 years. Doing more of the same will not ensure that Vietnam remains an inclusive society and high-growth economy. It now faces the more complex demands of a transition to a modern industrialized country. Moreover, it faces a changing domestic and external environment: rapid demographic change, a labor market exposed to increased global competition, new health challenges from noncommunicable diseases, and shifting societal expectations. Looking forward to 2035, Vietnam faces a twin agenda on social inclusion: one unfinished and one emerging.

The *unfinished inclusion agenda* is ensuring equality of opportunity for all. While Vietnam has made long strides in lifting living standards since *Đổi Mới*, some groups remain marginalized, and wide gaps in opportunity persist between children in poor and wealthy households. An ethnic minority child is four times more likely than a Kinh child to die before her first birthday, and more than half the children with severe disabilities never attend school. Such exclusion starkly contrasts with the rising fortunes of those at the top. As malnutrition among ethnic minority children remained nearly unchanged, the number of millionaires in Vietnam tripled over the last decade.

The *emerging inclusion agenda* is supporting the growing middle class and an aging population to manage risks and pursue opportunities. As countries move from lower-middle toward upper-middle and ultimately high-income status, social policy must respond to the needs of a growing, increasingly urban, middle class. By 2035, with more than half the population reaching the global middle class, Vietnamese social policy must shift its primary focus to helping the middle class maximize productivity and manage the risks that could set back social and economic progress.

The middle class will have several features. First, it will expect government to deliver quality services and provide citizens with greater voice and choice. Second, it will be subject to new challenges: changing family structures and rapid aging, a growing burden of lifestyle diseases, complex labor markets that require sophisticated labor institutions and regulation, and a higher and differently skilled workforce to meet economic needs. Third, with a more open and marketized economy it will face risks such as unemployment, rising inequality, wage and price shocks, and the need for constant skill upgrading. These create fiscal risks as government seeks to expand the coverage and quality of education to higher levels, widen social security, and provide affordable universal health coverage—all placing new demands on social policies and institutions.

Demographic changes also shape the emerging inclusion agenda. Vietnam is one of the fastest aging populations in the world. Around 2035, the old-age dependency ratio—the number of people 65 years of age or older for every 100 people aged 15–64—will have risen to 21.8 from 9.6 today, and the working-age population will begin to decline in absolute terms. This sharp shift in the country's demographic profile will reverberate throughout the economy and generate new challenges in social services, particularly for health, pensions, and old-age care.

Underpinning both the unfinished agenda and the emerging agenda is the need for a new vision of the role of social policy. One key message of this chapter is that the social sectors are very much *productive* sectors that are central to realizing the goals of knowledge-based and globally competitive upper-middle-income economies. Education is an important contributor to productivity growth. Labor market institutions are a key mechanism to balance productivity growth and societal welfare and thus sustain growth. Robust pension systems can free household consumption to play a central role in the new growth model. Reforming *hộ khẩu* (household registration) policy is critical to realizing the full potential of structural change in Vietnam's economy from low productivity rural employment to formal sector urban work. And an adequate social safety net allows people to take entrepreneurial risks confident that they will not face destitution if their business fails.

If the twin agenda is fulfilled, Vietnam's landscape of social inclusion in 2035 will look very different. For the unfinished inclusion agenda, the vision is as follows:

- *Take down the barriers to opportunity for ethnic minorities.* Targeted initiatives in education, nutrition, and sanitation can close the large gaps in opportunities for ethnic minority children. An approach of experimentation and evaluation, building on new insights from behavioral economics, can develop effective interventions in these areas. Policy actions can also be made more effective through greater voice for ethnic minority individuals.
- *Make people with disabilities full participants in society.* Vietnam has made strong commitments to the inclusion of people with disabilities but lags severely in implementation. Following the example of other countries, it can realize these promises by regularly monitoring commitments and by creating opportunities for people with disabilities and their families to be their own advocates through civil society organizations.
- *Delink the household registration system from access to public services.* At least 5 million Vietnamese lack permanent registration in their place of residence and thus have limited access to public services, including schooling, health care, and such administrative services as registering a

vehicle and applying for a birth certificate. While the force of the system has waned, it remains a source of inequality of opportunity and an effective tax on migration. Phased reform of the *hộ khẩu* system would place all citizens on an equal footing.

- *Reduce gender gaps.* More opportunities are needed for women in public leadership roles and could be created by eliminating gender discrimination in the retirement age and using affirmative action as a short-term measure. Also critical is reducing the imbalance in the sex ratio at birth (SRB), now one of the world's highest, with 114 boys born for every 100 girls. The preference for sons could be reduced through expanding the pension system, reforming the population policy, and campaigning to highlight the value of daughters.

For the emerging inclusion agenda, the vision is as follows:

- *Establish effective representation of workers through independent unions.* Vietnam needs to move toward an industrial relations system suited to a mature market economy, where the interests of workers, employers, and the state are more properly represented in a true bargaining process, following the recent commitments in a Trans-Pacific Partnership (TPP) side agreement. In addition, labor market regulations can better balance the protection of workers with the flexibility needed to promote a vibrant formal sector.
- *Ensure that nearly all children complete upper secondary school with job-relevant skills.* One policy priority will be ending the exam-based allocation of upper secondary school places and replacing it with universal secondary-school attendance. Another is to continuously improve the quality and relevance of what students learn, to help them develop the noncognitive and complex problem-solving skills they need for a competitive labor market.
- *Achieve universal health coverage and reorient the health delivery system.* Ensuring access to good quality health services without imposing financial hardship will entail both reforming the insurance regime and shifting health care from its focus on hospitals and toward high-quality primary care at the center of an integrated system.
- *Expand the pension system to cover most of the population.* Given the challenges of rapid aging, including those without any coverage in the informal sector, will be possible only through a diversified system and a major reform to make it financially sustainable, including raising the retirement age.

The Situation of Social Inclusion in Vietnam

Overall Situation

Vietnam faces many challenges for social inclusion. The country now faces the complex demands of a transition to a modern industrialized economy. Moreover, it faces a changing domestic and external environment: rapid demographic change, a labor market exposed to increased global competition, new health challenges from noncommunicable diseases, and shifting societal expectations. Ethnic minorities, people with disabilities, and migrant workers are disadvantaged and face barriers to sharing in the country's overall success. Access to basic social services has increased dramatically, but service quality is still wanting. Although Vietnam has managed to avoid an explosion of extreme inequality, growing inequities are increasingly a concern. Meanwhile, the growing dangers of climate change and environmental pollution disproportionately impact vulnerable groups, undermining the nation's poverty reduction achievements.

Social Development Trends

Looking forward to 2035, it is expected that economic growth will continue to lift people out of poverty, and economic opportunities, particularly in the private sector, will expand, and migration to urban areas will continue. High returns to education in urban areas will provide one pathway to a better life for millions of Vietnamese. Nevertheless, there are many reasons for concern about the country's social development. Domestic violence remains prevalent across the country, and illicit behavior is common. Traditional social values are weaker than in the past, and social tethers to one's community are fraying. Social trust that was the most important factor for community solidarity and social cohesion is now declining.

Poverty has plummeted in Vietnam over the past two decades, whichever of four poverty measurements are used (figure 6.1). Revisions to methodology and poverty lines (dashed lines) make it difficult to compare trends across years. Apparent upward bumps in poverty reflect points where the General Statistics Office–World Bank and the Ministry of Labour, Invalids, and Social Affairs (MOLISA) poverty lines were increased to reflect rising living standards and an evolving understanding of what constitutes "basic needs" in Vietnam. More than half of Vietnamese lived on less than $1.90 a day in 1993, while today such extreme poverty has been all but eliminated.

FIGURE 6.1 Poverty has plummeted in Vietnam in the past two decades

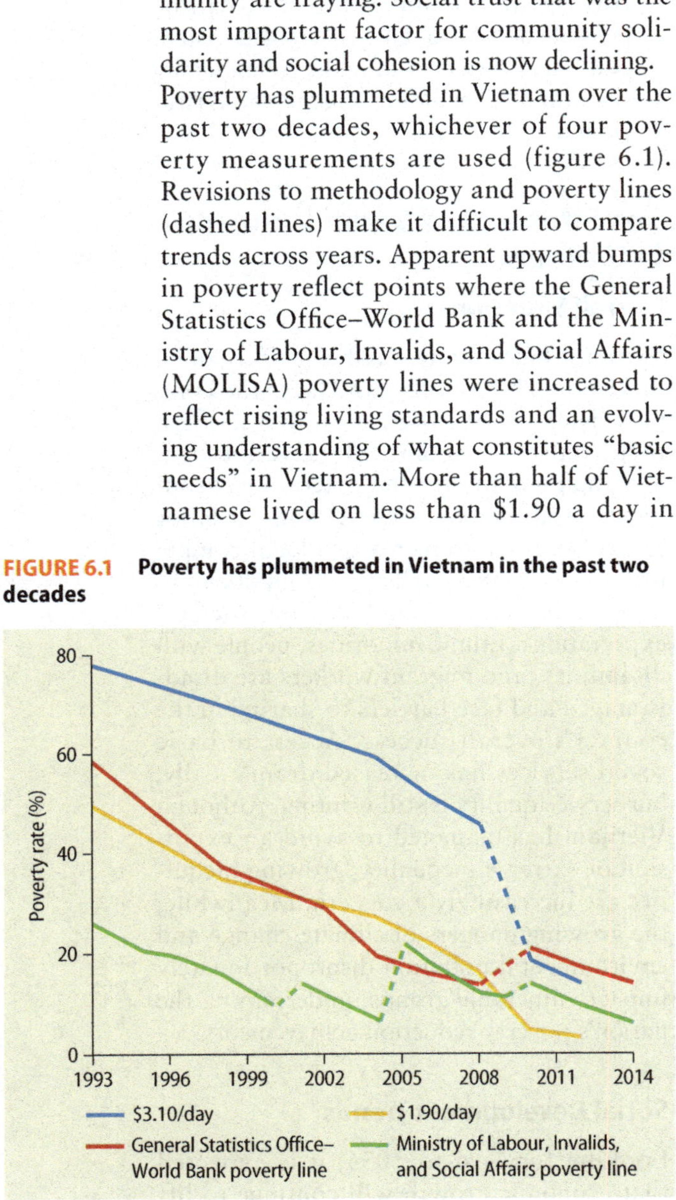

Source: Analysis of Vietnam Living Standards Surveys and Vietnam Household Living Standards Surveys, various years.
Note: Dotted lines indicate periods when substantial changes were made to poverty lines and/or methodology.

Unlike many other countries, Vietnam has achieved rapid growth without large increases in inequality in outcomes (figure 6.2). But a single measure like the Gini is an imperfect summary of broader distributional changes in the country, primarily the gap between those at the bottom and those in the middle of the distribution, and that between the middle and the top. The first gap is largely congruent with the divide between ethnic minorities and the Kinh majority. Ethnic minorities, who make up some 15 percent of the population, have historically been the poorest Vietnamese. Although they have made relative gains in welfare, as the large majority of Kinh have moved above the poverty line, the remaining poor increasingly comprise ethnic minorities. On the second gap, the few data suggest that the number of wealthy in Vietnam has increased sharply in the last decade—by one estimate, the number of U.S. dollar millionaires tripled between 2004 and 2014 and now exceeds 10,000—but that increase is typical of other countries experiencing similar GDP per capita growth during the period.

Vietnam's record on poverty reduction is matched by similar accomplishments across a range of social indicators (table 6.1). These gains stem from the mix of Vietnam's overall economic growth and the government's record of effective service delivery.

FIGURE 6.2 Vietnam has managed to contain the rise in inequality even as its economy grew rapidly

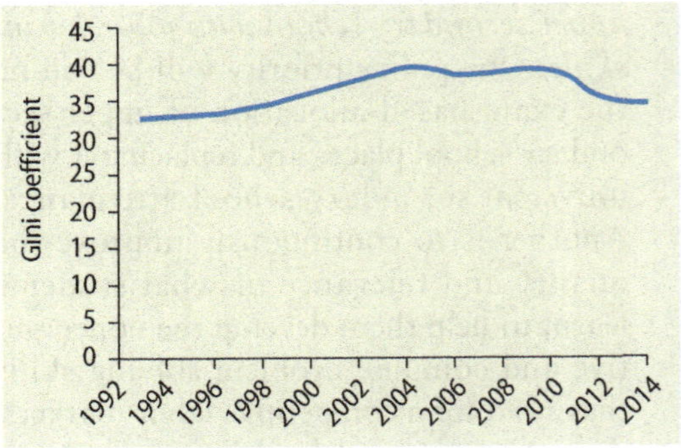

Source: Analysis of income data from Vietnam Living Standards Survey and Vietnam Household Living Standards Survey, various years.

TABLE 6.1 Vietnam has experience dramatic improvements in a range of social indicators

	1993	Circa 2012
Education		
Percentage of 15–24-year-olds who have not completed primary school	24	6
Primary enrollment rate (net)		
Female	87	93
Male	86	92
Lower secondary enrollment rate (net)		
Female	29	83
Male	31	80
Upper secondary enrollment rate (net)		
Female	6	64
Male	8	56
Health		
Infant mortality (per 1,000 live births)	33	19
Under-5 mortality (per 1,000 live births)	45	24
Incidence of stunting (low height for age), Under-5	61	23
Incidence of underweight (low weight for age), Under-5	37	12
Life expectancy at birth (years)	71	76
Access to household infrastructure		
Percentage using electricity as main source of lighting	48	98
Percentage with access to an improved water source	67	95
Rural	60	94
Urban	91	98
Percentage with access to clean water		70
Rural	17	61
Urban	60	90
Percentage with access to sanitation facilities	43	75
Rural	36	67
Urban	68	93
Ownership of assets		
Percentage of households with assets		
TV	22	92
Fan	31	88
Refrigerator	4	49
Car	0	1
Motorbike	11	80

Sources: Vietnam Living Standards Survey 2003, Multiple Indicator Cluster Survey 2011, and Vietnam Household Living Standards Survey 2012.

Subjective measures show that Vietnamese are pleased with public amenities influenced by government policy (figure 6.3). The greatest standouts are schools and affordable housing, where Vietnam ranks sixth and third among 143 surveyed countries. Air and water quality are less satisfactory.

Policy Issues

Vietnam's vision for social inclusion in 2035, across the twin agendas, reflects expected changes across six thematic areas:

Social policy will shift from quantity to quality. While issues of access and coverage will remain, quality will be the leitmotif. In education, this includes a higher performing education system that raises learning outcomes for all students and provides the relevant and increasingly complex skills needed by the economy for progression up the value chain. In health, it refers especially to high-quality services for the poor. In the labor market, the quality of institutions involved in wage bargaining, dispute resolution, and employment protection will become increasingly important.

FIGURE 6.3 Vietnamese citizens express high rates of satisfaction with public amenities

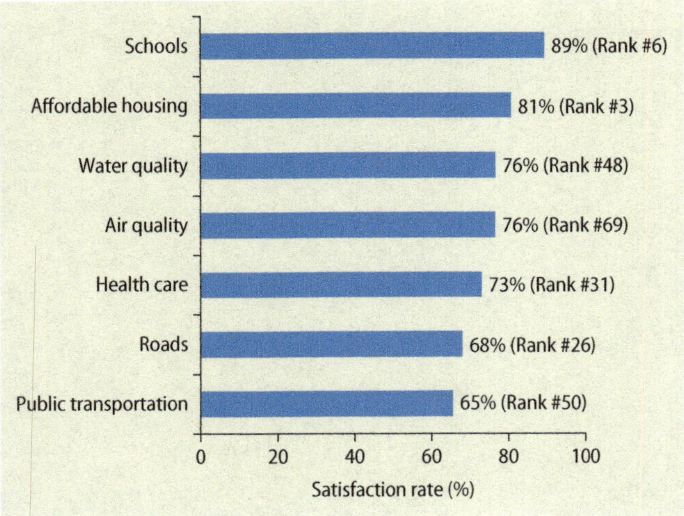

Source: Analysis of Gallup World Poll 2014.
Note: Vietnam's ranking in the survey is noted in parenthesis.

In social protection, the capacity of the system to collect revenue efficiently and provide better client services will demand institutional reform. In each of these domains, better quality will require enhanced mechanisms for accountability of service providers to the public and to the state.

Social service delivery and labor markets will demand greater efficiency. The challenges of meeting growing societal expectations while maintaining fiscal discipline will become more acute and may require more public resources. The bigger challenge is to derive better outcomes through efficiency gains—thus the need for robust systems to monitor human development outcomes relative to the costs of service provision.

The state's role in the social sectors will change. As the economy, labor market, and social services evolve, the state will need to diversify its functions. In some policy areas, it will need to do more (for example, strengthening the social safety net and financial support in old age). In others it will need to shift its role more to setting and enforcing the "rules of the game" and letting market forces play a stronger role (for instance, in labor markets and private provision of social services). In other areas, the state may need to retreat to functions more typical of a mature market economy (for example, reorienting *hộ khẩu* to a simple population registration function, and allowing independent worker representation in industrial relations). State–private sector relations will also become more complex: the state will continue to play a key financing role but provision should migrate more to the private sector. This will require the state to recalibrate its functions across the social sectors between provider, financier, and regulator.

A more diverse range of stakeholders will balance their interests and build social consensus as the country deepens sectoral reforms. The successes in Vietnam's first wave of reforms in social sectors have produced a new set of vested interests, which are often central to further reforms but may also resist them. The challenges of social sector reform require careful balancing of the interests of well-connected and vocal "insiders" and those of dispersed and less influential "outsiders."

Social policies will be reoriented to rapidly changing demographics. The dramatic falling fertility, increased longevity, greater mobility of people, urbanization, and rapidly shifting burden of disease from communicable to noncommunicable diseases are all reshaping the demographic landscape. Aging will accelerate, the working-age population will start to shrink, as will the size of cohorts of children entering school, and demand for new types of health services will escalate. New pressures will arise: old age financial protection and long-term care, higher-productivity workers as the demographic dividend fades, and new approaches to urban management to ensure livable and harmonious cities.

Finally, as Vietnam seeks to achieve its vision for social policy in 2035, it will need to keep social spending sustainable. This is one of the defining challenges of fiscal and macroeconomic management in middle-income countries. Global experience suggests that the social sectors will account for a growing share of public spending. Nearly all countries that have transitioned from low to upper-middle income devote a growing share of public spending to social sectors. In the initial phases, spending growth is often focused on education as the system expands coverage to a growing youth cohort. But as countries grow and age, spending on health and social security almost invariably increases as a share of total public spending.

The Unfinished Agenda: Marginalized Groups and Equality of Opportunity

Equity is a deeply held value of the Vietnamese people. In the nation's Declaration of Independence, Ho Chi Minh said, "All the peoples on earth are equal from birth." The Preamble to the Constitution sets the goal of "a prosperous people and a strong, democratic, equitable and civilized country," and Article 50 stipulates "the State shall create equal opportunities for citizens to enjoy social welfare." Surveys of Vietnamese citizens find widespread concern with inequality.

Vietnam's move away from collectivism and toward a market economy has created incentives that allow talented, entrepreneurial, and hard-working individuals to flourish but also inevitably lead to some inequality in outcomes. Inequality of outcomes can be understood as the result of interaction between opportunities, effort, and luck. Opportunities are individual circumstances at birth outside our control that influence outcomes. Examples include gender, ethnic group, place of birth, and the income or education levels of parents. Effort refers to action on the part of an individual. Luck also plays a part.

While inequality of outcomes is expected in a market economy, inequality of opportunity is inherently unfair and incompatible with Vietnamese ideals. Equality of opportunity prevails when the outcomes are independent of circumstances at birth—a "level playing field." Profound inequality of opportunity remains in Vietnam, particularly for three marginalized groups—ethnic minorities, people with disabilities, and urban migrants—which collectively include one in four Vietnamese.

Ethnic Minorities

Situation

The Constitution strongly commits to equality for ethnic minorities. Article 5 proclaims all ethnicities to be equal, prohibits discrimination by ethnicity, asserts the right of ethnic minorities to use their own languages, and commits the state to implementing a policy of comprehensive development for ethnic minorities. Other parts of the Constitution specifically prioritize ethnic minorities in policies for health care and education.

Members of Vietnam's 52 ethnic minorities have made substantial gains in welfare over time but remain much more likely to be poor than members of the Kinh and Hoa ethnic majority (figure 6.4).[1] Using the GSO–WB poverty line, in 2014 the poverty rate had fallen to 6.3 percent among the Kinh and Hoa while standing at 57.8 percent among ethnic minorities. Poverty rates for minority groups range from 38 percent among the San Diu to 93 percent among the Hmong (figure 6.5).

FIGURE 6.4 Vietnam's 52 ethnic minorities are much more likely to be poor than the Kinh–Hoa ethnic majority

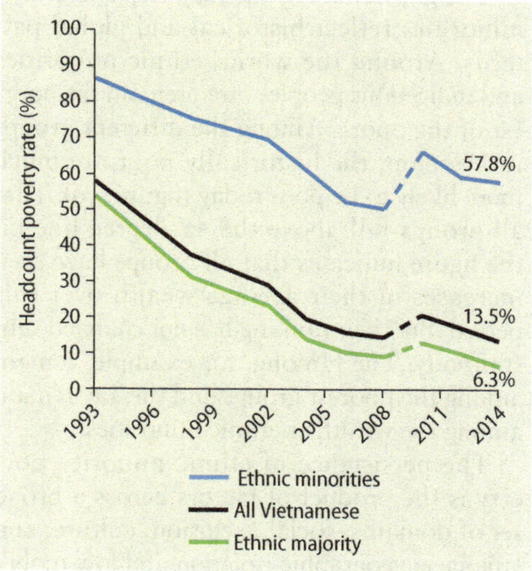

Source: Calculations based on the Vietnam Household Living Standards Survey.
Note: General Statistics Office–World Bank poverty line. Dotted lines represent periods when substantial changes were made to survey or poverty methodologies. The poverty rates before 2010 are not comparable to the rates of 2010 and later.

FIGURE 6.5 Poverty rates vary by ethnic group, 2009

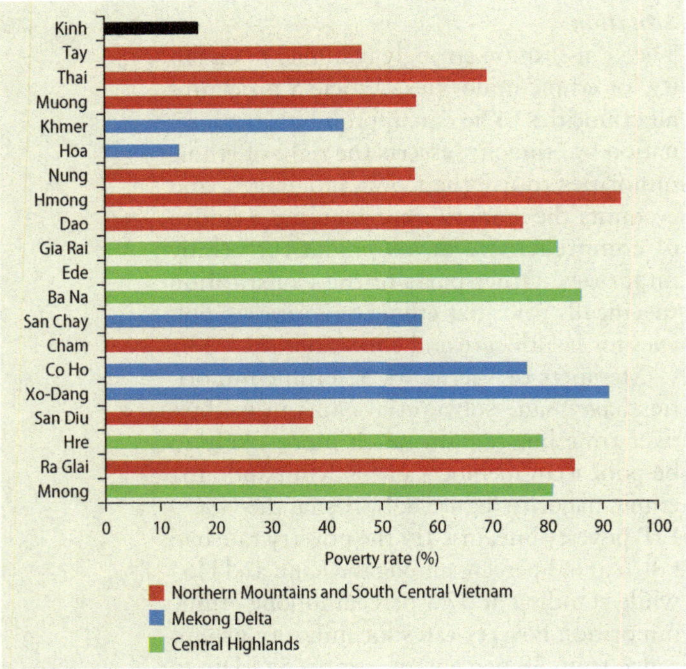

Source: Calculations based on the Vietnam Household Living Standards Survey.
Notes: Poverty rates using the General Statistics Office–World Bank poverty line. Only the largest groups in Vietnam are represented, in order of decreasing size from top to bottom. Colors indicate primary geographic region of each group. Estimates are based on poverty mapping methods using the 2009 Population and Housing Census.

FIGURE 6.6 The historically poor in Vietnam are much more likely to be poor today

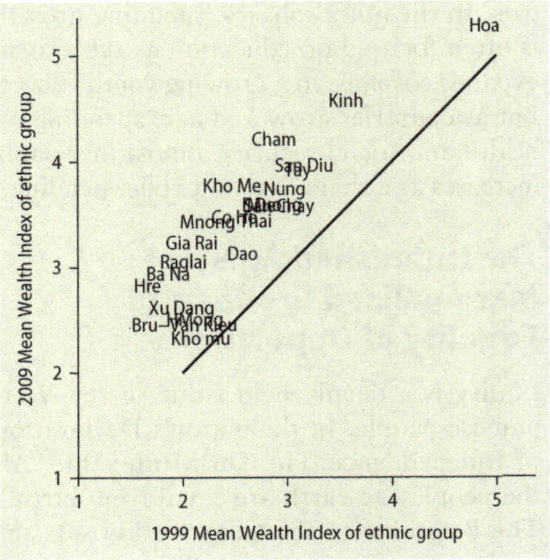

Source: Calculations based on the Population and Housing Censuses of 1999 and 2009.
Note: By ethnic group with at least 0.5 percent of the national population in 2009.

The gaps between the majority and ethnic minorities reflect historical and global patterns. Around the world, ethnic minorities and indigenous peoples often remain the poorest of the poor.[2] Among the different groups in Vietnam, the historically poor are much more likely to be poor today (figure 6.6). That all groups fall above the 45-degree line on the figure indicates that all groups have seen increases in their average wealth over this period. But their ranking has not changed substantially. The Hmong, for example, remain among the poorest groups and the Tay remain among the wealthier ethnic minorities.

The persistence of ethnic minority poverty is the product of factors across a broad set of domains: social exclusion, culture, and language; geographic isolation and low mobility; limited access to high-quality land; low education levels; and poor health and nutrition, often reflecting limited access to services.[3]

The first set of factors consists of social exclusion as well as cultural and language barriers, which may prevent ethnic minorities from better integrating into society. Language constraints create difficulty for ethnic minorities in accessing public services and information. Ethnic minority women are reluctant to use free services. There may also be cultural barriers to economic advancement, such as social pressure against excess economic accumulation and cultural perceptions of social obligations (VASS 2009 and World Bank 2009b). More recent qualitative work has emphasized the commonalities between Kinh–Hoa and ethnic minority attitudes (World Bank 2012c).

The importance of language as a barrier may be fading, with a rapid rise in self-reported literacy among ethnic minorities. In 2009, 94 percent of those aged 10–14 were reported as literate, compared with 74 percent of those 30–34. This matches trends in schooling: in 2012, 89 percent of ethnic minority individuals aged 15–20 had completed primary school, compared with just 45 percent in 1989. Due to the successful push to expand primary education, language will likely be much less of a barrier for ethnic minorities in the future.

Attitudes toward and treatment of the ethnic minorities are related barriers. Studies in many countries have shown that unconscious or implicit biases, usually favoring one's own group, are pervasive among all human beings. Thus even Kinh who do not see themselves as prejudiced may have unconscious biases that affect the way they treat ethnic minorities. Qualitative work has found that many Kinh hold negative stereotypes toward ethnic minorities and view them as "backward." For example, one survey by the Institute of Ethnic Minority Affairs found that the staff of banks in Dak Lak believed that Ede were not creditworthy for loans (World Bank 2009b).

A second set of factors is geographic isolation, limited market access, and disconnection from economic growth centers, particularly for those living in the Northern Mountains.[4] One study found that location accounts for 21 percent of the overall difference in consumption levels between minority and majority households. But geography by itself has only limited explanatory power, as ethnic minority groups in the Mekong Delta and Central Highlands regions—which are less isolated and more economically connected—still have high poverty rates, while the Kinh in the Northern Mountains have much lower poverty (map 6.1).

MAP 6.1 Geography alone does not explain poverty in Vietnam

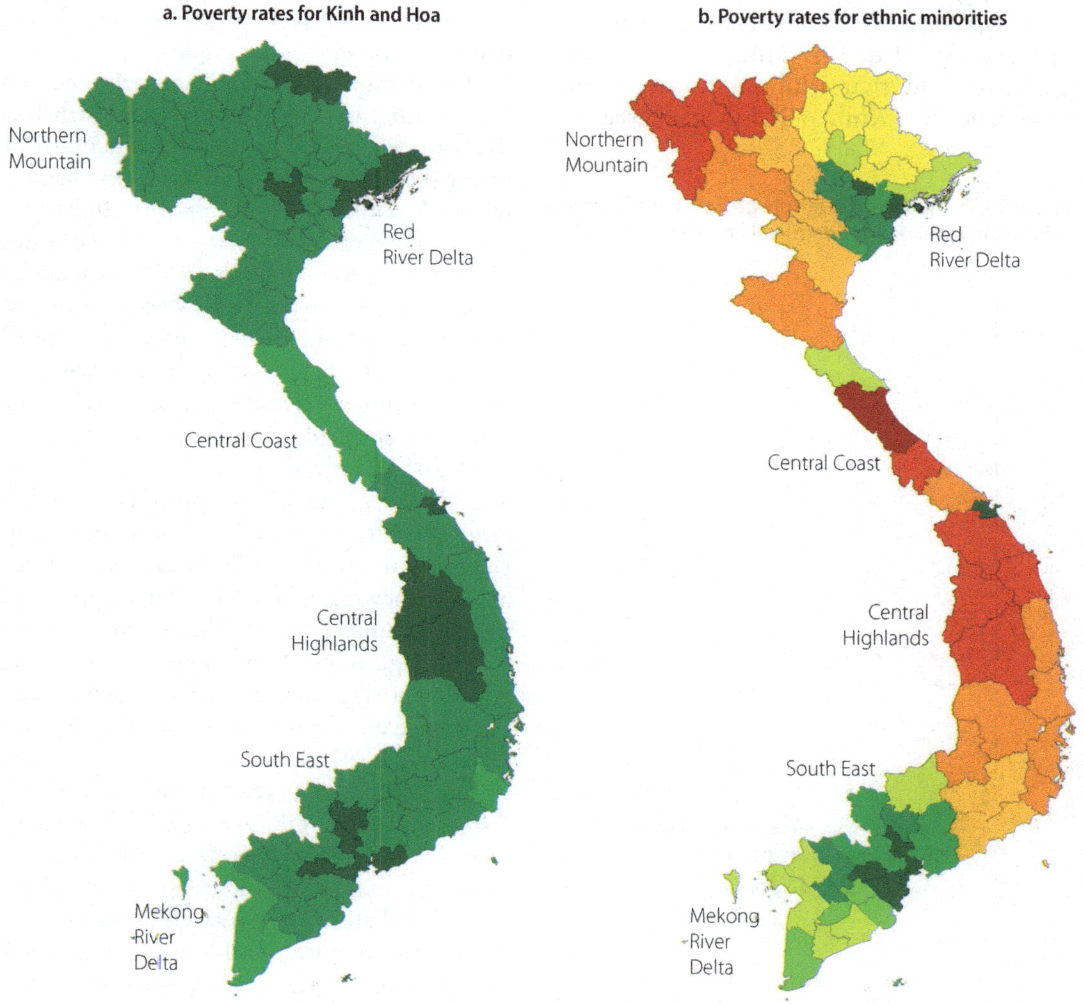

Source: World Bank 2012c. Estimates are based on the Population and Housing Census 2009 and the Vietnam Household Living Standards Survey 2010.

Geographic movement allows people to integrate with a country's broader economic success. Ethnic groups with higher migration rates are economically more successful (figure 6.7). Geographic movement allows people to integrate in a country's broader economic success, but ethnic minorities migrate at half the rate of Kinh-Hoa (Coxhead, Nguyen, and Linh 2015). This may stem from limited information—particularly for those in mountainous and remote areas—higher costs due to distance, potential discrimination by employers, thin migrant networks (as few ethnic minorities are already in cities), less education, and limited language ability. But these factors are in flux. It is likely that by 2035 migration will continue rising among ethnic minorities, increasingly offering a pathway out of poverty.

A third set of factors relates to limited access to good quality land. Surveys consistently show that ethnic minorities hold more land than Kinh and Hoa (in aggregate, annual cropland, perennial cropland, and forestry land), but their cropland is largely unirrigated and of low quality, unlike Kinh-Hoa land. Historically, land among many communities has been held communally, and even following the transition to a market-based land system in 1993, some ethnic households have not been willing to sell. Much forest land—the bulk of land held by many ethnic minorities—has not been formally allocated, rendering it hard for households to use land as collateral or sell their land-use rights (VASS 2009). Finally, agricultural extension services for ethnic minorities in mountainous areas are often inappropriate, having been designed for lowland cultivation (Jamieson, Le, and Rambo 1998; Oxfam and Action Aid 2008; World Bank 2009b). All these factors help keep ethnic minority households dependent on low-value staple crops.

FIGURE 6.7 Individual ethnic groups with higher migration rates are economically more successful

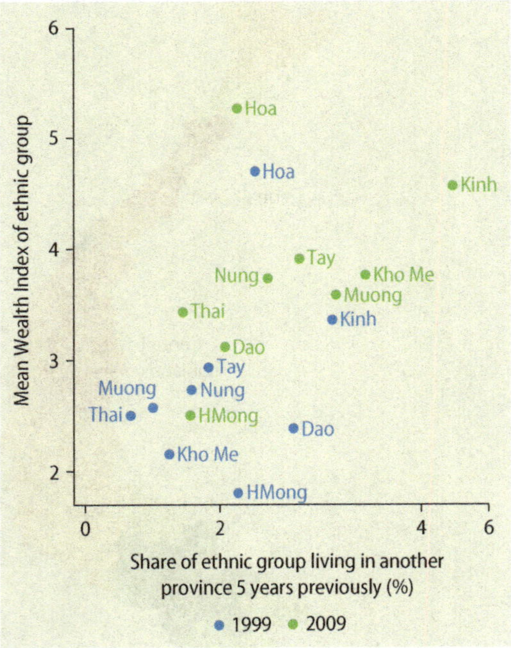

Source: Calculations based on the Population and Housing Censuses 1999 and 2009.
Note: By ethnic group with at least 0.5 percent of the national population in 2009. Blue dots correspond to 1999, and green dots correspond to 2009.

A fourth set of factors is related to education. Ethnic minority children are still less likely to be enrolled in school, particularly at upper secondary level, and education attainment is low among ethnic minority adults educated when ethnic minority enrollment rates were much lower. In 1989, just 20 percent of ethnic minority 6-year-olds were enrolled in school and only a bare majority were enrolled at age 10—the peak age for attendance. Few attended lower secondary, and only a very tiny share enrolled in upper secondary.

By 2012 nearly all ethnic minority children ages 7–9 were enrolled in primary school, a large majority attended lower secondary, and roughly one-third enrolled in upper secondary. But they lagged the Kinh's near-universal primary completion rate (figure 6.8).

Although some ethnic minorities start late, enrollment rates through primary school and the first years of lower secondary through age 13 are not far below those of the Kinh. But from age 14 (the last year of lower secondary) a steep fall-off in ethnic minority enrollment begins, and relatively few children from ethnic minorities make the jump to upper secondary.

Enrolled ethnic minority children perform worse than majority children, scoring lower on mathematics and reading tests than Kinh children (figure 6.9a). The disparities are very large before children start primary school. Language appears to be an important factor in the poorer performance (Glewwe, Chen, and Katare 2012). Despite their lower starting point, ethnic minority students show substantial learning gains—particularly in Vietnamese language (figure 6.9b).

A final set of factors consists of nutrition and health. Poor nutrition in the first years of life can have strong effects on learning and on later-life outcomes. The most important measure of malnutrition is the proportion of under-5 children who are stunted.[5] Stunting generally reflects malnutrition as a consequence of chronic illness or failure to receive adequate nutrition over a long period.

FIGURE 6.8 Ethnic minority children lag the Kinh's near-universal primary completion rate

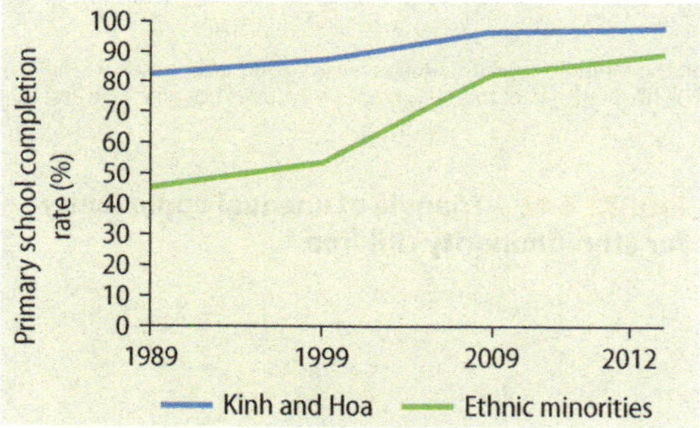

Source: Calculations based on the Vietnam Household Living Standards Survey 2012 and the Population and Housing Censuses 1989, 1999, and 2009.
Note: The lines represent those ages 15–20 years completing primary school in 1989, 1999, and 2009 for the Kinh and the Hoa versus the ethnic minorities as a whole.

Ethnic minorities have seen little improvement in the under-5 malnutrition rates and worsening infant mortality rates. Malnutrition rates in 2014 were twice as high among ethnic minorities as among the Kinh and Hoa (figure 6.10a). Infant mortality rates are low for the country's income level but are four times as high among ethnic minorities (figure 6.10b).

Three policy directions

Vietnam has pursued many programs and policies to promote ethnic minority development. These programs can be categorized by their form of targeting: by location, by household economic status, and by ethnic minority (Nguyen and Baulch 2007). Many programs targeted at poor locations and to poor households disproportionately target ethnic minority households de facto because of their high poverty rates and location in poorer areas. Many of the area-based programs focus on rural infrastructure, which research in Vietnam and worldwide has shown to be effective at reducing poverty in remote areas, where many ethnic minorities live. The analysis thus far suggests several areas of focus for a long-term agenda to boost the economic prospects of ethnic minorities.

Policy should be driven by the insight that, over the long term, migration will likely be a pathway to economic integration for many ethnic minorities. Vietnamese language

FIGURE 6.9 Ethnic minority children score lower on tests than Kinh but show large gains with time in school

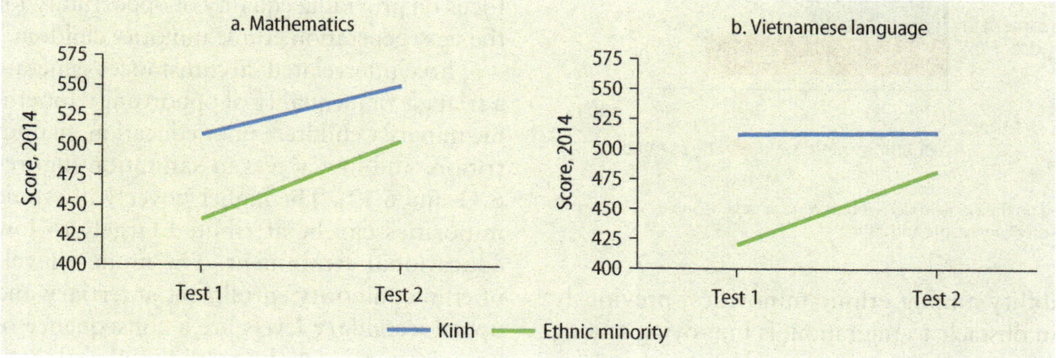

Source: Rolleston 2014.
Note: Scores represent successive tests in grade 5. Young Lives, a longitudinal study, was conducted in Ethiopia, India, Peru, and Vietnam.

FIGURE 6.10 Large gaps in child health and nutrition by ethnicity persist

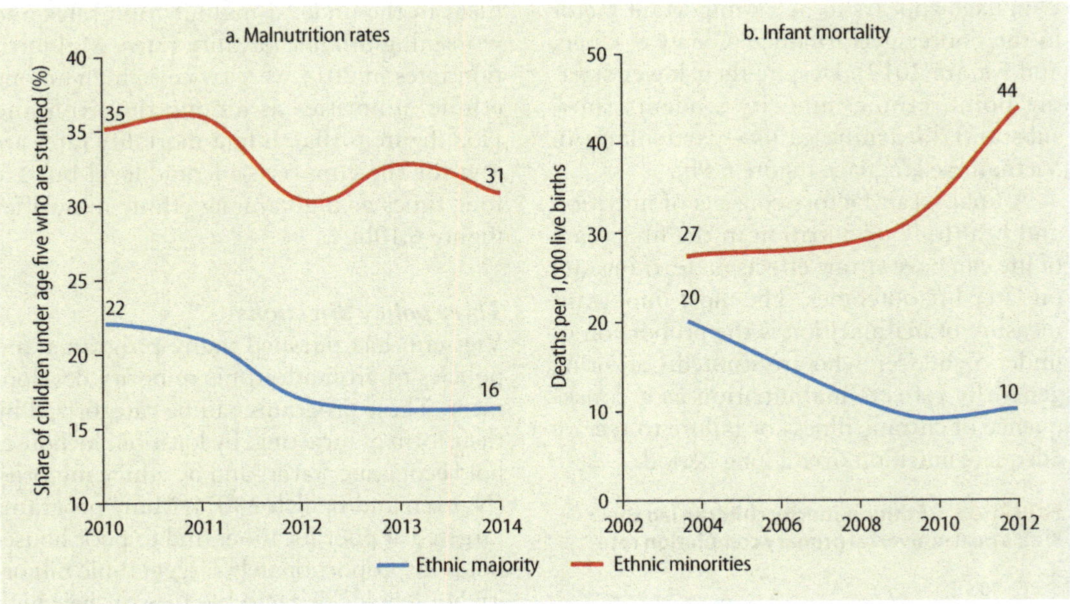

Source: Calculations based on the National Institute of Nutrition Surveys and the Multiple Indicator Cluster Survey 2006, 2011, and 2014 reports.
Note: For the nutrition figures the ethnic majority group includes only the Kinh, while in the infant mortality figures it includes both the Kinh and Hoa.

FIGURE 6.11 Ethnic minority children face inequality of opportunity, 2010–14

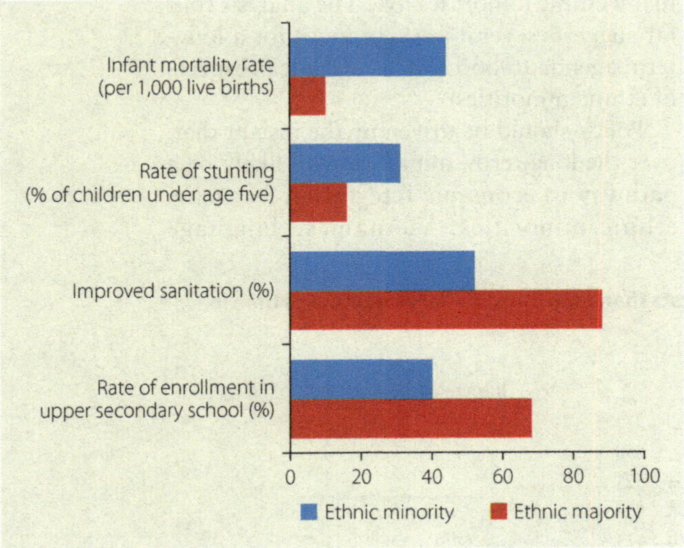

Source: Calculations based on the Vietnam Household Living Standards Survey 2014 and the Multiple Indicator Cluster Survey 2011 and 2014.

ability among ethnic minorities, previously an obstacle to migration, is improving among the younger generation, and over time ethnic minorities will develop migrant networks that will ease the path of future migrants.

FIGURE 6.12 Triangle of unequal opportunity for ethnic minority children

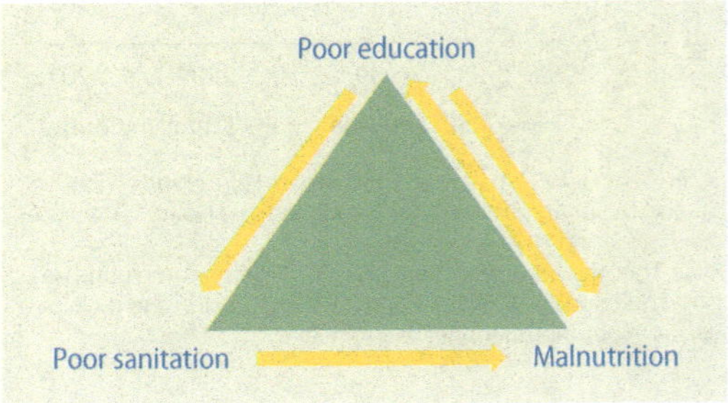

The prospect of migration points to a need to focus on providing equality of opportunity for the next generation ethnic minority children.

Three interrelated circumstances generate a triangle of inequality of opportunity for ethnic minority children: poor education, malnutrition, and low access to sanitation (figures 6.11 and 6.12). The higher poverty of ethnic minorities can be attributed largely to low educational attainment. The modest levels of ethnic minority enrollment at tertiary and upper secondary levels are a consequence of many factors, including childhood malnutrition, which is in turn driven by a set of causes including poor sanitation. Completing the cycle, children who grow up in poor households are much more likely to drop out of school early, be malnourished, and lack adequate sanitation. In these three areas, policy interventions could close the opportunity gap.

Improving education access for ethnic minority children is the first policy priority to boost equality of opportunity. Ethnic minority children do learn in school, but they start school less prepared to learn and drop out earlier. Few go on to upper secondary school and a very few attend university. These issues could be addressed by expanding current government initiatives. High-quality early childhood education programs can boost preparation, particularly for ethnic minority children. Placing teaching assistants who know the local language in the first few years of primary school can ease the transition for children who do not learn Vietnamese at home. And financially supporting ethnic minority children can raise attendance rates in upper secondary school.

Improving nutrition is a second priority. Early childhood nutrition has substantial effects on early cognitive development and readiness to learn in school. Despite existing programs, high rates of malnutrition persist among ethnic minority children. Two of the most important factors in undernutrition are inadequate knowledge about the benefits of exclusive breastfeeding, complementary feeding practices, and micronutrients, and the lack of time women have for childcare and for themselves during pregnancy.

The third policy priority is sanitation. A major driver of malnutrition is lack of improved sanitation facilities. In Vietnam, stunting rates are high precisely among the ethnic minority communities that are most likely to lack improved sanitation facilities (Quattri and Smets 2014). Poor access to sanitation is also one factor behind the high levels of infant mortality among ethnic minorities. A national sanitation program can achieve universal usage of improved sanitation. Policies, targets, and incentives under such a future program should be aligned to promote community-wide behavior change, including targeted support for the poor, such as low-interest household financing and/or targeted output-based subsidies. Affordable and accessible toilets provided through local private suppliers can move more people from open defecation and unimproved sanitation to improved sanitation. Community mobilization and behavioral-change communications can support a new social norm within communities.

In developing education, sanitation, and nutrition programs for ethnic minority children—and programs to address ethnic minority poverty more generally—the government could benefit from experimenting, monitoring, and evaluating, since in many cases the evidence on "what works" is thin. Pilot approaches could be carefully evaluated before programs are expanded to scale. And for all three points of the triangle, initiatives could draw on promising new insights from behavioral economics. Choices about sending children to school, feeding infants, and constructing latrines are determined by a variety of factors other than cost–benefit calculations. Interventions in all three areas that seek to "nudge" behavior can be effective and cost-efficient.

Policies and programs also need to tackle prejudice and help ethnic minority voices be heard. Although the legal framework is adequate in recognizing equality of status between ethnic minorities and Kinh, prejudice against minorities is still common (World Bank 2009a). Education can be the basic platform, focusing on appreciating and respecting the diversity of Vietnamese ethnicity and culture.

Conspicuously lacking is a strong ethnic minority presence in the Committee for Ethnic Minority Affairs. Local authorities, even in mainly ethnic minority areas, are typically Kinh. Vietnam can benefit from having ethnic minority civil society organizations take part in developing and implementing policy.

People with Disabilities

Like ethnic minorities, people with disabilities lack full opportunity. Vietnam has a substantial population of people with disabilities, in part a legacy of conflict. They face obstacles in accessing transport, education, health care, social assistance, infrastructure, culture and sports, and information and communications (NCCD 2010). In Vietnam, disability is highly correlated with poverty (Mont and Nguyen 2011).

People with disabilities merit particular consideration in a vision of social inclusion for several reasons. First, the number of people with disability is likely to increase rapidly as the old-age population expands. Second, as Vietnam reaches upper-middle income, it will face rising expectations on the part of people with disability and their families for greater inclusion. Third, given its rising level of resources, it should realize its commitment to inclusion for people with disabilities.

The government has made a number of commitments to advancing the rights of people with disabilities. Foremost among these are the Law on Persons with Disabilities, passed in 2010, and the United Nations (UN) Convention on the Rights of Persons with Disabilities, which Vietnam ratified in 2015. Protection of people with disabilities is also enshrined in the Vietnamese Constitution. Vietnam's Law on Persons with Disabilities and the Convention are based on similar principles. The Convention's purpose is "to promote, protect and ensure the full and equal enjoyment of all human rights and fundamental freedoms by all persons with disabilities, and to promote respect for their inherent dignity." The Law on Persons with Disabilities guarantees the following rights to people with disabilities:

- Participate on an equal basis in social activities.
- Live independently and integrate into the community.
- Enjoy exemption from or reduction of certain contributions to social activities.
- Be provided with health care, functional rehabilitation, education, vocational training, employment, legal assistance, access to public facilities, means of transport, information technology, and cultural, sports, tourist, and other services suitable to their forms and degrees of disability.

Many people with disabilities around the world have been hidden from society and sometimes segregated in residential institutions and special schools. But global policy has recently shifted toward including them in society, making them subjects of the law with clearly defined rights rather than objects of charity. This approach recognizes that disability is the result not of impairment but of the interaction between a person and his or her environment. For example, a person in a wheelchair might have difficulties finding a job not because of her condition but because of such barriers as staircases in the workplace. A child with disability might have difficulties going to school due to the attitudes of teachers and school officials who cannot adapt to students with particular needs. Closely related is the understanding that there is tremendous diversity in the set of situations that people with disability face, depending both on the domain and severity of their disability and the environment in which they live.

Disability-related issues

The above commitments and guarantees as implemented are too wide for full treatment here. The discussion focuses on four issues: incidence, attitudes to people with disabilities, access to education, and jobs.

The incidence of disability among those age 5 and older is substantial and rising, with estimates ranging from 7.8 percent (analysis of 2009 census) to 15.3 percent (2006 VHLSS) (VHLSS 2006). Separate administrative recognition of persons with disability is made by commune-level examination councils, with a much more thorough assessment than is possible in the census or VHLSS. The census data are used for most of the analysis in this report because they are the most recent nationally representative data on disability and allow fine-grained analysis, though the census disability classification has limitations.

Disability rates are low for children and young adults but rise rapidly after age 40, and particularly after age 65. Two-thirds of those at age 80 report having some form of disability (figure 6.13). The combination of age-specific-disability patterns and the aging of Vietnam's population means that this fraction will rise over the coming decades, to 12 million people

FIGURE 6.13 Disability rises quickly after age 65, with two-thirds of those age 80 reporting some form of disability

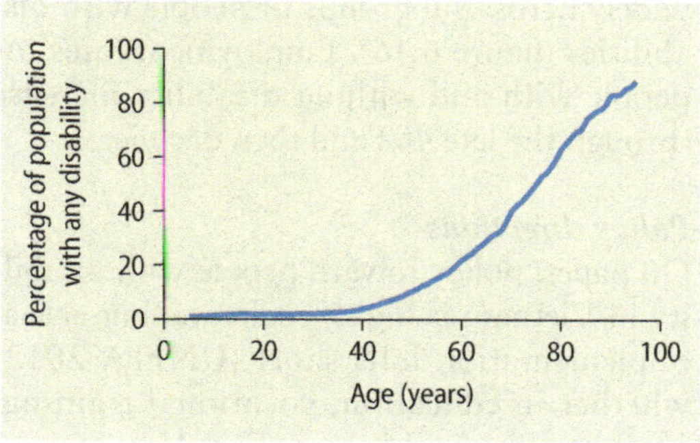

Source: Calculations based on the Population and Housing Census 2009.

FIGURE 6.14 Wealthier countries are more likely to report being a good place to live for people with intellectual disabilities, 2014

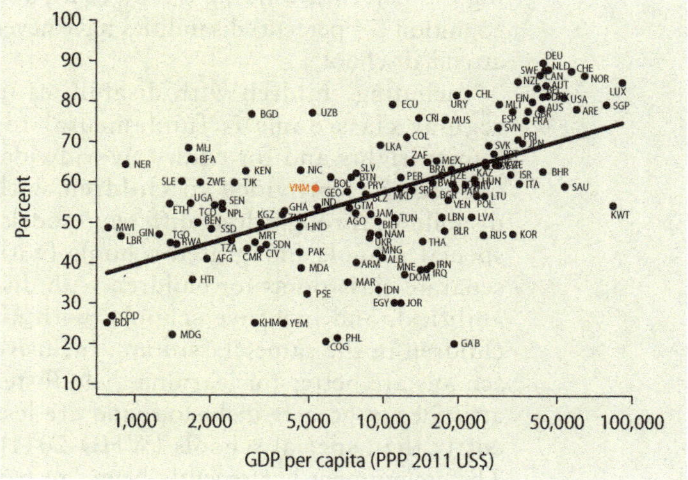

Source: Gallup World Poll 2014.

FIGURE 6.15 Most children with severe disabilities in Vietnam never attend school, 2009

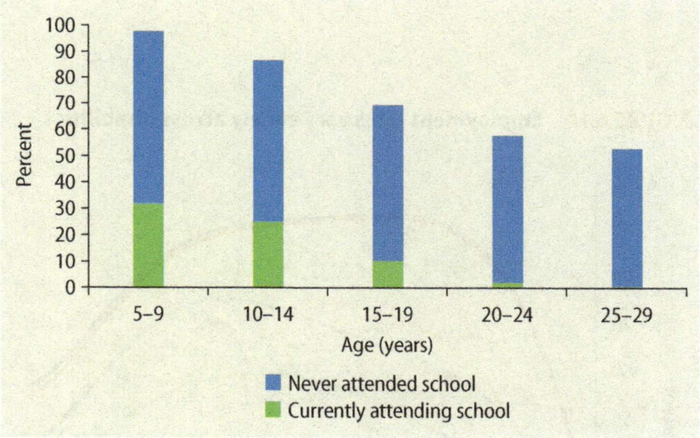

Source: Calculations based on the Population and Housing Census 2009.

(12.3 percent of the over-6 population) by 2035 under one scenario.[6] The projected surge in the older population will also mean a larger population of people with disability.

Limited research suggests that attitudes toward people with disabilities in Vietnam have generated exclusion but may be becoming more conducive to greater inclusion. A detailed qualitative survey in Thai Binh, Quang Nam, Da Nang, and Dong Nai found that attitudes toward people with disability were generally negative and that people with disability were often excluded from local activities (Le, Khuat, and Nguyen 2008). It documented discrimination in schools and at work, among other places.[7] In a more recent survey, 93 percent responded affirmatively when asked if they would like to make friends with a person with disability (Kham 2014). But this survey also showed evidence of the attitudes in the earlier study: just 43 percent said that they would work alongside a person with disabilities.

"Is the city or area where you live a good place or not a good place to live for people with intellectual disabilities?" Affirmative replies to that Gallup World Poll question, when plotted against gross domestic product (GDP) per capita, show that people in wealthier countries are more likely to report that where they live is a good place for people with disabilities (figure 6.14). Vietnam ranks above other countries at its income level but substantially below wealthier countries.

Children with disabilities who do not attend school are very likely to face real barriers to being part of society at later ages. Whether children with disabilities attend school indicates the degree to which people with disabilities are integrated into society. Most children with severe disabilities in Vietnam never attend school (figure 6.15). More than 53 percent of children age 10–14 with severe vision disability and nearly three-quarters of those 10–14 with hearing (73 percent), walking (72 percent), and cognition (74 percent) disabilities have never attended school.

Including children with disabilities in regular classrooms is fundamental for human rights and for equity. Worldwide, education is provided to children with disabilities through three different models: special schools, integrated schools (with separate classrooms for children with disabilities), and inclusive schools (with all children in the same classroom). Inclusive schools are better for learning, help foster attitudes of greater inclusion, and are less costly than special schools (WHO 2011). The government has recently begun to pay more attention to providing teacher training and moved toward an inclusive school approach.

Employment offers people with disabilities the opportunity to fully participate in society and to develop their talents and capabilities. They sometimes face obstacles, including discrimination by employers and inaccessible work environments. Employment rates vary widely across subgroups of people with disabilities (figure 6.16). Employment rates for people with and without disability increase through the late 40s and then decline.

FIGURE 6.16 Employment rates vary widely across disabilities

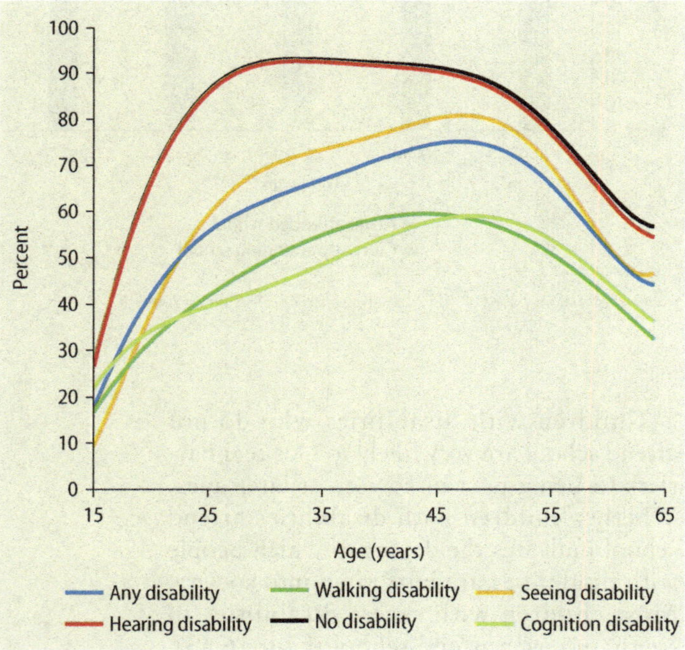

Source: Calculations based on the Population and Housing Census 2009.

Policy directions

On paper, policy toward people with disability in Vietnam is highly inclusive, but actual implementation falls short (UNFPA 2012) whether in education, vocational training, employment, health care, social assistance, cultural and sport activities, or transport and public accessibility. The broad agenda for disability policy is thus to fulfill the commitments across all the areas that the country has already made in its laws, the Constitution, and the UN Convention.

Looking to 2035, creating a mechanism to regularly monitor implementation (a commitment under the Convention) can be a practical step. The National Coordinating Council on Disability (NCCD) study, last conducted in 2010, should be updated once every year or two, including a regular, comparable assessment of attitudes toward people with disabilities. Better monitoring can help the Council and other advocates maintain long-term focus.

Creating space for civil society organizations for people with disabilities could foster implementation. In other countries, people with disabilities and their families advocate through their own organizations. These campaigns have guided governments on policy implementation and ensured follow-through on commitments.

Migrants

Migrants are essential in Vietnam's economic transformation. The movement of people out of areas with less opportunity to places with greater possibilities for more economically productive lives is an important driver of economic growth, generating "agglomeration effects" from greater production density.

An increasing number of Vietnamese are migrants. According to the 2009 census, 4.3 percent of the population over age five (3.4 million people) lived in a different province from five years earlier, up from 2.5 percent in 1989 and 2.9 percent in 1999. An additional 2.2 percent of the population, accounting for 1.7 million people, moved across districts within a province. In urban areas, 7.7 percent of the population consisted of interprovincial migrants, with 12.5 percent of urban households having at least one migrant.

Hộ khẩu policy and impacts

Hộ khẩu (household registration system) restricts access to services for some urban migrants, reducing equality of opportunity and slowing structural transformation. It was introduced in 1957 explicitly to restrain the movement of migrants into cities.[8] The essential component is a household registration booklet (*sổ hộ khẩu*) that records details of all household members. Originally, the system was tied to the ration system, and before 1986 a combination of government employment policies and the link to rations tightly controlled migration.

The 2007 Law on Residence eased *hộ khẩu* restrictions. The law lessened the requirements for temporary residents applying for permanent registration in centrally administered cities and removed geographic restrictions for registration of births, the requirement of employment for the registration, and the requirement that a letter of release be obtained from the migrant's original commune or district. But local authorities differ in interpreting and enforcing the law. And *hộ khẩu* remains important through its link to access to public services and as a requirement for many administrative procedures (Marx and Fleischer 2010).

But in 2014 *hộ khẩu* restrictions were strengthened through further amendments to the Law on Residence. Among other measures, applicants for permanent residence in four cities—Ho Chi Minh City, Hai Phong, Da Nang, and Can Tho—must now have lived there for at least two years without interruption (against one year under the previous law). A separate law requires at least three years of residence to apply for residence in Hanoi.

Recent studies have found that obtaining temporary residence status is generally not difficult, but there are high hurdles to obtaining permanent residence, particularly in Hanoi and Ho Chi Minh City (Giang 2014). Some people have lived in Ho Chi Minh City as temporary residents for many years but been unable to obtain permanent status, obstacles to which include inability to provide the required paperwork, as well as cost. Numerous respondents in one qualitative study reported that substantial informal payments were required—most commonly in Hanoi and Ho Chi Minh City—in the range of 3 million–10 million Vietnamese dong (around $150–500). Some with "connections" reported not paying anything.

More than 5 million people lack permanent registration status where they live. The 2015 Household Registration and Service Access Survey, conducted only in Hanoi, Ho Chi Minh City, Binh Duong, Da Nang, and Dak Nong, found large fractions of the population without permanent registration, particularly in Ho Chi Minh City (36 percent) and Binh Duong (72 percent) (figure 6.17) (World Bank 2016). In major urban centers, the Vietnamese without permanent registration face difficulties accessing services for health, utilities, schooling, and social protection, as well as challenges in employment and social networks.[9]

Evidence also points to some poor children not attending school for lack of registration. Net school enrollment rates are lower at every level for children without permanent registration (figure 6.18). Enrollment rates are very low for children without permanent registration at the upper secondary level. They are also particularly low for children without permanent registration who have been at their current location for less than six months. Multivariate analysis shows that the gap persists even when controlling for socioeconomic status. Urban schools, often overcrowded, give priority to residents

FIGURE 6.17 Percentage of population without permanent registration in four major urban centers

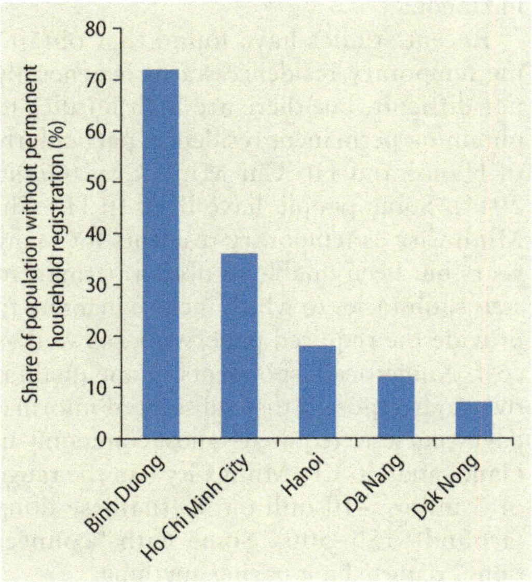

Source: World Bank 2016
Notes: Number of people per city: Bin Duong, 1.4 million; Ho Chi Minh City, 2.9 million; Hanoi, 1.3 million; Da Nang, 120,000; Dak Nong, 40,000.

FIGURE 6.18 Net school enrollment rate by school level and *hộ khẩu* status

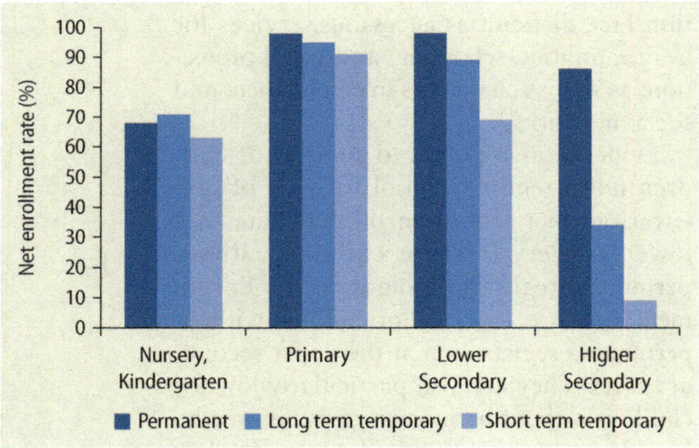

Source: Household Registration Survey 2015.
Note: "Long-term temporary" migrants are those without permanent registration status who have been living in their current location for more than six months. "Short-term temporary" migrants are those without permanent registration status who have been living in their current location for six months or less.

(Institute of Sociology 2015). Unregistered children and those with temporary residence are sometimes required to pay higher fees to attend public schools, must pay to attend private schools, or do not attend school at all (Oxfam and ActionAid 2012).

Access to health care, pensions, and support for poor households also present challenges for those without permanent registration. Those without permanent registration are less likely to seek professional care when ill and less likely to have health insurance (Haughton 2010). Without permanent registration, children under 6 struggle to get health insurance. Those without local *hộ khẩu* are also ineligible to receive social pensions for the elderly or support for poor households (Institute of Sociology 2015). Those without permanent registration face difficulties with such administrative procedures as registering vehicles, obtaining birth and marriage licenses, and applying for bank loans or business licenses (Institute of Sociology 2015).

Finally, unregistered workers receive lower wages than comparable registered workers. Controlling for other characteristics, unregistered workers have wages 8–9 percent lower. Differences in unobserved characteristics could explain the gap, as could legal vulnerability, which increases employer power in wage negotiations with unregistered workers.

While the registration system seems to have less force than it used to, it remains a source of inequality of opportunity, increasing the cost of migration to major cities. How much it discourages migration is unclear, however: the presence of large numbers of people in Hanoi and Ho Chi Minh City without permanent registration shows that many migrants continue to arrive, despite the costs.

Why does *hộ khẩu* persist when its original purpose no longer applies? Some fear that loosening *hộ khẩu* will increase the flow of migrants to the main urban centers and aggravate urban crowding. In a 2010 news story concerning possible changes to the rules in Hanoi, the Minister of Justice was quoted as saying, "To reduce migration is necessary to reduce the population growth of the capital, to limit traffic congestion, and to reduce the grubbiness of the capital" (VTC News 2010). Municipal officials worry that providing full service access to migrants will attract more migrants and put more pressure on already constrained urban infrastructure. The Ministry of Public Security, which administers *hộ khẩu,* opposes relaxing the system because it sees it as an instrument of security and control. The system also employs Ministry of Public Security officers and provides opportunities for informal payments (Institute of Sociology 2015).

Three policy directions
The broad objective of policy reform should loosen the link between service access and registration status:

1. One option is to reduce the barriers to obtaining permanent registration. Many countries require local registration to access services, and proof of residence, such as a property title or lease, to obtain local residence. What distinguishes Vietnam's *hộ khộu* from the typical system is that permanent registration is only possible after residence of 2–3 years, and both the payment and document requirements for permanent registration are substantial. The problems the system creates for service access would be reduced if these requirements were lessened. A package of reforms along these lines could include eliminating the residence period requirement for permanent registration or lowering it to six months, reducing the document requirements for permanent registration, and strictly regulating payments for permanent registration and cracking down on informal payments. These changes could be made as part of a renewed effort of broader administrative reform.
2. A second option is to eliminate the differences in service access based on registration. If temporary registration were treated as equivalent to permanent registration for services access, the gap in access between temporary and permanent residents would cease to exist.
3. A third long-term option is to replace *hộ khẩu* with a national identification card in a unified national database. The database could include place of residence and allow individuals to change their listed residence at will. Local service access could be determined on the basis of residence as specified in the national database.

Gender Equality and Fertility

Vietnam has achieved impressive outcomes on gender equality. Gender differences in school enrollment and attainment are minimal, and the gender wage gap is modest. But women remain outliers in private- and public-sector leadership positions, and the SRB has increased precipitously.

First, there are sharp gender differences in business and in government and political spheres, where the leadership is overwhelmingly male. In the last decade and a half, the share of women in the National Assembly has been declining. Few chairs of National Assembly committees are female. A large share of the civil service is comprised of women, but their representation in leadership positions is low. There is a target that all ministries should have at least one female vice minister, but the system for that is yet to be developed. Women's representation also remains low in key bodies of the Communist Party: the Politburo, the Central Committee, and the Secretariat. As of 2015, women constituted only 18.3 percent of Party leadership in communes, 14.2 percent in districts, and 11.3 percent in provinces.

Measures to boost women's leadership could focus on equalizing retirement ages in the labor code, using affirmative action as a short-term measure to ensure that qualified women are fast tracked to management positions, adopting a long-term program to identify potential women leaders early in their public career, and addressing gender stereotypes that limit women's career choices. This demands a long-term approach to update the education system and curricula and to promote healthier views of masculinity and gender roles in the media, and perhaps social media.

A second concern is the SRB, which surged after 1999 (figure 6.19). Sex-selective abortion is a form of gender discrimination and a threat to gender equity over the long term. Vietnam's level of the SRB, measured as the number of male births per 100 female births, was in the normal range of 105–106 in 1979 and 1989. With the spread of ultrasound technology that allows parents to identify the sex of the child, the SRB has risen rapidly, reaching nearly 114 in 2013, placing it with India and China among countries with the highest SRB. This imbalance will result in a large number of surplus men starting in approximately 20 years, which may result in an increased level of antisocial behavior, violence, and human trafficking.

Apart from the introduction of ultrasound technology, the high SRB is due to the traditional high value of Vietnamese families for sons, partly because sons traditionally have the main responsibility for taking care of parents in old age and worshipping their ancestors. Population policy is also likely to be a contributing factor.

The "one- or two-child policy" has its origins in policies targeting reduced population growth as far back as 1961. A policy decision in 1989 (largely reiterated in 1993) stipulated one or two children per family, born three to five years apart, and recommended the age of marriage. Although the program was rooted in a principal of volunteerism, coercive elements were sometimes apparent locally.

Changing demand for children is another factor. As in other fast-developing countries, a typical couple now wants fewer children. With declines in child mortality, a large number of children is no longer necessary to ensure that some children survive to care for their parents. Additionally, as economic opportunities have improved overall, the value of parents' time—particularly for women—has increased, making the child care commitment required for a large family less attractive. Finally, with rising incomes, families are investing more in each child (for higher "quality" children in economic terms). This increases the cost of each child and further discourages large families.

The upshot has been a dramatic decline in the total fertility rate, which reached the replacement rate (2.1) in 2005 (see figure 6.19). The rate appears to have increased slightly in recent years, however, possibly due to changes in 2011 in the messaging of the government's family planning campaign, which families may have perceived as loosening the two-child limit.

The government is considering issuing a new population law, further loosening or even abandoning the two-child policy. Although the impact is highly uncertain, the slight increase in the total fertility rate in 2012–14, possibly reflecting a perceived policy shift, suggests that full elimination may well increase fertility. The change would likely be modest, since the broader economic dynamics of fertility are more important determining factors than the two-child policy.

Removing the two-child policy will probably reduce the SRB somewhat. Given the option to have a larger number of children, couples with strong preferences for a male child may be less likely to abort a first or second child. Easing of the two-child policy,

FIGURE 6.19 Vietnam runs close to India and China as having the world's highest sex ratio at birth

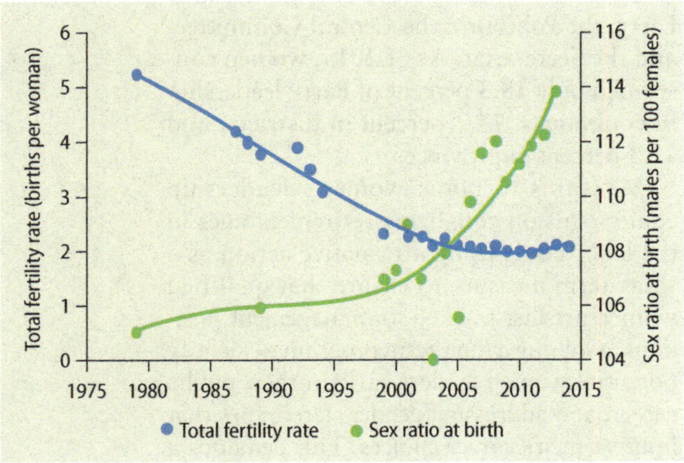

Source: Compilation from General Statistics Office of Vietnam estimates from Population and Housing Censuses and annual Population Change and Family Planning Surveys.

however, will most likely not reverse the sex ratio trend completely. Government laws to prohibit sex identification of fetuses (to reduce sex-selective abortion) have not proven effective. Very large majorities of women in the later stages of pregnancy know the sex of their fetuses. The imbalance in the SRB will probably only change markedly as parent preferences evolve.

Government policy may be able to speed this evolution through various measures. One approach is public campaigns to emphasize the value of daughters. A second approach—relevant to the discussion on pensions later in this chapter—is to ensure that the government provides sufficient old-age support to lessen the concern of parents about having a male offspring to support them in their later years.

It is important to note that besides the marginalized groups considered above, there are many other disadvantaged individuals who should be considered under social inclusion policies, although they are not given separate treatment in this report. These include child workers, people reintegrated after rehabilitation, and the victims of trafficking. Other populations of marginalized or vulnerable groups include the victims of disasters and climate change (and the elderly, who are considered in the next section).

The Emerging Agenda: Middle-Class Inclusion in a Market Economy

The second element of Vietnam's social inclusion vision for 2035 is the emerging agenda of supporting the growing middle class to maximize their productivity, manage risks, and pursue opportunities in a market economy. As countries move from lower- to upper-middle and ultimately high income, social policy must respond to a growing, increasingly urban, middle class, whose needs are very different from those of the mass of rural poor who characterized Vietnam in the past. By 2035, Vietnam will be overwhelmingly a middle-class society. Its focus of social policy will have shifted dramatically.

But what is the middle class? It has multiple definitions, each with its own strengths. One group of measure uses relative definitions, for example, the middle three quintiles of the income distribution within a country or people earning 75–125 percent of median income (Birdsall, Carroll, and Stefano 2000; Easterly 2001). A second set uses absolute terms, such as an income of \$2–\$13 a day for a developing world middle class and an income of \$10–\$100 a day for a global middle class (see for example, Banerjee and Duflo 2008; Ravallion 2009; Kharas 2010). A third type combines relative and absolute measures, including people consuming \$10 or more a day but also falling below the 90th percentile of the income distribution. Other indicators of the middle class are sociological, such as education, occupation, or lifestyle. Each approach has its utility, some for domestic analysis over time and some for cross-country comparisons.

The middle class is a driver of economic growth, social stability, and broader development.[10] Cross-country analysis points to a variety of channels through which a larger middle class affects development. Middle-class households tend to accumulate more human capital and have higher financial savings—both critical inputs to sustained economic growth. Middle classes are also stronger markets for consumer durables and thus a source of domestic consumption growth. Finally, worldwide they have pressed for greater accountability and quality in public service delivery, which in turn can improve efficiency and socioeconomic outcomes.

By a simple projection, in 2035 more than half of Vietnamese people will be members of the "global middle class" (\$15 or more per day consumption in 2011 PPP terms) (figure 6.20).

These gains are shifting expectations and generating new challenges. For example, most people will aspire to wage jobs. They will also expect the state to provide a minimum standard of services, financial protection, and decent work, with affordable health care, old-age protection, and basic working

FIGURE 6.20 By 2035, more than half the Vietnamese will have entered the global middle class

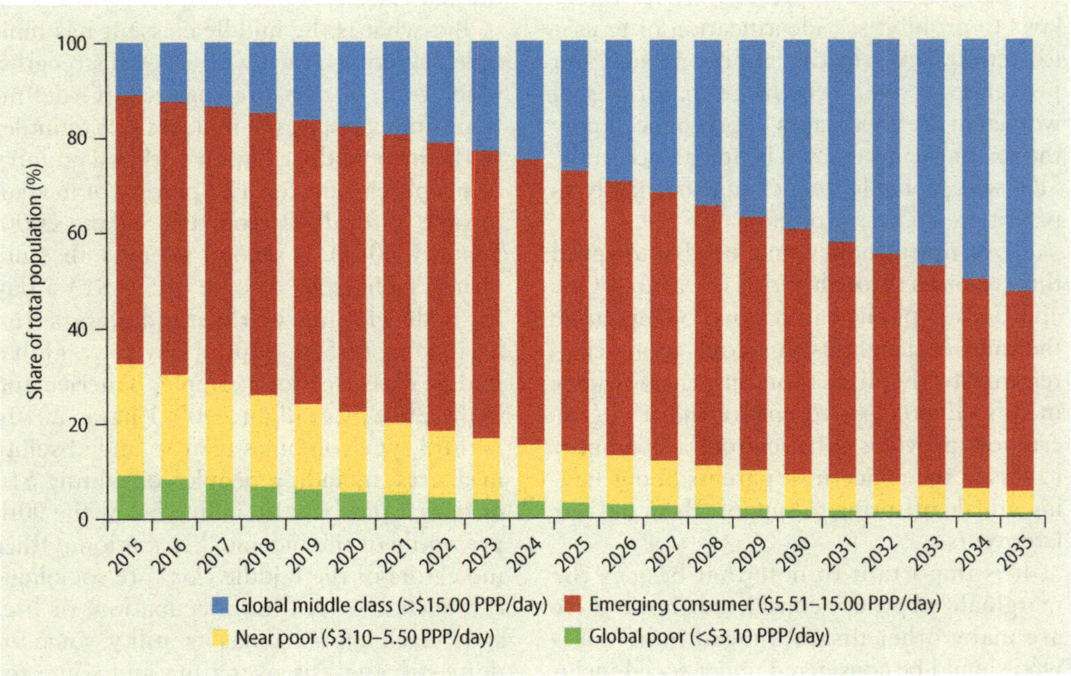

Source: Calculations based on the Vietnam Household Living Standards Survey 2014.
Note: Figures reflect the projected distribution of per capita consumption. Projections assume 4 percent annual growth in per capita consumption.

protections. Globally, the rise of the middle class has also meant greater demand for voice, such as independent worker representation in the workplace, citizen oversight of public services, and broader civic participation. Middle classes also tend to place a strong weight on avoiding high-income inequality.

The growing middle class also faces new risks. Health risks from urban and sedentary living will increase, and new health risks such as dementia will develop as people live longer. The risks of losing formal sector jobs may increase in the face of global competition and increased economic volatility, and risks of workplace conflict may worsen as the rapid increase in wages tapers.

What are the key public policy challenges in meeting these rising expectations? The first section looks at challenges in the labor market and balancing the interests of workers and employers in ways that share the fruits of growth, sustain competitiveness, and promote social harmony. The next focuses on Vietnam's education system and key challenges in promoting a system better suited to the needs of an upper-middle-income country. The following section discusses Vietnam's social protection system: first, looking at its pension system and the challenges of balancing coverage expansion, financial protection in old age, and fiscal sustainability in a rapidly aging society; and second, discussing the challenges of building an effective, equitable, and sustainable safety net. The final section reviews the challenges facing the health sector as it seeks to ensure universal coverage of health care at affordable levels, and reorient the health delivery system to the lifestyle diseases that dominate among the growing, and increasingly urban and aging, middle class.

The Labor Market

The jobs landscape has shifted over the last 25 years. While jobs were once entirely in family farming, collectives, and state-owned enterprises

(SOEs), more than half of jobs are now in manufacturing and services, household enterprises outside agriculture, and private domestic and foreign-owned firms. In 1989 nearly three-quarters (71 percent) of employed Vietnamese worked primarily in agriculture, fishing, or forestry, and private employment was almost nonexistent. Today agriculture, fishing, and forestry account for 46 percent of jobs, and one in 10 Vietnamese workers—about 5 million—holds a wage job with a private firm.[11]

The expansion of private sector wage jobs is fundamental to improving living standards. Family farms, household enterprises, SOEs, and the government will continue to be a source of livelihoods for many workers. But only private sector wage jobs promise the potential for the rapid productivity gains needed to lift large numbers of Vietnamese workers into the ranks of the global middle class.

Private sector job growth is determined by many factors. The primary driver is the business environment for private companies. For private companies to flourish, they need a government that sets clear and fair "rules of the game" that allow markets to function and allocate land, labor, and finance. Among the many other factors that can influence job growth are the education of the labor force, infrastructure, and government corruption.

Labor regulations and institutions can also be an important determinant of private sector wage growth. Labor market policies have the potential to help people grasp economic opportunities in a risky world but need to be well calibrated to help households and society manage the risks. Labor market policies can mitigate the effects of earnings and employment losses, provide voice to workers, and facilitate the movement of labor and human capital to where they are most efficiently deployed. Conversely, inappropriate policies may increase individual and societal labor market risks. At the individual level, risks of job loss or sustained informality may increase, while at a societal level they may result in slow formalization of employment, mismatches between earnings and productivity growth, or labor unrest. Poor policies may also inhibit structural transformation by reducing movement of workers across geography, sectors, and types of work.

Vietnam's labor market policies may be an emerging constraint to private sector wage job growth. In the most recent data from 2009, although just 1 percent of firms identified labor regulations as the chief constraint to firm growth, an additional 28 percent identified them as a minor or moderate constraint (World Bank 2014a). Since that time, employment protection legislation has become significantly more restrictive. Vietnam faces the danger that overly strict regulations could weigh on wage and job growth. Regulations often benefit insiders—workers who hold wage jobs—while smothering the creation of new jobs that would generate opportunity for outsiders. As the ranks of wage workers increase, insiders will become an increasingly powerful voice in favor of maintaining policies that are to their advantage. This could make it difficult to change overly strict policies in the future.

Structure

Despite the rapid changes that have taken place in the last quarter-century, nearly half of Vietnamese workers still work primarily in family farming, including fishing and forestry (figure 6.21). That share has dropped steadily since the start of the new millennium, at 1.6 percent a year, as workers from that sector move into nonfarm household enterprise and wage work. Household enterprises have generated a large boost in living standards for millions of Vietnamese but are limited in their potential for productivity growth. The future growth of Vietnam's middle class will depend principally on the growth of wage jobs, which is heavily influenced by labor regulations and institutions.

Regulations and institutions

Labor market regulations cover three subjects: the minimum wage, employment protection legislation, and industrial relations.

The minimum wage is intended to guarantee basic living standards for workers. The 2012 Labor Code states, "The minimum wage is the lowest payment for an employee

FIGURE 6.21 Even with rapid change over the last 25 years, family farming still employs the largest share of Vietnamese workers

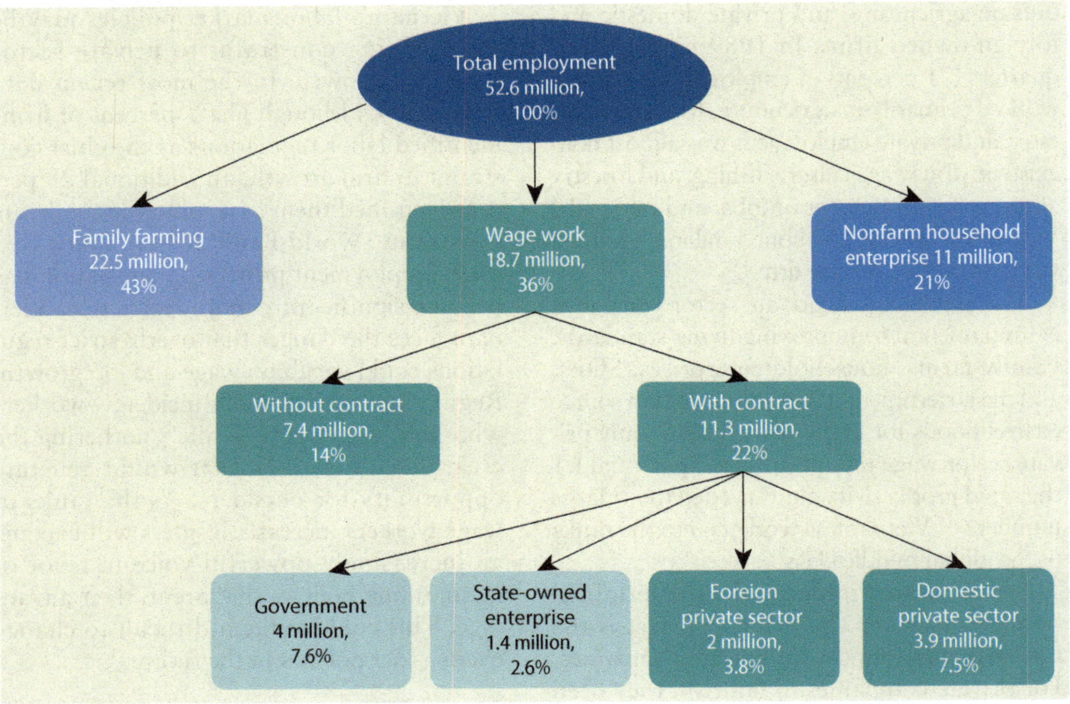

Source: Calculations based on the Labor Force Survey 2014.
Note: In this breakdown, family–farm or nonfarm–household–enterprise wage workers are classified under "wage worker." Nearly all such workers are without a contract.

who performs the simplest job in normal working conditions and must ensure the employee's minimum living needs and his/her family." Minimum wage legislation has direct implications for the 22 percent of Vietnamese workers who hold "formal" wage jobs—those with the job contract required by the Labor Code. The minimum wage also forms the basis to calculate wage scales for government staff/public-sector workers; wage scales for the payment of social insurance, unemployment insurance, and health insurance for workers of SOEs (and often private firms in practice); allowances for redundant workers due to restructuring of SOEs; and pensions, allowances for veterans, and some social transfers. Currently, the minimum wage for each district is set by the national government at one of four levels. A separate and lower minimum wage—known as the reference wage or basic wage—still applies to government workers.

The theoretical impact of changes in the minimum wage on employment is uncertain. Absent strict enforcement, if the minimum wage exceeds worker productivity, employers may hire workers informally without a contract to evade minimum wage restrictions. Economic theory shows that in a perfectly competitive labor market with both a formal sector covered by minimum wage laws and an uncovered informal sector, the effect of an increase in the minimum wage will be to shift employment from the formal to the informal sector. In the real world, labor markets are not perfectly competitive—large firms in particular can exert market power—and thus the impact of the minimum wage is less clear cut. Theories of efficiency wages suggest that paying workers more induces higher effort, makes them more productive, and/or reduces worker turnover. In the presence of either market power or efficiency wages, changes in the minimum wage at low levels can have little, no, or even positive effects on employment.

Nonetheless economic theory unambiguously predicts that an overly high minimum wage, if enforced, will reduce formal employment. Increases in the minimum wage can also increase wages higher up the wage scale—and possibly reduce employment—if some workers are paid multiples of the minimum wage. Given that Vietnam has attracted foreign direct investment (FDI) in part because of its low wages, there is a risk that very high minimum wages will discourage further FDI and the jobs it creates.

Outside the government sector, Vietnam's minimum wages have risen rapidly in recent years, outstripping productivity growth in the state, nonstate domestic, and FDI sectors (figure 6.22). The government's stated ambition is to raise minimum wages to allow households to reach the minimum monthly living standard by 2018.[12] This would imply further large increases.

Vietnam's private sector minimum wage is now somewhat high relative to other countries. A key benchmark of minimum wages is the relationship to median wages. For Vietnam, the picture differs sharply between the government and private sectors (figure 6.23). Vietnam's reference wage is low by global and regional standards at about 30 percent of median wage, while the private sector minimum wage is high, with the average ratio of minimum to median wage about 58 percent.

Vietnam's minimum wage increases may have depressed formal employment growth somewhat. Minimum wage changes in 2006–10 were associated with slower private sector employment growth in the domestic private sector. Increases in the minimum wage in 2001–2012 raised average wages and moderately lowered firm employment in private firms and SOEs (Del Carpio et al. 2013; Hansen, Rand, and Torm 2015a). The sharp increases in the minimum wage in 2011–13 substantially boosted wages at the low end of the distribution but only in SOEs and foreign-invested private firms. This suggests that the minimum wage is not fully enforced in the domestic private sector (Hansen, Rand, and Torm 2015b). Overall, 8 percent of full-time workers are paid less than the minimum wage.

FIGURE 6.22 The nongovernment minimum wage in Vietnam is high relative to the median wage, compared with other countries

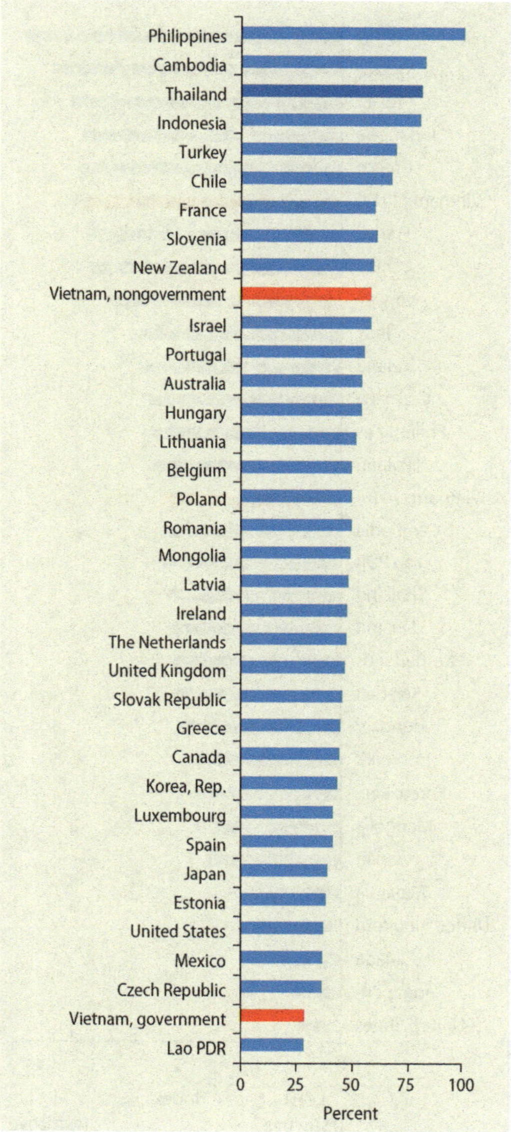

Source: World Bank 2014a, and World Bank and Ministry of Planning and Investment of Vietnam calculations based on the Labor Force Survey 2013.

Note: Full-time workers; 2008 for Lao PDR; 2009 for Cambodia, Mongolia, and Thailand; and 2010 for China, Indonesia, and the Philippines; average minimum wages for China and Vietnam. The nongovernment sector includes state-owned enterprises and domestic and foreign-owned private firms.

The second type of labor market regulation—employment protection legislation—establishes terms for hiring and dismissing

FIGURE 6.23 Vietnam—following labor code changes in 2012—is more restrictive in hiring and dismissing workers than France and China

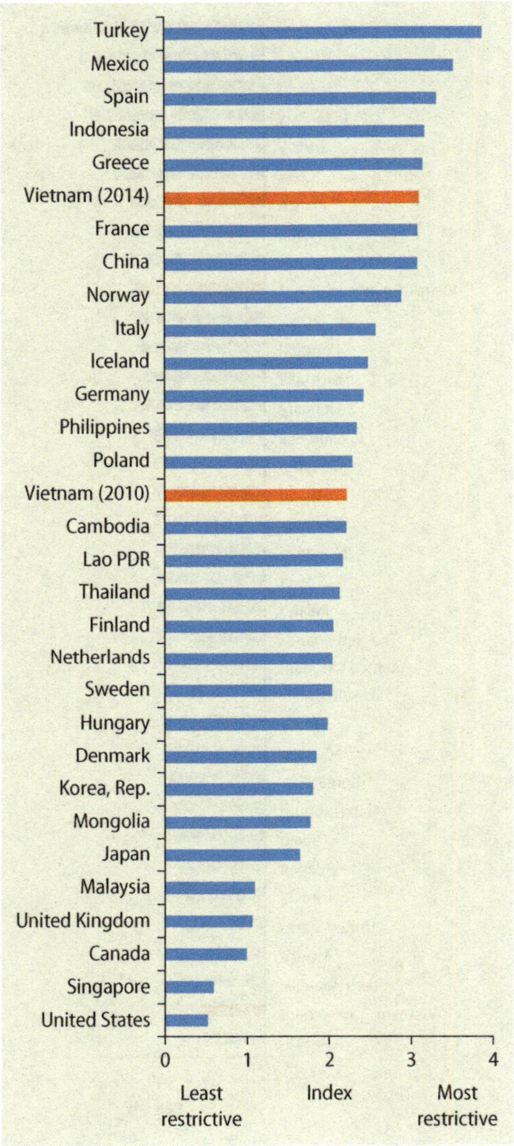

Source: Calculations based on the World Bank (2014a) and the Organisation for Economic Co-operation and Development Indicators of Employment Protection for 2010.
Note: The index has three components: protections of permanent workers against individual dismissal, additional requirements for collective dismissal, and regulations and restrictions on temporary forms of employment. The value ranges from zero (least restrictive) to six (most restrictive).

workers by employers. The intent is to provide some level of job security. Because overly restrictive employment protection legislation makes it harder to dismiss unproductive employees and to reduce employment during times of reduced demand, it may discourage firms from hiring workers in the first place. This reduces both overall formal sector employment and productivity.

The Organisation for Economic Co-operation and Development (OECD) calculates an employment protection legislation index that compares some of the most critical employment protection legislation components and the costs they put on employers. The index shows that changes to the Vietnam Labor Code in 2012 made Vietnam more restrictive than France (figure 6.23).

The most dramatic impacts from the 2012 reform were on fixed-term contract regulations, reflecting new regulations to outsource contracts (limited to a maximum cumulative duration of 12 months) and labor leasing enterprises. These reforms moved Vietnam from having moderately stringent restrictions on temporary forms of employment to being very restrictive.

Evidence from other countries shows that restrictive employment protection legislation is often associated with lower formal sector employment, especially of young workers, women, new entrants to the labor market, and unskilled workers (OECD 2004; Heckman and Pages 2004; Perry et al. 2007; Packard, Koettl, and Montenegro 2012; World Bank 2014a). These groups tend to be among the first to be laid off when labor costs rise or to be blocked from entry altogether. More restrictive employment protection legislation raises the share of self-employment and decreases dependent employment in low- and middle-income countries (Betcherman, Luinstra, and Ogawa 2001; Haltiwanger, Scarpetta, and Vodopivec 2003).

An important complement to more flexible employment protection legislation is active and passive labor market interventions. Both remain underdeveloped in Vietnam. Protecting workers in flexible labor markets requires both active labor market programs like training and job search assistance, and passive benefits such as severance pay and unemployment insurance. With China and Thailand, Vietnam is one of only three developing countries in East Asia and Pacific

(EAP) with a national unemployment insurance system, but coverage remains modest at under 20 percent of the workforce. At the same time, unemployment benefits in Vietnam are relatively generous. At 60 percent of average monthly earnings in the six months before unemployment, the replacement rate (the portion of income replaced by benefits) is higher than in China or Thailand, and relatively high globally for middle-income countries.

Active labor market programs are limited in low- and middle-income countries in the EAP region. But even there Vietnam is somewhat of an outlier as it has very few such programs. Those that it does have, as for public employment or to support employment changes for laborers in rural areas, often have low coverage and funding.

Vietnam's industrial relations system—the third segment—exhibits the legacy of a planned economy and faces growing challenges to adapt to its central function in a market economy. A basic shortcoming is the lack of clearly demarcated functions among labor unions (where membership is high), employers, and the state. This limits the force of industrial relations as an economic and social mediator, and places undue pressure on regulatory measures.[13]

Many observers have highlighted profound weaknesses in Vietnam's industrial relations system (Chi and van den Broek 2013; van Gramberg, Teicher, and Nguyen 2013; Schweisshelm 2014, for example). All labor unions fall under the umbrella of the Vietnam General Confederation of Labour (VGCL), which operates under the leadership of the Communist Party of Vietnam. The Confederation and its affiliated unions fulfill different roles that can result in conflicts of interest. First, enterprise-level unions have traditionally been close to management. Second, unions act as a transmission belt between the Communist Party and working people and are supposed to represent the people in government decision making. Third, unions are tasked with representing workers' interests in relation to firm management and providing welfare services to workers. This last function is at times subsidiary to other duties of union representatives.

The roles for employers' associations like the Vietnam Chamber of Commerce and Industry and the Vietnam Cooperative Alliance are similarly complex. In line with their original mandate, these associations are often more experienced in promoting the policies of the state and the Communist Party and in fostering trade activities than in engaging in industrial relations. In addition, state-designated employers' associations fail to represent the interest of all relevant employers, including foreign investors (Ly Khanh 2015). Finally, the capacity of the government to monitor the enforcement of labor legislation and to negotiate and implement collective agreements remains limited (Clarke, Lee, and Chi 2007).[14]

A symptom of these weaknesses is the high number of "wildcat" strikes. While Vietnam's Labor Code explicitly regulates strikes, official procedures are so cumbersome and the role of labor unions is so unclear that apparently no strike has ever taken place that was strictly in accordance with the Labor Code. Instead, strikes have been "wildcat"—spontaneous work stoppages bypassing official procedures (Schweisshelm 2014; Tran 2012). Such strikes have increased notably since the mid-2000s, though with considerable volatility from year to year and with the bulk of strikes in the foreign-invested sector, indicative of the underdeveloped nature of other mechanisms to resolve labor disputes. The capacity of mediators and arbitrators appears particularly weak (figure 6.24).

The 2012 legislative reforms attempted to address some of the weaknesses, with formal procedures to settle industrial relations disputes, a more active role in facilitating collective bargaining for the government, and a tripartite National Wage Council. Yet they did not resolve fundamental issues over the roles of labor unions and employers' associations. Well-functioning institutions for collective bargaining and dispute resolution are still missing.

Minimum wages adjustments and more stringent employment policy legislation have

FIGURE 6.24 The high frequency of wildcat strikes is a symptom of a weak industrial relations system

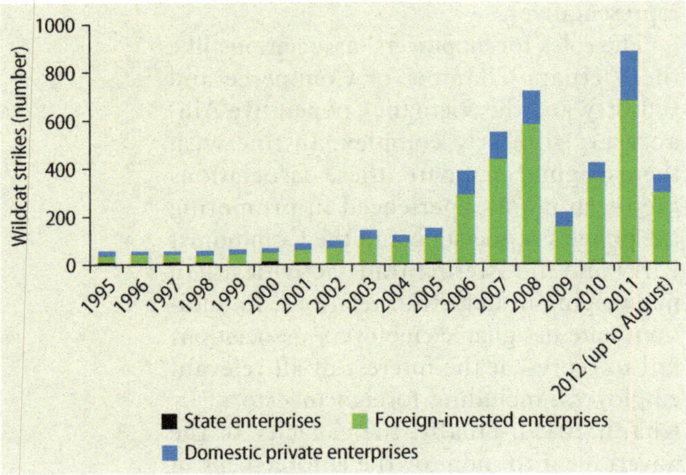

Source: Tran 2012.
Note: "Wildcat" strikes are spontaneous work stoppages bypassing official procedures (Schweisshelm 2014).

been used to address insufficient power of workers to negotiate adequate wages and assure decent work conditions. This has created one-size-fits-all regulatory parameters that fail to respond to the varying interests of workers and employers and are not necessarily appropriate for all sectors, locations, or types of work.

Policy directions

Whether Vietnam can realize the further transformation of its labor market will depend on its policies—whether the country addresses weaknesses that are already apparent before moving from farms to factories and firms. One concept is "flexicurity," striking a balance between flexible labor regulation that maximizes productivity growth and creative destruction and the needs of workers for decent employment that is fairly compensated. Put another way, Vietnam should aim to protect workers rather than jobs as it deepens its structural transformation.

The minimum wage will be most effective if it is determined primarily with reference to productivity and competitiveness factors. To date, Vietnam has taken a "living wage" approach to minimum wage setting, with a primary focus on the cost of living. Shifting to a wage floor approach that emphasizes productivity and competitiveness as the drivers of minimum wage adjustments should be considered while the market economy matures. Factors such as price growth and relative earnings could remain factors but productivity would become a more crucial factor in minimum wage determination. Other policy instruments are more effective—possibly in combination with the minimum wage—to assure that people who work are able to live above the poverty line. To achieve this shift in approach, in the short run, Vietnam's private sector would benefit from moderating the rate of minimum wage adjustments. In the medium term, existing plans to anchor minimum wage adjustments to real productivity growth should be put into place. A number of factors are taken into account in setting minimum wages in other countries (table 6.2).

Vietnam could also benefit from streamlining its employment policy legislation regulations to promote greater labor market flexibility. It should consider loosening regulation of labor leasing enterprises and of temporary and outsourcing contracts. It could look more closely at the interaction between employer-provided severance and unemployment insurance—generally more efficient in pooling risks related to job loss. Their potential substitutability is apparently already recognized in Vietnam's labor code.

To ensure that increased flexibility in the regulated labor market is accompanied by adequate security for workers, Vietnam should gradually expand coverage of unemployment insurance and active labor market programs. This can enhance labor market efficiency and worker welfare (World Bank 2012b). But Vietnam needs to keep close track of the fiscal impacts. It should also monitor the labor tax wedge and explore options of financing unemployment insurance, active labor market programs, and other initiatives out of general tax revenue.

The government might approach its industrial relations challenges over three stages. In the short term, it should continue strengthening efforts (such as the VGCL's attempts to form enterprise unions independent

TABLE 6.2 Countries have different criteria in setting minimum wages

Economy	Approach	Key criteria
Australia	Wage floor	Productivity, business competitiveness, relative standards of living, workforce participation rate.
Korea, Rep.	Wage floor	Cost of living, economic growth rate, average wage level, labor productivity, unemployment rate, consumer price index, and income distribution. No fixed weight for factors and relevance of each determined within wage council debate and varies in time.
Taiwan, China	Wage floor	Conditions of national economic development, price index, national income and average individual income, labor productivity of different industries and employment situation, workers' wages in different industries, survey and statistical figures on household income and expenditures.
United States	Wage floor	Manufacturing productivity, affordability to employers, cost of living, wage levels.
United Kingdom	Wage floor	Pay differentials, inflation, business costs, competitiveness, employment, economic conditions.
France	Living wage	Overall wages and income CPI economic conditions, needs of workers and families.
Hong Kong SAR, China	Wage floor	General economic conditions, latest economic performance and forecasts, labor market conditions, labor demand and supply, wage level and distribution, wage differentials and employment characteristics, competitiveness, productivity growth, labor costs, operating characteristics of enterprises, entrepreneurship, business sentiment and solvency, relative economic freedom and competitiveness, standards of living, changes in employment and earnings and inflation.

Source: Hong Kong SAR, China, Provisional Minimum Wage Commission 2010.

from management) to increase the capacity of unions and employers' federations through awareness campaigns, and training in collective bargaining, among others.

In the medium term, Vietnam should consider more specific measures. The VGCL and its affiliated unions could bar company executives and managers from key union positions (like being head of an enterprise union). This would follow the example of other countries where company managers cannot hold top union positions or even union membership. Vietnam should continue simplifying regulations to resolve industrial relation disputes. It could also consider institutional reforms that allow the creation of firm-level works councils or labor-management councils, as in many European countries and the Republic of Korea. And, it should look to develop labor mediation and arbitration systems that provide channels beyond the court system to resolve labor disputes when workplace institutions are unable to resolve matters amicably.

In the long term, Vietnam should consider fundamental institutional reforms to create an industrial relations system suited to the needs of a mature market economy. One goal should be to develop collective bargaining where the interests of workers, employers, and the state are more properly represented in a true bargaining process.

Vietnam has already made strong commitments along those lines in the United States–Vietnam Plan for the Enhancement of Trade and Labor Relations, a side agreement to the TPP. The main provision is as follows:

> Viet Nam shall ensure that its laws and regulations permit workers, without distinction, employed by an enterprise to form a grassroots labour union (*to chuc cua nguoi lao dong*) of their own choosing without prior authorization.... A grassroots labour union registered with the competent government body shall have the right autonomously to elect its representatives, adopt its constitution and rules, organize its administration, including managing its finances and assets, bargain collectively, and organize and lead strikes and other collective actions.

Further, Vietnam agreed that within five years grassroots unions may form organizations "across enterprises and at the levels above the enterprise, including the sectoral and regional levels." If fully implemented, these measures will address many of the weaknesses in the current industrial relations system.

Education

Education is the most critical component of equality of opportunity. In Vietnam's increasingly market-oriented economy, the prospects for success in life are far greater for those with a high-quality education. Despite great gains over time in educational attainment among Vietnamese of all income levels, large gaps remain in the education experience of children by socioeconomic status. A child from a wealthy family in Hanoi or Ho Chi Minh City will typically receive high-quality instruction through upper secondary school, supplemented by private tutoring, and complete a university degree, either in Vietnam or abroad. In contrast, a child from a poor rural family is unlikely to advance past lower secondary (figure 6.25).

Advances in education are also critical to Vietnam's overall economic success. High-income countries have workforces with high levels of advanced skills gained through education. These skills are essential to growth (Acemoglu and Autor 2012). The many specific skills combine in complementary ways with technology, and the educational foundations of the workforce allow individuals to change and adapt more quickly as changes in technology and the demands of work accelerate. These basic facts underlie the massive rising global demand for education (Garcia de León, Heckmann, and Gonzalez 2012).

Vietnam is rightly proud of its achievements in expanding education coverage, with quality and equity, over the past 20 years. This is an excellent start toward creating the adaptable, skilled workforce it needs to become and stay a high-income country. But it is not enough. Too many students fail to graduate high school, and too few continue

FIGURE 6.25 A large gap in upper secondary school attendance remains between the poorest and richest 20 percent

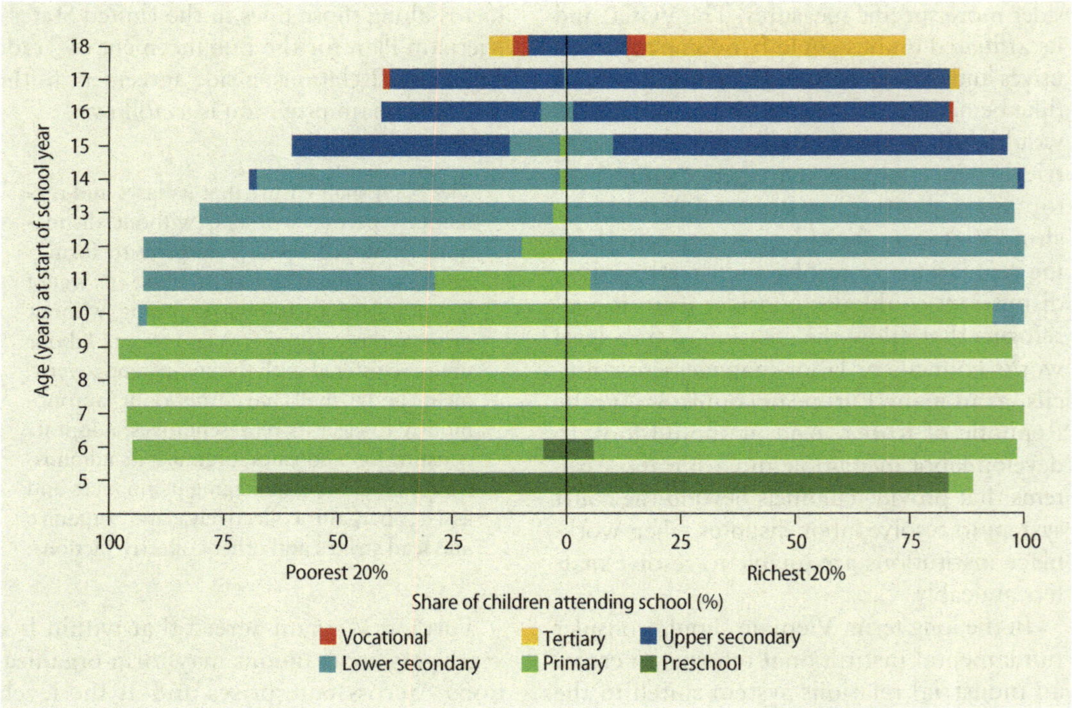

Source: Calculations based on the Population and Housing Census 1989 and the Vietnam Household Living Standards Survey 2012.

to tertiary education. Those who continue do not, as a rule, receive a high-quality education that is relevant for a modern labor market.

In short, the Vietnamese education system is inclusive, high quality, and largely equitable through lower secondary education. But it then becomes exclusive, mid-quality, and inequitable. It provides students with excellent foundations for success, but fails to build on them.

Public policy for education should promote universal high school completion. The excellent foundations of public basic education in Vietnam should channel students into a dynamic tertiary system. This system should offer students a wide range of choices—increasingly presented by private providers—that respond to their demands and aspirations. (This section focuses more on the basic education system and makes recommendations for policy directions; chapter 3 on innovation considers the tertiary education system more closely.)

The current education system

Over the past 25 years, Vietnam has expanded education access, achieving universal primary education and increasing enrollments in lower secondary, upper secondary, and tertiary education (figure 6.26).

Challenges remain after basic education. The poorer a student's family, the less likely she or he is to finish high school or continue to tertiary education. Dropping out disproportionately affects students from poorer families, and after age 14 the poor start to rapidly disappear from the education system. In the last year of junior secondary school, when students are 14 years old, there are 67 students from the bottom income quintile for every 100 enrolled students from the top quintile. By age 16, just two years later, 24 of the poor students are no longer in school, dropping the share to 43 poor students per 100 rich students. These ratios continue to worsen for high school graduation and tertiary enrollment.

FIGURE 6.26 Over the past 25 years, Vietnam has greatly expanded access to education

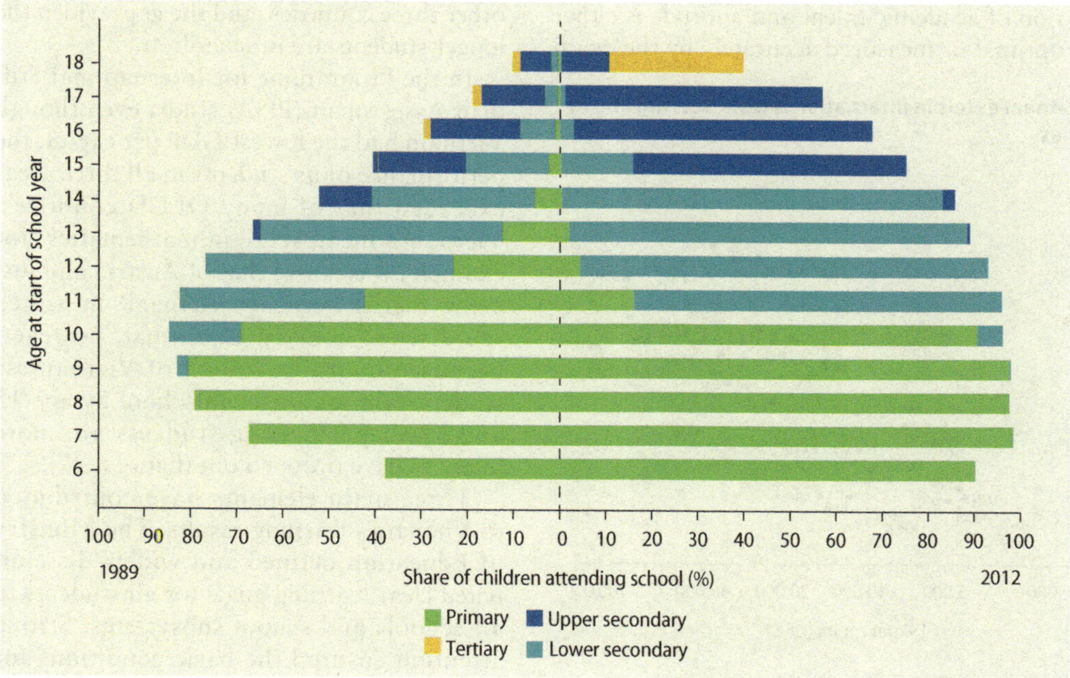

Source: Calculations based on the Population and Housing Census 1989 and the Vietnam Household Living Standards Survey 2012.

Vietnamese basic education policy has overemphasized the continued development of students seen as having more traditional academic ability and underemphasized those seen as having less. A key bottleneck is at the end of lower secondary school due to the exam-based system to allocate places in academic high schools. Policy puts the onus on the student to demonstrate sufficient academic talent to merit a place in upper secondary education. This policy prevents marginal students from entering upper secondary school. The policy also appears to have a strong indirect effect on students' decisions to drop out and parents' support and influence on these decisions.

Research confirms that the exam-based system of progression makes the path for ambitious students of moderate academic talent and achievement more arduous. Parents sometimes discourage further schooling of students who are having difficulty achieving top or even average grades (Duc and Tam 2013). Social attitudes and policy orientation choose to cast academic upper secondary school as a precious good not to be "wasted" on the less talented. Two problems stand out. First, it is unclear that the traditional definition of academic talent and aptitude is either optimal or measured accurately by the exam system. Second, in a "normal" distribution about 50 percent of students are below average by definition. This has led to a failure to sufficiently develop the potential of a large share of students, and a tolerance for dropping out and short educational careers.

Demand-side issues affect children continuing school beyond junior secondary. Affordability for less well-off households is a challenge, along with the opportunity cost of having young adults in school rather than at work. Poor families may also have concerns about the relevance and usefulness for job success of schooling at the senior secondary and tertiary levels.

Vietnamese schools are extremely good at achieving basic learning outcomes. Students in the Young Lives study documented learning gains and other characteristics from birth through age 15 for compatible cohorts of children in four countries (Ethiopia, India, Peru, and Vietnam). Children in all four countries show similar levels of cognitive development at age 5, but by age 8, after only three years in school, wide gaps emerge in their performance on standardized tests. At young ages, even the poorest students in Vietnam outperform the average students in the other three countries, and the gaps widen the longer students are in school.

In the Programme for International Student Assessment (PISA) study, even though Vietnam had the lowest GDP per capita, the performance of its students in all three areas exceeded that of many OECD countries. Vietnam's mean score in mathematics, for example, was above that of Austria and just below that of Germany. Vietnam's measured scores were boosted somewhat, however, because about one-fourth of Vietnamese students are no longer in school by age 15 and lower-performing students are more likely to have dropped out (figure 6.27).

Three main elements have contributed to Vietnam's learning results. The Ministry of Education defined and widely disseminated clear learning goals for all students to all schools and school subsystems. Strong attention ensured the basic conditions for performance through, for example, the

FIGURE 6.27 Vietnam excels in international tests, scoring above many rich countries

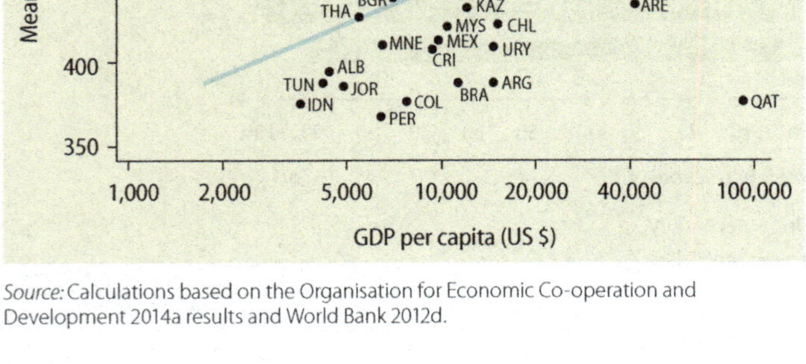

Source: Calculations based on the Organisation for Economic Co-operation and Development 2014a results and World Bank 2012d.

Fundamental School Quality Level (FSQL) audit system introduced in 2003 and used to compare primary school performance. The system maintained basic standards for quality, such as low absenteeism.

Regardless of a young person's socioeconomic status, investment in early childhood education can improve educational outcomes throughout a student's school career. Early childhood education programs can benefit disadvantaged children by preparing them for primary school. In Vietnam, there are crèches for children between three months and three years old and kindergartens for children between three and six years old. Early childhood education institutions are either public (the majority), semi-public, or private. Preschools all follow the same government regulations regarding organizational structures, curriculum, class size, and teacher qualifications. The objective of Vietnam's early childhood education institutions is to help children prepare for school by developing their physical, emotional, and intellectual abilities (UNESCO IBE 2011).

The government is committed to improving access to and the quality of early childhood education programs to ensure that students can enroll in full-day, full-year preschools. The government approved universal early childhood education for 5-year-old children (Decision 239) to raise enrollment in early childhood education institutions to 95 percent, raise attendance to 90 percent, and reduce malnutrition to below 10 percent by 2015. The program also aims to increase school readiness by expanding coverage to disadvantaged children and to improve the quality of early childhood education institutions by constructing infrastructure, providing teaching and learning materials, promoting teacher training, and providing lunches to disadvantaged students. The curriculum was changed from being teacher- to child-led to improve learning outcomes.

While access to basic education is nearly universal in Vietnam, supplemental tutoring is pervasive and a source of inequality of opportunity. Spending on tutoring increases as the student progresses through the education system, with 32 percent of students in primary schools receiving paid supplementary education, 46 percent in lower secondary schools, and 63 percent in upper secondary schools (Dang 2013). Some 27 percent of households pay for tutoring—15 percent in the poorest income quintile and 30 percent in wealthier quintiles (Dang 2013). Kinh families on average spend 80 percent more on private tutoring than ethnic minority families. The gap between rich and poor household spending on tutoring may be correlated with lower scores on entrance exams for disadvantaged students.

Most students attend supplementary education classes arranged by the students' schools, although urban areas have education centers. Six percent of students attend private tutoring classes not organized by their schools. The gap in supplementary education attendance between urban and rural students ranges from 4 percent in preschool to 23 percent in primary school (Dang 2013). Vietnamese students spent an average of 89 hours in tutoring in 2006, with urban students spending twice as much time as rural students. This disparity in attendance between rural and urban students may worsen educational outcomes for poor, rural students.

Policy directions

Vietnam is in strong position but will need to respond to new conditions. Its trends in education coverage place it along the same trajectory as Korea. Both countries are above the global trend line for attainment. But for Vietnam to develop educationally as Korea did will require new ways of thinking about education policy. The trends affecting Vietnam's education policies for the next two decades will be:

- The substitution of technology for human labor for routine tasks and for the increasing cognitive and skill demands of remunerative work.
- The global tendency toward higher levels of education in the workforce and the

FIGURE 6.28 Vietnam can follow the Republic of Korea's path in high school completion rates

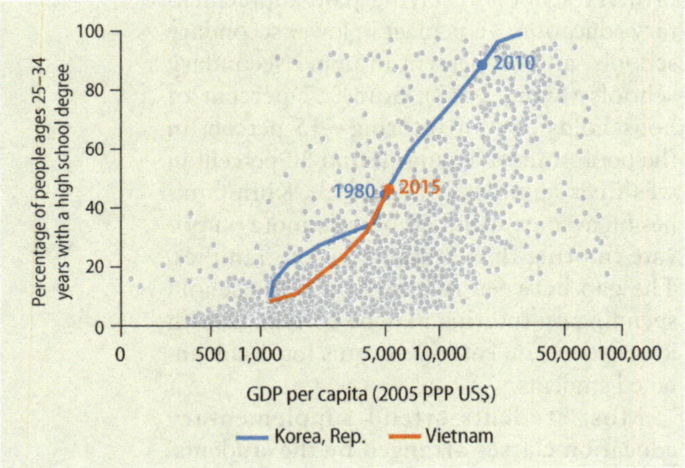

Source: Calculations based on Barro and Lee 2010 and World Development Indicators.

long-term persistence of returns to higher levels of education.

- The transition of Vietnam from a rural, lower-income, agricultural society to an urban, modern, middle-class economy.

As Vietnam moves toward 2035, basic education policy will need to focus on making all high school graduates ready for college—preparing them to succeed in education beyond high school. This workforce will allow Vietnam to raise productivity amid increasing global competition and rapidly changing knowledge and technology. The overall policy goal is to build on Vietnam's current advantages to produce a globally competent, adaptable, and high-quality workforce, through two avenues: universalizing high school completion and adopting greater elements of inquiry-based learning.

Too many students leave before receiving a high school diploma. Initial gains in equity of learning outcomes are dissipated when students from poorer families leave school with no diploma and few options for tertiary study. These problems are more prevalent among the country's ethnic minority students and families. Universal high school completion will reverse this trend.

Ending the exam-based allocation of upper secondary school places and replacing it with universal secondary school attendance is a priority. This matches global experience of universal high school completion as countries grow richer (figure 6.28). It will also mean that upper secondary schools will have cohorts with a greater range of abilities.

Serious consideration should also be given to a medium- to long-term transformation of the two separate subsystems (academic and technical/vocational upper secondary school) into a single system offering two tracks to a high school diploma. One track would be pursued by those who expect to continue to tertiary education. The other would be for those who may not or who seek only limited formal education beyond high school. The potential for housing both systems in common secondary school buildings should be explored.

Funding is too limited to expand both the academic and technical and vocational education training systems to full national coverage. This model would be especially advantageous for rural, isolated communities, which could see efficiency and social gains from a single high school for all high school-aged youth. Modulating course difficulty and content could be done as well or better in a single school. The policy would have the added effect of ending what is widely viewed as lower-value education and/or a distant second option for those without the talent to pursue academic secondary education.

The second avenue—inquiry-based learning—entails continuously improving the quality and relevance of what students learn. The Vietnamese school system excels at accomplishing straightforward tasks. But it needs to develop behavioral and complex problem-solving skills demanded by the modern world of work. These include broader generic skills such as communication, teamwork, problem-solving, and self-regulation, allied to a rigorous approach to content, enabling students to become skilled and flexible learners.

Some of the groundwork for pedagogical change has been put in place. The Vietnam Escuela Nueva Program provides more than 1,500 schools nationwide with much pedagogical autonomy to encourage student-centered pedagogy and locally initiated professional development for teachers. Building on this experience, the National Assembly has approved a fundamental reform of education to revise the curriculum and textbooks in all subjects for grades 1–12, aiming to replace rote learning with competency-based education.

To be successful, this sweeping change will require a clear idea of the attributes of the ideal graduate, continuous development of content that develops acquisition of factual knowledge along with the broader generic skills, creation of an expanded national learning assessment system of high technical quality that is carefully aligned with the revised curriculum, and strong education research capacity and the ability to move from research to policy.

Implementation of the revised curriculum will require efforts to ensure that teachers understand its goals. This is a large task, partly reconceptualizing what it means to teach and to learn. It requires that teachers understand and teach in a way that promotes the relatively complex goals in the competency-based curriculum. Continuous professional development, mentoring by master teachers, experimentation, and analyses are standard in the high-income OECD countries that are Vietnam's educational peers. Vietnam now needs the same type of system.

Health Care

As Vietnam moves to middle-class status by 2035, average citizens will increasingly aspire to a long and healthy life, to enjoy time with their family, and to take part in the country's growing affluence. Any perceived shortcomings in the health system—quality, cost, or responsiveness—are likely to spark public debate. There may also be growing impatience with gaps between the health care afforded by the rich and what is available to the rest of the population.

High expectations reflect the substantial risks that individuals face when they encounter the health system—the risk that if they get sick they will not be able to get the care they need, and the risk that falling ill will cost them money they cannot afford. The responsibility to manage and mitigate these risks will be a key challenge for policy makers. For these reasons, health system performance is likely to be an increasingly important factor in broader perceptions of government efficacy.

The major policy challenge facing Vietnam's health system over the next 20 years will be to achieve universal health coverage—that is, to ensure that everyone has access to good quality services without suffering financial hardship. Vietnam's 1992 Constitution also highlights this objective. Two big policy challenges will have to be met: in service delivery, transitioning to a health system centered on primary care; in health financing, besides resolving efficiency and equity challenges, stabilizing high total health expenditure and cutting out-of-pocket (OOP) spending. An important question on the latter is how the current pace of insurance enrollment can be accelerated, since by some estimates it may not be rapid enough to achieve 100 percent coverage by 2035. Other challenges are to involve the private sector more in the delivery of health care, and the state more in financing of aged and long-term care (ALTC).

Vietnam can build on many past successes as it looks toward 2035. For many years, it has enjoyed health outcomes better than what its income level would suggest. But past accomplishments do not guarantee continued success. For example, many countries that have done well on maternal and child health have struggled to make progress on addressing noncommunicable diseases (NCDs). Robust economic growth does not automatically translate into improved health outcomes. In fact, the global evidence suggests that higher income does not have a major role in "producing" better health, which relies instead on the wider application of health-improving knowledge and technology, especially in personal behavior and medical care.

Strengthening service delivery: Moving from hospitals to primary care

In recent years, Vietnam has been very successful at improving health outcomes for the majority of the population, and basic indicators such as life expectancy are generally better than in other countries at similar levels of development (figure 6.29). It is one of 10 high-performing countries on the health-related Millennium Development Goals. Nationally, infant, child, and maternal mortality all declined by roughly half over 2000–12, but in mountainous, rural areas child and maternal mortality rates are three to four times higher than on the rural plains and in urban areas. Child malnutrition is still high in areas with a concentration of ethnic minorities.

Yet for most of the population the major health challenge will be to address NCDs and injuries. Smoking rates, especially among men, are high. Emerging issues such as obesity loom.

Today's service delivery shortcomings are grounded in two interrelated problems: hospitals are doing too much and "grassroots" primary care (at district level and below) is doing too little. Vietnam has a hospital-centric system in which referrals and self-referrals to overcrowded facilities at the central and provincial levels are largely a result of low public confidence in the quality of a fragmented primary care health system that is ill-prepared to address the challenge of NCDs. There is a split between the preventive health system that primarily implements vertical programs and a curative system largely responsible for treating illness, but not detecting or preventing it. And for many patients, the first point of contact to seek health advice is the private pharmacy chain, not connected to the public service delivery or health insurance system at all.

Hospitals overadmit, overtest, and overprescribe, having received the autonomy and incentives to raise revenue from nonpublic sources under the policy of "socialization," including patient charges. Hospital-accountability safeguards are largely absent, however. A lack of system-wide capital planning is resulting in large inefficiencies due to overinvestment.

In recent years, inpatient stays have been growing nearly twice as fast as outpatient visits, and Vietnam's rate of hospital admissions and average length of stay are higher than the regional average. Inpatient spending is more than three times higher than outpatient spending. And in most hospitals well over half of patients either came directly or without any referral from a lower-level facility. At least one-fifth of inpatient admissions are "ambulatory care sensitive"—they could have been handled in an outpatient setting.

The need to shift service delivery to the grassroots is not only good for health, but will also be pro-poor. While the poorest 20 percent account for about one-third of commune visits, the richest 20 percent are responsible for nearly half the visits to central level hospitals (figure 6.30). Thus any attempt to

FIGURE 6.29 Vietnam needs to sustain its progress in raising life expectancy of its citizens

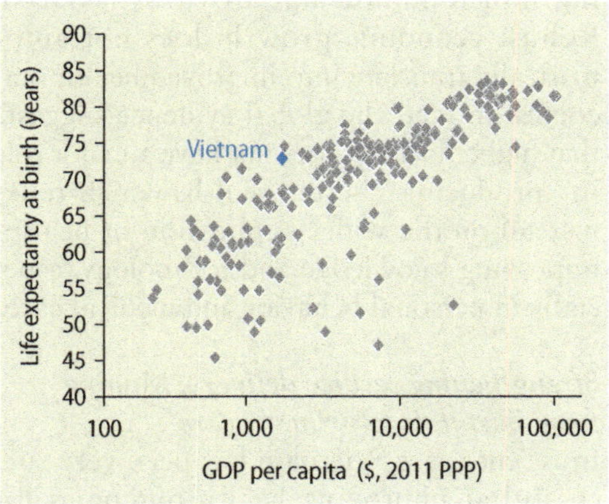

Source: World Development Indicators.

FIGURE 6.30 The poor use grassroots health care, while the rich use higher level hospitals

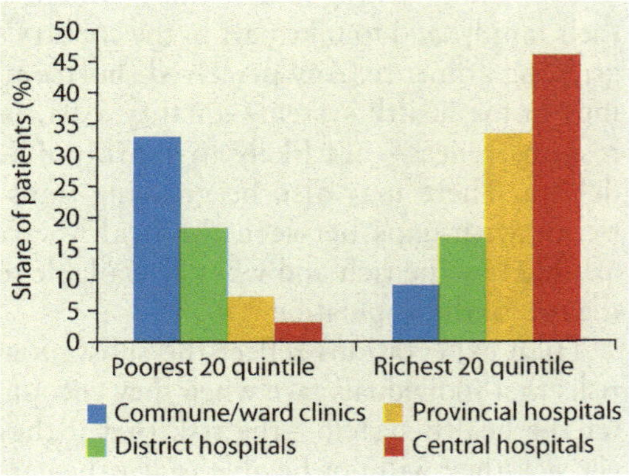

Source: Analysis of Vietnam Household Living Standards Survey 2012.

address inequality of opportunity in access to health care services should begin at the grassroots level.

Strengthening service delivery for primary care is arguably the most important task facing health policy makers over the next 20 years. For reasons of both quality and cost, a strong primary care function based on a continuous doctor–patient relationship is central to a modern, efficient health system. The evidence supporting this approach is abundant (Starfield, Shi, and Macinko 2005, for example). International evidence shows that a disease profile dominated by NCDs requires more complex case management and coordination of care, and primary care level plays a critical role in the process. A large majority (up to 80 percent) of NCD patients need lower-level care because their conditions can be controlled with self-management. Only about 5 percent of patients with NCDs require complex case management delivered by specialized or hospital-based care.

Global experience also suggests that countries seeking to make significant progress to address NCDs must rely more on public health and primary care than on hospital services. A few key interventions have been responsible for much of the significant longevity gains achieved by advanced health systems over the past 50 years (this period is instructive because it corresponds with a rise in life expectancy from the low 70s to over 80 years of age, which is also the task now facing Vietnam). First, there has been a large decline in smoking, with the most important policy in this regard being sharp increases in tobacco taxes. It is hard to envision Vietnam remaining a high performer without stronger anti-tobacco measures to help reduce smoking. Second, drugs to help treat risk factors for cardiovascular disease, such as hypertension and diabetes, most commonly managed and prescribed through primary care, have had a major impact. These two areas should be prioritized, due to their relatively lower cost as well as high impact.

More complex services that have had a significant health impact elsewhere will also warrant scaling up, albeit over a longer-term horizon. These include more advanced procedures to address heart disease, neonatal intensive care units for low-birth-weight infants, and screening programs to ensure early diagnosis and treatment of certain cancers (for example, breast and cervical). These interventions will be more costly on a population-wide scale than primary care services and are less likely to be pro-poor in the near term. Thus, while some pilots and centers of excellence may be valuable for learning purposes, scaling up can arguably wait until greater progress is made on public health and primary care agendas.

What steps are required for Vietnam to strengthen primary care over the next two decades, with the long-term aim of the population trusting their primary care providers? In the short term, it should build consensus on the importance of primary care, and set the broad parameters of organizational design and financing. It should also experiment and pilot, possibly with a focus on key diseases such as hypertension and diabetes. Over the medium to long term it will be important to revamp human resources policies and programs, resource allocation including provider payment, "gate-keeping" modalities (from the primary health care level), and coordination of care between primary and secondary levels, irrespective of the model of primary care delivery (solo or group practices, and so on).

It also needs to launch new graduate and post-graduate training programs and retrain existing cadres. Vietnam has the second lowest nurse-to-doctor ratio among more than 25 countries in Asia, suggesting a bias toward physician-based health care. A basic road map to strengthen primary care involves many steps (figure 6.31).

Thailand has been successful in shifting the focus of service delivery from tertiary level hospital-based care toward grassroots-based primary care. A key objective of the Universal Coverage Scheme (UCS), launched in 2001, was to strengthen the health system by placing a greater emphasis on primary care. Service delivery reform efforts through the UCS emphasized the development of family medicine, and primary care units at

FIGURE 6.31 Creating a basic road map to strengthen primary care entails many steps

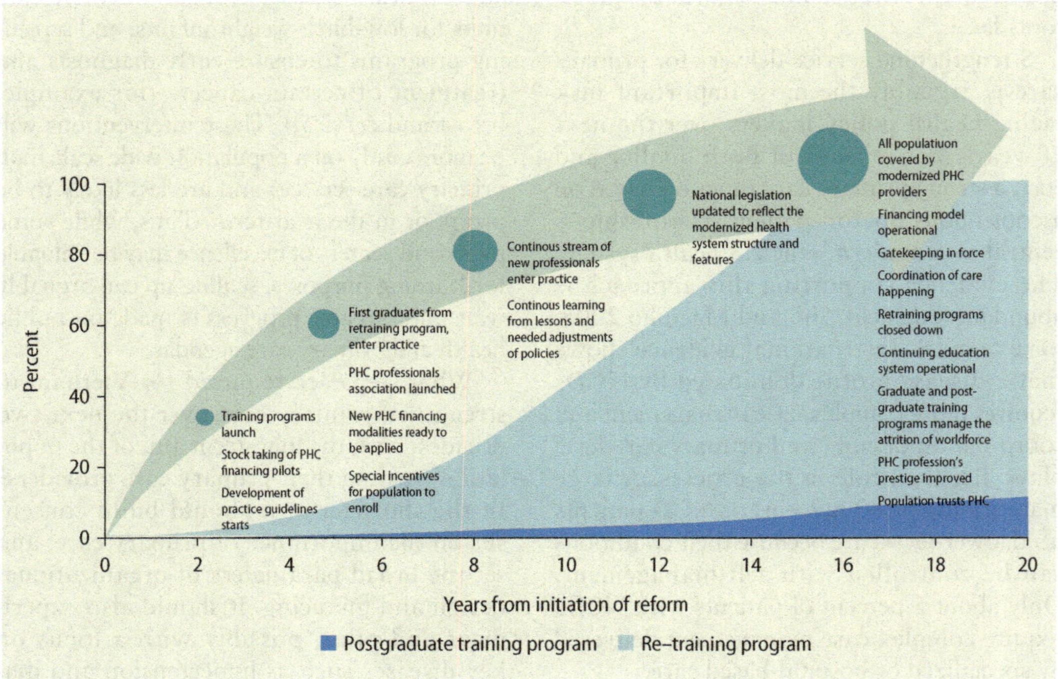

Source: World Bank and Development Research Center of the State Council, China 2013.
Note: PHC = primary health care.

the district level were strengthened. One of the main pillars of the approach was the use of strategic purchasing by the National Health Security Office (NHSO). The NHSO required all contracted hospitals to set up a primary care unit for designated population catchment sizes and areas, and to form district-level provider networks that would deliver primary care services and arrange patient referrals to secondary and tertiary-care services. This helped to shift the focus of care from specialists working in hospitals to family practitioners with stronger links to the community. There have been challenges in implementation, however, including a shortage of doctors to staff primary care units despite a policy of mandatory rural service for all health professional graduates. This constraint was addressed by rotating hospital doctors to work in clinics, as well as training a cadre of nurses and health workers to serve as the backbone of service delivery at the primary care level.

The hospital agenda is also critical. A key challenge is to exert greater influence over hospital accountability and efficiency through a more active strategic purchasing agency (Vietnam Social Security [VSS] or another body). This will require a shift from simply paying the bills submitted by providers to using information to ensure that patient care and cost-effectiveness are emphasized over hospital revenue maximization. For their part, patients need recourse to grievance-redress mechanisms.

Finally, there is a public health agenda related to urbanization. Most urban populations have better access to care and health outcomes than their rural counterparts, but with wider variation, and the urban poor face health risks the rural poor do not, including those related to air quality, road traffic safety, water, sanitation, and solid waste management, in addition to infectious diseases such as dengue and tuberculosis. Governments—especially municipal ones—need to manage and reduce these risks. More broadly, multisectoral advocacy for "health in all policies" should become a common undertaking of the Ministry of Health and others.

Financing health: Improving efficiency and equity

The major policy challenge facing Vietnam's health system over the next 20 years will be to achieve universal health coverage—that is, to ensure that everyone has access to good quality services without suffering financial hardship. Health system performance has relevance for the broader economy. There is now very strong evidence that conditions during early childhood—and especially child nutrition—have a strong impact on a wide range of economic and social indicators later in life, including schooling, learning, employment, and productivity. Ultimately, this also has implications for economic growth. Increasingly the health of older adults will also matter for economic performance, as Vietnam's aging population will pose new challenges to maintaining a healthy and productive workforce and mitigating the impact of a rising dependency ratio.

Since 2000, the government health budget has increased from 1.5 to 2.5 percent of GDP, and the share of total health expenditures paid out of pocket (OOP) has declined from about two-thirds to one-half. Over the same period, insurance enrollment has increased sharply, from less than 15 percent in 2000 to about 70 percent today, reflecting the government's incremental expansion that has targeted key vulnerable groups including the poor, children, and ethnic minorities.

Vietnam now spends a larger share of its income on health than almost any other country in developing Asia (figure 6.32a), yet households can be driven into poverty by unpredictable medical bills or discouraged from seeking necessary care at all due to high costs (figure 6.32b)—one of the pitfalls of high private OOP spending. The future is likely to see growing pressure to absorb it into the public purse.

Aging will impose additional cost pressures on the health system, accounting for up to one-third of the growth of health spending. Other factors, such as expanded insurance coverage and technology adoption, are likely to be more important. Because demographic change cannot be avoided while the other two drivers are amenable to policy intervention, rapidly rising health expenditures are not inevitable, but the risk should be managed carefully.

The health financing agenda for Vietnam over the next 20 years will be to stabilize the share of GDP spent on health near its current

FIGURE 6.32 Out-of-pocket health expenses push many Vietnamese into poverty

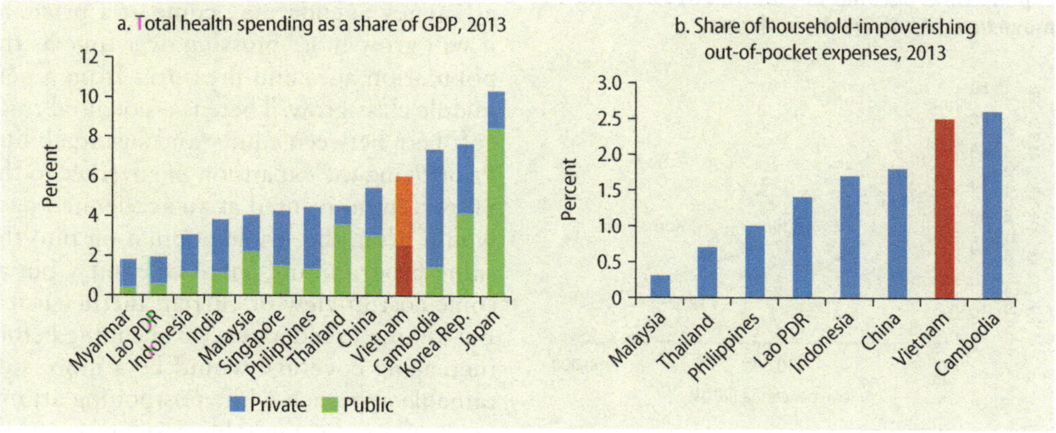

Source: World Development Indicators.

Source: Vietnam Household Living Standards Survey 2012 and Rannan-Eliya et al. 2013.

level while reducing reliance on OOP expenditures (figure 6.33). This will require crowding OOP through some combination of government spending and insurance contributions.

Some insights into what can be achieved can be gleaned by looking back at the performance of countries that had similar indicators in the 1990s to Vietnam today. Over almost 20 years, the average increase in total health expenditure among this group was a modest 0.7 percent of GDP (table 6.3).[15] For Vietnam, maintaining total health expenditures near 6 percent of GDP in 2035 would represent an above average achievement. On OOP spending, the average change among the comparator group (which, like Vietnam today, started with an OOP share near 50 percent) was a decrease of 9 percentage points.[16] An ambitious target for Vietnam would be a 20 percentage point decrease, to just under 30 percent. Ideally most remaining OOP expenses in 2035 will be for less cost-effective services and concentrated among the better-off.

A key agenda item as Vietnam seeks to reduce its reliance on OOP spending will be to expand insurance coverage to the roughly 30 percent of the population currently uninsured (figure 6.34). Many of these households include nonpoor informal sector workers, as the better off are covered through their formal sector contributions while a fraction of the poor

FIGURE 6.33 Reliance on out-of-pocket health expenditures declines as countries develop and move toward universal health care

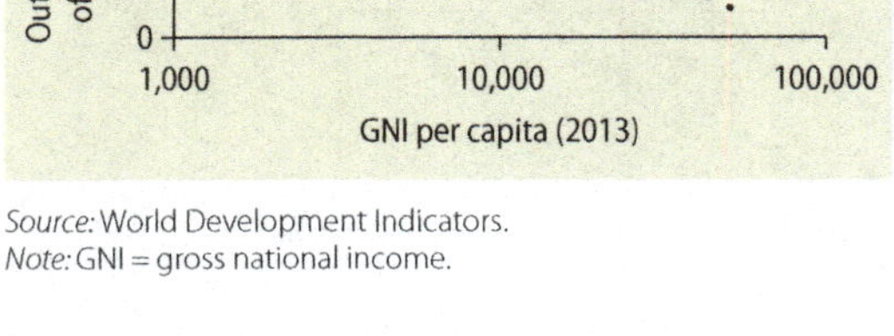

Source: World Development Indicators.
Note: GNI = gross national income.

are beneficiaries of premium subsidies paid by government. But many poor and vulnerable are not insured, because MOLISA's targeting approach is not perfect and the poverty line is low, excluding many poor households (as measured by comprehensive household surveys). An additional coverage challenge is that there are migrant workers who may be registered in their home district but do not have effective access where they live and work.

The current approach to expanding insurance coverage may not be adequate to achieve 100 percent coverage by 2035. Vietnam is relying on individual or household contributions alongside the gradual transition to a larger formal workforce. But this is a slow process, and some Ministry of Health projections have self-paying enrollees increasing by about 2 percentage points a year through 2020, which would not give full coverage in 20 years given today's low starting point.

Over the long term, how should new enrollees be funded? One option would be to offer premium subsidies to the uninsured, as it already attempts to do for some groups such as the poor and near-poor. A potentially much quicker route to a higher coverage alternative would be to allocate general tax revenue to cover the uninsured (table 6.4).

Expanded insurance coverage is a priority with longer-term impact, and more immediate inefficiencies should arguably be addressed first. These span a wide range of issues, from provider payment to pharmaceuticals to accountability. Delaying the efficiency agenda may come at a price, as it will grow more pressing over time as the population ages and pressures from a new middle class grow. There is a potential tradeoff here between equity and sustainability. Prioritizing the expansion of coverage to the 30 percent uninsured at an accelerated pace would bring the whole population into the same program and enhance equity, but at some cost in view of current inefficiencies. But aiming to reduce excess spending before increasing coverage would be a more sustainable approach while postponing attainment of a more equitable system. A middle road is also possible.

TABLE 6.3 Comparator countries averaged a 0.7 percent increase in total health expenditure, with out-of-pocket expenses decreasing 9 percent, 1990–2015

Indicator	Vietnam today	Average 20-year performance (1990s–present) of countries similar to Vietnam today	Potential 2035 target for a high-performing Vietnam
Life expectancy at birth	73.0 years	+4.1 years	+6.0 years (to reach 79.0 years)
Out-of-pocket spending as a share of total health expenditure	49%	−9.0%	−20% (to reach 29%)
Total health expenditure as a share of GDP	6.0%	+0.7%	0.0% (to remain at 6.0%)

Source: Information compiled from various sources.
Note: The similar indicators of the comparator countries are from the 1990s.

FIGURE 6.34 The current approach to expanding insurance coverage is unlikely to achieve 100 percent coverage by 2035

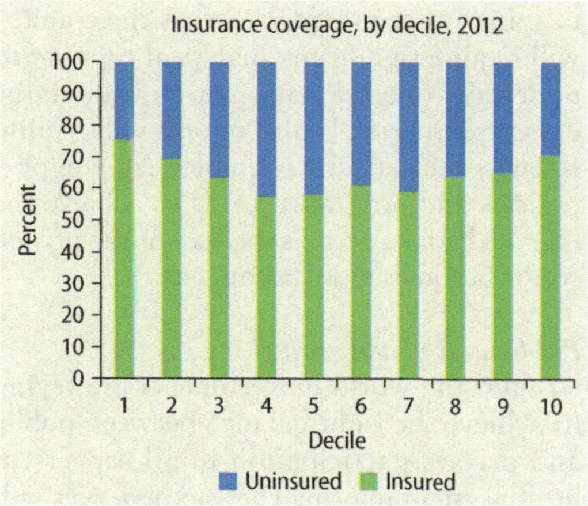

Source: Analysis of Vietnam Household Living Standards Survey 2012.

Perhaps the most important near-term area for efficiency gains is to rationalize the pharmaceutical system. In the past, hospitals have purchased drugs at widely varying prices, and the high costs are passed on to the government or the population. Centralized procurement and better use of state purchasing power to negotiate prices under a framework contract with pharmaceutical companies would help reduce costs. Vietnam has started to implement reforms in this area, but sustained effort will be required. There may be some tension with industrial policy priorities aimed at supporting domestic production. But from a health system perspective, lower prices are an obvious objective. Contracting private pharmacies can also be part of the solution (see the next subsection). Lastly, overconsumption of drugs is also a problem, and steps to enforce rational prescription patterns and address self-medication would help.

An additional area is to reform provider payments, including a shift toward a more strategic purchasing agency instead of a relatively passive payer of services. A transition from input-based financing from the Ministry of Health toward output-based payment by VSS is planned in the near term, and an initial move away from open-ended fee-for-service payment has begun as piloting of case-based payments is underway. But the provider payment environment remains fragmented and there is work to be done before incentives to oversupply are brought under control. In some cases, VSS has provided the wrong incentives—for example, by reimbursing pharmaceutical costs that vary widely for the same drug from one hospital to the next for no transparent reason. There is also presently an unequal treatment of provinces (and insured population groups) due to VSS allocation formulas. Enhancing the capacity of VSS (or an alternative purchaser) will be a critical part of strengthening provider payment.

A further move to reduce reliance on OOP and to improve efficiency entails strengthening the accountability of health care providers, in two broad approaches. The first is to rely on stronger stewardship by the Ministry of Health and VSS, with a clear delegation of responsibilities (for instance, a well-defined benefit package), coherent payment system,

TABLE 6.4 Alternative routes to 100 percent insurance coverage

Approach	Financing mechanism	Country examples	Advantages (for Vietnam)	Disadvantages (for Vietnam)
"Slower route"	Insurance contributions	Vietnam Philippines	More gradual approach means lower short-term fiscal burden Allows time to address existing inefficiencies before expanding coverage	Leaves many—including many of the poor—without insurance coverage for longer
"Faster route"	General tax revenue	Thailand Mexico	Achieves 100 percent insurance coverage sooner, including of the poor	Larger short-term fiscal burden Allows less time to address existing inefficiencies before expanding coverage

Source: World Bank and Ministry of Planning and Investment of Vietnam compilation.

strong information requirements by which providers report on their health care activities, and enforcement mechanisms. The second is to empower the population to hold providers accountable, which may be particularly important to discourage providers from extracting informal OOP from patients. Recent survey evidence indicates that 22 percent of respondents in Vietnam reported paying a bribe at a health facility within the previous 12 months, placing Vietnam in the bottom half of the nearly 100 countries under study.

A final priority to improve efficiency is to strengthen capital planning for infrastructure and equipment. The health financing agenda described here has obvious links with the service delivery reforms presented earlier. In particular, a stronger primary care system will promote efficiency. But it is also true that better primary care will help aid financial protection by keeping patients away from expensive (and frequently unnecessary) hospital care. Likewise, improving the efficiency of health expenditures will be essential to respond to the demand for more and better quality services.

Stepping back from all the potential reforms already discussed, it is clear that in the future Vietnam will be managing a more complex health system. An integrated primary care system requires strong information flows. Engaging the private sector will require a robust regulatory function. Emerging public health challenges, whether homegrown or from abroad, will require robust responses. Keeping a lid on pharmaceutical costs will require an ability to negotiate complex contracts with drug companies. Ensuring quality of care and efficiency of provision by hospitals and other providers across the country will require significant analytical capacity to undertake operational research using large datasets. In brief, health reform will require strong state capacity to implement complex policies and programs if it is to achieve the intended goals, even as the role of the private sector becomes more prominent.

Public and private roles

Around the world, governments are trying to achieve the right balance between public and private participation in all aspects of health system reform. These experiences will be directly relevant to Vietnam as it charts a path toward 2035.

Global patterns indicate that public financing must play the dominant role in paying for health care. In the majority of high-income countries, public spending accounts for at least 75 percent of total health expenditures. Many middle-income countries are headed in the same direction. This pattern has a strong economic rationale: people do not know when they might fall sick and how much it will cost if they do, and once ill they are not in a good position to judge where to seek care, what treatment is required, or in some cases even whether the doctor can be trusted. A reliance on private financing for health also tends to result in significant inequalities between rich and poor. These considerations will pose limits to how far a policy of "social mobilization" can go. As elsewhere, a predominant government role in health financing can also be expected in Vietnam.

Public funds do not need to flow exclusively to public providers, and thus a greater public–private mix is possible in service delivery, where private health care providers play a central role in many advanced health systems, especially at primary care level (table 6.5). In Vietnam, VSS has started to contract some private hospitals. In the years ahead, these relationships could be broadened and deepened, including by extending the approach to the outpatient setting.

There is no clear evidence from international experience that either public or private provision is "better"—what matters most is strong accountability, which requires clear delegation of tasks, adequate financing of service provision, collection and analysis information about what providers are doing, and enforcement of rules. Regulatory and supervisory authorities must play a key role in the oversight of public and private providers. (Vietnam's early experience with public–private purchasing arrangements for capital equipment at hospitals reveals some of the pitfalls of engaging the private sector without suitable accountability. Indeed, by obscuring the line between public and private, they could be discouraging the emergence of a robust private sector.)

An additional role for the private sector is delivery of health care services that cannot be afforded by government for the whole population. This may include high-cost interventions such as cardiology and oncology, for which there is demand from the better-off population (and who may otherwise seek treatment abroad). Private insurance, perhaps largely employer-based, may evolve further to help finance this care. Nonmedical aspects of health care provision, such as hoteling amenities, may become a common feature of these packages. Importantly, this will allow the government to focus its limited resources on a more cost-effective universal basic package for everyone else. As Vietnam grows more affluent, it should be presumed that eventually these services will also be funded by government for the broader population.

The private sector may have a comparative advantage in procuring and distributing pharmaceutical products. In many countries, government has curtailed its role in the direct procurement of drugs, including supply chain management, and instead contracts with private pharmacies to provide medicines to the population. This may be a particularly important step in Vietnam given the large inefficiencies in pharmaceutical procurement.

A broader development strategy to promote the private sector and job creation can sometimes come in conflict with health system objectives. For example, enacting measures to promote the domestic pharmaceutical industry at a cost of higher drug prices that are ultimately funded by the public purse will not be beneficial to the health sector. Similarly, an administratively complex health system may generate employment

TABLE 6.5 International experience indicates that strong accountability matters most in delivering health care—not public or private provision

Public/private sphere	Advanced systems (OECD countries)	Vietnam today
Health financing	Out-of-pocket spending share: 14% Private health insurance share: 6%	Out-of-pocket spending share: 49% Private health insurance share: <2%
Primary care provision	Private provision is more common in more than two thirds of countries	Mostly public provision
Hospital care provision	Public provision is most common. In a few countries, private not-for-profit is common. Private for-profit hospitals are relatively rare	Mostly public provision, but with public–private purchasing arrangements in some hospitals

Sources: World Development Indicators; Paris, Devaux, and Wei 2010.
Note: OECD = Organisation for Economic Co-operation and Development.

opportunities, but not in a productive way. Health policy makers should seek to avoid these pitfalls.

As Vietnam charts a path toward a stronger health system by 2035, a central challenge will be the difficult political economy of health reform. From tobacco lobbies to pharmaceutical companies to medical workers themselves, there are vested interests in the sector that can be expected to resist certain reforms. Doctors in particular are typically a well-educated and well-connected elite, many of whom prefer the prestige of using advanced equipment at a big-city hospital rather than taking blood pressure and writing prescriptions in a remote rural post. But Vietnam has made impressive strides in the past decade or more, providing an important foundation for further progress to come.

Aged and long-term care: An emerging need

Formal ALTC systems in the developing EAP remain nascent, but Vietnam, like other rapidly aging countries, will need to grapple with what is the appropriate and sustainable role of the state in an area that has traditionally been the domain of families, communities, and the health system.[17] Vietnam shows great demand for ALTC of different forms, from low-level social support to self-care activities of daily living—with which almost half of people 70 and over in Vietnam report having difficulties (HelpAge International 2015). And about two-thirds of adults expect government to be their primary source of support in old age (Jackson and Peter 2015). Proactive policy choices in the ALTC domain are therefore important, but require careful thought with respect to their interaction with informal care systems and existing formal health and welfare systems.

ALTC systems should be built around home- and community-based care ("aging in place")—as borne out globally—while a segment of older people receive residential care. More humane and fiscally sustainable, aging in place is also consistent with the expressed preferences of older people in the EAP region, in order to sustain family and social networks. One framework for ALTC policy is the "continuum of care," in which the large majority of older people in need of care receive it in the home (through some form of outreach services, often coordinated by social affairs-type agencies and/or community-based organizations), those with somewhat higher needs access community-based care, and only a small portion require residential care.

The continuum of care in ALTC as people move from modest to more intensive care needs also creates new demands for coordination, both within the state sector and between the state and nonstate sectors. Within the state sector, there is typically an institutional transition from welfare-type ministries (like MOLISA in Vietnam) managing ALTC at lower levels of care to health ministries as older people require more intensive medical intervention and eventually facility-based or institutional care. The boundaries between aged care and long-term care services are often blurred, and it requires close cross-agency cooperation to ensure that services are coordinated well across the continuum of care. In addition, the likelihood of a substantial role for nonstate providers in the ALTC sector will place new demands on the state for standard setting, human resource development in the caring industry, and regulation of quality and market rules.

The state cannot assume the full financing burden of ALTC. There will be a need to prioritize people and services for public support, but along what lines? For example, should priority for state financing for example be on the basis of level of frailty and disability, and/or focused primarily on the poorest? Should public financing come entirely from general revenue or is there a potential role for dedicated long-term care insurance (and how might that be afforded given the already high share of social contributions in Vietnam)? Should public financing be focused primarily on the supply side of the ALTC system or is there a role for financing on the demand side and letting elderly people and their families choose the type of care most suited to their situation? At this early stage in developing ALTC in Vietnam, the answers are unknown, but it is important to have the questions expressed.

Still, Vietnam needs to develop ALTC policy directions, ideally combined with well-evaluated pilots to test the culturally appropriate delivery models and better understand the market segments. As part of piloting, a critical challenge is to develop sustainable financing models, for the state and for citizens.

Social Protection

Vietnam's social protection system is in a transitional phase as it moves from being primarily reliant on informal, traditional sources of support toward a greater and more coherent role for the state. As countries transition from low to upper-middle income, their social protection systems typically grow in terms of GDP and public spending share. While social protection spending tends to rise over time and as countries get richer, falling rates of absolute poverty also drive a reorientation of social protection spending toward higher (and wider coverage) spending on social insurance, and a stronger link between social assistance and active labor programs.

Part of this social protection reform agenda is driven by the fact that Vietnam is at a demographic turning point, facing a slowdown in the growth of the labor force and a sharp expansion of the old-age population. The old-age dependency ratio—the ratio of older dependents to the working-age population—has been roughly constant for decades in Vietnam but will climb from 9.6 to 21.7 between 2015 and 2035 and continue to rise in the following decades. In other words, Vietnam will soon have many more old-age people to support for every person of working age (figure 6.35). Expanding social insurance coverage is both vital and challenging in light of the society's rapid aging.

Looking ahead to 2035, for Vietnam two strategic questions emerge for the social protection system:

1. How will Vietnam create a social protection system geared toward the risks faced by all people in a middle-class market society, as opposed to the current system that serves largely those at the top and bottom of the distribution in a fragmented manner? And what financing strategies can make this a reality?
2. How will Vietnam assure adequate financial protection for its growing old-age population in a fiscally sustainable way?

FIGURE 6.35 The old-age dependency ratio will increase rapidly

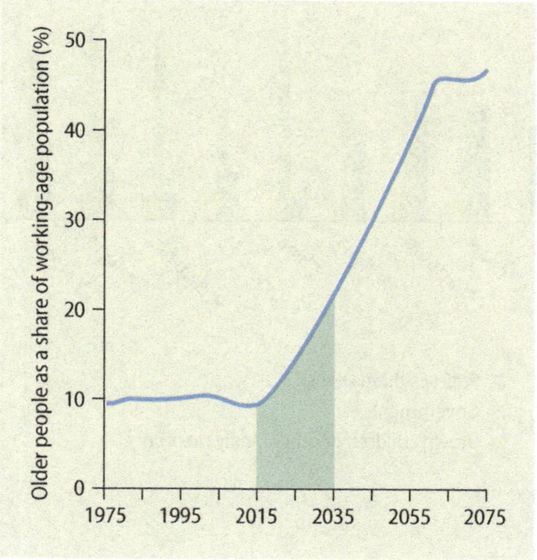

Source: United Nations 2015.

What is the desirable and sustainable social contract, with respect to social protection, between the Vietnamese state and its citizens and how will it differ from today? The period until 2035 will see a fundamental rebalancing of the relative roles of citizens and the state in social protection, driven by demographics in a low-fertility, aging society. It is also likely to be driven by changing social attitudes, increased wealth combined with greater income volatility, urbanization, and greater mobility of people, all of which change the expectations of citizens, especially among the younger generations. For example, more than 60 percent of the Vietnamese people expect the state to be their primary source of support in old age, an expectation that the country is not in a position to meet (figure 6.36).

FIGURE 6.36 The Vietnamese people expect the state to be their primary source of support in old age

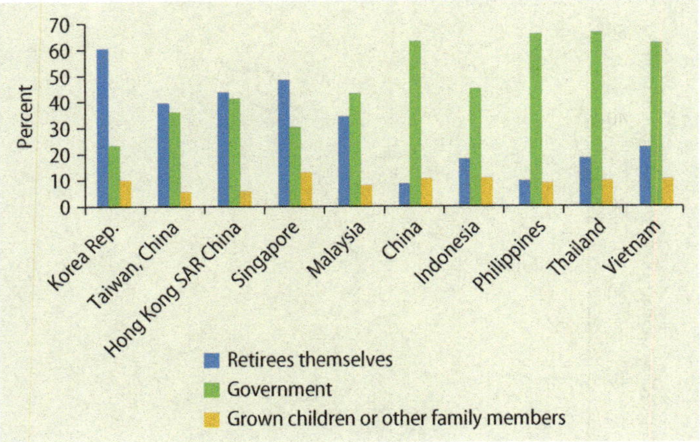

Source: Jackson and Peter 2015.

How do the tax and transfer system figure in the government's redistribution policies? And how do such policies interact with economic growth? In many countries, social protection addresses inequality, and tax/transfer systems are the primary vehicle for redistributive public policies. In Vietnam, the explicit and implicit subsidies accruing to public and formal private sector workers through pensions more than offset the targeted distribution through social assistance. Achieving sensible redistribution through social protection can foster social stability, address inequality, and help sustain economic growth.

Looking ahead to 2035, the institutional set-up, policy mix, coverage, financing, and delivery platforms of the social protection system in Vietnam are likely be fundamentally transformed. With respect to the policy mix, a well-functioning social protection system in an upper-middle-income country should perform three functions effectively—*protection* (of the poor and vulnerable), *prevention/mitigation* of risk for the whole population, and *promotional* policies to sustain productive movement out of poverty and into more efficient labor markets. At present, Vietnam does a fragmented and incomplete job on protection due to an underdeveloped, underfunded, and piecemeal safety net; does a very partial job on prevention due to low coverage of social insurance; and has an unclear strategy on promotional policies, where the system is also underfunded and fragmented, and in a transitional state between area-based antipoverty approaches and household-focused interventions. Articulation between the three functions of social protection is weak, so that social protection programs do not operate as an integrated and coherent system. For Vietnam, reform is needed in all three areas to achieve the kind of system that will be expected by its citizens.

The dramatic demographic changes that the country will soon encounter, with emerging fiscal risks, suggest that an immediate priority will be developing a strategy to achieve adequate and sustainable old-age protection.

Status and issues: The pension system

Against pension systems elsewhere in the EAP region and globally, Vietnam's system stands out on several aspects. First, contributory coverage is low, though on the global relationship between share of working-age population participating in contributory pension schemes and GDP per capita, Vietnam is around where one might expect given its high labor market informality (according to the World Bank Pension Database). At the end of 2013, social insurance covered about 10.9 million people in the compulsory scheme and 176,000 people in the voluntary scheme. This is just 20 percent of the total workforce, with coverage heavily concentrated among the top 40 percent of the distribution (figure 6.37).

Second, in terms of public spending on pensions, Vietnam is slightly below the global average for its share of population 60 years and older (figure 6.38), and the risk is that it will move quickly to the right in the figure due to rapid aging, just as it faces financing constraints on increased spending.

Third, on "generosity" within the contributory pension system, Vietnam is an outlier within the EAP region and globally, and continues to have high replacement rates, a product of high accrual rates in its pension system. This situation will improve somewhat as a result of the 2014 reforms, which reduced annual accrual rates[18]—though the adjustments only become fully effective from 2022—and still fall short of making the system sustainable. A complicating factor is that Vietnamese workers have typically contributed against a minimum base salary, so people combine high replacement rates with low absolute value of pensions. The 2014 reforms aim to broaden the compensation base on which contributions are levied, but achieving the desired outcome will require significant improvements in social insurance administration.

Vietnam has a high social contribution rate for pensions (table 6.6). In the region, the only country with a higher contribution rate is China, and more competitive parts of China have lower rates (for example, coastal prefectures of Guangdong). Some of its neighbors' lower contribution rates are helped by heavy public subsidies that match worker contributions.

FIGURE 6.37 Pension coverage should increase as Vietnam moves to upper-middle-income status, 2013

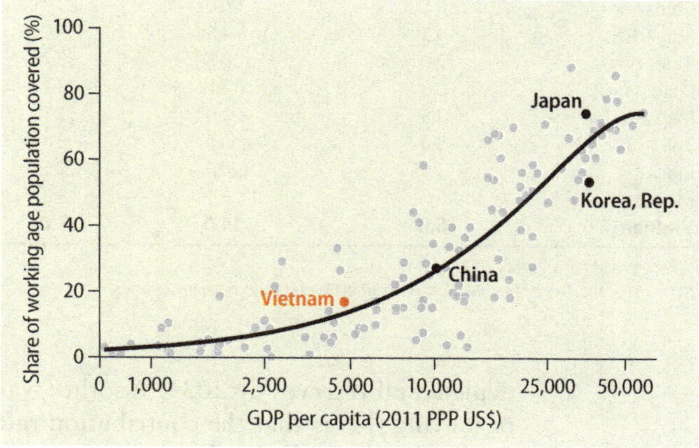

Source: World Bank 2014b.

Even with the 2014 reforms, the current pension system is not sustainable. Prior to the reform, the pension fund was projected to enter into deficit from 2021 and to have

FIGURE 6.38 Vietnam currently has low pension spending, but this is expected to rise quickly in coming years

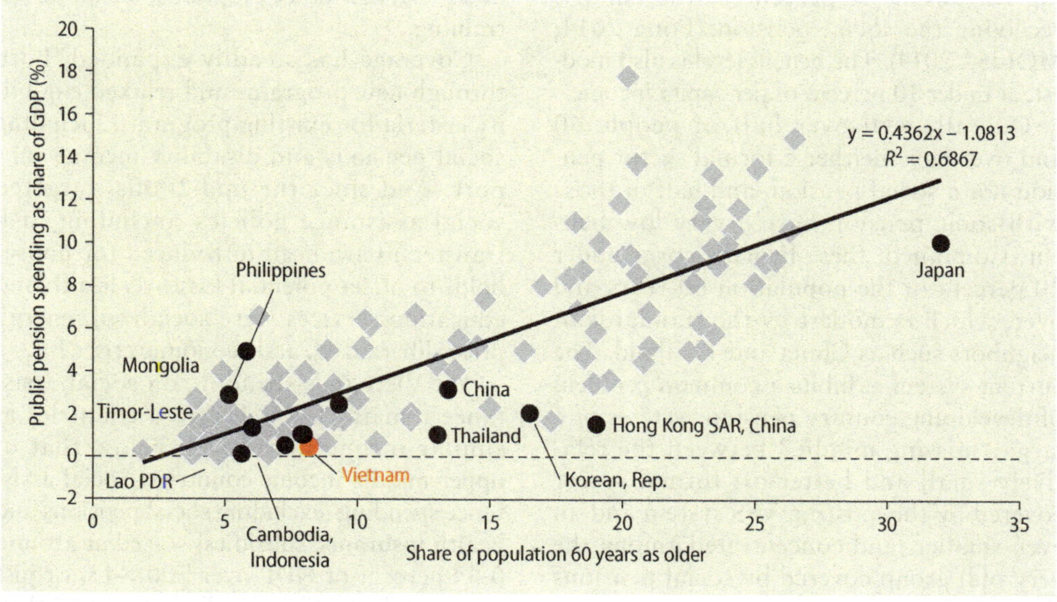

Source: World Bank 2014b and United Nations 2015.

TABLE 6.6 Vietnam has a high social contribution rate for pensions

Country	Employee	Employer	Total
China	8.0	20.0	28.0
Korea, Rep.	4.5	4.5	9.0
Indonesia	2.0	3.7	5.7
Philippines	3.3	7.1	10.4
Malaysia	11.5	11.0	22.5
Thailand	3.0	3.0	6.0
Brazil	7.65	20.0	27.65
Mexico	1.7	6.9	8.6
Vietnam	**8.0**	**14.0**	**22.0**

Source: World Bank 2014b.
Note: For China, this is the maximum rate. Many prefectures have lower rates.

FIGURE 6.39 Vietnam has a large "missing middle" of old-age support

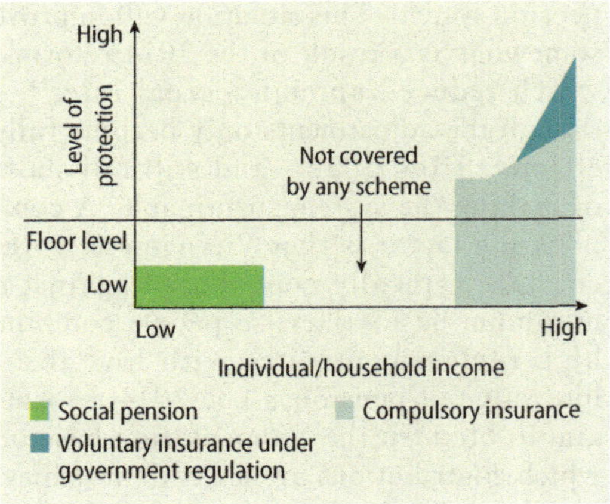

Source: Galian 2014.

depleted all reserves by 2034. Another way of putting this is that the contribution rate required to keep the fund in balance would have had to rise to almost 30 percent of salary by 2035, and to 80 percent of salary by 2080. This would clearly not be sustainable from a competitiveness perspective and would imply major subsidies from the budget. The 2014 reforms help but do not go far or fast enough.

Vietnam also has a social pension, tightly targeted for those age 60–79 and pension-tested from age 80. As of the end of 2013, there were 95,635 people aged 60–79 (or about 1.3 percent of people aged 60–79) and 1,410,064 people aged 80 and over (accounting for about 79 percent of the cohort) receiving the social pension (Long 2014; MOLISA 2014). The benefit level is also modest, at under 10 percent of per capita income.

Overall, well over half of people 60 and over have neither a formal sector pension nor a social pension, and half of those with some pension have a very low benefit. Combined, these benefits cover under 20 percent of the population 60 years and over, which is modest by the standards of neighbors such as China and Thailand. The current system exhibits a common problem of developing country pension systems of a large "missing middle" between the relatively small and better-off formal sector covered by the existing VSS system and an even smaller (and concentrated among the very old) group covered by social pensions (figure 6.39).

Status and issues: Safety net programs

Household- and individual-based cash transfer programs have expanded sharply over the past 15 years. The social assistance system is no longer a simple last-resort income support system for people who cannot work and do not have family support. In particular, it has evolved from reliance mainly on area-based development and antipoverty programs (emphasizing in-kind and programs targeting the poorest communes) to the current mix of area- and household-targeted antipoverty and social assistance programs, including job training.

Coverage has steadily expanded, both through new programs and relaxed eligibility criteria for existing programs, including social pensions and disability income support. And since the mid-2000s, targeted social assistance policies (including cash transfers) have been introduced for households to offset potential losses as health and education services were socialized, energy prices liberalized, and economic crises hit.

Yet Vietnam's spending on social assistance remains low relative to countries at similar incomes, and well below that of upper-middle-income countries. Social assistance spending (excluding social pensions and health insurance subsidies) stayed at around 0.69 percent of GDP over 2008–13, or just over half the EAP regional average and below half the global average among lower-middle-income countries (about 1.5 percent).

On coverage and generosity, social assistance in Vietnam was in the mid-range to cover the bottom quintile in the late 2000s, at just over 50 percent including social pensions (figure 6.40). This is well below some neighbors but mid-range among Association of Southeast Asian Nations. But coverage and generosity vary hugely across provinces, with some covering only a few percent of households, and others a third or more. Average benefit levels were in line or slightly above those of EAP neighbors, at about 26 percent of pretransfer levels in 2008.

Thus in the past 15 years, the social assistance system has become broader and somewhat more protective, but also more complex and fragmented, and changes have been introduced in an ad hoc manner. For example, at least five government decisions provide cash transfers for school-related expenses, excluding provincial programs.

Delivery systems are much below the quality expected from a country at Vietnam's development level. For example, Vietnam has a well-established mechanism to identify the poor but with methodological and governance-related deficits. Commune authorities conduct a poverty census every five years, updated annually. But implementation is uneven, standard rules and procedures are not strictly followed locally, and quality control of data is not rigorous, though preparations for the 2015 census suggest that this should improve in the current round. Nor is there a valid national or provincial household database for all assistance programs, causing government agencies to duplicate beneficiary lists for each program. Mechanisms for benefit payments, and monitoring and oversight of social assistance, are also inadequate. Payments are typically handled by districts and commune officials through visits to beneficiaries, and some education benefit payments are handled by schools, which are just not equipped to do this. (One recent promising reform was to assign VN Post as a payment provider for social insurance benefits nationwide and selected social assistance benefits in four provinces.)

FIGURE 6.40 Social assistance coverage and generosity vary across provinces but were in line with or slightly above East Asia Pacific neighbors

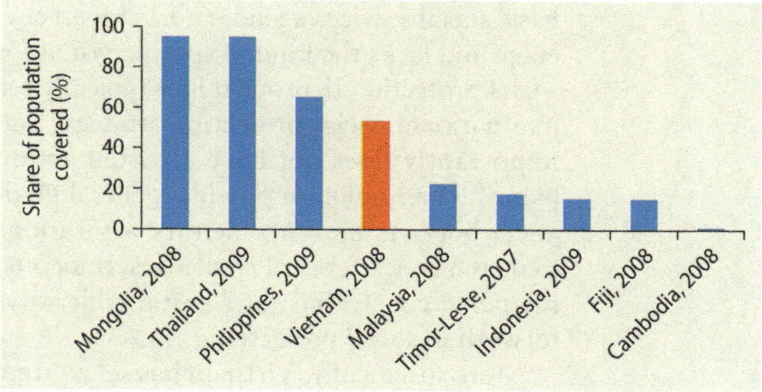

Source: Galian 2014.

Service delivery is also disconnected. There is no local, institutional structure that effectively links beneficiaries of cash transfers to supply-side health, education, and poverty reduction services, for example, through village/commune social collaborators who can provide support through case management and counseling services. While there is strong local monitoring, oversight at the provincial or central level is weak and mechanisms for bottom-up information management are underdeveloped due to the absence of an integrated management information system. Beneficiary-level information is not yet readily available beyond the commune. This restricts the ability of higher levels of government to monitor program performance and improve local accountability.

In short, Vietnam is transitioning from area-based antipoverty interventions toward household-focused cash transfers, and both types coexist. But the shift is piecemeal: it lacks clear vision of future priorities and instruments of support, duplicates social assistance transfers and support and area-based programs, and induces policy incoherence across agencies and levels of government.[19]

Policy directions: General

The social protection sector in Vietnam lacks a well-defined and evidence-based strategy that sets goals and targets. While Resolution is on Social Policies for 2012–20 (June 2012) sets out a wide-ranging social protection and basic social services agenda, it has broad coverage and lacks the kind of specific vision for social protection that one might typically see in a national social protection strategy, and importantly does not have a costed action plan.[20] The resolution provides general guidance, but acts more to identify aspirations than as a concrete set of challenges, tradeoffs, financing constraints, and sustainable ways forward in social protection.

More specifically, Vietnam has set a target of 50 percent coverage of pensions by 2020, but the strategy to realize it remains unclear. The target is unlikely to be reached under the current policy and financing approach. Essentially, Vietnam is "losing the race" between pension coverage expansion and rapid aging, on several fronts.

First, Vietnam's recent modest performance in expansion of contributory scheme participation suggests that a target closer to 30 percent is more likely realistic by 2020, and even that will need continued improvements in program administration by VSS. The bigger question is whether the existing combination of a purely contributory model for the formal pension scheme and a low coverage social pension approach will ever be sufficient to achieve widespread coverage beyond the formal sector. Global experience suggests this is unlikely and that Vietnam risks stagnating its pension coverage expansion at about 30 percent of the labor force in the contributory scheme and a further 20 percent of elderly in social pensions of some form. This is a common middle-income country challenge.

A second goal of the government is to achieve sustainability in its existing formal sector pension system. The goal is linked to the first goal of coverage expansion in that controlling deficits in the existing pension system is essential to creating the fiscal space for general revenue to fund old-age support. The recent social insurance reforms are a move in the right direction, but the slow pace of phase-in, alongside failure to move far enough (for example, on accrual rates) or at all in some cases (for instance, retirement ages) suggests that the pension fund will struggle to sustain balance, and will squeeze fiscal space to finance the coverage expansion agenda.

Even with 2014's social insurance reforms, the formal pension scheme remains unsustainable and will need further adjustment, without which the pension system will most likely reach a crisis during the 2020s. The central question is whether further reforms are politically possible.

On the safety net, Resolution 15 provides some general directions, with a specific target for 2.5 million beneficiaries of regular social allowances by 2020 (of which 30 percent are to be elderly). This is broadly the same target group size as currently receives benefits. Where the document is less clear is on the relative balance between poor households, meritorious people (who may or may not be poor), and other household characteristics (with or without children, disabilities, and so on).

Policy directions: Expanding pension coverage

A first step in social insurance coverage expansion is achieving higher participation rates in the formal private sector. In Vietnam, even higher inclusion of formal sector workers has proved challenging, with only two-thirds of formal private sector employees participating in social insurance (as against around 90 percent of FDI and 93 percent for state-owned sectors) (Vietnam Social Security 2013). The "low hanging fruit" of coverage expansion is thus achieving fuller coverage of formal sector workers. But this cannot happen without major improvements in social security administration, and the current rate of pension contributions creates incentives to evade. The feasibility of targets will also be affected by the demand side with respect to migrants, who may generally prefer to trade off higher salaries for less social insurance coverage.

A bigger challenge is extending coverage to the informal sector. International experience offers a range of approaches, all of which suggest that it would be very challenging to achieve wide pension coverage of informal sector workers through a purely contributory approach. This has also been the case with the expansion of health insurance in Vietnam. Three main options, which need not be mutually exclusive, are expanding social pensions, matching defined contribution (MDC) schemes, and adopting a hybrid of MDC and the basic pension.

Expanding social pensions is the easiest way to expand coverage and has achieved high coverage in a number of countries, including Thailand.[21] But it involves tradeoffs between coverage, degree of financial protection to the elderly, and fiscal costs. While Vietnam already has a universal social pension, the current threshold of 80 years old is very high, and contrasts with a typical threshold in countries with social pensions of closer to 65 years old. A key consideration is fiscal affordability. Projections suggest that a pension-tested elderly social pension at the level of the poverty line for people 65+ years of age would cost about 0.7 percent of GDP for the remainder of the decade, rising over 2020–2035 as the number of elderly rises sharply (Long 2014).

MDC schemes are usually voluntary, relying on incentives rather than a mandate (see Hinz et al. 2013). Most countries using MDCs sustain the subsidy for the entire contribution period of the worker. Given subsidy-matching costs, MDC pensions are subject to the same questions on whether to make the program universal for informal workers or targeted in some way. MDC schemes are more administratively demanding than social pensions, but have achieved some notable successes in expanding coverage, particularly in Korea, where coverage more than doubled between 1995 and 1999.

China has rolled out an innovative hybrid of the MDC scheme and the basic pension. The hybrid is voluntary and is not part of the formal sector pension schemes. Each contributor has an individual account, with a public subsidy partially matching a small yearly contribution. After 15 years of contributions, the worker is entitled to a monthly basic pension of around 220,000 Vietnamese dong equivalent (about US$10). The scheme thus blends incentives to contribute during the working life with a modest basic pension after retirement.[22]

Pension reform faces tradeoffs between adequacy, coverage, and sustainability and a potential tradeoff between the system's sustainability and the labor market impacts of high social insurance contribution rates and other factors like low retirement ages. To date, Vietnam has sought adequacy of pensions among a limited group of public servants and formal sector workers, but achieved this at the expense of low coverage and poor sustainability. The commitment to expand coverage and to improve the social insurance system's sustainability under the 2014 Law indicate a welcomed rebalancing of the historical tradeoffs.

The coverage expansion targets that Vietnam has set are ambitious. Few developing countries have achieved such a scale-up without publicly financed incentives to participate for the informal sector. Public subsidies will almost certainly be necessary to induce informal sector workers to join contributory schemes voluntarily (as has been seen with health insurance contributions for the near poor), and mandating their participation will most likely not work. Innovation will be needed to achieve substantial coverage expansion.

If Vietnam is serious about coverage expansion of its pension system, it will also require deeper parametric reforms of the existing pension system. It cannot afford both its formal sector pension and the new subsidies that will most likely be needed to expand coverage to informal workers without further reforms of the existing system. These reforms include gradual increases in official retirement age (which has not kept pace with increased longevity), increasing penalties for early retirement, more disciplined implementation of pension indexation on the basis of prices, further reduction in the annual accrual rate while broadening the base for collections to full compensation, reduction in special categories of privileged pensioner, and better provisioning for financing.

Achievements in reforming the pension policy will be hard to implement unless Vietnam modernizes its social insurance administration—as recognized in the Vietnam Social Services Modernization Strategy 2016–20. Higher public subsidies, as Vietnam's health insurance reform demonstrated, do not suffice. Vietnams' social services standards must also improve. Recent progress in the social services, with moves to reform its business processes, consolidate its information technology systems, and improve its client orientation, need sustained investment and high-level political support.

Policy directions: Reforming the social safety net

The overall policy mix of social services needs reform, along several dimensions. Underserved groups loom large for protection against risks and vulnerabilities in old age, consistent with the demographic profile. But investing early in young children's nutrition and early childhood development is also important. Today, no programs target households with children age 0–3 years.

Addressing the widening disparity between regions and groups through a more coherent policy for poor areas and for poor people is another dimension. Area- and household-based protective and promotional policies should be designed as a coherent package of support that addresses multiple vulnerabilities. Programs targeted to poor areas should continue. But the design of these area-based programs must shift from a simple infusion of productive assets or local infrastructure development to community-driven income generation.

Another need is a more coherent approach to household-based transfers, with a more comprehensive package of support. Consolidated policies could have common objectives and could target similar groups. Multiple education subsidies are an example.

Strengthening multidimensionality is a further dimension, based on the growing recognition of the need to address multiple deprivations captured by monetary and nonmonetary indicators, allowing poverty to be determined by comparing the household score on composite indicators with an income threshold. In addition, households with specific nonmonetary deprivations (for example, a child of school-going age not enrolled in school, inadequate housing) can be identified. The general approach was recently endorsed by the government. The most appropriate approach would be to use this information to provide customized and comprehensive packages of support. A sequenced approach would be desirable, initially emphasizing simplicity in design and implementation. The final dimension in the overall policy mix is to hugely expand the active labor market component of the social protection system in order to ease movement of people between rural and urban areas, and to match workers to jobs.

The second set of reforms touches on overhauling delivery systems for social assistance programs to realize greater efficiency and welfare impact, along two tracks. Track one requires improving systems to identify beneficiaries, better targeting through the poverty census, and systematic enrollment procedures for social assistance programs and beneficiary management, benefit payments (improving current cash payments by using third-party agents for greater transparency and accountability, eventually moving to electronic payments), community mobilization and social work networks, feedback/grievance redress, monitoring and evaluation, and management information systems.

Track two entails consolidating delivery systems across programs: information consolidation through digitized household and individual information in the national beneficiary database; and process consolidation, that is, relying on the same systems to deliver different programs, including a national beneficiary database, management information system, third-party payment agency (or electronic payments in the long run), collaborator network in the short term, and social workers in the long term.

An overarching question in the third and final set of reforms is the appropriate role of the state and citizens/families in providing social protection support of different forms. What is the emerging social contract in Vietnam and how is it likely to evolve over the coming two decades? The assumption of the family as the permanent primary source of support is increasingly open to question, with about two-thirds of adults expecting government to be their primary source of support in old age (Jackson and Peter 2015). Among nonfamily providers, the government will remain paramount in the short and long terms—even if nonstate providers are gradually expected to play more of a role—staying the primary financer and provider for both social insurance and social safety nets to 2035 and beyond.

In areas where the government collaborates with the for-profit and the not-for-profit private sector and civil society organizations, the regulatory and contracting framework needs to focus on their participation to ensure basic service standards, fiduciary compliance, and performance monitoring. Social protection is an area where collaboration with social partners such as unions, citizen groups, and employer associations is vital, more so when difficult social insurance reforms are needed.

The national level of social support will need a stronger coordinating mechanism across agencies to develop a more coherent strategy for reforms, linking social insurance and social assistance, which currently operate in silos. A fundamental reappraisal of the roles (policies, financing, and implementation) of national and subnational governments is needed, including implications for fiscal equalization.

The political economy risks of social protection reform in Vietnam must not be forgotten. First, insiders in the civil service and formal sector are a vocal and influential group. Those who stand to gain are disbursed, lack influence, and are not well organized. Second, if the social insurance system shifts more to general revenue and aims for greater spatial equalization, richer areas may object to greater cross-subsidization of poorer areas. Third is the relative lack of voice among safety net beneficiaries, which may mean a steady state of social safety net spending that is less than desirable, and results in an overall social protection system where public subsidies are less progressive than desirable. A related question is the optimal degree of targeting that promotes efficiency and maximizes poverty reduction while not being so narrow that popular and political support for social safety nets programs is undermined. Finally, there will be a need to overcome entrenched attitudes that social protection spending is a drag on growth. In fact, empirical studies from the International Monetary Fund find that redistribution—when sensibly done—accounts for around 0.5 percent additional GDP growth a year (Ostry, Berg, and Tsangarides 2014). Higher social protection spending has also been found in developing countries to be associated with higher average growth in the 1990s and 2000s (Zaman and Tiwari 2012).

Finally, a big challenge in realizing the social protection reform agenda, especially in social insurance, will be how to finance what will almost inevitably be expanding public spending. This will require fresh thinking on the right financing mix that balances sustainability, system coverage, and labor competitiveness, among others. Overall, general revenue financing of social protection will be more important, both within traditionally contributory programs like pensions (just as for health insurance) and in somewhat higher spending on social safety nets. This will require wider reform of Vietnam's tax structure, as there is no scope for further increases in social insurance taxes without risking compromising the country's long-term competitiveness.

Notes

1. The Kinh and Hoa, having comparable poverty levels and social indicators, are often grouped together. The Kinh are the largest ethnic minority group, accounting for

approximately 75 percent of the Vietnamese population.

2. For example, in the United States, poverty rates are 26 percent among Native Americans and 28 percent among African Americans, compared with 11 percent among whites. See Hall and Patrinos (2012) for analysis of poverty of ethnic minorities and indigenous peoples around the world.
3. The causes of poverty of ethnic minorities in Vietnam has been the subject of a large number of studies, for example, ADB (2003), DFID and UNDP (2003), Oxfam and ActionAid (2009), and World Bank (2009b, 2012c). Studies carrying out statistical decompositions of majority–minority differences in consumption or earnings include Van de Walle and Gunewardena (2000), Baulch, Pham, and Reilly (2008), Baulch et al. (2010), and Dang (2012).
4. Ethnic minorities are concentrated principally in the Northern Mountains and Central Highlands, with a smaller concentration in the Mekong Delta.
5. Stunting means the height-for-age is more than two standard deviations below the median for a reference population.
6. These projections assume that age-specific-disability rates remain constant over time. This is an approximation. Because disability among the current old-age population includes war-related injuries, rates of disability among the old-age population may fall over time.
7. NCCD (2010) conveys a similar message.
8. The prime minister enacted document no. 495/TTg, which restricted movement. Hanoi and Hai Phong then introduced *hộ khẩu*. The system was formally extended to the entire country in 1964.
9. The most detailed analysis on these issues is based on the 2009 Urban Poverty Survey conducted in Hanoi and Ho Chi Minh City, updated by more recent qualitative work.
10. ADB (2013) has a useful summary of the literature on these characteristics and impacts of middle classes globally and in Asia.
11. The figures for 1989 are based on an analysis of the population and housing census and those for "today" on the 2014 labor force survey.
12. The Institute for Workers and Trade Unions (2014) study set this level.
13. In 2013, labor force membership was 76 percent in the public sector and 33 percent in the private sector. Only China is higher, at 79 percent in 2010. Korea, Indonesia, Malaysia, and the Philippines were in the very low double digits in recent years. (World Bank staff calculations based on the Labor Force Survey 2013, and World Bank 2012a.
14. This includes MOLISA, particularly the local Departments of Labor, Invalids, and Social Affairs.
15. But the average increase in total health expenditure among this group varied widely. Several countries saw total expenditures rise by more than 2.5 percent of GDP, while others witnessed a decline.
16. The top performer was Thailand with a decline of 30 percentage points (its OOP share is now below 15 percent), but several countries experienced an increase over the same period.
17. See World Bank (2015) regional aging study.
18. In the late 2000s, the average annual accrual rates in defined benefit pension schemes were 1.7 percent for the world, 1.8 percent for the EAP region, but only 1 percent in China and Korea, against 2.25 percent for men and 2.75 percent for women in Vietnam, post-2014 reforms (World Bank Pensions database).
19. For the GIZ, see Giang et al. 2011.
20. The 2010 draft national social protection strategy was never formally endorsed.
21. For a global review, see Holzmann, Robalino, and Takayama 2009; Palacios and Sluchynskyy 2006.
22. For more detail on the Chinese pension system, see Dorfman et al. 2013.

References

Acemoglu, Daron, and David Autor. 2012. "What Does Human Capital Do?" *Journal of Economic Literature* 50 (2): 426–63.

ADB (Asian Development Bank) 2013. *ADB Annual Report 2013*. Manila: ADB.

Banerjee, Abhijit, and Esther Duflo. 2008. "What is Middle Class about the Middle Classes around the World?" *Journal of Economic Perspectives* 22 (2): 3–28.

Barro, Robert, and Jong-Wha Lee. 2010. "A New Data Set of Educational Attainment in the World, 1950–2010." *Journal of Development Economics* 104 (1): 184–198.

Baulch, Bob, Hoa Thi Minh Nguyen, Phuong Thi Thu Phuong, and Hung Hung Thai Pham. 2010. "Ethnic Poverty in Vietnam." Working Paper 169, Chronic Poverty Research Centre, Manchester, UK.

Baulch, Bob, Hung Pham, and B. Reilly. 2008. *Decomposing the Ethnic Gap in Living Standards in Rural Vietnam: 1993 to 2004*. Brighton, UK: Institute of Development Studies, University of Sussex.

Betcherman, Gordon, Amy Luinstra, and Makoto Ogawa. 2001. "Labor Market Regulation: International Experience in Promoting Employment and Social Protection." Social Protection Discussion Paper 128, World Bank, Washington, DC.

Birdsall, Nancy, Graham Carol, and Pettinato Stefano. 2000. "Stuck in The Tunnel: Is Globalization Muddling the Middle Class?" Working Paper 14, Brookings Institution, Center on Social and Economic Dynamics, Washington, DC.

Chi, Do Quynh, and Di van den Broek. 2013. "Wildcat Strikes: A Catalyst for Union Reform in Vietnam?" *Journal of Industrial Relations* 55 (1): 783–99.

Clarke, Simon, Chang-Hee Lee, and Do Quynh Chi. 2007. "From Rights to Interests: The Challenge of Industrial Relations in Vietnam." *Journal of Industrial Relations* 49 (1): 545–68.

Coxhead, Ian, Nguyen Viet Cuong, and Linh Hoang Vu. 2015. *Migration in Vietnam: New Evidence from Recent Surveys*. Hanoi: World Bank.

Dang, Hai anh. 2012. "Vietnam: A Widening Poverty Gap for Ethnic Minorities." In *Indigenous Peoples, Poverty, and Development*, edited by Hall, G., and H. A. Patrinos, 1-35, Cambridge, UK: Cambridge University Press.

———. 2013. "Private Tutoring in Vietnam: A Review of Current Issues and its Major Correlates." Policy Research Working Paper 6618, World Bank, Washington, DC.

Del Carpio, X., C. Nguyen, H. Nguyen, and L. C. Wang. 2013. *The Impacts of Minimum Wages on Employment, Wages and Welfare: The Case of Vietnam*. Washington, DC: World Bank East Asia Pacific Social Protection and Labor Unit.

DFID (Department for International Development) and UNDP (United Nations Development Programme). 2003. *Poverty Reduction in the Northern Mountains: A Synthesis of Participatory Poverty Assessments in Lao Cai and Ha Giang Province and Regional VHLSS Data*. Hanoi: DFID and UNDP.

Dorfman, Mark, Robert Holzmann, Philip O'Keefe, Dewen Wang, Yvonne Sin, and Richard Hinz. 2013. *China's Pension System: A Vision*. Washington, DC: World Bank.

Duc, Le Thuc, and Tran Ngo Minh Tam. 2013. "Why Children in Vietnam Drop out of School and What They Do After That." Young Lives Working Paper 102, Oxford, UK.

Easterly, W. 2001. "The Middle Class Consensus and Economic Development." *Journal of Economic Growth* 6 (1) 317–35.

Galian, Carlos. 2014. Social Protection Assessment for Vietnam. Draft unpublished mimeo. World Bank, Hanoi.

Gallup World Poll (data). 2014. Washington, DC. http://www.gallup.com/services/170945/world-poll.aspx.

Garcia de León, Pedro, Corinne Heckmann, and Gara Rojas González. 2012. "How Is the Global Talent Pool Changing?" Organisation for Economic Co-operation and Development (OECD) Education Indicators in Focus 05, OECD, Paris.

Giang, Nguyen, Le Duong, Le Bach, Tran Giang Linh, and Nguyen Thi Phuong Thao. 2011. *Social Protection for Rural-Urban Migrants in Vietnam: Current Situation, Challenges, and Opportunities*. CSP Research Report 08, Institute for Social Development Studies, Hanoi.

Giang, N. T. 2014. "Briefing on hộ khẩu-related Issues of the Migrant Population in Go Vap, District 12, and Binh Tan." Unpublished manuscript, Ho Chi Minh City.

Glewwe, Paul, Qihui Chen, and Bhagyashree Katare. 2012. "What Determines Learning among Kinh and Ethnic Minority Students in Vietnam? An Analysis of the Round 2 Young Lives Data." Young Lives Working Paper 80, Oxford, UK.

Hall, Gillette, and Harry Patrinos. 2012. *Indigenous Peoples, Poverty, and Development*. New York: Cambridge University Press.

Haltiwanger, John, Stefano Scarpetta, and Milan Vodopivec. 2003. *How Institutions Affect Labor Market Outcomes: Evidence from Transition Countries*. Washington, DC: World Bank Economist Forum.

Hansen, Henrik, John Rand, and Nina Torm. 2015a. "Effects of Minimum Wages on Manufacturing Firms in Vietnam." International Labour Organization (ILO) Working Paper, ILO, Geneva, Switzerland.

———. 2015b. "The Impact of Minimum Wage Adjustments on Vietnamese Workers' Hourly Wages." International Labour Organization (ILO) Working Paper.

HelpAge International. 2015 *Community-based social care in East and Southeast Asia*. HelpAge Briefing, Chang Mai. Thailand.

Haughton, Jonathan. 2010. *Urban Poverty Assessment in Ha Noi and Ho Chi Minh City*. Hanoi: UNDP.

Heckman, James, and Carmen Pages. 2004. "Introduction." In *Law and Employment: Lessons from Latin America and the Caribbean*, edited by James Heckman and Carmen Pages. NBER Conference Report, 1-107. Chicago, IL: University of Chicago Press.

Hinz, Richard, Robert Holzmann, David Tuesta, and Noriyuki Takayama. 2013. *Matching Contributions for Pensions: A Review of International Experience*. Washington, DC: World Bank.

Holzmann, Robert, David Robalino, and Noriyuki Takayama. 2009. *Closing the Coverage Gap: The Role of Social Pensions and Other Retirement Income Transfers*. Washington, DC: World Bank.

International Labour Organization Financial and Actuarial Services. 2013. ILO, Vietnam, Hanoi.

Institute of Sociology. 2015. *Household Registration System in Vietnam from Multidirectional Perspectives*. Unpublished manuscript. Hanoi, August 2015.

Jackson, Richard, and Tobias Peter. 2015. *From Challenge to Opportunity: Wave 2 of the East Asia Retirement Survey*. Alexandria, VA: Global Aging Institute.

Jamieson, N. L., T. C. Le, and A. T. Rambo. 1998. "The Development Crisis in Vietnam's Mountains." East-West Center Special Report 6, East-West Center, Honoluu, HI.

Kham, Tran. 2014. "Social Construction of Disability and its Potential Impacts to Welfare Practice in Vietnamese Contexts." *Springeplus* 3 (1): 325.

Kharas, Homi. 2010. "The Emerging Middle Class in Developing Countries." Working Paper 285, OECD Development Centre Paris, Paris.

Labor Force Survey. 2013. Labor Force Survey Database. General Statistics Office. Hanoi.

Labor Force Survey. 2014. Labor Force Survey Database. General Statistics Office. Hanoi.

Le, D. B., H. T. Khuat, and V. D. Nguyen. 2008. *People with Disabilities in Vietnam: Findings from a Social Survey at Thai Binh, Quang Nam, Da Nang and Dong Nai*. Hanoi: National Political Publishing House.

Long, G. T. 2014. *Expansion of Pension Coverage to the Informal Sector: International Experiences and Options for Vietnam*. Mimeo for UNFPA and ILO. Hanoi.

Ly Khanh, Trinh. 2015. "The Right to Strike in Vietnam's Private Sector." *Asian Journal of Law and Society* 2 (1): 115–35.

Marx, Veronique, and Katherine Fleischer. 2010. *Internal Migration: Opportunities and Challenges for Socio-economic Development in Viet Nam*. Hanoi: United Nations.

MICS (Multiple Indicator Cluster Survey), 2011. MICS database. General Statistics Office, Hanoi.

MICS (Multiple Indicator Cluster Survey), 2014. MICS database. General Statistics Office, Hanoi.

MOLISA (Ministry of Labour, Invalids, and Social Affairs). 2014. "Thực hiện chính sách ASXH đối với NCT" [Implementation of Social Protection Policies for Older People]. Presentation at the National Assembly Committee for Social Affairs, September 15, 2014. Hanoi, Vietnam.

Mont, Daniel, and Cuong Nguyen. 2011. "Disability and Poverty in Vietnam." *World Bank Economic Review* 25 (2): 323–35.

National Institute of Nutrition Surveys (database). Hanoi: Ministry of Health. http://viendinhduong.vn/news/en/158/110/a/national-institute-of-nutrition.aspx.

NCCD (National Coordinating Council on Disability). 2010. Annual Report on Status of People with Disabilities in Vietnam, Hanoi. December 2010.

Nguyen, P., and B. Baulch. 2007. *A Review of Ethnic Minority Programmes and Policies in Vietnam*. Hanoi: Centre for Analysis and Forecasting, Vietnam Academy of Social Sciences.

OECD (Organisation for Economic Co-operation and Development). 2004. *Employment Outlook*. Paris: OECD.

———. 2010. Indicators of Employment Protection. Paris: OECD. http://www.oecd.org/employment/emp/oecdindicatorsofemploymentprotection.htm

———. 2014a. *PISA 2012 Results in Focus: What 15-Year-Olds Know and What They Can Do with What They Know*. Paris: OECD.

———. 2014b. *Social Cohesion Policy Review of Vietnam*. Paris: OECD.

Ostry, Jonathan, Andrew Berg and Charalambos Tsangarides. 2014. *Redistribution, Inequality and Growth*. International Monetary Fund Staff

Discussion Note, SDN/14/02. Washington, DC. International Monetary Fund.

Oxfam and ActionAid. 2008. *Participatory Poverty Monitoring in Rural Communities in Vietnam: Synthesis Report*. Hanoi: Oxfam and ActionAid.

———. 2009. *The Impacts of the Global Financial Crisis on Socio-economic Groups in Vietnam*. Monitoring report. Hanoi: Oxfam and ActionAid.

———. 2012. *Participatory Monitoring of Urban Poverty in Viet Nam: Five-Year Synthesis Report (2008–2012)*. Hanoi: Oxfam and ActionAid.

Packard, Truman, Johannes Koettl, and Claudio Montenegro. 2012. *In from the Shadow: Integrating Europe's Informal Labor*. Washington, DC: World Bank.

Palacios, Robert, and Edward Whitehouse. 2006. *The Role of Social Pensions*. Washington, DC: World Bank.

Palacios, Robert, and Oleksiy Sluchynskyy. 2006. Social Pensions Part 1: Their Role in the Overall Pension System. World Bank Social Protection Discussion Paper No. 0601, Washington TC, World Bank.

Paris, V., M. Devaux, and L. Wei. 2010. "Health System Institutional Characteristics: A Survey of 29 OECD Countries." Health Working Paper 50, OECD, Paris.

Perry, Guillermo, William Maloney, Omar Arias, Pablo Fajnzylber, Andrew Mason, and Jaime Saavedra-Chanduvi. 2007. *Informality: Exit and Exclusion*. Latin American and the Caribbean Regional Study, World Bank, Washington, DC.

Population and Housing Census. 1989. Census Database. General Statistics Office, Hanoi.

Population and Housing Census. 1999. Census Database. General Statistics Office, Hanoi.

Population and Housing Census. 2009. Census Database. General Statistics Office, Hanoi.

Provisional Minimum Wage Commission, Hong Kong SAR, China. 2010. Report of the Provisional Minimum Wage Commission. Hong Kong SAR, China. http://www.mwc.org.hk/en/downloadable_materials/PMWC_Report.pdf

Quattri, M., and S. Smets. 2014. "Lack of Community-Level Improved Sanitation Is Associated with Stunting in Rural Villages of Lao PDR and Vietnam." Submitted for the 37th WEDC International Conference "Sustainable Water and Sanitation Services for All in a Fast Changing World," September 15-19, 2014. Hanoi.

Rannan-Eliya, Ravi, Chamara Anuranga, Adilius Manual, Ruwani Wickramasinghe, Prasadini Perera, Shanaz Saleem, Jayalal Chandrasiri, Indra Pathmanathan, and Institute for Health Systems Research Core team 2013. *Malaysia Healthcare Demand Analysis: Inequalities in Healthcare Demand and Simulation of Trends and Impact of Potential Changes in Healthcare Spending*. Report prepared for the Ministry of Health, Malaysia, by Health Policy Research Associates and Institute for Health Systems Research, Columbo, Sri Lanka.

Ravallion, Martin. 2009. "The Developing World's Bulging (But Vulnerable) Middle Class." Policy Research Working Paper 4816, World Bank, Washington, DC.

Rolleston, Caine. 2014. "Learning Profiles and the 'Skills Gap' in Four Developing Countries: A Comparative Analysis of Schooling and Skills Development." *Oxford Review of Education* 40 (1): 63–86.

Schweisshelm, Erwin. 2014. *Trade Unions in Transition: Changing Industrial Relations in Vietnam*. Hanoi: Friedrich-Ebert-Stiftung Briefing Paper.

Starfield, B., L. Shi, and J. Macinko. 2005. "Contribution of Primary Care to Health Systems and Health." *Milbank Quarterly* 83 (3): 457–502.

Tran, Ngoc Dien. 2012. *Industrial Relations and Strikes in Vietnam*. Presentation to Labour Market and Industrial Relations in Vietnam Conference, Nuremberg, 8-9 October 2012. http://studylib.net/doc/9725561/1.2.-industrial-relations-in-the-market-mechanism-in-vietnam.

UN (United Nations). 2015. United Nations World Population Prospects 2015 Revision (database). New York: UN. http://esa.un.org/unpd/wpp/.

UNDP (United Nations Development Programme). 2010. *2009 Urban Poverty Assessment in Hanoi and Ho Chi Minh City*. Hanoi: UNDP.

UNESCO-IBE (United Nations Educational, Scientific, and Cultural Organization International Bureau of Education). 2011. *World Data on Education*. New York: UNESCO-IBE. http://www.ibe.unesco.org/fileadmin/user_upload/Publications/WDE/2010/pdfversions/Myanmar.pdf.

UNFPA (United Nations Population Fund). 2012. People with Disabilities in Vietnam: Key Findings from the 2009 Vietnam Population and Housing Census. Hanoi. UNFPA.

Van de Walle, Dominique, and Dileni Gunewardena. 2000. "Sources of Ethnic Inequality in Vietnam." *Journal of Development Economics* 65 (1): 177–207. http://ssrn.com/abstract=244564.

Van Gramberg, Bernadine, Julian Teicher, Tien Nguyen. 2013. Industrial disputes in Vietnam: the tale of the wildcat. Asian Pacific Journal of Human Resources. Volume 51, Issue 2, April 2013, Pages 248–268. Wiley, Australia.

VASS (Vietnam Academy of Social Sciences). 2009. *Participatory Poverty Assessment: 2008 Synthesis Report*. Hanoi: VASS.

VHLSS (Vietnam Household Living Standard Survey), various years (2002, 2004, 2006, 2008, 2010, 2012, 2014). VHLSS database. General Statistics Office, Hanoi.

Vietnam Social Security. 2013. Vietnam Social Security 2012–13 Annual Report. Hanoi, Vietnam Social Security.

VLSS (Vietnam Living Standard Survey), various years (1993, 1998). VLSS database. General Statistics Office, Hanoi.

WHO (World Health Organization). 2011. *World Report on Disability.* Geneva: WHO.

World Bank. 2009a. *Country Social Analysis: Ethnicity and Development in Vietnam*. Washington, DC: World Bank.

———. 2009b. *Vietnam Enterprise Survey*. Washington, DC: World Bank.

———. 2012a. *World Development Report 2013: Jobs*. Washington, DC: World Bank.

———. 2012b. *Addressing Vulnerability in East Asia: A Regional Study*. Washington, DC: World Bank.

———. 2012c. *Well Begun, Not Yet Done: Vietnam's Remarkable Progress on Poverty Reduction and the Emerging Challenges*. Washington, DC: World Bank.

———. 2012d. *World Development Indicators 2012*. Washington, DC: World Bank.

———. 2014a. *East Asia Pacific at Work: Employment, Enterprise, and Well-being*. Washington, DC: World Bank.

———. 2014b. Pensions Database. World Bank, Washington, DC. http://go.worldbank.org/IRHX8QBQU0.

———. 2015. *Live Long and Prosper: Aging in East Asia Pacific*. Washington, DC: World Bank.

———. 2016. *Vietnam's Household Registration System*. Hanoi: Hong Duc Publishing House. June.

World Bank and DRC (Development Research Center of the State Council, China). 2013. *China 2030: Building a Modern, Harmonious, and Creative Society*. Washington DC. World Bank.

World Bank. World Development Indicators 2013. World Bank, Washington DC.

Zaman, Hassan, and Sailesh Tiwari. 2012. *Can Social Protection Spending Contribute to Economic Growth?* Unpublished manuscript. Washington, DC. World Bank.

7

Building Modern Institutions for an Effective State

Main Messages

Institutional change is fundamental in economic development. A strong relationship exists between the level of development and the quality of institutions that provide security, regulate economic activity, enforce the rule of law, and enable the public to take part in governmental decision making. But there is no single path to achieving modern institutions, and every country must devise solutions to institutional problems suited to its specific historical, political, and cultural conditions.

Evidence from many countries indicates that state effectiveness, or the capacity of government to set objectives and attain them, is closely associated with economic growth in the long run. The development of state capacity rests on three supporting pillars: a coherent, disciplined, and meritocratic bureaucracy; adherence to market rationality in policy making; and mechanisms to ensure broad public participation in setting goals and making decisions.

Vietnam's existing institutional structure has facilitated three decades of growth and development, but signs of needed change are surfacing. Success was due in large part to an increasing reliance on markets in economic decision making. But sustaining past growth rates will not be easy. Productivity growth has fallen sharply and the economy remains dependent on small-scale production and foreign-invested firms for exports and jobs. Corruption is deteriorating and the rule of law is weak, with a critical gap between the laws and their implementation. This aspect has to be addressed to underpin the "level playing field" that is essential for the market to work and for efficiency within government. A strong rule of law also constrains domination of the economy and society by the state and its officials.

Vietnamese institutions suffer from two fundamental problems: constraints on autonomous private sector activity and weak capacity and accountability. Achieving a clear boundary between private business and state officials will be crucial to creating an environment conducive to long-term investment in capital and to technology-intensive industries. Commercialization of state agencies has created powerful incentives for public officials to exploit their authority over market regulation, law enforcement, and the allocation of property rights to lock in benefits for themselves and their networks. The government suffers from vertical and horizontal fragmentation, with responsibility for policy making and implementation divided among numerous agencies at the central and provincial level. Fragmentation results in gridlock and creates opportunities for individual agencies to bargain for policies that serve their particular interests, often leading to decisions that are suboptimal from the perspective of society as a whole. Government effectiveness is also undermined by nepotism and corruption in the state human resource management system.

These problems are evident in applications of the law. Vietnam has made progress in establishing the legal and regulatory foundations of a market economy and has taken steps to strengthen property rights. But major issues remain, particularly on allocating and enforcing land-use rights. The dependence of local governments on revenue from land sales has prompted them to capitalize on their power to expropriate land and control prices. Land disputes are the dominant source of complaints against government, and most consist of disagreements over amounts of compensation for expropriated land. Bias in the design and implementation of economic regulations, often in favor of state-owned or state-connected firms, is a product of close relationships between authorities and businesses, and reflects limited capacity within state agencies to formulate regulations that are consistent with sound economic principles.

The weak accountability also means that the state is inefficient. Vietnam has high rates of citizen participation in nonstate organizations, but the ability of citizens to participate in governmental affairs is bounded. Lack of transparency reduces government accountability and discourages participation. While the confidence and professionalism of the National Assembly are on the rise, the influence of the executive branch on the legislature is still predominant. The role of local councils is restricted to oversight, and even this function is constrained by intersecting relationships with the executive and party organizations.

Looking toward 2035, a modern, prosperous Vietnam will rest on three pillars—a state that sets, enforces, and abides by law, a full-fledged market economy, and an evolved democratic society where the rule of law governs all social interactions. Accordingly, institutional modernization entails a comprehensive reform of the state as well as the relationships between the state and the market and the state and the society. The state can become more effective through a coherent and disciplined government; market rationality applied to economic policy making; and accountability through greater public involvement in decision making and strong accountability mechanisms.

The government will need to be more rationally organized, with greater coherence among state institutions and a lean public administration based on meritocracy. The decentralization of authority will be improved through clearer functional assignments with corresponding adjustments in the intergovernmental financial framework. These changes will increase accountability and overcome present inefficiencies in coordination and the use of public resources. The center of government should be strengthened to improve policy coordination and oversight of policy execution by public agencies. There will be an efficient allocation of powers among central agencies to have greater effectiveness and accountability. Public administration practices will be reformed to ensure that merit drives the deployment of human resources by the state. The National Assembly will be a professional body, democratically elected, consisting of full-time deputies, fully representing the people and supported by expert staff. The judiciary will be similarly strengthened to function as a body that is independent in carrying out justice, and with enough capacity to settle increasingly complex disputes.

State–market relations will have a clearer division between the public and private spheres. It will be necessary to build a state that promotes long-term development and a dynamic and competitive market economy that actively participates in the global value chains with a strong private sector as the growth engine. This will occur through adoption of conflict-of-interest provisions and as a function of political leadership that will be sensitive to the particular challenges Vietnam has in separating the two spheres. The state will continue to disengage from its role as a participant in the economy through state-owned enterprises (SOEs) and closely linked private companies. It will focus on providing a level playing field for the economy, with more secure and transparent property rights, particularly around land issues. A more capable, trained, meritocratic judiciary will be developed to enforce rules to keep the playing field level.

State–society relations should provide for a stronger voice of citizens and the public. The role of social organizations representing the people as important partners of the state needs to be strengthened. The state will need to provide a comprehensive legal framework and space for the citizens to exercise fundamental rights, including the right to information, the right to associations, the right to hold demonstrations, and other basic democratic rights. The state will also adopt legislation requiring public bodies to be transparent and provide mechanisms for citizens to interact with the state.

Taken together, a state can only function effectively when it focuses on facilitating, regulating, and nurturing a safe and healthy environment for development, but does not direct the market and society.

The Role of Institutions

Institutions, defined broadly as the rules of the game for interaction in society, play a fundamental role in any country's economic growth and overall development performance.[1] Institutions embody formal and informal rules devised by people that constrain or condition human activity and hence provide incentives that influence human behavior. Since institutions influence or even shape behavior, the extent to which they prompt or discourage growth-enhancing or other socially desirable activity is critical to whether a country achieves better economic or social outcomes.

Institutions that encourage socially constructive behavior—such as healthy competition among firms or cooperation among individuals and groups—help promote economic growth and other desirable outcomes. Dysfunctional institutions—such as those that reward corruption, collusion, nondisclosure of public information, or other forms of counter-productive behavior—discourage productivity-enhancing investment from investors and citizens and create opportunities for rent seeking. Poorly formed institutions often result in one group exploiting another. Recent scholarship has documented the close relationship between institutions such as property rights enforcement and the rule of law and economic performance. Predictable and just rules of the game reduce uncertainty and thus encourage individuals and businesses to invest for the long term rather than seek quick returns.

The relationship is strong between institutional quality and the level of development. Political and economic institutions vary considerably. Prosperous countries have developed institutions that provide security, enforce the rule of law (including for contracts), protect property rights, control corruption, and foster broad participation in the economy and the society. Data from the Worldwide Governance Indicators (WGI) project, which collects annual information on six dimensions of governance, reveal a strong relationship between the quality of governance over the long period and prosperity as measured by gross domestic product (GDP) per capita (figure 7.1).[2] This is especially so among countries with limited natural resource endowments such as Japan, the Republic of Korea, and Singapore, which have developed successfully thanks to enabling institutions. In broad terms, institutions that promote openness and inclusiveness of a country's economy and society are integral to prosperity.[3] Outliers tend to be countries with large

FIGURE 7.1 There is a long-term correlation between good governance and prosperity, 1996–2013

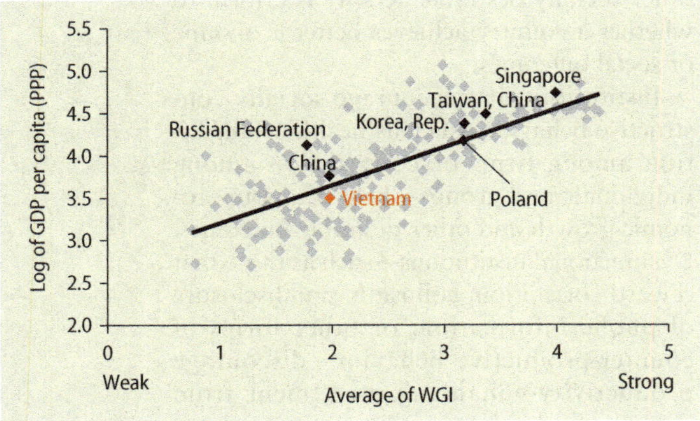

Sources: World Development Indicators; International Monetary Fund 2015 (for Taiwan, China only); Worldwide Governance Indicators database.
Note: "Log of GDP per capita (PPP)" is the average of GDP per capita in PPP from 1996 to 2013. The original unit of GDP per capita is current international dollars, transformed into a log scale. "Average of WGI" is the average of the six Worldwide Governance Indicators good governance indicators in 1996–2003. The scale of the scores has been transformed from −2.5 (weak)/+2.5 (strong) into 0 (weak)/5 (strong). PPP = purchasing power parity.

natural resource endowments that achieve relatively high middle incomes even without deeper institutional reform. The regularity of this relationship suggests that a prosperous Vietnam in 2035 will possess modern institutions that meet the needs of a middle-class society for security, equity, fairness, and public participation.

The close relationship between open, inclusive institutions and economic prosperity should also not be taken to imply a direct line of causality from institutional reform to higher rates of economic growth. While there are good reasons to believe that improvements to institutional quality are good for growth, causality may also run in the opposite direction—that is, from prosperity to institutional development. In 2035 a majority of Vietnamese people will have joined the ranks of the middle class and thus possess enough resources and autonomy from government to demand better public services, less arbitrary regulation, and greater public participation and supervision in decision making and the implementation of policies and laws. A larger proportion of the population will have attended university or undergone other forms of tertiary education, and will therefore most likely have a greater awareness of the rights and obligations of citizenship. Universities will train more of the skilled professionals that Vietnam needs to run a modern bureaucracy, well-developed legal and judicial institutions, and an active civil society.

While the relationship between government and growth is not linear, one consistently important element is government effectiveness, defined as the capability of the state to formulate and implement policy and law. The WGI government effectiveness indicator is most closely associated with the rate of growth among developing countries—at least those that are not dependent on oil for export revenues (Pincus 2015). This indicator, which measures the quality of the bureaucracy and specific public sector outcomes relating to service delivery and infrastructure development, captures the capacity of government to set clear objectives and meet them. The idea of state effectiveness recalls Max Weber's classic formulation of an effective bureaucracy: fixed jurisdictions (to prevent overlapping authority); hierarchical organization; meticulous record keeping; meritocracy; full-time employment; and rule-based authority. These features are echoed elsewhere, from Confucian political philosophy to modern public administration theory (box 7.1).

State effectiveness entails not only the ability to make rules and formulate plans but also the capacity to realize plans and achieve concrete outcomes over the long term. A despotic state could impose its will on the population; but, if its policies do not make economic sense or fail to mobilize public support, it is unlikely that they will generate positive outcomes for more than a limited period of time. Scrapping fiscal rules and ignoring market signals, or consistently overriding the aspirations of the people, are likely to reduce the effectiveness of the state. Peter Evans captures multidimensional state effectiveness in his "hybridity" model (Evans 2005). According to him, the development of state capacity requires a balance between three separate—and at times contradictory—components: the above-mentioned Weberian bureaucratic capacity based on hierarchy, unified jurisdiction, meritocracy, and rule-based authority; the use of market signals to

BOX 7.1 State effectiveness and development: Confluence of Eastern and Western thought

Economists who have studied in the Western tradition look to Adam Smith for the first definitive statement of the role of the state in economic development. For Smith, the proper realm of state action was limited to defense, justice, the rule of law, the establishment of public institutions, and the provision of public goods (Smith 1904). While often cited as an advocate for a limited state, Smith made it clear that state action included public education, control of monopolies, and other forms of business regulations. He understood the importance of an effective state to economic prosperity (Viner 1927).

Vietnamese economists have recourse to an older tradition, which is similar in many ways to the ideal state described by Smith. Confucian political philosophy is based on the creation and maintenance of a meritocratic bureaucracy, legal protection for property rights and contracts, military defense, and public works, with water control the most important among the latter. The aim of government was to protect the general welfare of the people through mechanisms like stabilizing food prices, redistributing rice to the poor, and providing famine relief (Nolan 2004). The ideal monarch was expected to govern virtuously and to give equal emphasis to administration and moral guidance.

The characteristics of modern bureaucracy described by Max Weber would not be unfamiliar to Chinese or Vietnamese officials under the ancien régime: fixed jurisdictions, hierarchical organization, meticulous record keeping, meritocracy, full-time employment (no moonlighting), and rule-based authority in which all citizens are subject to the same treatment (Weber 1946). Like the philosopher–officials of ancient China, Weber had in mind an ideal type of a properly functioning state, a model that governments in the real world may aspire to but rarely achieve. Rules are often unclear and designed to serve special interests; appointments are made on the basis of patronage rather than merit; hierarchical structures are undermined by politics and clientelism; and overlapping responsibilities create confusion and lead to power struggles. The philosopher–kings of the Confucian ideal were challenged in practice by regional aristocrats and warlords in China, the Republic of Korea, and Vietnam.

Source: Pincus 2015.

allocate resources and fiscal discipline to match policies with financial capacity; and popular participation to ensure that policies and programs are aligned with the needs and aspirations of citizens.

The three components, together, strengthen state capacity while narrowing the space for policies to benefit officials at the expense of the public good. The crucial point that Evans makes—and one directly relevant to Vietnam's program of developing modern institutions—is that all three legs of this public administration tripod are necessary to achieve satisfactory levels of state effectiveness. This is directly related to Vietnam's institutional modernization agenda. Reforming state structures but rejecting market discipline, or assigning a larger role to the market mechanism while insulating government decision making from the community, is unlikely to generate positive outcomes.

Institutional reform does not occur in a vacuum, but is rather shaped by the interests of influential groups in society. In their influential work *Why Nations Fail*, Acemoglu and Robinson stress that the development of "inclusive institutions"—those that serve the mass of the population rather than a small elite—is not an automatic process (Acemoglu and Robinson 2012). The origins of inclusive institutions lie in political settlements in which elites agree to share power rather than lose it. These settlements arise out of shifting political coalitions and a healthy dose of good luck. For present-day middle-income countries like Vietnam, the main lesson from these historical analyses is that the development of well-functioning modern institutions is not an inevitable consequence of economic growth. Much depends on the alignment and relative bargaining power of interest groups within and outside government, the assessment of these groups of how institutional change is likely to affect them, and their willingness to accept compromise to manage risk and achieve their political aims. The state's domination (including in nominally independent businesses and organizations) and the relative weakness of civil society organizations have threatened to push institutional reform off the agenda. Modernizing the country's institutions, even in the context of rapid economic growth, will require greater tolerance for market-driven activity and deeper involvement of citizens in the process of making policies and laws that have widespread effects for the population.

Diagnosing Vietnam's Institutional Challenges

Demonstrable Achievements

Vietnam's institutional framework has been gradually reformed and has facilitated rapid social and economic development over 30 years. The country has transitioned from central planning to market forces as the primary means of resource allocation. Accomplishing this without a major economic crisis helped empower Vietnam's ascent in just 25 years from one of the poorest countries in the world to lower middle income. Specific achievements have been presented in the previous chapters—achievements all the more remarkable given that Vietnam endured nearly half a century of war and destruction before peace was secured in the 1980s.

Vietnam's success is largely owing to reforms that allowed market forces to enter production, distribution, and trade. Before *Đổi Mới* (economic reforms instituted by the Party Congress in 1986), the private business sector was targeted for "re-education." The private sector, as the 10th Party Congress confirmed in 2006, has become "one of the sources of momentum of the economy" alongside the state. In the 1990s Vietnam liberalized trade, and in 2007 it joined the World Trade Organization. There are now roughly a half million registered private firms and thousands of foreign-invested enterprises. The 2013 Constitution reaffirmed that markets allocate resources and reemphasized that national sovereignty rests with the people. It also established the legal foundations for democratic society, holding the state accountable to its citizens and making it subject to the law.

Over the past three decades, Vietnam's government has demonstrated the capacity to formulate effective policies and achieve objectives. The country's record of sustained economic growth and poverty reduction with narrow disparities in income and access to services are exemplary, particularly when compared with countries of similar income. Government agencies can mobilize the state to achieve specific targets like rural electrification and immunization. Maternal mortality and under-5 mortality rates have been reduced by two-thirds since 2002.

Vietnam's success is also a result of the reform of the state toward greater adherence to the rule of law, although efforts to reform the organization and operation of the state (such as legislative, administrative, and judicial reforms) have not always kept pace with the requirements of economic reforms. The 1992 Constitution brought about changes in the organization and operation of the center of government.[4] Administrative reforms started in 1994 have changed procedures to reduce cumbersome interactions of citizens and businesses with government. In 2001 a Comprehensive Administrative Reform Program was issued for the first time while legislative and judicial reform strategies were launched in 2005. The 2013 Constitution continues the process of legislative, executive, and judicial reforms, establishes the principle of a socialist state governed by rule of law and of the people, by the people, and for the people, which also responds to the needs of developing a market economy, accelerating industrialization, modernization, and international integration. While the legal framework still pays inadequate attention to the direct democratic rights of the people, there are laws regulating most of the important economic, political, cultural, and social activities and the organization of the public sector.[5] The policy- and law-making process has been gradually improved toward greater use of evidence and employing more democratic norms, including consultations with beneficiary groups and greater use of impact assessments.[6]

Major Challenges

State effectiveness

Vietnam's capacity to sustain this rapid development is in question. The economic gains of the state–market reforms are not yielding structural changes tied to sustained growth—particularly for a lower-middle-income country. GDP growth has fallen steadily since the late-1990s, with labor productivity and total factor productivity growth also trending downward. Indeed, total factor productivity growth came to a standstill after 2000, with higher capital investment and faster rates of increase in the labor force generating slower rates of economic growth. Economic growth continues to rely heavily on small-scale agriculture production and foreign-invested firms in manufacturing. Large private domestic firms, 30 years after introducing *Đổi Mới*, are few in number, with very few in manufacturing. The economy is dominated by state-owned, state-controlled, and state-connected firms.[7] Moreover, few large manufacturing firms can manage technologically and managerially complex processes, realize economies of scale, control costs and quality, and compete in domestic and foreign markets. This reflects the weaknesses of the country's institutions.

Vietnam consistently ranks in the bottom third in global indicators of corruption—and lacks progress in addressing the problem (figure 7.2). Most firms (51–70 percent) reported having to pay bribes to access government services between 1996 and 2014, and firms stating that informal payments were normal practice saw an uptick (Vietnam Province Competitiveness Index 2006–2014). Of citizens and civil servants, over four-fifths rated corruption as

FIGURE 7.2 Corruption is a continuing challenge

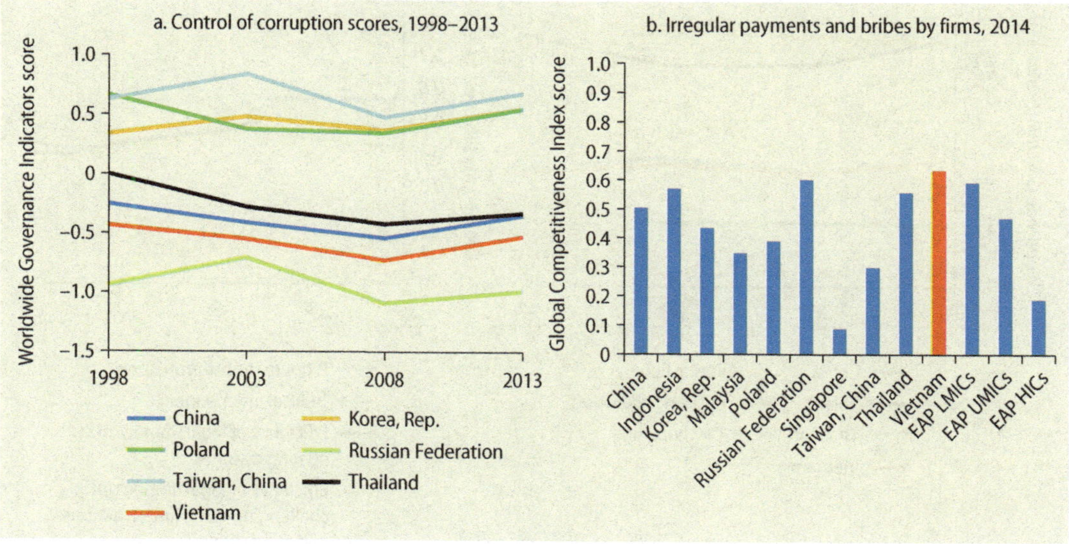

Sources: a. Worldwide Governance Indicators; b. World Economic Forum 2015.
Note: Panel a. 2.5 = best, −2.5 = worst. Indicators for each country are a blend of up to 24 perception- and experience-based indicators. Panel b. 0 = best, 1 = worst. The data are based on an opinion survey of business executives. Group averages are based on the countries with data (18 EAP countries); EAP = East Asia and Pacific; HICs = high-income countries; LMICs = lower-middle-income countries; UMICs = upper-middle-income countries.

a serious issue (World Bank 2013b); 92 percent identified corruption as a problem in the public sector (Transparency International 2013).

Corruption is a serious economic problem even if Vietnam has sustained high rates of growth in the early stages of development. As in other East Asian economies, Vietnam's corruption has coexisted with high rates of investment and strong export performance. This paradox has led observers to argue that corruption facilitates growth by providing a path around the slow-moving bureaucracy. Surveys indicate tolerance of corruption in Vietnamese society, suggesting that corruption is not a major impediment but part of doing business. This does not mean that corruption is costless. It has negative long-term effects on market efficiency and investment. As the middle class grows in Vietnam, corruption will increasingly affect political stability; perceptions of inequality and unfairness in the use of public power can lead to social tensions that undermine the state's legitimacy.

Vietnam faces a core challenge in developing the rule of law. A strong rule-of-law state means that broadly accepted laws constrain the behavior of all actors—including those with political power. Fair and open rules accepted and adhered to by all are intrinsic to functioning markets, and systematic enforcement of the law promotes fairness and social cohesion. Through its 2013 Constitution and market-focused laws such as the Law on Enterprises, Vietnam has established a legislative basis for a rule-based state, but implementation is weak. Less than 10 percent of firms surveyed over the past nine years believe that central laws will be consistently applied in the provinces (Vietnam Province Competitiveness Index 2006–2014). Based on global governance indicators, Vietnam lags its neighbors and peers on the rule of law (figure 7.3a). Perception-based surveys of business executives suggest that important elements in the rule of law have been weakening over the past five years, while long-term trends show no signs of improvement (figure 7.3b).

FIGURE 7.3 Rule of law continues to be weak

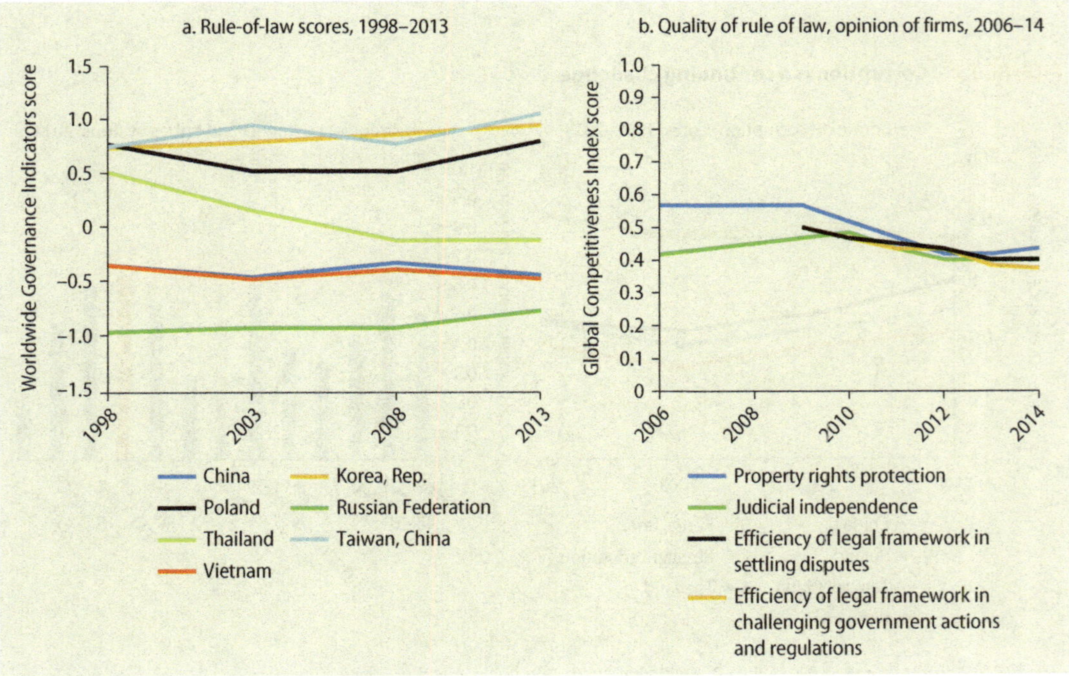

Sources: a. Worldwide Governance Indicators; b. World Economic Forum 2015.
Note: Panel a. −1.5 = worst, 1.5 = best. Indicators for each country are a blend of up to 24 perception- and experience-based indicators. Panel b. 0 = worst, 1 = best. The data are based on an opinion survey of business executives.

Vietnam has two basic challenges in instituting the rule of law: state domination over the private sector and fragmented state institutions with weak capacity. These two factors are interrelated. The absence of independent economic interests has reduced external pressure for institutional reform, while commercial interests within the state are left to pursue policies that deliver economic benefits to them but often at the expense of the government's capacity to act as an impartial regulator and supplier of public goods and services.

Weaknesses in the operations of government have emerged as important checks on investment and growth. Regulations are unclear or contradictory. State agencies have conflicting mandates because they often serve as regulators but also have their own commercial interests. The judiciary is politicized and law enforcement is selective. Endemic corruption pervades the public sector.

Moving forward, the quality of institutions will be increasingly important. For the Vietnamese economy to transition from small farms and workshops to large, capital- and technology-intensive manufacturing, public institutions must create a stable, low-risk economic environment.

Building a more effective state requires balance—to set clear boundaries between business and government officials, to institute bureaucratic coherence while maximizing capacity, to apply market rationality to economic policy making, and to ensure public participation in policies and programs. These four conditions present challenges in Vietnam. Connections to the state are integral to success in business. Government institutions are fragmented vertically—local authorities either resist or go against directives from the center—and horizontally—assigned and assumed mandates and power splinter agencies at every level of government. Market rationality does not guide public policy, with regulations favoring state-owned or state-connected enterprises and property rights unevenly enforced. Although the stature of legislative bodies is increasing, government decision making remains shielded from public scrutiny. And in the past decade, the space of civil society organizations—social and professional—has narrowed.

Commercialization of the State

The prospect for building modern institutions in Vietnam depends on the degree of distinction in terms of benefits among private enterprises, SOEs, and state officials. As in all countries, influential groups have accumulated political and economic power that they seek to preserve by influencing government decisions. But in Vietnam economic success stemming from state relations appears to be unusually high. Citizens consistently report that connections to the state are necessary to succeed in business and that vested interests' power is on the rise (figure 7.4).

The interconnectedness between the state sector and entrepreneurial business class was born out of economic reforms. The Communist Party, in the four-decade struggle for independence, was highly effective at mobilizing the state. With victory in 1975 the Party mobilized capacity to build a centralized, planned economy. But the system teetered on the brink of collapse in a few years. State companies, local authorities, and other state agencies began working around the planned economy to acquire inputs, pay workers, and provide essential goods to their communities.

Đổi Mới grew out of these off-plan (fence-breaking) activities. Markets for food, consumer goods, construction materials, and financial instruments such as gold, money, credit, and foreign exchange replaced the planned-economy instruments. But because the control of resources was vested in the state, the reform represented less a shift from the *state* to *markets* than a *marketization of the state*. Millions of household microenterprises grew in the space created by the reforms, but they operated at the fringe of the economy. SOEs (including equitized firms that retained a close relationship with the state), politically connected private firms, and foreign-invested enterprises continued to dominate the economy (Pincus 2015).

FIGURE 7.4 Where private business interest ends and government begins is still being negotiated in Vietnam

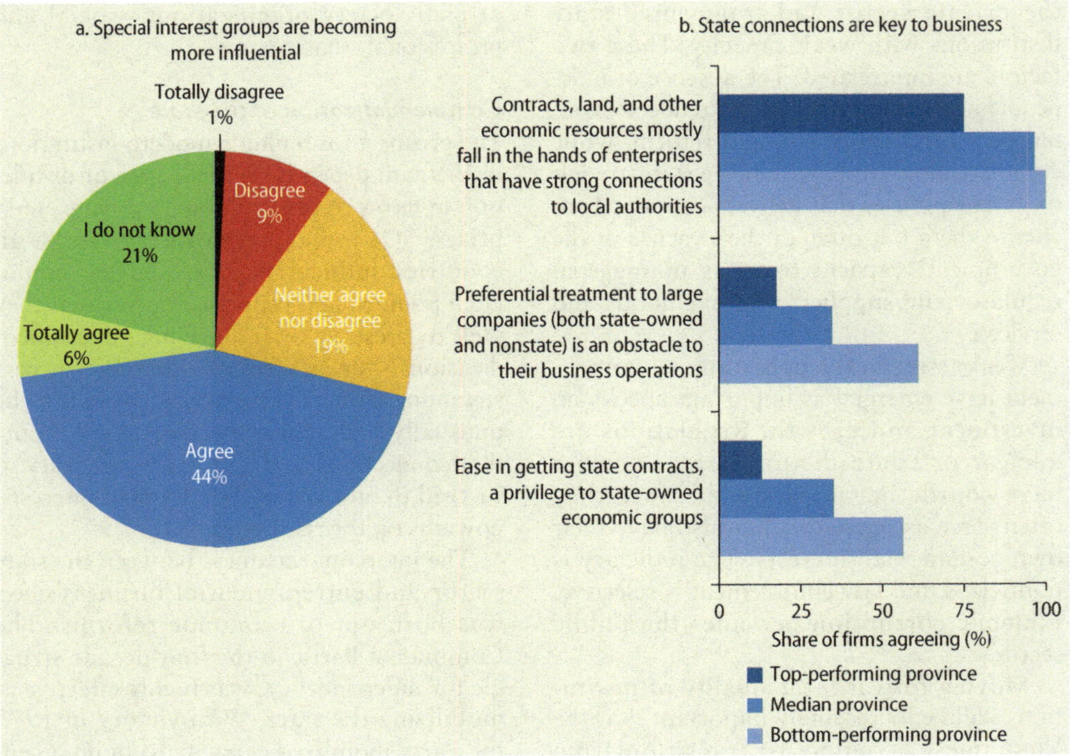

Sources: a. World Bank 2013b; b. Provincial Competitive Index 2013.
Note: Data based on a survey of firms.

The confluence of commercial interests and state power produces rents that reinforce and perpetuate the system. Rents were clear cut in the early days of reforms. Agile entrepreneurs in the government or with government connections secured subsidized goods and other privileges. Subsequent legislation has done little to demarcate the public–private boundaries and stem these advantages. Relations with state agencies provide government contracts, access to land and credit, and access to state-controlled markets. Insiders use their market position and political access to sustain the rents. And the transition—expected to reduce rent-seeking opportunities—offered further opportunities to manipulate the social and political environment. In the words of one scholar, "What occurred was the development of a business class within the state" (London 2009). Connections to the state raise the risks for private firms. They discourage large investments in land, plants, skills, equipment, and technologies. State commercialization has effectively crowded out large, genuinely private firms.

The direct involvement of the state in the economy declined in the 2000s. Next-generation reforms allowed private enterprises to emerge, diminishing the state's direct, formal, and dominant role in the economy. By the end of 2014, 3,166 SOEs accounted for 20 percent of total capital assets, marking a decline from 66 percent in 2001. Their share in total employment fell from 55 to 11 percent in the same period (GSO Enterprise Surveys 2001–2014). But this reduction came through equitization, merely shifting the connection to public officials (Gainsborough 2009).

The state remains a producer of many goods and services without a strong public goods rationale. It mostly closed small SOEs, then equitized large-scale SOEs in the mid-2000s. But the global financial crisis halted any momentum to reduce the level of state ownership. Although the pace accelerated in 2013–14, firms with 50 percent or more state ownership have remained essentially the same (CIEM and World Bank 2015). The state has tried to promote efficiency as well as upward and downward production links in SOEs by creating "general corporations" and "state economic groups." Where there are monopolies or a lack of public goods justification, state economic groups play an outsized role. Critical sectors such as telecommunications, banking, and insurance are dominated by SOEs, even though the private sector could provide much needed competition for them.

The legal framework does not provide explicit advantages to SOEs. The Law on Enterprises, amended in 2005, called for equitizing SOEs and stipulated that their operations must be carried out under the same rules as private businesses. Subsequent prime ministerial decisions and government decrees require greater transparency and a clear separation of the state's ownership and regulatory functions. State shares in more than 1,000 equitized entities have been transferred to the State Capital Investment Corporation, separating ownership rights from the ministries and regulatory agencies.

SOEs nonetheless enjoy preferential treatment by the state—including access to credit, soft budget constraints, and direct administrative interventions. The share of total bank credits to SOEs is 30 percent above the share of private firms.[8] The National Assembly's Economic Commission reported in 2013 that SOEs face a soft budget constraint and documented the Ministry of Finance covering loan defaults in 2010–14, including those of Vinashin and Song Da Corporation. In early 2015 the Ministry of Transport banned Vietnam Airlines' pilots from moving to private aviation companies, a decision that insulated Vietnam Airlines management from wage competition—and violated the rights of pilots under the country's labor code.

SOEs are not subject to the same market discipline as private firms. Annualized SOE growth rates in 2005–12 were 50 percent higher than those of the private sector. The global financial crisis did not affect SOE performance but stalled private sector growth after 2009. In this same period, the SOE turnover-to-asset and output-to-asset ratios lagged those of the private and the foreign-invested sectors. While making direct comparisons is complicated by sector-specific factors, these figures suggest that SOEs were able to access financing to sustain operations based on nonmarket criteria. SOEs have privileged access to finance. They receive a disproportionate share of financing from the state banks, favorable terms to restructure, implicit (such as Vinashin's unguaranteed loans) and explicit government guarantees, and outright capital injections (CIEM and World Bank 2015). Special terms like interest-free loans cover sensitive expenditures or social insurance payments. These benefits are not codified but are provided ad hoc. SOE compliance with financial and nonfinancial transparency regulations also compares poorly with the private sector (World Bank 2013a).

Preferential access to information aids rent seeking and provides other advantages. Insider information on opportunities and upcoming policy changes allows connected businesses to preempt or outmaneuver their competitors. Low transparency in government reinforces this. The nexus between connections and sensitive information comes through clearly in the PCI. In one province over half the surveyed firms said that relationships were important to access provincial documents regulating commercial matters (figure 7.5).

State commercialization and rent-seeking behavior undermine state capacity. The blurred state–market line imposes static inefficiencies on the economy since high-cost producers are rewarded at the expense of consumers and efficient firms. Efficient firms also avoid investing because of regulatory risks and elite capture, deepening the inefficiencies. Public officials have powerful incentives to

FIGURE 7.5 Transparency and preferential access to information are major hindrances to economic efficiency

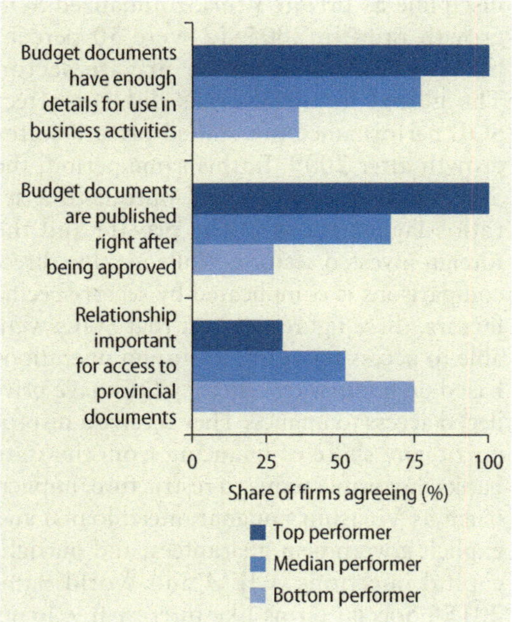

Source: Provincial Competitive Index 2013.
Note: Data based on a survey of 8,093 firms.

exploit their regulatory powers to lock in long-term benefits for themselves, their families, and their networks. This abuse of public authority undermines the legitimacy of state institutions.

Vietnam's fragmented government structure

Vietnam's horizontal and vertical fragmentation of power creates overlapping mandates, conflicting rules and decisions, and bargaining in the bureaucracy. The Office of the Government, the Ministry of Finance, and the Ministry of Planning are the most powerful entities.[9] They formulate policies, often deploying interministerial task forces to achieve consensus. In theory the Communist Party oversees cohesive planning. In practice the power splinters across agencies and between the center and the provinces. The absence of a clear hierarchy and distribution of authority creates incentives for agencies to resist decisions perceived to be against their interests. The result is gridlock and decisions contrary to the society's point of view.

The political power of local authorities complicates policing the public–private boundary. The system bears a striking resemblance to the fragmented authoritarianism framework developed by Lieberthal and Oksenberg to describe policy making in China (Lieberthal and Oksenberg 1988). Budgetary and regulatory decentralization have empowered provincial leaders to the extent that they wield considerable influence over the decisions of the central government. Reforms in the 1980s increased provincial representation in the Party's Central Committee from 101 to 176 members between 1976 and 1996. Provincial party leaders now make up the largest single voting bloc of the Central Committee. Local power brokers have repeatedly demonstrated their capacity to block central directives, such as when SOEs and local governments halted an attempt by Hanoi to rationalize the port system in Ho Chi Minh City (Overview of this report).[10] Their capacity to veto or delay decisions affords bargaining power to extract resources from the center, to obtain other privileges, or to simply block central directives against their interests. They also have forced through decisions regardless of economic logic. They compelled the national airline to serve small provincial capitals justifying building of airports. Local leaders have strong local roots and loyalties. As of November 2011 only eight provincial secretaries and about 10 percent of senior provincial officials served in areas in which they did not have extensive local ties (Pincus et al. 2012).

Vietnam is one of the most fiscally decentralized countries in the region, with provinces accounting for more than half of government spending. Its unusual budget process nests provincial budgets in the central budget. This process complicates tracking expenditures, compresses budget review time, and countervails coherence in planning and execution—making it difficult for central institutions to set policy and to monitor and enforce delivery standards.[11] Indeed, the center's interest in maintaining local authorities' support prevents ministries from acting consistently.

Fewer than 10 percent of firms surveyed for the PCI over the past nine years believe that the central laws would be consistently applied in the provinces.

Fragmented authority contributes to excessive capital investment in the provinces. Virtually every coastal province has its own deep seaport and nearly all provinces have an airport with arrangements for at least a few flights a week by the national airline, often operating at a loss. Similarly, about 260 industrials parks are spread across nearly all of the country's 63 provinces, with plans to build 239 more by 2020. Yet the average occupancy rate of the existing parks is well below half. The investments were financed by the central government to impose greater discipline on local capital investment decisions, with little success.

Fragmentation also occurs horizontally. State actors often reinterpret, ignore, or even run against overall state policy objectives. Horizontal fragmentation delays issuing and implementing regulations. The central government issued about half of 2014's required regulations but only 20 percent of them were issued on time.[12]

Overlapping mandates and redundancies in the government are by far the most complicating factors. Multiple agencies can claim the authority to make or influence decisions, giving rise to interagency bargaining that slows down decision making and often leads to poor outcomes.

Unmeritocratic administration

The public administration system is not meritocratic. A basic element of state effectiveness is the extent to which the functions of government are carried out by capable public servants who demonstrate high standards of ethical behavior, who are motivated, and who are assigned discrete tasks within a clear chain of command. International experience indicates that developing a meritocratic system takes a long time and responds to particular political imperatives.[13] While issues of low pay, and skill shortages in fields like information technology and policy analysis are a challenge in most developing countries, two specific features of Vietnam's system have slowed progress in developing a meritocratic system. First, despite the enactment of reforms mandating open recruitment for technical positions in 2008, recruitment and promotion are still conducted based on patronage relationships or seniority rather than merit. Second, human resource management is itself fragmented, with responsibility assigned to three entities within the government plus the Central Committee Secretariat and Organization Commission of the Party (Phuc 2015).

The state personnel system is undermined by corruption. Nothing destroys bureaucratic capacity more quickly than distributing jobs based on connection and side payments rather than merit. While the problem is difficult to measure, perceptions are that corruption plays a major role in public sector human resource practices. For instance, 60 percent of the population consistently report that bribes are paid for government jobs (figure 7.6a). Personal connections are also perceived by the public and by firms as the main factor of success, followed by material incentives (figure 7.6b). Recent discussions in the Vietnamese press about the rise of the appointment of children of senior party officials to high posts in local and national government (*con ông cháu cha*) have highlighted concerns over widespread nepotism in public sector recruitment at all levels.

Market rationality in regulation and enforcement

The state has made progress in building the system of rules regulating the modern market economy, but the lack of consistency, objectivity, and fairness in enforcement is a significant problem. Vietnam's business environment, in such measures as the Ease of Doing Business indicators and the yearly PCI surveys, has improved in the past decade. The legal infrastructure of the market economy is now largely in place, having enacted laws on land, enterprise, investment, bankruptcy, intellectual property, civil and penal proceedings, commercial arbitration, and real property trading as well as civil and penal codes.[14]

FIGURE 7.6 Corruption in public administration is a widespread concern

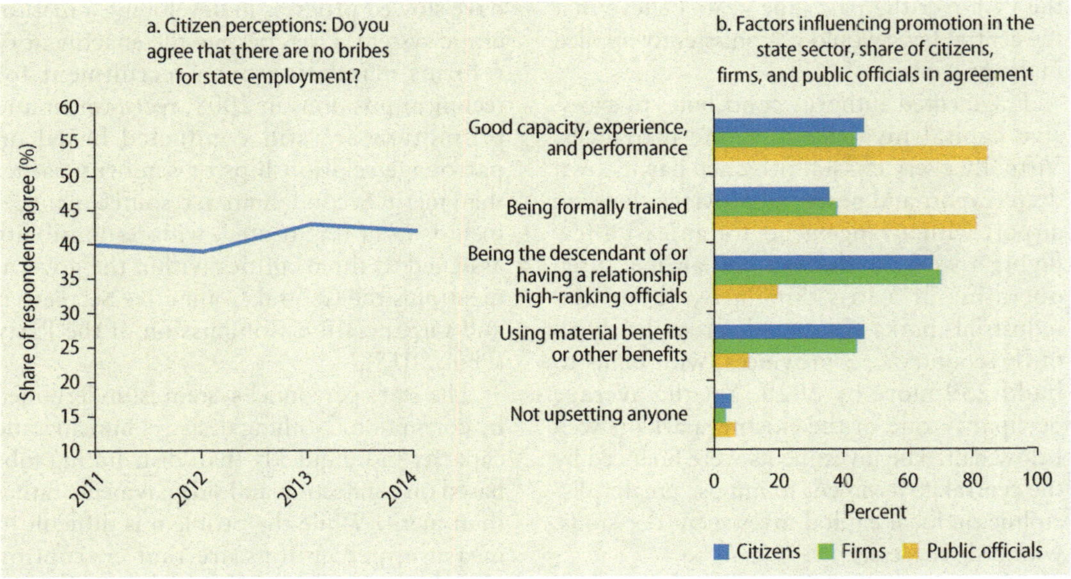

Sources: a. Centre for Community Support and Development Studies, Centre for Research and Training of the Viet Nam Fatherland Front, and United Nations Development Programme 2015; b. World Bank and Government Inspectorate of Vietnam 2016.

This has simplified administrative procedures and shortened waiting times to register a business or secure an electricity connection. But the regulatory system lacks coherence and the enforcement of regulatory rules is neither impartial nor fair. The governance of land markets presents the most serious problems. Land's legal framework consists of 21 laws, and hundreds of instructions, resolutions, circulars, and decisions. Vietnam lags other Southeast Asian countries in the time required to pay taxes, to register property, or to get a construction permit. The transfer of land-use rights and the conversion of use rights are allowed but difficult to execute—except when a state actor has interests and intervenes.

Vietnam has introduced important reforms to strengthen property rights. A major effort is underway to provide land-use certificates. And the provinces have developed property registration systems to protect the rights of those holding the rights to land use. Systematically registering use rights and compiling and integrating technical and normative documents (such as land-use plans and physical parameters) in the Ministry of Natural Resources and Environment have improved property cadasters. However, the quality of the property records differs widely across the 63 provinces. The 2013 Land Law articulates a clear framework for the disposition of real property, such as leases, exchanges, and mortgages. Use-right terms, including for agriculture, have been extended to encourage investment. And, market mechanisms such as auctions must set prices when the government confers long-term use rights.

Government action affects the holders of use rights. Land remains one of the challenging issues in the state–citizen relationship. Of the 700,000 registered complaints between 2009 and 2011, 70 percent were land issues. Nearly three-quarters of these dealt with compensation, land acquisition, and disagreements over resettlement terms (Government Inspectorate of Vietnam 2012; MONRE 2012). Though weak, Vietnam's property-rights protection is on par with the average of other East Asian lower-middle-income countries (figure 7.7).

Developing land provides a major stream of revenue in provinces and in local communities but also causes most disputes. Land transactions, as a result of the 2003 decentralization, now account for 20–30 percent of local revenue.[15] Property taxes in many developed countries serve as an important source of local revenue and encourage broader provision of public goods. In Vietnam, the local governments raise revenue by selling land. This provides incentives for local governments to use—if not abuse—key powers in land administration, including:

- Expropriating land for vaguely defined public purposes, including industrial and residential development. Between 2001 and 2010, 1 million hectares of agricultural land were converted to industrial or urban residential use (World Bank 2011).
- Using provincial land-price tables to expropriate land—typically 30–60 percent below the market price—and thus creating elite capture of rents or a dual-priced system (MONRE 2012). The 2013 Land Law bars this practice and requires auctions but uptake has been slow.
- Affecting land and land-use values through planning, conversion, and granting the spatial use of land plots.

FIGURE 7.7 A comparative assessment shows relatively weak protection of property rights in Vietnam

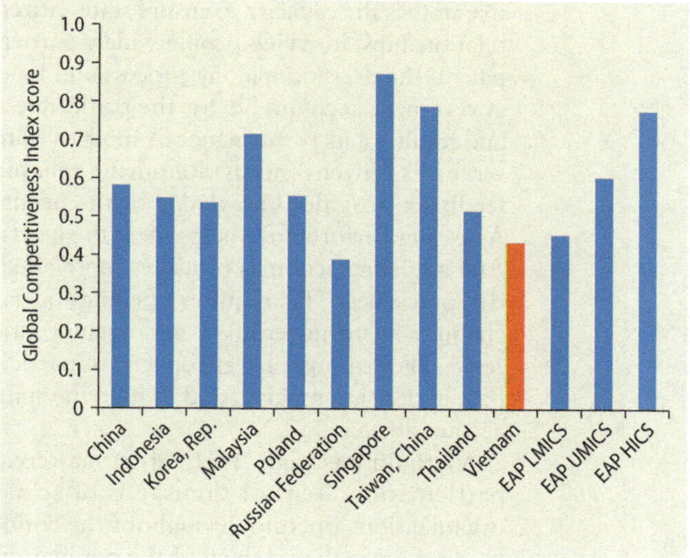

Source: World Economic Forum 2015.
Note: 0 = worst, 1 = best. Data based on an opinion survey of business executives. Group averages are based on the countries with data (18 EAP countries). EAP = East Asia and Pacific; HICs = high-income countries; LMICs = lower-middle-income countries; UMICs = upper-middle-income countries.

Persistent bias in treating businesses and individuals extends beyond land markets to other forms of regulation. Although equal treatment of all market participants is guaranteed under the Constitution and the Enterprise Law, these basic principles are violated in sectoral legislation. Laws construe entry barriers and restrict the business model. The Law on Investment also introduces specific conditions on some 267 sectors. Matters are made worse by implementing agencies' inconsistent legal interpretations and by exceptions and special provisions granted to targeted sectors and entities. Regulatory inconsistency allows the authorities to favor state-owned and state-connected enterprises. These complex and profuse regulations hinder market rationality from entering economic governance.

Government agencies do not have the analytical capacity to incorporate sound economic principles in new regulations. Evidence-based regulatory impact assessments are lacking (Institute of Legal Science 2014, 113–14). Limited understanding of economic principles constrains regulatory agencies, with new rules quickly withdrawn when heavy costs are imposed on firms or consumers. These costs can be predicted. Regulators need a firmer grasp of microeconomics and a willingness to involve independent experts in the consultation process.

These problems are even more serious given the increasingly complex commercial disputes and the limited capacity of the judicial system. Vietnam's formal legal framework has developed quickly to meet the needs of an open, mixed economy. But the justice system, unable to handle increasingly sophisticated and complex commercial cases, contributes to poor enforcement. Demands for adjudication and for conflict resolution are increasing rapidly. Between 2006 and 2013 civil cases doubled and economic cases spiked by 750 percent.[16] In contrast, resources have remained constant, with only a modest increase in the total number of courts and judges over the past 10 years. Training for judges and for other officials to apply the updated legal framework has been insufficient.

Accountability of the State to Citizens

An element that is indispensable in an effective state is the capacity to ensure state–citizen relationships, in which people widely participate in the decision-making process and hold government accountable for the truthfulness and results of its performance. A modern state serves its citizens' needs. Requiring reliable feedback provides knowledge of the needs. Assessing performance helps meet the needs. And adjusting activities produces more effective outcomes. This requires opening formal channels to the government and opening citizens' space to organize effectively, to participate in decision making, and to hold the state accountable.

Vietnam has high levels of formal civic participation. Tens of thousands of social organizations operate throughout the country, and more than a third of the population is a member of one or more group.[17] Citizen organizations support government social programs, provide services when the government is unable or unwilling to do so, advocate for specific constituencies, and monitor the authorities' actions. New non-mass organizations, a notable trend, increased more than 40 percent from 2008 to 2014 (figure 7.8). They span credit, sports, culture, business, and elderly groups.

FIGURE 7.8 Membership of mass organizations and other voluntary groups is growing

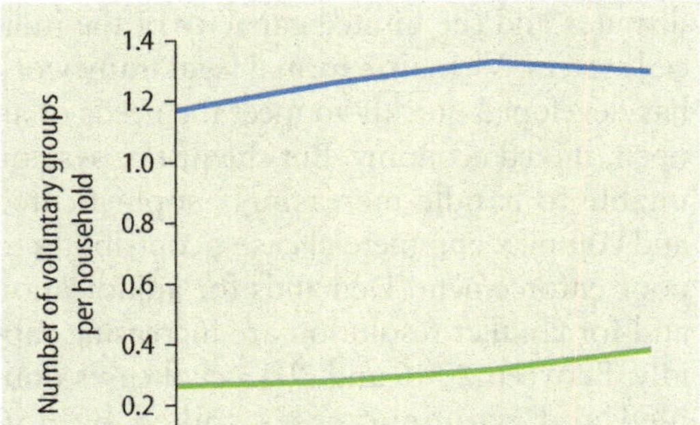

Source: Markussen 2015.

Acting as facilitator and enabler, civil society organizations can become the "space where we act for common good" (Putnam 1993; World Economic Forum 2013).

Despite a large number of formal civic organizations, in practice citizens' exercise of their rights, particularly their participation in the affairs of state, is constrained. The government has few formal channels to consult with civil society organizations on policy and planning. And it rarely consults in a substantive way. Civil society organizations are not seen as active or successful in influencing public policies and in holding the state and private sector accountable. Yet the correlation between stakeholder policy consultation and effective implementation is strong. This could be the case in Vietnam.[18]

Limited transparency hinders the ability of citizens to hold government accountable. Vietnam's governance practices, like many countries with a legacy of state-dominated development, have not encouraged openness and public discussion of state activities. The low uptake of current legislation requiring public disclosure, particularly in the land and SOE sectors, is a cause for concern (see World Bank 2014, 2015a). This profoundly affects the accountability of the state to its citizens and the development of a democratic society. It also undermines the market efficiencies. Incoherent land use imposes costs on most market participants because unpredictable changes increase the risk of doing business. It also favors insiders (figure 7.9).

The National Assembly's role has been strengthened, but there is room for improvement for it to fully exercise its legislative and oversight functions to the government. Though now debating and reviewing legislation more substantively, it is not empowered to formulate policy or to supervise the government. Major limitations are its irrational structure, the undemocratic election with bias to a weighing structure of representativeness, and the high turnover between sessions (first-term deputies now have 70 percent of the seats). Full-time deputies increased 4–5 percentage points in the last three sessions. Two-thirds are

FIGURE 7.9 Vietnam has low levels of transparency

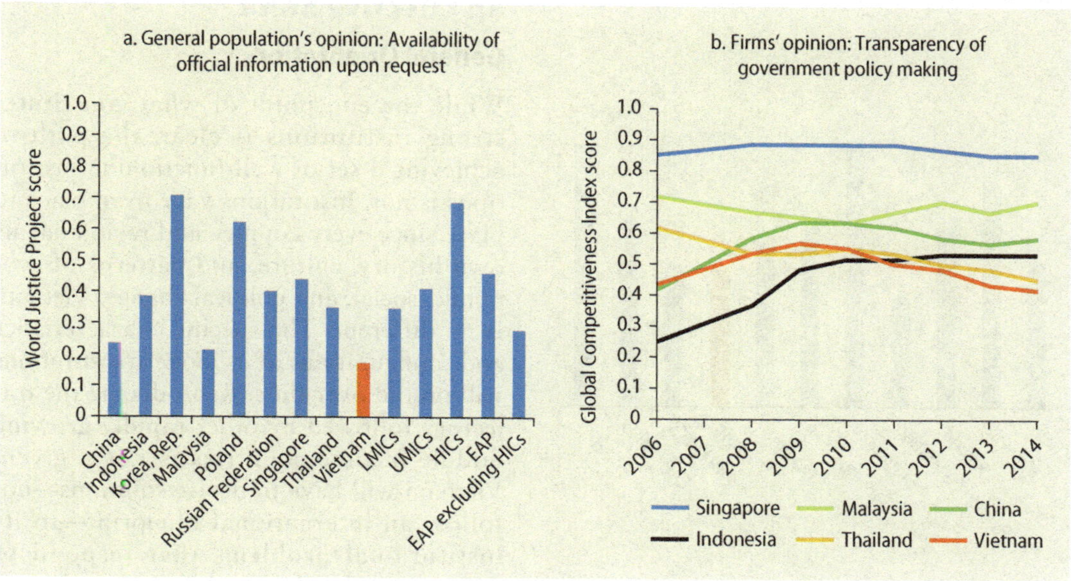

Sources: a. World Justice Project 2014; b. World Economic Forum 2015.
Note: Panel a, 0 = worst, 1 = best. The data are based on a general population poll and legal professionals carried out the assessment. Group averages are based on the countries with data (15 EAP countries). Panel b, 0 = worst, 1 = best. Data based on an opinion survey of business executives. EAP = East Asia and Pacific; HICs = high-income countries; LMICs = lower-middle-income countries; UMICs = upper-middle-income countries.

part-time and are drawn from the executive at the national or provincial level or from budgetary institutions. This creates bias toward accepting whatever the executive proposes. Compared internationally, Vietnam scores poorly on the effectiveness of its legislature (figure 7.11a) in limiting government powers.

The People's Councils lack the independence to provide oversight of the People's Committees in the provinces. An array of intersecting relationships and reporting requirements constrain the Councils. This involves the central government, the Local People's Committee, the Vietnam Fatherland Front, the Council's own party organization, and the Standing Committee of the National Assembly. The Councils' supervisory function is limited to compliance with national policies and laws. It does not touch on the performance of local governments in implementing policies and programs. Local public meetings, mandated under various "grassroots democracy" decrees since 1998, have not changed government structures. Citizens interact with the state much as they had before the reforms, with additional meetings and budget-information requirements.

Vietnam lacks a key element of a well-functioning judiciary—judicial independence from the executive. A well-functioning court system has to be independent from the executive and from political and commercial interest groups. It is only then that it can be considered an objective arbitrator. Judicial appointments are subject to political and administrative pressures, and the hierarchical system contributes to this dependence. Many executive operations do not fall under judicial supervision, but the courts are beholden to the executive to administer the courts. There are no important instances of the court's ruling against major state policies, and only rare cases of judgments against public officials. The independence of Vietnam's judiciary ranks below that of its regional peers (figure 7.10).

Individuals and firms are reluctant to use the court system. An average of 60 percent of firms were willing to use provincial courts in

FIGURE 7.10 Comparative ratings show relatively low judicial independence in Vietnam

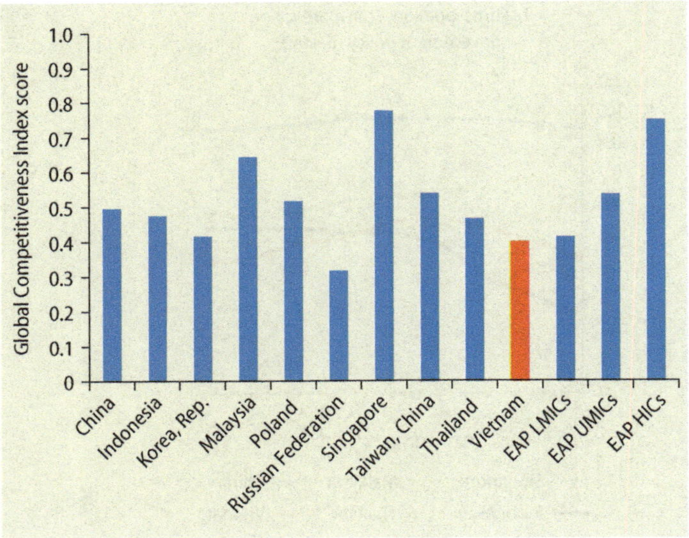

Source: World Economic Forum 2015.
Note: 0 = lowest, 1 = highest. Data based on an opinion survey of business executives. EAP = East Asia and Pacific; HICs = high-income countries; LMICs = lower-middle-income countries; UMICs = upper-middle-income countries.

the event of a dispute, but only 22 percent had actually done so (PCI 2013). Individuals are even less likely to use the courts (Anderson, Garrido, and Phung 2009). While the overall number of cases is increasing, there is likely further unmet demand for adjudication. The formal judicial system, costly and time consuming, should not be the only means of dispute resolution. Alternative dispute resolution mechanisms, including mediation, are needed. But confidence in the judicial system as a last resort is critical to the functioning of the other means of dispute resolution. Lack of confidence in the courts is damaging to Vietnam.

Improving state effectiveness will require strong legislative and judicial institutions to hold government accountable. Vietnam's legislature and judiciary are less effective in imposing limits on the actions of the state than corresponding institutions in neighboring Southeast Asian countries (World Justice Project 2014). And they score far below the average of lower-middle-income countries (figure 7.11). Government officials, in the absence of a strong and independent legislature and judiciary, will not confront meaningful curbs on arbitrary and self-interested decision making.

Toward Modern Institutions for an Effective State

General Orientation

While the end point of what constitutes strong institutions is clear, the path to achieving a set of well-functioning institutions is not. Institutions vary from place to place since every country and region has its own history, culture, and patterns of economic, social, and political change. Vietnam is no different. The specific characteristics and configurations of its modern institutions will unfold over time. Reproducing the trajectory followed by other rapidly growing middle-income countries is not a given. Vietnam will have to devise solutions—not follow an international blueprint—to its institutional problems that respond to national and local priorities. Another important issue when switching from the current institutions to modern institutions is the restructuring of economic and political interests. Political institutions should be reformed to enable well-functioning socioeconomic institutions.

As Vietnam becomes more prosperous, citizens and businesses will increasingly demand that the state facilitates growth, delivers services, and provides opportunities. Middle-class growth will increase the demand for higher-value goods and services and supply skilled professionals and workers to domestic firms, to the government, and to civil society. Incomes will rise. So too will the expectations for goods and services, including public sector services like health care, education, and public administration. Failure to meet these expectations can result in frustration and social tensions. Albert Hirschman famously described a "tunnel effect," in which some groups in society do not feel that they are making progress ("moving through the tunnel"), leading to feelings of disappointment and disaffection. The inclusiveness of growth—and the performance of the state in providing services, justice, and a fair environment for individuals and businesses—maintains political stability and social cohesion. Tolerance of poor performance and lack of probity will only decline.

FIGURE 7.11 Vietnam's legislature and judiciary do not constitute strong checks on the executive

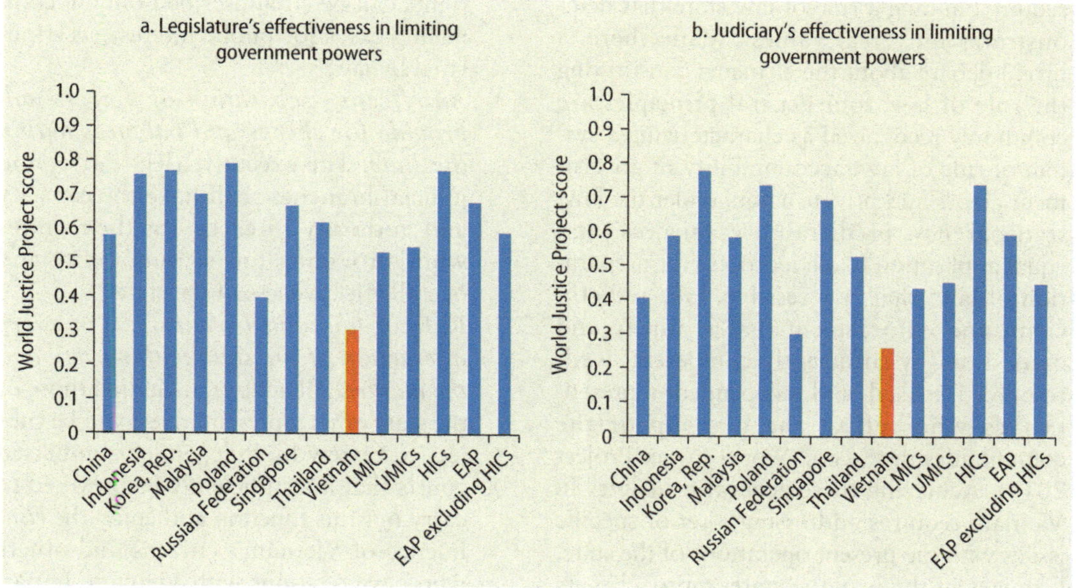

Source: World Justice Project 2014.
Note: Panel a, 0 = worst, 1 = best. The data are based on a general population poll and legal professionals carried out the assessment. Group averages are based on the countries with data available (15 EAP countries). Panel b, 0 = lowest, 1 = highest. The data are based on a general population poll and legal professionals carried out the assessment. EAP = East Asia and Pacific; HICs = high-income countries; LMIC = lower-middle-income countries; UMICs = upper-middle-income countries.

The 2013 Constitution confirms that sovereignty rests with the people and establishes the market as the driving force behind economic development. Building strong and competent government agencies will be the first challenge. And adhering to market principles in economic policy and encouraging robust political and social institutions will be the second. Together they can gather the people's energy and creativity to design the instruments, implement the plans, and monitor the performance of government policies and programs.

Institutional modernization will require continuous reform of the state structure and of the relationships between the state and the market, and between the state and the society. The state can improve its effectiveness by instituting a highly disciplined and coherent government, applying market principles in all economic decisions, and enhancing accountability by enlarging space for people's participation in the decision-making process with more effective accountability mechanisms. Government fragmentation should be reduced both horizontally and vertically; public and private boundaries should be clearly defined; and regulatory and economic roles of the government should be separated. The authority of the legislature, executive, and judiciary needs to be clearly defined to ensure that each branch operates in accordance with its functions and with sufficient autonomy. Economic management must be based on market principles. The state needs to guarantee the protection of property rights, including clearer definition and limitation of cases where these rights may be overridden. Nongovernmental organizations, including social and professional organizations, should play a more active role in overseeing the operation of the government and can collaborate more robustly with state entities in their operations and in the delivery of public goods.

Modernizing institutions in Vietnam will require building a rule-of-law state that demonstrates universal values. While there is broad debate about the elements constituting the rule of law, four general principles are commonly recognized as characterizing a system of rule of law: accountability of government actors and private actors under the law; transparency, predictability, fairness, and equal application to all; a process for preparation of laws that is accessible, fair, and efficient; and enforcement that is timely and carried out by sufficiently competent, well-resourced, ethical, and independent representatives who reflect the makeup of the communities they serve (World Justice Project 2014). Achieving these general principles in Vietnam requires addressing a set of specific issues with the present operations of the state. Changes in the way the state approaches its operations will provide a framework for full application of the rule of law, and condition the development of specific institutions to achieve the vision for 2035 laid out below. In the context of Vietnam, the following eight requirements are crucial to the development of a rule of law state with a vision toward 2035:

1. *Full implementation of the principle of people's sovereignty in the state's organizations and operations will be ensured.* The state must be truly of the people, by the people, and for the people, serving the needs of the people and public interest and being held accountable for this. The enforcement of state power is for the public interest, within the legal framework. The state will be clean, strong, and effectively prevent and control corruption as well as manifestations of state capture. This will guarantee the legitimacy of the state.
2. *State power must be clearly delineated by law.* All functions, powers, and roles of the state and its agencies must be governed by law, and any arbitrary actions by state agencies or officials are precluded. Implementing the principle that citizens can do everything not prohibited by law, the state agencies and their officials can do only what is allowed by law. And human rights can be circumscribed only in compelling cases for public interest, as stipulated by law.
3. *An effective separation of powers will provide for checks and balances within the state.* The executive, legislative, and judicial branches shall have the capacity and authority to carry out their duties while providing for accountability and overall effectiveness of the state.
4. *Rule of law will be enforced in every interaction of the state with society and the market.* All actions, including those of the state or its representatives, will be subject to review by independent, unbiased courts that are sufficiently empowered to carry out this function and enjoy the confidence of Vietnam's citizens and others who have relations with Vietnam. In particular, individual property rights are to be ensured.
5. *Individual accountability of officials will be defined and upheld.* Individual accountability of public servants is to be clearly determined, with a corresponding reward or sanction for individual performance; there shall be progressively higher levels of accountability for higher-level officials.
6. *The legal system will be fair, transparent, practical, uniform, stable, accessible, effective, efficient, and predictable.* Laws will be a means to help the state govern and a tool for citizens to control the exercise of state power.
7. *The roles of central and subnational governments will be clearly determined by law*, focusing on advancing the autonomy and accountability of local governments and gradually implementing the principle of local self-government, especially at grassroots levels.
8. *International agreements will be fully observed.* The state will actively participate in global governance mechanisms to contribute to common world development and protect national interests. Vietnam will be a reliable friend and partner and a responsible member of the international community.

Building a Rationally Organized State with a Meritocratic Bureaucracy

Tackling fragmentation

Reducing public sector fragmentation is integral to modernization. Eliminating overlapping jurisdictions will reduce vertical and horizontal fragmentation and decrease the scope to bargain and foot-drag in the bureaucracy. A guiding principle should be to see that responsibility and authority for public sector functions are assigned to a single agency. Delegation of tasks between and among levels of government will continue, but through specified mechanisms and on the basis of objective performance targets.

A more coherent approach will address outstanding issues in Vietnam's decentralization policies. Clearer functional assignments should lead to four corresponding adjustments in the intergovernmental financial framework. First, the nested budgeting system should be reformed to achieve closer links between financing and functional responsibilities. To raise accountability for performance, these links should be made transparent to citizens and businesses in a given locality and to the central government and the oversight agencies, such as the Supreme Audit. Second, a closer match between functions and finances should then inform capital investment plans, providing greater discipline in sectors where subnational governments spend and making more explicit responsibility for the recurrent costs that ensue when assets are built. Third, increased financial management accountability at the subnational levels should be combined with policy incentives to increase own-source revenues at the local level. In addition to providing greater authority with greater clarity in responsibilities for services, building a stronger direct link between subnational taxes and government outputs helps strengthen accountability. Finally, the capacity of the central government to monitor performance of subnational governments and to coordinate among them would need to be enhanced.

A strengthened center of government will serve Vietnam well in addressing vertical and horizontal fragmentation (figure 7.12). The main functions include strategic planning, coordinating and monitoring performance, and ensuring accountability. The building blocks of a coherent national bureaucracy are rationalization of the personnel system, improved management information systems, and public finance reforms. These components link concrete objectives to the resources needed to achieve them and the performance of responsible administrators. Results-based management methods and robust information systems can deliver substantial improvements to evidence-based policy formulation and implementation. A more effective center of government function does not mean a reversal of decentralization. It should yield greater clarity on the roles and tasks assigned to subnational government agencies and their relationship to the execution of national policies. Clear responsibilities increase accountability while preserving the authority of decentralized decision makers to be responsive to the citizen's needs. Hiring based on competencies, competitive compensation, and rigorous performance evaluation increases accountability and reduces scope for corruption, while careful economic assessment of policy impact narrows the scope for self-interested behavior and improves the quality of regulation.

The ability of the government to manage its resources efficiently and effectively is integral to the state's overall effectiveness.

FIGURE 7.12 A strengthened center will serve Vietnam well in streamlining resources and operations

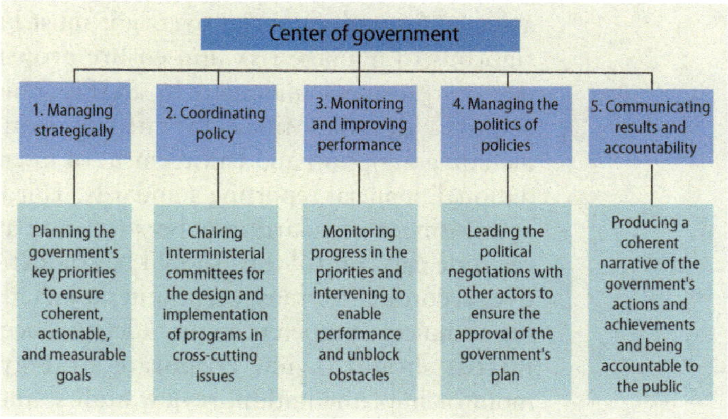

Source: Adapted from Dương and Cương 2015.

Vietnam has a comprehensive legal framework and a record of implementing essential public financial management functions: fiscal controls and commitment limits, a budgeting process and a corresponding set of institutions, and basic transparency measures. Achieving stronger links between government spending and clearly defined results will be a challenge. Financial systems that provide timely and reliable financial information will be essential. A comprehensive Government Financial Management Information Platform is needed to achieve proper integration of related databases for revenues, expenditures, assets, and liabilities—as is the development of analytical tools for consolidated statements.

Managing state assets well is of particular importance—including SOEs and government shares in equitized firms. First, the state, acting on behalf of the people, must responsibly deploy its assets to serve public purposes, from maximizing financial benefit and managing associated risks to analyzing the public goods rationale behind continued state ownership (and resulting influence over management) in any particular enterprise. Different countries have adopted varying institutional forms including decentralized control through line agencies, centralization in one government agency, and various special-purpose entities (to contract out asset management). What is important is ensuring that basic policy objectives are agreed, executed, and widely communicated. The rationale for state enterprises needs to be clearly articulated as a guide to investment and divestiture of state assets.[19] Second, financial oversight must be rigorous to manage risk and ensure proper use of resources managed by SOEs. This requires detailed financial information, including adoption and enforcement of international financial reporting standards. Third, appointment of board members (insofar as the state can control this) should be competitive, according to transparent criteria including technical competence and independence. Boards should review corporate strategy, monitor implementation, review audits, and take action to redress issues. Fourth, regulatory functions should be kept separate from ownership and management to promote competition and accountability. Fifth, SOEs should be encouraged to list on international stock markets that set high compliance standards.

Meritocracy in public administration

Vietnam will need to strengthen meritocracy and ensure optimal integrity in public administration through a rigorous position-based system, salary reform, and organizational reform. The Government's Public Administration Reform (PAR) Master Program up to 2020 sets out a vision of a capable public sector that supports the market economy, citizens' rights, and access to quality services. The PAR Master Program is structured around six interlinked reform areas: institutions, public finance, administrative procedures, organization of government, government systems—including e-governance—and human resources—including performance management and accountability. The program connects public sector functions to the positions needed, civil service recruitment, promotion, compensation, and performance evaluation. Key features include open recruitment for civil service positions, separation of political and administrative spheres, modernization of compensation, improved talent management, and a robust performance appraisal system (box 7.2).

An institutional approach will be needed to counter the vested interests in the current system and ingrain the principle of meritocracy into the public service. There will be resistance to change because the control of recruitment, selection, and promotion often holds the key to redistributing power and rents controlled by the state. And that very power, constituting a rent in its own right, triggers informal payments and patronage (and feeding into the ethos that factors other than merit drive human resource decisions). While overcoming this resistance will necessarily take a long time, the many public servants moving toward retirement present Vietnam with an opportunity to revitalize the civil service (table 7.1).

BOX 7.2 Other countries' experience in managing talent in the civil service

Talent management concerns recruiting, selecting, training, developing, and retaining public employees. A good example of a deliberate strategy is the Ministry of International Trade and Industry (MITI) in Japan, running Japanese industrial policy well in the 1960s and 1970s. MITI recruited top graduates from the most prestigious universities. Applicants had to pass difficult civil service entrance exams. In Southeast Asia, Thailand, Singapore, and Malaysia have crafted more general frameworks to manage talent.

	Singapore	Malaysia	Thailand
Talent recruitment	Open recruitment (new graduates and midcareer entrants) Preservice bonded scholarships Green harvesting Scouting/headhunting	Open recruitment (new graduates and midcareer entrants) Preservice bonded scholarships Scouting/headhunting Recruitment for administrative and diplomatic service	Open recruitment (new graduates) Preservice bonded scholarships Public Service Executive Development Program
Talent development	Allocated training hours Roadmaps for special schemes (management associates, administrative service, and high potential schemes)	Allocated training hours Administrative and diplomatic scheme, high-performing-officer scheme	Allocated training hours High-potential performance system scheme New-wave-leadership development
Talent retention	Competitive salaries pegged to market pay structure Performance-based bonus payouts Performance-based promotions High-pay structure for administrative officers	Base pay coupled with types of allowances Performance-based promotions Incremental fixed-pay structure Opportunities for postgraduate studies	Fast-stream track Performance-based system Higher pay (about 1 percent higher for high-potential officers) Perks in health care and pension schemes

TABLE 7.1 A demographic snapshot of the civil service
Percent

Age	2005	2012
Younger than 30 years	23.8	18.0
Between 30 and 50 years	65.6	60.0
Older than 50 years	10.6	22.0

Source: Phuc 2015.

New systems and responsibilities need to be established to begin changing the incentives in the public service. These should include:

- A legal framework to promote professional criteria and to safeguard the recruitment, selection, and promotion processes from bribery, patronage, and other types of rent seeking.
- A separation of political and administrative spheres to reset the business climate—for instance, arm's-length relations between the government and the Communist Party.
- An internal code of conduct to recruit, select, and promote (as embedded in the 2008 Civil Service Law) that is vested in an agency reporting to the highest political levels and that the National Assembly can hold accountable through audits and queries.
- Supplementing stronger central policy and monitoring capacity with more devolved personnel management, relying on a running-cost system in which managers

choose their own staff mix to deliver programs in a hard budget constraint and to ensure due process.
- A sequenced hiring process to foster scrutiny and fairness—with clear job descriptions and required knowledge and skills; a standard system to advertise and apply; procedures to evaluate, select, appoint, and promote candidates; and required notification of results to all candidates.

Accountability within government

Independence of the legislature and judiciary will give rise to greater accountability and performance. Much of Vietnam's progress in the past 30 years was based on informal consensus-building within decision-making structures. By 2035 consensus building will be formalized in state institutions. Stronger checks and balances will increase the accountability of state agencies and their officials, primarily in the executive. The scope for self-interested behavior among government officials will be reduced and a clearer separation will be achieved between government and business.

By 2035 the National Assembly will realize its constitutional role as the supreme representative of the people, exercising legislative and oversight functions. Internal ruling party mechanisms help to fill this gap at present. As the country modernizes, the National Assembly will provide an independent check on executive power. It will be composed of full-time deputies who, with the support of technical experts, take responsibility to draft, debate, and enact laws while preparing budgets and monitoring the government's performance. National Assembly oversight, as the representative chamber of the people, will encompass all the operations of government. As a step toward that goal, consideration should be given to increasing the number of full-time deputies (that is, not having regular employment in executive bodies) in the National Assembly to over half in the next sessions. Analytical and technical capacity will be developed in the National Assembly's specialized thematic committees. It will draw on research and analysis conducted by scholars and other independent experts. The National Assembly will realize in full its right of legislative initiative. Deputies will be held accountable to their constituents through regular elections and through public forums held at the constituency level.

By 2035 the judiciary will be autonomous from the executive and will implement its responsibilities in a professional and responsible manner. The selection and promotion of judges and other personnel will be conducted by a judicial oversight body composed of members primarily drawn from the judiciary itself and independent of the executive. Selection of judges will be carried out on the basis of national examinations, drawing on a pool of experienced legal practitioners. Court administration—clerical staffing, maintaining courthouses, financial management, and case tracking and management—will continue to be performed by the executive. But the judiciary will be empowered to take action against staff if administrative underperformance hinders the judicial process. At the same time, a long-term, large-scale program to train judges on ethics, case management, and substantive law (particularly relating to sophisticated market transactions) will build professionalism within the judiciary. Rigorous laws and enforcement mechanisms to ensure ethical conduct and counter conflict of interest among judges will be put in place. These measures will provide for a judiciary that is capable of carrying out key functions in the society and in the economy: protection of human and civil rights, resolution of commercial and other disputes, and provision of a check on the powers of the executive and legislature. In successfully carrying out these functions, the judiciary can be expected to encourage greater confidence of the citizens and the firms in its capacity to arbitrate fairly among interests.

Collective responsibility mechanisms need to change to ones of individual responsibility, particularly in the case of leadership positions. A key constraint in public administration is the lack of mechanisms to hold individuals accountable, and the lack of clarity in handling individual and collective responsibilities, as well as political and legal accountability. Rigorous mechanisms should be put in place to sanction policy makers who commit mistakes and cause severe damage to society. It is necessary to reform policy-making processes to avoid getting views of individuals and agencies on matters outside of their sphere of responsibility. It is also very important to strengthen administrative discipline in the public service sector.

Vietnam should seek to keep pace with its middle-income peers in using information and communications technology (ICT) to enhance the effectiveness of the state through relatively low-cost mechanisms to monitor compliance. Information generated through automation can be harnessed to improve the evidence base to plan and set policy. ICT tools can make possible more efficient communication and transactions between government agencies, businesses, and citizens. The efficiency and probity of transactions involving government agencies can be improved through e-filing of key documents such as tax declarations. Digital identification systems enable government services to track recipients more accurately and efficiently, leading to better coverage and less leakage. ICT is also used extensively to reflect feedback from the people on activities performed by the state—for example, the level of service satisfaction. User-feedback mechanisms help improve the public's confidence in the ability of the state to serve the people and businesses.

Applying Market Rationality to Economic Policy Making

Vietnam aspires to be a fully fledged market economy and to be recognized as such by international partners. The legal framework for a market economy has been put in place incrementally, from amendments to the Law on Enterprise in 1999, 2005, and 2014 to enshrining the principle of equal treatment of all sectors of the economy in the 2013 Constitution. By 2035 Vietnam aspires to having a level playing field among economic actors and a clear separation between the government's regulatory and commercial activities. This will involve changes in two major respects: providing for the security of property rights and transforming the role of the state in the economy from a producer to a regulator and facilitator.

Addressing commercialization of the public sector must be made a priority if Vietnam is to modernize its government institutions. Agencies that are directly or indirectly involved in economic regulation should not be permitted to engage in business of any kind. This avoids the appearance and reality of conflicts of interest. More difficult to observe, and therefore to control, is the exercise of state power for state-connected companies and individuals that do not have an overt relationship with the state. Powerful conglomerates have emerged in recent years that have benefitted from state connections. Because of their dependence on the government, they do not represent genuinely private businesses that have an interest in impartial regulation and the distribution of state benefits based on fair and transparent criteria. Creating the space for a genuinely independent private sector to flourish will require political commitment at the highest levels of government and reduced state control over business and professional organizations, including the Vietnam Chamber of Commerce and Industry. Allowing these organizations to operate as authentic representatives of independent business interests would give voice to the domestic private sector and enable these groups to play a more proactive role in monitoring government policy.

Political leadership will need to better enforce the boundary between the public and the private sector. Over the long term, accountability mechanisms and greater transparency can be expected to create an environment that lessens the opportunities for, and impact of, the use of public power for private gain. In the short term greater discipline is needed in policing that boundary to ensure that rents are not captured solely for private benefit. Formal mechanisms to identify and enforce conflict-of-interest provisions for public officials are an important step in strengthening this boundary.

By 2035 the state's main role in the economy will be to facilitate the development and smooth functioning of markets and to provide public goods. The state's portfolio of SOEs will be substantially reduced, and will focus on enterprises in markets deemed to be natural monopolies or involved in the provision of public goods such as energy, health and educational institutions, and management of transportation infrastructure. The state will progressively divest its holdings in enterprises in which it can demonstrate no public interest. Commercial SOEs will be run on a fully commercial basis, meaning that they will be subject to the same market discipline as private sector entities, with no privileges—regulatory exemptions, subsidies, or preferential treatment in state contracting. SOEs not involved with public goods provision will be allowed to fail. The state will seek to manage its ownership stake though professional fund-management structures. This will provide careful monitoring of fiscal performance and risks to raise the effectiveness in the use of state assets.

A successful market is built on security of property rights, especially to land. Clarity in defining property rights and impartial and rigorous enforcement reduce investment risks and promote longer time horizons and therefore the potential for more capital- and technology-intensive ventures. Ensuring the broad distribution of property rights, including to disadvantaged segments of the population, promotes social inclusion and reduces economic exploitation. Confidence in property markets increases the number and density of transactions, resulting in more accurate pricing and lower costs. One of the most important roles of the state is thus to enforce the rules of the game, with regard to the array of ownership rights, including possession, use, and disposition.

Reforms to protect the security of property rights should focus on transparency in assigning and converting land-use rights. Reducing rent-seeking opportunities linked to the conversion of land-use rights from agricultural to commercial and residential use will be a challenge. Publication of information on land transactions, including auctions, should be mandatory. Information from property cadasters—including the description of each property, rights held over the property, and any restrictions on use—should be made available to the public. Land-use planning should be fully open to public consultation and changes in land-use regimes should be carried out in a planned fashion with a lead time for public review, rather than ad hoc. Oversight mechanisms should be strengthened. Finally, rules on government acquisition of land should be strengthened to ensure that citizens can only be dispossessed of their land to serve a demonstrated public need. Compensation rates should be related to market prices. Looking ahead to 2035, additional strengthening of the legal framework for property rights may include provision of full, fee-simple ownership rights. In addition, commercial investments should be acquired to obtain land through voluntary transactions rather than involving the state.

The state will have an active policy of promoting the innovation and skills needed for the Vietnam of tomorrow. The state will act to match demand for different skills in Vietnam's changing economy with the provision of tertiary and vocational training. It will maintain a National Skills Council to track the changing skill demands and to enact programs or to contract with the private sector to meet demand. Greater autonomy for tertiary education institutions and stronger links between universities and the private sector would help achieve a better match between the demand and supply of skills. The state will also finance and facilitate private investment in research and development activities to promote innovation in the economy.

Enhancing State Accountability to the People

There is a conceptual link between corruption and the combination of monopoly power and discretionary authority without accountability.[20] Following this simple formulation, controlling corruption should consider reducing monopoly over power and instances where there is bureaucratic discretion without sufficient accountability. Strengthening checks and balances among the branches of the state and between the national and subnational governments as mentioned above will help reduce monopoly power and increase accountability. Improving transparency, protecting the right to information by the people, can be expected to result in strengthened accountability of state institutions to the people.

Establishing a right to information is essential to create more space and opportunity for the public to participate meaningfully in the affairs of state. Two major reforms likely to be adopted soon in Vietnam will contribute to democratic society's development. First, Vietnam is on the threshold of passing a Right to Access to Information Law. This will provide a powerful tool to open state institutions to greater participation and public accountability. It is a well-established principle in economics that restricting access to information imposes costs on society, as information asymmetries give rise to market distortions. Analogously, unequal access to information has negative social and political consequences, such as reducing levels of trust and raising the costs of cooperation. Corruption also thrives when information is costly or difficult to obtain. A basic principle is that information should be publicly available unless there is a compelling rationale for nondisclosure, such as national security or privacy concerns.

Improvements to the enabling environment for citizens' organizations are also under consideration. A stronger legal framework is needed to allow citizens to form organizations that enrich the life of the community or that address the interests and concerns of their members. Limits on the ability of people to form voluntary organizations increases the burden on government since state agencies move to fill the gap left by their absence. For example, local businesses can form voluntary groups to keep their neighborhoods clean, manage public spaces, and so forth. Professional organizations can work to uphold standards of service and inform the government of inconsistencies in regulations or enforcement. Religious groups can help increase access to education and health services. The draft Law on Associations provides for sharp improvements to help develop independent civil society organizations. It is likely to be adopted in the near future.

Stronger support for the participation of citizens' organizations in decision making is needed. The Law on Promulgation of Legal Normative Documents provides a starting point for participation and access to information. Yet the mechanisms to realize the law's objectives are not in place. In addition to information, specific procedures to channel input from citizens' organizations into decision making and feedback on government performance are needed. Consultative mechanisms and public access to deliberative meetings of governments at all levels should be enhanced. Social, cultural, and professional societies can contribute in important ways to the review of draft legislation, the impact of regulations, policy formulation and implementation, and the delivery of public services.

Building modern institutions is a long-term, complex endeavor, but there are steps in the short to medium term that Vietnam can undertake to move toward the aspirational vision outlined above. Having a clear vision for what Vietnam wants to look like in 2035 is important as a reference point for a program of reforms. But a vision is not a plan of action, nor is it necessarily a clear guide to the steps to be taken since institutional improvement almost never occurs in a linear sequence toward desired results. Political realities, the interplay of interests among stakeholders, external factors, and the complexity of institutional change mean that success rarely lies simply in charting a straight path toward an end goal of a substantially different institutional framework. Identifying the steps that should be undertaken now to reach the goals for 2035 needs to build on analysis of present weaknesses, prioritization of what changes are important in terms of working toward the desired end goal, as well as sensitivity to what is likely to work given the present balance of interests.

Consideration of these factors combined with the preceding analysis and vision-setting point to three types of steps that Vietnam can consider in the short to medium term to move toward developing modern institutions:

1. Reforms to improve the effectiveness of key state structures
2. Changes in incentives (reward and sanction mechanisms) to improve the accountability, discipline, and behavioral culture of different actors in the state–society relationship, above all leaders and public servants therein
3. Mechanisms to manage the shifting relationship between the state and the private sector and the associated rents to ensure broader goals of continued legitimacy of the state and the promotion of productivity-enhancing behavior

Notes

1. There is widespread consensus around the importance of institutions to achieving sustained growth. See, for instance, North 1990, Acemoglu and Robinson 2012, and Fukuyama 2011.
2. The six dimensions of governance are voice and accountability; political stability and absence of violence; government effectiveness; regulatory quality; rule of law; and control of corruption. See http://info.worldbank.org/governance/wgi/index.aspx#home for more information.
3. Institutional economists have developed categories of countries as either "open access orders" or "limited access orders," with the former corresponding to states where meaningful participation in the economy and society is broad-based. Acemoglu and Robinson (2012) identify countries' political and economic institutions as either inclusive or exclusive, and stress the interaction of both types of institutions as well as political power. They argue that inclusiveness of both political and economic institutions is a necessary condition for sustained prosperity.
4. The number of government agencies was reduced from 70 before the *Đổi Mới* to 30 currently (including 22 ministerial-level agencies and 8 government agencies).
5. The number of laws and ordinances passed by the National Assembly, the National Assembly's Standing Committee promulgated in the 29 years of *Đổi Mới* (from January 1, 1987, to June 30, 2015), is 8 times more than the number of laws and ordinances issued in 41 years before the *Đổi Mới*. Specifically, between September 2, 1945, and December 30, 1986, Vietnam enacted 63 laws and ordinances, while the number is 524 between January 1, 1987, and June 30, 2015.
6. That is evident in the laws on legal document promulgation issued in 2008 and 2015.
7. Through direct relationships with SOEs and government officials.
8. A recent joint study by the Central Institute for Economic Management and the World Bank (CIEM and World Bank 2015).
9. Dunleavy and Rhodes (1990) define the core executive in this functional way: "all those organizations and structures which primarily serve to pull together and integrate central government policies, or act as final arbiters within the executive of conflicts between different elements of the government machine."
10. See Nguyen and Pincus 2011.
11. For a full discussion, see World Bank 2015b.
12. Ministry of Justice, Monitoring Report on Law Implementation of 2014, numbered 64/BC-BTP, dated March 18, 2015.
13. For instance, the introduction of meritocracy in Scandinavia emerged as the absolute kings had an incentive to establish a bureaucracy that would be rule-based, capable, and independent from anything but the absolute monarch, and that could control the nobility and the landed gentry. In the Republic of Korea, the legitimacy of the state depended on a capable and neutral public service when the meritocracy gained a foothold in the 1980s.
14. For example, while the Company Law of 1990 requires that a person, to start a business, go through multiple steps and months to complete the procedures, the Enterprise Law of 2014 stipulates that an individual application for starting up a business has to be processed within 3 days.
15. In 2010, 87 percent of revenue associated with land came from use-right allocations (World Bank 2014).
16. In 2006 the court system at all levels received and handled 63,079 civil cases, 64,058 family and marriage cases, and 1,979 economic cases. In 2013 the numbers increased to 94,963, 145,797, and 14,767, respectively.
17. See Markussen 2015.
18. For the global evidence see for example, the classic study by Schmitter and Lehmbruch (1979).

And for the Vietnam specific evidence see Malesky and Taussig (forthcoming).

19. New Zealand, for instance, directs its SOEs to be (i) as profitable and efficient as comparable businesses in the private sector; (ii) good employers; and (iii) socially responsible, by paying attention to local communities' needs and interests.
20. Robert Klitgaard first developed a general "formula" identifying circumstances, which, taken together, contribute to the emergence of corruption: Corruption = Monopoly + Discretion – Accountability

References

Acemoglu, Daron, and James Robinson. 2012. *Why Nations Fail: The Origins of Power, Prosperity, and Poverty*. New York: Green Business.

Anderson, James, Maria Delfina Alcaide Garrido, and Tuyet Thi Phung. 2009. *Vietnam Development Report 2010: Modern Institutions*. Washington, DC: World Bank.

CECODES (Centre for Community Support and Development Studies), VFF-CRT (Centre for Research and Training of the Viet Nam Fatherland Front), and UNDP (United Nations Development Programme). 2015. "The Viet Nam Governance and Public Administration Performance Index (PAPI) 2014: Measuring Citizens' Experiences." A Joint Policy Research Paper by the CECODES, VFF-CRT, and UNDP, Hanoi.

CIEM (Central Institute for Economic Management) database. Ministry of Planning and Investment, Hanoi. http://www.ciem.org.vn/en/hoptacquocte/duanciem/tabid/303/articletype/ArticleView/articleId/942/default.aspx.

CIEM and World Bank. 2015. *Are There Preferential Treatments of SOEs: Review of Regulatory Framework and Evidence from Practice*. Hanoi: CIEM and World Bank.

Dunleavy, P., and R. A. W. Rhodes. 1990. "Core Executive Studies in Britain." *Public Administration* 68 (1): 3–28.

Dương, Thị Thanh Mai, and Dr. Nguyễn Văn Cương. 2015. "Policy Making and Enforcement in Vietnam: Context, Expected Transformation, and Vision to 2035." Background paper for Vietnam 2035 Report.

Evans, Peter. 2005. "Harnessing the State: Rebalancing Strategies for Monitoring and Motivation." In *States and Development: Historical Antecedents of Stagnation and Advance*, edited by Matthew Lange, and Dietrich Rueschemeyer, 26–47. Political Evolution and Institutional Change. New York: Palgrave Macmillan Ltd.

Fukuyama, F. 2011. *The Origins of Political Order*. New York: Farrar, Straus, and Giroux.

Gainsborough, M. 2009. "Privatization as State Advance: Private Indirect Government in Vietnam." *New Political Economy* 14 (2): 257–74.

Global Competitiveness Index (database). World Economic Forum with Columbia University, New York. http://www.gaportal.org/global-indicators/global-competitiveness-index.

Government Inspectorate of Vietnam. 2012. Annual Report on Anticorruption to the National Assembly, October 2012.

Hirschman, Albert O., and Michael Rothschild. 1973. "The Changing Tolerance for Income Inequality in the Course of Economic Development." *Quarterly Journal of Economics* 87(4): 544–66.

IMF (International Monetary Fund). 2015. *World Economic Outlook*. Washington, DC: IMF. https://www.imf.org/external/pubs/ft/weo/2015/02/weodata/index.aspx.

Institute of Legal Science. 2014. "A Study on the Present State of Policy Analysis in Law Making Process in Vietnam." Background paper, Ministry of Justice, Hanoi.

Klitgaard, Robert. 1988. *Controlling Corruption*. Berkeley: University of California Press.

Lieberthal, Kenneth, and Michel Oksenberg. 1988. *Policy Making in China: Leaders, Structures, and Processes*. Princeton, NJ: Princeton University Press.

London, Jonathan. 2009. "Viet Nam and the Making of Market-Leninism." *The Pacific Review* 22 (3): 373–97.

Malesky, Edmund, and Markus Taussig. 2016. "Opening Factory Doors to Government Regulations: An Experiment on Participation by Firms in the Design of Labor Protections in Vietnam." Workshop presentation.

Markussen, Thomas. 2015. "Social and Political Capital in Rural Viet Nam." Working Paper 2015/087, United Nations University World Institute for Development Economics Research, Helsinki.

MONRE (Ministry of Natural Resources and Environment). 2012. *MONRE Review Report on the implementation of the 2003 Land Law, No. 193/BC-BTNMT*. September 6, MONRE.

Nguyen, Xuan Thanh, and Jonathan Pincus. 2011. *Ho Chi Minh City Sea Port Relocation: A Case Study of Institutional Fragmentation*. Ho Chi Minh City: Fulbright Economics Teaching Program.

Nolan, Peter. 2004. *China at the Crossroads*. Cambridge, UK: Polity.

North, Douglass. 1990. *Institutions, Institutional Change and Economic Performance (Political Economy of Institutions and Decisions)*. Cambridge, UK: Cambridge University Press.

PCI (Provincial Competitive Index) database. 2013. *Vietnam Chamber of Commerce and Industry (VCCI) and United States Agency for International Development*. Hanoi. english/pcivietnam.org.

Phuc, Thang Van. 2015. "Developing a Modern Civil Service Institution and Capacity of Civil Servants Based on the Actual Situation in Vietnam." Background paper for Vietnam 2035 Report.

Pincus, Jonathan, Vu Thanh Tu Anh, Pham Duy Nghia, Ben Wilkinson, and Nguyen Xuan Thanh. 2012. "Structural Reform for Growth, Equity, and National Sovereignty." Ash Center for Democratic Governance, Harvard Kennedy School. A Policy Discussion Paper Prepared for the Vietnam Executive Leadership Program (VELP), Harvard Kennedy School, February 13–17.

Pincus, Jonathan. 2015. "Vietnam: Building Capacity in a Fragmented, Commercialized State." Background paper for Vietnam 2035 Report.

Putnam, Robert. 1993. *Making Democracy Work: Civic Traditions in Modern Italy*. Princeton, NJ: Princeton University Press.

Schmitter, Philippe, and Gerhard Lehmbruch. 1979. *Trends toward Corporatist Intermediation*. London: Sage.

Smith, Adam. 1904. *An Inquiry Into Nature and Causes of the Wealth of Nations*. Edited by Edwin Cannan. London: Methuen and Company. http://www.econlib.org/library/Smith/smWN0.html.

Transparency International. 2013. "Global Corruption Barometer." http://www.transparency.org

Vietnam Province Competitiveness Index. 2006–2014. www.pcivietnam.vn.

Viner, Jacob. 1927. "Adam Smith and Laissez Faire." *Journal of Political Economy* 35 (2): 198–232.

Weber, Max. 1946. *From Max Weber: Essays in Sociology*. Edited by Hans Heinrich Gerth and C. Wright Mills. Oxford: Oxford University Press.

World Bank. World Development Indicators (WDI) database. Washington, DC: World Bank. http://data.worldbank.org/data-catalog/world-development-indicators.

———. World Governance Indicators (WGI) database. Washington, DC: World Bank. http://info.worldbank.org/governance/wgi/index.aspx#home.

———. 2011. *Compulsory Land Acquisition and Voluntary Land Conversion in Vietnam: The Conceptual Approach, Land Valuation and Grievance Redress Mechanisms*. Washington, DC: World Bank.

———. 2013a. *Recognizing and Reducing Corruption Risks in Land Management in Vietnam, 2013*. Washington, DC: World Bank.

———. 2013b. *Corruption from the Perspective of Citizens, Firms, and Public Officials: Results of Sociological Surveys. Second Edition*. Washington, DC: World Bank.

———. 2014. *Land Transparency Study*. Washington, DC: World Bank.

———. 2015a. "Transparency of State-owned Enterprises in Vietnam: Current Status and Ideas for Reform." Policy Note, World Bank, Washington, DC.

———. 2015b. *Making the Whole Greater Than the Sum of the Parts: A Review of Fiscal Decentralization in Viet Nam—Summary Report*. Washington, DC: World Bank.

World Bank and Government Inspectorate of Vietnam. 2016. *Managing Conflict of Interest in the Public Sector: Law and Practice in Vietnam*. Draft Report. Washington, DC: World Bank and Government Inspectorate of Vietnam.

World Economic Forum. 2013. *The Future Role of Civil Society*. Geneva: World Economic Forum.

———. 2015. *Global Competitiveness Report, 2013–14 and 2014–15*. Geneva: World Economic Forum.

World Justice Project. 2014. *The Rule of Law Index® 2014*. Washington, DC: World Justice Project.

Made in United States
Orlando, FL
04 November 2026

90201385R00223